Software Engineering Project Management

Second Edition

Software Engineering Project Management

Second Edition

Edited by Richard H. Thayer
Foreword by Edward Yourdon

Original contributions by

Bill Brykczynski
Alan M. Davis
Robert H. Dunn
Richard E. Fairley
John E. Gaffney, Jr.

John M. Glabas
Patricia W. Hurst
Deanna B. Legg
Reginald N. Meeson, Jr.

Richard D. Stutzke
Richard H. Thayer
Heinz Weihrich
David A. Wheeler
Edward Yourdon

IEEE
COMPUTER
SOCIETY

Los Alamitos, California

Washington • Brussels • Tokyo

IEEE Computer Society Order Number BP08000
ISBN 0-8186-8000-8
Library of Congress Number 97-20500

Additional copies may be ordered from:

IEEE Computer Society	IEEE Service Center	IEEE Computer Society
Customer Service Center	445 Hoes Lane	Asia/Pacific Office
10662 Los Vaqueros Circle	P.O. Box 1331	Watanabe Bldg., 1-4-2
P.O. Box 3014	Piscataway, NJ 08855-1331	Minami-Aoyama
Los Alamitos, CA 90720-1314	Tel: + 1-732-981-0060	Minato-ku, Tokyo 107-0062
Tel: + 1-714-821-8380	Fax: + 1-732-981-9667	JAPAN
Fax: + 1-714-821-4641	mis.custserv@computer.org	Tel: + 81-3-3408-3118
E-mail: cs.books@computer.org		Fax: + 81-3-3408-3553
		tokyo.ofc@computer.org

Printed in the United States of America by Edwards Brothers Incorporated

IEEE
COMPUTER
SOCIETY

Contributors of Original Papers

Mr. Bill Brykczynski, Institute for Defense Analyses, 1801 N. Beauregard Street, Alexandria, VA 22311-1772, USA

Ms. Mary Beth Chrissis, Software Engineering Institute (SEI), Carnegie Mellon University, Pittsburgh, PA 15213-3890, USA **

Dr. Bill Curtis, TeraQuest Metrics, Inc., P.O. Box 200490, Austin, TX, 78720-0490, USA **

Dr. Alan M. Davis, University of Colorado at Colorado Springs, 1867 Austin Bluffs Parkway, Suite 200, Colorado Springs, CO 80933-7150, USA

Mr. Jon K. Digerness, North Coast Graphics, 7418 Kanai Avenue, Citrus Heights, CA 95621 (illustrator)

Mr. Robert H. Dunn, Systems for Quality Software, 107 Buck Hill Road, Easton, CT 06612, USA

Dr. Richard E. Fairley, Colorado Technical University, 4435 N. Chestnut Street, Colorado Springs, CO 80907-3896, USA

Dr. Stuart R. Faulk, Department of Computer and Information Science, Deschutes Hall, University of Oregon, Eugene, OR 97403, USA **

Mr. John E. Gaffney, Jr., Lockheed Martin Company, Air Traffic Management, Rockville, MD 20850, USA

Mr. John M. Glabas, Information Systems Division, California State Comptroller's Office, 300 Capitol Mall, Sacramento, CA 95819, USA

Ms. Patricia W. Hurst, Fastrak Training, Inc., 9175 Guilford Rd., Suite 300, Columbia, MD 21046, USA

Mr. Frank S. Ingrassia (deceased) *

Ms. Deanna B. Legg, 8900 Camp Far West Read, Sheridan, CA 95681, USA

Dr. Reginald Meeson Jr., Institute for Defense Analyses, 1801 N Beauregard Street, Alexandria, VA 22311-1772, USA

Mr. Mark C. Paulk, Software Engineering Institute (SEI), Carnegie Mellon University, Pittsburgh, PA 15213-3890, USA **

Dr. Roger S. Pressman, R.S. Pressman & Associates, Inc., 620 East Slope Drive, Orange, CT 06477, USA **

Dr. Winston W. Royce (deceased) *

Dr. Richard D. Stutzke, Science Applications International Corporation (SAIC), 6725 Odyssey Dr., Huntsville, AL 35806, USA

Dr. Richard H. Thayer, Department of Computer Science, California State University at Sacramento, Sacramento, CA 95819, USA

Mr. Charles V. Weber, Lockheed Martin Federal Systems Company, 6304 Spine Road Boulder, CO 80301, USA **

Dr. Heinz Weihrich, McLaren School of Business, University of San Francisco, 2130 Fulton Street, San Francisco, CA 94117-1080, USA

Mr. David Wheeler, Institute for Defense Analyses, 1801 N Beauregard Street, Alexandria, VA 22311-1772, USA

Mr. Edward Yourdon, 161 West 86th Street, Suite 9A, New York, NY 10024, USA

** Author of an original paper in *Software Engineering*, M. Dorfman and R.H. Thayer, eds., IEEE Computer Soc. Press, Los Alamitos, Calif., 1997.

* Author of an original paper in *Software Engineering Project Management*, 1ˢᵗ ed., R.H. Thayer, ed., IEEE Computer Soc. Press, Los Alamitos, Calif., 1988.

Foreword

Edward Yourdon
Author and Consultant
New York, NY

In the past several years, a lot of attention has been focused on the tools, techniques, and methods necessary to solve the "software crisis." As reported in Wayt Gibbs' paper, in this tutorial, the software crisis is a term used to describe the recurring system development problems where software problems cause the system to be late, over cost, and/or not responsive to the user's needs and requirements. Papers and reports abound with description of new methodologies and software tools developed in university and corporation laboratories. Many claim that theirs is the only methodology necessary for the project to be successful, or that their tool will reduce cost or produce an improved product (usually without adequate proof). Much of this discussion has centered around what is sometime termed a "silver bullet,"[1] in other words, the tool or technique that can solve the software crisis.

I would like to propose that the silver bullet (or bullets if you prefer) exists, and it is software engineering project management. A properly managed project, in a mature software engineering environment, managed by a competent manager, can repeatedly deliver a software system on time, within cost, and satisfactory to the user. Good project management environments can compensate when things go wrong, for example, adjust the delivery schedule under changing conditions, select appropriate people for the job at hand, provide clear and unambiguous direction, monitor progress and job completion status, and take appropriate action when controlling metrics indicate plans are not being followed. See the paper by Mark Paulk, Bill Curtis, Mary Beth Chrissis, and Charles Weber for a description of a mature software engineering environment.

This *Software Engineering Project Management* tutorial, by Richard Thayer, provides a broad but detailed look at the functions and activities necessary for the proper management of a software development project. Chapters 1 through 3 provide a description of issues that the project manager must face, a general description of management and project management,

and a description of software engineering. The first paper of the tutorial, on general management by Heinz Weihrich, provides a management model that can be adapted by any manager to his management task. Thayer's and Fred Brook's papers provide overviews on how to manage software projects.

Chapters 4 through 10 provide the details necessary to successfully manage a software project.

Chapters 4 and 5 cover project planning with emphasis on accurate cost and schedules estimating. The first paper by Stuart Faulk on "Software Requirements" describes the technical goals of a project. Ed Goldberg's seminar viewgraphs deal with a method of establishing company policies for developing a quality software system. Thayer and Richard Fairley's papers on work breakdown structure and software risk management emphasize some essential project management tools. The new *IEEE Standard on Software Project Management Plans* as described by John Glabas and Richard Fairley provides the necessary outline needed to develop a software engineering project management plan. The papers by Richard Stutzke and John Gaffney provide an overview of software cost modeling, and the paper by Legg describes in simple terms how to implement COCOMO, the world's most popular software cost technique. COCOMO 2.0 is documented by Barry Boehm and the staff at the Center of Software Engineering.

Chapter 6 describes the three types of software project organizations and how to select the appropriate one for the project. Robert Youker's paper defines these development organizations—functions, project, and matrix. Lynn Stuckenbruck describes ways of correctly implementing the matrix organization that is probably the most used project organization in the software industry. Marilyn Mantei describes in considerable detail the types of team organizations.

Chapter 7 tells about staffing a project and how to enlist enthusiastic people in your project. The chapter begins with a very fine paper by Robert Zawacki on "How to Pick Eagles" and terminates with a paper called "Trial by Firing: Saga of a Rookie Manager" by Al Davis. Marie Moneysmith, in a very short paper, points out that the annual performance review is a har-

---

[1] Frederick P. Brooks, "No Silver Bullets: Essence and Accidents of Software Engineering," *Computer*, Apr. 1987.

rowing experience for both employee and the manager.

Chapter 8 provides guidance on how to direct and lead an organization to a successful conclusion of its project. One of the most important concepts all managers should use is how to delegate their work. This is well described in Eugene Raudsepp's paper "Delegate Your Way to Success." Also well documented is the concept that "Excitement and Commitment" are the "Keys to Project Success." by Gary Powell and Barry Posner. Motivating people is a highly important aspect of management and is well described by K. Whitaker.

And Chapter 9 and 10 delineate all of the control mechanisms necessary to control a project. Pat Hurst begins the first chapter with a paper on "Thread of Control," which provides a short overview on project control and project control tools. Two other papers that describe controlling mechanisms are "Software Quality Assurance" by Robert Dunn and the landmark paper by Ed Bersoff on "Configuration Management." Three more important control mechanisms are "Software Peer Reviews" by David Wheeler, Reginald Meeson, Jr., and Bill Brykczynski; "Software Management Metrics" by Herman Schultz; and "The Unit Development Folder" by Frank Ingrassia.

Richard and Mildred Thayer round off the *Tutorial* with a very detailed glossary.

Give it some thought. Could software engineering project management along with a good management process and solid environment be our "silver bullet"?

Dr. Winston W. Royce (1929–1995) was one of the leaders in software development in the second half of the 20th century. He wrote the Foreword for the first edition of this Tutorial. It is reprinted here in his memory.

Foreword for the First Edition of

Software Engineering Project Management

Winston W. Royce, Director
Lockheed Software Technology Center

Project management is a discipline that surely existed from the beginning of our civilization. Slowly through the millennia, and more rapidly within the last century, an immense body of management knowledge has arisen. Management is a discipline that must redefine itself to deal with the continuing changes arising within human institutions. For project management, technology is probably the principal driving force for such redefinition. To service the newest technological breakthrough, project management must adapt.

For example, at the midpoint of this century, the need for a new form of project management tailored to digital computer programming slowly became evident. The need to program digital computers had made its first appearance, and such programming had seemed a simple, almost self-managing, activity. A common task of the day had been programming analog computers; digital programming, by comparison, had seemed simpler and less frequently needed. However, as the incredible diversity and raw power of a properly programmed digital computer proved itself, this wrong initial impression was quickly corrected.

The term "software engineering" arose in the late 1960s and early 1970s. "Software engineering" is new enough that it is still struggling for a clear, single meaning, much as the definition of "software" struggled during its first ten years to the present meaning.

Software engineering, a discipline invented by human beings (exhibiting both their creative spark and frailties) has driven project management up new, uncharted pathways and forced its redefinition—and it continues to do so today. For all who contribute to the charting of these new pathways, it is an exhilarating experience.

This tutorial on software engineering project management collects the major published material, either by republication here or by inclusion in the complete set of references. The reader will note that many sides of the major issues are presented, for consensus has not yet been achieved. While existing, complete, and definitive solutions for the best method to achieve software engineering project management are still evolving, this tutorial is an important milestone along this uncharted pathway.

Preface

Software Engineering Project Management

The purpose of this tutorial is to assemble under one cover a sufficient body of knowledge about managing a successful software engineering project. The following quote from Heinz Weihrich outlines the basic ideas behind this tutorial.

> All managers carry out the functions of *planning, organizing, staffing, leading,* and *controlling,* although the time spent in each function will differ and the skills required by managers at different organizations and organizational levels vary. ... This concept is sometimes called the *universality of management* in which managers perform the same functions regardless of their place in the organizational structure or the type of enterprise in which they are managing. [1]

This tutorial is about the adaptation of this management theory to project management and reflects the practice and methods of software engineering project management. This tutorial is intended for:

- *New managers*—The tutorial delivers the necessary information to manage a software development project.

- *Experienced managers*—The tutorial presents the state of the practice in software engineering management techniques.

- *Software engineers, programmers, analysts, and other computer personnel*—The tutorial contains a general description of—and problems in—software engineering project management, plus a number of methodologies and techniques for managing a software development project. It will also serve as a guide or goal for the future of these specialists in project management.

- *College-level students*—The tutorial offers sufficient background and instructional material to serve as a main or supplementary text for a course in software engineering project management.

This book presents a top-down, practical view of software engineering project management. This top-down structure was used as a framework for selecting appropriate reprints and in assembling original material that will explain as specifically as possible how project managers manage a software project.

One of the major premises of this tutorial is that managing a software development project is no different than managing anything else. The functions are the same—planning, organizing, staffing, directing, and controlling—only the activities to implement these functions differ. Therefore, where a software project paper was not available to address a topic, a paper on general management or management of a hardware project was substituted.

The chapters of this tutorial are arranged into two general groups. The first group contains Chapters 1, 2, and 3 and provides the background for software engineering project management. Chapter 1 is a general introduction to management. Chapter 2 provides a general description of software engineering and software engineering problems for the reader who may be unfamiliar with how large, custom-made, computer systems are built. Also included is a paper on the Software Engineering Institute (SEI) Capability Maturity Model (CMM). Chapter 3 presents a general overview of project management and how it fits into the concept of software engineering, including a paper on process models.

The second group of papers, Chapters 4 through 10, focuses on the five functions of general management: planning, organizing, staffing, directing, and controlling. Each chapter describes one function and the project management activities that support that function. In two cases, the activities of project management were split between two chapters. For example, under planning (Chapters 4 and 5), we describe requirements and goals, policies, decision making, estimating project costs and schedules, and docu-

---

[1] Weihrich, H., "Management Science, Theory, and Practice," in *Software Engineering Project Management*, 2nd ed., R.H. Thayer, ed., IEEE Computer Society Press, Los Alamitos, Calif., 1997.

menting a project plan. Under organizing (Chapter 6), we describe the various organizational structures, different responsibilities and authority relationships, and project teams that are used to organize a software engineering project.

Chapter 7, on staffing, suggests how to fill the organizational structure with people who are qualified to perform their duties. Training of employees is also discussed. In Chapter 8, we discuss directing (sometimes called leading), which concerns itself with motivation, delegating, conflict resolution, and the leadership of software people. Chapters 9 and 10, on controlling, take into consideration standards, Unit Development Folders (UDFs), reviews, walkthroughs and inspections, configuration management, audits, and other means necessary to ensure that a project is on schedule, within cost, and meets the customer's requirements. Chapter 11 is a wrap-up to the tutorial and was written after the foreword by Edward Yourdon was written.

This tutorial concludes with a glossary of over 250 software engineering project management and software engineering terms.

Every attempt was made to obtain tutorial papers that would provide a basic understanding of the various facets of software engineering project management. Papers selected generally were broad in coverage. When possible, secondary sources were selected—sources that summarized earlier papers or studies.

This tutorial is different. Instead of just collecting and organizing existing project management papers, this tutorial builds a framework of software engineering project management activities based on the planning, organizing, staffing, directing, and controlling model. This framework then had to then be filled with papers or articles on project management. Because of *universality of management theory*, management papers from other disciplines could be used. Despite this broadening of the search area, there were (and still are) management areas and activities that were not covered adequately by existing papers. To make up this deficiency, researchers and authors in the field of software engineering and project management contributed original papers to fill in the holes. Other papers that were written for or used in the tutorial's sister tutorials—*Software Engineering* and *Software Requirements Engineering*—were also used to fill in the gaps (although every attempt was made to keep this to a minimum).

An effort was made to use current papers for every important topic; that is, those published later than 1986. However, in many instances this was not possible, and papers in this tutorial range from 1971 through 1997. Regardless of the year the article was written or published, these papers reflect the latest state of the practice in software engineering project management.

This tutorial is one of a set of tutorials on "software system engineering" published by the IEEE Computer Society Press:

- *Software Engineering*, M. Dorfman and R.H. Thayer, eds., IEEE Computer Society Press, Los Alamitos, Calif., 1997
- *Software Requirements Engineering*, R.H. Thayer and M. Dorfman, eds., IEEE Computer Society Press, Los Alamitos, Calif., 1997
- *Software Engineering*—A European Perspective, R.H. Thayer and A.D. McGettrick, eds., IEEE Computer Society Press, Los Alamitos, Calif., 1993

Acknowledgments

Few successful endeavor has ever been made by one person alone and this tutorial is no exception. I would like to thank the people and organizations that supported me in this effort.

- The individuals on the list titled "Contributors of Original Papers" and the IEEE members who reviewed the original manuscript.

- Mrs. Mildred C. Thayer who did major proofreading and helped gather the terms for the Project Management Glossary.

- Ms. Ali McAlester from the Information Technology Associates Company Scheme (ITACS), University of Strathclyde, Glasgow, Scotland who typed many of the original papers and the chapter introductions.

- Mr. Jon K. Digerness and Ms. Bonnie J. Nieland, North Coast Graphics, Citrus Heights, CA.

- Dr. Merlin Dorfman (Cisco Systems) and Dr. Richard E. Fairley (Colorado Technical University) who acted as unofficial reviewer of the tutorial. Mr. James (Jim) Tozza who helped with the mechanics of producing readable copy.

- Ms. Lisa O'Conner (Tutorial Production Editor), Ms. Cheryl Baltes (Development Editor), and Dr. William (Bill) Sanders, (Managing Editor), all with the IEEE Computer Society Press.

- Ms. Louise D. Burnham, Copy Editor, Tucson, AZ.

- University of Stirling Library, Scotland, where the editor did much of his literature search

Richard H. Thayer, PhD
California State University, Sacramento
Sacramento, California 95819

Contents

Chapter 1

Introduction to Management

1. Chapter Introduction

Management can be defined as all the activities and tasks undertaken by one or more persons for the purpose of planning and controlling the activities of others in order to achieve an objective or complete an activity that could not be achieved by the others acting independently [1]. Management as defined by well-known authors in the field of management [2]–[6] contains the following components:

- Planning
- Organizing
- Staffing
- Directing (Leading)
- Controlling

For definitions of these terms see Table 1.1.

WELL CHAPS...THE MISSION OF THE TEAM IS TO CATCH AND ELIMINATE THE NOTORIOUS COMPUTER BUG—ULTIMA RECTALGIA COMPUPESTI

Table 1.1. Major management functions.

Activity	Definition or Explanation
Planning	Predetermining a course of action for accomplishing organizational objectives
Organizing	Arranging the relationships among work units for accomplishment of objectives and the granting of responsibility and authority to obtain those objectives
Staffing	Selecting and training people for positions in the organization
Directing	Creating an atmosphere that will assist and motivate people to achieve desired end results
Controlling	Establishing, measuring, and evaluating performance of activities toward planned objectives

From Weihrich [7] comes a definition of management:

All managers carry out the functions of planning, organizing, staffing, leading, and controlling, although the time spent in each function will differ and the skills required by managers at different organizational levels vary. Still, all managers are engaged in getting things done through people. ... The managerial activities, grouped into the managerial functions of planning, organizing, staffing, leading, and controlling, are carried out by all managers, but the practices and methods must be adapted to the particular tasks, enterprises, and situation.

This concept is sometimes called the *universality of management* in which managers perform the same functions regardless of their place in the organizational structure or the type of enterprise in which they are managing.

The statement from Weihrich means that

- management performs the same functions regardless of its position in the organization or the enterprise managed, and
- management functions and fundamental activities are characteristic duties of managers; management practices, methods, detailed activities, and tasks are particular to the enterprise or job managed.

Therefore, the functions and general activities of management can be universally applied to managing any organization or activity. Recognition of this con-

cept is crucial to the improvement of software engineering project management, for it allows us to apply the wealth of research in management sciences to improving the management of software engineering projects [8]. Additional discussion on the universality of management can be found in [9].

This chapter and introduction is important to the readers of this tutorial. The basic assumption of this tutorial on software engineering project management is based on a scientific management approach as follows:

1. Management consists of planning, organizing, staffing, directing, and controlling.

2. The concepts and activities of management applies to all levels of management, as well as to all types of organizations and activities managed.

Based on these two assumptions, this tutorial

- is divided into chapters, based on planning, organizing, staffing, directing, and controlling, and
- includes articles from other disciplines that illustrate the concepts of management that can be applied to software engineering project management.

2. Chapter Overview

The two articles contained in this chapter introduce management and show that the management of any endeavor (like a software engineering project) is the same as managing any other activity or organization. The first article, by Heinz Weihrich, sets the stage by defining management and the major functions of management. The second article, by Alec MacKenzie, is a condensed and comprehensive overview of management from the *Harvard Business Review*.

3. Article Descriptions

The first article in this chapter is extracted from an internationally famous book, *Management* by Weihrich, 10th edition [10], and adapted specifically by Weihrich for this tutorial. Earlier editions of this book were written by Harold Koontz and Cyril O'Donnell from the University of California, Los Angeles; Weihrich joined them as a co-author with the 7th edition. Both Koontz and O'Donnell are now deceased, leaving Weihrich to be the author of future editions. In this article, Weihrich

1. defines and describes the nature and purpose of management,
2. states that management applies to all kinds of organizations and to managers at all organizational levels,
3. defines the managerial functions of planning, organizing, staffing, leading [directing], and controlling,
4. states that managing requires a systems approach and that practice always takes into account situations and contingencies, and
5. recognizes that the aim of all managers is to be productive—that is, to carry out their activities effectively and efficiently and to create a "surplus."

Weihrich introduced the term "leading" to replace the term "directing" used by Koontz and O'Donnell in their earlier books. The articles by Richard Thayer will stay with the older term "directing."

The last article by Alec MacKenzie is also a clas-

sic. It is still the most comprehensive yet condensed description of management in existence. MacKenzie presents a top-down description of management starting with the elements of management—ideas, things, and people—and ending with a detailed description of general management activities—all on one foldout page.

References

1. Koontz, H., C. O'Donnell, and H. Weihrich, *Management*, 7th ed., McGraw-Hill, New York, N.Y., 1980.

2. Koontz, H., C. O'Donnell, and H. Weihrich, *Management*, 7th ed., McGraw-Hill, New York, N.Y., 1980.

3. Cleland, D.I. and W.R. King, *Management: A Systems Approach*, McGraw-Hill, New York, N.Y., 1972.

4. MacKenzie, R.A., "The Management Process in 3-D," *Harvard Business Review*, Nov.-Dec. 1969, pp. 80–87.

5. Blanchard, B.S. and W.J. Fabrycky, *System Engineering and Analysis*, 2nd ed., Prentice Hall, Englewood Cliffs, N.J., 1990.

6. Kerzner, H., *Project Management: A Systems Approach to Planning, Scheduling, and Controlling*, 3rd ed., Van Nostrand Reinhold, New York, N.Y., 1989.

7. Koontz, H. and C. O'Donnell, *Principles of Management: An Analysis of Managerial Functions*, 5th ed., McGraw-Hill, New York, N.Y., 1972.

8. Thayer, R.H. and A.B. Pyster, "Guest Editorial: Software Engineering Project Management," *IEEE Transactions on Software Engineering*, Vol. SE-10, No. 1, Jan. 1984.

9. Fayol, H., *General and Industrial Administration*, Sir Isaac Pitman & Sons, London, UK, 1949.

10. Weihrich, H. and H. Koontz, *Management: A Global Perspective*, 10th ed., McGraw-Hill, New York, NY, 1993.

Management: Science, Theory, and Practice[1]

Heinz Weihrich
University of San Francisco
San Francisco, California

One of the most important human activities is managing. Ever since people began forming groups to accomplish aims they could not achieve as individuals, managing has been essential to ensure the coordination of individual efforts. As society has come to rely increasingly on group effort and as many organized groups have grown larger, the task of managers has been rising in importance. The purpose of this book is to promote excellence of all persons in organizations, but especially managers, aspiring managers, and other professionals.

Definition of Management: Its Nature and Purpose

Management is the process of designing and maintaining an environment in which individuals, working together in groups, accomplish efficiently selected aims. This basic definition needs to be expanded:

1. As managers, people carry out the managerial functions of planning, organizing, staffing, leading, and controlling.

2. Management applies to any kind of organization.

3. It applies to managers at all organizational levels.

4. The aim of all managers is the same: to create a surplus.

5. Managing is concerned with productivity; that implies effectiveness and efficiency.

The Functions of Management

Many scholars and managers have found that the analysis of management is facilitated by a useful and clear organization of knowledge. As a first order of knowledge classification, we have used the five functions of managers: planning, organizing, staffing, leading, and controlling. Thus, the concepts, principles, theory, and techniques are organized around these functions and become the basis for discussion.

This framework has been used and tested for many years. Although there are different ways of organizing managerial knowledge, most textbook authors today have adopted this or a similar framework even after experimenting at times with alternative ways of structuring knowledge.

Although the emphasis in this article is on managers' tasks in designing an internal environment for performance, it must never be overlooked that managers must operate in the external environment of an enterprise as well as in the internal environment of an organization's various departments. Clearly, managers cannot perform their tasks well unless they understand, and are responsive to, the many elements of the external environment—economic, technological, social, political, and ethical factors that affect their areas of operations.

Management as an Essential for Any Organization

Managers are charged with the responsibility of taking actions that will make it possible for individuals to make their best contributions to group objectives. Management thus applies to small and large organiza-

---

[1] This paper has been modified for this book by Heinz Weihrich from Chapter 1 of *Management: A Global Perspective*, 10th ed. by Heinz Weihrich and Harold Koontz, McGraw-Hill, Inc., New York, N.Y., 1993. Reproduced by permission of McGraw-Hill, Inc.

tions, to profit and not-for-profit enterprises, to manufacturing as well as service industries. The term "enterprise" refers to business, government agencies, hospitals, universities, and other organizations, because almost everything said in this book refers to business as well as nonbusiness organizations. Effective managing is the concern of the corporation president, the hospital administrator, the government first-line supervisor, the Boy Scout leader, the bishop in the church, the baseball manager, and the university president.

Management at Different Organizational Levels

Managers are charged with the responsibility of taking actions that will make it possible for individuals to make their best contributions to group objectives To be sure, a given situation may differ considerably among various levels in an organization or various types of enterprises. Similarly, the scope of authority held may vary and the types of problems dealt with may be considerably different. Furthermore, the person in a managerial role may be directing people in the sales, engineering, or finance department. But the fact remains that, as managers, all obtain results by establishing an environment for effective group endeavor.

All managers carry out managerial functions. However, the time spent for each function may differ. Figure 1[2] shows an approximation of the relative time spent for each function. Thus, top-level managers spend more time on planning and organizing than lower level managers. Leading, on the other hand, takes a great deal of time for first-line supervisors. The difference in time spent on controlling varies only slightly for managers at various levels.

All Effective Managers Carry Out Essential Functions

All managers carry out the functions of *planning, organizing, staffing, leading,* and *controlling*, although the time spent in each function will differ and the skills required by managers at different organizational levels vary. Still, all managers are engaged in getting things done through people. Although the managerial concepts, principles, and theories have general validity, their application is an art and depends on the situation. Thus, managing is an art using the underlying sciences. Managerial activities are common to all managers, but the practices and methods must be adapted to the particular tasks, enterprises, and situations.

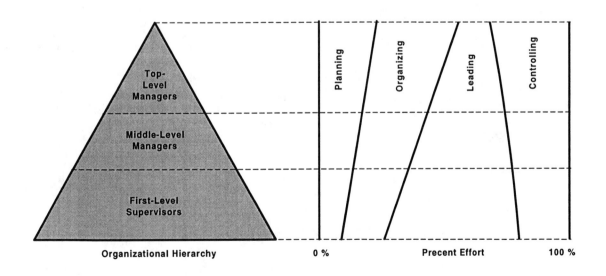

Figure 1. Time spent in carrying out managerial functions.

[2] This figure is partly based on and adapted from T.A. Money, T.H. Jerdee, and S.J. Carroll's "The Job(s) of Management," *Industrial Relations,* Feb. 1965, pp. 97–110.

5

This concept is sometimes called the *universality of management* in which managers perform the same functions regardless of their place in the organizational structure or the type of enterprise in which they are managing.

Managerial Skills and the Organizational Hierarchy

Robert L. Katz identified three kinds of skills for administrators.[3] To these may be added a fourth—the ability to design solutions.

1. *Technical skill* is knowledge of and proficiency in activities involving methods, processes, and procedures. Thus it involves working with tools and specific techniques. For example, mechanics work with tools, and their supervisors should have the ability to teach them how to use these tools. Similarly, accountants apply specific techniques in doing their job.

2. *Human skill* is the ability to work with people; it is cooperative effort; it is teamwork; it is the creation of an environment in which people feel secure and free to express their opinions.

3. *Conceptual skill* is the ability to see the "big picture," to recognize significant elements in a situation, and to understand the relationships among the elements.

4. *Design skill* is the ability to solve problems in ways that will benefit the enterprise. To be effective, particularly at upper organizational levels, managers must be able to do more than see a problem. If managers merely see the problem and become "problem watchers," they will fail. They must have, in addition, the skill of a good design engineer in working out a practical solution to a problem.

The relative importance of these skills may differ at various levels in the organization hierarchy. As shown in Figure 2, technical skills are of greatest importance at the supervisory level. Human skills are also helpful in the frequent interactions with subordinates. Conceptual skills, on the other hand, are usually not critical for lower level supervisors. At the middle-management level, the need for technical skills decreases; human skills are still essential; and the conceptual skills gain in importance. At the top-management level, conceptual and design abilities and human skills are especially valuable, but there is relatively little need for technical abilities. It is assumed,

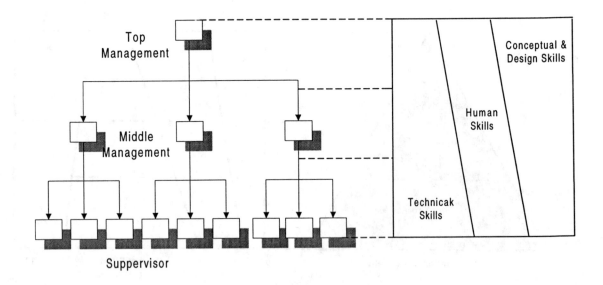

Figure 2. Skills versus management levels.

[3] R.L. Katz, "Skills of an Effective Administrator," *Harvard Business Review*, Jan.–Feb., 1955, pp. 33–42, and R.L. Katz, "Retrospective Commentary," *Harvard Business Review*, Sept.–Oct. 1974, pp. 101–102.

especially in large companies, that chief executives can utilize the technical abilities of their subordinates. In smaller firms, however, technical experience may still be quite important.

The Aim of All Managers

Nonbusiness executives sometimes say that the aim of business managers is simple—to make a profit. But profit is really only a measure of a *surplus* of sales dollars (or in any other currency) over expense dollars. In a very real sense, in all kinds of organizations, whether commercial and noncommercial, the logical and publicly desirable aim of all managers should be a surplus—managers must establish an environment in which people can accomplish group goals with the least amount of time, money, materials, and personal dissatisfaction, or where they can achieve as much as possible of a desired goal with available resources. In a nonbusiness enterprise such as a police department, as well as in units of a business (such as an accounting department) that are not responsible for total business profits, managers still have budgetary and organizational goals and should strive to accomplish them with the minimum of resources.

Productivity, Effectiveness, and Efficiency

Another way to view the aim of all managers is to say that they must be productive. After World War II the United States was the world leader in productivity. But in the late 1960s productivity began to decelerate. Today government, private industry, and universities recognize the urgent need for productivity improvement. Until very recently we frequently looked to Japan to find answers to our productivity problem, but this overlooks the importance of effectively performing fundamental managerial and nonmanagerial activities.

Definition of productivity. Successful companies create a surplus through productive operations. Although there is not complete agreement on the true meaning of productivity, we will define it as *the output-input ratio within a time period with due consideration for quality.* It can be expressed as follows:

$$\text{Productivity} = \frac{\text{output}}{\text{input}} \text{ within a time period,}$$

quality considered

Thus, productivity can be improved by increasing outputs with the same inputs, by decreasing inputs but maintaining the same outputs, or by increasing output

and decreasing inputs to change the ratio favorably. In the past, productivity improvement programs were mostly aimed at the worker level. Yet, as Peter F. Drucker, one of the most prolific writers in management, observed, "The greatest opportunity for increasing productivity is surely to be found in knowledge, work itself, and especially in management."[4]

Definitions of effectiveness and efficiency. Productivity implies effectiveness and efficiency in individual and organizational performance. *Effectiveness* is the achievement of objectives. *Efficiency* is the achievement of the ends with the least amount of resources. To know whether they are productive, managers must know their goals and those of the organization.

Managing: Science or Art?

Managing, like so many other disciplines—medicine, music composition, engineering, accountancy, or even baseball—is in large measure an art but founded on a wealth of science. It is making decisions on the basis of business realities. Yet managers can work better by applying the organized knowledge about management that has accrued over the decades. It is this knowledge, whether crude or advanced, whether exact or inexact, that, to the extent it is well organized, clear, and pertinent, constitutes a science. Thus, managing as practiced is an art; the organized knowledge underlying the practice may be referred to as a science. In this context science and art are not mutually exclusive but are complementary.

As science improves so should the application of this science (the art) as has happened in the physical and biological sciences. This is true because the many variables with which managers deal are extremely complex and intangible. But such management knowledge as is available can certainly improve managerial practice. Physicians without the advantage of science would be little more than witch doctors. Executives who attempt to manage without such management science must trust to luck, intuition, or to past experiences.

In managing, as in any other field, unless practitioners are to learn by trial and error (and it has been said that managers' errors are their subordinates' trials), there is no place they can turn for meaningful guidance other than the accumulated knowledge underlying their practice.

---

[4] P.F. Drucker, *Management, Tasks, Responsibilities, Practices,* Harper & Row, New York, 1973, p. 69.

The Elements of Science

Science is organized knowledge. The essential feature of any science is the application of the scientific method to the development of knowledge. Thus, we speak of a science as having clear concepts, theory, and other accumulated knowledge developed from hypotheses (assumptions that something is true), experimentation, and analysis.

The Scientific Approach

The scientific approach first requires clear *concepts*— mental images of anything formed by generalization from particulars. These words and terms should be exact, relevant to the things being analyzed, and informative to the scientist and practitioner alike. From this base, the *scientific method* involves determining facts through observation. After classifying and analyzing these facts, scientists look for causal relationships. When these generalizations or hypotheses are tested for accuracy and appear to be true, that is, to reflect or explain reality, and therefore to have value in predicting what will happen in similar circumstances. They are called *principles*. This designation does not always imply that they are unquestionably or invariably true, but that they are believed to be valid enough to be used for prediction.

Theory is a systematic grouping of interdependent concepts and principles that form a framework for a significant body of knowledge. Scattered data, such as what we may find on a blackboard after a group of engineers has been discussing a problem, are not information unless the observer has knowledge of the theory that will explain relationships. Theory is, as C.G. Homans has said, "in its lowest form a classification, a set of pigeonholes, a filing cabinet in which fact can accumulate. Nothing is more lost than a loose fact."

The Role of Management Theory

In the field of management, then, the role of theory is to provide a means of classifying significant and pertinent management knowledge. In designing an effective organization structure, for example, a number of principles are interrelated and have a predictive value for managers. Some principles give guidelines for delegating authority; these include the principle of delegating by results expected, the principle of equality of authority and responsibility, and the principle of unity of command.

Principles in management are fundamental truths (or what are thought to be truths at a given time), explaining relationships between two or more sets of variables, usually an independent variable and a dependent variable. Principles may be *descriptive* or *predictive,* and are not prescriptive. That is, they describe how one variable relates to another—what will happen when these variables interact. They do not prescribe what we should do. For example, in physics, if gravity is the only force acting on a falling body, the body will fall at an increasing speed; this principle does not tell us whether anyone should jump off the roof of a high building. Or take the example of Parkinson's law: Work tends to expand to fill the time available. Even if Parkinson's somewhat frivolous principle is correct (as it probably is), it does not mean that a manager should lengthen the time available for people to do a job.

To take another example, in management the principle of unity of command states that the more often an individual reports to a single superior, the more that individual is likely to feel a sense of loyalty and obligation, and the less likely it is that there will be confusion about instruction. The principle merely predicts. It in no sense implies that individuals should never report to more than one person. Rather, it implies that if they do so, their managers must be aware of the possible dangers and should take these risks into account in balancing the advantages and disadvantages of multiple command.

Like engineers who apply physical principles to the design of an instrument, managers who apply theory to managing must usually blend principles with realities. A design engineer is often faced with the necessity of combining considerations of weight, size, conductivity, and other factors. Likewise, a manager may find that the advantages of giving a controller authority to prescribe accounting procedures throughout an organization outweigh the possible costs of multiple authority. But if they know theory, these managers will know that such costs as conflicting instructions and confusion may exist, and they will take steps—such as making the controller's special authority crystal clear to everyone involved—to minimize or outweigh any disadvantages.

Management Techniques

Techniques are essentially ways of doing things, methods of accomplishing a given result. In all *fields of practice* they are important. They certainly are in managing, even though few really important managerial techniques have been invented. Among them are budgeting, cost accounting, network planning and control techniques like the Program Evaluation and Review Technique (PERT) or the critical path method (CPM), rate-of-return-on-investment control, various devices of organizational development, managing by objectives, total quality management (TQM). Techniques normally reflect theory and are a means of helping managers undertake activities most effectively.

The Systems Approach to Operational Management

An organized enterprise does not, of course, exist in a vacuum. Rather, it depends on its external environment; it is a part of larger systems such as the industry to which it belongs, the economic system, and society. Thus, the enterprise receives inputs, transforms them, and exports the outputs to the environment, as shown by the very basic model in Figure 3. However, this simple model needs to be expanded and developed into a model of operational management that indicates how the various inputs are transformed through the managerial functions of planning, organizing, staffing, leading, and controlling. Clearly, any business or other organization must be described by an open-system

model that includes interactions between the enterprise and its external environment.

Inputs and Stakeholders

The inputs from the external environment may include people, capital, and managerial skills, as well as technical knowledge and skills. In addition, various groups of people make demands on the enterprise. For example, employees want higher pay, more benefits, and job security. On the other hand, consumers demand safe and reliable products at a reasonable price. Suppliers want assurance that their products will be bought. Stockholders want not only a high return on their investment but also security for their money. Federal, state, and local governments depend on taxes paid by the enterprise, but they also expect the enterprise to comply with their laws. Similarly, the community demands that enterprises be "good citizens," providing the maximum number of jobs with a minimum of pollution. Other claimants to the enterprise may include financial institutions and labor unions; even competitors have a legitimate claim for fair play. It is clear that many of these claims are incongruent, and it is the managers' job to integrate the legitimate objectives of the claimants.

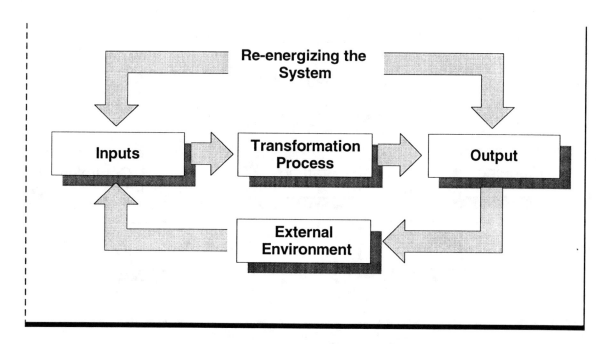

Figure 3. Input-output model.

The Managerial Transformation Process

Managers have the task of transforming inputs, effectively and efficiently, into outputs. Of course, the transformation process can be viewed from different perspectives. Thus, one can focus on such diverse enterprise functions as finance, production, personnel, and marketing. Writers on management look on the transformation process in terms of their particular approaches to management. Specifically, as you will see, writers belonging to the human behavior school focus on interpersonal relationships; social systems theorists analyze the transformation by concentrating on social interactions; and those advocating decision theory see the transformation as sets of decisions. However we believe that the most comprehensive and useful approach for discussing the job of managers is to use the managerial functions of planning, organizing, staffing, leading, and controlling as a framework for organizing managerial knowledge (see Figure 4).

The Communication System

Communication is essential to all phases of the managerial process: It integrates the managerial functions and links the enterprise with its environment. A communication system is a set of information providers and information recipients and the means of transferring information from one group to another group with the understanding that the messages being transmitted will be understood by both groups. For example, the objectives set in planning are communicated so that the appropriate organization structure can be devised. Communication is essential in the selection, appraisal, and training of managers to fill the roles in this structure. Similarly, effective leadership and the creation of an environment conducive to motivation depend on communication. Moreover, it is through communication that one determines whether events and performance conform to plans. Thus, it is communication that makes managing possible.

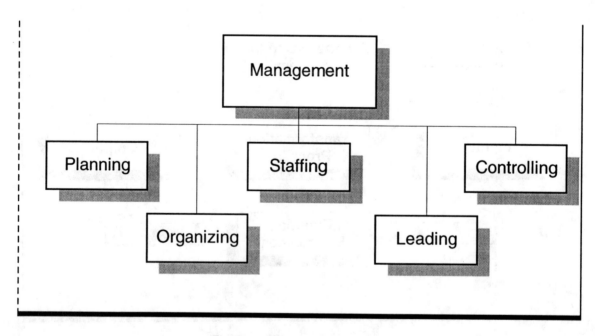

Figure 4. Management model.

The second function of the communication system is to link the enterprise with its external environment, where many of the claimants are. Effective managers will regularly scan the external environment. While it is true that managers may have little or no power to change the external environment, they have no alternative but to respond to it. For example, one should never forget that the customer, who is the reason for the existence of virtually all businesses, is outside a company. It is through the communication system that the needs of customers are identified; this knowledge enables the firm to provide products and services at a profit. Similarly, it is through an effective communication system that the organization becomes aware of competition and other potential threats and constraining factors.

Outputs

Managers must secure and utilize inputs to the enterprise, to transform them through the managerial functions—with due consideration for external variables—to produce outputs.

Although the kinds of outputs will vary with the enterprise, they usually include a combination of products, services, profits, satisfaction, and integration of the goals of various claimants to the enterprise. Most of these outputs require no elaboration, and only the last two will be discussed.

The organization must indeed provide many "satisfactions" if it hopes to retain and elicit contributions from its members. It must contribute to the satisfaction not only of basic material needs (for example, earning money to buy food and shelter or having job security) but also of needs for affiliation, acceptance, esteem, and perhaps even self-actualization.

Another output is goal integration. As noted above, the different claimants to the enterprise have very divergent—and often directly opposing—objectives. It is the task of managers to resolve conflicts and integrate these aims. This is not easy, as one former Volkswagen executive discovered. Economics dictated the construction of a Volkswagen assembly plant in the United States. However, an important claimant, German labor, out of fear that jobs would be eliminated in Germany, opposed this plan. This example illustrates the importance of integrating the goals of various claimants to the enterprise, which is indeed an essential task of any manager.

Re-energizing the System or Providing Feedback to the System

Finally, we should notice that in the systems model of operational management, some of the outputs become inputs again. Thus, the satisfaction of employees becomes an important human input to the enterprise. Similarly, profits, the surplus of income over costs, are reinvested in cash and capital goods, such as machinery, equipment, buildings, and inventory.

The Functions of Managers

Managerial functions provide a useful framework for organizing management knowledge. There have been no new ideas, research findings, or techniques that cannot readily be placed in the classifications of planning, organizing, staffing, leading, and controlling.

Planning

Planning involves selecting missions and objectives and the actions to achieve them; it requires decision making, that is, choosing future courses of action from among alternatives. There are various types of plans, ranging from overall purposes and objectives to the most detailed actions to be taken, such as to order a special stainless steel bolt for an instrument or to hire and train workers for an assembly line. No real plan exists until a decision—a commitment of human or material resources or reputation—has been made. Before a decision is made, all we have is a planning study, an analysis, or a proposal, but not a real plan.

Organizing

People working together in groups to achieve some goal must have roles to play, much like the parts actors fill in a drama, whether these roles are ones they develop themselves, are accidental or haphazard, or are defined and structured by someone who wants to make sure that people contribute in a specific way to group effort. The concept of a "role" implies that what people do has a definite purpose or objective; they know how their job objective fits into group effort, and they have the necessary authority, tools, and information to accomplish the task.

Organizing, then, is that part of managing that involves establishing an intentional structure of roles for people to fill in an organization. It is intentional in the sense of making sure that all the tasks necessary to accomplish goals are assigned and, it is hoped, assigned to people who can do them best. Imagine what would have happened if such assignments had not been made in the program of flying the special aircraft Voyager around the globe without stopping or refueling. The purpose of an organization structure is to help in creating an environment for human performance. It is, then, a management tool and not an end in and of itself. Although the structure must define the tasks to be done, the roles so established must also be designed in light of the workers' abilities and motivations.

Staffing

Staffing involves filling, and keeping filled, the positions in the organization structure. This is done by identifying workforce requirements, inventorying the people available, recruiting, selecting, placing, promoting, planning the career, compensating, and training or otherwise developing both candidates and current job holders to accomplish their tasks effectively and efficiently.

Leading

Leading is influencing people so that they will contribute to organization and group goals; it has to do predominantly with the interpersonal aspect of managing. All managers would agree that their most important problems arise from people—their desires and attitudes, their behavior as individuals and in groups— and that effective managers also need to be effective leaders. Since leadership implies followership and people tend to follow those who offer a means of satisfying their own needs, wishes, and desires, it is understandable that leading involves motivation, leadership styles and approaches, and communication.

Controlling

Controlling is the measuring and correcting of activities of subordinates, to ensure that events conform to plans. It measures performance against goals and plans, shows where negative deviations exist, and, by putting in motion actions to correct deviations, helps ensure accomplishment of plans. Although planning must precede controlling, plans are not self-achieving. The plan guides managers in the use of resources to accomplish specific goals. Then activities are checked to determine whether they conform to plans.

Control activities generally relate to the measurement of achievement. Some means of controlling, like the budget for expense, inspection records, and the record of labor hours lost, are generally familiar. Each measures and shows whether plans are working out. If deviations persist, correction is indicated. But what is corrected. Nothing can be done about reducing scrap, for example, or buying according to specifications, or handling sales returns unless one knows who is responsible for these functions. (Compelling events to conform to plans means locating the persons who are responsible for results that differ from planned action and then taking the necessary steps to improve performance. Thus, controlling what people do controls outcomes.

Coordination, the Essence of Managership

Some authorities consider coordination to be an additional function of management. It seems more accurate, however, to regard it as the essence of managership, for managing's purpose is to harmonize individual efforts in the accomplishment of group goals. Each of the managerial functions is an exercise contributing to coordination.

Even in the case of a church or a fraternal organization, individuals often interpret similar interests in different ways, and their efforts toward mutual goals do not automatically mesh with the efforts of others. It thus becomes the central task of the manager to reconcile differences in approach, timing, effort, or interest, and to harmonize individual goals to contribute to organization goals.

Summary

Management is the process of designing and maintaining an environment in which individuals, working together in groups, accomplish efficiently selected aims. Managers are charged with the responsibility of taking actions that will make it possible for individuals to make their best contributions to group objectives. Managing as practiced is an art; the organized knowledge underlying the practice may be referred to as a science. In this context science and art are not mutually exclusive but are complementary.

All managers carry out the functions of *planning, organizing, staffing, leading,* and *controlling,* although the time spent in each function will differ and the skills required by managers at different organizational levels vary. Managerial activities are common to all managers, but the practices and methods must be adapted to the particular tasks, enterprises, and situations. *The universality of management* states that managers perform the same functions regardless of their place in the organizational structure or the type of enterprise in which they are managing.

R. Alec Mackenzie

The management process in 3-D

A diagram showing the activities, functions, and basic elements of the executive's job

Foreword

To many businessmen who are trying to keep up with management concepts, the literature must sometimes seem more confusing than enlightening. In addition to reflecting differences of opinion and semantics, it generally comes to the reader in fragments. The aim of this diagram is not to give the executive new information, but to help him put the pieces together.

Mr. Mackenzie is Vice President of The Presidents Association, Inc., an organization affiliated with the American Management Association. He has had extensive experience in planning, organizing, and teaching seminars for businessmen here and abroad. He is coauthor with Ted W. Engstrom of *Managing Your Time* (Zondervan Publishing House, 1967).

The chart of "The Management Process," facing this page, begins with the three basic elements with which a manager deals: ideas, things, and people. Management of these three elements is directly related to conceptual thinking (of which planning is an essential part), administration, and leadership. Not surprisingly, two scholars have identified the first three types of managers required in organizations as the planner, the administrator, and the leader.[1]

Note the distinction between leader and manager. The terms should not be used interchangeably. While a good manager will often be a good leader, and vice versa, this is not necessarily the case. For example:

☐ In World War II, General George Patton was known for his ability to lead and inspire men on the battlefield, but not for his conceptual abilities. In contrast, General Omar Bradley was known for his conceptual abilities, especially planning and managing a campaign, rather than for his leadership.

Similarly in industry, education, and government it is possible to have an outstanding manager who is not capable of leading people but who, if he recognizes this deficiency, will staff his organization to compensate for it. Alternatively, an entrepreneur may possess charismatic qualities as a leader, yet may lack the administrative capabilities required for overall effective management; and he too must staff to make up for the deficiency.

We are not dealing here with leadership in general. We are dealing with leadership as a *function of management*. Nor are we dealing with administration in general but, again, as a function of management.

The following definitions are suggested for clarity and simplicity:

○ *Management*—achieving objectives through others.

1. See H. Igor Ansoff and R.G. Brandenburg, "The General Manager of the Future," *California Management Review*, Spring 1969, p. 61.

Exhibit I. The management process

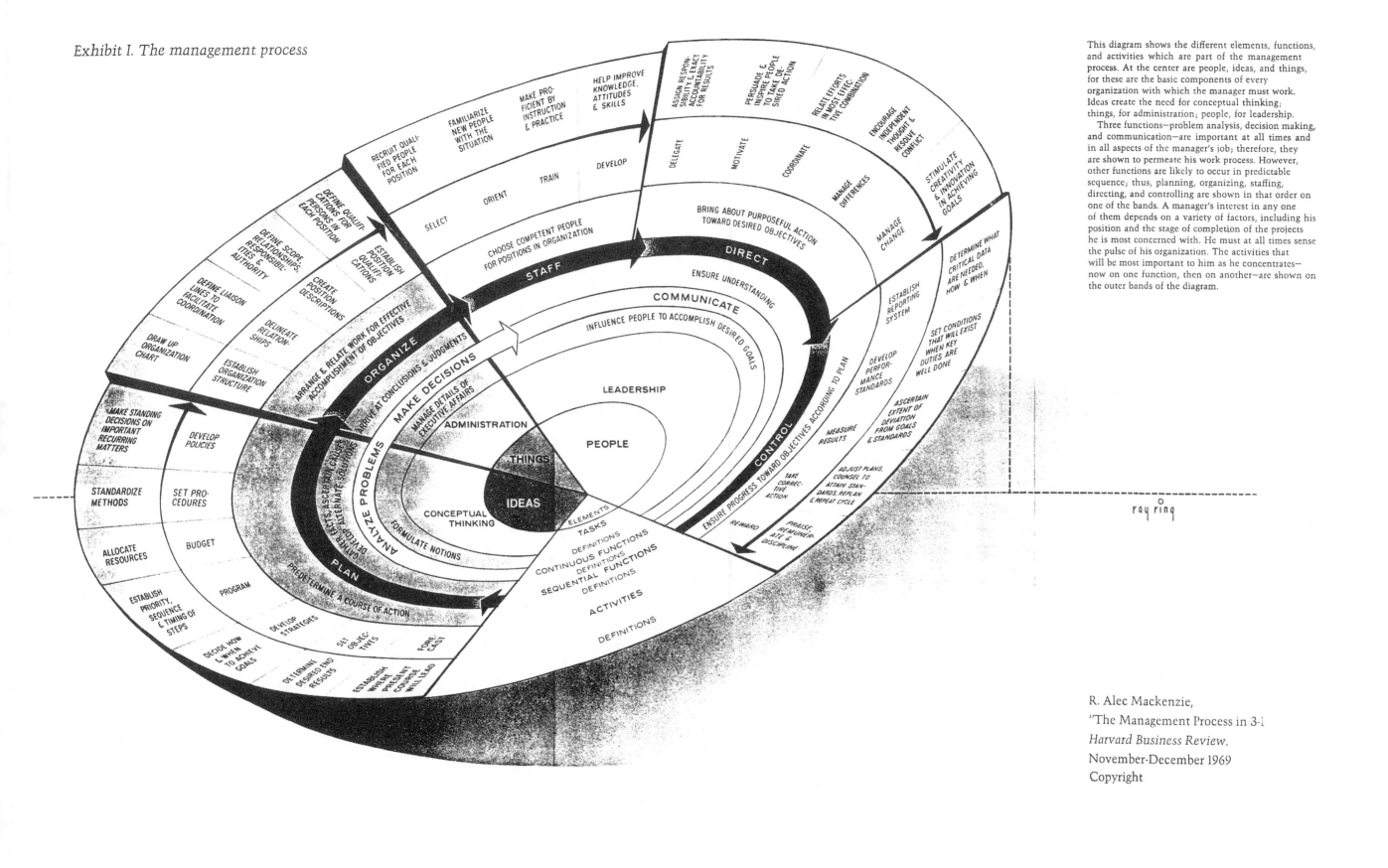

This diagram shows the different elements, functions, and activities which are part of the management process. At the center are people, ideas, and things, for these are the basic components of every organization with which the manager must work. Ideas create the need for conceptual thinking; things, for administration; people, for leadership.

Three functions—problem analysis, decision making, and communication—are important at all times and in all aspects of the manager's job; therefore, they are shown to permeate his work process. However, other functions are likely to occur in predictable sequence; thus, planning, organizing, staffing, directing, and controlling are shown in that order on one of the bands. A manager's interest in any one of them depends on a variety of factors, including his position and the stage of completion of the projects he is most concerned with. He must at all times sense the pulse of his organization. The activities that will be most important to him as he concentrates— now on one function, then on another—are shown on the outer bands of the diagram.

R. Alec Mackenzie,
"The Management Process in 3-1
Harvard Business Review,
November-December 1969
Copyright

O *Administration*—managing the details of executive affairs.

O *Leadership*—influencing people to accomplish desired objectives.

Functions described

The functions noted in the diagram have been selected after careful study of the works of many leading writers and teachers.[2] While the authorities use different terms and widely varying classifications of functions, I find that there is far more agreement among them than the variations suggest.

Arrows are placed on the diagram to indicate that five of the functions generally tend to be "sequential." More specifically, in an undertaking one ought first to ask what the purpose or objective is which gives rise to the function of *planning*; then comes the function of *organizing*—determining the way in which the work is to be broken down into manageable units; after that is *staffing*, selecting qualified people to do the work; next is *directing*, bringing about purposeful action toward desired objectives; finally, the function of *control* is the measurement of results against the plan, the rewarding of the people according to their performance, and the replanning of the work to make corrections —thus starting the cycle over again as the *process repeats itself*.

Three functions—analyzing problems, making decisions, and communicating—are called "general" or "continuous" functions because they occur throughout the management process rather than in any particular sequence. For example, many decisions will be made throughout the planning process as well as during the organiz-

2. The following studies were particularly helpful: Harold Koontz, *Toward a Unified Theory of Management* (New York, McGraw-Hill Book Company, 1964); Philip W. Shay, "The Theory and Practice of Management," Association of Consulting Management Engineers, 1967; Louis A. Allen, *The Management Profession* (New York, McGraw-Hill Book Company, 1964), a particularly useful analysis of managerial functions and activities; Ralph C. Davis, *Fundamentals of Top Management* (New York, Harper & Brothers, 1951); Harold F. Smiddy, "GE's Philosophy & Approach for Manager Development," General Management Series # 174, American Management Association, 1955; George R. Terry, *Principles of Management* (Homewood, Illinois, Richard D. Irwin, Inc., 1956); William H. Newman, *Administrative Action* (Englewood Cliffs, N.J., Prentice-Hall, Inc., 1950); Lawrence A. Appley, *Values in Management* (New York, American Management Association, 1969); Ordway Tead, *Administration: Its Purpose and Performance* (New York, Harper & Brothers, 1959); Peter F. Drucker, *The Practice of Management* (New York, Harper & Row, 1954).

ing, directing, and controlling processes. Equally, there must be communication for many of the functions and activities to be effective. And the active manager will be employing problem analysis throughout all of the sequential functions of management.

In actual practice, of course, the various functions and activities tend to merge. While selecting a top manager, for example, an executive may well be planning new activities which this manager's capabilities will make possible, and may even be visualizing the organizational impact of these plans and the controls which will be necessary.

Simplified definitions are added for each of the functions and activities to ensure understanding of what is meant by the basic elements described.

Prospective gains

Hopefully, this diagram of the management process will produce a variety of benefits for practitioners and students. Among these benefits are:

O A unified concept of managerial functions and activities.

O A way to fit together all generally accepted activities of management.

O A move toward standardization of terminology.

O The identifying and relating of such activities as problem analysis, management of change, and management of differences.

O Help to beginning students of management in seeing the "boundaries of the ballpark" and sensing the sequential relationships of certain functions and the interrelationships of others.

O Clearer distinctions between the leadership, administrative, and strategic planning functions of management.

In addition, the diagram should appeal to those who, like myself, would like to see more emphasis on the "behaviorist" functions of management, for it elevates staffing and communicating to the level of a function. Moreover, it establishes functions and activities as the two most important terms for describing the job of the manager.

Chapter 2

Software Engineering Process

1. Chapter Introduction

Software can be considered a product of engineering just like an airplane, automobile, television, or any other object that requires a high degree of skill to turn a raw material into a usable product.

Friedrich Bauer coined the term *software engineering* in 1967 at a pre-conference meeting in Germany for a NATO conference on issues in developing large-scale software systems. (For a detailed description on how it came about see the article by Bauer in the IEEE tutorial on *software engineering* [1] and forward to the *European version* [2].) Software engineering was first applied as a technology in the mid-1970s and was accepted as a job title in the late 1970s.

Today, most software positions (programmer or engineer) are advertised as "software engineers."

Software engineering can be defined as two things:

- The practical application of computer science, management, and other sciences to the analysis, design, construction, and maintenance of software and the documentation necessary to use, operate, and maintain the delivered software system

- An engineering science that applies the concept of analysis, design, coding, testing, documentation, and management to the successful completion of large, custom-built computer programs

NOW... DOES ANYBODY KNOW WHERE WE ARE GOING?

The purpose of software engineering was to introduce an engineering discipline to software development. It is applied to try to solve or reduce the problems of late deliveries, cost overruns, and failure to meet requirements that have plagued software projects since the early 1960s.

2. Chapter Overview

This chapter begins with an excellent overview of the major issues of software development written from a very commercial viewpoint (in contrast to a typical military-industrial viewpoint) in a recent edition of *Scientific American*. In addition, Peter Neumann, a "collector" of software engineering "horror" stories, lists a number of them in an article in the *Communications of the ACM*. This article is followed by a description of software engineering written by a leading software engineering author, Roger Pressman. The last article in the chapter is a description of the Software Engineering Institute's Capability Maturity Model—a device for separating good software engineering development institutions (called "mature" organizations) from inferior software engineering development organizations.

3. Article Descriptions

The first article in this chapter describes many of the major issues in developing software engineering—many issues that could be directly attributed to poor management of a software system. This article, by Wayt Gibbs, recently appeared in an issue of *Scientific American*. The article describes the software crisis, a term that had been previously reserved for major software development problems in the Department of Defense.

The Gibbs article defines and presents essentially all the major issues currently plaguing software development and software maintenance. The article is a "popular" rather than technical article in the sense that it is journalistic in style and focuses on popular perceptions of software as "black magic," but raises many issues that software professionals need to be familiar with. It is also worth noting that many of the problems described are partly or largely due to non-software issues such as politics, funding, and external constraints, yet the software professional needs to know that problems unrelated to software engineering must be overcome if software projects are to be successful.

It is not unexpected that the term "software crisis" originated with the military and/or aerospace industry, for that is where the first large, complex, usually real-time, software systems were first developed. More recently, as civilian and commercial software systems have approached and exceeded military systems in size, complexity, and performance requirements, the "software crisis" has occurred in these environments as well. It is noteworthy that the *Scientific American* article mentions military systems only peripherally.

The article begins with a discussion of the highly publicized and software-related failure of the baggage system at the new Denver International Airport. As of the date of the article, the opening date of the airport had been delayed four times, by nearly a year at a cost to the airport authority of over $1 million a day.

Nearly as visible in recent months, and also mentioned in the article, are failures of software development for the Department of Motor Vehicles (DMV) of the State of California as well as the advanced air traffic control system of the US Federal Aviation Administration (FAA). The DMV project involved attempts to merge existing, separately developed systems that managed driver's licenses and vehicle registrations in the State of California. The project was finally scrapped after several years of failed development efforts at a total loss in excess of $40 million.

As has been pointed out in the Sacramento press [3], the State of California has had problems with computer projects in excess of $1 billion in value, and which resulted from the acquisition policies of the State of California (how contractors and consultants are selected and managed by the State), hardware-software integration difficulties, and from causes strictly related to software development.

In the second article, "Software Engineering," Pressman discusses technical and management aspects of software engineering. Having surveyed existing high-level models of the software development process (linear sequential, prototyping, incremental, evolutionary, and formal), he discusses management of people, the software project, and the software process. Quality assurance and configuration management are equally as important as technical and management issues. Pressman further reviews some of the principles and methods that form the foundation of the current practice of software engineering, and concludes with a prediction that three issues—reuse, re-engineering, and a new generation of tools—will dominate software engineering for the next ten years or so.

Pressman is the author of one of our most prominent books on software engineering: *Software Engineering: A Practitioner's Approach*, McGraw-Hill, the 4th edition to be published in 1997 [4].

The third article is a description of the Software Engineering Institute's Capability Maturity Model (CMM) written by some of the original authors of the model from the Software Engineering Institute (SEI),

Pittsburgh, PA. The article is an update of a 1993 article [5] that introduced the SEI's Capability Maturity model for Software, Version 1.1, describing its rationale and contents.

This article on CMM is included because of the frequency with which it is referred to in many current articles on project management, many of which are contained in this tutorial.

The CMM, and the software engineering improvement efforts it fostered, represent perhaps the most important real change in the past 20 years in the way large-scale, critical software is developed. Until the mid-1980s, efforts to improve the quality of software products and the cost and schedule of developing the products were focused almost entirely on technology (methods and tools) and people (hiring, educating, and training). A third aspect, the process by which software is developed and maintained, was neglected. Its recognition as a factor of equal importance to the other two is largely due to the SEI.

The CMM is the result of approximately seven years of work on quantitative methods by which a software developer, or a potential customer of the developer, could determine the maturity of the developer's process. The US Department of Defense (DoD) sponsored the SEI's work; the SEI in turn convinced the DoD that process maturity should be a factor in the selection of contractors who will develop their software.

The CMM defines five levels of process maturity through which a software developer must move in order to become truly effective:

1. *Initial:* ad hoc, chaotic; process not defined and followed
2. *Repeatable:* basic software management processes in place, defined and followed at the project level
3. *Defined:* standard process defined at organization (company or division) level and tailored for use by specific projects
4. *Managed:* measurements taken and used to improve product quality
5. *Optimizing:* measurements used to improve process; error prevention

The CMM has become a driving force in the US and around the world for the improvement of software development processes. Many companies and US government agencies strive to improve their software engineering through the use of the goals and activities associated with this model. At the present time, achievement of level 3 is the goal of many development organizations, although some have achieved level 4 and a handful are reported to be at level 5.

References

1. Dorfman, M, and R.H. Thayer (eds.), *Software Engineering*, IEEE Computer Society Press, Los Alamitos, Calif., 1997.

2. Thayer, R.H. and A.D. McGettrick (eds.), *Software Engineering—An European Perspective*, IEEE Computer Society Press, Los Alamitos, Calif., 1992.

3. "State Fears a Computer Nightmare: Costly 'Screw-Ups' Found in Many Government Projects," *Sacramento Bee*, Sacramento, Calif., June 16, 1994.

4. Pressman, R.S., *Software Engineering: A Practitioner's Approach*, 4th ed., McGraw-Hill, NY, 1997.

5. Paulk, M.C., B. Curtis, M.B. Chrissis, and C.V. Weber, "Capability Maturity Model, Version 1.1," *IEEE Software*, Vol. 10, No. 4, July 1993, pp. 18–27.

Software's Chronic Crisis

by W. Wayt Gibbs, *staff writer*

Denver's new international airport was to be the pride of the Rockies, a wonder of modern engineering. Twice the size of Manhattan, 10 times the breadth of Heathrow, the airport is big enough to land three jets simultaneously—in bad weather. Even more impressive than its girth is the airport's subterranean baggage-handling system. Tearing like intelligent coal-mine cars along 21 miles of steel track, 4,000 independent "telecars" route and deliver luggage between the counters, gates and claim areas of 20 different airlines. A central nervous system of some 100 computers networked to one another and to 5,000 electric eyes, 400 radio receivers and 56 bar-code scanners orchestrates the safe and timely arrival of every valise and ski bag.

At least that is the plan. For nine months, this Gulliver has been held captive by Lilliputians—errors in the software that controls its automated baggage system. Scheduled for take-off by last Halloween, the airport's grand opening was postponed until December to allow BAE Automated Systems time to flush the gremlins out of its $193-million system. December yielded to March. March slipped to May. In June the airport's planners, their bond rating demoted to junk and their budget hemorrhaging red ink at the rate of $1.1 million a day in interest and operating costs, conceded that they could not predict when the baggage system would stabilize enough for the airport to open.

To veteran software developers, the Denver debacle is notable only for its visibility. Studies have shown that for every six new large-scale software systems that are put into operation, two others are canceled. The average software development project overshoots its schedule by half; larger projects generally do worse. And

some three quarters of all large systems are "operating failures" that either do not function as intended or are not used at all.

The art of programming has taken 50 years of continual refinement to reach this stage. By the time it reached 25, the difficulties of building big software loomed so large that in the autumn of 1968 the NATO Science Committee convened some 50 top programmers, computer scientists and captains of industry to plot a course out of what had come to be known as the software crisis. Although the experts could not contrive a road map to guide the industry toward firmer ground, they did coin a name for that distant goal: software engineering, now defined formally as "the application of a systematic, disciplined, quantifiable approach to the development, operation and maintenance of software."

A quarter of a century later software engineering remains a term of aspiration. The vast majority of computer code is still handcrafted from raw programming languages by artisans using techniques they neither measure nor are able to repeat consistently. "It's like musket making was before Eli Whitney," says Brad J. Cox, a professor at George Mason University. "Before the industrial revolution, there was a nonspecialized approach to manufacturing goods that involved very little interchangeability and a maximum of craftsmanship. If we are ever going to lick this software crisis, we're going to have to stop this hand-to-mouth, every-programmer-builds-everything-from-the-ground-up, preindustrial approach."

The picture is not entirely bleak. Intuition is slowly yielding to analysis as programmers begin using quantitative measurements of the quality of the software they produce to improve the way they produce it. The mathematical foundations of programming are solidifying as researchers work on ways of expressing program designs in algebraic forms that make it easier to avoid serious mistakes. Academic computer scientists are starting to address their failure to produce a solid corps of software professionals. Perhaps most important, many in the industry are turning their attention toward inventing the technology and market structures needed to support interchangeable, reusable software parts.

"Unfortunately, the industry does not uniformly apply that which is well-known best practice," laments Larry E. Druffel, director of Carnegie Mellon University's Software Engineering Institute. In fact, a research innovation typically requires 18 years to wend its way into the repertoire of standard programming techniques. By combining their efforts, academia, industry and government may be able to hoist software development to the level of an industrial-age engineering discipline within the decade. If they come up short, society's headlong rush into the information age will be halting and unpredictable at best.

Shifting Sands

"We will see massive changes [in computer use] over the next few years, causing the initial personal computer revolution to pale into comparative insignificance," concluded 22 leaders in software development from academia, industry and research laboratories this past April. The experts gathered at Hedsor Park, a corporate retreat near London, to commemorate the NATO conference and to analyze the future directions of software. "In 1968 we knew what we wanted to build but couldn't," reflected Cliff Jones, a professor at the University of Manchester. "Today we are standing on shifting sands."

The foundations of traditional programming practices are eroding swiftly, as hardware engineers churn out ever faster, cheaper and smaller machines. Many fundamental assumptions that programmers make—for instance, their acceptance that everything they produce will have defects—must change in response. "When computers are em-

SOFTWARE IS EXPLODING in size as society comes to rely on more powerful computer systems (*top*). That faith is often rewarded by disappointment as most large software projects overrun their schedules (*middle*) and many fail outright (*bottom*)—usually after most of the development money has been spent.

bedded in light switches, you've got to get the software right the first time because you're not going to have a chance to update it," says Mary M. Shaw, a professor at Carnegie Mellon.

"The amount of code in most consumer products is doubling every two years," notes Remi H. Bourgonjon, director of software technology at Philips Research Laboratory in Eindhoven. Already, he reports, televisions may contain up to 500 kilobytes of software; an electric shaver, two kilobytes. The power trains in new General Motors cars run 30,000 lines of computer code.

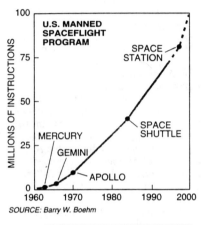

SOURCE: Barry W. Boehm

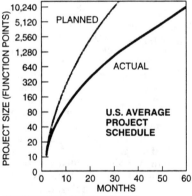

SOURCE: Software Productivity Research

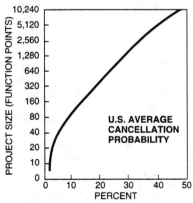

SOURCE: Software Productivity Research

Getting software right the first time is hard even for those who care to try. The Department of Defense applies rigorous—and expensive—testing standards to ensure that software on which a mission depends is reliable. Those standards were used to certify *Clementine,* a satellite that the DOD and the National Aeronautics and Space Administration directed into lunar orbit this past spring. A major part of the Clementine mission was to test targeting software that could one day be used in a space-based missile defense system. But when the satellite was spun around and instructed to fix the moon in its sights, a bug in its program caused the spacecraft instead to fire its maneuvering thrusters continuously for 11 minutes. Out of fuel and spinning wildly, the satellite could not make its rendezvous with the asteroid Geographos.

Errors in real-time systems such as *Clementine* are devilishly difficult to spot because, like that suspicious sound in your car engine, they often occur only when conditions are just so [see "The Risks of Software," by Bev Littlewood and Lorenzo Strigini; SCIENTIFIC AMERICAN, November 1992]. "It is not clear that the methods that are currently used for producing safety-critical software, such as that in nuclear reactors or in cars, will evolve and scale up adequately to match our future expectations," warned Gilles Kahn, the scientific director of France's INRIA research laboratory, at the Hedsor Park meeting. "On the contrary, for real-time systems I think we are at a fracture point."

Software is buckling as well under tectonic stresses imposed by the inexorably growing demand for "distributed systems": programs that run cooperatively on many networked computers. Businesses are pouring capital into distributed information systems that they hope to wield as strategic weapons. The inconstancy of software development can turn such projects into Russian roulette.

Many companies are lured by goals that seem simple enough. Some try to reincarnate obsolete mainframe-based software in distributed form. Others want to plug their existing systems into one another or into new systems with which they can share data and a friendlier user interface. In the technical lingo, connecting programs in this way is often called systems integration. But Brian Randell, a computer scientist at the University of Newcastle upon Tyne, suggests that "there is a better word than integration, from old R.A.F. slang: namely, 'to graunch,' which means 'to make to fit by the use of excessive force.'"

It is a risky business, for although

21

software seems like malleable stuff, most programs are actually intricate plexuses of brittle logic through which data of only the right kind may pass. Like handmade muskets, several programs may perform similar functions and yet still be unique in design. That makes software difficult to modify and repair. It also means that attempts to graunch systems together often end badly.

In 1987, for example, California's Department of Motor Vehicles decided to make its customers' lives easier by merging the state's driver and vehicle registration systems—a seemingly straightforward task. It had hoped to unveil convenient one-stop renewal kiosks last year. Instead the DMV saw the projected cost explode to 6.5 times the expected price and the delivery date recede to 1998. In December the agency pulled the plug and walked away from the seven-year, $44.3-million investment.

Sometimes nothing fails like success. In the 1970s American Airlines constructed SABRE, a virtuosic, $2-billion flight reservation system that became part of the travel industry's infrastructure. "SABRE was the shining example of a strategic information system because it drove American to being the world's largest airline," recalls Bill Curtis, a consultant to the Software Engineering Institute.

Intent on brandishing software as effectively in this decade, American tried to graunch its flight-booking technology with the hotel and car reservation systems of Marriott, Hilton and Budget. In 1992 the project collapsed into a heap of litigation. "It was a smashing failure," Curtis says. "American wrote off $165 million against that system."

The airline is hardly suffering alone. In June IBM's Consulting Group released the results of a survey of 24 leading companies that had developed large distributed systems. The numbers were unsettling: 55 percent of the projects cost more than expected, 68 percent overran their schedules and 88 percent had to be substantially redesigned.

The survey did not report one critical statistic: how reliably the completed programs ran. Often systems crash because they fail to expect the unexpected. Networks amplify this problem. "Distributed systems can consist of a great set of interconnected single points of failure, many of which you have not identified beforehand," Randell explains. "The complexity and fragility of these systems pose a major challenge."

The challenge of complexity is not only large but also growing. The bang that computers deliver per buck is doubling every 18 months or so. One result is "an order of magnitude growth in system size every decade—for some industries, every half decade," Curtis says. To keep up with such demand, programmers will have to change the way that they work. "You can't build skyscrapers using carpenters," Curtis quips.

Mayday, Mayday

When a system becomes so complex that no one manager can comprehend the entirety, traditional development processes break down. The Federal Aviation Administration (FAA) has faced this problem throughout its decade-old attempt to replace the nation's increasingly obsolete air-traffic control system [see "Aging Airways," by Gary Stix; SCIENTIFIC AMERICAN, May].

The replacement, called the Advanced Automation System (AAS), combines all the challenges of computing in the 1990s. A program that is more than a million lines in size is distributed across hundreds of computers and embedded into new and sophisticated hardware, all of which must respond around the clock to unpredictable real-time events. Even a small glitch potentially threatens public safety.

To realize its technological dream, the FAA chose IBM's Federal Systems Company, a well-respected leader in software development that has since been purchased by Loral. FAA managers expected (but did not demand) that IBM would use state-of-the-art techniques to estimate the cost and length of the project. They assumed that IBM would screen the requirements and design drawn up for the system in order to catch mistakes early, when they can be fixed in hours rather than days. And the FAA conservatively expected to pay about $500 per line of computer code, five times the industry average for well-managed development processes.

According to a report on the AAS project released in May by the Center for Naval Analysis, IBM's "cost estimation and development process tracking used inappropriate data, were performed inconsistently and were routinely ignored" by project managers. As a result, the FAA has been paying $700 to $900 per line for the AAS software. One reason for the exorbitant price is that "on average every line of code developed needs to be rewritten once," be-

moaned an internal FAA report.

Alarmed by skyrocketing costs and tests that showed the half-completed system to be unreliable, FAA administrator David R. Hinson decided in June to cancel two of the four major parts of the AAS and to scale back a third. The $144 million spent on these failed programs is but a drop next to the $1.4 billion invested in the fourth and central piece: new workstation software for air-traffic controllers.

That project is also spiraling down the drain. Now running about five years late and more than $1 billion over budget, the bug-infested program is being scoured by software experts at Carnegie Mellon and the Massachusetts Institute of Technology to determine whether it can be salvaged or must be canceled outright. The reviewers are scheduled to make their report in September.

Disaster will become an increasingly common and disruptive part of software development unless programming takes on more of the characteristics of an engineering discipline rooted firmly in science and mathematics [see box on page 92]. Fortunately, that trend has already begun. Over the past decade industry leaders have made significant progress toward understanding how to measure, consistently and quantitatively, the chaos of their development processes, the density of errors in their products and the stagnation of their programmers' productivity. Researchers are already taking the next step: finding practical, repeatable solutions to these problems.

Proceeds of Process

In 1991, for example, the Software Engineering Institute, a software think tank funded by the military, unveiled its Capability Maturity Model (CMM). "It provides a vision of software engineering and management excellence," beams David Zubrow, who leads a project on empirical methods at the institute. The CMM has at last persuaded many programmers to concentrate on measuring the process by which they produce software, a prerequisite for any industrial engineering discipline.

Using interviews, questionnaires and the CMM as a benchmark, evaluators can grade the ability of a programming team to create predictably software that meets its customers' needs. The CMM uses a five-level scale, ranging from chaos at level 1 to the paragon of good management at level 5. To date, 261 organizations have been rated.

"The vast majority—about 75 percent—are still stuck in level 1," Curtis reports. "They have no formal process, no measurements of what they do and no way of knowing when they are on the wrong track or off the track altogether." (The Center for Naval Analysis concluded that the AAS project at IBM Federal Systems "appears to be at a low 1 rating.") The remaining 24 percent of projects are at levels 2 or 3.

Only two elite groups have earned the highest CMM rating, a level 5. Motorola's Indian programming team in Bangalore holds one title. Loral's (formerly IBM's) on-board space shuttle software project claims the other. The Loral team has learned to control bugs so well that it can reliably predict how many will be found in each new version of the software. That is a remarkable feat, considering that 90 percent of American programmers do not even keep count of the mistakes they find, according to Capers Jones, chairman of Software Productivity Research. Of those who do, he says, few catch more than a third of the defects that are there.

Tom Peterson, head of Loral's shuttle software project, attributes its success to "a culture that tries to fix not just the bug but also the flaw in the testing process that allowed it to slip through." Yet some bugs inevitably escape detection. The first launch of the space shuttle in 1981 was aborted and delayed for two days because a glitch prevented the five on-board computers from synchronizing properly. Another flaw, this one in the shuttle's rendezvous program, jeopardized the *Intelsat-6* satellite rescue mission in 1992.

Although the CMM is no panacea, its promotion by the Software Engineering Institute has persuaded a number of leading software companies that quantitative quality control can pay off in the long run. Raytheon's equipment division, for example, formed a "software engineering initiative" in 1988 after flunking the CMM test. The division began pouring $1 million per year into refining rigorous inspection and testing guidelines and training its 400 programmers to follow them.

Within three years the division had jumped two levels. By this past June, most projects—including complex radar and air-traffic control systems—were finishing ahead of schedule and under budget. Productivity has more than doubled. An analysis of avoided rework costs revealed a savings of $7.80 for every dollar invested in the initiative. Impressed by such successes, the U.S. Air Force has mandated that all its software developers must reach level 3 of the CMM by 1998. NASA is reportedly considering a similar policy.

Mathematical Re-creations

Even the best-laid designs can go awry, and errors will creep in so long as humans create programs. Bugs squashed early rarely threaten a project's deadline and budget, however. Devastating mistakes are nearly always those in the initial design that slip undetected into the final product.

Mass-market software producers, because they have no single customer to please, can take a belated and brute-force approach to bug removal: they release the faulty product as a "beta" version and let hordes of users dig up the glitches. According to Charles Simonyi, a chief architect at Microsoft, the new version of the Windows operating system will be beta-tested by 20,000 volunteers. That is remarkably effective, but also expensive, inefficient and—since mass-produced PC products make up less than 10 percent of the $92.8-billion software market in the U.S.—usually impractical.

Researchers are thus formulating several strategies to attack bugs early or to avoid introducing them at all. One idea is to recognize that the problem a system is supposed to solve always changes as the system is being built. Denver's airport planners saddled BAE with $20 million worth of changes to the design of its baggage system long after construction had begun. IBM has been similarly bedeviled by the indecision of FAA managers. Both companies naively assumed that once their design was approved, they would be left in peace to build it.

Some developers are at last shedding that illusion and rethinking software as something to be grown rather than built. As a first step, programmers are increasingly stitching together quick prototypes out of standard graphic interface components. Like an architect's scale model, a system prototype can help clear up misunderstandings between customer and developer before a logical foundation is poured.

Because they mimic only the outward behavior of systems, prototypes are of little help in spotting logical inconsistencies in a system's design. "The vast majority of errors in large-scale software are errors of omission," notes Laszlo A. Belady, director of Mitsubishi Electric Research Laboratory. And models do not make it any easier to detect bugs once a design is committed to code.

When it absolutely, positively has to be right, says Martyn Thomas, chairman of Praxis, a British software company, engineers rely on mathematical analysis to predict how their designs will behave in the real world. Unfortunately, the mathematics that describes physical systems does not apply within the synthetic binary universe of a computer program; discrete mathematics, a far less mature field, governs here. But using the still limited tools of set theory and predicate calculus, computer scientists have contrived ways to translate specifications and programs into the language of mathematics, where they can be analyzed with theoretical tools called formal methods.

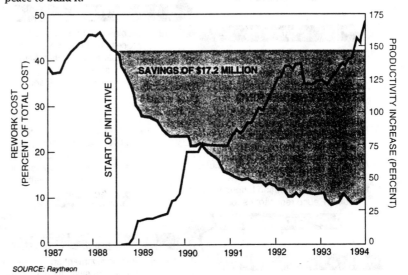

SOURCE: Raytheon

RAYTHEON HAS SAVED $17.2 million in software costs since 1988, when its equipment division began using rigorous development processes that doubled its programmers' productivity and helped them to avoid making expensive mistakes.

Progress toward Professionalism

ENGINEERING EVOLUTION PARADIGM

SCIENCE

Skilled craftsmen
Established procedure
Pragmatic refinement
Training in mechanics
Economic concern for cost
and supply of materials
Manufacture for sale

PRODUCTION

Virtuosos and talented amateurs
Design uses intuition and brute force
Haphazard progress
Knowledge transmitted slowly
and casually
Extravagant use of materials
Manufacture for use rather than
for sale

CRAFT

COMMERCIALIZATION

PROFESSIONAL ENGINEERING

Educated professionals
Analysis and theory
Progress relies on science
Analysis enables new applications
Market segmentation by product
variety

Engineering disciplines share common stages in their evolution, observes Mary M. Shaw of Carnegie Mellon University. She spies interesting parallels between software engineering and chemical engineering, two fields that aspire to exploit on an industrial scale the processes that are discovered by small-scale research.

Like software developers, chemical engineers try to design processes to create safe, pure products as cheaply and quickly as possible. Unlike most programmers, however, chemical engineers rely heavily on scientific theory, mathematical modeling, proven design solutions and rigorous quality-control methods—and their efforts usually succeed.

Software, Shaw points out, is somewhat less mature, more like a cottage industry than a professional engineering discipline. Although the demand for more sophisticated and reliable software has boosted some large-scale programming to the commercial stage, computer science (which is younger than many of its researchers) has yet to build the experimental foundation on which software engineering must rest.

CHEMICAL ENGINEERING

1774: Joseph Priestley isolates oxygen
1808: John Dalton publishes his atomic theory
1887: George E. Davis identifies functional operations
1922: Hermann Staudinger explains polymerization

1775: French Academy offers reward
for method to convert brine (salt)
to soda ash (alkali)

SCIENCE

PRODUCTION

COMMERCIALIZATION

PROFESSIONAL ENGINEERING

1915: Arthur D. Little refines and
demonstrates unit operations
1994: Du Pont operates chemical megaplants

CRAFT

1823: Nicolas Leblanc's industrial alkali
process first put into operation
1850s: Pollution of British Midlands
by alkali plants
1857: William Henry Perkin founds synthetic
dye industry

1300s: Alchemists discover alcohol
1700s: Lye boiled to make soap
Most dyes made from vegetables

SOFTWARE ENGINEERING

1956: IBM invents FORTRAN
1968: Donald E. Knuth publishes his theory of algorithms
and data structures
1972: Smalltalk object-oriented language released
1980s: Formal methods and notations refined

1970s: Structured programming methods
gain favor
1980s: Fourth-generation languages released
1990s: Reuse repositories founded

SCIENCE

PRODUCTION

COMMERCIALIZATION

PROFESSIONAL ENGINEERING

1994: Isolated examples only of
algorithms, data structures,
compiler construction

CRAFT

1980s: Most government and management
information systems use some
production controls

Some safety-critical systems (such
as in defense and transportation) use
rigorous controls

1950s: Programs are small and intuitive
1970s: SABRE airline reservation
system is rare success
1990s: Most personal computer software
is still handcrafted

Praxis recently used formal methods on an air-traffic control project for Britain's Civil Aviation Authority. Although Praxis's program was much smaller than the FAA's, the two shared a similar design problem: the need to keep redundant systems synchronized so that if one fails, another can instantly take over. "The difficult part was guaranteeing that messages are delivered in the proper order over twin networks," recalls Anthony Hall, a principal consultant to Praxis. "So here we tried to carry out proofs of our design, and they failed, because the design was wrong. The benefit of finding errors at that early stage is enormous," he adds. The system was finished on time and put into operation last October.

Praxis used formal notations on only the most critical parts of its software, but other software firms have employed mathematical rigor throughout the entire development of a system. GEC Alsthom in Paris is using a formal method called "B" as it spends $350 million to upgrade the switching- and speed-control software that guides the 6,000 electric trains in France's national railway system. By increasing the speed of the trains and reducing the distance between them, the system can save the railway company billions of dollars that might otherwise need to be spent on new lines.

Safety was an obvious concern. So GEC developers wrote the entire design and final program in formal notation and then used mathematics to prove them consistent. "Functional tests are still necessary, however, for two reasons," says Fernando Mejia, manager of the formal development section at GEC. First, programmers do occasionally make mistakes in proofs. Secondly, formal methods can guarantee only that software meets its specification, not that it can handle the surprises of the real world.

Formal methods have other problems as well. Ted Ralston, director of strategic planning for Odyssey Research Associates in Ithaca, N.Y., points out that reading pages of algebraic formulas is even more stultifying than reviewing computer code. Odyssey is just one of several companies that are trying to automate formal methods to make them less onerous to programmers. GEC is collaborating with Digilog in France to commercialize programming tools for the B method. The beta version is being tested by seven companies and institutions, including Aerospatiale, as well as France's atomic energy authority and its defense department.

On the other side of the Atlantic, formal methods by themselves have yet to catch on. "I am skeptical that Americans are sufficiently disciplined to apply formal methods in any broad fashion," says David A. Fisher of the National Institute of Standards and Technology (NIST). There are exceptions, however, most notably among the growing circle of companies experimenting with the "clean-room approach" to programming.

The clean-room process attempts to meld formal notations, correctness proofs and statistical quality control with an evolutionary approach to software development. Like the microchip manufacturing technique from which it takes its name, clean-room development tries to use rigorous engineering techniques to consistently fabricate products that run perfectly the first time. Programmers grow systems one function at a time and certify the quality of each unit before integrating it into the architecture.

Growing software requires a whole new approach to testing. Traditionally, developers test a program by running it the way they intend it to be used, which often bears scant resemblance to real-world conditions. In a clean-room process, programmers try to assign a probability to every execution path—correct and incorrect—that users can take. They then derive test cases from those statistical data, so that the most common paths are tested more thoroughly. Next the program runs through each test case and times how long it takes to fail. Those times are then fed back, in true engineering fashion, to a model that calculates how reliable the program is.

Early adopters report encouraging results. Ericsson Telecom, the European telecommunications giant, used clean-room processes on a 70-programmer project to fabricate an operating system for its telephone-switching computers. Errors were reportedly reduced to just one per 1,000 lines of program code; the industry average is about 25 times higher. Perhaps more important, the company found that development productivity increased by 70 percent, and testing productivity doubled.

No Silver Bullet

Then again, the industry has heard tell many times before of "silver bullets" supposedly able to slay werewolf projects. Since the 1960s developers have peddled dozens of technological innova-

tions intended to boost productivity—many have even presented demonstration projects to "prove" the verity of their boasts. Advocates of object-oriented analysis and programming, a buzzword du jour, claim their approach represents a paradigm shift that will deliver "a 14-to-1 improvement in productivity," along with higher quality and easier maintenance, all at reduced cost.

There are reasons to be skeptical. "In the 1970s structured programming was also touted as a paradigm shift," Curtis recalls. "So was CASE [computer-assisted software engineering]. So were third-, fourth- and fifth-generation languages. We've heard great promises for technology, many of which weren't delivered."

Meanwhile productivity in software development has lagged behind that of more mature disciplines, most notably computer hardware engineering. "I think of software as a cargo cult," Cox says. "Our main accomplishments were imported from this foreign culture of hardware engineering—faster machines and more memory." Fisher tends to agree: adjusted for inflation, "the value added per worker in the industry has been at $40,000 for two decades," he asserts. "We're not seeing any increases."

"I don't believe that," replies Richard A. DeMillo, a professor at Purdue University and head of the Software Engineering Research Consortium. "There has been improvement, but everyone uses different definitions of productivity." A recent study published by Capers Jones—but based on necessarily dubious historical data—states that U.S. programmers churn out twice as much code today as they did in 1970.

The fact of the matter is that no one really knows how productive software developers are, for three reasons. First, less than 10 percent of American companies consistently measure the productivity of their programmers.

Second, the industry has yet to settle on a useful standard unit of measurement. Most reports, including those published in peer-reviewed computer science journals, express productivity in terms of lines of code per worker per month. But programs are written in a wide variety of languages and vary enormously in the complexity of their operation. Comparing the number of lines written by a Japanese programmer using C with the number produced by an American using Ada is thus like comparing their salaries without converting from yen to dollars.

25

Third, Fisher says, "you can walk into a typical company and find two guys sharing an office, getting the same salary and having essentially the same credentials and yet find a factor of 100 difference in the number of instructions per day that they produce." Such enormous individual differences tend to swamp the much smaller effects of technology or process improvements.

After 25 years of disappointment with apparent innovations that turned out to be irreproducible or unscalable, many researchers concede that computer science needs an experimental branch to separate the general results from the accidental. "There has always been this assumption that if I give you a method, it is right just because I told you so," complains Victor R. Basili, a professor at the University of Maryland. "People are developing all kinds of things, and it's really quite frightening how bad some of them are," he says.

Mary Shaw of Carnegie Mellon points out that mature engineering fields codify proved solutions in handbooks so that even novices can consistently handle routine designs, freeing more talented practitioners for advanced projects. No such handbook yet exists for software, so mistakes are repeated on project after project, year after year.

DeMillo suggests that the government should take a more active role. "The National Science Foundation should be interested in funding research aimed at verifying experimental results that have been claimed by other people," he says. "Currently, if it's not groundbreaking, first-time-ever-done research, program officers at the NSF tend to discount the work." DeMillo knows whereof he speaks. From 1989 to 1991 he directed the NSF's computer and computation research division.

Yet "if software engineering is to be an experimental science, that means it needs laboratory science. Where the heck are the laboratories?" Basili asks. Because attempts to scale promising technologies to industrial proportions so often fail, small laboratories are of limited utility. "We need to have places where we can gather data and try things out," DeMillo says. "The only way to do that is to have a real software development organization as a partner."

There have been only a few such partnerships. Perhaps the most successful is the Software Engineering Laboratory, a consortium of NASA's Goddard Space Flight Center, Computer Sciences Corp.

and the University of Maryland. Basili helped to found the laboratory in 1976. Since then, graduate students and NASA programmers have collaborated on "well over 100 projects," Basili says, most having to do with building ground-support software for satellites.

Just Add Water

Musket makers did not get more productive until Eli Whitney figured out how to manufacture interchangeable parts that could be assembled by any skilled workman. In like manner, software parts can, if properly standardized, be reused at many different scales. Programmers have for decades used libraries of subroutines to avoid rewriting the same code over and over. But these components break down when they are moved to a different programming language, computer platform or operating environment. "The tragedy is that as hardware becomes obsolete, an excellent expression of a sorting algorithm written in the 1960s has to be rewritten," observes Simonyi of Microsoft.

Fisher sees tragedy of a different kind. "The real price we pay is that as a specialist in any software technology you cannot capture your special capability in a product. If you can't do that, you basically can't be a specialist." Not that some haven't tried. Before moving to NIST last year, Fisher founded and served as CEO of Incremental Systems. "We were truly world-class in three of the component technologies that go into compilers but were not as good in the other seven or so," he states. "But we found that there was no practical way of selling compiler components; we had to sell entire compilers."

So now he is doing something about that. In April, NIST announced that it was creating an Advanced Technology Program to help engender a market for component-based software. As head of the program, Fisher will be distributing $150 million in research grants to software companies willing to attack the technical obstacles that currently make software parts impractical.

The biggest challenge is to find ways of cutting the ties that inherently bind programs to specific computers and to other programs. Researchers are investigating several promising approaches, including a common language that could be used to describe software parts, programs that reshape components to match any environment, and components that have lots of optional features a user can turn on or off.

Fisher favors the idea that components should be synthesized on the fly. Programmers would "basically capture how to do it rather than actually doing it," producing a recipe that any computer could understand. "Then when you want to assemble two components, you would take this recipe and derive compatible versions by adding additional elements to their interfaces. The whole thing would be automated," he explains.

Even with a $150-million incentive and market pressures forcing companies to find cheaper ways of producing software, an industrial revolution in software is not imminent. "We expect to see only isolated examples of these technologies in five to seven years—and we may not succeed technically either," Fisher hedges. Even when the technology is ready, components will find few takers unless they can be made cost-effective. And the cost of software parts will depend less on the technology involved than on the kind of market that arises to produce and consume them.

Brad Cox, like Fisher, once ran a software component company and found it hard going. He believes he has figured out the problem—and its solution. Cox's firm tried to sell low-level program parts analogous to computer chips. "What's different between software ICs [integrated circuits] and silicon ICs is that silicon ICs are made of atoms, so they abide by conservation of mass, and people therefore know how to buy and sell them robustly," he says. "But this interchange process that is at the core of all commerce just does not work for things that can be copied in nanoseconds." When Cox tried selling the parts his programmers had created, he found that the price the market would bear was far too low for him to recover the costs of development.

The reasons were twofold. First, recasting the component by hand for each customer was time-consuming; NIST hopes to clear this barrier with its Advanced Technology Program. The other factor was not so much technical as cultural: buyers want to pay for a component once and make copies for free.

"The music industry has had about a century of experience with this very problem," Cox observes. "They used to sell tangible goods like piano rolls and sheet music, and then radio and television came along and knocked all that into a cocked hat." Music companies adapted to broadcasting by setting up agencies to collect royalties every time a song is aired and to funnel the money back to the artists and producers.

Cox suggests similarly charging users each time they use a software compo-

26

A Developing World

Since the invention of computers, Americans have dominated the software market. Microsoft alone produces more computer code each year than do any of 100 nations, according to Capers Jones of Software Productivity Research in Burlington, Mass. U.S. suppliers hold about 70 percent of the worldwide software market.

But as international networks sprout and large corporations deflate, India, Hungary, Russia, the Philippines and other poorer nations are discovering in software a lucrative industry that requires the one resource in which they are rich: an underemployed, well-educated labor force. American and European giants are now competing with upstart Asian development companies for contracts, and in response many are forming subsidiaries overseas. Indeed, some managers in the trade predict that software development will gradually split between Western software engineers who design systems and Eastern programmers who build them.

"In fact, it is going on already," says Laszlo A. Belady, director of Mitsubishi Electric Research Laboratory. AT&T, Hewlett-Packard, IBM, British Telecom and Texas Instruments have all set up programming teams in India. The Pact Group in Lyons, France, reportedly maintains a "software factory" in Manila. "Cadence, the U.S. supplier of VLSI design tools, has had its software development sited on the Pacific rim for several years," reports Martyn Thomas, chairman of Praxis. "ACT, a U.K.-based systems house, is using Russian programmers from the former Soviet space program," he adds.

So far India's star has risen fastest. "Offshore development [work commissioned in India by foreign companies] has begun to take off in the past 18 to 24 months," says Rajendra S. Pawar, head of New Delhi-based NIIT, which has graduated 200,000 Indians from its programming courses. Indeed, India's software exports have seen a compound annual growth of 38 percent over the past five years; last year they jumped 60 percent—four times the average growth rate worldwide.

About 58 percent of the $360-million worth of software that flowed out of India last year ended up in the U.S. That tiny drop hardly makes a splash in a $92.8-billion market. But several trends may propel exports beyond the $1-billion mark as early as 1997.

The single most important factor, Pawar asserts, is the support of the Indian government, which has eased tariffs and restrictions, subsidized numerous software technology parks and export zones, and doled out five-year tax exemptions to software exporters. "The opening of the Indian economy is acting as a very big catalyst," Pawar says.

It certainly seems to have attracted the attention of large multinational firms eager to reduce both the cost of the software they need and the amount they build in-house. The primary cost of software is labor. Indian programmers come so cheap—$125 per unit of software versus $925 for an American developer, according to Jones—that some companies fly an entire team to the U.S. to work on a project. More than half of India's software exports come from such "body shopping," although tightened U.S. visa restrictions are stanching this flow.

Another factor, Pawar observes, is a growing trust in the quality of overseas project management. "In the past two years, American companies have become far more comfortable with the offshore concept," he says. This is a result in part of success stories from leaders like Citicorp, which develops banking systems in Bombay, and Motorola, which has a top-rated team of more than 150 programmers in Bangalore building software for its Iridium satellite network.

Offshore development certainly costs less than body shopping, and not merely because of saved airfare. "Thanks to the time differences between India and the U.S., Indian software developers can act the elves and the shoemaker," working overnight on changes requested by managers the previous day, notes Richard Heeks, who studies Asian computer industries at the University of Manchester in England.

Price is not everything. Most Eastern nations are still weak in design and management skills. "The U.S. still has the best system architects in the world," boasts Bill Curtis of the Software Engineering Institute. "At large systems, nobody touches us." But when it comes to just writing program code, the American hegemony may be drawing to a close.

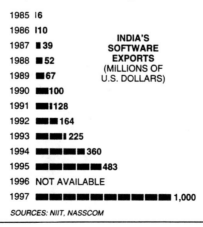

Year	India's Software Exports (Millions of U.S. Dollars)
1985	6
1986	10
1987	39
1988	52
1989	67
1990	100
1991	128
1992	164
1993	225
1994	360
1995	483
1996	NOT AVAILABLE
1997	1,000

SOURCES: NIIT, NASSCOM

nent. "In fact," he says, "that model could work for software even more easily than for music, thanks to the infrastructure advantages that computers and communications give us. Record players don't have high-speed network links in them to report usage, but our computers do."

Or will, at least. Looking ahead to the time when nearly all computers are connected, Cox envisions distributing software of all kinds via networks that link component producers, end users and financial institutions. "It's analogous to a credit-card operation but with tentacles that reach into PCs," he says. Although that may sound ominous to some, Cox argues that "the Internet now is more like a garbage dump than a farmer's market. We need a national infrastructure that can support the distribution of everything from Grandma's cookie recipe to Apple's window managers to Addison-Wesley's electronic books." Recognizing the enormity of the cultural shift he is proposing, Cox expects to press his cause for years to come through the Coalition for Electronic Markets, of which he is president.

The combination of industrial pro-cess control, advanced technological tools and interchangeable parts promises to transform not only how programming is done but also who does it. Many of the experts who convened at Hedsor Park agreed with Belady that "in the future, professional people in most fields will use programming as a tool, but they won't call themselves programmers or think of themselves as spending their time programming. They will think they are doing architecture, or traffic planning or film making."

That possibility begs the question of who is qualified to build important systems. Today anyone can bill herself as a software engineer. "But when you have 100 million user-programmers, frequently they will be doing things that are life critical—building applications that fill prescriptions, for example," notes Barry W. Boehm, director of the Center for Software Engineering at the University of Southern California. Boehm is one of an increasing number who suggest certifying software engineers, as is done in other engineering fields.

Of course, certification helps only if programmers are properly trained to begin with. Currently only 28 universities offer graduate programs in software engineering; five years ago there were just 10. None offer undergraduate degrees. Even academics such as Shaw, DeMillo and Basili agree that computer science curricula generally provide poor preparation for industrial software development. "Basic things like designing code inspections, producing user documentation and maintaining aging software are not covered in academia," Capers Jones laments.

Engineers, the infantry of every industrial revolution, do not spontaneously generate. They are trained out of the bad habits developed by the craftsmen that preceded them. Until the lessons of computer science inculcate a desire not merely to build better things but also to build things better, the best we can expect is that software development will undergo a slow, and probably painful, industrial evolution.

FURTHER READING

ENCYCLOPEDIA OF SOFTWARE ENGINEERING. Edited by John J. Marciniak. John Wiley & Sons, 1994.

SOFTWARE 2000: A VIEW OF THE FUTURE. Edited by Brian Randell, Gill Ringland and Bill Wulf. ICL and the Commission of European Communities, 1994.

FORMAL METHODS: A VIRTUAL LIBRARY. Jonathan Bowen. Available in hypertext on the World Wide Web as http://www.comlab.ox.ac.uk/archive/formal-methods.html

Peter G. Neumann

SYSTEM DEVELOPMENT WOES

inside RISKS

Addendum, March 1997: These problems are getting worse rather than better. For example, Major system development difficulties have been recently experienced in projects to modernize the air-traffic control system, the National Crime Information system (NCIC), and the Internal Revenue Service. See Peter G. Neumann, *Computer-Related Risks*, Addison-Wesley, 1995, for a broader context.

Complex computer systems are rarely developed on time, within budget, and up to spec. Here are just a few examples from the RISKS archives. We welcome more recent updates, as well as genuine success stories.

• Virginia acquired a new system for distributing child-support checks, but experienced massive delays, confusion, lost checks, delayed payments, and improper seizure of tax refunds. Operations costs were expected to be triple the original estimates. (See the *Richmond Times-Dispatch,* June 8, 1987, p. B1, from Nick Condyles in *Softw. Eng. Notes (SEN)* 12, 3.)

• Bank of America spent $23M on an initial 5-year development of MasterNet, a new computerized trust accounting and reporting system. After abandoning the old system, they spent $60M more trying to make the new system work, and finally gave up. Departed customer accounts may have exceeded billions of dollars. (See *SEN 12, 4; 13, 1; 13, 2,* contributed by Rodney Hoffman, who also contributed the following 5 items, abstracted from *Business Week,* November 7, 1988; see *SEN 14, 1.*)

• Allstate Insurance began in 1982 to build an $8M computer to automate its business, with Electronic Data Systems providing software. The supposedly 5-year effort continued until at least 1993, with a cost approaching $100M.

• Richmond, Virginia hired Arthur Young in 1984 to develop a $1.2M billing and information system for its water and gas utilities. After spending almost $1M, Richmond canceled the contract for nondelivery. A.Y. retaliated with a $2M breach-of-contract suit.

• Business Men's Assurance began a one-year project in 1985 to build a $.5M system to help minimize the risk of buying insurance policies held by major insurers. After spending $2M, the completion date was slipped to 1990.

• Oklahoma hired a major accounting firm in 1983 to design a $.5M system to handle its workers' compensation claims. Two years and more than $2M later, the system still didn't work. It was finally finished in 1987 for nearly $4M.

• Blue Cross and Blue Shield United of Wisconsin hired EDS in late 1983 to build a $200M computer system. It was delivered on time in 18 months, but didn't work, issuing $60M in overpayments and duplicate checks. By the time it was finished in 1987, Blue Cross had lost 35,000 policy holders.

• The U.S. Office of Surface Mining spent $15M on a computer system intended to prevent violators of strip-mine laws from getting new permits. The system could not keep identities straight, and the GAO called it a failure. (See *The*

Washington Times, February 15, 1989, from Joseph M. Beckman in *SEN 14,* 2.)

• Thousands of Los Angeles County homeowners were billed retroactively for up to $15,000 in additional property taxes, resulting from a 1988 glitch in an $18M computer system that was subsequently rewritten from scratch. The county was unable to collect $10M in taxes. (See the *Los Angeles Daily News,* February 25, 1991, summarized in *SEN 16,* 2.)

• The B-1 bomber required an additional $1B to improve its ineffective air-defense software, but software problems prevented it from achieving its goals.

• The software for the modernization of the Satellite Tracking Control Facility was about seven years behind schedule, about $300M over budget, and provided less capability than required.

• The Airborne Self-Protection Jammer (ASJP), an electronic air-defense system installed in over 2,000 Navy fighters and attack planes, was $1B over budget, 4 years behind schedule, and only "marginally operationally effective and marginally operationally suitable."

• General Bernard Randolph, commander of the Air Force Systems Command: "We have a perfect record on software schedules—we have never made one yet and we are always making excuses." (Gary Chapman reported in *SEN 15,* 1, on these 4 items.)

• The C-17 cargo plane being built by Douglas Aircraft had a $500M overrun because of problems in its avionics software. A GAO report noted that there were 19 on-board computers, 80 microprocessors, and six different programming languages. It stated that "The C-17 is a good example of how *not* to approach software development when procuring a major weapons system." This was noted by James Paul in *SEN 17,* 3. Also see James H. Paul and Gregory C. Simon, "Bugs in the system: Problems in federal government computer software development and regulation," U.S. Government Printing Office, Washington, D.C., September 1989. The report takes to task the waterfall model and the system and software procurement process. "Software is now the choke point in large systems... Government policies on everything from budgeting to intellectual property rights have congealed over time in a manner almost perfectly designed to thwart the development of quality software." Paul told *Science,* "The federal procurement system is like a software system with bugs. (See *SEN 15,* 1.)

Email to "risks-request @ csl.sri.com" for on-line access to RISKS issues and archives. For RISKS by fax, phone 310-455-9300 or fax 310-455-2364.

Software Engineering

Roger S. Pressman, PhD

As software engineering approaches its fourth decade, it suffers from many of the strengths and some of the frailties that are experienced by humans of the same age. The innocence and enthusiasm of its early years have been replaced by more reasonable expectations (and even a healthy cynicism) fostered by years of experience. Software engineering approaches its mid-life with many accomplishments already achieved, but with significant work yet to do.

The intent of this paper is to provide a survey of the current state of software engineering and to suggest the likely course of the aging process. Key software engineering activities are identified, issues are presented, and future directions are considered. There will be no attempt to present an indepth discussion of specific software engineering topics. That is the job of other papers presented in this book.

1.0 Software Engineering—Layered Technology[1]

Although hundreds of authors have developed personal definitions of software engineering, a definition proposed by Fritz Bauer [1] at the seminal conference on the subject still serves as a basis for discussion:

> [Software engineering is] the establishment and use of sound engineering principles in order to obtain economically software that is reliable and works efficiently on real machines.

Almost every reader will be tempted to add to this definition. It says little about the technical aspects of software quality; it does not directly address the need for customer satisfaction or timely product delivery; it omits mention of the importance of measurement and metrics; it does not state the importance of a mature process. And yet, Bauer's definition provides us with a baseline. What are the "sound engineering principles" that can be applied to computer software development? How do we "economically" build software so that it is

"reliable"? What is required to create computer programs that work "efficiently" on not one but many different "real machines"? These are the questions that continue to challenge software engineers.

Software engineering is a layered technology. Referring to Figure 1, any engineering approach (including software engineering) must rest on an organizational commitment to quality. Total quality management and similar philosophies foster a continuous process improvement culture, and it is this culture that ultimately leads to the development of increasingly more mature approaches to software engineering. The bedrock that supports software engineering is a quality focus.

The foundation for software engineering is the process layer. Software engineering process is the glue that holds the technology layers together and enables rational and timely development of computer software. Process defines a framework for a set of *key process areas* [2] that must be established for effective delivery of software engineering technology. The key process areas form the basis for management control of software projects, and establish the context in which technical methods are applied, deliverables (models, documents, data reports, forms, and so on) are produced, milestones are established, quality is ensured, and change is properly managed.

Software engineering methods provide the technical "how to's" for building software. Methods encompass a broad array of tasks that include: requirements analysis, design, program construction, testing, and maintenance. Software engineering methods rely on a set of basic principles that govern each area of the technology and include modeling activities, and other descriptive techniques.

Software engineering tools provide automated or semi-automated support for the process and the methods. When tools are integrated so that information created by one tool can be used by another, a system for the support of software development, called *computer aided software engineering* (CASE), is established. CASE combines software, hardware, and a software engineering database (a repository containing important information about analysis, design, program construction, and testing) to create a software engineering environment that is analogous to CAD/CAE (computer aided design/engineering) for hardware.

---

1 Portions of this paper have been adapted from *A Manager's Guide to Software Engineering* [19] and *Software Engineering: A Practitioner's Approach* (McGraw-Hill, 4th ed., 1997) are used with permission.

Reprinted from *Software Engineering*, M. Dorfman and R.H. Thayer, eds., 1997 pp. 57–74.
Copyright © 1997 by The Institute of Electrical and Electronics Engineers, Inc. All rights reserved.

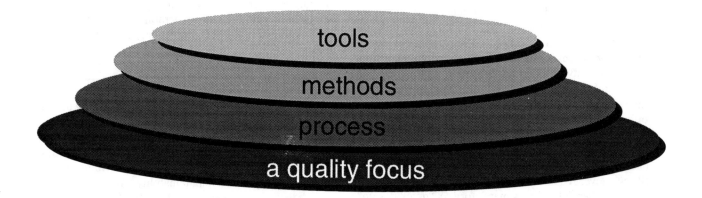

Figure 1. Software engineering layers.

2.0 Software Engineering Process Models

Software engineering incorporates a development strategy that encompasses the process, methods, and tools layers described above. This strategy is often referred to as a *process model* or a *software engineering paradigm.* A process model for software engineering is chosen based on the nature of the project and application, the methods and tools to be used, and the controls and deliverables that are required. Four classes of process models have been widely discussed (and debated). A brief overview of each is presented in the sections that follow.

2.1 Linear, Sequential Models

Figure 2 illustrates the *linear sequential* model for software engineering. Sometimes called the "classic life cycle" or the "waterfall model," the linear sequential model demands a systematic, sequential approach to software development that begins at the system level and progresses through analysis, design, coding, testing, and maintenance. The linear sequential model is the oldest and the most widely used paradigm for software engineering. However, criticism of the paradigm has caused even active supporters to question its efficacy. Among the problems that are sometimes encountered when the linear sequential model is applied are:

1. Real projects rarely follow the sequential flow that the model proposes. Although the linear model can accommodate iteration, it does so indirectly. As a result, changes can cause confusion as the project team proceeds.

2. It is often difficult for the customer to state all requirements explicitly. The linear sequential model requires this and has difficulty accommodating the natural uncertainty that exists at the beginning of many projects.

3. The customer must have patience. A working version of the program(s) will not be available until late in the project time-span. A major blunder, if undetected until the working program is reviewed, can be disastrous.

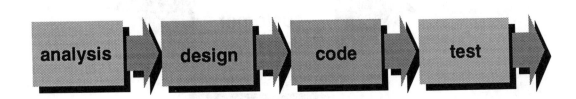

Figure 2.The linear, sequential paradigm.

2.2 Prototyping

Often, a customer defines a set of general objectives for software, but does not identify detailed input, processing, or output requirements. In other cases, the developer may be unsure of the efficiency of an algorithm, the adaptability of an operating system, or the form that human-machine interaction should take. In these, and many other situations, a *prototyping paradigm* may offer the best approach.

The prototyping paradigm (Figure 3) begins with requirements gathering. Developer and customer meet and define the overall objectives for the software, identify whatever requirements are known, and outline areas where further definition is mandatory. A "quick design" then occurs. The quick design focuses on a representation of those aspects of the software that will be visible to the customer/user (for example, input approaches and output formats). The quick design leads to the construction of a prototype. The prototype is evaluated by the customer/user and is used to refine requirements for the software to be developed. Iteration occurs as the prototype is tuned to satisfy the needs of the customer, while at the same time enabling the developer to better understand what needs to be done.

Ideally, the prototype serves as a mechanism for identifying software requirements. If a working prototype is built, the developer attempts to make use of existing program fragments or applies tools (report generators, window managers, for instance) that enable working programs to be generated quickly.

Both customers and developers like the prototyping paradigm. Users get a feel for the actual system and developers get to build something immediately. Yet, prototyping can also be problematic for the following reasons:

1. The customer sees what appears to be a working version of the software, unaware that the prototype is held together "with chewing gum and baling wire" or that in the rush to get it working we haven't considered overall software quality or long term maintainability. When informed that the product must be rebuilt, the customer cries foul and demands that "a few fixes" be applied to make the prototype a working product. Too often, software development management relents.

2. The developer often makes implementation compromises in order to get a prototype working quickly. An inappropriate operating system or programming language may be used simply because it is available and known; an inefficient algorithm may be implemented simply to demonstrate capability. After a time, the developer may become familiar with these choices and forget all the reasons why they were inappropriate. The less-than-ideal choice has now become an integral part of the system.

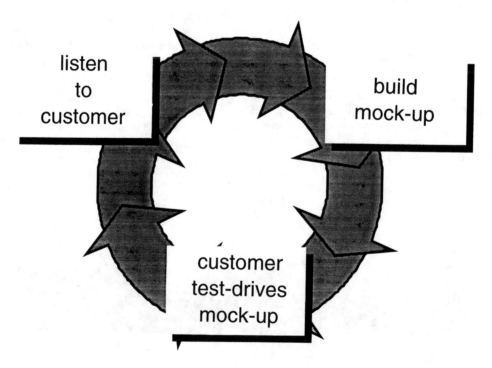

Figure 3. The prototyping paradigm.

Although problems can occur, prototyping is an effective paradigm for software engineering. The key is to define the rules of the game at the beginning; that is, the customer and developer must both agree that the prototype is built to serve as a mechanism for defining requirements. It is then discarded (at least in part) and the actual software is engineered with an eye toward quality and maintainability.

2.3 Incremental Models

Incremental development, like the prototyping approach, is used when requirements are less than certain and when other project risks (such as staffing availability or the delivery date) create potential management problems. Rather than developing a project plan that focuses on a major long term deliverable system, the incremental model defines the project as a series of increments. Each increment produces a deliverable 'product.'

When an incremental model is used, the first increment is often a *core product*. That is, basic requirements are addressed, but many supplementary features (some known, others unknown) remain undelivered. The core product is used by the customer (or undergoes detailed review). As a result of use and/or evaluation, a plan is developed for the next increment. The plan addresses the modification of the core product to better meet the needs of the customer and the delivery of additional features and functionality. This process is repeated following the delivery of each increment, until the complete product is produced.

The incremental process model, like prototyping (Section 2.2) and evolutionary approaches (Section 2.4), is iterative in nature. However, the incremental model focuses on the delivery of an operational product with each increment. Early increments are 'stripped down' versions of the final product, but they do provide capability that serves the user and also provide a platform for evaluation by the user.

Incremental development is particularly useful when staffing is unavailable for a complete implementation by the business deadline that has been established for the project. Early increments can be implemented with fewer people. If the core product is well received, then additional staff (if required) can be added to implement the next increment. In addition, increments can be planned to manage technical risks. For example, a major system might require the availability of new hardware that is under development and whose delivery date is uncertain. It might be possible to plan early increments in a way that avoids the use of this hardware, thereby enabling partial functionality to be delivered to end-users without inordinate delay.

2.4 Evolutionary Models

The *evolutionary paradigm,* also called the *spiral model* [3] couples the iterative nature of prototyping with the controlled and systematic aspects of the linear model. Using the evolutionary paradigm, software is developed in a series of incremental releases. During early iterations, the incremental release might be a prototype. During later iterations, increasingly more complete versions of the engineered system are produced.

Figure 4 depicts a typical evolutionary model. Each pass around the spiral moves through six task regions:

- **customer communication**—tasks required to establish effective communication between developer and customer

- **planning**—tasks required to define resources, timelines and other project related information

- **risk assessment**—tasks required to assess both technical and management risks

- **engineering**—tasks required to build one or more representations of the application

- **construction and release**—tasks required to construct, test, install and provide user support (for example, documentation and training)

- **customer evaluation**—tasks required to obtain customer feedback based on evaluation of the software representations created during the engineering stage and implemented during the installation stage.

Each region is populated by a series of tasks that are adapted to the characteristics of the project to be undertaken.

The spiral model is a realistic approach to the development of large scale systems and software. It uses an "evolutionary" approach [4] to software engineering, enabling the developer and customer to understand and react to risks at each evolutionary level. It uses prototyping as a risk reduction mechanism, but more importantly, enables the developer to apply the prototyping approach at any stage in the evolution of the product. It maintains the systematic stepwise approach suggested by the classic life cycle, but incorporates it into an iterative framework that more realistically reflects the real world. The spiral model demands a direct consideration of technical risks at all stages of the project, and if properly applied, should reduce risks before they become problematic.

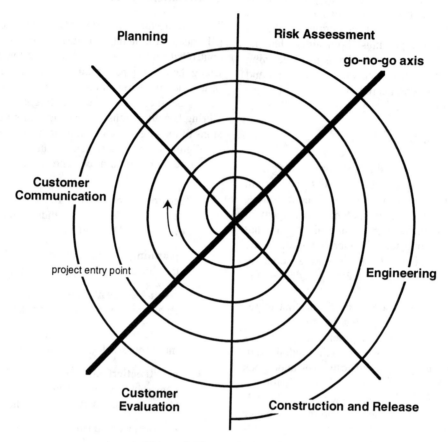

Figure 4. The evolutionary model.

But like other paradigms, the spiral model is not a panacea. It may be difficult to convince customers (particularly in contract situations) that the evolutionary approach is controllable. It demands considerable risk assessment expertise, and relies on this expertise for success. If a major risk is not discovered, problems will undoubtedly occur. Finally, the model itself is relatively new and has not been used as widely as the linear sequential or prototyping paradigms. It will take a number of years before efficacy of this important new paradigm can be determined with absolute certainty.

2.5 The Formal Methods Model

The formal methods paradigm encompasses a set of activities that leads to formal mathematical specification of computer software. Formal methods enable a software engineer to specify, develop, and verify a computer-based system by applying a rigorous, mathematical notation. A variation on this approach, called *cleanroom engineering* [5, 6], is currently applied by a limited number of companies.

When formal methods are used during development,

they provide a mechanism for eliminating many of the problems that are difficult to overcome using other software engineering paradigms. Ambiguity, incompleteness, and inconsistency can be discovered and corrected more easily—not through ad hoc review, but through the application of mathematical analysis. When formal methods are used during design, they serve as a basis for program verification and therefore enable the software engineer to discover and correct errors that might otherwise go undetected.

Although not yet a mainstream approach, the formal methods model offers the promise of defect-free software. Yet, concern about its applicability in a business environment has been voiced:

1. The development of formal models is currently quite time-consuming and expensive.

2. Because few software developers have the necessary background to apply formal methods, extensive training is required.

3. It is difficult to use the models as a communication mechanism for technically unsophisticated customers.

These concerns notwithstanding, it is likely that the formal methods approach will gain adherents among software developers that must build safety-critical software (such as developers of aircraft avionics and medical devices) and among developers that would suffer severe economic hardship should software errors occur.

3.0 The Management Spectrum

Effective software project management focuses on the three P's: *people, problem,* and *process.* The order is not arbitrary. The manager who forgets that software engineering work is an intensely human endeavor will never have success in project management. A manager who fails to encourage comprehensive customer communication early in the evolution of a project risks building an elegant solution for the wrong problem. Finally, the manager who pays little attention to the process runs the risk of inserting competent technical methods and tools into a vacuum.

3.1 People

The cultivation of motivated, highly skilled software people has been discussed since the 1960s [see 7, 8, 9]. The Software Engineering Institute has sponsored a *people management maturity model* "to enhance the readiness of software organizations to undertake increasingly complex applications by helping to attract, grow, motivate, deploy, and retain the talent needed to improve their software development capability." [10]

The people management maturity model defines the following key practice areas for software people: recruiting, selection, performance management, training, compensation, career development, organization, and team and culture development. Organizations that achieve high levels of maturity in the people management area have a higher likelihood of implementing effective software engineering practices.

3.2 The Problem

Before a project can be planned, objectives and scope should be established, alternative solutions should be considered, and technical and management constraints should be identified. Without this information, it is impossible to develop reasonable estimates of the cost, a realistic breakdown of project tasks, or a manageable project schedule that provides a meaningful indication of progress.

The software developer and customer must meet to define project objectives and scope. In many cases, this activity occurs as part of structured customer communication process such as *joint application design* [11, 12]. Joint application design (JAD) is an activity that occurs

in five phases: project definition, research, preparation, the JAD meeting, and document preparation. The intent of each phase is to develop information that helps better define the problem to be solved or the product to be built.

3.3 The Process

A software process (see discussion of process models in Section 2.0) can be characterized as shown in Figure 5. A few *framework activities* apply to all software projects, regardless of their size or complexity. A number of *task sets*—tasks, milestones, deliverables, and quality assurance points—enable the framework activities to be adapted to the characteristics of the software project and the requirements of the project team. Finally, umbrella activities—such as software quality assurance, software configuration management, and measurement—overlay the process model. Umbrella activities are independent of any one framework activity and occur throughout the process.

In recent years, there has been a significant emphasis on process "maturity." [2] The Software Engineering Institute (SEI) has developed a comprehensive assessment model that is predicated on a set of software engineering capabilities that should be present as organizations reach different levels of process maturity. To determine an organization's current state of process maturity, the SEI uses an assessment questionnaire and a five-point grading scheme. The grading scheme determines compliance with a *capability maturity model* [2] that defines key activities required at different levels of process maturity. The SEI approach provides a measure of the global effectiveness of a company's software engineering practices and establishes five process maturity levels that are defined in the following manner:

Level 1: Initial—The software process is characterized as ad hoc, and occasionally even chaotic. Few processes are defined, and success depends on individual effort.

Level 2: Repeatable—Basic project management processes are established to track cost, schedule, and functionality. The necessary process discipline is in place to repeat earlier successes on projects with similar applications.

Level 3: Defined—The software process for both management and engineering activities is documented, standardized and integrated into an organization-wide software process. All projects use a documented and approved version of the organization's process for developing and maintaining software. This level includes all characteristics defined for level 2.

35

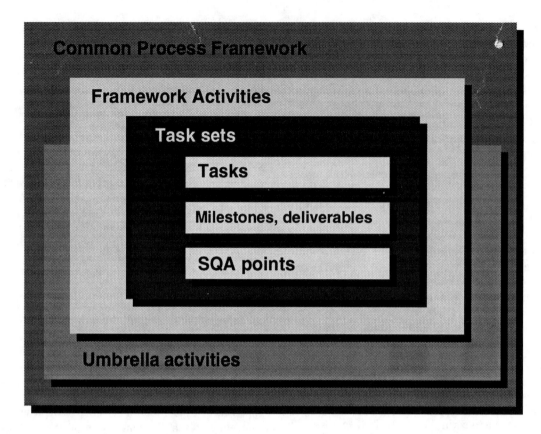

Figure 5. A common process framework.

Level 4: Managed—Detailed measures of the software process and product quality are collected. Both the software process and products are quantitatively understood and controlled using detailed measures. This level includes all characteristics defined for level 3.

Level 5: Optimizing—Continuous process improvement is enabled by quantitative feedback from the process and from testing innovative ideas and technologies. This level includes all characteristics defined for level 4.

The five levels defined by the SEI are derived as a consequence of evaluating responses to the SEI assessment questionnaire that is based on the CMM. The results of the questionnaire are distilled to a single numerical grade that provides an indication of an organization's process maturity.

The SEI has associated *key process areas* (KPAs) with each of the maturity levels. The KPAs describe those software engineering functions (for example, software project planning and requirements manage-

ment) that must be present to satisfy good practice at a particular level. Each KPA is described by identifying the following characteristics:

- *goals*—the overall objectives that the KPA must achieve

- *commitments*—requirements (imposed on the organization) that must be met to achieve the goals, provide proof of intent to comply with the goals

- *abilities*—those things that must be in place (organizationally and technically) that will enable the organization to meet the commitments

- *activities*—the specific tasks that are required to achieve the KPA function

- *methods for monitoring implementation*—the manner in which the activities are monitored as they are put into place

- *methods for verifying implementation*—the manner in which proper practice for the KPA can be verified.

36

Eighteen KPAs (each defined using the structure noted above) are defined across the maturity model and are mapped into different levels of process maturity.

Each KPA is defined by a set of *key practices* that contribute to satisfying its goals. The key practices are policies, procedures, and activities that must occur before a key process area has been fully instituted. The SEI defines *key indicators* as "those key practices or components of key practices that offer the greatest insight into whether the goals of a key process area have been achieved." Assessment questions are designed to probe for the existence (or lack thereof) of a key indicator.

4.0 Software Project Management

Software project management encompasses the following activities: measurement, project estimating, risk analysis, scheduling, tracking, and control. A comprehensive discussion of these topics is beyond the scope of this paper, but a brief overview of each topic will enable the reader to understand the breadth of management activities required for a mature software engineering organizations.

4.1 Measurement and Metrics

To be most effective, software metrics should be collected for both the process and the product. Process-oriented metrics [14, 15] can be collected during the process and after it has been completed. Process metrics collected during the process focus on the efficacy of quality assurance activities, change management, and project management. Process metrics collected after a project has been completed examine quality and productivity. Process measures are normalized using either lines of code or function points [13], so that data collected from many different projects can be compared and analyzed in a consistent manner. Product metrics measure technical characteristics of the software that provide an indication of software quality [15, 16, 17, 18]. Measures can be applied to models created during analysis and design activities, the source code, and testing data. The mechanics of measurement and the specific measures to be collected are beyond the scope of this paper.

4.2 Project Estimating

Scheduling and budgets are often dictated by business issues. The role of estimating within the software process often serves as a "sanity check" on the predefined deadlines and budgets that have been established by management. (Ideally, the software engineering organization should be intimately involved in establishing deadlines and budgets, but this is not a perfect or fair world.)

All software project estimation techniques require that the project have a bounded scope, and all rely on a high level functional decomposition of the project and an assessment of project difficulty and complexity. There are three broad classes of estimation techniques [19] for software projects:

- **Effort estimation techniques.** The project manager creates a matrix in which the left hand column contains a list of major system functions derived using functional decomposition applied to project scope. The top row contains a list of major software engineering tasks derived from the common process framework. The manager (with the assistance of technical staff) estimates the effort required to accomplish each task for each function.

- **Size-Oriented Estimation.** A list of major system functions derived using functional decomposition applied to project scope. The "size" of each function is estimated using either lines of code (LOC) or function points (FP). Average productivity data (for instance, function points per person month) for similar functions or projects are used to generate an estimate of effort required for each function.

- **Empirical Models.** Using the results of a large population of past projects, an empirical model that relates product size (in LOC or FP) to effort is developed using a statistical technique such as regression analysis. The product size for the work to be done is estimated and the empirical model is used to generate projected effort (for example, [20]).

In addition to the above techniques, a software project manager can develop estimates by analogy. That is, by examining similar past projects and projecting effort and duration recorded for these projects to the current situation.

4.3 Risk Analysis

Almost five centuries have passed since Machiavelli said: "I think it may be true that fortune is the ruler of half our actions, but that she allows the other half to be governed by us ... [fortune] is like an impetuous river ... but men can make provision against it by dykes and banks." Fortune (we call it risk) is in the back of every software project manager's mind, and that is often where it stays. And as a result, risk is never adequately addressed. When bad things happen, the manager and the project team are unprepared.

In order to "make provision against it," a software project team must conduct risk analysis explicitly. Risk analysis [21, 22, 23] is actually a series of steps that enable the software team to perform risk identification, risk assessment, risk prioritization, and risk management. The goals of these activities are: (1) to identify those risks that have a high likelihood of occurrence, (2) to assess the consequence (impact) of each risk should it occur, and (3) to develop a plan for mitigating the risks when possible, monitoring factors that may indicate their arrival, and developing a set of contingency plans should they occur.

4.4 Scheduling

The process definition and project management activities that have been discussed above feed the scheduling activity. The common process framework provides a work breakdown structure for scheduling. Available human resources, coupled with effort estimates and risk analysis provide the task interdependencies, parallelism, and time lines that are used in constructing a project schedule.

4.5 Tracking and Control

Project tracking and control is most effective when it becomes an integral part of software engineering work. A well-defined process framework should provide a set of milestones that can be used for project tracking. Control focuses on two major issues: quality and change.

To control quality, a software project team must establish effective techniques for software quality assurance, and to control change, the team should establish a software configuration management framework.

5.0 Software Quality Assurance

In his landmark book on quality, Philip Crosby [24] states:

> The problem of quality management is not what people don't know about it. The problem is what they think they do know ...
>
> In this regard, quality has much in common with sex. Everybody is for it. (Under certain conditions, of course.) Everyone feels they understand it. (Even though they wouldn't want to explain it.) Everyone thinks execution is only a matter of following natural inclinations. (After all, we do get along somehow.) And, of course, most people feel that problems in these areas are caused by other people. (If only *they* would take the time to do things right.)

There have been many definitions of software quality proposed in the literature. For our purposes, software quality is defined as: *Conformance to explicitly stated functional and performance requirements, explicitly documented development standards, and implicit characteristics that are expected of all professionally developed software.*

There is little question that the above definition could be modified or extended. If fact, a definitive definition of software quality could be debated endlessly. But the definition stated above does serve to emphasize three important points:

1. Software requirements are the foundation from which *quality* is assessed. Lack of conformance to requirements is lack of quality.

2. A mature software process model defines a set of development criteria that guide the manner in which software is engineered. If the criteria are not followed, lack of quality will almost surely result.

3. There is a set of *implicit requirements* that often goes unmentioned (for example, the desire for good maintainability). If software conforms to its explicit requirements, but fails to meet implicit requirements, software quality is suspect.

Almost two decades ago, McCall and Cavano [25, 26] defined a set of quality factors that were a first step toward the development of metrics for software quality. These factors assessed software from three distinct points of view: (1) product operation (using it); (2) product revision (changing it), and (3) product transition (modifying it to work in a different environment, that is, "porting" it). These factors include:

- *Correctness.* The extent to which a program satisfies its specification and fulfills the customer's mission objectives.

- *Reliability.* The extent to which a program can be expected to perform its intended function with required precision.

- *Efficiency.* The amount of computing resources and code required by a program to perform its function.

- *Integrity.* Extent to which access to software or data by unauthorized persons can be controlled.

- *Usability.* Effort require to learn, operate, prepare input and interpret output of a program.

- *Maintainability.* Effort require to locate and fix

an error in a program. [Might be better termed "correctability".]

- *Flexibility.* Effort required to modify an operational program.

- *Testability.* Effort required to test a program to insure that it performs its intended function.

- *Portability.* Effort required to transfer the program from one hardware and/or software system environment to another.

- *Reusability.* Extent to which a program [or parts of a program] can be reused in other applications—related to the packaging and scope of the functions that the program performs.

- *Interoperability.* Effort required to couple one system to another.

The intriguing thing about these factors is how little they have changed in almost 20 years. Computing technology and program architectures have undergone a sea change, but the characteristics that define high quality software appear to be invariant. The implication: an organization that adopts factors such as those described above will build software today that will exhibit high quality well into the first few decades of the 21st century. More importantly, this will occur regardless of the massive changes in computing technologies that are sure to come over that period of time.

Software quality is designed into a product or system. It is not imposed after the fact. For this reason, *software quality assurance* (SQA) actually begins with the set of *technical methods and tools* that help the analyst to achieve a high quality specification and the designer to develop a high quality design.

Once a specification (or prototype) and design have been created, each must be assessed for quality. The central activity that accomplishes quality assessment is the *formal technical review.* The formal technical review (FTR)—conducted as a *walkthrough* or an *inspection* [27]—is a stylized meeting conducted by technical staff with the sole purpose of uncovering quality problems. In many situations, formal technical reviews have been found to be as effective as testing in uncovering defects in software [28].

Software testing combines a multistep strategy with a series of test case design methods that help ensure effective error detection. Many software developers use software testing as a quality assurance "safety net." That is, developers assume that thorough testing will uncover most errors, thereby mitigating the need for other SQA activities. Unfortunately, testing, even when performed well, is not as effective as we might like for all classes of errors. A much better strategy is to find and correct errors (using FTRs) before getting to testing.

The degree to which formal *standards and proce-* *dures* are applied to the software engineering process varies from company to company. In many cases, standards are dictated by customers or regulatory mandate. In other situations standards are self-imposed. An assessment of compliance to standards may be conducted by software developers as part of a formal technical review, or in situations where independent verification of compliance is required, the SQA group may conduct its own *audit*.

A major threat to software quality comes from a seemingly benign source: *changes.* Every change to software has the potential for introducing error or creating side effects that propagate errors. The *change control* process contributes directly to software quality by formalizing requests for change, evaluating the nature of change, and controlling the impact of change. Change control is applied during software development and later, during the software maintenance phase.

Measurement is an activity that is integral to any engineering discipline. An important object of SQA is to track software quality and assess the impact of methodological and procedural changes on improved software quality. To accomplish this, *software metrics* must be collected.

Record keeping and recording for software quality assurance provide procedures for the collection and dissemination of SQA information. The results of reviews, audits, change control, testing, and other SQA activities must become part of the historical record for a project and should be disseminated to development staff on a need-to-know basis. For example, the results of each formal technical review for a procedural design are recorded and can be placed in a "folder" that contains all technical and SQA information about a module.

6.0 Software Configuration Management

Change is inevitable when computer software is built. And change increases the level of confusion among software engineers who are working on a project. Confusion arises when changes are not analyzed before they are made, recorded before they are implemented, reported to those who should be aware that they have occurred, or controlled in a manner that will improve quality and reduce error. Babich [29] discusses this when he states:

> The art of coordinating software development to minimize ... confusion is called *configuration management.* Configuration management is the art of identifying, organizing, and controlling modifications to the software being built by a programming team. The goal

is to maximize productivity by minimizing mistakes.

Software configuration management (SCM) is an umbrella activity that is applied throughout the software engineering process. Because change can occur at any time, SCM activities are developed to (1) identify change, (2) control change, (3) ensure that change is being properly implemented and (4) report change to others who may have an interest.

A primary goal of software engineering is to improve the ease with which changes can be accommodated and reduce the amount of effort expended when changes must be made.

7.0 The Technical Spectrum

There was a time—some people still call it "the good old days"—when a skilled programmer created a program like an artist creates a painting: she just sat down and started. Pressman and Herron [30] draw other parallels when they write:

> At one time or another, almost everyone laments the passing of the good old days. We miss the simplicity, the personal touch, the emphasis on quality that were the trademarks of a craft. Carpenters reminisce about the days when houses were built with mahogany and oak, and beams were set without nails. Engineers still talk about an earlier era when one person did all the design (and did it right) and then went down to the shop floor and built the thing. In those days, people did good work and stood behind it.
>
> How far back do we have to travel to reach the good old days? Both carpentry and engineering have a history that is well over 2,000 years old. The disciplined way in which work is conducted, the standards that guide each task, the step by step approach that is applied, have all evolved through centuries of experience. *Software engineering* has a much shorter history.

During its short history, the creation of computer programs has evolved from an art form, to a craft, to an engineering discipline. As the evolution took place, the free form style of the artist was replaced by the disciplined methods of an engineer. To be honest, we lose something when a transition like this is made. There's a certain freedom in art that can't be replicated in engineering. But we gain much, much more than we lose.

As the journey from art to engineering occurred, basic principles that guided our approach to software problem analysis, design, and testing slowly evolved. And at the same time, methods were developed that embodied these principles and made software engineering tasks more systematic. Some of these "hot, new" methods flashed to the surface for a few years, only to disappear into oblivion, but others have stood the test of time to become part of the technology of software development.

In this section we discuss the basic principles that support the software engineering methods and provide an overview of some of the methods have already "stood the test of time" and others that are likely to do so.

7.1 Software Engineering Methods—The Landscape

All engineering disciplines encompass four major activities: (1) the definition of the problem to be solved, (2) the design of a solution that will meet the customer's needs; (3) the construction of solution, and (4) the testing of the implemented solution to uncover latent errors and provide an indication that customer requirements have been achieved. Software engineering offers a variety of different methods to achieve these activities. In fact, the methods landscape can be partitioned into three different regions:

- conventional software engineering methods
- object-oriented approaches
- formal methods

Each of these regions is populated by a variety of methods that have spawned their own culture, not to mention a sometimes confusing array of notation and heuristics. Luckily, all of the regions are unified by a set of overriding principles that lead to a single objective: to create high quality computer software.

Conventional software engineering methods view software as an information transform and approach each problem using a input-process-output viewpoint. Object-oriented approaches consider each problem as a set of classes and work to create a solution by implementing a set of communicating objects that are instantiated from these classes. Formal methods describe the problem in mathematical terms, enabling rigorous evaluation of completeness, consistency, and correctness.

Like competing geographical regions on the world map, the regions of the software engineering methods map do not always exist peacefully. Some inhabitants of a particular region cannot resist religious warfare.

Like most religious warriors, they become consumed by dogma and often do more harm that good.

The regions of the software engineering methods landscape can and should exist peacefully, and tedious debates over which method is best seem to miss the point. Any method, if properly applied within the context of a solid set of software engineering principles, will lead to higher quality software than an undisciplined approach.

7.2 Problem Definition

A problem cannot be fully defined and bounded until it is communicated. For this reason, the first step in any software engineering project is customer communication. Techniques for customer communication [11, 12] were discussed earlier in this paper. In essence, the developer and the customer must develop an effective mechanism for defining and negotiating the basic requirements for the software project. Once this has been accomplished, requirements analysis begins. Two options are available at this stage: (1) the creation of a prototype that will assist the developer and the customer in better understanding the system to be build, and/or (2) the creation of a detailed set of analysis models that describe the data, function and behavior for the system.

7.2.1 Analysis Principles

Today, analysis modeling can be accomplished by applying one of a number of different methods that populate the three regions of the software engineering methods landscape. Yet all methods conform to a set of analysis principles [31]:

1. **The data domain of the problem must be modeled.** To accomplish this, the analyst must define the data objects (entities) that are visible to the user of the software and the relationships that exist between the data objects. The content of each data object (the objects attributes) must also be defined.

2. **The functional domain of the problem must be modeled.** Software functions transform the data objects of the system and can be modeled as a hierarchy (conventional methods), as services to classes within a system (the object-oriented view), or as a succinct set of mathematical expressions (the formal view).

3. **The behavior of the system must be represented.** All computer-based systems respond to external events and change their state of operation as a consequence. Behavioral modeling indicates the externally observable states of operation of a system and how transition occurs between these states.

4. **Models of data, function, and behavior must be partitioned.** All engineering problem solving is a process of elaboration. The problem (and the models described above) are first represented at a high level of abstraction. As problem definition progresses, detail is refined and the level of abstraction is reduced. This activity is called partitioning.

5. **The overriding trend in analysis is from essence toward implementation.** As the process of elaboration progresses, the statement of the problem moves from a representation of the essence of the solution toward implementation-specific detail. This progression leads us from analysis toward design.

7.2.2 Analysis Methods

A discussion of the notation and heuristics of even the most popular analysis methods is beyond the scope of this paper. The problem is further compounded by the three different regions of the methods landscape and the local issues that are specific to each. Therefore, all that we can hope to accomplish in this section is to note similarities among the different methods and regions:

- All analysis methods provide a notation for describing data objects and the relationships that exist between them.

- All analysis methods couple function and data and provide a way for understanding how function operates on data.

- All analysis methods enable an analyst to represent behavior at a system level, and in some cases, at a more localized level.

- All analysis methods support a partitioning approach that leads to increasingly more detailed (and implementation specific models).

- All analysis methods establish a foundation from which design begins, and some provide representations that can be directly mapped into design.

For further information on analysis methods in each of the three regions noted above, the reader should review work by Yourdon [32], Booch [33], and Spivey [34].

7.3 Design

M.A. Jackson [35] once said: "The beginning of wisdom for a computer programmer [software engineer] is to recognize the difference between getting a program to work, and getting it *right*." Software design is a set of basic principles and a pyramid of modeling methods that provide the necessary framework for "getting it right."

7.3.1 Design Principles

Like analysis modeling, software design has spawned a collection of methods that populate the conventional, object-oriented, and formal regions that were discussed earlier. Each method espouses its own notation and heuristics for accomplishing design, but all rely on a set of fundamental principles [31] that are outlined in the paragraphs that follow:

1. **Data and the algorithms that manipulate data should be created as a set of interrelated abstractions.** By creating data and procedural abstractions, the designer models software components that have characteristics that lead to high quality. An abstraction is self contained; it generally implements one well constrained data structure or algorithm; it can be accessed using a simple interface; the details of its internal operation need not be known for it to be used effectively; it is inherently reusable.

2. **The internal design detail of data structures and algorithms should be hidden from other software components that make use of the data structures and algorithms.** Information hiding [36] suggests that modules be "characterized by design decisions that (each) hides from all others." Hiding implies that effective modularity can be achieved by defining a set of independent modules that communicate with one another only that information that is necessary to achieve software function. The use of information hiding as a design criterion for modular systems provides greatest benefits when modifications are required during testing and later, during software maintenance. Because most data and procedures are hidden from other parts of the software, inadvertent errors (and resultant side effects) introduced during modification are less likely to propagate to other locations within the software.

3. **Modules should exhibit independence.** That is, they should be loosely coupled to each other and to the external environment and should exhibit functional cohesion. Software with *effective modularity,* that is, independent modules, is easier to develop because function may be compartmentalized and interfaces are simplified (consider ramifications when development is conducted by a team). Independent modules are easier to maintain (and test) because: secondary effects caused by design/code modification are limited; error propagation is reduced; reusable modules are possible.

4. **Algorithms should be designed using a constrained set of logical constructs.** This design approach, widely know as structured programming [37], was proposed to limit the procedural design of software to a small number of predictable operations. The use of the structured programming constructs (sequence, conditional, and loops) reduces program complexity and thereby enhances readability, testability and maintainability. The use of a limited number of logical constructs also contributes to a human understanding process that psychologists call chunking. To understand this process, consider the way in which you are reading this page. You do not read individual letters; but rather, recognize patterns or chunks of letters that form words or phrases. The structured constructs are logical chunks that allow a reader to recognize procedural elements of a module, rather than reading the design or code line by line. Understanding is enhanced when readily recognizable logical forms are encountered.

7.3.2 The Design Pyramid

Like analysis, a discussion of even the most popular design methods is beyond the scope of this paper. Our discussion here will focus on a set of design activities that should occur regardless of the method that is used.

Software design should be accomplished by following a set of design activities that are illustrated in Figure 6. *Data design* translates the data model created during analysis into data structures that meet the needs of the problem. *Architectural design* differs in intent depending upon the designer's viewpoint. Conventional design creates hierarchical software architectures, while object-oriented design views architecture as the message network that enables objects to communicate. *Interface design* creates implementation models for the human-computer interface, the external system interfaces that enable different applications to interoperate, and the internal interfaces that enable program data to be communicated among software components. Finally, procedural design is conducted as algorithms are created to implement the processing requirements of program components.

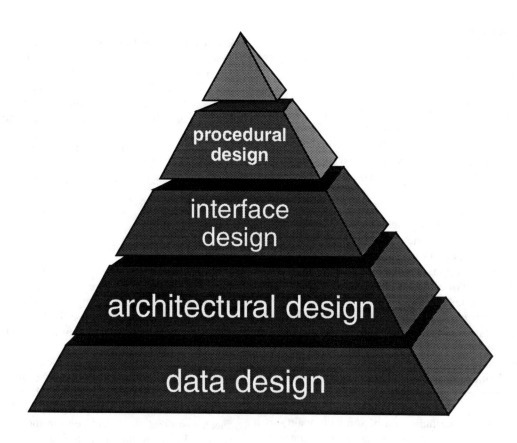

Figure 6. The design pyramid.

Like the pyramid depicted in Figure 6, design should be a stable object. Yet, many software developers do design by taking the pyramid and standing it on its point. That is, design begins with the creation of procedural detail, and as a result, interface, architectural, and data design just happen. This approach, common among people who insist upon coding the program with no explicit design activity, invariably leads to low quality software that is difficult to test, challenging to extend, and frustrating to maintain. For a stable, high quality product, the design approach must also be stable. The design pyramid provides the degree of stability necessary for good design.

7.4 Program Construction

The glory years of third generation programming languages are rapidly coming to a close. Fourth genera-tion techniques, graphical programming methods, component-based software construction, and a variety of other approaches have already captured a signifi-cant percentage of all software construction activities, and there is little debate that their penetration will grow.

And yet, some members of the software engineering community continue to debate 'the best programming language.' Although entertaining, such debates are a waste of time. The problems that we continue to en-counter in the creation of high quality computer-based systems have relatively little to do with the means of construction. Rather, the challenges that face us can only be solved through better or innovative approaches to analysis and design, more comprehensive SQA tech-niques, and more effective and efficient testing. It is for this reason that construction is not emphasized in this paper.

7.5 Software Testing

Glen Myers [38] states a number of rules that can serve well as testing objectives:

1. Testing is a process of executing a program with the intent of finding an error.
2. A good test case is one that has a high probability of finding an as-yet undiscovered error.
3. A successful test is one that uncovers an as-yet undiscovered error.

These objectives imply a dramatic change in viewpoint. They move counter to the commonly held view that a successful test is one in which no errors are found. Our objective is to design tests that systematically uncover different classes of errors and to do so with a minimum amount of time and effort.

If testing is conducted successfully (according to the objective stated above), it will uncover errors in the software. As a secondary benefit, testing demonstrates that software functions appear to be working according to specification, that performance requirements appear to have been met. In addition, data collected as testing is conducted provides a good indication of software reliability and some indication of software quality as a whole. But there is one thing that testing cannot do: *testing cannot show the absence of defects, it can only show that software defects are present.* It is important to keep this (rather gloomy) statement in mind as testing is being conducted.

7.5.1 Strategy

A strategy for software testing integrates software test case design techniques into a well-planned series of steps that result in the successful construction of software. It defines a *template* for software testing—a set of steps into which we can place specific test case design techniques and testing methods.

A number of software testing strategies have been proposed in the literature. All provide the software developer with a template for testing and all have the following generic characteristics:

- Testing begins at the module level and works incrementally "outward" toward the integration of the entire computer-based system.
- Different testing techniques are appropriate at different points in time.
- Testing is conducted by the developer of the software and (for large projects) an independent test group.
- Testing and debugging are different activities, but debugging must be accommodated in any testing strategy.

A strategy for software testing must accommodate low-level tests that are necessary to verify that a small source code segment has been correctly implemented, intermediate-level tests designed to uncover errors in the interfaces between modules, and high level tests that validate major system functions against customer requirements. A strategy must provide guidance for the practitioner and a set of milestones for the manager. Because the steps of the test strategy occur at a time when deadline pressure begins to rise, progress must be measurable and problems must surface as early as possible.

7.5.2 Tactics

The design of tests for software and other engineered products can be as challenging as the initial design of the product itself. Recalling the objectives of testing, we must design tests that have the highest likelihood of finding the most errors with a minimum amount of time and effort.

Over the past two decades a rich variety of test case design methods have evolved for software. These methods provide the developer with a systematic approach to testing. More importantly, methods provide a mechanism that can help to ensure the completeness of tests and provide the highest likelihood for uncovering errors in software.

Any engineered product (and most other things) can be tested in one of two ways: (1) knowing the specified function that a product has been designed to perform, tests can be conducted that demonstrate each function is fully operational; (2) knowing the internal workings of product, tests can be conducted to ensure that "all gears mesh"; that is, internal operation performs according to specification and all internal components have been adequately exercised. The first test approach is called *blac- box testing* and the second, *white box testing* [38].

When computer software is considered, black-box testing alludes to tests that are conducted at the software interface. Although they are designed to uncover errors, black-box tests are also used to demonstrate that software functions are operational; that input is properly accepted, and output is correctly produced; that the integrity of external information (such as data files) is maintained. A black-box test examines some aspect of a system with little regard for the internal logical structure of the software.

White box testing of software is predicated on close examination of procedural detail. Logical paths through the software are tested by providing test cases that exercise specific sets of conditions and/or loops. The status of the program may be examined at various points to determine if the expected or asserted status corresponds to the actual status.

8.0 The Road Ahead and The Three R's

Software is a child of the latter half of the 20th century—a baby boomer. And like its human counterpart, software has accomplished much while at the same time leaving much to be accomplished. It appears that the economic and business environment of the next ten years will be dramatically different than anything that baby boomers have yet experienced. Staff downsizing, the threat of outsourcing, and the demands of customers who won't take "slow" for an answer require significant changes in our approach to software engineering and a major reevaluation of our strategies for handling hundreds of thousands of existing systems [39].

Although many existing technologies will mature over the next decade, and new technologies will emerge, it's likely that three existing software engineering issues—I call them the three Rs—will dominate the software engineering scene.

8.1 Reuse

We must build computer software faster. This simple statement is a manifestation of a business environment in which competition is vicious, product life cycles are shrinking, and time to market often defines the success of a business. The challenge of faster development is compounded by shrinking human resources and an increasing demand for improved software quality.

To meet this challenge, software must be constructed from reusable components. The concept of software reuse is not new, nor is a delineation of its major technical and management challenges [40]. Yet without reuse, there is little hope of building software in time frames that shrink from years to months.

It is likely that two regions of the methods landscape may merge as greater emphasis is placed on reuse. Object-oriented development can lead to the design and implementation of inherently reusable program components, but to meet the challenge, these components must be demonstrably defect free. It may be that formal methods will play a role in the development of components that are proven correct prior to their entry in a component library. Like integrated circuits in hardware design, these "formally" developed components can be used with a fair degree of assurance by other software designers.

If technology problems associated with reuse are overcome (and this is likely), management and cultural challenges remain. Who will have responsibility for creating reusable components? Who will manage them once they are created? Who will bear the additional costs of developing reusable components? What incentives will be provided for software engineers to use them? How will revenues be generated from reuse? What are the risks associated with creating a reuse culture? How will developers of reusable component be compensated? How will legal issues such as liability and copyright protection be addressed? These and many other questions remain to be answered. And yet, component reuse is our best hope for meeting the software challenges of the early part of the 21st century.

8.2 Reengineering

Almost every business relies on the day to day operation of an aging software plant. Major companies spend as much of 70 percent or more of their software budget on the care and feeding of legacy systems. Many of these systems were poorly designed more than a decade ago and have been patched and pushed to their limits. The result is a software plant with aging, even decrepit systems that absorb increasingly large amounts of resource with little hope of abatement. The software plant must be rebuilt and that demands a reengineering strategy.

Reengineering takes time; it costs significant amounts of money, and it absorbs resources that might be otherwise occupied on immediate concerns. For all of these reasons, reengineering is not accomplished in a few months or even a few years. Reengineering of information systems is an activity that will absorb software resources for many years.

A paradigm for reengineering includes the following steps:

- *inventory analysis*—creating a prioritized list of programs that are candidates for reengineering

- *document restructuring*—upgrading documentation to reflect the current workings of a program

- *code restructuring*—recoding selected portions of a program to reduce complexity, ready the code for future change and improve understandability.

- *data restructuring*—redesigning data structures to better accommodate current needs; redesign the algorithms that manipulate these data structures

- *reverse engineering*—examine software internals to determine how the system has been constructed

- *forward engineering*—using information obtained from reverse engineering, rebuild the application using modern software engineering practices and principles.

8.3 Retooling

To achieve the first two R's, we need a third R—a new

generation of software tools. In retooling the software engineering process, we must remember the mistakes of the 1980s and early 1990s. At that time, CASE tools were inserted into a process vacuum, and failed to meet expectations. Tools for the next ten years will address all aspects of the methods landscape. But they should emphasize reuse and reengineering.

9.0 Summary

As each of us in the software business looks to the future, a small set of questions is asked and re-asked. Will we continue to struggle to produce software that meets the needs of a new breed of customers? Will generation X software professionals repeat the mistakes of the generation that preceded them? Will software remain a bottleneck in the development of new generations of computer-based products and systems? The degree to which the industry embraces software engineering and works to instantiate it into the culture of software development will have a strong bearing on the final answers to these questions. And the answers to these questions will have a strong bearing on whether we should look to the future with anticipation or trepidation.

References

[1] Naur, P. and B. Randall (eds.), "Software Engineering: A Report on a Conference Sponsored by the NATO Science Committee," NATO, 1969.

[2] Paulk, M. et al, "Capability Maturity Model for Software," Software Engineering Institute, Carnegie Mellon University, Pittsburgh, PA, 1993.

[3] Boehm, B., "A Spiral Model for Software Development and Enhancement," *Computer*, Vol. 21, No. 5, May 1988, pp. 61-72.

[4] Gilb, T., *Principles of Software Engineering Management*, Addison-Wesley, 1988.

[5] Mills, H.D., M. Dyer, and R. Linger, "Cleanroom Software Engineering," *IEEE Software*, Sept. 1987, pp. 19-25.

[6] Dyer, M., *The Cleanroom Approach to Quality Software Development*, Wiley, 1992.

[7] Cougar, J and R. Zawacki, *Managing and Motivating Computer Personnel*, Wiley, 1980.

[8] DeMarco, T. and T. Lister, *Peopleware*, Dorset House, 1987.

[9] Weinberg, G., *Understanding the Professional Programmer*, Dorset Hosue, 1988.

[10] Curtis, B., "People Management Maturity Model," *Proc. Intl. Conf. Software Engineering*, Pittsburgh, 1989.

[11] August, J.H., *Joint Application Design*, Prentice Hall, 1991.

[12] Wood, J., and D. Silver, *Joint Application Design*, Wiley, 1989.

[13] Dreger, J. B., *Function Point Analysis*, Prentice-Hall, 1989.

[14] Hetzel, B., *Making Software Measurement Work*, QED Publishing, 1993.

[15] Jones, C., *Applied Software Measurement*, McGraw-Hill, 1991.

[16] Fenton, N.E., *Software Metrics*, Chapman & Hall, 1991.

[17] Zuse, H., *Software Complexity*, W. deGruyer & Co., Berlin, 1990.

[18] Lorenz, M. and J. Kidd, *Object-Oriented Software Metrics*, Prentice-Hall, 1994.

[19] Pressman, R.S., *A Manager's Guide to Software Engineering*, McGraw-Hill, 1993.

[20] Boehm, B., *Software Engineering Economics*, Prentice-Hall, 1981.

[21] Charette, R., *Application Strategies for Risk Analysis*, McGraw-Hill, 1990.

[22] Jones, C., *Assessment and Control of Software Risks*, Yourdon Press, 1993.

[24] Crosby, P., *Quality is Free*, McGraw-Hill, 1979.

[25] McCall, J., P. Richards, and G. Walters, "Factors in Software Quality," three volumes, NTIS AD-A049-014, 015, 055, November, 1977.

[26] Cavano, J.P. and J.A. McCall, "A Framework for the Measurement of Software Quality," *Proc. ACM Software Quality Assurance Workshop*, , 1978, pp. 133-139.

[27] Freedman, D and G. Weinberg, *The Handbook of Walkthroughs, Inspections and Technical Reviews*, Dorset House, 1990.

[28] Gilb, T. and D. Graham, *Software Inspection*, Addison-Wesley, 1993.

[29] Babich, W., *Software Configuration Management*, Addison-Wesley, 1986.

[30] Pressman, R. and S. Herron, *Software Shock*, Dorset House, 1991.

[31] Pressman, R., *Software Engineering: A Practitioner's Approach*, 3rd edition, McGraw-Hill, 1992.

[32] Yourdon, E., *Modern Structured Analysis*, Yourdon Press, 1989.

[33] Booch, G., *Object-Oriented Analysis & Design*, Benjamin-Cummings, 1994.

[34] Spivey, M., *The Z Notation*, Prentice-Hall, 1992.

[35] Jackson, M., *Principles of Program Design*, Academic Press, 1975.

[36] Parnas, D.L., "On Criteria to be used in Decomposing Systems into Modules," *Comm. ACM*, Vol. 14, No. 1, Apr. 1972, pp. 221-227.

[37] Linger, R., H. Mills, and B. Witt, *Structured Programming*, Addison-Wesley, 1979.

[38] Myers, G., *The Art of Software Testing*, Wiley, 1979.

[38] Beizer, B., *Software Testing Techniques*, 2nd edition, VanNostrand Reinhold, 1990.

[39] Pressman, R., "Software According to Nicollo Machiavelli," *IEEE Software*, Jan. 1995.

[40] Tracz, W., *Software Reuse: Emerging Technology,* IEEE Computer Society Press, 1988.

The Capability Maturity Model for Software

Mark C. Paulk

Software Engineering Institute
Carnegie Mellon University
Pittsburgh, PA 15213-3890

Bill Curtis

TeraQuest Metrics, Inc.
P.O. Box 200490
Austin, TX 78720-0490

Mary Beth Chrissis

Software Engineering Institute
Carnegie Mellon University
Pittsburgh, PA 15213-3890

Charles V. Weber

Lockheed Martin Federal Systems Company
6304 Spine Road
Boulder, CO 80301

Abstract

This paper provides an overview of the latest version of the Capability Maturity Model[SM] for Software, CMM[SM] v1.1. CMM v1.1 describes the software engineering and management practices that characterize organizations as they mature their processes for developing and maintaining software. This paper stresses the need for a process maturity framework to prioritize improvement actions, describes the five maturity levels, key process areas, and their common features, and discusses future directions for the CMM.

Keywords: capability maturity model, CMM, software process improvement, process capability, maturity level, key process area, software process assessment, software capability evaluation.

1   Introduction

After decades of unfulfilled promises about productivity and quality gains from applying new software methodologies and technologies, organizations are realizing that their fundamental problem is the inability to manage the software process. In many organizations, projects are often excessively late and over budget, and the benefits of better methods and tools cannot be realized in the maelstrom of an undisciplined, chaotic project.

In November 1986, the Software Engineering Institute (SEI), with assistance from the Mitre Corporation, began developing a process maturity framework that would help organizations improve their software process. In September 1987, the SEI released a brief description of the process maturity framework, which was later expanded in Watts Humphrey's book, *Managing the Software Process* [Humphrey89]. Two methods, software process assessment[1] and software capability evaluation[2] were developed to appraise software process maturity.

After four years of experience with the software

---

[1] A software process assessment is an appraisal by a trained team of software professionals to determine the state of an organization's current software process, to determine the high-priority software process-related issues facing an organization, and to obtain the organizational support for software process improvement.

[2] A software capability evaluation is an appraisal by a trained team of professionals to identify contractors who are qualified to perform the software work or to monitor the state of the software process used on an existing software effort.

Reprinted from *Software Engineering*, M. Dorfman and R.H. Thayer, eds., 1997, pp. 427–438.

process maturity framework, the SEI evolved the maturity framework into the Capability Maturity Model for Software (CMM or SW-CMM[3]). The CMM presents sets of recommended practices in a number of key process areas that have been shown to enhance software process capability. The CMM is based on knowledge acquired from software process assessments and extensive feedback from both industry and government.

The CMM provides software organizations with guidance on how to gain control of their processes for developing and maintaining software and how to evolve toward a culture of software engineering and management excellence. The CMM was designed to guide software organizations in selecting process improvement strategies by determining current process maturity and identifying the most critical issues for software quality and process improvement. By focusing on a limited set of activities and working aggressively to achieve them, an organization can steadily improve its organization-wide software process to enable continuous and lasting gains in software process capability.

The initial release of the CMM, version 1.0, was reviewed and used by the software community during 1991 and 1992. The current version of the CMM, version 1.1, was released in 1993 [Paulk95a] and is the result of extensive feedback from the software community. The CMM has evolved significantly since 1986 [Paulk95b], and the SEI is currently working on version 2.

1.1   Immature Versus Mature Software Organizations

Setting sensible goals for process improvement requires an understanding of the difference between immature and mature software organizations. In an immature software organization, software processes are generally improvised by practitioners and their management during the course of the project. Even if a software process has been specified, it is not rigorously followed or enforced. The immature software organization is reactionary, and managers are usually focused on solving immediate crises (better known as fire fighting). Schedules and budgets are routinely exceeded because they are not based on realistic esti-

mates. When hard deadlines are imposed, product functionality and quality are often compromised to meet the schedule.

In an immature organization, there is no objective basis for judging product quality or for solving product or process problems. Therefore, product quality is difficult to predict. Activities intended to enhance quality such as reviews and testing are often curtailed or eliminated when projects fall behind schedule.

On the other hand, a mature software organization possesses an organization-wide ability for managing software development and maintenance processes. The software process is accurately communicated to both existing staff and new employees, and work activities are carried out according to the planned process. The mandated processes are usable and consistent with the way the work actually gets done. These defined processes are updated when necessary, and improvements are developed through controlled pilot-tests and/or cost benefit analyses. Roles and responsibilities within the defined process are clear throughout the project and across the organization.

In a mature organization, managers monitor the quality of the software products and the process that produced them. There is an objective, quantitative basis for judging product quality and analyzing problems with the product and process. Schedules and budgets are based on historical performance and are realistic; the expected results for cost, schedule, functionality, and quality of the product are usually achieved. In general, a disciplined process is consistently followed because all of the participants understand the value of doing so, and the necessary infrastructure exists to support the process.

1.2   Fundamental Concepts Underlying Process Maturity

A *software process* can be defined as a set of activities, methods, practices, and transformations that people use to develop and maintain software and the associated products (for instance, project plans, design documents, code, test cases, and user manuals). As an organization matures, the software process becomes better defined and more consistently implemented throughout the organization.

Software process capability describes the range of expected results that can be achieved by following a software process. An organization's software process capability is one way of predicting the most likely outcome to expect from the next software project the organization undertakes.

Software process performance represents the actual results achieved by following a software process. Thus, software process performance focuses on

---

[3] A number of CMMs inspired by the CMM for Software have now been developed, including the Systems Engineering CMM [Bate95] and the People CMM [Curtis95]. Additional CMMs are being developed on software acquisition and integrated product development. To minimize confusion, we are starting to use SW-CMM to distinguish the original CMM for Software, but since this paper focuses on software engineering, we will use the CMM acronym.

the results achieved, while software process capability focuses on results expected.

Software process maturity is the extent to which a specific process is explicitly defined, managed, measured, controlled, and effective. Maturity implies a potential for growth in capability and indicates both the richness of an organization's software process and the consistency with which it is applied in projects throughout the organization.

As a software organization gains in software process maturity, it institutionalizes its software process via policies, standards, and organizational structures. Institutionalization entails building an infrastructure and a corporate culture that supports the methods, practices, and procedures of the business so that they endure after those who originally defined them have gone.

2 The Five Levels of Software Process Maturity

Continuous process improvement is based on many small, evolutionary steps rather than revolutionary innovations. The staged structure of the CMM is based on principles of product quality espoused by Walter Shewart, W. Edwards Deming, Joseph Juran, and Philip Crosby. The CMM provides a framework for organizing these evolutionary steps into five maturity levels that lay successive foundations for continuous process improvement. These five maturity levels define an ordinal scale for measuring the maturity of an organization's software process and for evaluating its software process capability. The levels also help an organization prioritize its improvement efforts.

A *maturity level* is a well-defined evolutionary plateau toward achieving a mature software process. Each maturity level comprises a set of process goals that, when satisfied, stabilize an important component of the software process. Achieving each level of the maturity framework establishes a higher level of process capability for the organization.

Organizing the CMM into the five levels shown in Figure 2.1 prioritizes improvement actions for increasing software process maturity. The labeled arrows in Figure 2.1 indicate the type of process capability being institutionalized by the organization at each step of the maturity framework.

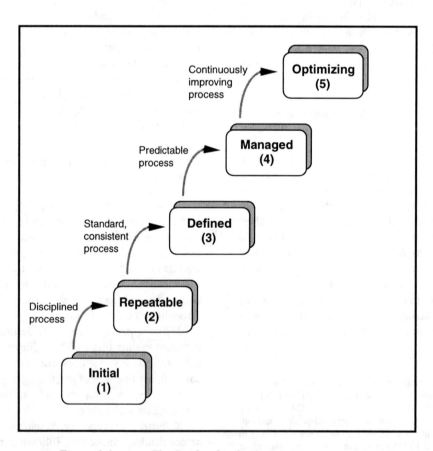

Figure 2.1   The five levels of software process maturity

The five levels can be briefly described as:

1) Initial   The software process is characterized as ad hoc, and occasionally even chaotic. Few processes are defined, and success depends on individual effort and heroics.

2) Repeatable   Basic project management processes are established to track cost, schedule, and functionality. The necessary process discipline is in place to repeat earlier successes on projects with similar applications.

3) Defined   The software process for both management and engineering activities is documented, standardized, and integrated into a standard software process for the organization. All projects use an approved, tailored version of the organization's standard software process for developing and maintaining software.

4) Managed   Detailed measures of the software process and product quality are collected. Both the software process and products are quantitatively understood and controlled.

5) Optimizing   Continuous process improvement is enabled by quantitative feedback from the process and from piloting innovative ideas and technologies.

These five levels reflect the fact that the CMM is a model for improving the capability of software organizations. The priorities in the CMM, as expressed by these levels, are not directed at individual projects. A project that is in trouble might well prioritize its problems differently than the taxonomy given by the CMM. Its solutions might be of limited value to the rest of the organization, because other projects might have different problems or because other projects could not take advantage of its solutions if they lack the necessary foundation to implement the solutions. The CMM focuses on processes that are of value across the organization.

2.1 Behavioral Characterization of the Maturity Levels

Maturity Levels 2 through 5 can be characterized through the activities performed by the organization to establish or improve the software process, by activities performed on each project, and by the resulting process capability across projects. A behavioral characterization of Level 1 is included to establish a base of comparison for process improvements at higher maturity levels.

2.1.1 Level 1—The Initial Level

At the Initial Level, the organization typically does not provide a stable environment for developing and maintaining software. Over-commitment is a characteristic of Level 1 organizations, and such organizations frequently have difficulty making commitments that the staff can meet with an orderly engineering process, resulting in a series of crises. During a crisis, projects typically abandon planned procedures and revert to coding and testing. Success depends on hav-

ing an exceptional manager and a seasoned and effective software team. Occasionally, capable and forceful software managers can withstand the pressures to take shortcuts in the software process; but when they leave the project, their stabilizing influence leaves with them. Even a strong engineering process cannot overcome the instability created by the absence of sound management practices.

In spite of this ad hoc, even chaotic, process, Level 1 organizations frequently develop products that work, even though they may exceed the budget and schedule. Success in Level 1 organizations depends on the competence and heroics of the people in the organization[4] and cannot be repeated unless the same competent individuals are assigned to the next project. Thus, at Level 1, capability is a characteristic of the individuals, not of the organization.

2.1.2 Level 2—The Repeatable Level

At the Repeatable Level, policies for managing a software project and procedures to implement those policies are established. Planning and managing new projects is based on experience with similar projects. Process capability is enhanced by establishing basic process management discipline on a project by project basis. Projects implement effective processes that are defined, documented, practiced, trained, measured, enforced, and able to improve.

Projects in Level 2 organizations have installed basic software management controls. Realistic project commitments are made, based on the results observed on previous projects and on the requirements of the current project. The software managers for a project

---

[4] Selecting, hiring, developing, and retaining competent people are significant issues for organizations at all levels of maturity, but they are largely outside the scope of the CMM.

track software costs, schedules, and functionality; problems in meeting commitments are identified when they arise. Software requirements and the work products developed to satisfy them are baselined, and their integrity is controlled. Software project standards are defined, and the organization ensures they are faithfully followed. The software project works with its subcontractors, if any, to establish an effective customer-supplier relationship.

Processes may differ among projects in a Level 2 organization. The organizational requirement for achieving Level 2 is that there are policies that guide the projects in establishing the appropriate management processes.

The software process capability of Level 2 organizations can be summarized as disciplined because software project planning and tracking are stable and earlier successes can be repeated. The project's process is under the effective control of a project management system, following realistic plans based on the performance of previous projects.

2.1.3   Level 3—The Defined Level

At the Defined Level, a standard process (or processes) for developing and maintaining software is documented and used across the organization. This standard process includes both software engineering and management processes, which are integrated into a coherent whole. This standard process is referred to throughout the CMM as the *organization's standard software process*. Processes established at Level 3 are used (and changed, as appropriate) to help the software managers and technical staff perform more effectively. The organization exploits effective software engineering practices when standardizing its software processes. A group such as a software engineering process group or SEPG is responsible for the organization's software process activities. An organization-wide training program is implemented to ensure that the staff and managers have the knowledge and skills required to fulfill their assigned roles.

Projects tailor the organization's standard software process to develop their own defined software process, which accounts for the unique characteristics of the project. This tailored process is referred to in the CMM as the *project's defined software process*. It is the process used in performing the project's activities. A defined software process contains a coherent, integrated set of well-defined software engineering and management processes. A well-defined process includes readiness criteria, inputs, standards and procedures for performing the work, verification mechanisms (such as peer reviews), outputs, and completion criteria. Because the software process is well defined,

management has good insight into technical progress on the project.

The software process capability of Level 3 organizations can be summarized as standard and consistent because both software engineering and management activities are stable and repeatable. Within established product lines, cost, schedule, and functionality are under control, and software quality is tracked. This process capability is based on a common, organization-wide understanding of the activities, roles, and responsibilities in a defined software process.

2.1.4   Level 4—The Managed Level

At the Managed Level, the organization sets quantitative quality goals for both software products and processes. Productivity and quality are measured for important software process activities across all projects as part of an organizational measurement program. An organization-wide software process database is used to collect and analyze the data available from the projects' defined software processes. Software processes are instrumented with well-defined and consistent measurements. These measurements establish the quantitative foundation for evaluating the projects' software processes and products.

Projects achieve control over their products and processes by narrowing the variation in their process performance to fall within acceptable quantitative boundaries. Meaningful variations in process performance can be distinguished from random variation (noise), particularly within established product lines. The risks involved in moving up the learning curve of a new application domain are known and carefully managed.

The software process capability of Level 4 organizations can be summarized as being quantified and predictable because the process is measured and operates within quantitative limits. This level of process capability allows an organization to predict trends in process and product quality within the quantitative bounds of these limits. Because the process is both stable and measured, when some exceptional circumstance occurs, the "special cause" of the variation can be identified and addressed. When the pre-defined limits are exceeded, actions are taken to understand and correct the situation. Software products are of predictably high quality.

2.1.5   Level 5—The Optimizing Level

At the Optimizing Level, the entire organization is focused on continuous process improvement. The organization has the means to identify weaknesses and strengthen the process proactively, with the goals of preventing defects and improving efficiency. Data on process effectiveness are used to perform cost/benefit analyses of new technologies and proposed changes to the organization's software process. Innovations that exploit the best software engineering practices are identified and transferred throughout the organization.

Software teams in Level 5 organizations analyze defects to determine their causes, evaluate software processes to prevent known types of defects from recurring, and disseminate lessons learned throughout the organization.

There is chronic waste, in the form of rework, in any system simply due to random variation. Organized efforts to remove waste result in changing the system by addressing "common causes" of inefficiency. While efforts to reduce waste occur at all maturity levels, it is the focus of Level 5.

The software process capability of Level 5 organizations can be characterized as continuously improving because Level 5 organizations are continuously striving to improve the range of their process capability, thereby improving the process performance of their projects. Improvements occur both by incremental advancements in the existing process and by innovations using new technologies and methods. Technology and process improvements are planned and managed as ordinary business activities.

2.2   Process Capability and the Prediction of Performance

An organization's software process maturity helps predict a project's ability to meet its goals. Projects in Level 1 organizations experience wide variations in achieving cost, schedule, functionality, and quality targets. Figure 2.2 illustrates the kinds of improvements expected in predictability, control, and effectiveness in the form of a probability density for the likely performance of a particular project with respect to targets, such as cycle time, cost, and quality.

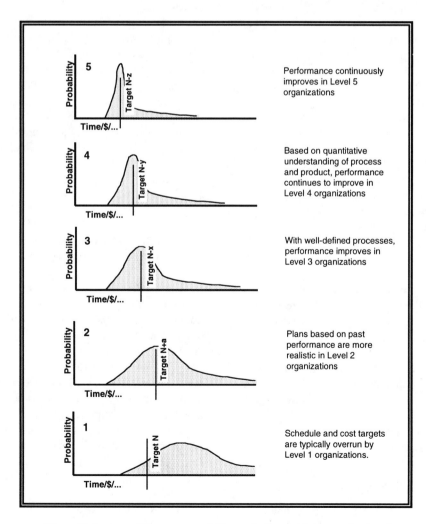

Figure 2.2   Process capability as indicated by maturity level

The first improvement expected as an organization matures is in predictability. As maturity increases, the difference between targeted results and actual results decreases across projects. For instance, Level 1 organizations often miss their originally scheduled delivery dates by a wide margin, whereas higher maturity level organizations should be able to meet targeted dates with increased accuracy.

The second improvement is in control. As maturity increases, the variability of actual results around targeted results decreases. For instance, in Level 1 organizations delivery dates for projects of similar size are unpredictable and vary widely. Similar projects in a higher maturity level organization, however, will be delivered within a smaller range.

The third improvement is in effectiveness. Targeted results improve as the maturity of the organization increases. That is, as a software organization matures, costs decrease, development time becomes shorter, and productivity and quality increase. In a Level 1 organization, development time can be quite long because of the amount of rework that must be performed to correct mistakes. In contrast, higher maturity level organizations have increased process effectiveness and reduced costly rework, allowing development time to be shortened.

The improvements in predicting a project's results represented in Figure 2.2 assume that the software project's outcomes become more predictable as noise, often in the form of rework, is removed from the software process. Unprecedented systems complicate the picture since new technologies and applications lower the process capability by increasing variability. Even in the case of unprecedented systems, the management and engineering practices characteristic of more mature organizations help identify and address problems earlier than for less mature organizations. In some cases a mature process means that "failed" projects are identified early in the software life cycle and investment in a lost cause is minimized.

The documented case studies of software process improvement indicate that there are significant improvements in both quality and productivity as a result of the improvement effort [Herbsleb94, Lawlis95, Goldenson95, Hayes95]. The return on investment seems to typically be in the 4:1 to 8:1 range for successful process improvement efforts, with increases in productivity ranging from 9-67 percent and decreases in cycle time ranging from 15-23 percent reported [Herbsleb94].

2.3   Skipping Maturity Levels

Trying to skip maturity levels may be counterproductive because each maturity level in the CMM forms a foundation from which to achieve the next level. The CMM identifies the levels through which an organization should evolve to establish a culture of software engineering excellence. Organizations can institute specific process improvements at any time they choose, even before they are prepared to advance to the level at which the specific practice is recommended. However, organizations should understand that the stability of these improvements is at greater risk since the foundation for their successful institutionalization has not been completed. Processes without the proper foundation fail at the very point they are needed most—under stress.

For instance, a well-defined software process that is characteristic of a Level 3 organization, can be placed at great risk if management makes a poorly planned schedule commitment or fails to control changes to the baselined requirements. Similarly, many organizations have collected the detailed data characteristic of Level 4, only to find that the data were uninterpretable because of inconsistent software processes.

At the same time, it must be recognized that process improvement efforts should focus on the needs of the organization in the context of its business environment, and higher-level practices may address the current needs of an organization or project. For example, when prescribing what steps an organization should take to move from Level 1 to Level 2, one frequent recommendation is to establish a software engineering process group (SEPG), which is an attribute of Level 3 organizations. While an SEPG is not a necessary characteristic of a Level 2 organization, they can be a useful part of the prescription for achieving Level 2.

3   Operational Definition of the Capability Maturity Model

The CMM is a framework representing a path of improvements recommended for software organizations that want to increase their software process capability. The intent is that the CMM is at a sufficient level of abstraction that it does not unduly constrain how the software process is implemented by an organization. The CMM describes what we would normally expect in a software process, regardless of how the process is implemented.

This operational elaboration of the CMM is designed to support the many ways it will be used. There are at least five uses of the CMM that are supported:

- Senior management will use the CMM to understand the activities necessary to launch a software process improvement program in their organization.

- Appraisal method developers will use the CMM to develop CMM-based appraisal methods that meet specific needs.

- Evaluation teams will use the CMM to identify the risks of selecting among different contractors for awarding business and to monitor contracts.

- Assessment teams will use the CMM to identify strengths and weaknesses in the organization.

- Technical staff and process improvement groups, such as an SEPG, will use the CMM as a guide to help them define and improve the software process in their organization.

Because of the diverse uses of the CMM, it must be decomposed in sufficient detail that actual process recommendations can be derived from the structure of the maturity levels. This decomposition also indicates the key processes and their structure that characterize software process maturity and software process capability.

3.1   Internal Structure of the Maturity Levels

Each maturity level, with the exception of Level 1, has been decomposed into constituent parts. The decomposition of each maturity level ranges from abstract summaries of each level down to their operational definition in the key practices, as shown in Figure 3.1. Each maturity level is composed of several key process areas. Each key process area is organized into five sections called common features. The common features specify the key practices that, when collectively addressed, accomplish the goals of the key process area.

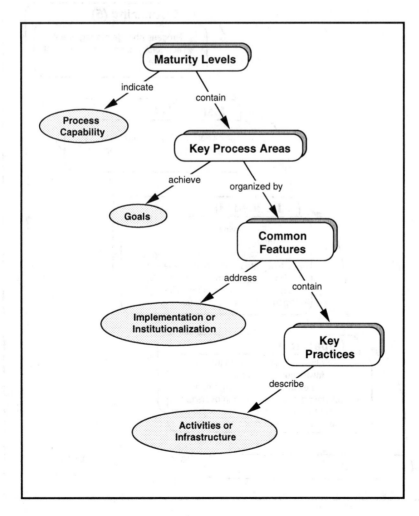

Figure 3.1   The CMM structure

3.2　Maturity Levels

A maturity level is a well-defined evolutionary plateau toward achieving a mature software process. Each maturity level indicates a level of process capability, as was illustrated in Figure 2.2. For instance, at Level 2 the process capability of an organization has been elevated from ad hoc to disciplined by establishing sound project management controls.

3.3　Key Process Areas

Except for Level 1, each maturity level is decomposed into several key process areas that indicate where an organization should focus on to improve its software process. Key process areas identify the issues that must be addressed to achieve a maturity level.

Each *key process area* identifies a cluster of related activities that, when performed collectively, achieve a set of goals considered important for enhancing process capability. The key process areas have been defined to reside at a single maturity level as shown in Figure 3.2. The path to achieving the goals of a key process area may differ across projects based on differences in application domains or environments. Nevertheless, all the goals of a key process area must be achieved for the organization to satisfy that key process area.

The adjective "key" implies that there are process areas (and processes) that are not key to achieving a maturity level. The CMM does not describe in detail all the process areas that are involved with developing and maintaining software. Certain process areas have been identified as key determiners of process capability, and these are the ones described in the CMM.

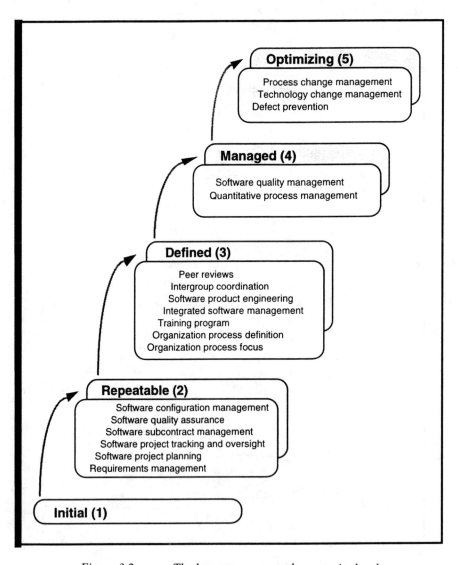

Figure 3.2　　The key process areas by maturity level

56

The key process areas are the requirements for achieving a maturity level. To achieve a maturity level, the key process areas for that level and the lower levels must be satisfied (or not applicable, such as Software Subcontract Management when there are no subcontractors).

The specific practices to be executed in each key process area will evolve as the organization achieves higher levels of process maturity. For instance, many of the project estimating capabilities described in the Software Project Planning key process area at Level 2 must evolve to handle the additional project data available at Level 3, as described in Integrated Software Management.

The key process areas at Level 2 focus on the software project's concerns related to establishing basic project management controls.

- Requirements Management: establish a common understanding between the customer and the software project of the customer's requirements that will be addressed by the software project. This agreement with the customer is the basis for planning and managing the software project.

- Software Project Planning: establish reasonable plans for performing the software engineering and for managing the software project. These plans are the necessary foundation for managing the software project.

- Software Project Tracking and Oversight: establish adequate visibility into actual progress so that management can take effective actions when the software project's performance deviates significantly from the software plans.

- Software Subcontract Management: select qualified software subcontractors and manage them effectively.

- Software Quality Assurance: provide management with appropriate visibility into the process being used by the software project and of the products being built.

- Software Configuration Management: establish and maintain the integrity of the products of the software project throughout the project's software life cycle.

The key process areas at Level 3 address both project and organizational issues, as the organization establishes an infrastructure that institutionalizes effective software engineering and management processes across all projects.

- Organization Process Focus: establish the organizational responsibility for software process activities that improve the organization's overall software process capability.

- Organization Process Definition: develop and maintain a usable set of software process assets that improve process performance across the projects and provides a basis for defining meaningful data for quantitative process management. These assets provide a stable foundation that can be institutionalized via mechanisms such as training.

- Training Program: develop the skills and knowledge of individuals so they can perform their roles effectively and efficiently. Training is an organizational responsibility, but the software projects should identify their needed skills and provide the necessary training when the project's needs are unique.

- Integrated Software Management: integrate the software engineering and management activities into a coherent, defined software process that is tailored from the organization's standard software process and related process assets. This tailoring is based on the business environment and technical needs of the project.

- Software Product Engineering: consistently perform a well-defined engineering process that integrates all the software engineering activities to produce correct, consistent software products effectively and efficiently. Software Product Engineering describes the technical activities of the project, for instance requirements analysis, design, code, and test.

- Intergroup Coordination: establish a means for the software engineering group to participate actively with the other engineering groups so the project is better able to satisfy the customer's needs effectively and efficiently.

- Peer Reviews: remove defects from the software work products early and efficiently. An important corollary effect is to develop a better understanding of the software work products and of the defects that can be prevented. The peer review is an important and effective engineering method that can be implemented via inspections, structured walkthroughs, or a number of other collegial review methods.

The key process areas at Level 4 focus on establishing a quantitative understanding of both the software process and the software work products being built.

- Quantitative Process Management: control process performance of the software project quantitatively. Software process performance represents the actual results achieved from following a software process. The focus is on identifying special causes of variation within a measurably stable process and correcting, as appropriate, the circumstances that drove the transient variation to occur.

- Software Quality Management: develop a quantitative understanding of the quality of the project's software products and achieve specific quality goals.

The key process areas at Level 5 cover the issues that both the organization and the projects must address to implement continuous and measurable software process improvement.

- Defect Prevention: identify the causes of defects and prevent them from recurring. The software project analyzes defects, identifies their causes, and changes its defined software process.

- Technology Change Management: identify beneficial new technologies (such as tools, methods, and processes) and transfer them into the organization in an orderly manner. The focus of Technology Change Management is on performing innovation efficiently in an ever-changing world.

- Process Change Management: continually improve the software processes used in the organization with the intent of improving software quality, increasing productivity, and decreasing the cycle time for product development.

3.4 Goals and Key Practices

Goals summarize the key practices of a key process area and can be used to determine whether an organization or project has effectively implemented the key process area. The goals signify the scope, boundaries, and intent of each key process area. Satisfaction of a key process area is determined by achievement of the goals.

Key practices describe the activities and infrastructure that contribute most to the effective implementation and institutionalization of the key process area. Each key practice consists of a single sentence, often followed by a more detailed description, which may include examples and elaboration. These key practices, also referred to as the top-level key practices, state the fundamental policies, procedures, and activities for the key process area. The components of the detailed description are frequently referred to as subpractices. The key practices describe "what" is to be done, but they should not be interpreted as mandating "how" the goals should be achieved. Alternative practices may accomplish the goals of the key process area. The key practices should be interpreted rationally to judge whether the goals of the key process area are effectively, although perhaps differently, achieved.

4   Future Directions of the CMM

Achieving higher levels of software process maturity is incremental and requires a long-term commitment to continuous process improvement. Software organizations may take ten years or more to build the foundation for, and a culture oriented toward, continuous process improvement. Although a decade-long process improvement program is foreign to most U.S. companies, this level of effort is required to produce mature software organizations.

The CMM is not a silver bullet and does not address all of the issues that are important for successful projects. For example, it does not currently address expertise in particular application domains, advocate specific software technologies, or suggest how to select, hire, motivate, and retain competent people. Although these issues are crucial to a project's success, they have not been integrated into the CMM.

The CMM has evolved since 1986 [Paulk95b] and will continue to evolve. Feedback from the use of the CMM in software process assessments, software capability evaluations, and process improvement programs, the continuing evolution of the field of software engineering, and the changing business environment all contribute to the need for a "living CMM." To achieve a reasonable balance between the need for stability by organizations using the CMM in software process improvement and the need for continual improvement, we anticipate a 5-year cycle for major revisions of the CMM. Version 2 of the CMM is planned for the 1997 time frame.

The SEI is also working with the International Standards Organization (ISO) in its efforts to build international standards for software process assessment, improvement, and capability determination [Dorling93, Konrad95]. This effort will integrate concepts from many different process improvement methods. The development of the ISO standards (and the contributions of other methods) will influence CMM v2, even as the SEI's process work will influence the activities of the ISO.

5   Conclusion

The CMM represents a "common sense engineering" approach to software process improvement. The maturity levels, key process areas, common features, and key practices have been extensively discussed and reviewed within the software community. While the CMM is not perfect, it does represent a broad consensus of the software community and is a useful tool for guiding software process improvement efforts.

The CMM provides a conceptual structure for improving the management and development of software products in a disciplined and consistent way. It does not guarantee that software products will be successfully built or that all problems in software engineering will be adequately resolved. However, current reports from CMM-based improvement programs indicate that it can improve the likelihood with which a software organization can achieve its cost, quality, and productivity goals.

The CMM identifies practices for a mature software process and provides examples of the state-of-the-practice (and in some cases, the state-of-the-art), but it is not meant to be either exhaustive or dictatorial. The CMM identifies the characteristics of an effective software process, but the mature organization addresses all issues essential to a successful project, including people and technology, as well as process.

6   References

Bate95   Roger Bate, et al, "A Systems Engineering Capability Maturity Model, Version 1.1," Software Engineering Institute, CMU/SEI-95-MM-003, Nov. 1995.

Dorling93   Alec Dorling, "Software Process Improvement and Capability dEtermination," *Software Quality J.*, Vol. 2, No. 4, Dec. 1993, pp. 209–224.

Curtis95   Bill Curtis, William E. Hefley, and Sally Miller, "People Capability Maturity Model," Software Engineering Institute, CMU/SEI-95-MM-02, Sept. 1995.

Goldenson95   Dennis R. Goldenson and James D. Herbsleb, "After the Appraisal: A Systematic Survey of Process Improvement, Its Benefits, and Factors that Influence Suc

cess," Software Engineering Institute, CMU/SEI-95-TR-009, Aug. 1995.

Hayes95   Will Hayes and Dave Zubrow, "Moving On Up: Data and Experience Doing CMM-Based Process Improvement," Software Engineering Institute, CMU/SEI-95-TR-008, Aug. 1995.

Herbsleb94   James Herbsleb, et al., "Benefits of CMM-Based Software Process Improvement: Initial Results," Software Engineering Institute, CMU/SEI-94-TR-13, Aug. 1994.

Humphrey89   W.S. Humphrey, *Managing the Software Process*, Addison-Wesley, Reading, Mass., 1989.

Konrad95   Michael D. Konrad, Mark C. Paulk, and Allan W. Graydon, "An Overview of SPICE's Model for Process Management," *Proc. 5th Int'l Conf. Software Quality*, 1995.

Lawlis95   Patricia K. Lawlis, Robert M. Flowe, and James B. Thordahl, "A Correlational Study of the CMM and Software Development Performance," *Crosstalk: The Journal of Defense Software Engineering*, Vol. 8, No. 9, Sept. 1995, pp. 21–25.

Paulk95a   Carnegie Mellon University, Software Engineering Institute (Principal Contributors and Editors: Mark C. Paulk, Charles V. Weber, Bill Curtis, and Mary Beth Chrissis), *The Capability Maturity Model: Guidelines for Improving the Software Process*, Addison-Wesley Publishing Company, Reading, Mass., 1995.

Paulk95b   Mark C. Paulk, "The Evolution of the SEI's Capability Maturity Model for Software," *Software Process: Improvement and Practice*, Pilot Issue, Spring 1995.

For Further Information

For further information regarding the CMM and its associated products, including training on the CMM and how to perform software process assessments and software capability evaluations, contact:

SEI Customer Relations
Software Engineering Institute
Carnegie Mellon University
Pittsburgh, PA 15213-3890
(412) 268-5800
Internet: customer-relations@sei.cmu.edu

Chapter 3

Software Engineering Project Management

1. Chapter Introduction

Project management is defined as a system of procedures, practices, technologies, and know-how that provides the planning, organizing, staffing, directing, and controlling necessary to successfully manage an engineering project. *Know-how* in this case means the skill, background, and wisdom necessary to apply effective knowledge effectively in practice. If the product of the project is software, the act of managing a software project is called *software development proj-ect management* or, more recently, *software engineering project management*. The manager of a software engineering project is called a *software engineering project manager*.

Software engineering projects are frequently part of a larger, more comprehensive system that includes equipment (hardware), facilities, personnel, and procedures, as well as software. Examples are aircraft systems, accounting systems, radar systems, inventory control systems, railroad switching systems, and so forth.

OKAY BOYS...FOLLOW ME.

These system engineering projects are typically managed by one or more system project managers (sometimes called program managers) who manage an organization comprising technically qualified engineers (all types), experts in the field of the application, scientific specialists, programmers, support personnel, and others. If the software to be delivered is a "stand-alone" software system (a system that does not interface with any other system) that is being developed for (or on) an existing or commercial "off-the-shelf" computer, the software engineering project manager can be the system project manager.

These system engineering projects are typically managed by one or more system project managers (sometimes called program managers) who manage an organization comprising technically qualified engineers (all types), experts in the field of the application, scientific specialists, programmers, support personnel, and others. If the software to be delivered is a "stand-alone" software system (a system that does not interface with any other system) that is being developed for (or on) an existing or commercial "off-the-shelf" computer, the software engineering project manager can be the system project manager.

2. Chapter Overview

The three articles contained in this chapter introduce software engineering project management. The first article by Fred Brooks sets the stage by defining the major issues of—and providing historic significance to—software engineering project management. The second article by Richard Thayer extrapolates from the general concepts of management as well as other articles and references and applies the concept of the universality of management to developing an overview of software engineering project management. The last article in this chapter is an overview of lifecycle models by Alan Davis.

3. Article Descriptions

No collection of articles on software engineering project management would be complete without including the classic of all classic software engineering articles, "The Mythical Man-Month," by Fred Brooks. Brooks could be considered the father of modern software engineering project management; his book *The Mythical Man-Month: Essays on Software Engineering*, 1975 [2] is still a best-seller today. This article (or better, the original book) should be required reading for all project managers.

Brooks is the source of such now-famous quotes and sayings as these:

- Adding manpower to a late software project makes it later.

- How does a project get to be a year late? …One day at a time.

- All programmers are optimists.

- The man-month as a unit for measuring the size of a job is a dangerous and deceptive myth.

Brooks completed a second edition of his classic book, *Mythical Man-Month*, in 1995 [2], which includes four new chapters. One of these chapters summarizes his understanding and beliefs of project management, some twenty years from when the initial book was written. It both supports and, in several cases, refutes some of his earlier beliefs.

In the next article in this chapter, Thayer expands on Alex MacKenzie's and other articles by applying the concept of the "universality of management" to developing an overview of software engineering project management. His article takes a top-down approach to establishing a set of project management and software engineering project management responsibilities, activities, and tasks that should be undertaken by any manager who is assigned the responsibility of managing a software engineering project. It covers the management functions of planning, organizing, staffing, directing, and controlling, and discusses in detail activities and tasks necessary to successfully manage a software development project.

The last article in this chapter is an overview of lifecycle development models by Alan Davis entitled "Software Life Cycle Models." Sometimes the term "life cycle" (or "lifecycle") is replaced with the term "process" (see discussion on the Capability Maturity Model in this book).

Davis discusses some of the more recent variations in lifecycle development models as well as the historic waterfall model developed by Winston Royce [3]. Because of the growing complexity of software systems, many practitioners feel the need to have different process models available than the conventional requirements, design, implementation, and testing model.

These alternative models are radically different from the conventional model and include such approaches as rapid prototyping, incremental development, evolutionary prototyping, and the reuse of previously developed software products. Davis points out that many of these alternative models are not yet standardized and are still being developed. (It should be noted that the current US Mil-Std 498, *Software Development and Documentation*, [4] recognizes, among others, three process models: the conventional waterfall, the incremental, and the evolutionary development model.) Davis' article includes a lengthy discussion of Barry Boehm's spiral model [5].

References

1. Brooks, F.P., Jr., *The Mythical Man-Month: Essays on Software Engineering*, Addison-Wesley, Reading, Mass., 1975.

2. Brooks, F.P., Jr., *The Mythical Man-Months: Essays on Software Engineering: Anniversary Edition*, Addison-Wesley, Reading, Mass., 1995.

3. Royce, W.W., "Managing the Development of Large Software Systems: Concepts and Techniques," *1970 WESCON Technical Articles*, Vol. 14, 1970.

4. Mil-Std-498, *Software Development and Documentation*, Department of Defense, 5 Dec 1995.

5. Boehm, B.W., "A Spiral Model of Software Development and Enhancement," *Computer*, Vol. 21, No. 5, May 1988, pp. 61–72. Reprinted in *Software Engineering*, M. Dorfman and R.H. Thayer, eds., IEEE Computer Society Press, Los Alamitos, Calif., 1997.

THE MYTHICAL
MAN-MONTH

The above is an extract from the *Mythical Man-Month* by Frederick P. Brooks, Jr., copyright © 1975 by Addison-Wesley Publishing Company, Inc., Reading, Massachusetts, pages 14-26, 88-94, 153-160, and 177. Reprinted with permission. The extract was prepared by the editors of *Datamation* and published in *Datamation*, December 1974, pages 44-52.

HOW DOES A PROJECT GET TO BE A YEAR LATE? . . . . . . ONE DAY AT A TIME.

By Frederick P. Brooks, Jr.

Dr. Brooks was part of the management team charged with developing the hardware for the IBM 360 system. In 1964 he became the manager of the Operating System/360 project; this trial by fire convinced him that managing a large software project is more like managing any other large undertaking than programmers believe and less like it than professional managers expect.

About his OS/360 project, he says: "Managing OS/360 development was a very educational experience, albeit a very frustrating one. The team, including F. M. Trapnell who succeeded me as manager, has much to be proud of. The system contains many excellences in design and execution, and it has been successful in achieving widespread use. Certain ideas, most noticeably device-independent input/ output and external library management, were technical innovations now widely copied. It is now quite reliable, reasonably efficient, and very versatile.

The effort cannot be called wholly successful, however. Any OS/ 360 user is quickly aware of how much better it should be. The flaws in design and execution pervade especially the control program, as distinguished from language compilers. Most of the flaws date from the 1964-1965 design period and hence must be laid to my charge. Furthermore, the product was late, it took more memory than planned, the costs were several times the estimate, and it did not perform very well until several releases after the first."

Analyzing the OS/360 experiences for management and technical lessons, Dr. Brooks put his thoughts into book form. Addison-Wesley Publishing Company (Reading, Mass.) will offer "The Mythical Man-Month: Essays on Software Engineering", from which this article is taken, sometime next month.

NO SCENE FROM PREHISTORY is quite so vivid as that of the mortal struggles of great beasts in the tar pits. In the mind's eye one sees dinosaurs, mammoths, and saber-toothed tigers struggling against the grip of the tar. The fiercer the struggle, the more entangling the tar, and no beast is so strong or so skillful but that he ultimately sinks.

Large-system programming has over the past decade been such a tar pit, and many great and powerful beasts have thrashed violently in it. Most have emerged with running systems—few have met goals, schedules, and budgets. Large and small, massive or wiry, team after team has become entangled in the tar. No one thing seems to cause the difficulty—any particular paw can be pulled away. But the accumulation of simultaneous and interacting factors brings slower and slower motion. Everyone seems to have been surprised by the stickiness of the problem, and it is hard to discern the nature of it. But we must try to understand it if we are to solve it.

More software projects have gone awry for lack of calendar time than for all other causes combined. Why is this case of disaster so common?

First, our techniques of estimating are poorly developed. More seriously, they reflect an unvoiced assumption which is quite untrue, i.e., that all will go well.

Second, our estimating techniques fallaciously confuse effort with progress, hiding the assumption that men and months are interchangeable.

Third, because we are uncertain of our estimates, software managers often

lack the courteous stubbornness required to make people wait for a good product.

Fourth, schedule progress is poorly monitored. Techniques proven and routine in other engineering disciplines are considered radical innovations in software engineering.

Fifth, when schedule slippage is recognized, the natural (and traditional) response is to add manpower. Like dousing a fire with gasoline, this makes matters worse, much worse. More fire requires more gasoline and thus begins a regenerative cycle which ends in disaster.

Schedule monitoring will be covered later. Let us now consider other aspects of the problem in more detail.

Optimism

All programmers are optimists. Perhaps this modern sorcery especially attracts those who believe in happy endings and fairy godmothers. Perhaps the hundreds of nitty frustrations drive away all but those who habitually focus on the end goal. Perhaps it is merely that computers are young, programmers are younger, and the young are always optimists. But however the selection process works, the result is indisputable: "This time it will surely run," or "I just found the last bug."

So the first false assumption that underlies the scheduling of systems programming is that *all will go well*, i.e., that *each task will take only as long as it "ought" to take*.

The pervasiveness of optimism among programmers deserves more than a flip analysis. Dorothy Sayers, in her excellent book, *The Mind of the*

Maker, divides creative activity into three stages: the idea, the implementation, and the interaction. A book, then, or a computer, or a program comes into existence first as an ideal construct, built outside time and space but complete in the mind of the author. It is realized in time and space by pen, ink, and paper, or by wire, silicon, and ferrite. The creation is complete when someone reads the book, uses the computer or runs the program, thereby interacting with the mind of the maker.

This description, which Miss Sayers uses to illuminate not only human creative activity but also the Christian doctrine of the Trinity, will help us in our present task. For the human makers of things, the incompletenesses and inconsistencies of our ideas become clear only during implementation. Thus it is that writing, experimentation, "working out" are essential disciplines for the theoretician.

In many creative activities the medium of execution is intractable. Lumber splits; paints smear; electrical circuits ring. These physical limitations of the medium constrain the ideas that may be expressed, and they also create unexpected difficulties in the implementation.

Implementation, then, takes time and sweat both because of the physical media and because of the inadequacies of the underlying ideas. We tend to blame the physical media for most of our implementation difficulties; for the media are not "ours" in the way the ideas are, and our pride colors our judgment.

Computer programming, however, creates with an exceedingly tractable medium. The programmer builds from pure thought-stuff: concepts and very flexible representations thereof. Because the medium is tractable, we expect few difficulties in implementation; hence our pervasive optimism. Because our ideas are faulty, we have bugs; hence our optimism is unjustified.

In a single task, the assumption that all will go well has a probabilistic effect on the schedule. It might indeed go as planned, for there is a probability distribution for the delay that will be encountered, and "no delay" has a finite probability. A large programming effort, however, consists of many tasks, some chained end-to-end. The probability that each will go well becomes vanishingly small.

The mythical man-month

The second fallacious thought mode is expressed in the very unit of effort used in estimating and scheduling: the man-month. Cost does indeed vary as

the product of the number of men and the number of months. Progress does not. *Hence the man-month as a unit for measuring the size of a job is a dangerous and deceptive myth.* It implies that men and months are interchangeable.

Men and months are interchangeable commodities only when a task can be partitioned among many workers *with no communication among them* (Fig. 1). This is true of reaping wheat or picking cotton; it is not even approximately true of systems programming.

When a task cannot be partitioned

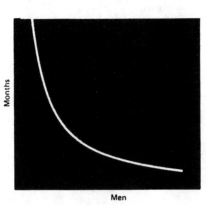

Fig. 1. The term "man-month" implies that if one man takes 10 months to do a job, 10 men can do it in one month. This may be true of picking cotton.

because of sequential constraints, the application of more effort has no effect on the schedule. The bearing of a child takes nine months, no matter how many women are assigned. Many software tasks have this characteristic because of the sequential nature of debugging.

In tasks that can be partitioned but which require communication among the subtasks, the effort of communication must be added to the amount of work to be done. Therefore the best that can be done is somewhat poorer than an even trade of men for months (Fig. 2).

The added burden of communication is made up of two parts, training and intercommunication. Each worker must be trained in the technology, the goals of the effort, the overall strategy, and the plan of work. This training cannot be partitioned, so this part of the added effort varies linearly with the number of workers.

V. S. Vyssotsky of Bell Telephone Laboratories estimates that a large project can sustain a manpower buildup of 30% per year. More than that strains and even inhibits the evolution of the essential informal structure and its communication pathways. F. J.

Corbató of MIT points out that a long project must anticipate a turnover of 20% per year, and new people must be both technically trained and integrated into the formal structure.

Intercommunication is worse. If each part of the task must be separately coordinated with each other part, the effort increases as $n(n-1)/2$. Three workers require three times as much pairwise intercommunication as two; four require six times as much as two. If, moreover, there need to be conferences among three, four, etc., workers to resolve things jointly, matters get worse yet. The added effort of communicating may fully counteract the division of the original task and bring us back to the situation of Fig. 3.

Since software construction is inherently a systems effort—an exercise in complex interrelationships—communication effort is great, and it quickly

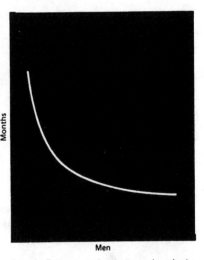

Fig. 2. Even on tasks that can be nicely partitioned among people, the additional communication required adds to the total work, increasing the schedule.

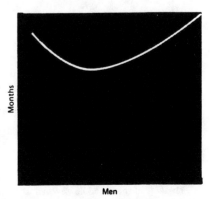

Fig. 3. Since software construction is complex, the communications overhead is great. Adding more men can lengthen, rather than shorten, the schedule.

dominates the decrease in individual task time brought about by partitioning. Adding more men then lengthens, not shortens, the schedule.

Systems test

No parts of the schedule are so thoroughly affected by sequential constraints as component debugging and system test. Furthermore, the time required depends on the number and subtlety of the errors encountered. Theoretically this number should be zero. Because of optimism, we usually expect the number of bugs to be smaller than it turns out to be. Therefore testing is usually the most mis-scheduled part of programming.

For some years I have been successfully using the following rule of thumb for scheduling a software task:

⅓ planning
⅙ coding
¼ component test and early system test
¼ system test, all components in hand.

This differs from conventional scheduling in several important ways:
1. The fraction devoted to planning is larger than normal. Even so, it is barely enough to produce a de-

of the schedule.

In examining conventionally scheduled projects, I have found that few allowed one-half of the projected schedule for testing, but that most did indeed spend half of the actual schedule for that purpose. Many of these were on schedule until and except in system testing.

Failure to allow enough time for system test, in particular, is peculiarly disastrous. Since the delay comes at the end of the schedule, no one is aware of schedule trouble until almost the delivery date. Bad news, late and without warning, is unsettling to customers and to managers.

Furthermore, delay at this point has unusually severe financial, as well as psychological, repercussions. The project is fully staffed, and cost-per-day is maximum. More seriously, the software is to support other business effort (shipping of computers, operation of new facilities, etc.) and the secondary costs of delaying these are very high, for it is almost time for software shipment. Indeed, these secondary costs may far outweigh all others. It is therefore very important to allow enough system test time in the original schedule.

two choices—wait or eat it raw. Software customers have had the same choices.

The cook has another choice; he can turn up the heat. The result is often an omelette nothing can save—burned in one part, raw in another.

Now I do not think software managers have less inherent courage and firmness than chefs, nor than other engineering managers. But false scheduling to match the patron's desired date is much more common in our discipline than elsewhere in engineering. It is very difficult to make a vigorous, plausible, and job-risking defense of an estimate that is derived by no quantitative method, supported by little data, and certified chiefly by the hunches of the managers.

Clearly two solutions are needed. We need to develop and publicize productivity figures, bug-incidence figures, estimating rules, and so on. The whole profession can only profit from sharing such data.

Until estimating is on a sounder basis, individual managers will need to stiffen their backbones, and defend their estimates with the assurance that their poor hunches are better than wish-derived estimates.

Regenerative disaster

What does one do when an essential software project is behind schedule? Add manpower, naturally. As Figs. 1 through 3 suggest, this may or may not help.

Let us consider an example. Suppose a task is estimated at 12 man-months and assigned to three men for four months, and that there are measurable mileposts A, B, C, D, which are scheduled to fall at the end of each month.

Now suppose the first milepost is not reached until two months have elapsed. What are the alternatives facing the manager?
1. Assume that the task must be done on time. Assume that only the first part of the task was misestimated. Then 9 man-months of effort remain, and two months, so 4½ men will be needed. Add 2 men to the 3 assigned.
2. Assume that the task must be done on time. Assume that the whole estimate was uniformly low. Then 18 man-months of effort remain, and two months, so 9 men will be needed. Add 6 men to the 3 assigned.
3. Reschedule. In this case, I like the advice given by an experienced hardware engineer, "Take no small slips." That is, allow enough time in the new schedule to ensure that the work can be carefully and

Fig. 4. Adding manpower to a project which is late may not help. In this case, suppose three men on a 12 man-month project were a month late. If it takes one of the three an extra month to train two new men, the project will be just as late as if no one was added.

tailed and solid specification, and not enough to include research or exploration of totally new techniques.
2. The *half* of the schedule devoted to debugging of completed code is much larger than normal.
3. The part that is easy to estimate, i.e., coding, is given only one-sixth

Gutless estimating

Observe that for the programmer, as for the chef, the urgency of the patron may govern the scheduled completion of the task, but it cannot govern the actual completion. An omelette, promised in ten minutes, may appear to be progressing nicely. But when it has not set in ten minutes, the customer has thoroughly done, and that rescheduling will not have to be done again.

4. Trim the task. In practice this tends to happen anyway, once the team observes schedule slippage. Where the secondary costs of delay are very high, this is the only feasible action. The manager's only alternatives are to trim it formally and carefully, to reschedule, or to watch the task get silently trimmed by hasty design and incomplete testing.

In the first two cases, insisting that the unaltered task be completed in four months is disastrous. Consider the regenerative effects, for example, for the first alternative (Fig. 4 preceding page). The two new men, however competent and however quickly recruited, will require training in the task by one of the experienced men. If this takes a month, *3 man-months will have been devoted to work not in the original estimate.* Furthermore, the task, originally partitioned three ways, must be repartitioned into five parts, hence some work already done will be lost and system testing must be lengthened. So at the end of the third month, substantially more than 7 man-months of effort remain, and 5 trained people and one month are available. As Fig. 4 suggests, the product is just as late as if no one had been added.

To hope to get done in four months, considering only training time and not repartitioning and extra systems test, would require adding 4 men, not 2, at the end of the second month. To cover repartitioning and system test effects, one would have to add still other men. Now, however, one has at least a 7-man team, not a 3-man one; thus such aspects as team organization and task division are different in kind, not merely in degree.

Notice that by the end of the third month things look very black. The March 1 milestone has not been reached in spite of all the managerial effort. The temptation is very strong to repeat the cycle, adding yet more manpower. Therein lies madness.

The foregoing assumed that only the first milestone was misestimated. If on March 1 one makes the conservative assumption that the whole schedule was optimistic one wants to add 6 men just to the original task. Calculation of the training, repartitioning, system testing effects is left as an exercise for the reader. Without a doubt, the regenerative disaster will yield a poorer product later, than would rescheduling with the original three men, unaugmented.

Oversimplifying outrageously, we state Brooks' Law:

Adding manpower to a late software project makes it later.

This then is the demythologizing of the man-month. The number of months of a project depends upon its sequential constraints. The maximum number of men depends upon the number of independent subtasks. From these two quantities one can derive schedules using fewer men and more months. (The only risk is product obsolescence.) One cannot, however, get workable schedules using more men and fewer months. More software projects have gone awry for lack of calendar time than for all other causes combined.

Calling the shot

How long will a system programming job take? How much effort will be required? How does one estimate?

I have earlier suggested ratios that seem to apply to planning time, coding, component test, and system test. First, one must say that one does *not* estimate the entire task by estimating the coding portion only and then applying the ratios. The coding is only one-sixth or so of the problem, and errors in its estimate or in the ratios could lead to ridiculous results.

Second, one must say that data for building isolated small programs are not applicable to programming systems products. For a program averaging about 3,200 words, for example, Sackman, Erikson, and Grant report an average code-plus-debug time of about 178 hours for a single programmer, a figure which would extrapolate to give an annual productivity of 35,800 statements per year. A program half that size took less than one-fourth as long, and extrapolated productivity is almost 80,000 statements per year.[1]. Planning, documentation, testing, system integration, and training times must be added. The linear extrapolation of such spring figures is meaningless. Extrapolation of times for the hundred-yard dash shows that a man can run a mile in under three minutes.

Before dismissing them, however, let us note that these numbers, although not for strictly comparable problems, suggest that effort goes as a power of size *even* when no communication is involved except that of a man with his memories.

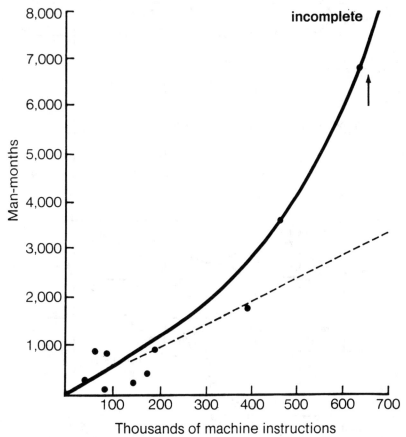

Fig. 5. As a project's complexity increases, the number of man-months required to complete it goes up exponentially.

Fig. 5 tells the sad story. It illustrates results reported from a study done by Nanus and Farr[2] at System Development Corp. This shows an exponent of 1.5; that is,

effort = (constant)×(number of instructions)[1.5]

Another SDC study reported by Weinwurm[3] also shows an exponent near 1.5.

A few studies on programmer productivity have been made, and several estimating techniques have been proposed. Morin has prepared a survey of the published data.[4] Here I shall give only a few items that seem especially illuminating.

Portman's data

Charles Portman, manager of ICL's Software Div., Computer Equipment Organization (Northwest) at Manchester, offers another useful personal insight.

He found his programming teams missing schedules by about one-half— each job was taking approximately twice as long as estimated. The estimates were very careful, done by experienced teams estimating man-hours for several hundred subtasks on a PERT chart. When the slippage pattern appeared, he asked them to keep careful daily logs of time usage. These showed that the estimating error could be entirely accounted for by the fact that his teams were only realizing 50% of the working week as actual programming and debugging time. Machine downtime, higher-priority short unrelated jobs, meetings, paperwork, company business, sickness, personal time, etc. accounted for the rest. In short, the estimates made an unrealistic assumption about the number of technical work hours per man-year. My own experience quite confirms his conclusion.

An unpublished 1964 study by E. F. Bardain shows programmers realizing only 27% productive time.[5]

Aron's data

Joel Aron, manager of Systems Technology at IBM in Gaithersburg, Maryland, has studied programmer productivity when working on nine large systems (briefly, *large* means more than 25 programmers and 30,-000 deliverable instructions). He divides such systems according to interactions among programmers (and system parts) and finds productivities as follows:

Very few interactions   10,000 instructions per man-year
Some interactions   5,000
Many interactions   1,500

The man-years do not include support and system test activities, only design and programming. When these figures are diluted by a factor of two to cover system test, they closely match Harr's data.

Harr's data

John Harr, manager of programming for the Bell Telephone Laboratories' Electronic Switching System, reported his and others' experience in a paper at the 1969 Spring Joint Computer Conference.[6] These data are shown in Table 1 and Figs. 6 and 7.

Of these, Fig. 6 is the most detailed and the most useful. The first two jobs are basically control programs; the second two are basically language translators. Productivity is stated in terms of debugged words per man-year. This includes programming, component test, and system test. It is not clear how much of the planning effort, or effort in machine support, writing, and the

	Prog. units	Number of programmers	Years	Man-years	Program words	Words/ man-yr.
Operational	50	83	4	101	52,000	515
Maintenance	36	60	4	81	51,000	630
Compiler	13	9	2¼	17	38,000	2230
Translator (Data assembler)	15	13	2½	11	25,000	2270

Table 1. Data from Bell Labs indicates productivity differences between complex problems (the first two are basically control programs with many modules) and less complex ones. No one is certain how much of the difference is due to complexity, how much to the number of people involved.

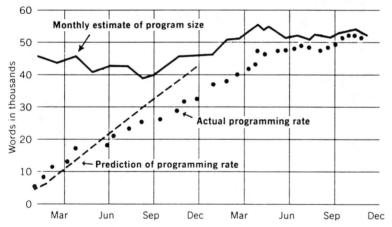

Fig. 6. Bell Labs' experience in predicting programming effort on one project.

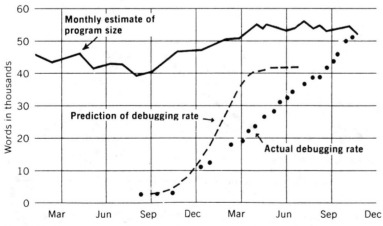

Fig. 7. Bell's predictions for debugging rates on a single project, contrasted with actual figures.

like, is included.

The productivities likewise fall into two classifications: those for control programs are about 600 words per man-year; those for translators are about 2,200 words per man-year. Note that all four programs are of similar size—the variation is in size of the work groups, length of time, and number of modules. Which is cause and which is effect? Did the control programs require more people because they were more complicated? Or did they require more modules and more man-months because they were assigned more people? Did they take longer because of the greater complexity, or because more people were assigned? One can't be sure. The control programs were surely more complex. These uncertainties aside, the numbers describe the real productivities achieved on a large system, using present-day programming techniques. As such they are a real contribution.

Figs. 6 and 7 show some interesting data on programming and debugging rates as compared to predicted rates.

OS/360 data
IBM OS/360 experience, while not available in the detail of Harr's data, confirms it. Productivities in range of 600-800 debugged instructions per man-year were experienced by control program groups. Productivities in the 2,000-3,000 debugged instructions per man-year were achieved by language translator groups. These include planning done by the group, coding component test, system test, and some support activities. They are comparable to Harr's data, so far as I can tell.

Aron's data, Harr's data, and the OS/360 data all confirm striking differences in productivity related to the complexity and difficulty of the task itself. My guideline in the morass of estimating complexity is that compilers are three times as bad as normal batch application programs, and operating systems are three times as bad as compilers.

Corbató's data
Both Harr's data and OS/360 data are for assembly language programming. Little data seem to have been published on system programming productivity using higher-level languages. Corbató of MIT's Project MAC reports, however, a mean productivity of 1,200 lines of debugged PL/I statements per man-year on the MULTICS system (between 1 and 2 million words) [7]

This number is very exciting. Like the other projects, MULTICS includes control programs and language transla-

tors. Like the others, it is producing a system programming product, tested and documented. The data seem to be comparable in terms of kind of effort included. And the productivity number is a good average between the control program and translator productivities of other projects.

But Corbató's number is *lines* per man-year, not *words!* Each statement in his system corresponds to about three-to-five words of handwritten code! This suggests two important conclusions:

• Productivity seems constant in terms of elementary statements, a conclusion that is reasonable in terms of the thought a statement requires and the errors it may include.
• Programming productivity may be increased as much as five times when a suitable high-level language is used. To back up these conclusions, W. M. Taliaffero also reports a constant productivity of 2,400 statements/year in Assembler, FORTRAN, and COBOL.[8] E. A. Nelson has shown a 3-to-1 productivity improvement for high-level language, although his standard deviations are wide.[9]

Hatching a catastrophe
When one hears of disastrous schedule slippage in a project, he imagines that a series of major calamities must have befallen it. Usually, however, the disaster is due to termites, not tornadoes; and the schedule has slipped imperceptibly but inexorably. Indeed, major calamities are easier to handle; one responds with major force, radical reorganization, the invention of new approaches. The whole team rises to the occasion.

But the day-by-day slippage is harder to recognize, harder to prevent, harder to make up. Yesterday a key man was sick, and a meeting couldn't be held. Today the machines are all down, because lightning struck the building's power transformer. Tomorrow the disc routines won't start testing, because the first disc is a week late from the factory. Snow, jury duty, family problems, emergency meetings with customers, executive audits—the list goes on and on. Each one only postpones some activity by a half-day or a day. And the schedule slips, one day at a time.

How does one control a big project on a tight schedule? The first step is to *have* a schedule. Each of a list of events, called milestones, has a date. Picking the dates is an estimating problem, discussed already and crucially dependent on experience.

For picking the milestones there is

only one relevant rule. Milestones must be concrete, specific, measurable events, defined with knife-edge sharpness. Coding, for a counterexample, is "90% finished" for half of the total coding time. Debugging is "99% complete" most of the time. "Planning complete" is an event one can proclaim almost at will.[10]

Concrete milestones, on the other hand, are 100% events. "Specifications signed by architects and implementers," "source coding 100% complete, keypunched, entered into disc library," "debugged version passes all test cases." These concrete milestones demark the vague phases of planning, coding, debugging.

It is more important that milestones be sharp-edged and unambiguous than that they be easily verifiable by the boss. Rarely will a man lie about mile-

> None love
> the bearer of bad news.
> *Sophocles*

stone progress, *if* the milestone is so sharp that he can't deceive himself. But if the milestone is fuzzy, the boss often understands a different report from that which the man gives. To supplement Sophocles, no one enjoys bearing bad news, either, so it gets softened without any real intent to deceive.

Two interesting studies of estimating behavior by government contractors on large-scale development projects show that:
1. Estimates of the length of an activity made and revised carefully every two weeks before the activity starts do not significantly change as the start time draws near, no matter how wrong they ultimately turn out to be.
2. *During* the activity, *over*estimates of duration come steadily down as the activity proceeds.
3. *Underestimates* do not change significantly during the activity until about three weeks before the scheduled completion.[11]

Sharp milestones are in fact a service to the team, and one they can properly expect from a manager. The fuzzy milestone is the harder burden to live with. It is in fact a millstone that grinds down morale, for it deceives one about lost time until it is irremediable. And chronic schedule slippage is a morale-killer.

"The other piece is late"
A schedule slips a day; so what? Who gets excited about a one-day slip? We can make it up later. And the other piece ours fits into is late anyway.

A baseball manager recognizes a nonphysical talent, *hustle,* as an essential gift of great players and great teams. It is the characteristic of running faster than necessary, moving sooner than necessary, trying harder than necessary. It is essential for great programming teams, too. Hustle provides the cushion, the reserve capacity, that enables a team to cope with routine mishaps, to anticipate and forfend minor calamities. The calculated response, the measured effort, are the wet blankets that dampen hustle. As we have seen, one *must* get excited about a one-day slip. Such are the elements of catastrophe.

But not all one-day slips are equally disastrous. So some calculation of response is necessary, though hustle be dampened. How does one tell which slips matter? There is no substitute for a PERT chart or a critical-path schedule. Such a network shows who waits for what. It shows who is on the critical path, where any slip moves the end date. It also shows how much an activity can slip before it moves into the critical path.

The PERT technique, strictly speaking, is an elaboration of critical-path scheduling in which one estimates three times for every event, times corresponding to different probabilities of meeting the estimated dates. I do not find this refinement to be worth the extra effort, but for brevity I will call any critical path network a PERT chart.

The preparation of a PERT chart is the most valuable part of its use. Laying out the network, identifying the dependencies, and estimating the legs all force a great deal of very specific planning very early in a project. The first chart is always terrible, and one invents and invents in making the second one.

As the project proceeds, the PERT chart provides the answer to the demoralizing excuse, "The other piece is late anyhow." It shows how hustle is needed to keep one's own part off the critical path, and it suggests ways to make up the lost time in the other part.

Under the rug

When a first-line manager sees his small team slipping behind, he is rarely inclined to run to the boss with this woe. The team might be able to make it up, or he should be able to invent or reorganize to solve the problem. Then why worry the boss with it? So far, so good. Solving such problems is exactly what the first-line manager is there for. And the boss does have enough real worries demanding his action that he doesn't seek others. So all the dirt gets swept under the rug.

But every boss needs two kinds of information, exceptions for action and a status picture for education.[12] For that purpose he needs to know the status of all his teams. Getting a true picture of that status is hard.

The first-line manager's interests and those of the boss have an inherent conflict here. The first-line manager fears that if he reports his problem, the boss will act on it. Then his action will preempt the manager's function, diminish his authority, foul up his other plans. So as long as the manager thinks he can solve it alone, he doesn't tell the boss.

Two rug-lifting techniques are open to the boss. Both must be used. The first is to reduce the role conflict and inspire sharing of status. The other is to yank the rug back.

Reducing the role conflict

The boss must first distinguish between action information and status information. He must discipline himself *not* to act on problems his managers can solve, and *never* to act on problems when he is explicitly reviewing status. I once knew a boss who invariably picked up the phone to give orders before the end of the first para-

A=APPROVAL
C=COMPLETED

*= REVISED PLANNED DATE
NE=NOT ESTABLISHED

PROJECT	LOCATION	COMMITMNT ANNOUNCE RELEASE	OBJECTIVE AVAILABLE APPROVED	SPECS AVAILABLE APPROVED	SRL AVAILABLE APPROVED	ALPHA TEST ENTRY EXIT	COMP TEST START COMPLETE	SYS TEST START COMPLETE	BULLETIN AVAILABLE APPROVED	BETA TEST ENTRY EXIT
OPERATING SYSTEM										
12K DESIGN LEVEL (E)										
ASSEMBLY	SAN JOSE	04/--/4 12/31/5	10/28/4 C	10/13/4 C 01/11/5	11/13/4 C 11/16/4 A	01/15/5 C 02/22/5				09/01/5 11/30/5
FORTRAN	POK	04/--/4 C 12/31/5	10/28/4 C	10/21/4 C 01/22/5	12/17/4 C 12/19/4 A	01/15/5 C 02/22/5				09/01/5 11/30/5
COBOL	ENDICOTT	04/--/4 C 12/31/5	10/25/4 C	10/15/4 C 01/20/5 A	11/17/4 C 12/08/4 A	01/15/5 C 02/22/5				09/01/5 11/30/5
RPG	SAN JOSE	04/--/4 C 12/31/5	10/28/4 C	09/30/4 C 01/05/5 A	12/02/4 C 01/18/5 A	01/15/5 C 02/22/5				09/01/5 11/30/5
UTILITIES	TIME/LIFE	04/--/4 C 12/31/5	06/24/4 C		11/20/4 C 11/30/4 A					09/01/5 11/30/5
SORT 1	POK	04/--/4 C 12/31/5	10/28/4 C	10/19/4 C 01/11/5	11/12/4 C 11/30/4 A	01/15/5 C 03/22/5				09/01/5 11/30/5
SORT 2	POK	04/--/4 C 06/30/6	10/28/4 C	10/19/4 C 01/11/5	11/12/4 C 11/30/4 A	01/15/5 C 03/22/5				03/01/6 05/30/6
44K DESIGN LEVEL (F)										
ASSEMBLY	SAN JOSE	04/--/4 C 12/31/5	10/28/4 C	10/13/4 C 01/11/5	11.13.4 C 11/18/4 A	02/15/5 C 03/22/5				09/01/5 11/30/5
COBOL	TIME/LIFE	04/--/4 C 06/30/6	10/28/4 C	10/15/4 C 01/20/5 A	11/17/4 C 12/06/4 A	02/15/5 C 03/22/5				03/01/5 05/30/6
NPL	HURSLEY	04/--/4 C 03/31/6	10/28/4 C							
2250	KINGSTON	03/30/4 C 03/31/6	11/05/4 C	10/06/4 C 01/04/5	01/12/5 C 01/29/5	01/04/5 C 01/29/5				01/03/6 NE
2280	KINGSTON	06/30/4 C 09/30/6	11/05/4 C			04/01/5 04/30/5				01/28/6 NE
200K DESIGN LEVEL (H)										
ASSEMBLY	TIME/LIFE		10/28/4 C							
FORTRAN	POK	04/--/4 C 06/30/6	10/28/4 C	10/16/4 C 01/11/5	11/11/4 C 12/10/4 A	02/15/5 C 03/22/5				03/01/6 05/30/6
NPL	HURSLEY	04/--/4 C	10/28/4 C			07/--/5				01/--/7
NPL H	POK	04/--/4 C	03/30/4 C			02/01/5 04/01/5				10/15/5 12/15/5

Fig. 8. A report showing milestones and status in a key document in project control. This one shows some problems in OS development: specifications approval is late on some items (those without "A"); documentation (SRL) approval is overdue on another; and one (2250 support) is late coming out of alpha test.

graph in a status report. That response is guaranteed to squelch full disclosure.

Conversely, when the manager knows his boss will accept status reports without panic or preemption, he comes to give honest appraisals.

This whole process is helped if the boss labels meetings, reviews, conferences, as *status-review* meetings versus *problem-action* meetings, and controls himself accordingly. Obviously one may call a problem-action meeting as a consequence of a status meeting, if he believes a problem is out of hand. But at least everybody knows what the score is, and the boss thinks twice before grabbing the ball.

Yanking the rug off

Nevertheless, it is necessary to have review techniques by which the true status is made known, whether cooperatively or not. The PERT chart with its frequent sharp milestones is the basis for such review. On a large project one may want to review some part of it each week, making the rounds once a month or so.

A report showing milestones and actual completions is the key document. Fig. 8 (preceding page), shows an excerpt from such a report. This report shows some troubles. Specifications approval is overdue on several components. Manual (SRL) approval is overdue on another, and one is late getting out of the first state (ALPHA) of the independently conducted product test. So such a report serves as an agenda for the meeting of 1 February. Everyone knows the questions, and the component manager should be prepared to explain why it's late, when it will be finished, what steps he's taking, and what help, if any, he needs from the boss or collateral groups.

V. Vyssotsky of Bell Telephone Laboratories adds the following observation:

I have found it handy to carry both "scheduled" and "estimated" dates in the milestone report. The scheduled dates are the property of the project manager and represent a consistent work plan for the project as a whole, and one which is a priori a reasonable plan. The estimated dates are the property of the lowest level manager who has cognizance over the piece of work in question, and represents his best judgment as to when it will actually happen, given the resources he has available and when he received (or has commitments for delivery of) his prerequisite inputs. The project manager has to keep his fingers off the estimated dates, and put the emphasis on getting accurate, unbiased estimates rather than palatable optimistic estimates or self-protective conservative ones. Once this is clearly established in everyone's mind, the project manager can see quite a ways into the future where he is going to be in trouble if he doesn't do something.

The preparation of the PERT chart is a function of the boss and the managers reporting to him. Its updating, revision, and reporting requires the attention of a small (one-to-three-man) staff group which serves as an extension of the boss. Such a "Plans and Controls" team is invaluable for a large project. It has no authority except to ask all the line managers when they will have set or changed milestones, and whether milestones have been met. Since the Plans and Controls group handles all the paperwork, the burden on the line managers is reduced to the essentials—making the decisions.

We had a skilled, enthusiastic, and diplomatic Plans and Controls group on the os/360 project, run by A. M. Pietrasanta, who devoted considerable inventive talent to devising effective but unobtrusive control methods. As a result, I found his group to be widely respected and more than tolerated. For a group whose role is inherently that of an irritant, this is quite an accomplishment.

The investment of a modest amount of skilled effort in a Plans and Controls function is very rewarding. It makes far more difference in project accomplishment than if these people worked directly on building the product programs. For the Plans and Controls group is the watchdog who renders the imperceptible delays visible and who points up the critical elements. It is the early warning system against losing a year, one day at a time.

Epilogue

The tar pit of software engineering will continue to be sticky for a long time to come. One can expect the human race to continue attempting systems just within or just beyond our reach; and software systems are perhaps the most intricate and complex of man's handiworks. The management of this complex craft will demand our best use of new languages and systems, our best adaptation of proven engineering management methods, liberal doses of common sense, and a God-given humility to recognize our fallibility and limitations.

References

1. Sackman, H., W. J. Erikson, and E. E. Grant, "Exploratory Experimentation Studies Comparing Online and Offline Programming Performance," *Communications of the ACM*, 11 (1968), 3-11.
2. Nanus, B., and L. Farr, "Some Cost Contributors to Large-Scale Programs," *AFIPS Proceedings, SJCC*, 25 (1964), 239-248.
3. Weinwurm, G. F., *Research in the Management of Computer Programming*. Report SP-2059, 1965, System Development Corp., Santa Monica.
4. Morin, L. H., *Estimation of Resources for Computer Programming Projects*, M. S. thesis, Univ. of North Carolina, Chapel Hill, 1974.
5. Quoted by D. B. Mayer and A. W. Stalnaker, "Selection and Evaluation of Computer Personnel," *Proceedings 23 ACM Conference*, 1968, 661.
6. Paper given at a panel session and not included in the *AFIPS Proceedings*.
7. Corbató, F. J., *Sensitive Issues in the Design of Multi-Use Systems*. Lecture at the opening of the Honeywell EDP Technology Center, 1968.
8. Taliaffero, W. M., "Modularity the Key to System Growth Potential," *Software*, 1 (1971), 245-257.
9. Nelson, E. A., *Management Handbook for the Estimation of Computer Programming Costs*. Report TM-3225, System Development Corp., Santa Monica, pp. 66-67.
10. Reynolds, C. H., "What's Wrong with Computer Programming Management?" in *On the Management of Computer Programming*. Ed. G. F. Weinwurm. Philadelphia: Auerbach, 1971, pp. 35-42.
11. King, W. R., and T. A. Wilson, "Subjective Time Estimates in Critical Path Planning—a Preliminary Analysis," *Management Sciences*, 13 (1967), 307-320, and sequel, W. R. King, D. M. Witterrongel, and K. D. Hezel, "On the Analysis of Critical Path Time Estimating Behavior," *Management Sciences*, 14 (1967), 79-84.
12. Brooks, F. P., and K. E. Iverson, *Automatic Data Processing, System/360 Edition*. New York: Wiley, 1969, pp. 428-430.

Dr. Brooks is presently a professor at the Univ. of North Carolina at Chapel Hill, and chairman of the computer science department there. He is best known as "the father of the IBM System/360," having served as project manager for the hardware development and as manager of the Operating System/360 project during its design phase. Earlier he was an architect of the IBM Stretch and Harvest computers.

At Chapel Hill he has participated in establishing and guiding the Triangle Universities Computation Center and the North Carolina Educational Computing Service. He is the author of two editions of "Automatic Data Processing" and "The Mythical Man-Month: Essays on Software Engineering" (Addison-Wesley), from which this excerpt is taken.

Software Engineering Project Management

Richard H. Thayer
California State University, Sacramento
Sacramento, CA 95819

Abstract

This article describes those management procedures, practices, technologies, and skills that are necessary to successfully manage—plan, organize, staff, direct, and control—a software engineering activity or enterprise. The universality of these concepts provides a management framework for adapting traditional management functions. From these management functions, this article derives the detailed activities and tasks that should be undertaken by a manager assigned to a software engineering project.

1. Introduction

This article is about management, the universality of management concepts, and the activities and tasks of software engineering project management.

Management involves the activities and tasks undertaken by one or more persons for the purpose of planning and controlling the activities of others in order to achieve objectives that could not be achieved by the others acting alone. Management functions can be categorized as planning, organizing, staffing, directing, and controlling.

Project management is a system of management procedures, practices, technologies, skill, and experience that are necessary to successfully manage an engineering project. If the product of a project is software, then the act of managing the project is called software engineering project management. The manager of a software engineering project is called a *software engineering project manager*, a *software project manager*, or in many cases just project manager.

Software engineering projects are frequently part of larger, more comprehensive projects that include equipment (hardware), facilities, personnel, and procedures, as well as software. Examples include aircraft systems, accounting systems, radar systems, inventory control systems, and railroad switching systems. These systems engineering projects are typically managed by one or more system project managers (sometimes called *program managers*) who manage projects composed of engineers, domain experts, sci-entific specialists, programmers, support personnel, and others. If the software to be delivered is a stand-alone software system (a system that does not involve development of other non-software components), the software engineering project manager may be called the system project manager.

Universality of management is a concept that comes from management science [Weihrich 1997], [Koontz and O'Donnell 1972], [Fayol 1949]:

- Management performs the same functions (planning, organizing, staffing, directing, and controlling) regardless of position in the organization or the enterprise managed.

- Management functions are characteristic duties of managers; management practices, methods, activities, and tasks are specific to the enterprise or job managed.

The universality of management concepts let us apply them to software engineering project management [Thayer and Pyster 1984].

This article describes the management functions necessary to plan, organize, staff, direct, and control an activity or enterprise. The universality of these concepts provides a management framework for adapting traditional management functions. From these management functions, this article derives the detailed activities and tasks that should be undertaken by a manager assigned to a software engineering project.

Section 2 lists some of the major issues of software engineering that pertain to project management. Section 3 partitions the functions of management into a detailed list of management activities. Sections 4 through 8 then partitions these management activities into the detailed activities and tasks of a software engineering project manager. Section 9 provides a summary of the article.

2. Major Issues of Software Engineering

Over 70 percent of software development organizations develop their software through ad hoc and unpredictable methods [Zubrow et al. 1995]. These organizations (considered to be "immature" according to the Software Engineering Institute's Capability Maturity Model) do not have an objective basis for determining software cost and schedule or judging software quality. Software development processes are generally improvised by practitioners and their management during the course of the project. The company does not have any standard practices or if they do, they are not followed. Each manager manages by using what worked best for himself during his last project. Proved software engineering techniques such as in-depth requirements analysis, inspections, reviews, testing, and documentation are reduced or eliminated when the project falls behind in cost, schedule, and/or the customer demands more functionality without a corresponding increase in budget. [Paulk et al. 1997]

The "software crisis" is identified by software that is late, over budget, and fails to meet the customer's system requirements [Gibbs 1994]. Many if not most of these problems have been blamed on inadequate or inferior software project management.

The importance of software project management is best illustrated in the following paragraphs extracted from the following Department of Defense (DoD) reports.

- A report from the STARS initiative (STARS: Software Technology for Adaptable, Reliable Systems) states, "The manager plays a major role in software and systems development and support. The difference between success or failure—between a project being on schedule and on budget or late and over budget—is often a function of the manager's effectiveness." [DoD Software Initiative 1983].

- A *Report to the Defense Science Board Task Force on Military Software* states that "... today's major problems with software development are not technical problems, but management problems." [Brooks 1987]

- This was reinforced by a General Accounting Office report that investigated the cost and schedule overrun of the C-17 and said, "... software development has clearly been a major problem during the first 6 years of the program. In fact, the C-17 is a good example of how not to manage software development...." [GAO/IMTEC-92-48 C-17 Aircraft Software]

3. Functions and Activities of Management

This article presents a top-down overview of software engineering project management responsibilities, activities, and tasks that should be undertaken by any manager who is assigned the responsibility of managing a software engineering project. A top-down approach is used to partition and allocate top-level functions to lower level activities and tasks.

Figure 1 depicts the classic management model as portrayed by such well-known authors in the field of management as Heinz Weihrich [1997], Harold Koontz and Cyril O'Donnell [1972], and others [Rue and Byars, 1983], [Cleland and King, 1972], [MacKenzie, 1969].

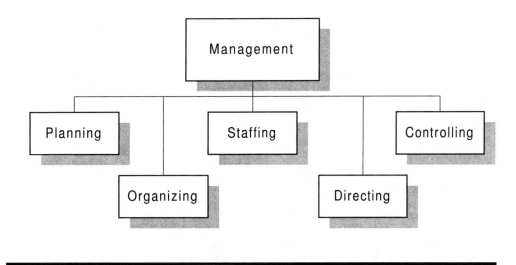

Figure 1. Classic management model.

According to this model, management is partitioned into five separate functions or components: planning, organizing, staffing, directing, and controlling (see Table 1 for definitions or explanations of these functions). All the activities of management—such as budgeting, scheduling, establishing authority and responsibility relationships, training, communicating, allocation of responsibility, and so forth—fall under one of these five headings.

In a later edition of Koontz and O'Donnell's classic reference [Koontz, O'Donnell, and Weihrich 1980], the function "directing" is called "leading." However, we will retain the original term in this article.

Each of the five principal functions of management can be further partitioned into a set of more detailed management activities. These activities can then be subdivided into more detailed tasks. These activities are the characteristic duties of managers and can be applied to the management of any organization or project. (The definitions or explanations of these activities can be found in Tables 2, 4, 7, 8, and 11.)

The detailed activities and tasks that are particular to a software engineering project are defined and discussed in Sections 3 through 8. Each of these sections defines and discusses one of the five management functions plus associated concerns. The management activities from Table 1 are partitioned into one or more levels of detailed tasks, which are then discussed and/or illustrated in the appropriate section.

4. Planning a Software Engineering Project

4.1 Introduction and Definitions

Planning a software engineering project consists of the management activities that lead to selection, among alternatives, of future courses of action for the project and a program for completing those actions.

Planning thus involves specifying the *goals* and *objectives* for a project and the *strategies, policies, plans,* and *procedures* for achieving them. "Planning is deciding in advance what to do, how to do it, when to do it, and who is to do it" [Koontz and O'Donnell 1972].

Every software engineering project should start with a good plan. Uncertainties and unknowns, both within the software project environment and from external sources make planning necessary. Planning focuses attention on project goals, actions necessary to reach those goals, and potential risks and problems that might interfere with attaining those goals.

4.2 Major Issues in Planning a Software Project

The major issues in planning for a software engineering project include the following:

- Software requirements are frequently incorrect and incomplete.

- Many software requirement specifications are unstable and are subject to frequent and major changes.

- Planning is often not attempted under the mistaken belief that it is a waste of time and the plans will change anyway.

- Planning schedule and cost are not updated and are based on marketing needs, not system requirements.

- It is difficult to estimate the size and complexities of the software project in order to make a realistic cost and schedule estimate.

- Cost and schedules are not reestimated when requirements or development environment change.

- Risk factors are not assessed or managed.

- Most software development organizations don't collect project data on past projects.

- Companies do not establish software development policies or processes.

Table 1. Major functions of management.

Activity	Definition or Explanation
Planning	Predetermining a course of action for accomplishing organizational objectives
Organizing	Arranging the relationships among work units for accomplishment of objectives and the granting of responsibility and authority to obtain those objectives
Staffing	Selecting and training people for positions in the organization
Directing	Creating an atmosphere that will assist and motivate people to achieve desired end results
Controlling	Establishing, measuring, and evaluating performance of activities toward planned objectives

It is difficult to prepare software requirements that are correct, complete, and clear [Davis 1990], [Faulk 1997]. As a result, the project may have incorrect or incomplete objectives. This vagueness can result in poor cost and schedule estimates, which are essential elements of a management plan.

In addition, when requirements change, often drastically, cost and schedule estimates remain unchanged. This is caused by the reluctance of project managers to ask their supervisors or the customer for more resources. In addition, when requirements change, often drastically, cost and schedule estimates remain unchanged. This is caused by the reluctance of project managers to ask their supervisors or the customer for more resources and the failure to recognize that even minor change can have a drastic effect on cost and schedule of the project.

More importantly, planning is often not done or is poorly done. Plans are often neglected and not updated as conditions change. Project plans are usually not deliverable items. To some managers, planning appears to be an unnecessary activity that can be discarded to save money for programming and testing. Even in Department of Defense (DoD) projects, where a planning document is usually required 30 days after award of contract, the project plan may receive only a superficial review. In many cases, it is allowed "to gather dust on a shelf" after it is produced.

Accurate budgets and schedules are hard to prepare. Most realistic cost estimates are based on past histories of cost and schedule for similar projects modified by the expected size and complexity of the proposed project. Accurate size estimates are extremely difficult to obtain in the planning stage of a project. The real culprit for inaccurate estimates is lack of relevant historical data on which to base the estimates.

Many project managers do not get a chance to make realistic attempts to create an accurate cost and schedule estimate. Outside forces, such as marketing or software contracts that have been bid too low, can establish a cost and schedule ceiling. This can be far from the probable cost of the software system. Many senior managers do not realize that forcing a low estimate will drive up the cost of a software system. This causes software developers to make many false starts trying to deliver against unrealistic, low cost goals. As a result they lose good software engineers who quit in frustration.

Risks are acceptable as long as their possible effects on the project are known, including likely outcomes if problems develop from the risks. Unfortunately many times project requirements and plans are based on assumptions that are not documented and/or known by the responsible managers. In these cases,

when a risk becomes a problem, it catches the development staff and management completely by surprise, resulting in late delivery and cost overruns.

Policies are the tools of upper management. Many major corporations operate without adequate policies for developing and managing software systems. This results in a lack of control in and around the project environment. For an exception, see the policies produced by TRW in [Goldberg 1978].

4.3 Planning Activities for a Software Project

Table 2 provides an outline of the activities that must be accomplished by software project managers in planning their projects. The project manager is responsible for developing numerous types of plans. Table 3 contains a list of general management plans that can be applicable to any software engineering project.

The balance of this section discusses in greater detail the activities outlined in Table 2.

4.3.1 Set Objectives and Goals for the Project. The first planning step for a software engineering project is to determine what the project must accomplish, when it must be accomplished, and what resources are necessary.

This involves analyzing and documenting the system and software requirements. The management requirements and constraints must be determined. Management constraints are often expressed as resource and schedule limitations.

Success criteria must also be specified. Success criteria would normally include delivery of a software system that satisfies the requirements, on time and within costs. However, there may be other criteria. For instance, success could include winning a follow-on contract. Other criteria might include increasing the size and scope of the present contract, or increasing the profit margin by winning an incentive award.

Success criteria might also be placed in a relative hierarchy of importance. For example being on time might be more important than being within budget.

4.3.2 Develop Project Strategies. Another planning activity is to develop and document a set of management *strategies* (sometimes called strategic policies) for a project. Strategies are defined as long-range goals and the methods to obtain those goals. These long-range goals are usually developed at a corporate level. The project manager can also have strategic plans within an individual project. This is particularly true if it is a large project. An example of a strategic plan might be to develop a new area of expertise or business for the organization by conducting a project in that area.

Table 2. Planning activities for software projects.

Activity	Definition or Explanation
Set objectives and goals	Determine the desired outcome for the project.
Develop strategies	Decide major organizational goals and develop a general program of action for reaching those goals.
Develop policies	Make standing decisions on important recurring matters to provide a guide for decision making.
Forecast future situations	Anticipate future events or make assumptions about the future; predict future results or expectations from courses of action.
Conduct a risk assessment	Anticipate possible adverse events and problem areas; state assumptions; develop contingency plans; predict results of possible courses of action.
Determine possible courses of action	Develop, analyze, and/or evaluate different ways to conduct the project.
Make planning decisions	Evaluate and select a course of action from among alternatives.
Set procedures and rules	Establish methods, guides, and limits for accomplishing the project activity.
Develop project plans	Establish policies, procedures, rules, tasks, schedules, and resources necessary to complete the project.
Prepare budgets	Allocate estimated costs to project functions, activities, and tasks.
Document project plans	Record policy decisions, courses of action, budget, program plans, and contingency plans.

Table 3. Types of plans for software projects.

Types of Plans	Definition or Explanation
Objectives	The project goals toward which activities are directed.
Strategic	The overall approach to a project that provides guidance for placing emphasis and using resources to achieve the project objectives.
Policies	Directives that guide decision making and project activities. Policies limit the freedom in making decisions but allow for some discretion.
Procedures	Directives that specify customary methods of handling activities; guides to actions rather than decision making. Procedures detail the exact manner in which a project activity must be accomplished and allow very little discretion.
Rules	Requirements for specific and definite actions to be taken or not taken with respect to particular project situations. No discretion is allowed.
Plan	An interrelated set of goals, objectives, policies, procedures, rules, work assignments, resources to be used, and other elements necessary to conduct a software project.
Budget	A statement of constraints on resources, expressed in quantitative terms such as dollars or staff-hours.

4.3.3 Develop Policies for the Project. Policies are predetermined management decisions. The project manager may establish policies for the project to provide guidance to supervisors and individual team members in making routine decisions. For example, it might be a policy of the project that status reports from team leaders are due in the project manager's office by close of business each Thursday. Policies can reduce the need for interaction on every decision and provide a sense of direction for the team members. In many cases, the project manager does not develop new policies for the project but follows the policies established at the corporate level.

4.3.4 Forecast Future Situations. Determining future courses of action will be based on the current status and environment as well as the project manager's vision of the future. The project manager is responsible for forecasting situations that might impact the software project.

Forecasting is addressed in two steps. Step (1) involves predicting the future environment of the project, and step (2) deals with how the project will respond to the predicted future. Step one involves prediction of future events such as availability of personnel, the inflation rate, availability of new computer hardware, and the impact these future events will have on the project. The second step involves the prediction of project results such as the specification of future project resource and fund expenditures. The project manager is also responsible for estimating risks and developing contingency plans for countering those risks.

4.3.5 Conduct a Risk Assessment for the Project. Risk is the likelihood of a specified hazardous, undesirable event occurring within a specified period or circumstance. The concept of risk has two elements: the frequency, or probability that a specified hazard might occur, and the consequences of it. Risk factors must be identified and forecasts must be prepared outlining situations that might adversely impact the software project. [Fairley and Rook 1996] and [Thayer and Fairley, Software Risks, 1997]. For example, suppose there is serious doubt that the software can be developed for the amount specified in the contract. Should this occur, the results would be a loss of profit for the development company.

Contingency plans specify the actions to be taken should a risk (a potential problem) become a real problem. The risk becomes a problem when a predetermined risk-indicator metric crosses a predetermined threshold. For example, suppose the budget has been overrun by 12 percent at software specifications review (SSR). The preset threshold metric was 10 percent; therefore, the appropriate contingency plan must be put into effect. [Boehm 1987]

4.3.6 Determine Possible Courses of Action. In most projects, there is more than one way to conduct the project—but not with equal cost, equal schedule, or equal risk. It is the project manager's responsibility to examine various approaches that could achieve the project objectives and satisfy the success criteria.

For example, one approach might be very costly in terms of personnel and machines yet reduce the schedule dramatically. Another approach might reduce both schedule and cost but take a severe risk of being unable to deliver a satisfactory system. A third approach might be to stretch the schedule, thereby reducing the cost of the project. The manager must examine each course of action to determine advantages, disadvantages, risks, and benefits. (See paper by Barry Boehm [1987] for a description of a software development lifecycle model that incorporates risk analysis and decision making.)

4.3.7 Make Planning Decisions for the Project. The project manager, in consultation with higher level management, the customer, and other appropriate parties is responsible for selecting the best course of action for meeting project goals and objectives. The project manager is responsible for making trade-off decisions involving cost, schedule, design strategies, and risks [Bunyard and Coward 1982].

The project manager is also responsible for approving the methods and tools, both technical and managerial, by which the project will be managed and the product developed. For example, will the requirements be documented using "structured analysis" methods or Peter Coad's "Object-Oriented Analysis" charts? Will testing be done top-down, bottom-up, or both? Which tools, techniques, and procedures will be used in planning the development schedule: PERT, CPM, workload chart, work breakdown structure (WBS) chart or Gantt chart [Cori 1985], [Thayer and Fairley, WBS, 1997]?

4.3.8 Set Procedures and Rules for the Project. The project manager establishes procedures and rules for the project. In contrast to policies, procedures establish customary methods and provide detailed guidance for project activities. Procedures detail the exact manner in which to accomplish an activity. For example, there may be a procedure for conducting design reviews.

In another contrast, a rule establishes specific and definite actions to be taken or not taken with respect to a given situation. A rule allows no discretion. For example, a rule might require two people to be on duty in the machine room at all times.

Process standards (in contrast to product standards) can be used to establish procedures. Process standards may be adopted from the corporate standards or written for a particular project. Process standards might cover topics such as reporting methods, reviews, and documentation preparation requirements.

4.3.9 Develop a Software Project Plan. A project plan specifies all of the actions necessary to successfully deliver a software product.

Typically, the plan specifies the following:

- The *tasks* to be performed by the software development staff in order to deliver the final software product. This usually requires the partitioning of the project activities into small, well-specified tasks. A useful tool for representing the partitioned project is the WBS.

- The *size* of the software system [Gaffney, *Size*, 1997].

- The *cost* and *resources* necessary to accomplish each project task [Boehm 1984], [Legg 1997], [Boehm, et al., COCOMO 2.0, 1994].

- The project *schedule* that specifies dependencies among tasks and establishes project milestones [Gaffney, *Schedule*, 1997]

For further discussion of project planning see [Miller 1978].

4.3.10 Prepare Budgets for the Project. Budgeting is the process of placing cost figures on the project plan [Stutzke 1997]. The project manager is responsible for determining the cost of the project and allocating the budget to project tasks. Cost is the common denominator for all elements of the project plan. Requirements for personnel, computers, travel, office space, equipment, and so forth can only be compared and cost trade-offs made when these requirements are measured in terms of their monetary value.

4.3.11 Document Project Plans. The project manager is responsible for documenting the project plan [Glabas and Fairley 1997]. He/She is also responsible for preparing other plans such as the software quality assurance plan, software configuration management plan, staffing plan, and the test plan. The project plan is the primary means of communicating with other entities that interface with the project.

5. Organizing a Software Engineering Project

5.1   Introduction and Definitions

Organizing a software engineering project involves developing an effective and efficient organizational structure for assigning and completing project tasks

and establishing the authority and responsibility relationships among the tasks.

Organizing involves itemizing the project activities required to achieve the project objectives and arranging these activities into logical clusters. It also involves assigning groups of activities to various organizational entities and delegating responsibility and authority needed to carry out the activities.

The purpose of an organizational structure is to "focus the efforts of many on a selected goal" [Donnelly, Gibson, and Ivancevich 1975].

5.2   Major Issues in Organizing

The major issues in organizing a software engineering project are as follows:

- It is difficult to determine the best organizational structure for a particular organization and/or environment (for example, project, functional, matrix) to manage the project.

- An organizational structure may leave responsibilities for some project activities and tasks undefined or unclear.

- A matrix organizational structure is not accepted by many software development personnel.

- Many team leaders are expected to perform technically as well as manage his/her team.

It is difficult to determine the best organizational structure for a project and for the organization conducting the project. According to Robert Youker [1977], there is a spectrum of organizational techniques for software projects, with formats ranging from functional to matrix to project. The project format creates centralized control over the project and makes the project manager responsible for all aspects of the project. Conversely, the functional organization distributes authority and control of a project among the functional elements involved.

The matrix organization incorporates elements of both the project and functional formats. Project managers are given authority over the project; the project members are drawn from their functional "homes" and assigned to the project for the duration of the project. In a matrix structure, conflicts can arise between the project manager, who is responsible for the project, and the functional managers, who provide the software engineers for the project. Matrix structures require special attention to overcome this "two-boss" phenomenon.

Software developers and many managers are frequently unsupportive of the matrix organizational structure. Software developers are not enthusiastic about the matrix because they are always being treated as "temporary" help and are rarely given responsibility for system delivery. Functional managers, especially long-time employees, view the new matrix organizations as usurping the power and authority once held by the managers under the functional project structure.

Papers by Lynn Stuckenbruck [1981], Robert Youker [1977], and Marilyn Mantei [1981] offer criteria for selecting a software project's appropriate organizational structure. Both Stuckenbruck and Youker indicate the need for top management to provide a clear charter for the matrix organization to define responsibilities. Authority must be defined for the project manager as well as for the roles of the functional departments.

The last issue is over the role of the team leader. A team is a group of five to fifteen software engineers working together toward a common goal. A team leader heads the team. Team leaders are generally senior project personnel with responsibility and authority for developing an assigned part of the overall software product. It is unfortunate that many top-level managers will sometimes expect team leaders to do their "share" of the technical effort in addition to managing the team. This of course has a major impact on the team leaders' management functions.

5.3   Organizing a Software Project

Table 4 outlines the activities that must be accomplished by the project manager in organizing a project.

The remainder of this section describes the activities in greater detail.

5.3.1 Identify and Group Project Tasks. The manager is responsible for reviewing the project requirements, defining the various tasks to be accomplished, and sizing and grouping those tasks into logical entities. Titles and organizational entities are assigned to the assembly of tasks; for example, analysis tasks, design tasks, coding tasks, and testing tasks. This information enables the project manager to select an organizational structure to control these groups. See Table 5 for an example of task identification and grouping.

The project manager must also identify the supporting tasks needed, both internal and external to the project. Examples of internal tasks are secretarial support, word processing support, financial monitoring, project administration, and project control. External to the project, there may be tasks associated with travel requirements, motor pools, security guards, computer operation support, and so on.

5.3.2 Select an Organizational Structure for the Project. After identifying and grouping project tasks, the project manager must select an organizational structure. A software development project can be organized using one of several different and overlapping organizational types, for example:

- Conventional organization structure—line or staff organization
- Project organization structure—functional, project, or matrix
- Team structure—Egoless, chief programmer, or hierarchical

Table 4. Organizing activities for a software Project.

Activity	Definition or Explanation
Identify and group project function, activities, and tasks	Define, size, and categorize the project work.
Select organizational structures	Select appropriate structures to accomplish the project and to monitor, control, communicate, and coordinate.
Create organizational positions	Establish title, job descriptions, and job relationships for each project role.
Define responsibilities and authority	Define responsibilities for each organizational position and the authority to be granted for fulfillment of those responsibilities.
Establish position qualifications	Define qualifications for persons to fill each position.
Document organizational decisions	Document titles, positions, job, descriptions, responsibilities, authorities, relationships, and position qualifications.

Table 5. A set of software engineering project tasks that have been grouped and assigned an organizational entity.

Project Tasks	Organizational Entity
Determine software system requirements	Software System Engineering
Partition and allocate software requirements to software components	
Develop software architectural design	
Identify and schedule tasks to be done	
Establish and maintain external and internal interfaces	
Control the software development process	
Verify and validate the software process and product	
Analyze software components for product 1 requirements	Software Engineering Applications Group 1
Design components of product 1	
Implement product 1 software components	
Prepare documents	
Support verification and validation	
Same tasks and activities as defined in Product 1.	Software Engineering Applications Group 2
Prepare software verification & validation plan	Software Verification & Validation
Conduct verification & validation activities	
Prepare and support software testing	
Establish software quality assurance plan	Software Quality Assurance
Conduct software quality activities	
Document results of software quality activities	

The project manager may not have the luxury of selecting the best project organizational type, since this may be determined by policy at the corporate level. Regardless of who does it, an organizational structure should match the needs and goals of the project with an environment that facilitates communication among the organizational entities.

The following paragraphs describe these organizational considerations.

5.3.2.1 Conventional Organizational Structures. A line organization has the responsibility and authority to perform the work that represents the primary mission of the larger organizational unit. In contrast, a staff organization is a group of functional experts that has responsibility and authority to perform special activities that help the line organization do its work. All organizations in a company are either line or staff. Figure 2 illustrates a line organization and is the organizational structure for the example in Table 5.[1]

---

[1] This can just as well be a staff organization, depending on the major activities and mission of the general management structure.

5.3.2.2 Software Project Structures. A project structure is a temporary organizational form established to develop and build a system that is too big to be done by one or, at most, a few people. In a software engineering project, the system to be built is a software system. A project structure can be superimposed on a line or staff organization.

Functional Project Organization: One type of project organization is a functional organization. This is a project structure built around a software engineering function or group of similar functions. A project is accomplished either within a functional unit or, if multifunctional, by two or more functional units. The project is accomplished by passing the work products from function to function as the project passes through the lifecycle phases. Figure 3 illustrates the tasks and lines of authority of a functional organization used to develop a software product.

In Figure 3, the software requirements specifications are prepared by the *software systems engineering group* under the supervision of the group leader. When finished, the system engineering group transfers

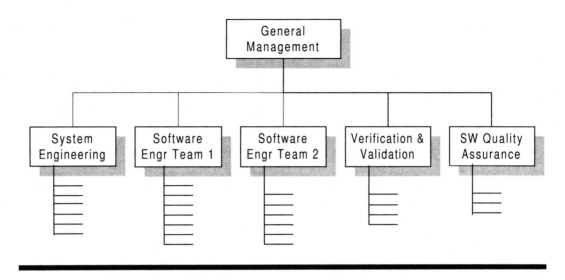

Figure 2. A line organization in a software development organization.

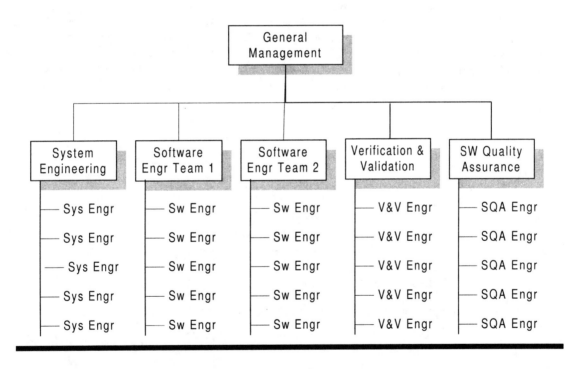

Figure 3. Functional project organization.

the requirement specifications to the *software engineering applications group* most familiar with the application. The software engineering applications group, using the requirement specifications, designs the software system under the supervision of the software engineering applications group leader. In this illustration, the applications group also programs the software system and then passes the finished code to the software verification and validation (V&V) engi-

neering group for testing. Software quality assurance (SQA) is provided as an oversight by the software quality assurance group. There is no single supervisor over the whole project, but generally there is a project coordinator or customer and/or user liaison.

The customer and/or user liaison does not supervise the staff or control the project. The project coordinator usually does not have the responsibility to hire, discharge, train, or promote people within the project. The user liaison coordinates the project, monitors the progress (reporting to top management when things do not go according to plan), and acts as a common interface with the user.

Project Organization: Another type of project organization is built around each specific project; a project manager is given the responsibility, authority, and resources for conducting the project [Middleton, 1967]. (The project organization is sometimes called a *projected* organization to get away from the term "project project organization."). The manager must meet project goals within the resources of the organization. The project manager usually has the responsibility to hire, discharge, train, and promote people within the project. Figure 4 illustrates the tasks and lines of authority of a project organization. Note that the software project manager has total control over the project and the assigned software personnel.

Matrix Project Organization: The third project organization is the *matrix* (sometimes called matrix project organization), which is a composite of the functional and the project organizations [Stuckenbruck 1981]. The project manager is given responsibility and authority for completing the project. The functional managers provide the resources

needed to conduct the project. In a matrix organization, the project manager usually does not have the authority to hire, discharge, train, or promote personnel within his project. Figure 5 illustrates the tasks and lines of authority in a matrix organization. Engineers labeled "A" are temporarily assigned to Project A, Engineers labeled "B" are temporarily assigned to Project B, Engineers labeled "C" are temporarily assigned to Project C.

In Figure 5, a project manager who supervises functional workers supervises each project. Typically the software project manager is responsible for the day-to-day supervision of the software project members, and the functional manager is responsible for the career, training, and well-being of those people.

Since each individual worker is "supervised" by two separate managers, the system is sometimes called the "two-boss" system.

5.3.2.3 Software Project Teams. Within the larger organizational structures discussed above, a software development project is typically organized around a number of software engineering teams. These teams usually consist of five to seven members. Examples of structures for these teams include egoless programming teams, chief programmer teams, and hierarchical teams [Mantei 1981].

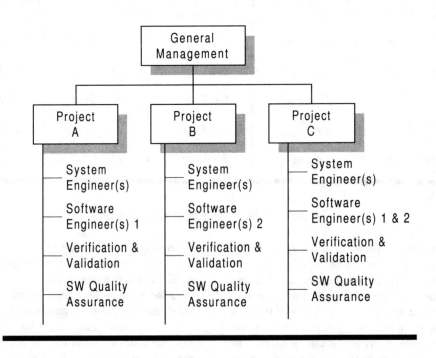

Figure 4. Project organization.

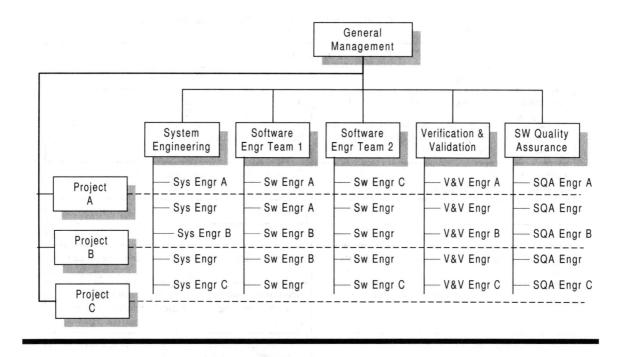

Figure 5. Matrix project organization.

Egoless Programming Team: The egoless team (also know as the democratic team) structure was introduced by Gerald Weinberg [Weinberg 1971]. An egoless team typically consists of ten or twelve members. Discussions and decisions are made by consensus. Group leadership responsibility rotates; there is no permanent central authority.

Chief Programmer Team: IBM in the now-famous New York Times Morgue Project [Baker 1972] first used the chief programmer team. The team consists of three or four permanently assigned team members—chief programmer, backup programmer, and program librarian—plus other auxiliary programmers and/or analysts who are added as needed. The chief programmer manages all the technical aspects and makes all the managerial and technical decisions. The librarian maintains all documents, code, and data, and performs all administrative work [Cooke 1976].

Hierarchical Team: A hierarchical structure (also known as a controlled decentralized) team is a structured organization in which the project leaders manage senior engineers (programmers), and senior engineers (programmers) manage junior engineers (programmers). The project team is called hierarchical because of its top-down flow of authority.

In today's environment, both egoless and chief programming teams are seldom used. Egoless teams can sometimes be found in research organizations.

Chief programmer teams, after a flurry of use in the 1970s, are seldom found because of the difficulties in recruiting and training "chief programmers." Therefore the most used method is the hierarchical team (usually called a project team).

One of the cardinal rules of project management is that on any team of five or more individuals, the team leader (manager) is a full-time job and should not be expect to carry any share of the "technical" work.

6.3.2.4 Strengths and Weaknesses of the Project Organization Types. In selecting an organizational structure, it is important that the needs of the project be matched to the various strengths and weaknesses of the organization type. Table 6 displays the advantages and disadvantages of the six organizational types.

The software engineering project is either a line or a staff organization. The project manager must decide if the project will operate as a functional, project, or matrix organization and if the project will use egoless, chief programmer, or project team types. The chief programmer and egoless teams are seldom used, but the librarian concept from the chief programmer team and the egoless technical reviews (walkthroughs) are frequently used by software engineering project teams.

The majority of software engineering projects in the aerospace industry use the matrix organization with project teams.

Table 6. Strengths and weaknesses of organizational models for software projects.

Functional Project Organization	
Strengths	**Weaknesses**
Organization already exists (quick start-up and phase-down).	No central position of responsibility or authority exists for the project.
Recruiting, training, and retention of functional specialists is easier.	Interface problems are difficult to solve.
Policies, procedures, standards, methods, tools, and techniques are already established.	Projects are difficult to monitor and control.

Project Organization	
Strengths	**Weaknesses**
A central position of responsibility and authority exists for the project.	Organization must be formed for each new project.
All system interfaces are centrally controlled.	Recruiting, training, and retention of functional specialists may be more difficult than for functional format.
Decisions can be made quickly.	Policies, procedures, standards, methods, tools, and techniques must be developed for each project.
Staff motivation is typically high.	

Matrix Project Organization	
Strengths	**Weaknesses**
Central position of responsibility and authority is improved, compared to functional format.	Responsibility for and authority over individual project members is shared between two or more managers—unlike project or functional formats.
Interfaces between functions can be controlled more easily than in functional format.	It's too easy to move people from one project to another—unlike project or functional formats.
Recruiting, training, and retention may be easier than in project format.	More organizational coordination is required than in project or functional formats.
It's easier to start and end a project than in project format.	Greater competition exists for resources among projects than in project or functional formats.
Policies, procedures, standards, methods, tools, and techniques are already established; unlike project organization.	
More flexible use of people is possible than in project or functional formats.	

6.3.3 Create Organizational Position for the Software Project. Once the tasks are identified, sized, and grouped, and the organizational structure has been specified, the project manager must create job titles and position descriptions. Personnel will be recruited for the project using the job titles and position descriptions. Some short examples of typical software engineering titles and position descriptions are illustrated below [*High Technology Careers* Magazine 1997]:

- *Project managers*—responsible for system development and implementation within major functional areas. Direct the efforts of software engineers, analysts, programmers, and other project personnel.
- *Software system engineers*—design and develop software to drive computer systems. Develop firmware, drivers, and specialized software such as graphics, communications controllers, operating systems, and user-

friendly interfaces. Work closely with hardware engineers and applications and systems programmers; requires understanding of all aspects of the product.

- *Scientific/engineering programmers, programmer-analysts*—perform detailed program design, coding, testing, debugging, and documentation of scientific/engineering computer applications and other applications that are mathematical in nature. May assist in overall system specification and design.

- *Software verification and validation engineers*—able to develop independent V&V plans, procedures, and tools. Able to develop test procedures and develop test cases for realtime and non-realtime software systems.

- *Software quality assurance engineers*—able to develop software development procedures and standards. Conducts audits of software systems and overview tests. Will work closely with independent V&V teams.

5.3.4 Define Responsibilities and Authority. Responsibility is the obligation to fulfill commitments. Authority is the right to make decisions and exert power. It is often stated that authority can be delegated but responsibility cannot. Koontz and O'Donnell [1972] support this view by defining responsibility as "the obligation owed by subordinates to their supervisors for exercising authority delegated to them in a way to accomplish results expected." Responsibility and authority for organizational activities or tasks should be assigned to the organizational position at the time it is created or modified. The project manager is assigned, and in turn assigns, the responsibilities and the corresponding authorities to the various organizational positions within the project.

5.3.5 Establish Position Qualifications. Position qualifications must be identified for each position in the project. Position qualifications are established by considering questions such as: What types of individuals do you need for your project? How much experience is necessary in the area of the application? How much education is required: BS in computer science, MS in artificial intelligence? How much training is required, either before or after the project is initiated? Does the applicant need to know Fortran, Lisp, or some other programming language? The establishment of proper and accurate position qualifications will make it possible for the manager to correctly staff the project.

Some short examples of typical position qualifications for software engineering titles and positions are included below.

- *Project managers*—background in successful systems implementation, advanced industrial knowledge, awareness of current computer technology, intimate understanding of user operations and problems, and proven management ability. Minimum requirements are four years of significant system development and project management experience.

- *Software system engineers*—seven years' experience in aerospace applications designing realtime control systems for embedded computers. Experience with Ada preferred. BS in computer science, engineering, or related discipline.

- *Scientific/engineering programmers, programmer-analysts*—three years' experience in programming aerospace applications, control systems, and/or graphics. One year minimum with Fortran, assembly, or C programming languages. Large-scale or mini/micro hardware exposure and system software programming experience desired. Minimum requirements include undergraduate engineering or math degree.

- *Verification and validation engineer*—minimum of three or more years experiences in one or more aspects of V&V for realtime systems. Must be able to work independently of the development teams. MS degree in software engineering preferred. Salary commensurate with experience.

- *Software quality assurance engineer*—minimum of three years experience working in a software QA environment. Some CM experience desirable. BS or MS in computer science with specialty in software engineering. Travel required.

5.3.6 Document Organizational Structures. Lines of authority, tasks, and responsibilities should be documented in the project plan. Justifications for decisions must be well documented and made available to guide staffing of the project.

6. Staffing a Software Engineering Project

6.1 Introduction and Definitions

Staffing a software engineering project consists of all the management activities that involve filling (and keeping filled) the positions that were established in the project organizational structure. This includes selecting candidates for the positions and training or otherwise developing them to accomplish their tasks effectively. Staffing also involves terminating project personnel when necessary.

Staffing is not the same as organizing; staffing involves filling the roles created in the project organizational structure through personnel selection, training, and development. The objective of staffing is to ensure that project roles are filled by personnel who are qualified (both technically and temperamentally) to occupy them.

6.2 Major Issues in Staffing

The major issues in staffing for a software engineering project are as follows:

- Project managers are frequently selected for their ability to program or perform engineering tasks rather than their ability to manage (few engineers make good managers).

- The productivity of programmers, analysts, and software engineers varies greatly from individual to individuals.

- There is a high turnover of staff on software projects especially those organized under a matrix organization.

- Universities are not producing a sufficient number of computer science graduates who understand the software engineering process or project management.

- Training plans for individual software developers are not developed or maintained.

It is common practice today to make project managers from those programmers and software engineers who have excelled at their technical activities. Unfortunately success as a software developer (for example, software engineer, programmer, or tester) does not always indicate potential as a project manager. Compounding this problem is the lack of training in project management techniques and procedures that can be made available to these budding project managers.

One of the major issues in staffing a project with capable people is that programmer and software engineer skills vary greatly from individual to individual. H. Sackman and others proved that the difference in productivity between programmers was as high as 26

to 1 [Sackman, H., et al. 1968]. In his book *Software Engineering Economics* Boehm [1981] reports differences in productivity due to personnel and/or team capability as high as 4 to 1. This inability to accurately predict the productivity of individuals in a project undermines our ability to accurately estimate the cost and schedule of software projects.

Experience is a valuable commodity in a software development activity. Unfortunately, acquiring this experience is hampered by the constant turnover of project personnel. In the days of people shortages, companies raid their rivals' workforce, resulting in people moving from one company to another and from one project to another. The use of the matrix organizational project format, discussed in the previous chapter, encourages the movement of software people from one project to another as priorities change within a company. In addition, many software people recognize that the only way to get a raise is to look for and accept a position in a different company (always good for a 10 percent raise). This entire turnover problem can sometimes greatly hinder the ability of software projects to deliver the system on time, at cost, and meet the system requirements.

Training in the technical skills to be applied to an assigned job is a necessary element of staffing. To ensure that training is properly applied to meet the short- and long-term needs of the individual and the organization, individual training plans are needed. Training plans are agreements between the individual and his/her manager as to what training (courses, seminars, study groups, tuition support) will be provided by the organization. In many if not most organizations, these plans are not realized, leaving the pairing of individuals and appropriate courses subject to a rather ad hoc approach.

Universities are not producing sufficient numbers of software engineers. Most of the computer science programs in the United States are turning out theoretical computer scientists at best, or merely programmers (coders) at worst. Most industry personnel and others involved in the hiring of new college graduates seek computer science graduates with education and experience in developing software systems—that is, software engineering skills [McGill 1984].

6.3 Staffing a Software Project

Table 7 outlines the activities and tasks that must be accomplished by project managers in project staffing. The remainder of this section discusses these activities in greater detail.

Table 7. Staffing activities for software projects.

Activity	Definition or Explanation
Fill organizational positions	Select, recruit, or promote qualified people for each project position.
Assimilate newly assigned personnel	Orient and familiarize new people with the organization, facilities, and tasks to be done on the project.
Educate or train personnel	Make up deficiencies in position qualifications through training and education.
Provide for general development	Improve knowledge, attitudes, and skills of project personnel.
Evaluate and appraise personnel	Record and analyze the quantity and quality of project work as the basis for personnel evaluations. Set performance goals and appraise personnel periodically.
Compensate	Provide wages, bonuses, benefits, or other financial remuneration commensurate with project responsibilities and performance.

6.3.1 Fill Organizational Positions in a Software Project. The project manager is responsible for filling the positions established during organizational project planning. In staffing any software project, the following factors should be considered. Deficiencies in any of these factors can be offset by strengths in other factors. For example, deficiencies in education can be offset by better experience, a particular type of training, or enthusiasm for the job. Serious deficiencies should be cause for corrective action.

- *Education*—Does the candidate have the minimum level of education for the job? Does the candidate have the proper education for future growth in the company?
- *Experience*—Does the candidate have an acceptable level of experience? Is it the right type and variety of experience?
- *Training*—Is the candidate trained in the language, methodology, and equipment to be used, and the application area of the software system?
- *Motivation*—Is the candidate motivated to do the job, work for the project, work for the company, and take on the assignment?
- *Commitment*—Will the candidate demonstrate loyalty to the project, to the company, and to the decisions made? [Powell and Posner 1984]?
- *Self-motivation*—Is the candidate a self-starter, willing to carry a task through to the end without excessive direction?
- *Group affinity*—Does the candidate fit in with the current staff? Are there potential conflicts that need to be resolved?

- *Intelligence*—Does the candidate have the capability to learn, to take difficult assignments, and adapt to changing environments?

6.3.1.1 Sources of Qualified Project Individuals. One source of qualified individuals is to transfer personnel from within the project itself. It is the project manager's prerogative to move people from one task to another within a project. Another source is transfers from other projects within the organization. This can be done anytime but often happens when another software engineering project is either phasing down or is canceled.

Other sources of qualified personnel are new hires from other companies through such methods as job fairs, referrals, headhunters, want ads, and unsolicited resumes. New college graduates can be recruited either through interviews on campus or through referrals from recent graduates who are now company employees.

If the project manager is unable to obtain qualified individuals to fill positions, one option is to hire unqualified but motivated individuals and train them for those vacancies.

6.3.1.2 Selecting a Productive Software Staff. Two metrics may indicate a productive software staff:

- *Amount of experience*—An experienced staff is more productive than an inexperienced staff [Boehm 1984]. Some of the best experience comes from having worked on software projects similar to the project being staffed.
- *Diversity of experience*—Diversity of experience is a reasonable predictor of productivity [Kruesi 1982]. It is better that the individuals

under consideration have done well in several jobs, rather than one job, over a given period of time.

Other qualities indicative of a highly productive individual are communications skills (both oral and written), a college degree (usually in a technical field), being a self-starter, and experience in the application area of the project.

6.3.2 Assimilate Newly Assigned Software Personnel. The manager is responsible not only for hiring the people but also for familiarizing them with any project procedures, facilities, and plans necessary to assure their effective integration into the project. In short, the project manager is responsible for introducing new employees to the company and the company to the employees.

Many large companies have formal orientation programs, many lasting several days. Orientation programs include the features and history of the company; the products or services that are the main sources of revenue for the company; general policies and procedures; organizational structure; company benefits; and the availability of in-company service organizations.

6.3.3 Educate or Train Personnel as Necessary. It is not always possible to recruit or transfer employees with exactly those skills needed for a particular project. Therefore, the manager is responsible for educating and training the personnel assigned to ensure that they can meet the project requirements.

Education differs from training. Education involves teaching the basics, theory, and underlying concepts of a discipline with a view toward a long-term payoff. Training means teaching a skill or knowledge of how to use, operate, or make something. The skill is typically needed in the near future and has a short-term payoff.

For example, managers should be educated in the management sciences and business techniques. They should be trained in management techniques and the duties of administration. Engineers, on the other hand, are educated in science, physics, and mathematics, but must be trained in the application domain. Everyone must be familiar with the procedures, tools, techniques, and equipment they operate and use.

Training methods include on-the-job training, formal company courses, courses through local universities and schools [Mills 1980], self-study, and in-house lectures.

Each individual within an organization must have a training plan that specifies career education and training goals and the steps each person will take in achieving those goals. To be successful, top management must actively support training programs.

Another technique is retraining into software engineering (sometimes called "retreading") of long-time, valuable employees with somewhat obsolete skills. Two organizations that have used this technique are the Israel Aircraft Industry [Ben-David et al. 1984] and Lockheed Missiles & Space Company [McGill 1984].

6.3.4 Provide for General Development of the Project Staff. In addition to education and training, the project manager must ensure that project staff grows with the project and company. The manager must ensure that their professional knowledge will increase and that they maintain a positive attitude toward the project, the company, and the customers.

One of the purposes of providing general development for the employee is to improve organizational effectiveness. For example, courses and degree programs at the local university in any worthwhile skill, funded by the company, will improve employee morale, aid in retaining employees, and broaden the skill base available to the company. Even indirect skills such as typing and communication should be enhanced.

6.3.5 Evaluate and Appraise Project Personnel. The project manager is also responsible for periodically evaluating and appraising personnel. An appraisal provides feedback to staff members concerning the positive and negative aspects of their performance. This feedback allows the staff member to strengthen good qualities and improve those that are negative. Appraisals should be done at regular intervals and should concentrate on the individual's performance and not on personality, unless personality issues interfere with performance [Moneysmith 1984].

One well-known evaluation technique that is applicable to project management is "management by objectives" [Maslow 1954]. At the beginning of the appraisal period, the individual and the project manager establish a set of verifiable objectives that the individual believes he/she can meet over the next reporting period. These measurable objectives are a verifiable goal that will form the basis of the next appraisal. This approach is superior to evaluation by personal traits and work characteristics, such as promptness, neatness, punctuality, golf scores, and so on.

6.3.6 Compensate the Project Personnel. The manager—sometimes directly, sometimes indirectly—is responsible for determining the salary scale and benefits of project personnel. Benefits take on many forms. Most benefits are monetary or can be equated to money. These include stock options, a company car, first-class tickets for all company trips, or a year-end bonus. Some benefits are nonmonetary but appeal to the self-esteem of the individual; examples are combat medals in the military, a reserved parking place at the company plant, or an impressive title on the door.

6.3.7 Terminate Project Assignments. The project manager is not only responsible for hiring people, but must also terminate people and assignments as necessary. "Terminate" includes reassignment of personnel at the end of a successful project (a pleasant termination) and dismissal of personnel due to project cancellation (an unpleasant termination). Termination can also occur by firing when an employee is determined to be unsatisfactory [Davis 1994].

Termination is important. Poor performers are not just failing to pull their weight; they frequently lower the morale of others on the project. Management may be seen as ineffective if such individuals are not dealt with. Other people resent it when another team member regularly shows up late, or is missing deadlines, for example.

6.3.8 Document Project Staffing Decisions. Project managers should document their staffing plan and evaluation and training policies for all to read. Each individual within an organization should have a personal training plan reflecting course work needed and progress made. Other staffing documents that might be produced include orientation plans and schedules, salary schedules, and promotion policies. The project manager and each individual employee should have a copy of his or her annual performance objectives signed by the employee and the project manager.

7. Directing a Software Engineering Project

7.1 Introduction and Definitions

Directing a software engineering project consists of the management activities that involve motivational and interpersonal aspects by which project personnel come to understand and contribute to the achievement of project goals. Once subordinates are trained and oriented, the project manager has a continuing responsibility for clarifying their assignments, guiding them toward improved performance, and motivating them to work with enthusiasm and confidence toward project goals.

Directing, like staffing, involves people. Directing is sometimes considered to be synonymous with leading (compare reference [Koontz and O'Donnell 1972] with reference [Koontz, O'Donnell, and Weihrich 1984]). Directing a project involves providing leadership, day-to-day supervision of personnel, delegating authority, coordinating activities, facilitating communications, resolving conflicts, managing change, and documenting important decisions.

7.2 Major Issues in Directing a Software Project

The major issues in directing a software engineering project are these:

- Failure to have effective communications between project and nonproject entities.

- Money is not a sufficient motivator for software developers.

- Companies and managers do not have the proper tools and techniques to motivate software engineers.

- Customers and manager do not recognize the potential software impact caused by a seemingly trivial change, for example, they believe it is "just a simple matter of programming."

One of the major goals of software engineering is to improve communication among the many organizations that are involved in developing a software system. Most software engineering documents are written in the English language, which is notoriously imprecise and ambiguous. Research in software engineering is concerned with developing tools and techniques that will ease communication of requirements specifications, design documents, and other software engineering documents.

Most software engineers are well paid, work in pleasant surroundings, and are reasonably satisfied with their position in life. According to Abraham Maslow's hierarchy of unfulfilled needs, the average software engineer is high on the ladder of satisfied needs [Maslow 1954]. Most software engineers are at the "esteem and recognition" level and are occasionally reaching to the "self-actualization" level. At this level, money alone is not a strong motivator. As a result, management is faced with the issue of how to motivate software engineers to produce more and better software (called software psychology in some circles), since money alone is not sufficient.

The opportunity to use modern tools and techniques is a strong motivator for many software engineers. Technology transfer is defined as the time interval between the development of a new product, tool, or technique and its use by the consumers. In their paper [Redwine and Riddle 1985], Sam Redwine and Bill Riddle estimated that this time can be on the order of 15–18 years. The cause of this technology transfer gap can be looked at from two viewpoints:

- The leadership team may be reluctant to introduce unfamiliar methods and tools because it may increase the risks to their projects.
- The use of unfamiliar methods and tools may make it more difficult for the leadership team to estimate project cost and schedule.
- A plan for improving technology transfer is discussed in paragraph 7.3.8, Resolve Conflicts.

Software developers are discouraged by the seeming lack of understanding on the part of managers and customers of the software development process. Software engineering is one of the most difficult jobs in the world today. There are no small or easy software jobs or changes. Software engineers under pressure to hurry up and finish that "simple change" become discouraged and may eventually "burn out" [Cherlin 1981].

7.3 Directing the Project Team

Table 8 outlines leadership activities and tasks that must be accomplished by project managers and team leaders. The remainder of this section discusses these activities in greater detail.

7.3.1 Provide Leadership to the Project Team. The project manager provides leadership to the project team by interpreting plans and requirements, to ensure that everybody on the project team is working toward common goals. Leadership results from the leader's power and ability to guide and influence individuals. The project manager's power can be derived from his/her leadership position; this is called positional power. The project manager's power can also be derived from his/her own "charm," sometimes called charisma; this is called personal power.

A good leader is able to align the personal goals of subordinates with organizational goals of the project. Problems can arise when the project manager who has only positional power comes into conflict with a subordinate who has personal power over the project members. For a discussion of different uses of power by managers see [Boyatzis 1971].

7.3.2 Supervise Project Personnel. The project manager is responsible for overseeing the project members' work and providing day-to-day supervision of project personnel. It is the project manager's responsibility to provide guidance and, when necessary, discipline project members to ensure that they fulfill their assigned duties.

Table 8. Directing activities for software projects.

Activity	Definition or Explanation
Provide leadership	Create an environment in which project members can accomplish their assignments with enthusiasm and confidence.
Supervise personnel	Provide day-to-day instructions, guidance, and discipline to help project members fulfill their assigned duties.
Delegate authority	Allow project personnel to make decisions and expend resources within the limitations and constraints of their roles.
Motivate personnel	Provide a work environment in which project personnel can satisfy their psychological needs.
Build teams	Provide a work environment in which project personnel can work together toward common project goals. Set performance goals for teams as well as for individuals.
Coordinate activities	Combine project activities into effective and efficient arrangements.
Facilitate communication	Ensure a free flow of correct information among project members.
Resolve conflicts	Encourage constructive differences of opinion and help resolve the resulting conflicts.
Manage changes	Stimulate creativity and innovation in achieving project goals.
Document directing decisions	Document decisions involving delegation of authority, communication and coordination, conflict resolution, and change management.

Supervisory responsibilities can involve such mundane tasks as "clocking in" the employees at the beginning of the work day, approving vacation time, reprimanding an individual for a missed appointment, or approving a deviation from company policy. At other times, the project manager can provide a crucial decision on a software design approach; make a well-reasoned argument to top management that results in procurement of better tools and work space; or be a sympathetic listener to a project member's personal problems.

7.3.3 Delegate Authority to the Appropriate Project Members.
The software engineering project manager is also responsible for delegating authority to the project staff. Tasks are assigned to subgroups, teams, and individuals, and authority is delegated to these teams so that they can accomplish their tasks in an efficient and effective manner. Typically, a good project manager will always delegate authority down through the lowest possible level of the project [Raudsepp 1981].

The proper delegation of the right kind of authority can free managers from time-consuming routine supervision and decisions, thus enabling them to concentrate on the important aspects of the project. The project manager should ensure that individual project members understand what authority is delegated for what responsibility. Project members should also clearly understand the scope, limitations, and purpose of the delegation.

7.3.4 Motivate Project Personnel.
The project manager is responsible for motivating and inspiring personnel to do their best. Several motivational techniques from mainstream management are applicable to software engineering projects, such as management by objective, Maslow's hierarchy of needs [Maslow 1954], Frederick Herzberg's hygiene factors [Herzberg, Mausner, and Snyderman 1959], and sometimes just the manager's charisma. The project manager should always acknowledge the special needs of the highly qualified, technically trained engineers and scientists who staff the project. Dollars will attract good software engineers to a company; dollars will not keep them. For a further discussion of motivating software development personnel see [Fitz-enz 1978]. For another paper with a unique method of motivating software people, see [Powell and Posner 1984].

The motivational models and techniques from Table 9 have been developed over the past 50 years and should be familiar to project managers. The following paragraphs describe several of these motivation techniques:

Table 9. Motivation models and techniques.

Motivation Model	Definition or Explanation
Frederick Taylor	Workers will respond to an *incentive wage*.
Elton Mayo	*Interpersonal (group) values* override *individual values*. Personnel will respond to group pressure.
Kurt Lewin	*Group forces* can overcome the interests of an *individual*.
Douglas McGregor	Managers must understand the nature of people in order to be able to motivate them.
Abraham Maslow	Human needs can be categorized in a hierarchy. Satisfied needs are *not* motivators.
Frederick Herzberg	A decrease in *environmental* factors is dissatisfying; an increase in environmental factors is *not* satisfying. A decrease in job content factors is *not* dissatisfying; an increase in job content factors is satisfying.
Chris Argyris	The greater the disparity between *company needs* and *individual needs* the greater the dissatisfaction of the employee.
Rensis Likert	*Participative management* is essential to personal motivation
Arch Patton	Executives are *motivated* by the challenge of work, status, the urge to achieve leadership, the lash of competition, fear, and money.
Theory Z	A combination of American and Japanese management style. People need goals and objectives, otherwise they can easily impede their own progress and the progress of their company.
Total quality management (TQM)	A strategy for continually improving performance at each level and area of responsibility.

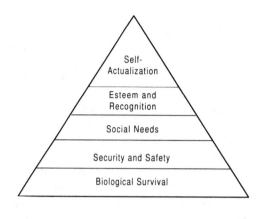

Figure 6. Maslow's hierarchy of human needs.

7.3.4.1 Hierarchy of Needs (Maslow). Satisfied needs are not motivators. For example, an individual who has adequate job security cannot be motivated by increased job security. Maslow's hierarchy of human needs in order of importance is listed below and in Figure 6 [Maslow 1954]:

- Biological survival needs—basics to sustain human life—food, water, shelter, and so forth
- Security and safety needs—freedom from physical danger
- Social needs—to belong; to be accepted by others
- Esteem and recognition needs—to be held in esteem by themselves and by others
- Self-actualization needs—to maximize one's potential and to accomplish something significant

7.3.4.2 McGregor's Theories X and Y. Douglas McGregor presented two theories concerning human nature called Theory X and Theory Y [McGregor 1960]. It should be noted that contrary to popular belief, McGregor did not favor one view over the other. He did not say that Theory Y was a better view than Theory X, only that there were two theories.

Theory X Assumptions:

- Human beings have an inherent dislike of work and will avoid it if they can.
- Because of this dislike of work, most people must be coerced, controlled, directed, and threatened with punishment to get them to put forth adequate effort toward the achievement of organizational objectives.

- Human beings prefer to be directed, wish to avoid responsibility, have relatively little ambition, and want security above all.

Theory Y Assumptions:

- The expenditure of physical and mental effort in work is as natural as in play or rest.
- External control and the threat of punishment are not the only means for achieving organizational objectives. People will exercise self-direction and self-control in the attainment of objectives to which they are committed.
- Commitment to objectives is a function of the rewards associated with their achievement.
- Motivated human beings not only accept responsibility but will also seek it.

7.3.4.3 Theory Z. Theory Z is a combination of American and Japanese management styles [Ouchi 1981]. The basic principles of Theory Z are [Arthur 1983] as follows:

- People need goals and objectives. Goals help to keep one on a forward track while minimizing the time lost to non-productivity.
- Motivation is essential for good performance and must be both positively and negatively reinforced by management. Optimal motivation is derived from both peer and managerial recognition and, to a lesser extent, from promotion and monetary reward.
- Merely having goals and motivation will not prevent people from making mistakes. Man-

paths that are in the best interests of the company.

- The best interests of any given company are achieved when each individual's work is standardized to ensure that similar goals are attained by similar means. In turn, any suggested improvement in one particular area of work automatically is incorporated into related areas.

- Goals must change as working conditions and corporate needs change. In anticipation of such change, Theory Z provides the mechanism for gradual change.

7.3.4.4 Total Quality Management (TQM). TQM can be thought by some to be a motivation technique for an organization or enterprise. TQM is a strategy for continually improving performance at each level and area of responsibility. Increasing user satisfaction is the overriding objective. TQM focuses on processes that create products. By delegating the authority to the lowest level to make decisions and improve quality, the TQM process provides a degree of motivation to the personnel implementing it. TQM is based on the work of Edward Deming [1986].

7.3.4.5 Job Factors for Computer Personnel. Table 10 provides a list of factors, in order of declining importance, that motivate computer personnel toward taking a job (left-hand column) and a list of factors that make a job dissatisfying to the job holder (right-hand column).

7.3.5 Build Software Project Teams. As discussed in Section 5, software is built by project teams. *Team building* is the process of improving the interrelationship between team members in order to improve the efficiency and effectiveness of the team as a whole. Techniques include, for example, team-building exercises, "off-site" meetings, and group dynamics to improve the team's capabilities so they can be more productive as a group.

7.3.6 Coordinate Project Activities. *Coordination* is the arrangement of project entities to work together toward common goals with minimum friction. Documents, policies, procedures, and so forth are viewed differently by various people. The task of the project manager is to reconcile differences in approach, effort, and schedule for the benefit of the project.

The project manager is responsible for coordinating the activities of the project to ensure that people understand and communicate with one another. The manager wants to ensure that other personnel in contact with the project are aware of the organizational structure, the task being performed, and what is expected from other organizations.

7.3.7 Facilitate Communication. Along with coordination, the project manager is responsible for facilitating communication both within the project and between the project and other organizations. *Facilitate* means to expedite, ease, and to assist in the progress of communication. *Communication* is the exchange of information among entities that are working toward common goals.

For example, the project manager should disseminate the staffing plans and project schedule throughout the organization when practical. Nothing can destroy the morale of an organization faster than false and misleading rumors. A good project manager will ensure that the project staff is kept well informed so that rumors are quickly dispelled.

Table 10. Job factors for software personnel.

Job Attractors	Job Dissatisfiers
Salary	Company mismanagement
Chance to advance	Poor work environment
Work environment	Little feeling of accomplishment
Location	Poor recognition
Benefits	Inadequate salary
Facilities/equipment	Poor chance to advance
Job satisfaction	Poor facilities/equipment
Company management	Poor benefits
Job responsibility	Poor career path definition

7.3.8 Resolve Conflicts. It is the project manager's responsibility to resolve conflicts among project staff members and between the staff and outside agencies in both technical and managerial matters. The project manager is not expected to be an expert in all aspects of the project, but should possess good judgment and problem-solving skills.

The project manager should reduce the opportunity for future conflict by removing potential sources of disagreement whenever possible, for example, team members with somewhat equal positions should have equal benefits, access to the manager, parking places, and so forth.

Another type of conflict that the project manager should watch for is the conflict between the employee's work activities and personal life. When this conflict reaches epic proportions it is called "burnout" [Cherlin 1981].

7.3.9 Manage Change that Impacts the Software Project. The project manager is responsible for encouraging independent thought and innovation in achieving project goals. A good manager must always accommodate change, when change is cost-effective and beneficial to the project [Kirchof and Adams 1986].

It is important that the project manager controls changes and not discourage cost-effective changes. Clearly, requirements, design, and the application for which the software system is built will change. There will be social changes. What is acceptable to build at one time will not necessarily be acceptable at another time. People change; newly graduated engineers will have new ideas, as they have been taught new ways to develop software systems. The bottom line is not to eliminate change but to control it. Edward Yourdon [1997] presents a simple step-by-step plan for the transfer of a new software technology (a change) into a software development organization:

- Explain the risks and benefits of the new method, tool, or technique.
- Provide training for the project team.
- Prototype the technique before it is used.
- Provide technical support throughout the project.
- Listen to the users' concerns and problems.
- Avoid concentrating on the technology at the expense of the project.

As another example of controlling (taking advantage of) change, staff turnover is usually considered a problem in most software development organizations. The paper by Kathryn Bartol and David Martin [1983] discusses how to make positive use of staff turnover.

7.3.10 Document Directing Decisions. The project manager must document all tasks, assignments of authority and responsibility, and the outcome of conflict resolution. In addition, all decisions concerning lines of communication and coordination must be documented.

8. Controlling a Software Engineering Project

8.1 Introduction and Definitions

Controlling is the collection of management activities used to ensure that the project goes according to plan. Performance and results are measured against plans, deviations are noted, and corrective actions are taken to ensure conformance of plans and actuals.

Control is a feedback system that provides information on how well the project is going. Control asks the questions—Is the project on schedule? Is it within cost? Are there any potential problems that will cause delays in meeting the requirement within the budget and schedule? Controls also provide plans and approaches for eliminating the difference between the plans and/or standards and the actuals or results.

The control process also requires organizational structure, communication, and coordination. For example, who is responsible for assessing progress? Who will take action on reported problems?

Controlling methods and tools must be objective. Information must be quantified. The methods and tools must point out deviations from plans without regard to the particular people or positions involved. Control methods must be tailored to individual environments and managers. The methods must be flexible and adaptable to deal with the changing environment of the organization. Control also must be economical; the cost of control should not outweigh its benefits.

Control must lead to corrective action—either to bring the actual status back to plan, to change the plan, or to terminate the project.

8.2 Major Issues in Controlling

The major issues in controlling a software engineering project are as follows:

- Many methods of controlling a software project rely on budget expenditures for measurement of "progress" without consideration of work accomplished.
- Visibility of progress in a software development is difficult to measure.
- Quality is not required, monitored or controlled.

- Often standards for software development and project management are not written or, if written, not enforced.
- The body of knowledge called software metrics (used to measure the productivity, quality, and progress of a software product) is not fully developed.

A major issue in controlling a software project involves reliance on budget expenditures for managing progress. For example, when a project manager is asked for the status of a software project, he or she will typically look at the resources expended. If three-quarters of project funds have been expended, the project manager will report that the project is three-quarters completed. The obvious problem is that the relationship between resources consumed and works actually accomplished is only a rough measure at best and completely incorrect at worst.

Other methods of determining progress have not progressed to the point where they are accurate and easy to use. Progress metrics such as the "earned-value method" and "binary tracking system" of monitoring software projects are two of the most accurate methods but are time-consuming and costly to implement.

Standard methods that can be used for measuring progress and products are either not written or, if written, not enforced. Standards are sometimes felt to be detrimental to software projects because they "stifle creativity." Therefore, it is not unusual for entire projects, including the project manager, to ignore the company standards in favor of local, ad hoc, and frequently inadequate, project control systems.

Users and buyers of software systems do not specify quality in their software system or in their request for proposals (RFP). Project managers do not feel obligated to build a quality product if the customer has not requested it, enforced it, or funded it specifically.

This is primarily because the body of knowledge known as "software metrics" is not fully developed. For example, software quality metrics are used to measure reliability, maintainability, usability, safety, and security of a software product. However, we do not know how to do a priori design of software systems that, when implemented, will have the desired quality attributes. This has resulted in emphasis being placed on the processes of software engineering in the belief that sound development processes will result in high quality products. The expenditure of budget is still the primary metric of progress in a software engineering project.

8.3 Controlling the Software Project

Table 11 outlines the project management activities that must be accomplished by project managers to control their projects. The remainder of this section discusses these activities. Figure 7 reflects the activities and their sequence in applying a control process to a software engineering project.

Table 11. Controlling activities for software projects.

Activity	Definition or Explanation
Develop standards of performance	Set goals that will be achieved when tasks are correctly accomplished.
Establish monitoring and reporting systems	Determine necessary data, who will receive it, when they will receive it, and what they will do with it to control the project.
Measure and analyze results	Compare achievements with standards, goals, and plans.
Initiate corrective actions	Bring requirements, plans, and actual project status into conformance.
Reward and discipline	Praise, remunerate, and discipline project personnel as appropriate.
Document controlling methods	Document the standards of performance, monitoring and control systems, and reward and discipline mechanisms.

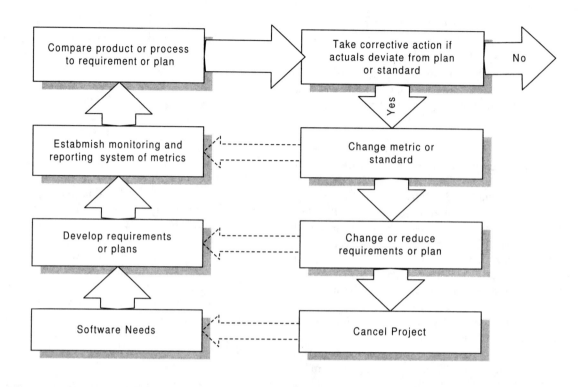

Figure 7. Project control.

8.3.1 Develop Standards of Performance. The project manager is responsible for developing and specifying standards of performance for the project. The project manager either develops standards and procedures for the project, adopts and uses standards developed by the parent organization, or uses standards developed by the customer or a professional society (see for example [IEEE Software Engineering Standards 1993]).

8.3.1.1 Standards. A standard is a documented set of criteria to specify, and determine the adequacy of, an action or object. A software engineering standard is a set of procedures that define the process for developing a software product and/or specifying the quality of a software product. See [Buckley 1987] for a discussion of implementing software engineering standards in a company.

Process and product standards are both important in developing high-quality software. Software engineering is primarily concerned with the process of developing software rather than the measurement of the product. This is because software quality metrics (measuring such quality attributes as software reliability, maintainability, portability, and other "-ilities") is not a well-developed science. Tools and techniques that do an effective job of measuring the quality of a software product are generally not avail-

able. Most software engineering standards are concerned with the process of developing software.

In addition to providing a gauge by which to measure the software engineering process, software engineering standards offer a substantial advantage for software engineering organizations. A good set of standards will do the following:

- Improve communications between team members.

- Ease transferring of staff among projects.

- Expedite the sharing of project experiences and project history.

- Reduce the need to retrain engineers, designers, and programmers.

- Make it easier to apply the best experience of successful projects.

- Simplify software implementation and software maintenance.

- Improve the control of projects since the standard for the process can be controlled.

- Enable software quality assurance to be applied.

8.3.1.2 Software Quality Assurance. Software quality assurance (SQA) is "a planned and systematic pattern of all actions necessary to provide adequate confidence that the item or product conforms to established technical requirements" [IEEE Std. 729-1983]. SQA includes the development process and management methods (requirements and design), standards, configuration management methods, review procedures, documentation standards, verification and validation, and testing specifications and procedures. SQA is one of the major control techniques available to the project manager [Dunn 1997].

8.3.1.3 Software Configuration Management. Software configuration management (SCM) is a method for controlling and reporting on software status. SCM is the discipline of identifying the configuration of a system at discrete points in time. This is done for the purpose of systematically controlling changes to this configuration and maintaining the integrity and traceability throughout the system lifecycle [Bersoff 1984].

8.3.1.4 Process and Product Metrics. A metric is a measure of the degree to which a process or product possesses a given attribute. Besides process and product metrics, other definitions of types of metrics are the following (adapted from [IEEE Std. 610.12-1990]):

- *Software quality metric*—A quantitative measure of the degree to which software possesses a given attribute that affects its quality. Examples are reliability, maintainability, and portability.

- *Software quantity metric*—A quantitative measure of some physical attribute of software. Examples are lines of code, function points, and pages of documentation.

- *Management metric*—A management indicator that can be used to measure management activities such as budget spent, value earned, cost overruns, and schedule delays.

In the early 1980s, the US Air Force's Rome Air Development Center (now known as Rome Laboratories) developed a set of software metrics called quality factors that represent the product attributes most desired by customers [RADC-TR-175]. These metrics have become part of our metrics environment and are used in many developments of software systems. These metrics are as follows:

- Correctness
- Efficiency
- Usability
- Maintainability
- Flexibility
- Reliability

- Integrity
- Survivability
- Reusability
- Expandability
- Portability
- Interoperability

Perhaps the most important software quality attribute is software reliability. Software reliability measures the extent to which the software will perform without any failures within a specified time period [RADC TR-85-37].

Other important attributes not on the RADC list include safety, security, complexity, and user friendliness.

An important set of metrics for software management was developed by the MITRE Corporation for the US Air Force Electronic System Division (now Electronic Systems Center) [Schultz 1988]. These ten metrics are considered by many to be the best set of management metrics available today. They are:

- Software size metric
- Software volatility metric
- Design complexity metric
- Design progress metric
- Testing progress metric
- Software personnel metric
- Computer resources utilization metric
- Schedule progress metric
- Computer Software Unit (CSU) development progress metric
- Incremental release content metric

Another set of management metrics was published by the US Air Force Systems Command (now part of the Air Force Material Command) in 1986 [AFSC Pamphlet 800-43 1986]. This set included the following:

- Computer resource utilization
- Software development manpower
- Requirements definition and stability
- Software progress (development and test)
- Cost and schedule deviations
- Software development tools

Measurement has been an integral part of the Software Engineering Institute's process improvement project. The first set of guidelines published by this project [Humphrey and Sweet 1987] included 10 metrics at process maturity level 2:

- Planned versus actual staffing profiles
- Software size versus time
- Statistics on software code and test errors
- Actual versus planned units designed

- Actual versus planned units completing unit testing
- Actual versus planned units integrated
- Target computer memory utilization
- Target computer throughput utilization
- Target computer I/O channel utilization
- Software build/release content

With the publication in 1993 of the Software Engineering Institute's Capability Maturity Model for Software [Paulk 1993], measurements became one of the "common features" that are part of every key process area.

8.3.2 Establish Monitoring and Reporting Systems. The project manager is responsible for establishing the methods of monitoring the software project and reporting project status. Monitoring and reporting systems must be specified in order to determine project status. The project manager needs feedback on the progress of the project and quality of the product to ensure that everything is going according to plan. The type, frequency, originator, and recipient of project reports must be specified. Status reporting tools to provide visibility of progress, and not just resources used or time passed, must be implemented.

Software methods, procedures, tools, and techniques must also be specified. Table 12 lists typical monitoring and reporting systems. Some tools that aid in controlling of a software engineering project are PERT and CPM, workload charts, and Gantt charts [Cori 1985]. The papers by Norm Howes [1984] and Pat Hurst [1997] presents the earned-value method of tracking a software engineering project.

8.3.2.1 Baseline Management System. This is a management and software lifecycle development strategy that integrates a series of lifecycle phases, reviews, and baseline documents into a system for managing a software engineering project. Specifically, it uses the waterfall lifecycle model to partition the project into manageable phases: requirements, design, implementation, and testing. It also establishes milestones, documents, and reviews at the end of each phase [Davis 1997].

Table 12. Methods of monitoring software projects.

Method	Definition or Explanation
Formal (milestone) reviews	Periodic, preplanned reviews of work products by developers, customers, users, and management in order to assess progress
Budget reviews	A comparison of estimated budget with actual expenditures in order to determine compliance with or deviations from plan
Independent auditing	An independent examination of a software project for the purpose of determining compliance with plans, specifications, and standards
Binary tracking system	A method of measuring progress on a work package by accepting only 0 or 100% completion
Software quality assurance (SQA)	A planned and systematic pattern of all actions necessary to provide adequate confidence that the development process and the work products of a software project conform to established standards
Unit development folder (UDF)	A specific form of development notebook that provides an orderly approach to the development process and the work products of a software project conform to established standards
Configuration management (CM)	A method for controlling and reporting on the status of work products generated by a software project
Testing	The controlled exercise of the program code in order to expose errors
Verification and validation	The process of assuring that each phase of the development life cycle correctly implements the specifications from the previous phase and that each software work product satisfy its requirements
Walk-throughs and inspections	Systematic examination of software work products by the producer's peers, conducted for the purpose of finding errors

Milestones: Milestones and milestone charts play a major part in the controlling process. A milestone is a discrete event; achievement of a milestone must be based on completion of one or more tangible work products. The purpose of milestones is to allow the project manager to partition a project into measurable units, each of which can be demonstrated to be complete. Examples of milestones are the completion of a software requirement specification, the completion of a software design, the completion of code, and of course the major milestone, the completion of the project.

Milestone Reviews: Reviews are analysis of project processes and products by customers, users, and management in order to assess progress. A milestone review is held at the end of each lifecycle phase of the project. For example, a preliminary design review (PDR) (sometimes called architectural design review) is held at the completion of the preliminary design phase.

Milestone reviews are usually chaired by the customer or higher level management. The project manager presents the current status and progress, the work done to date, the money expended, the current schedule, and any management and technical problems that may have surfaced since the last review. The review is a success when the customer or top management gives permission for the project manager to proceed to the next phase.

Baseline: A baseline is an agreed-on technical configuration at some point in the software project. Baselines are typically agreed on between developers, customers, and managers, and are controlled and maintained by a software configuration management board. Baselines are normally established at the end of a successful milestone review. Baselines commonly used by the Department of Defense are functional, allocated, and product baselines [Mil-Std-498 1995].

8.3.3 Measure and Analyze Results. The project manager is responsible for measuring the results of the project both during and at the end of the project. For instance, actual phase deliverables should be measured against planned phase deliverables. The measured results can be management (process) results and/or technical (product) results. An example of a process result would be the status of the project schedule. An example of a product result would be the degree to which the design specifications correctly interpreted the requirement specifications. Some of the tools and methods for measuring results are described in the following paragraphs.

8.3.3.1 Binary Tracking and Work Product Specifications. Specification of the work to be accomplished in completing a function, activity, or task. A work package specifies the objectives of the work, staffing, the expected duration, the resources, the re-

sults, and any other special considerations for the work. Work packages are normally small tasks that can be assigned to two or three individuals to be completed in two to three weeks. A series of work packages makes up a software project.

The "98 percent completion syndrome" is a cynical view of the method of determining project status by looking at the project as a whole and trying to determine what percent is complete. For example, given a six-week project, an immature project team will report that the project is 98 percent complete in the final week of the project with only "one or two bugs to find and fix." The project manager continues to report 98 percent complete for the next six or more weeks until the project is finally completed long after its estimated due date. The real issue is that nobody knew the real status of the project.

Binary tracking is the concept that a work package is either done or not done (that is, assigned a numeric "1" or "0"). Binary tracking of work packages is a reasonably accurate means of tracking the completion of a software project. For example, if a project has 880 work packages and 440 are completed at the end of the fifth week, the project is 50 percent complete, not 98 percent complete.

Binary tracking is also a major support tool to the earned-value concept (see Howes [1984] for a good description of the earned-value concept).

8.3.3.2 Unit Development Folders. The unit development folder (sometimes called software development folder) is a specific form of development notebook that has proven to be useful and effective in collecting and organizing software products as they are produced. The purpose of the UDF is to provide an orderly approach to the development of a program unit and to provide management visibility and control over the development process [Ingrassia 1988].

8.3.3.3 Walkthroughs and Inspections. Walkthroughs and inspections are reviews of a software product (design specifications, code, test procedures, and so on) conducted by the peers of the group being reviewed [Ackerman 1997], [Wheeler, Meeson, and Brykczynski 1997]. Walkthroughs are a critique of a software product by the producer's peers for the sole purpose of finding errors (see Weinberg [1971] for a description of an egoless review). The inspection system is another peer review developed by Michael Fagan [Fagan 1976], [Fagan 1986] of IBM in 1976. Inspections are typically more structured than walkthroughs.

8.3.3.4 Independent Auditing. The software project audit is an independent review of a software project to determine compliance with software requirements, specifications, baselines, standards, policies, and software quality assurance plans.

An independent audit is an audit done by an outside organization not associated with the project [Bernstein 1981]. On the positive side, an independent team can provide a totally unbiased opinion. Where there is a need for expert knowledge, the independent team can supplement existing talent.

The negative side of the independent audit is that the audit team needs to be brought up to speed on the project. An audit team requires ongoing involvement to be effective.

8.3.3.5 Verification and Validation. Verification and validation is one of the most capable methods of determining whether the product is correct. Verification is assuring that each phase of the lifecycle correctly interprets the specification from the previous phase. Validation is assuring that each completed software product satisfies its requirements [Fujii and Wallace 1997].

8.3.3.6 Testing. Testing is the controlled exercise of the program code in order to expose errors. Unit testing is the testing of one unit of code (usually a module) by the programmer who programmed the unit. Integration testing is the testing of each unit or element in combination with other elements to show the existence of errors between the units or elements. System testing is the controlled exercise of the completed system. In each case, it is important to develop test plans, test procedures, test cases, and test results [ANSI/IEEE Std 829-1983].

8.3.3.7 Software Configuration Audit. Software configuration audits provide the mechanism for determining the degree to which the current software system mirrors the software system contained in the baseline and the requirements document [Bersoff 1984].

8.3.4 Initiate Corrective Actions for the Project. If standards and requirements are not being met, the project manager must initiate corrective action. For instance, the project manager can change the plan or standard, use overtime or other procedures to get back on plan, or change the requirements, for example, deliver less.

The project manager might change the plans or standards if apparently the original plans or standards cannot be met. This might involve requiring a larger budget, more people, or more checkout time on the development computer. It also might require reducing the standards (and, indirectly, the quality) by reducing the number of walkthroughs or reducing the review of all software modules to only the critical software modules.

It is sometimes possible to get back on schedule by increasing the resources. This increases the resources requirements plan. It is also sometimes possible to keep the original cost by stretching out the schedule or reducing the functionality of the software system.

An example of changing the requirements involves delivering software that does not completely meet all the functional requirements that were laid out in the original software requirements specifications.

8.3.5 Reward and Discipline the Project Members. The project manager should reward people who meet their standards and plans, and discipline those who, without good reason, do not. This should not be confused with the rewards and discipline given to workers for performing their assigned duties; that is a function of staffing. The system of rewards and discipline discussed here is a mechanism for controlling ability to meet a plan or standard.

8.3.6 Document Controlling Methods. The project manager must document all standards, software quality procedures, metrics, and other means of measuring production and products. In addition, the manager must establish metrics for determining when corrective action should be initiated and determine in advance possible corrective action that can be taken.

9. Summary

Software engineering procedures and techniques do not alone guarantee a successful project. A good project manager can sometimes overcome or work around deficiencies in organization, staffing, budgets, standards, or other shortcomings. A poor manager stumbles over every problem, real or imaginary—no number of rules, policies, standards, or techniques will help. The methods and techniques discussed in this article, in the hands of a competent project manager, can significantly improve the probability of a successful project.

In this and in many other documents, the terms "project management" and "software engineering project management" are used interchangeably. This is because the management of software engineering projects and other types of projects require many of the same tools, techniques, approaches, and methods of mainstream management. The functions and general activities of management are the same at all levels; only the detailed activities and tasks are different.

References

[Ackerman 1997] Ackerman, F.A., "Software Inspections and the Cost-Effective Production of Reliable Software," in *Software Engineering*, M. Dorfman and R.H. Thayer, eds., IEEE Computer Soc. Press, Los Alamitos, Calif., 1997, pp. 235–255.

[AFSC Pamphlet 800-43 1986] *Air Force Systems Command Software Management Indicators: Management Insight*, AFSC Pamphlet 800-43, HQ AFSC, Andrews AFB, DC, Jan. 31, 1986.

[ANSI/IEEE Std 829-1983] ANSI/IEEE Std. 829-1983, *IEEE Standard for Software Test Documents*, IEEE, New York, N.Y., 1987, approved by American National Standards Institute Aug. 19, 1983.

[Arthur 1983] Arthur, L.J., *Programmer Productivity: Myths, Methods, and Murphology*, John Wiley & Sons, New York, N.Y., 1983.

[Baker 1972] Baker, F. Terry, "Chief Programmer Team Management of Production Programming," *IBM System J.*, Vol. 11, 1972, pp. 56-73.

[Bartol and Martin 1983] Bartol, K.M., and D.C. Martin, "Managing the Consequences of DP Turnover: A Human Resources Planning Perspective," *Proc. 20th ACM Computer Resources Planning Perspective*, ACM Press, New York, N.Y., 1983, pp. 79–86. Reprinted in *Software Engineering Project Management*, 2nd ed., R.H. Thayer, ed., IEEE Computer Soc. Press, Los Alamitos, Calif., 1997.

[Ben-David, et al. 1984] Ben-David, A., M. Ben-Porath, J. Loeb, and M. Rich, "An Industrial Software Engineering Retraining Course: Development Considerations and Lessons Learned," *IEEE Trans. Software Eng.*, Vol. SE-10, No. 1, Nov. 1984, pp. 748–755.

[Bernstein 1981] Bernstein, L., "Software Project Management Audits," *J. Systems and Software*, Elsevier North Holland, 1981, pp. 281–287. Reprinted in *Software Engineering Project Management*, 2nd ed., R.H. Thayer, ed., IEEE Computer Soc. Press, Los Alamitos, Calif., 1997.

[Bersoff 1984] Bersoff, E.H., "Elements of Software Configuration Management," *IEEE Trans. Software Eng.*, Vol. SE-10, No. 1, Jan. 1984, pp. 79–87. Reprinted in *Software Engineering Project Management*, 2nd ed., R.H. Thayer, ed., IEEE Computer Soc. Press, Los Alamitos, Calif., 1997.

[Boehm 1981] Boehm, B.W., *Software Engineering Economics*, Prentice-Hall, Englewood Cliffs, N.J., 1981.

[Boehm 1984] Boehm, B.W., "Software Engineering Economics," *IEEE Trans. Software Eng.*, Vol. SE-10, No. 1, Jan. 1984, pp. 4–21. Reprinted in *Tutorial: Software Engineering Project Management*, R.H. Thayer, ed., IEEE Computer Soc. Press, Los Alamitos, Calif., 1988, pp. 239–256.

[Boehm 1987] Boehm, B.W., *Tutorial: Software Risk Management*, IEEE Computer Soc. Press, Los Alamitos, Calif., 1989.

[Boehm 1988] Boehm, B.W., "A Spiral Model of Software Development and Enhancement," *Computer*, May 1988, pp. 61–72. Reprinted in *Software Engineering*, M. Dorfman and R.H. Thayer, eds., IEEE Computer Soc. Press, Los Alamitos, Calif., 1997, pp. 415–426.

[Boehm et al., COCOMO 2.0, 1994] Boehm, B., B. Clark, E. Horowitz, C. Westland, R. Madachy, and R. Selby, "Cost Models for Future Software Life Cycle Process: COCOMO 2.0," in *Software Engineering Project Management*, 2nd ed., R.H. Thayer, ed., IEEE Computer Soc. Press, Los Alamitos, Calif., 1997.

[Boyatzis 1971] Boyatzis, R.E., "Leadership: The Effective Use of Power," Management of Personnel Quarterly, Bureau of Industrial Relations, 1971, pp. 1–8. Reprinted in *Software Engineering Project Management*, 2nd ed., R.H. Thayer, ed., IEEE Computer Soc. Press, Los Alamitos, Calif., 1997.

[Brooks 1987] "Report on the Defense Science Board Task Force on Military Software," Office of the Undersecretary of Defense for Acquisition, Dept. of Defense, Washington, D.C., Sept. 1987.

[Buckley 1987] Buckley, F.J., "Establishing Software Engineering Standards in an Industrial Organization," in *Tutorial: Software Engineering Project Management*, R.H. Thayer, ed., IEEE Computer Soc. Press, Los Alamitos, Calif., 1988, pp. 424–429.

[Bunyard and Coward 1982] Bunyard, J.M., and J.M. Coward, "Today's Risks in Software Development—Can They be Significantly Reduced?" in "Concepts," *J. Defense Systems Acquisition Management*, Vol. 5, No. 4, Aug. 1982, pp. 73–94. Reprinted in *Tutorial: Software Engineering Project Management*, R.H. Thayer, ed., IEEE Computer Soc. Press, Los Alamitos, Calif., 1988, pp. 75–90.

[Cherlin 1981] Cherlin, M., "Burnout: Victims and Avoidance's," *Datamation*, July 1981, pp. 92–99.

[Cleland and King, 1972] Cleland, D.I., and W.R. King, *Management: A Systems Approach*, See Table 5-1: Major Management Functions as Seen by Various Authors, McGraw-Hill, New York, N.Y., 1972.

[Cook 1976] Cooke, L.H., Jr., "The Chief Programmer Team Administrator," *Datamation*, June 1976, pp. 85–86.

[Cori 1985] Cori, K.A., "Fundamentals of Master Scheduling for the Project Manager," *Project Management J.*, June 1985, pp. 78–89. Reprinted *in Software Engineering Project Management*, 2nd ed., R.H. Thayer, ed., IEEE Computer Soc. Press, Los Alamitos, Calif., 1997.

[Davis 1990] Davis, A.M., "The Analysis and Specification of System and Software Requirements," in *System and Software Requirements Engineering*, R.H. Thayer and M. Dorfman, eds., IEEE Computer Soc. Press, Los Alamitos, Calif., 1990.

[Davis 1994] Davis, A., "Trial by Firing: Saga of a Rookie Manager," *IEEE Software*, Sept. 1994, pp. 109–110. Reprinted in *Software Engineering Project Management*, 2nd ed., R.H. Thayer, ed., IEEE Computer Soc. Press, Los Alamitos, Calif., 1997.

[Davis 1997] Davis, A., "Life Cycle Models," in *Software Engineering Project Management*, 2nd ed., R.H. Thayer, ed., IEEE Computer Soc. Press, Los Alamitos, Calif., 1997.

[Deming 1986] Deming, W.E., *Out of the Crisis*, MIT Center for Advanced Engineering Study, Cambridge, Mass., 1986.

[DoD Software Initiative 1983] *Strategy for a DoD Software Initiative*, Dept. of Defense Report, Oct. 1, 1982. (An edited public version was published in *Computer*, Nov. 1983.)

[Donnelly, Gibson, and Ivancevich 1975] Donnelly Jr., J.H., J.L. Gibson, and J.M. Ivancevich, *Fundamentals of Management: Functions, Behavior, Models*, revised edition, Business Publications, Inc., Dallas, TX, 1975.

[Dunn 1997] Dunn, R.H., "Software Quality Assurance," in *Software Engineering Project Management*, 2nd ed., R.H. Thayer, ed., IEEE Computer Soc. Press, Los Alamitos, Calif., 1997.

[Fagan 1976] Fagan, M.E., "Design and Code Inspections to Reduce Errors in Program Development," *IBM Systems J.*, Vol. 15, No. 3, 1976, pp. 182–211.

[Fagan 1986] Fagan, M.E., "Advances in Software Inspections," *IEEE Trans. Software Eng.*, Vol. SE-12, No. 7, July 1986, pp. 744–751. Reprinted in *Tutorial: Software Engineering Project Management*, R.H. Thayer, ed., IEEE Computer Soc. Press, Los Alamitos, Calif., 1988, pp. 416–423.

[Fairley and Rook 1997] Fairley, R.E., and P. Rook, "Risk Management for Software Development," in *Software Engineering*, M. Dorfman and R.H. Thayer, eds., IEEE Computer Soc. Press, Los Alamitos, Calif., 1997, pp. 387–403.

[Faulk 1997] Faulk, S., "Software Requirements: A Tutorial," in *Software Engineering*, M. Dorfman and R.H. Thayer, eds., IEEE Computer Society Press, Los Alamitos, Calif., 1997, pp. 82–103. Reprinted in *Software Engineering Project Management*, 2nd ed., R.H. Thayer, ed., IEEE Computer Soc. Press, Los Alamitos, Calif., 1997.

[Fayol 1949] Fayol, H., *General and Industrial Administration*, Sir Isaac Pitman & Sons, Ltd., London, 1949.

[Fitz-enz 1978] Fitz-enz, J., "Who is the DP Professional?" *Datamation*, Sept. 1978, pp. 125–128. Reprinted in *Software Engineering Project Management*, 2nd ed., R.H. Thayer, ed., IEEE Computer Soc. Press, Los Alamitos, Calif., 1997.

[Fujii and Wallace 1997] Fujii, R., and D.R. Wallace, "Software Verification and Validation, in *Software Engineering*, M. Dorfman and R.H. Thayer, eds., IEEE Computer Soc. Press, Los Alamitos, Calif., 1997, pp. 220–234.

[Gaffney, Schedule, 1997] Gaffney, J.E., "How to Estimate Schedule," in *Software Engineering Project Management*, 2nd ed., R.H. Thayer, ed., IEEE Computer Soc. Press, Los Alamitos, Calif., 1997.

[Gaffney, Size, 1997] Gaffney, J.E., "How to Estimate Software System Size," in *Software Engineering Project Management*, 2nd ed., R.H. Thayer, ed., IEEE Computer Soc. Press, Los Alamitos, Calif., 1997.

[GAO/IMTEC-92-48 C-17 Aircraft Software] "Embedded Computer Systems: Significant Software Problems on C-17 Must be Addressed?" General Accounting Office GAO/IMTEC-92-48, Gaithersburg, MD 20877, May 1992.

[Gibbs 1994] Gibbs, W.W., "Software's Chronic Crisis," in *Software Engineering Project Management*, 2nd ed., R.H. Thayer, ed., IEEE Computer Soc. Press, Los Alamitos, Calif., 1997.

[Glabas and Fairley 1997] Glabas, J.M., and R.E. Fairley, "IEEE Guide to Software Project Management Plans," in *Software Engineering Project Management*, 2nd ed., R.H. Thayer, ed., IEEE Computer Soc. Press, Los Alamitos, Calif., 1997.

[Goldberg 1978] Goldberg, E.A., "Applying Corporate Software Development Policies," TRW, Defense and Space Systems Group, Jan. 1978. Reprinted in *Software Engineering Project Management*, 2nd ed., R.H. Thayer, ed., IEEE Computer Soc. Press, Los Alamitos, Calif., 1997.

[Herzberg, Mausner, and Snyderman 1959] Herzberg, F., B. Mausner, and B.B. Snyderman, *The Motivation to Work*, John Wiley & Sons, New York, N.Y., 1959.

[High Technology Careers Magazine 1997] *High Technology Careers Magazine*, Vol. 13, No. 1, Jan. /Mar. 1997.

[Howes 1984] Howes, N.R., "Managing Software Development Projects for Maximum Productivity," *IEEE Trans. Software Eng.*, Vol. SE-10, No. 1, Jan. 1984, pp. 27–35. Reprinted in *Tutorial: Software Engineering Project Management*, R.H. Thayer, ed., IEEE Computer Soc. Press, Los Alamitos, Calif., 1988, pp. 446–454.

[Humphrey and Sweet 1987] Humphrey, W.S., and W.L. Sweet, *A Method for Assessing the Software Development Capability of Contractors*, CMU/SEI-87-TR-23, Carnegie Mellon Univ., Software Eng. Inst., Pittsburgh, Pa., Sept. 1987.

[Hurst 1997] Hurst, R.W., "Software Project Management: Threads of Control," in *Software Engineering Project Management*, 2nd ed., R.H. Thayer, ed., IEEE Computer Soc. Press, Los Alamitos, Calif., 1997.

[IEEE Software Engineering Standards 1993] Hardbound Edition of *Software Engineering Standards*, IEEE, New York, N.Y., 1993.

[IEEE Std 610.12-1990] IEEE Std. 610.12-1990, *Glossary of Software Engineering Terminology*, IEEE Press, Piscataway, N.J., 1990.

[IEEE Std 729-1983] ANSI/IEEE Std. 729-1983, *IEEE Standard Glossary of Software Engineering Terminology*, IEEE, New York, N.Y., 1983.

[Ingrassia 1988] Ingrassia, F.S., "The Unit Development Folder (UDF): A Ten-Year Perspective," in *Tutorial: Software Engineering Project Management*, R.H. Thayer, ed., IEEE Computer Society Press, Los Alamitos, Calif., 1988, pp. 405–415. Reprinted in *Software Engineering Project Management*, 2nd ed., R.H. Thayer, ed., IEEE Computer Soc. Press, Los Alamitos, Calif., 1997.

[Kirchof and Adams 1986] Kirchof, N.S., and J.R. Adams, "Conflict Management for Project Managers: An Overview," extracted from *Conflict Management for Project Managers*, Project Management Inst., Feb. 1986, pp. 1–13. Reprinted in *Software Engineering Project Management*, 2nd ed., R.H. Thayer, ed., IEEE Computer Soc. Press, Los Alamitos, Calif., 1997.

[Koontz and O'Donnell 1972] Koontz, H., and C. O'Donnell, *Principles of Management: An Analysis of Managerial Functions*, 5th ed., McGraw-Hill, New York, N.Y., 1972.

[Koontz, O'Donnell, and Weihrich 1980] Koontz, H., C. O'Donnell, and H. Weihrich, *Management*, 7th ed., McGraw-Hill, New York, N.Y., 1980.

[Koontz, O'Donnell, and Weihrich 1984] Koontz, H., C. O'Donnell, and H. Weihrich, *Management*, 8th ed., McGraw-Hill, New York, N.Y., 1984.

[Kruesi 1982] Kruesi, B., seminar on "Software Psychology," California State University, Sacramento, Fall 1982.

[Legg 1997] Legg, D.B., Legg, "How to Estimate Software Costs Using COCOMO," in *Software Engineering Project Management*, 2nd ed., R.H. Thayer, ed., IEEE Computer Soc. Press, Los Alamitos, Calif., 1997.

[MacKenzie, 1969] MacKenzie, R.A., "The Management Process in 3-D," *Harvard Business Review*, Vol. 47, No. 6, Nov. -Dec. 1969, pp. 80–87. Reprinted in *Software Engineering Project Management*, 2nd ed., R.H. Thayer, ed., IEEE Computer Soc. Press, Los Alamitos, Calif., 1997.

[Mantei 1981] Mantei, M., "The Effect of Programming Team Structures on Programming Tasks," *Comm. ACM*, Vol. 24, No. 3, Mar. 1981, pp. 106–113. Reprinted in *Software Engineering Project Management*, 2nd ed., R.H. Thayer, ed., IEEE Computer Soc. Press, Los Alamitos, Calif., 1997.

[Maslow 1954] Maslow, A.H., *Motivation and Personality*, Harper & Brothers, New York, N.Y. 1954.

[McGill 1984] McGill, J.P., "The Software Engineering Shortage: A Third Choice," *IEEE Trans. Software Eng.*, Vol. SE-10. No. 1, Jan. 1984, pp. 42–48. Reprinted in *Tutorial: Software Engineering Project Management*, R.H. Thayer, ed., IEEE Computer Soc. Press, Los Alamitos, Calif., 1988, pp. 330–337.

[McGregor 1960] McGregor, D., *The Human Side of Enterprise*, McGraw-Hill, New York, N.Y. 1960.

[Middleton, 1967] Middleton, C.J., "How to Set Up a Project Organization," *Harvard Business Review*, Nov.–Dec. 1967, pp. 73–82. Reprinted *in Tutorial: Software Engineering Project Management*, R.H. Thayer, ed., IEEE Computer Soc. Press, Los Alamitos, Calif., 1988, pp. 277–286.

[Miller 1978] Miller, W.B., "Fundamentals of Project Management," *J. Systems Management*, Vol. 29, No. 11, Issue 211, Nov. 1978, pp. 22–29. Reprinted *in Tutorial: Software Engineering Project Management*, R.H. Thayer, ed., IEEE Computer Soc. Press, Los Alamitos, Calif., 1988, pp. 178–185.

[Mills 1980] Mills, H.D., "Software Engineering Education," *Proc. IEEE*, Vol. 68, No. 9, Sept. 1980, pp. 1,158–1,162.

[Mil-Std-498 1995] *Software Development and Documentation*, Dept. of Defense, Dec. 5, 1995.

[Moneysmith 1984] Moneysmith, M., "I'm OK—and You're Not," *Savvy*, Apr. 1984, pp. 37–38. Reprinted in *Software Engineering Project Management*, 2nd ed., R.H. Thayer, ed., IEEE Computer Soc. Press, Los Alamitos, CA, 1997.

[Ouchi 1981] Ouchi, W., *Theory Z: How American Business Can Meet the Japanese Challenge*, Addison-Wesley, Reading, Mass., 1981.

[Paulk, et al. 1993] Paulk, M.C., B. Curtis, M.B. Chrissis, and C.V. Weber, *Key Practices of the Capability Maturity Model*, Version 1.1, CMU/SEI-93-TR-25, Carnegie Mellon Univ., Software Eng. Inst., Pittsburgh, Pa., Feb. 1993.

[Paulk, et al. 1997] Paulk, M.C., B. Curtis, M.B. Chrissis, and C.V. Weber, "The Capability Maturity Model for Software," in *Software Engineering*, M. Dorfman and R.H. Thayer, eds., IEEE Computer Society Press, Los Alamitos, Calif., 1997, pp. 427–438. Reprinted in *Software Engineering Project Management*, 2nd edition, R.H. Thayer, ed., IEEE Computer Soc. Press, Los Alamitos, Calif., 1997.

[Powell and Posner 1984] Powell, G.N., and B.Z. Posner, "Excitement and Commitment: Keys to Project Success," *Project Management J.*, Dec. 1984, pp. 39–46. Reprinted in *Software Engineering Project Management*, 2nd ed., R.H. Thayer, ed., IEEE Computer Soc. Press, Los Alamitos, Calif., 1997.

[RADC TR-85-37] Bowen, T.P., G.B. Wigle, and J.T. Tsai, *Specification of Software Quality Attributes*: Vol. 1, *Final Technical Report*; Vol. 2, *Software Quality Specifications Guidebook*; Vol. 3, *Software Quality Evaluation Guidebook*; RADC TR-85-37, prepared by Boeing Aerospace Co. for Rome Air Development Center, Griffiss AFB, N.Y., Feb. 1985.

[RADC-TR-175] *Software Quality Measures for Distributed Systems* (Vol. I), *Software Quality Measures for Distributed Systems: Guide Book for Software Quality Measurements* (Vol. II), and *Software Quality Measures for Distributed Systems: Impact on Software Quality* (Vol. III), TR RADC-TR-175, Rome Air Development Center, Griffiss AFB, N.Y., 1983.

[Raudsepp 1981] Raudsepp, E., "Delegate Your Way to Success," *Computer Decisions*, Mar. 1981, pp. 157–164. Reprinted in *Software Engineering Project Management*, 2nd ed., R.H. Thayer, ed., IEEE Computer Soc. Press, Los Alamitos, Calif., 1997.

[Redwine and Riddle 1985] Redwine, S.T. Jr., and W. E. Riddle, "Software Technology Maturation, *Proc. 8th Int'l Conf. Software Eng.*, IEEE Computer Soc. Press, Los Alamitos, Calif., 1985, pp. 189–200.

[Rue and Byars, 1983] Rue, L.W., and L.L. Byars, *Management: Theory and Application*, Richard D. Irwin, Inc., Homewood, Ill., 1983.

[Sackman, H. et al 1968] Sackman, H., W.J. Erikson, and E.E. Grant, "Exploratory Experimental Studies Comparing On-Line and Off-Line Programming Performance," *Comm. ACM*, Vol. 11, No. 1, Jan. 1968, pp. 3–11. Reprinted in *Tutorial: Software Engineering Project Management*, R.H. Thayer, ed., IEEE Computer Soc. Press, Los Alamitos, Calif., 1988, pp. 321–329.

[Schultz 1988] Schultz, H.P., *Software Management Metrics*, ESD TR-88-001, prepared by The MITRE Corporation for the US Air Force, Electronic Systems Division, Hanscom AFB, Mass., 1988. Extract printed in *Software Engineering Project Management*, 2nd ed., Thayer, R.H., ed., IEEE Computer Soc. Press, Los Alamitos, Calif., 1997.

[Stuckenbruck 1981] Stuckenbruck, L.C., "The Matrix Organization," *A Decade of Project Management*, Project Management Institute, 1981, pp. 157–169. Reprinted in *Software Engineering Project Management*, 2nd ed., R.H. Thayer, ed., IEEE Computer Soc. Press, Los Alamitos, Calif., 1997.

[Thayer and Fairley, Software Risks, 1997] Thayer, R.H., and R.E. Fairley, "Risk Management for Software Projects," in *Software Engineering Project Management*, 2nd ed., R.H. Thayer, ed., IEEE Computer Soc. Press, Los Alamitos, Calif., 1997.

[Thayer and Fairley, WBS, 1997] Thayer, R.H., and R.E. Fairley, The Work Breakdown Structure (WBS)," in *Software Engineering Project Management*, 2nd ed., R.H. Thayer, ed., IEEE Computer Soc. Press, Los Alamitos, Calif., 1997.

[Thayer and Pyster 1984] Thayer, R.H., and A.B. Pyster, "Guest Editorial: Software Engineering Project Management," *IEEE Trans. Software Eng.*, Vol. SE-10, No. 1, Jan. 1984.

[Weihrich 1997] Weihrich, H., "Management Science, Theory, and Practice," in *Software Engineering Project Management*, 2nd ed., R.H. Thayer, ed., IEEE Computer Soc. Press, Los Alamitos, Calif., 1997.

[Weinberg 1971] Weinberg, G., *The Psychology of Computer Programming*, Van Nostrand Reinhold, New York, N.Y., 1971.

[Wheeler, Meeson, and Brykczynski 1997] Wheeler, D.A., R.N. Meeson, Jr., and B. Brykczynski, "Software Peer Review," in *Software Engineering Project Management*, 2nd ed., R.H. Thayer, ed., IEEE Computer Soc. Press, Los Alamitos, Calif., 1997.

[Youker 1977] Youker, R., "Organizational Alternatives for Project Management," *Project Management Quarterly*, Vol. VIII, No. 1, Mar. 1977, pp. 18–24. Reprinted in *Software Engineering Project Management*, 2nd ed., R.H. Thayer, ed., IEEE Computer Soc. Press, Los Alamitos, Calif., 1997.

[Yourdon 1997] Yourdon, E., "Inserting a New Technology into a Software Project," in *Software Engineering Project Management*, 2nd ed., R.H. Thayer, ed., IEEE Computer Soc. Press, Los Alamitos, Calif., 1997.

[Zubrow, et al. 1995] Zubrow, D., J. Herbsleb, W. Hayes, D. Goldenson presentation: "Process Maturity Profile of the Software Community 1995 Update," Nov. 1995, based on data up to Sept. 1995 for most recent assessment of 440 organizations: ML1–70.2%; ML2–18.4%; ML3–10.2%; ML4–1%; ML5–0.2%—Source: e-mail, Mark Paulk, Software Engineering Institute, Feb. 14, 1996.

Software Life Cycle Models

Alan M. Davis

University of Colorado at Colorado Springs
Center for Software Systems Engineering
1867 Austin Bluffs Parkway; Suite 200
Colorado Springs, CO 80933-7150
adavis@vivaldi.uccs.edu
http://mozart.uccs.edu/adavis/adavis.html

Abstract

The first software life cycle, the waterfall, was defined by Winston Royce in the early 1970s. Since then many development teams have followed this model. In the past 10–15 years, the waterfall model has come under attack for being too constraining and too rigid for modern software development projects. In its stead, many new life cycle models have been proposed, including models that purport to develop software more rapidly, or more incrementally, or in an evolutionary manner, or they precede full-scale development with some kind of rapid prototype. This paper explores the world of life cycle models, and emphasizes that they are not particularly different from one another. Instead, they provide different views of the same basic software development process.

Introduction

Software permeates every aspect of our lives. We trust software in systems to monitor our health, maintain our nuclear power stations, shepherd our astronauts in space, drive our trains, and help us pilot aircraft. It is no wonder that so much emphasis has been placed on the software industry lately to ensure that the software being produced is of the highest possible quality.

It is generally believed that a relationship exists between the quality of a product and the quality of the process that produced it. A quality software development process is neither necessary nor sufficient to produce quality products, but clearly it is easier to hone your products if your process is well understood. A life cycle model defines the stages or phases through which a software development project moves; it is thus a primary element of software process. The classic waterfall model for the software life cycle (see Figure 1) was defined in 1970 by Winston Royce [ROY70] as a first attempt to harness software process. For almost twenty years it served as the primary life cycle model in use in the software industry.

Since the late 1980s, many software development teams have expressed frustration with the waterfall model. In many cases, the frustration was justified; in other cases, the frustration was caused by individuals failing to read and/or understand Royce's original paper. Increasing demand for satisfactory software solutions with tight development budgets and tight development schedules fueled the fire, and caused projects to try to escape what they perceived as the overly constraining waterfall model. In response to these pressures, many alternative ways of looking at software life cycles have been proposed, including prototyping, incremental development, and evolutionary development.

The following sections define a software life cycle model, introduce choices of life cycle models, and present an approach for contrasting and evaluating life cycle models.

Definition of a Life Cycle Model

A *software life cycle model* is a view of the activities that occur during software development. Just as a human life cycle model (for example, infant, child, adolescent, adult, senior citizen) helps us understand the basic activities and characteristics of humans as they progress, the software life cycle model helps us understand the basic activities and characteristics of software as it develops. Notice that humans progress from birth to death whether or not we describe it using a life cycle model. Similarly, software progresses from idea inception through deployment and eventual death whether or not we describe it using a life cycle model. A software life cycle model is thus a way we look at software development; it is not a way to develop software.

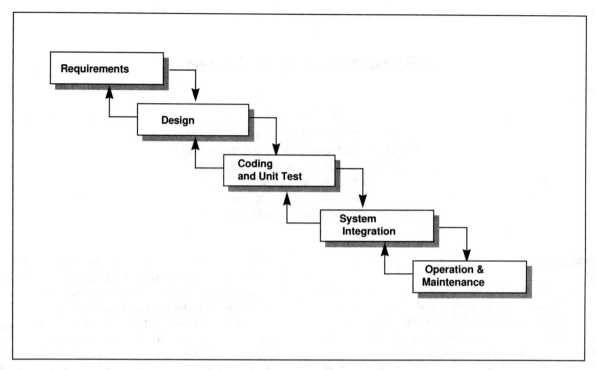

Figure 1. Royce's waterfall chart.

A software life cycle model

- describes the major phases of software development,
- defines the primary functions expected to be performed during those phases,
- helps managers track progress, and
- provides a framework for the definition of a detailed software development process.

Choices for Life Cycle Models

Since a life cycle model is a way of looking at and talking about software development, it is possible to take many such views of any single software development effort. It makes no sense then for a project to make a decision concerning which one life cycle model it will adhere to. The software life cycle models presented here are more complementary than exclusionary. There are many options, such as the following:

- Waterfall model
- Incremental model
- Evolutionary model
- Prototyping model
- Spiral model
- Concurrent model

Waterfall Model

The waterfall model was originally documented for software in 1970 by Royce [ROY70]. It is the most basic of all life cycle models, and in fact serves as the building block for most other life cycle models. The *waterfall model* view of software development is very simple; it says that software development can be thought of as a simple sequence of phases, as shown in Figure 1. Each phase has a set of well-defined goals, and the activities within any phase contribute to the satisfaction of that phase's goals or perhaps a subsequent phase's goals. Arrows show the flow of information among the phases. The forward arrows show the normal flow; the backward arrows represent feedback. Royce did not say that "only requirements activities may occur during the requirements phase" nor that "only design activities may occur during the design phase," and so forth. Furthermore, he said nothing about whether a trip through all the phases would build an entire system, or just part of it.

There is nothing sacred about the names for the phases. The requirements phase has been called elicitation, system analysis, requirements analysis, or requirements specification; the preliminary design phase has been called high-level design, top-level design, software architectural definition, design specification or just "design;" the detailed design phase is often called program design, module design, lower level design, algorithmic design, or just "design," and so on [COM91].

The waterfall life cycle model captures some very basic tenets:

- Plan a project before you embark on it.
- Define a system's desired external behavior before designing its internal architecture.
- Document the results of each activity.
- Design a system before you code it.
- Test a system after you build it.

One of the most important contributions of the waterfall model is for management. It enables managers to track development progress, albeit on a very gross scale.

Incremental Development Model

Risks associated with development of large, complex systems are enormous. One way to reduce the risk is to build only a part of a system, reserving other features for subsequent releases. *Incremental development* [HIR85] is the process of constructing ever-increasing subsets of a system's requirements. See Figure 2. Typically, a requirements document is written that captures all of the requirements for the full system (Let's call this the "wish-list" document). There are two ways to handle the requirements for the series of incremental products [LEF98]. One is to write separate requirements documents for each in-cremental product, suitably cross-referenced to the full "wish-list" document. The other is to maintain just one document, annotating each requirement to indicate the product increment in which the requirement will be met.

Notice that incremental development is 100 percent compatible with the waterfall model. Incremental development does not demand any specific way of looking at the development of any one increment. Thus, the waterfall model could be used to manage each development effort, as shown in Figure 3.

The incremental development model provides some significant benefits to projects:

- Building a smaller system is always less risky than building a larger system.
- By deploying part of the functionality, it is easier to determine whether the requirements planned for the subsequent release are correct.
- If a major mistake is made, only the latest iteration need be discarded.
- As described in [DAV88], reducing the time to develop a system (in this case an increment of the system) decreases the likelihood that user requirements will change during the development.
- If a major mistake is made, the previous increment can be used.
- Development mistakes made in one increment can be fixed before the next increment starts.

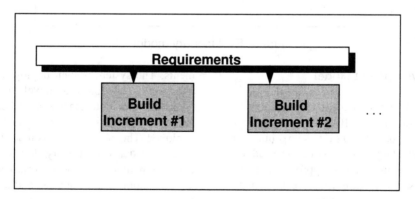

Figure 2. Incremental development model.

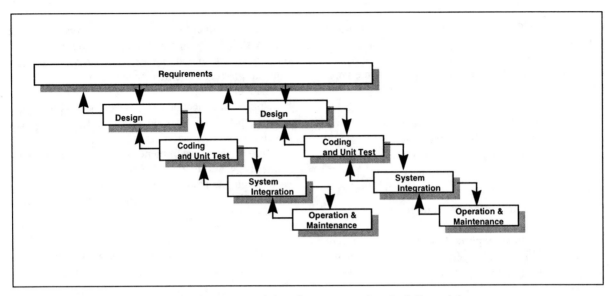

Figure 3. Incremental development and waterfall models.

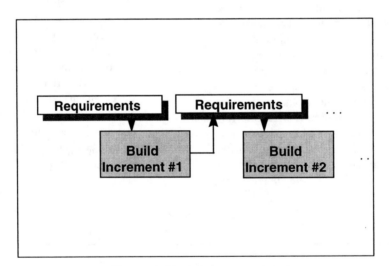

Figure 4. Evolutionary model.

Evolutionary Development Model

Like the incremental development model, the *evolutionary development* model [GID84] (sometimes called an evolutionary prototyping [DAV95]) builds a series of successively larger versions of the product. However, whereas the incremental approach presupposes that the full set of requirements are known up front, the evolutionary model assumes that the requirements are not fully known at project inception.

In the evolutionary model, shown in Figure 4, the requirements are carefully examined, and only those that are well understood are selected for the first increment. The developers construct a partial implementation of the system that meets only these require-

ments. The system is then deployed, the users use it, and provide feedback to developers. Based on this feedback, the requirements specification is updated, and a second version of the product is developed and deployed. The process repeats indefinitely.

Notice that evolutionary development is 100 percent compatible with the waterfall model. Evolutionary development does not demand any specific way of looking at the development of any one increment. Thus, the waterfall model could be used to manage each development effort in a manner identical to that shown in Figure 3 for incremental development. Obviously, incremental and evolutionary development can be combined as well. All one has to do is build a subset of the known requirements (incremental), and understand up front that many new requirements are likely to be uncovered when the system is deployed (evolutionary).

Requirements Prototyping Model

Requirements prototyping is the creation of a partial implementation of a system, for the express purpose of learning about the system's requirements [DAV95]. (Note that for the purposes of this discussion, I am excluding architectural prototypes, which are part of the design phase). A prototype is constructed in as quick a manner as is possible. It is given to users, customers, or representatives of either, to enable them to experiment with the prototype. These individuals then provide feedback about what they liked and disliked about the prototype to the developers, who cap

ture what was learned in documenting the actual requirements specification for the real system development. The first documented use of this type of prototyping was done by Gomaa and Scott [GOM81]. Prototyping can be used as part of the requirements phase (to ascertain requirements) or just before the requirements phase (as a precursor to requirements). In either case, prototyping can serve its role immediately before a waterfall development (see Figure 5), or immediately before any or all of the incremental developments in incremental or evolutionary models (see Figure 6).

Prototyping has been used often in the 1990s because requirements specifications for complex systems tend to be relatively difficult to read. Many users and customers find it much easier to provide feedback suitability based on manipulating a prototype rather than reading a lengthy, potentially ambiguous requirements specification.

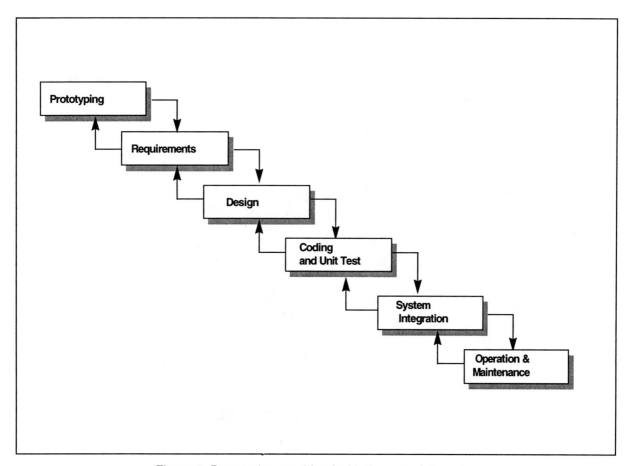

Figure 5. Prototyping combined with the waterfall model.

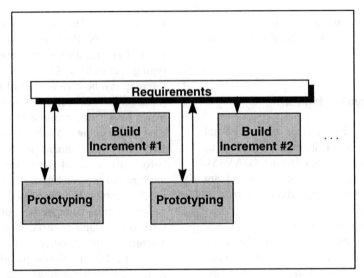

Figure 6. Prototyping combined with incremental or evolutionary models.

Unlike evolutionary models where the best-understood requirements are incorporated, a prototype generally constructs the poorest-understood requirements. For if you were to build the well-understood requirements, the customer would respond with "yeah, so?" and nothing would be learned from the experience.

Spiral Model

The spiral model [BOE88] of the software process (see Figure 7) is a meta-life cycle model. In this model, development effort is iterative. As soon as one development effort completes, another begins. Furthermore, every time you perform development, you should follow these four steps:

1. Determine what you want to achieve.

2. Determine the alternative routes you can take to achieve these goals. For each, analyze the risks and payoffs, and select the best one.

3. Follow the approach selected in step 2.

4. Assess what you have done.

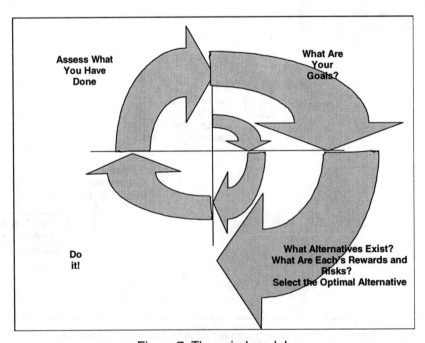

Figure 7. The spiral model.

The radial dimension in Figure 7 reflects cumulative costs incurred by the project.

Let us look at a particular scenario. Let's say that on this project, we are trying to solve a particular set of customer problems. During the first trip around the spiral, we analyze the situation and determine that the biggest risk is the user interface. After careful analysis of the alternative ways of addressing this (for example, build the system and hope for the best, write a requirements specification and hope the customer understands, and build a prototype), we determine that the best course of action is to build a prototype. We do so. Then we provide the prototype to the customer who provides us with useful feedback. Now, we start the second trip around the spiral. This time we decide that the biggest risk is that we fear many new requirements will become apparent only after the system is deployed. We analyze the alternative routes, and decide the best approach is to build an increment of the system that satisfies only the well-understood requirements. We do so. After deployment, the customer provides us with feedback that says we were correct with those requirements, but 50 new requirements now arise in the customers' heads. And the third trip around the spiral starts.

The spiral model captures some very basic tenets:

- Decide what problem you want to solve before trying to solve it.

- Examine your alternative (multiple) actions and select the one that is most suitable.

- Assess what you have done and what you have learned after you do something.

- Don't be so naïve as to think that the system you are building will be *the* system the customer needs, and

- Understand what level of risk you are willing to tolerate.

Many adherents to the spiral model have mistakenly thought that the figure in Boehm's original spiral model article [BOE88] was *the* spiral model, as opposed to an *example* (or instance) of the spiral model. Notice that the spiral model does *not* say you must do prototyping, nor does it say you must do the loop any specific number of times.

The spiral model is not an alternative to the waterfall model; they are completely compatible! If you take a waterfall model as shown in Figure 8a, and bend it as shown in Figure 8b, it becomes one part of a trip around the spiral as shown in Figure 8c. Similarly, the spiral model is completely compatible with the incremental and evolutionary models. Figure 9 shows a spiral model that realizes either incremental or evolutionary models as a series of waterfall models. Finally, the spiral model is obviously compatible with prototyping. Prototyping simply adds an extra loop to the spiral before any increment.

Concurrent Model

Like the spiral model, the concurrent model [KEL91, SIT94] provides a metadescription of the software process. The *concurrent model* uses Harel statecharts [HAR87] to show how multiple software development activities can occur concurrently. Whereas the spiral model's primary contribution is in the fact that software activities occur repeatedly, the concurrent model's primary contribution is its ability to describe multiple software activities occurring simultaneously.

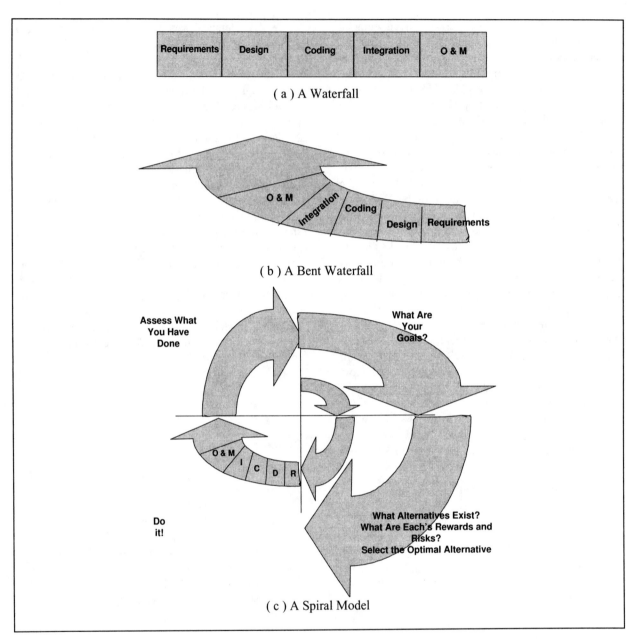

Figure 8. Transforming a waterfall model into one trip around the spiral model.

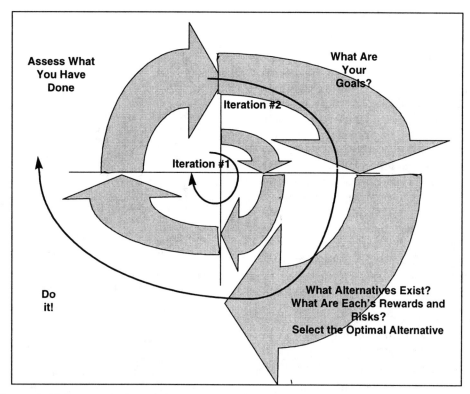

Figure 9. Using a spiral model to represent incremental or evolutionary development.

It is no surprise to anybody who has been involved with software that diverse activities occur at the same time. Let us discuss a few such cases:

- Requirements are usually "baselined" [BER80] when a majority of the requirements become well understood, and it is time to devote considerable effort to design. However, once design begins, changes to requirements are common and frequent (after all, real problems do change, and our understanding of problems evolves as well). It is unwise to stop design dead in its tracks when requirements change; instead, there is a need to update and re-baseline the requirements while design progresses. Of course, depending on the impact of the requirements change, design may be unaffected, mildly affected, or required to start all over from scratch.

- During architectural design, it is possible that some components become well defined be

fore the entire architecture is stabilized. In such cases, it may be possible to start detailed design on those stable components. Similarly, during detailed design, it might be possible to proceed with coding and maybe even unit testing or integration testing prior to completing detailed design on all components.

- On some projects, multiple releases of a product are being developed concurrently. For example, it is not unusual to be doing maintenance of release 1 of a product, and at the same time be doing testing on release 2, while doing coding on release 3, while doing design on release 4, and requirements specification on release 5.

In all of the above cases, diverse activities *are* occurring simultaneously. Choosing to monitor a project using concurrent modeling techniques enables you to understand what a project's true status is.

Selecting Life Cycle Models

Although all the life cycle models described above are compatible with each other, a project must decide which views are most useful in their unique situations. The most comprehensive study of factors that influence this choice was conducted by Linda Alexander [ALE91]. Alexander proposed 23 project- and application-specific criteria, and the creation of templates that describe "ideal profiles" (with respect to these 23 criteria) of projects suitable for each life cycle model. After creating a profile for the project in question, the project manager need only find the "ideal profiles" that most closely match it. This method offers great potential although the actual "ideal profiles" provided in Alexander's paper would need to be tailored to today's knowledge of life cycle model characteristics.

The criteria included in the Alexander study include the following:

- Maturity of application (relates to the likelihood that many requirements will become known only after system use)
- Problem and solution complexity
- Usefulness of early (partial) functionality
- Expected frequency and magnitude of requirements changes
- Funding availability, and its profile as a function of time
- Developers' access to users
- Fuzziness of known requirements

Others might include

- risk tolerance,
- criticality of meeting schedule and budget, and
- degree of slack built into schedules and budgets.

Acknowledgments

The author would like to thank Dr. Ed Bersoff and Mr. Edward Comer for helping to write an earlier version of this paper, and Mr. Naoki Tamura for reviewing and commenting on this paper, and the El Pomar Foundation for their generous financial support.

References

[ALE91 Alexander, L. and A. Davis, "Criteria for the Selection of a Software Process Model," *Proc. 15th IEEE Int'l Conf. Computer Software and Applications* (COMPSAC '91), IEEE CS Press, Los Alamitos, Calif., 1991, pp. 521–528.

[BER80] Bersoff, E. et al., *Software Configuration Management*, Prentice Hall, Englewood Cliffs, N.J., 1980.

[BOE88] Boehm, B.W., "A Spiral Model of Software Development and Enhancement," *Computer*, May 1988, pp. 61-72.

[COM91] Comer, E., "Alternative Software Life Cycle Models," in *Aerospace Software Engineering: A Collection of Concepts*, C. Anderson and R. Thayer, eds., American Institute of Aeronautics, Inc., 1991; reprinted in *Software Engineering*, M. Dorfman and R. Thayer, eds., IEEE CS Press, Los Alamitos, Calif., 1997, pp. 404–414.

[DAV88] Davis, A.M., E.H. Bersoff, and E.R. Comer, "A Strategy for Comparing Alternative Software Development Life Cycle Models," *IEEE Trans. Software Eng.*, Vol. 14, No. 10, Oct. 1988, pp. 1,453–1,461.

[DAV95] Davis, A., "Software Prototyping," *Advances in Computers,* Vol. 40, 1995, pp. 39–63.

[GID84] Giddings, R.V., "Accommodating Uncertainty in Software Design," *Comm. ACM*, Vol. 27, No. 5, May 1984, pp. 428–434.

[GOM81] Gomaa, H., and D. Scott, "Prototyping as a Tool in the Specification of User Requirements," *Proc. 5th IEEE Int'l Conf. Software Eng.*, IEEE CS Press, Los Alamitos, Calif., 1981, pp. 333–342.

[HAR87] Harel, D., "Statecharts: A Visual Formalism for Complex Systems," *Science of Computer Programming, 8*, 1987, pp. 231–274.

[HIR85] Hirsch, E., "Evolutionary Acquisition of Command and Control Systems," *Program Manager*, Nov.-Dec. 1985, pp. 18–22.

[KEL91] Kellner, M., "Software Process Modeling Support for Management Planning and Control," *Proc. 1st Int'l Conf. Software Process*, IEEE CS Press, Los Alamitos, Calif., 1991, pp. 8–28.

[LEF98] Leffingwell, D., A. Davis, and E. Yourdon, *Smart Requirements*, Prentice Hall, Englewood Cliffs, N.J., 1998.

[LEH76] Lehman, M., "Programs, Cities, and Students—Limits to Growth?" Inaugural Lecture, Imperial College of Science and Technology, London (May 14, 1974); reprinted in Belady, L., and M. Lehman, "A Model of Large Program Development," *IBM Systems J.,* Vol. 15, No. 3, Mar. 1976, pp. 225–252.

[ROY70] Royce, W.W., "Managing the Development of Large Software Systems: Concepts and Techniques," *Proc. 1970 WESCON Technical Papers*, Vol. 14, 1970.

[SHA96] Shaw, M. and D. Garlan, *Software Architecture*, Prentice Hall, Englewood Cliffs, N.J., 1996.

[SIT94] Sitaram, P. and A. Davis, "A Concurrent Model of Software Development," *ACM Software Eng. Notes*, Vol. 19, No. 2, Apr. 1994, pp. 38–51.

Chapter 4

Planning a Software Engineering Project

1. Chapter Introduction

Planning a software engineering project is defined as all the management activities that lead to the selection, among alternatives, of future courses of action for the project and a program for executing them. Planning involves selecting the objectives and goals of the project and the strategies, policies, programs, and procedures for achieving them. "Planning is deciding in advance what to do, how to do it, when to do it, and who is to do it" [1].

Planning for a software engineering project can be partitioned into 11 general management activities (see Table 4.1). Its definition or an amplifying description follows each activity in the table.

AHH...LET IT GO; EXPERIENCED PEOPLE DON'T NEED A PLAN.

115

Table 4.1. Planning activities for software projects.

Activity	Definition or Explanation
Set objectives and goals	Determine the desired outcome for the project.
Develop strategies	Decide major organizational goals and develop a general program of action for reaching those goals.
Develop policies	Make standing decisions on important recurring matters to provide a guide for decision making.
Set procedures and rules	Establish methods, guides, and limits for accomplishing the project activity.
Develop project plans	Establish policies, procedures, rules, tasks, schedules, and resources necessary to complete the project.
Determine possible courses of action	Develop, analyze, and/or evaluate different ways to conduct the project.
Prepare budgets	Allocate estimated costs to project functions, activities, and tasks.
Conduct a risk assessment	Anticipate possible adverse events and problem areas; state assumptions; develop contingency plans; predict results of possible courses of action.
Make planning decisions	Evaluate and select a course of action from among alternatives.
Forecast future situations	Anticipate future events or make assumptions about the future; predict future results or expectations from courses of action.
Document project plans	Record policy decisions, courses of action, budget, program plans, and contingency plans.

2. Chapter Overview

The nine articles in this chapter cover many aspects of planning a software engineering project. The portion of planning that covers software cost and schedule estimation is covered in Chapter 5.

Planning or lack of planning is the major issue in software engineering development. It has given rise to more articles than all the other functions of managing a software development project combined.

The activities listed in Table 4.1 were used as an outline to identify a spectrum of articles on planning activities. Remember that because of the universality of management concept, these articles do not have to be exactly about software engineering project management or even project management.

These activities are discussed and illustrated in one or more of the articles described below.

3. Article Descriptions

The objectives or goals of a software engineering project can usually be found in the software require-
ments specifications and the project management plans. Usually we think of software requirements as being part of the software development process, rather than the management process. However, the objectives of a software engineering project are both technical and managerial. Without an accurate and detailed software requirements specification, the manager cannot possibly accurately schedule and estimate the cost of the project.

The first article in this chapter, by Stuart Faulk of the Department of Computer and Information Science, University of Oregon, is an overview of software requirements in engineering. In this article, which was originally published in the *Software Engineering* tutorial [2], Faulk shows that "requirements problems are persistent, pervasive, and costly," and he describes the difficulties that arise in the development and documentation of software requirements. By illustrating a disciplined approach to solve requirements problems, Faulk summarizes current and emerging methods for software requirements engineering, and concludes with a general observation that while it may be impossible to do a perfect job of software requirements, a careful, systematic approach, carried out by properly trained and supported people, can contribute to a successful software development.

Note: Only technical requirements should be documented in a software requirements specification [3]. Non-technical requirements belong in the project management plan (see John Glabas and Richard Fairley's article on "A Guide for Preparing Software Project Management Plans" in this chapter).

The next article, by William Miller, is an overview on planning a project and provides an excellent description on how to implement the plan (called a "program of action" in the management sciences; not to be confused with a "computer program"). He describes how to plan a generic project that could apply equally well to the development of a software engineering product. To Miller, project planning has essentially one purpose: to establish a foundation for execution and successful completion of the project. He discusses who is responsible for the plan, what the planning process is, what goes into a plan, and the planning document itself. The final part of the article also covers controlling the project according to the plan (an activity discussed in Chapter 8 of this tutorial).

The third article is a series of slides on *software development policies* and *software engineering standards*, prepared and presented by Ed Goldberg of TRW, Inc. for an early AIAA Software Management Conference. The slides describe a set of software engineering policies within the SEID (System Engineering and Integration Division) of TRW. These policies are generic to any large software development organization and therefore can be used as a model for other software development groups. This list of software engineering policies and standards, prepared by TRW, are still in use today (the *Tutorial* author is told), and have been copied by a number of other institutions and agencies.

One of the major issues in software engineering today is how and when to introduce a new technology into a company or software project. Ed Yourdon presents "Inserting New Technology into a Software Project" for implementing new software development technologies into software development organizations. The article provides insight into the problems encountered in trying to implement new techniques.

In recent correspondence to the *Tutorial* author, a reader had the following comment about the Yourdon article.

> This article makes many good points. I know, because of something I lived through about 15 years ago. I was one of the lead designers on a project that grew to

about 70 people in the design stage and would grow to several hundred for the implementation. The organization's history was of making incremental change to a very large product and did not have good design skills or knowledge of new design technologies. One of the more junior designers convinced some gullible management that the project could be done quicker, at lower cost resulting in a higher quality, less costly to maintain product [if a new technology was adopted]. In fact two new technologies were introduced through classes. One was Yourdon Data Flow and the other was a top-down refinement process—complete with programs to process it (though they were not debugged and it turned out either took forever or failed on our large design). Naturally we still had to document the design using the company's standard process. Well, this meant writing the design down three different ways, and with no automated tools to match them. After the project was about a year on this path it was hardly started technically and the whole thing went up in smoke. I found the data flow was reasonable on a small unrelated project that I was working on at the same time. However, too much was introduced too fast and on too many people. *Had the Yourdon article been around perhaps we would not have done things this way.* [emphasis by the *Tutorial* author].

The fifth article, by Kent Cori, debates the necessity of having a master project schedule. He prescribes a method for defining project objectives, breaking down the work to be accomplished into manageable pieces, sequencing the work activities, and estimating activity duration. This article also surveys and compares five popular scheduling techniques—*milestone charts, Gantt charts, full-wall scheduling,* and *precedence networks* (CPA and PERT).

One of the more effective planning tools in project management is the work breakdown structure (more commonly called a WBS). This article, written by the author and Richard E. Fairley of Colorado Technical University, defines a WBS, describes three modes of representation—process, product, and a hybrid WBS—and then presents an example of a process WBS.

In another article by the *Tutorial* author and Fairley, "Software Risk Management," the concept of identifying and resolving risk is discussed. This article is a rewrite of two Department of Defense (DoD) articles [4], [5] in order to make the articles more general and more applicable to software. The article emphasizes that there is a basic difference between risk management and traditional project management. The goal of traditional project management is to control pervasive risks by using systematic procedures to support the development of a software project. Risk management augments traditional project management by identifying potential problems and solutions on specific projects. "When a project is successful, it is not because there were no problems but that the problems were overcome." [6]

This risk article attempts to explain in its simplest form risks and risk management. The article covers

- risk assessment and identification
- risk analysis
- risk handling

Also included is a way of calculating the optimum level of risk that can be accepted.

To summarize this chapter, John Glabas and Richard Fairley discuss the "IEEE Guide to Preparing Software Project Management Plans," which is based on the latest draft IEEE standard for project management plans [7]. This article delineates the contents of a software engineering project plan and can be used as a checklist for planning activities. As a famous philosopher once said, "A plan in the mind of man is not a plan at all," emphasizing the need to document the plan.

References

1. Koontz, H. and C. O'Donnell, *Principles of Management: An Analysis of Managerial Functions*, 5th ed., McGraw-Hill, New York, N.Y., 1972.

2. Dorfman, M., and R.H. Thayer, eds., *Software Engineering*, IEEE Computer Society Press, Los Alamitos, Calif., 1997.

3. ANSI/IEEE Std. 830-1984, *IEEE Standard for Software Requirements Specifications*, IEEE, NY, 1984.

4. *System Engineering Management Guide*, Defense Systems Management College, Superintendent of Documents, US Government Printing Office, Washington, D.C., Jan.1990.

5. *Risk Management: Concepts and Guidance*, Defense Systems Management College, Superintendent of Documents, US Government Printing Office, Washington, D.C., Mar. 1989.

6. Rook, P., "Controlling Software Projects," *Software Engineering Journal*, Jan. 1986, pp. 7–16. Reprinted in *Software Engineering Project Management*, 2nd ed., R.H. Thayer, ed., IEEE Computer Society Press, Los Alamitos, Calif., 1997.

7. P1058.1, *IEEE Standard for Software Project Management Plans* (Draft), IEEE Computer Society, Washington, DC, 1997.

Software Requirements: A Tutorial

Stuart R. Faulk

"The hardest single part of building a software system is deciding precisely what to build. No other part of the conceptual work is as difficult as establishing the detailed technical requirements . . . No other part of the work so cripples the resulting system if done wrong. No other part is as difficult to rectify later."

[Brooks 87]

1. Introduction

Deciding precisely what to build and documenting the results is the goal of the requirements phase of software development. For many developers of large, complex software systems, requirements are their biggest software engineering problem. While there is considerable disagreement on how to solve the problem, few would disagree with Brooks' assessment that no other part of a development is as difficult to do well or as disastrous in result when done poorly. The purpose of this tutorial is to help the reader understand why the apparently simple notion of "deciding what to build" is so difficult in practice, where the state of the art does and does not address these difficulties, and what hope we have for doing better in the future.

This paper does not survey the literature but seeks to provide the reader with an understanding of the underlying issues. There are currently many more approaches to requirements than one can cover in a short paper. This diversity is the product of two things: different views about which of the many problems in requirements is pivotal, and different assumptions about the desirable characteristics of a solution. This paper attempts to impart a basic understanding of the requirements problem and its many facets, as well as the trade-offs involved in attempting a solution. Thus forearmed, readers can assess the claims of different requirements methods and their likely effectiveness in addressing the readers' particular needs.

We begin with basic terminology and some historical data on the requirements problem. We examine the goals of the requirements phase and the problems that can arise in attempting those goals. As in Brooks's article [Brooks 87], much of the discussion is moti-vated by the distinction between the difficulties inherent in what one is trying to accomplish (the "essential" difficulties) and those one creates through inadequate practice ("accidental" difficulties). We discuss how a disciplined software engineering process helps address many of the accidental difficulties and why the focus of such a disciplined process is on producing a written specification of the detailed technical requirements. We examine current technical approaches to requirements in terms of the specific problems each approach seeks to address. Finally, we examine technical trends and discuss where significant advances are likely to occur in the future.

2. Requirements and the Software Life Cycle

A variety of software life-cycle models have been proposed with an equal variety of terminology. Davis [Davis 88] provides a good summary. While differing in the detailed decomposition of the steps (for example, prototyping models) or in the surrounding management and control structure (for example, to manage risk), there is general agreement on the core elements of the model. Figure 1 [Davis 93] is a version of the common model that illustrates the relationship between the software development stages and the related testing and acceptance phases.

When software is created in the context of a larger hardware and software system, system requirements are defined first, followed by system design. System design includes decisions about which parts of the system requirements will be allocated to hardware and which to software. For software-only systems, the life-cycle model begins with software requirements analysis. From this point on, the role of software requirements in the development model is the same whether or not the software is part of a larger system, as shown in Figure 2 [Davis 93]. For this reason, the remainder of our discussion does not distinguish whether or not software is developed as part of a larger system. For an overview of system versus software issues, the reader is referred to Dorfman and Thayer's survey [Thayer 90].

Reprinted from *Software Engineering*, M. Dorfman and R.H. Thayer, eds., 1997, pp. 128–149.
Copyright © 1997 by The Institute of Electrical and Electronics Engineers, Inc. All rights reserved.

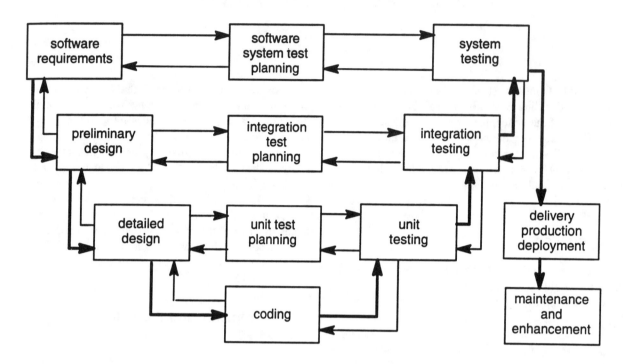

Figure 1. Software life cycle

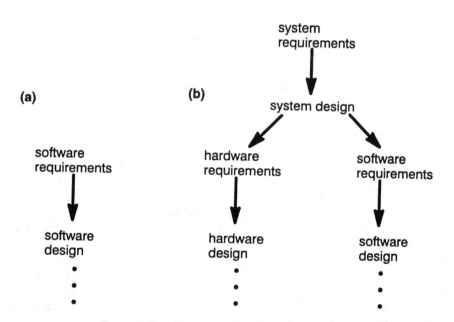

Figure 2. Development paths: (a) software, (b) systems

In a large system development, the software requirements specification may play a variety of roles:

- For customers, the requirements typically document what should be delivered and may provide the contractual basis for the development.

- For managers, it may provide the basis for scheduling and a yardstick for measuring progress.

- For the software designers, it may provide the "design-to" specification.

- For coders, it defines the range of acceptable implementations and is the final authority on the outputs that must be produced.

- For quality assurance personnel, it is the basis for validation, test planning, and verification.

The requirements may also used by such diverse groups as marketing and governmental regulators.

It is common practice (for example, see [Thayer 90]) to classify software requirements as "functional" or "nonfunctional." While definitions vary somewhat in detail, "functional" typically refers to requirements defining the acceptable mappings between system input values and corresponding output values. "Nonfunctional" then refers to all other constraints including, but not limited to, performance, dependability, maintainability, reusability, and safety.

While widely used, the classification of requirements as "functional" and "nonfunctional" is confusing in its terminology and of little help in understanding common properties of different kinds of requirements. The word "function" is one of the most overloaded in computer science, and its only rigorous meaning, that of a mathematical function, is not what is meant here. The classification of requirements as functional and non-functional offers little help in understanding common attributes of different types of requirements since it partitions classes of requirements with markedly similar qualities (for example, output values and output deadlines) while grouping others that have commonality only in what they are not (for example, output deadlines and maintainability goals).

A more useful distinction is between what can be described as "behavioral requirements" and "developmental quality attributes" with the following definitions [Clements 95]:

- *Behavioral requirements*—Behavioral requirements include any and all information necessary to determine if the runtime behavior

of a given implementation is acceptable. The behavioral requirements define all constraints on the system outputs (for example, value, accuracy, timing) and resulting system state for all possible inputs and current system state. By this definition, security, safety, performance, timing, and fault tolerance are all behavioral requirements.

- *Developmental quality attributes*— Developmental quality attributes include any constraints on the attributes of the system's static construction. These include properties like testability, changeability, maintainability, and reusability.

Behavioral requirements have in common that they are properties of the runtime behavior of the system and can (at least in principle) be validated objectively by observing the behavior of the running system, independent of its method of implementation. In contrast, developmental quality attributes are properties of the system's static structures (for example, modularization) or representation. Developmental quality attributes have in common that they are functions of the development process and methods of construction. Assessment of developmental quality attributes are necessarily relativistic—for example, we do not say that a design is or is not maintainable but that one design is more maintainable than another.

3. A Big Problem

Requirements problems are persistent, pervasive, and costly. Evidence is most readily available for the large software systems developed for the US government, since the results are a matter of public record. As soon as software became a significant part of such systems, developers identified requirements as a major source of problems. For example, developers of the early Ballistic Missile Defense System noted that:

In nearly every software project that fails to meet performance and cost goals, requirements inadequacies play a major and expensive role in project failure [Alford 79].

Nor has the problem mitigated over the intervening years. A recent study of problems in mission-critical defense systems identified requirements as a major problem source in two thirds of the systems examined [GAO 92]. This is consistent with results of a survey of large aerospace firms that identified requirements as the most critical software development problem [Faulk 92]. Likewise, studies by Lutz

[Lutz 92] identified functional and interface requirements as the major source of safety-related software errors in NASA's Voyager and Galileo spacecraft.

Results of industry studies in the 1970s described by Boehm [Boehm 81], and since replicated a number of times, showed that requirements errors are the most costly. These studies all produced the same basic result: The earlier in the development process an error occurs and the later the error is detected, the more expensive it is to correct. Moreover, the relative cost rises quickly. As shown in Figure 3, an error that costs a dollar to fix in the requirements phase may cost $100 to $200 to fix if it is not corrected until the system is fielded or in the maintenance phase.

The costs of such failures can be enormous. For example, the 1992 GAO report notes that one system, the Cheyenne Mountain Upgrade, will be delivered eight years late, exceed budget by $600 million, and have less capability than originally planned, largely due to requirements-related problems. Prior GAO reports [GAO 79] suggest that such problems are the norm rather than the exception. While data from private industry is less readily available, there is little reason to believe that the situation is significantly different.

In spite of presumed advances in software engineering methodology and tool support, the requirements problem has not diminished. This does not mean that the apparent progress in software engineering is illusory. While the features of the problem have not changed, the applications have grown significantly in capability, scale, and complexity. A reasonable conclusion is that the growing ambitiousness of our software systems has outpaced the gains in requirements technology, at least as such technology is applied in practice.

4. Why Are Requirements Hard?

It is generally agreed that the goal of the requirements phase is to establish and specify precisely what the software must do without describing how to do it. So simple seems this basic intent that it is not at all evident why it is so difficult to accomplish in practice. If what we want to accomplish is so clear, why is it so hard? To understand this, we must examine more closely the goals of the requirements phase, where errors originate, and why the nature of the task leads to some inherent difficulties.

Most authors agree in principle that requirements should specify "what" rather than "how." In other words, the goal of requirements is to understand and specify the *problem* to be solved rather than the *solution*. For example, the requirements for an automated teller system should talk about customer accounts, deposits, and withdrawals rather than the software algorithms and data structures. The most basic reason for this is that a specification in terms of the problem captures the actual requirements without overconstraining the subsequent design or implementation. Further, solutions in software terms are typically more complex, more difficult to change, and harder to understand (particularly for the customer) than a specification of the problem.

Unfortunately, distinguishing "what" from "how" itself represents a dilemma. As Davis [Davis 88], among others, points out, the distinction between what and how is necessarily a function of perspective. A specification at any chosen level of system decomposition can be viewed as describing the "what" for the next level. Thus customer needs may define the "what" and the decomposition into hardware and software the corresponding "how." Subsequently, the behavioral requirements allocated to a software component define its "what," the software design, the "how," and so on. The upshot is that requirements cannot be effectively discussed at all without prior agreement on which system one is talking about and at what level of decomposition. One must agree on what constitutes the problem space and what constitutes the solution space—the analysis and specification of requirements then properly belongs in the problem space.

Stage	Relative Repair Cost
Requirements	1–2
Design	5
Coding	10
Unit test	20
System test	50
Maintenance	200

Figure 3: Relative cost to repair a software error in different stages

In discussing requirements problems, one must also distinguish the development of large, complex systems from smaller efforts (for example, developments by a single or small team of programmers). Large system developments are multiperson efforts. They are developed by teams of tens to thousands of programmers. The programmers work in the context of an organization typically including management, systems engineering, marketing, accounting, and quality assurance. The organization itself must operate in the context of outside concerns also interested in the software product, including the customer, regulatory agencies, and suppliers.

Even where only one system is intended, large systems are inevitably multiversion as well. As the software is being developed, tested, and even fielded, it evolves. Customers understand better what they want, developers understand better what they can and cannot do within the constraints of cost and schedule, and circumstances surrounding development change. The results are changes in the software requirements and, ultimately, the software itself. In effect, several versions of a given program are produced, if only incrementally. Such unplanned changes occur in addition to the expected variations of planned improvements.

The multiperson, multiversion nature of large system development introduces problems that are both quantitatively and qualitatively different from those found in smaller developments. For example, scale introduces the need for administration and control functions with the attendant management issues that do not exist on small projects. The quantitative effects of increased complexity in communication when the number of workers rises are well documented by Brooks [Brooks 75]. In the following discussion, it is this large system development context we will assume, since that is the one in which the worst problems occur and where the most help is needed.

Given the context of multiperson, multiversion development, our basic goal of specifying what the software must do can be decomposed into the following subgoals:

1. Understand precisely what is required of the software.

2. Communicate the understanding of what is required to all of the parties involved in the development.

3. Provide a means for controlling the production to ensure that the final system satisfies the requirements (including managing the effects of changes).

It follows that the source of most requirements errors is in the failure to adequately accomplish one of these goals, that is:

1. The developers failed to understand what was required of the software by the customer, end user, or other parties with a stake in the final product.

2. The developers did not completely and precisely capture the requirements or subsequently communicate the requirements effectively to other parties involved in the development.

3. The developers did not effectively manage the effects of changing requirements or ensure the conformance of down-stream development steps including design, code, integration, test, or maintenance to the system requirements.

The end result of such failures is a software system that does not perform as desired or expected, a development that exceeds budget and schedule or, all too frequently, failure to deliver any working software at all.

4.1 Essential Difficulties

Even our more detailed goals appear straightforward; why then do so many development efforts fail to achieve them? The short answer is that the mutual satisfaction of these goals, in practice, is inherently difficult. To understand why, it is useful to reflect on some points raised by Brooks [Brooks 87] on why software engineering is hard and on the distinction he makes between essential difficulties—those inherent in the problem, and the accidental difficulties—those introduced through imperfect practice. For though requirements are inherently difficult, there is no doubt that these difficulties are many times multiplied by the inadequacies of current practice.

The following essential difficulties attend each (in some cases all) of the requirements goals:

- *Comprehension.* People do not know what they want. This does not mean that people do not have a general idea of what the software is for. Rather, they do not begin with a precise and detailed understanding of what functions belong in the software, what the output must be for every possible input, how long each operation should take, how one decision will affect another, and so on.

Indeed, unless the new system is simply a reconstruction of an old one, such a detailed understanding at the outset is unachievable. Many decisions about the system behavior will depend on other decisions yet unmade, and expectations will change as the problem (and attendant costs of alternative solutions) is better understood. Nonetheless, it is a precise and richly detailed understanding of expected behavior that is needed to create effective designs and develop correct code.

- *Communication.* Software requirements are difficult to communicate effectively. As Brooks points out, the conceptual structures of software systems are complex, arbitrary, and difficult to visualize. The large software systems we are now building are among the most complex structures ever attempted. That complexity is arbitrary in the sense that it is an artifact of people's decisions and prior construction rather than a reflection of fundamental properties (as, for example, in the case of physical laws). To make matters worse, many of the conceptual structures in software have no readily comprehensible physical analogue so they are difficult to visualize.

In practice, comprehension suffers under all of these constraints. We work best with regular, predictable structures, can comprehend only a very limited amount of information at one time, and understand large amounts of information best when we can visualize it. Thus the task of capturing and conveying software requirements is inherently difficult.

The inherent difficulty of communication is compounded by the diversity of purposes and audiences for a requirements specification. Ideally, a technical specification is written for a particular audience. The brevity and comprehensibility of the document depend on assumptions about common technical background and use of language. Such commonality typically does not hold for the many diverse groups (for example, customers, systems engineers, managers) that must use a software requirements specification.

- *Control.* Inherent difficulties attend control of software development as well. The arbitrary and invisible nature of software makes it difficult to anticipate which requirements will be met easily and which will decimate the project's budget and schedule if, indeed, they can be fulfilled at all. The low fidelity of software planning has become a cliche, yet the requirements are often the best available basis for planning or for tracking to a plan.

This situation is made incalculably worse by software's inherent malleability. Of all the problems bedeviling software managers, few evoke such passion as the difficulties of dealing with frequent and arbitrary changes to requirements. For most systems, such changes remain a fact of life even after delivery. The continuous changes make it difficult to develop stable specifications, plan effectively, or control cost and schedule. For many industrial developers, change management is the most critical problem in requirements.

- *Inseparable concerns.* In seeking solutions to the foregoing problems, we are faced with the additional difficulty that the issues cannot easily be separated and dealt with, piecemeal. For example, developers have attempted to address the problem of changing requirements by baselining and freezing requirements before design begins. This proves impractical because of the comprehension problem—the customer may not fully know what he wants until he sees it. Similarly, the diversity of purposes and audiences is often addressed by writing a different specification for each. Thus there may be a system specification, a set of requirements delivered to customer, a distinct set of technical requirements written for the internal consumption of the software developers, and so on. However, this solution vastly increases the complexity, provides an open avenue for inconsistencies, and multiplies the difficulties of managing changes.

These issues represent only a sample of the inherent dependencies between different facets of the requirements problem. The many distinct parties with an interest in a system's requirements, the many different roles the requirements play, and the interlocking nature of software's conceptual structures, all introduce dependencies between concerns and impose conflicting constraints on any potential solution.

The implications are twofold. First we are constrained in the application of our most effective strategy for dealing with complex problems—divide and conquer. If a problem is considered in isolation, the solution is likely to aggravate other difficulties. Effective solutions to most requirements difficulties must simultaneously address more than one problem. Second, developing practical solutions requires making difficult trade-offs. Where different problems have conflicting constraints, compromises must be made. Because the trade-offs result in different gains or losses to the different parties involved, effective compromises require negotiation. These issues are considered in more detail when we discuss the properties of a good requirements specification.

4.2 Accidental Difficulties

While there is no doubt that software requirements are inherently difficult to do well, there is equally no doubt that common practice unnecessarily exacerbates the difficulty. We use the term "accidental" in contrast to "essential," not to imply that the difficulties arise by chance but that they are the product of common failings in management, elicitation, specification, or use of requirements. It is these failings that are most easily addressed by improved practice.

- *Written as an afterthought*. It remains common practice that requirements documentation is developed only after the software has been written. For many projects, the temptation to rush into implementation before the requirements are adequately understood proves irresistible. This is understandable. Developers often feel like they are not really doing anything when they are not writing code; managers are concerned about schedule when there is no visible progress on the implementation. Then too, the intangible nature of the product mitigates toward early implementation. Developing the system is an obvious way to understand better what is needed and make visible the actual behavior of the product. The result is that requirements specifications are written as an afterthought (if at all). They are not created to guide the developers and testers but treated as a necessary evil to satisfy contractual demands.

Such after-the-fact documentation inevitably violates the principle of defining what the system must do rather than the how since it is a specification of the code as written. It is produced after the fact so it is not planned or managed as an essential part of the development but is thrown together. In fact, it is not even available in time to guide implementation or manage development.

- *Confused in purpose*. Because there are so many potential audiences for a requirements specification, with different points of view, the exact purpose of the document becomes confused. An early version is used to sell the product to the customer, so it includes marketing hype extolling the product's virtues. It is the only documentation of what the system does, so it provides introductory, explanatory, and overview material. It is a contractual document, so it is intentionally imprecise to allow the developer latitude in the delivered product or the customer latitude in making no-cost changes. It is the vehicle for communicating decisions about software details to designers and coders, so it incorporates design and implementation. The result is a document in which it is unclear which statements represent real requirements and which are more properly allocated to marketing, design, or other documentation. It is a document that attempts to be everything to everyone and ultimately serves no one well.

- *Not designed to be useful*. Often, in the rush to implementation, little effort is expended on requirements. The requirements specification is not expected to be useful and, indeed, this turns out to be a self-fulfilling prophecy. Because the document is not expected to be useful, little effort is expended on designing it, writing it, checking it, or managing its creation and evolution. The most obvious result is poor organization. The specification is written in English prose and follows the author's stream of consciousness or the order of execution [Heninger 80].

The resulting document is ineffective as a technical reference. It is unclear which statements represent actual requirements. It is unclear where to put or find particular requirements. There is no effective procedure for ensuring that the specification is consistent or complete. There is no systematic way to manage requirements changes. The specification is difficult to use and difficult to maintain. It quickly becomes out of date and loses whatever usefulness it might originally have had.

- *Lacks essential properties.* Lack of forethought, confusion of purpose, or lack of careful design and execution all lead to requirements that lack properties critical to good technical specifications. The requirements, if documented at all, are redundant, inconsistent, incomplete, imprecise, and inaccurate.

Where the essential difficulties are inherent in the problem, the accidental difficulties result from a failure to gain or maintain intellectual control over what is to be built. While the presence of the essential difficulties means that there can be no "silver bullet" that will suddenly render requirements easy, we can remove at least the accidental difficulties through a well thought out, systematic, and disciplined development process. Such a disciplined process then provides a stable foundation for attacking the essential difficulties.

5. Role of a Disciplined Approach

The application of discipline in analyzing and specifying software requirements can address the accidental difficulties. While there is now general agreement on the desirable qualities of a software development approach, the field is insufficiently mature to have standardized the development process. Nonetheless, it is useful to examine the characteristics of an idealized process and its products to understand where current approaches are weak and which current trends are promising. In general, a complete requirements approach will define:

- *Process*: The (partially ordered) sequence of activities, entrance and exit criteria for each activity, which work product is produced in each activity, and what kind of people should do the work.

- *Products*: The work products to be produced and, for each product, the resources needed to produce it, the information it contains, the expected audience, and the acceptance criteria the product must satisfy.

Currently, there is little uniformity in different author's decomposition of the requirements phase or in the terminology for the activities. Davis [Davis 88] provides a good summary of the variations. Following Davis's integrated model and terminology [Davis 93],

the requirements phase consists of two conceptually distinct but overlapping activities corresponding to the first two goals for requirements enumerated previously:

1. *Problem analysis*: The goal of problem analysis is to understand precisely what problem is to be solved. It includes identifying the exact purpose of the system, who will use it, the constraints on acceptable solutions, and the possible trade-offs between conflicting constraints.

2. *Requirements specification*: The goal of requirements specification is to create a document, the Software Requirements Specification (SRS), describing exactly what is to be built. The SRS captures the results of problem analysis and characterizes the set of acceptable solutions to the problem.

In practice, the distinction between these activities is conceptual rather than temporal. Where both are needed, the developer typically switches back and forth between analysis of the problem and documentation of the results. When problems are well understood, the analysis phase may be virtually nonexistent. When the system model and documentation are standardized or based on existing specifications, the documentation paradigm may guide the analysis [Hester 81].

5.1 Problem Analysis

Problem analysis is necessarily informal in the sense that there is no effective, closed-end procedure that will guarantee success. It is an information-acquiring, -collating, and -structuring process through which one attempts to understand all the various parts of a problem and their relationships. The difficulty in developing an effective understanding of large, complex software problems has motivated considerable effort to structure and codify problem analysis.

The basic issues in problem analysis are:

- How to effectively elicit a complete set of requirements from the customer or other sources?

- How to decompose the problem into intellectually manageable pieces?

- How to organize the information so it can be understood?

- How to communicate about the problem with all the parties involved?

- How to resolve conflicting needs?
- How to know when to stop?

5.2 Requirements Specification

For substantial developments, the effectiveness of the requirements effort depends on how well the SRS captures the results of analysis and how useable the specification is. There is little benefit to developing a thorough understanding of the problem if that understanding is not effectively communicated to customers, designers, implementors, testers, and maintainers. The larger and more complex the system, the more important a good specification becomes. This is a direct result of the many roles the SRS plays in a multiperson, multiversion development [Parnas 86]:

1. The SRS is the primary vehicle for agreement between the developer and customer on exactly what is to be built. It is the document reviewed by the customer or his representative and often is the basis for judging fulfillment of contractual obligations.

2. The SRS records the results of problem analysis. It is the basis for determining where the requirements are complete and where additional analysis is necessary. Documenting the results of analysis allows questions about the problem to be answered only once during development.

3. The SRS defines what properties the system must have and the constraints on its design and implementation. It defines where there is, and is not, design freedom. It helps ensure that requirements decisions are made explicitly during the requirements phase, not implicitly during programming.

4. The SRS is the basis for estimating cost and schedule. It is management's primary tool for tracking development progress and ascertaining what remains to be done.

5. The SRS is the basis for test plan development. It is the tester's chief tool for determining the acceptable behavior of the software.

6. The SRS provides the standard definition of expected behavior for the system's maintainers and is used to record engineering changes.

For a disciplined software development, the SRS is the primary technical specification of the software and the primary control document. This is an inevitable result of the complexity of large systems and the need to coordinate multiperson development teams. To ensure that the right system is built, one must first understand the problem. To ensure agreement on what is to be built and the criteria for success, the results of that understanding must be recorded. The goal of a systematic requirements process is thus the development of a set of specifications that effectively communicate the results of analysis.

Requirement's accidental difficulties are addressed through the careful analysis and specification of a disciplined process. Rather than developing the specification as an afterthought, requirements are understood and specified before development begins. One knows what one is building before attempting to build it. The SRS is the primary vehicle for communicating requirements between the developers, managers, and customers, so the document is designed to be useful foro that purpose. A useful document is maintained.

6. Requirements for the Software Requirements Specification

The goals of the requirements process, the attendant difficulties, and the role of the requirements specification in a disciplined process determine the properties of a "good" requirements specification. These properties do not mandate any particular specification method but do describe the characteristics of an effective method.

In discussing the properties of a good SRS, it is useful to distinguish semantic properties from packaging properties [Faulk 92]. Semantic properties are a consequence of what the specification says (that is, its meaning or semantics). Packaging properties are a consequence of how the requirements are written—the format, organization, and presentation of the information. The semantic properties determine how effectively an SRS captures the software requirements. The packaging properties determine how useable the resulting specification is. Figure 4 illustrates the classification of properties of a good SRS.

An SRS that satisfies the semantic properties of a good specification is:

- *Complete.* The SRS defines the set of acceptable implementations. It should contain all the information needed to write software that is acceptable to the customer and no more. Any implementation that satisfies every statement in the requirements is an acceptable product. Where information is not available before development begins, areas of incompleteness must be explicitly indicated [Parnas 86].

127

SRS Semantic Properties	SRS Packaging Properties
Complete	Modifiable
Implementation independent	Readable
Unambiguous and consistent	Organized for reference and review
Precise	
Verifiable	

Figure 4. Classification of SRS properties

- *Implementation independent.* The SRS should be free of design and implementation decisions unless those decisions reflect actual requirements.

- *Unambiguous and consistent.* If the SRS is subject to conflicting interpretation, the different parties will not agree on what is to be built or whether the right software has been built. Every requirement should have only one possible interpretation. Similarly, no two statements of required behavior should conflict.

- *Precise.* The SRS should define exactly the required behavior. For each output, it should define the range of acceptable values for every input. The SRS should define any applicable timing constraints such as minimum and maximum acceptable delay.

- *Verifiable.* A requirement is verifiable if it is possible to determine unambiguously whether a given implementation satisfies the requirement or not. For example, a behavioral requirement is verifiable if it is possible to determine, for any given test case (that is, an input and an output), whether the output represents an acceptable behavior of the software given the input and the system state.

An SRS[1] that satisfies the packaging properties of a good specification is:

- *Modifiable.* The SRS must be organized for ease of change. Since no organization can be equally easy to change for all possible changes, the requirements analysis process must identify expected changes and the relative likelihood of their occurrence. The specification is then organized to limit the effect of likely changes.

- *Readable.* The SRS must be understandable by the parties that use it. It should clearly relate the elements of the problem space as understood by the customer to the observable behavior of the software.

- *Organized for reference and review.* The SRS is the primary technical specification of the software requirements. It is the repository for all the decisions made during analysis about what should be built. It is the document reviewed by the customer or his representatives. It is the primary arbitrator of disputes. As such, the document must be organized for quick and easy reference. It must be clear where each decision about the requirements belongs. It must be possible to answer specific questions about the requirements quickly and easily.

To address the difficulties associated with writing and using an SRS, a requirements approach must provide techniques addressing both semantic and packaging properties. It is also desirable that the conceptual structures of the approach treat the semantic and packaging properties as distinct concerns (that is, as independently as possible). This allows one to change the presentation of the SRS without changing its meaning.

In aggregate, these properties of a good SRS represent an ideal. Some of the properties may be unachievable, particularly over the short term. For example, a common complaint is that one cannot develop complete requirements before design begins because the customer does not yet fully understand what he wants or is still making changes. Further, different SRS "requirements" mitigate toward conflicting solutions. A commonly cited example is the use of English prose to express requirements. English is readily understood but notoriously ambiguous and imprecise. Conversely, formal languages are precise and unambiguous, but can be difficult to read.

Although the ideal SRS may be unachievable, possessing a common understanding of what constitutes

---

1. Reusability is also a packaging property and becomes an attribute of a good specification where reusability of requirements specifications is a goal.

an ideal SRS is important [Parnas 86] because it:

- provides a basis for standardizing an organization's processes and products,

- provides a standard against which progress can be measured, and,

- provides guidance—it helps developers understand what needs to be done next and when they are finished.

Because it is so often true that (1) requirements cannot be fully understood before at least starting to build the system, and (2) a perfect SRS cannot be produced even when the requirements are understood, some approaches advocated in the literature do not even attempt to produce a definitive SRS. For example, some authors advocate going directly from a problem model to design or from a prototype implementation to the code. While such approaches may be effective on some developments, they are inconsistent with the notion of software development as an engineering discipline. The development of technical specifications is an essential part of a controlled engineering process. This does not mean that the SRS must be entire or perfect before anything else is done but that its development is a fundamental goal of the process as a whole. That we may currently lack the ability to write good specifications in some cases does not change the fact that it is useful and necessary to try.

7. State of the Practice

Over the years, many analysis and specification techniques have evolved. The general trend has been for software engineering techniques to be applied first to coding problems (for example, complexity, ease of change), then to similar problems occurring earlier and earlier in the life cycle. Thus the concepts of structured programming led eventually to structured design and analysis. More recently, the concepts of object-oriented programming have led to object-oriented design and analysis. The following discussion characterizes the major schools of thought and provides pointers to instances of methods in each school. The general strengths and weaknesses of the various techniques are discussed relative to the requirements difficulties and the desirable qualities of analysis and specification methods.

It is characteristic of the immature state of requirements as a discipline that the more specific one gets, the less agreement there is. There is not only disagreement in terminology, approach, and the details of different methods, there is not even a commonly accepted classification scheme. The following general

groupings are based on the evolution of the underlying concepts and the key distinctions that reflect paradigmatic shifts in requirements philosophy.

7.1 Functional Decomposition

Functional decomposition was originally applied to software requirements to abstract from coding details. Functional decomposition focuses on understanding and specifying what processing the software is required to do. The general strategy is to define the required behavior as a mapping from inputs to outputs. Ideally, the analysis proceeds top down, first identifying the function associated with the system as a whole. Each subsequent step decomposes the set of functions into steps or sub-functions. The result is a hierarchy of functions and the definitions of the functional interfaces. Each level of the hierarchy adds detail about the processing steps necessary to accomplish the more abstract function above. The function above controls the processing of its subfunctions. In a complete decomposition, the functional hierarchy specifies the "calls" structure of the implementation. One example of a methodology based on functional decomposition is Hamilton and Zeldin's Higher Order Software [Hamilton 76].

The advantage of functional decomposition is that the specification is written using the language and concepts of the implementors. It communicates well to the designers and coders. It is written in terms of the solution space so the transition to design and code is straightforward.

Common complaints are that functional specifications are difficult to communicate, introduce design decisions prematurely, and difficult to use or change. Because functional specifications are written in the language of implementation, people who are not software or systems experts find them difficult to understand. Since there are inevitably many possible ways of decomposing functions into subfunctions, the analyst must make decisions that are not requirements. Finally, since the processing needed in one step depends strongly on what has been done the previous step, functional decomposition results in components that are closely coupled. Understanding or changing one function requires understanding or changing all the related functions.

As software has increased in complexity and become more visible to nontechnical people, the need for methods addressing the weaknesses of functional decomposition has likewise increased.

7.2 Structured Analysis

Structured analysis was developed primarily as a

means to address the accidental difficulties attending problem analysis and, to a lesser extent, requirements specification, using functional decomposition. Following the introduction of structured programming as a means to gain intellectual control over increasingly complex programs, structured analysis evolved from functional decomposition as a means to gain intellectual control over system problems.

The basic assumption behind structured analysis is that the accidental difficulties can be addressed by a systematic approach to problem analysis using [Svoboda 90]:

- a common conceptual model for describing all problems,
- a set of procedures suggesting the general direction of analysis and an ordering on the steps,
- a set of guidelines or heuristics supporting decisions about the problem and its specification, and
- a set of criteria for evaluating the quality of the product.

While structured analysis still contains the decomposition of functions into subfunctions, the focus of the analysis shifts from the processing steps to the data being processed. The analyst views the problem as constructing a system to transform data. He analyzes the sources and destinations of the data, determines what data must be held in storage, what transformations are done on the data, and the form of the output.

Common to the structured analysis approaches is the use of data flow diagrams and data dictionaries. Data flow diagrams provide a graphic representation of the movement of data through the system (typically represented as arcs) and the transformations on the data (typically represented as nodes). The data dictionary supports the data flow diagram by providing a repository for the definitions and descriptions of each data item on the diagrams. Required processing is captured in the definitions of the transformations. Associated with each transformation node is a specification of the processing the node does to transform the incoming data items to the outgoing data items. At the most detailed level, a transformation is defined using a textual specification called a "MiniSpec." A MiniSpec may be expressed in several different ways including English prose, decision tables, or a procedure definition language (PDL).

Structured analysis approaches originally evolved for management information systems (MIS). Examples of widely used strategies include those described by DeMarco [DeMarco 78] and Gane and Sarson [Gane

79]. "Modern" structured analysis was introduced to provide more guidance in modeling systems as data flows as exemplified by Yourdon [Yourdon 89]. Structured analysis has also been adapted to support specification of embedded control systems by adding notations to capture control behavior. These variations are collectively known as structured analysis/real-time (SA/RT). Major variations of SA/RT have been described by Ward and Mellor [Ward 86] and Hatley and Pirbhai [Hatley 87]. A good summary of structured analysis concepts with extensive references is given by Svoboda [Svoboda 90].

Structured analysis extends functional decomposition with the notion that there should be a systematic (and hopefully predictable) approach to analyzing a problem, decomposing it into parts, and describing the relationships between the parts. By providing a well-defined process, structured analysis seeks to address, at least in part, the accidental difficulties that result from ad hoc approaches and the definition of requirements as an afterthought. It seeks to address problems in comprehension and communication by using a common set of conceptual structures—a graphic representation of the specification in terms of those structures—based on the assumption that a decomposition in terms of the data the system handles will be clearer and less inclined to change than one based on the functions performed.

While structured analysis techniques have continued to evolve and have been widely used, there remain a number of common criticisms. When used in problem analysis, a common complaint is that structured analysis provides insufficient guidance. Analysts have difficulty deciding which parts of the problem to model as data, which parts to model as transformations, and which parts should be aggregated. While the gross steps of the process are reasonably well defined, there is only very general guidance (in the form of heuristics) on what specific questions the analyst needs to answer next. Similarly, practitioners find it difficult to know when to stop decomposition and addition of detail. In fact, the basic structured analysis paradigm of modeling requirements as data flows and data transformations requires the analyst to make decisions about intermediate values (for example, form and content of stored data and the details of internal transformations) that are not requirements. Particularly in the hands of less experienced practitioners, data flow models tend to incorporate a variety of detail that properly belongs to design or implementation.

Many of these difficulties result from the weak constraints imposed by the conceptual model. A goal of the developers of structured analysis was to create a very general approach to modeling systems; in fact, one that could be applied equally to model human enterprises, hardware applications, software applications of different kinds, and so on. Unfortunately, such generality can be achieved only by abstracting away any semantics that are not common to all of the types of systems potentially being modeled. The conceptual model itself can provide little guidance relevant to a particular system. Since the conceptual model applies equally to requirements analysis and design analysis, its semantics provide no basis for distinguishing the two. Similarly, such models can support only very weak syntactic criteria for assessing the quality of structured analysis specifications. For example, the test for completeness and consistency in data flow diagrams is limited to determining that the transformations at each level are consistent in name and number with the data flows of the level above.

This does not mean one cannot develop data flow specifications that are easy to understand, communicate effectively with the user, or capture required behavior correctly. The large number of systems developed using structured analysis show that it is possible to do so. However, the weakness of the conceptual model means that a specification's quality depends largely on the experience, insight, and expertise of the analyst. The developer must provide the necessary discipline because the model itself is relatively unconstrained.

Finally, structured analysis provides little support for producing an SRS that meets our quality criteria. Data flow diagrams are unsuitable for capturing mathematical relations or detailed specifications of value, timing, or accuracy so the detailed behavioral specifications are typically given in English or as pseudocode segments in the MiniSpecs. These constructs provide little or no support for writing an SRS that is complete, implementation independent, unambiguous, consistent, precise, and verifiable. Further, the data flow diagrams and attendant dictionaries do not, themselves, provide support for organizing an SRS to satisfy the packaging goals of readability, ease of reference and review, or reusability. In fact, for many of the published methods, there is no explicit process step, structure, or guidance for producing an SRS, as a distinct development product, at all.

7.3 Operational Specification

The operational[2] approach focuses on addressing two of the essential requirements dilemmas. The first is that we often do not know exactly what should be built until we build it. The second is the problem inherent in moving from a particular specification of

requirements (what to build) to a design that satisfies those requirements (how to build it). The closer the requirements specification is to the design, the easier the transition, but the more likely it is that design decisions are made prematurely.

The operational approach seeks to address these problems, among others, by supporting development of executable requirements specifications. Key elements of an operational approach are: a formal specification language and an engine for executing well-formed specifications written in the language. Operational approaches may also include automated support for analyzing properties of the formal specification and for transforming the specification into an equivalent implementation. A good description of the operational approach, its rationale, and goals is given by Zave [Zave 82].

The underlying reasoning about the benefits of the operational approach is as follows:

- Making the requirements specification itself executable obviates the dilemma that one must build the system to know what to build. The developer writes the requirements specification in a formal language. The specification may then be executed to validate that the customer's needs have been captured and the right system specified (for example, one can apply scenarios and test cases). The approach is presumed to require less labor and be more cost-effective than conventional prototyping because a separate requirements specification need not be produced; the specification and the "prototype" are the same thing.

- Operational specifications allow the developer to abstract from design decisions while simplifying the transition from requirements to design and implementation. Transition to design and implementation is both simple and automatable because the behavioral requirements are already expressed in terms of computational mechanisms. During design, one makes decisions concerning efficiency, resource management, and target language realization that are abstracted from the operational specification.

For general applications, operational approaches have achieved only limited success. This is at least in part due to the failure to achieve the necessary semantic distinction between an operational computational model and conventional programming. The benefits of the approach are predicated on the assumption that the

---

2. We use the term "operational" here specifically to denote approaches based on executable specifications in the sense of Zave [Zave 82]. The term is sometimes used to contrast with axiomatic specification–that is not the meaning here.

operational model can be written in terms of the problem domain, without the need to introduce conceptual structures belonging to the solution domain. In practice, this goal has proven elusive. To achieve generality, operational languages have typically had to introduce implementation constructs. The result is not a requirements specification language but a higher-level programming language. As noted by Parnas [Parnas 85b] and Brooks [Brooks 87], the specification ends up giving the solution method rather than the problem statement. Thus, in practice, operational specifications do not meet the SRS goal of implementation independence.

The focus of operational specification is on the benefits of early simulation rather than on the properties of the specification as a reference document. Since executability requires formality, operational specifications necessarily satisfy the SRS semantic properties of being unambiguous, consistent, precise, and verifiable. The ability to validate the specification through simulation also supports completeness. However, as discussed, these properties have not been achieved in concert with implementation independence. Further, the methods discussed in the literature put little emphasis on the communication or packaging qualities of the specification, except as these qualities overlap with desirable design properties. Thus, there may be some support for modifiability but little for readability or organizing an SRS for reference and review.

7.4 Object Oriented Analysis (OOA)

There is currently considerable discussion in the literature, and little agreement, on exactly what should and should not be considered "object oriented." OOA has evolved from at least two significant sources: information modeling and object oriented design. Each has contributed to current views of OOA, and the proponents of each emphasize somewhat different sets of concepts. For the purposes of this tutorial, we are not interested in which method is by some measure "more object oriented" but in the distinct contributions of the object-oriented paradigm to analysis and specification. For an overview of OOA concepts and methods, see Balin's article [Balin 94]; Davis's book [Davis 93] includes both discussion and examples. Examples of recent approaches self-described as object oriented include work by Rumbaugh [Rumbaugh 91], Coad and Yourdon [Coad 91], Shlaer and Mellor [Shlaer 88], and Selic, Gullekson, and Ward [Selic 94].

OOA techniques differ from structured analysis in their approach to decomposing a problem into parts and in the methods for describing the relationships between the parts. In OOA, the analyst decomposes the problem into a set of interacting objects based on the entities and relationships extant in the problem domain. An object encapsulates a related set of data, processing, and state (thus, a significant distinction between object-oriented analysis and structured analysis is that OOA encapsulates both data and related processing together). Objects provide externally accessible functions, typically called services or methods. Objects may hide information about their internal structure, data, or state from other objects. Conversely, they may provide processing, data, or state information through the services defined on the object interface. Dynamic relationships between objects are captured in terms of message passing (that is, one object sends a message to invoke a service or respond to an invocation). The analyst captures static relationships in the problem domain using the concepts of aggregation and classification. Aggregation is used to capture whole/part relationships. Classification is used to capture class/instance relationships (also called "is-a" or inheritance relationships).

The structural components of OOA (for example, objects, classes, services, aggregation) support a set of analytic principles. Of these, two directly address requirements problems:

1. From information modeling comes the assumption that a problem is easiest to understand and communicate if the conceptual structures created during analysis map directly to entities and relationships in the problem domain. This principle is realized in OOA through the heuristic of representing problem domain objects and relationships of interest as OOA objects and relationships. Thus an OOA specification of a vehicle registration system might model vehicles, vehicle owners, vehicle title, and so on [Coad 90] as objects. The object paradigm is used to model both the problem and the relevant problem context.

2. From early work on modularization by Parnas [Parnas 72] and abstract data types, by way of object-oriented programming and design, come the principles of information hiding and abstraction. The principle of information hiding guides one to limit access to information on which other parts of the system should not depend. In an OO specification of requirements, this principle is applied to hide details of design and implementation. In OOA, behavior requirements are specified in terms of the data and services provided on the object interfaces; how those services are implemented is encapsulated by the object.

The principle of abstraction says that only the relevant or essential information should be presented. Abstraction is implemented in OOA by defining object interfaces that provide access only to essential data or state information encapsulated by an object (conversely hiding the incidentals).

The principles and mechanisms of OOA provide a basis for attacking the essential difficulties of comprehension, communication, and control. The principle of problem-domain modeling helps guide the analyst in distinguishing requirements (what) from design (how). Where the objects and their relationships faithfully model entities and relationships in the problem, they are understandable by the customer and other domain experts; this supports early comprehension of the requirements.

The principles of information hiding and abstraction, with the attendant object mechanisms, provide mechanisms useful for addressing the essential problems of control and communication. Objects provide the means to divide the requirements into distinct parts, abstract from details, and limit unnecessary dependencies between the parts. Object interfaces can be used to hide irrelevant detail and define abstractions providing only the essential information. This provides a basis for managing complexity and improving readability. Likewise objects provide a basis for constructing reusable requirements units of related functions and data.

The potential benefits of OOA are often diluted by the way the key principles are manifest in particular methods. While the objects and relations of OOA are intended to model essential aspects of the application domain, this goal is typically not supported by a corresponding conceptual model of the domain behavior. As for structured analysis, object-modeling mechanisms and techniques are intentionally generic rather than application specific. One result is insufficient guidance in developing appropriate object decompositions. Just as structured analysis practitioners have difficulty choosing appropriate data flows and transformations, OOA practitioners have difficulty choosing appropriate objects and relationships.

In practice, the notion that one can develop the structure of a system, or a requirements specification, based on physical structure is often found to be oversold. It is true that the elements of the physical world are usually stable (especially relative to software details) and that real-world-based models have intuitive appeal. It is not, however, the case that everything that must be captured in requirements has a physical analog. An obvious example is shared state information. Further, many real-world structures are themselves arbitrary and likely to change (for example, where two hardware functions are put on one physical platform to reduce cost). While the notion of basing requirements structure on physical structure is a useful heuristic, more is needed to develop a complete and consistent requirements specification.

A further difficulty is that the notations and semantics of OOA methods are typically based on the conceptual structures of software rather than those of the problem domain the analyst seeks to model. Symptomatic of this problem is that analysts find themselves debating about object language features and their properties rather than about the properties of the problem. An example is the use of message passing, complete with message passing protocols, where one object uses information defined in another. In the problem domain it is often irrelevant whether information is actively solicited or passively received. In fact there may be no notion of messages or transmission at all. Nonetheless one finds analysts debating about which object should initiate a request and the resulting anomaly of passive entities modeled as active. For example, to get information from a book one might request that the book "read itself" and "send" the requested information in a message. To control an aircraft the pilot might "use his hands and feet to 'send messages' to the aircraft controls which in turn send messages to the aircraft control surfaces to modify themselves" [Davis 93]. Such decisions are about OOA mechanisms or design, not about the problem domain or requirements.

A more serious complaint is that most current OOA methods inadequately address our goal of developing a good SRS. Most OOA approaches in the literature provide only informal specification mechanisms, relying on refinement of the OO model in design and implementation to add detail and precision. There is no formal basis for determining if a specification is complete, consistent, or verifiable. Further, none of the OOA techniques discussed directly address the issues of developing the SRS as a reference document. The focus of all of the cited OOA techniques is on problem analysis rather than specification. If the SRS is addressed at all, the assumption is that the principles applied to problem understanding and modeling are sufficient, when results are documented, to produce a good specification. Experience suggests otherwise. As we have discussed, there are inherent trade-offs that must be made to develop a specification that meets the needs of any particular project. Making effective trade-offs requires a disciplined and thoughtful approach to the SRS itself, not just the problem. Thus, while OOA provide the means to address packaging issues, there is typically little methodological emphasis on issues like modifiability or organization of a specification for reference and review.

7.5 Software Cost Reduction (SCR) Method

Where most of the techniques thus far discussed focus on problem analysis, the requirements work at the US Naval Research Laboratory (NRL) focused equally on issues of developing a good SRS. NRL initiated the Software Cost Reduction (SCR) project in 1978 to demonstrate the feasibility and effectiveness of advanced software engineering techniques by applying them to a real system, the Operational Flight Program (OFP) for the A-7E aircraft. To demonstrate that (then-academic) techniques such as information hiding, formal specification, abstract interfaces, and cooperating sequential processes could help make software easier to understand, maintain, and change, the SCR project set out to reengineer the A-7E OFP.

Since no existing documentation adequately captured the A-7E's software requirements, the first step was to develop an effective SRS. In this process, the SCR project identified a number of properties a good SRS should have and a set of principles for developing effective requirements documentation [Heninger 80]. The SCR approach uses formal, mathematically based specifications of acceptable system outputs to support development of a specification that is unambiguous, precise, and verifiable. It also provided techniques for checking a specification for a variety of completeness and consistency properties. The SCR approach introduced principles and techniques to support our SRS packaging goals, including the principle of separation of concerns to aid readability and support ease of change. It also includes the use of a standard structure for an SRS specification and the use of tabular specifications that improve readability, modifiability, and facilitate use of the specification for reference and review.

While other requirements approaches have stated similar objectives, the SCR project is unique in having applied software engineering principles to develop a standard SRS organization, a specification method, review method [Parnas 85a], and notations consistent with those principles. The SCR project is also unique in making publicly available a complete, model SRS of a significant system [Alspaugh 92].

A number of issues were left unresolved by the original SCR work. While the product of the requirements analysis was well documented, the underlying process and method were never fully described. Since the original effort was to reengineer an existing system, it was not clear how effective the techniques would be on a new development. Since the developers of the A-7E requirements document were researchers, it was also unclear whether industrial developers would find the rather formal method and notation useable, readable, or effective. Finally, while the A-7E

SRS organization is reasonably general, many of the specification techniques are targeted to real-time, embedded applications. As discussed in the following section, more recent work by Parnas [Parnas 91], NRL [Heitmeyer 95a,b], and others [Faulk 92] has addressed many of the open questions about the SCR approach.

8. Trends and Emerging Technology

While improved discipline will address requirement's accidental difficulties, addressing the essential difficulties requires technical advances. Significant trends, in some cases backed by industrial experience, have emerged over the past few years that offer some hope for improvement:

- *Domain specificity*: Requirements methods will provide improved analytic and specification support by being tailored to particular classes of problems. Historically, requirements approaches have been advanced as being equally useful to widely varied types of applications. For example, structured analysis methods were deemed to be based on conceptual models that were "universally applicable" (for example, [Ross 77]); similar claims have been made for object-oriented approaches.

Such generality comes at the expense of ease of use and amount of work the analyst must do for any particular application. Where the underlying models have been tailored to a particular class of applications, the properties common to the class are embedded in the model. The amount of work necessary to adapt the model to a specific instance of the class is relatively small. The more general the model, the more decisions that must be made, the more information that must be provided, and the more tailoring that must be done. This provides increased room for error and, since each analyst will approach the problem differently, makes solutions difficult to standardize. In particular, such generality precludes standardization of sufficiently rigorous models to support algorithmic analysis of properties like completeness and consistency.

Similar points have been expressed in a recent paper by Jackson [Jackson 94]. He points out that some of the characteristics separating real engineering disciplines from what is euphemistically described as "software engineering" are well-understood procedures, mathematical models, and standard designs specific to narrow classes of applications. Jackson points out the need for software methods based on the conceptual structures and mathematical models of behavior inherent in a given problem domain (for example, publication, command and control, accounting, and so on). Such common underlying constructs can provide the engineer guidance in developing the specification for a particular system.

- *Practical formalisms*: Like so many of the promising technologies in requirements, the application of formal methods is characterized by an essential dilemma. On one hand, formal specification techniques hold out the only real hope for producing specifications that are precise, unambiguous, and demonstrably complete or consistent. On the other, industrial practitioners widely view formal methods as impractical. Difficulty of use, inability to scale, readability, and cost are among the reasons cited. Thus, in spite of significant technical progress and a growing body of literature, the pace of adoption by industry has been extremely slow.

In spite of the technical and technical transfer difficulties, increased formality is necessary. Only by placing behavioral specification on a mathematical basis will we be able to acquire sufficient intellectual control to develop complex systems with any assurance that they satisfy their intended purpose and provide necessary properties like safety. The solution is better formal methods—methods that are practical given the time, cost, and personnel constraints of industrial development.

Engineering models and the training to use them are de rigueur in every other discipline that builds large, complex, or safety-critical systems. Builders of a bridge or skyscraper who did not employ proven methods or mathematical models to predict reliability and safety would be held criminally negligent in the event of failure. It is only the relative youth of the software discipline that permits us to get away with less. But, we cannot expect great progress overnight. As Jackson [Jackson 94] notes, the field is sufficiently immature that "the prerequisites for a more mathematical approach are not in place." Further, many of those practicing our craft lack the background required of licensed engineers in other disciplines [Parnas 89]. Nonetheless, sufficient work has been done to show that more formal approaches are practical and effective in industry. For an overview of formal methods and their role in practical developments, refer to Rushby's summary work [Rushby 93].

- *Improved tool support*: It remains common to walk into the office of a software develop-

ment manager and find the shelves lined with the manuals for CASE tools that are not in use. In spite of years of development and the contrary claims of vendors, many industrial developers have found the available requirements CASE tools of marginal benefit.

Typically, the fault lies not so much with the tool vendor but with the underlying method or methods the tool seeks to support. The same generality, lack of strong underlying conceptual model, and lack of formality that makes the methods weak limits the benefits of automation. Since the methods do not adequately constrain the problem space and offer little specific guidance, the corresponding tool cannot actively support the developer in making difficult decisions. Since the model and SRS are not standardized, its production eludes effective automated support. Since the underlying model is not formal, only trivial syntactic properties of the specification can be evaluated. Most such tools provide little more than a graphic interface and requirements database.

Far more is now possible. Where the model, conceptual structures, notations, and process are standardized, significant automated support becomes possible. The tool can use information about the state of the specification and the process to guide the developer in making the next step. It can use standardized templates to automate rote portions of the SRS. It can use the underlying mathematical model to determine to what extent the specification is complete and consistent. While only the potential of such tools has yet been demonstrated, there are sufficient results to project the benefits (for example, [Heitmeyer 95b], [Leveson 94]).

- *Integrated paradigms*: One of the Holy Grails of software engineering has been the integrated software development environment. Much of the frustration in applying currently available methods and tools is the lack of integration, not just in the tool interfaces, but in the underlying models and conceptual structures. Even where an approach works well for one phase of development, the same techniques are either difficult to use in the next phase or there is no clear transition path. Similarly tools are either focused on a small subset of the many tasks (for example, analysis but not documentation) or attempt to address the entire life cycle but support none of it well. The typical development employs a hodgepodge of software engineering methodologies and ad hoc techniques. Developers often build their own software to bridge the gap between CASE platforms.

In spite of a number of attempts, the production of a useful, integrated set of methods and supporting environment has proven elusive. However, it now appears that there is sufficient technology available to provide, if not a complete solution, at least the skeleton for one.

The most significant methodological trend can be described as convergent evolution. In biology, convergent evolution denotes a situation where common evolutionary pressures lead to similar characteristics (morphology) in distinct species. An analogous convergence is ongoing in requirements. As different schools of thought have come to understand and attempt to address the weaknesses and omissions in their own approaches, the solutions have become more similar. In particular, the field is moving toward a common understanding of the difficulties and common assumptions about the desired qualities of solutions. This should not be confused with the bandwagon effect that often attends real or imaginary paradigm shifts (for example, the current rush to object-oriented everything). Rather, it is the slow process of evolving common understanding and changing conventional practices.

Such trends and some preliminary results are currently observable in requirements approaches for embedded software. In the 1970s, the exigencies of national defense and aerospace applications resulted in demand for complex, mission-critical software. It became apparent early on that available requirements techniques addressed neither the complexity of the systems being built nor the stringent control, timing, and accuracy constraints of the applications. Developers responded by creating a variety of domain-specific approaches. Early work by TRW for the US Army on the Ballistic Missile Defense system produced the Software Requirements Engineering Method (SREM) [Alford 77] and supporting tools. Such software problems in the Navy led to the SCR project. Ward, Mellor, Hatley, and Pirbhai ([Ward 86], [Hatley 87]) developed extensions to structured analysis techniques targeted to real-time applications. Work on the Israeli defense applications led Harel to develop statecharts [Harel 87] and the supporting tool Statemate.

The need for high-assurance software in mission-

and safety-critical systems also led to the introduction of practical formalisms and integrated tools support. TRW developed REVS [Davis 77] and other tools as part of a complete environment supporting SREM and other phases of the life cycle. The SCR project developed specification techniques based on mathematical functions and tabular representations [Heninger 80]. These allowed a variety of consistency and completeness checks to be performed by inspection. Harel introduced a compact graphic representation of finite state machines with a well-defined formal semantics. These features were subsequently integrated in the Statemate tool that supported symbolic execution of statecharts for early customer validation and limited code generation. All of these techniques began to converge on an underlying model based on finite state automata.

More recent work has seen continuing convergence toward a common set of assumptions and similar solutions. Recently, Ward and colleagues have developed the Real-Time Object-Oriented Modeling (ROOM) method [Selic 94]. ROOM integrates concepts from operational specification, object-oriented analysis, and statecharts. It employs an object-oriented modeling approach with tool support. The tool is based on a simplified statechart semantics and supports symbolic execution and some code generation. The focus of ROOM currently remains on problem modeling and the transition to design, and execution rather than formal analysis.

Nancy Leveson and her colleagues have adapted statecharts to provide a formally based method for embedded system specification [Jaffe 91]. The approach has been specifically developed to be useable and readable by practicing engineers. It employs both the graphical syntax of statecharts and a tabular representation of functions similar to those used in the SCR approach. Its underlying formal model is intended to support formal analysis of system properties, with an emphasis on safety. The formal model also supports symbolic execution. These techniques have been applied to develop a requirements specification for parts of the Federal Aviation Administration's safety-critical Traffic Alert and Collision Avoidance System (TCAS) [Leveson 94].

Extensions to the SCR work have taken a similar direction. Parnas and Madey have extended the SCR approach to create a standard mathematical model for embedded system requirements [Parnas 91]. Heitmeyer and colleagues at NRL have extended the Parnas/Madey work by defining a corresponding formal model for the SCR approach [Heitmeyer 95b]. This formal model has been used to develop a suite of prototype tools supporting analysis of requirements properties like completeness and consistency [Heitmeyer

95a]. The NRL tools also support specification-based simulation and are being integrated with other tools to support automated analysis of application-specific properties like safety assertions. Concurrent work at the Software Productivity Consortium by Faulk and colleagues [Faulk 92] has integrated the SCR approach with object-oriented and graphic techniques and defined a complete requirements analysis process including a detailed process for developing a good SRS. These techniques have been applied effectively in development of requirements for Lockheed's avionics upgrade on the C-130J aircraft [Faulk 94]. The C-130J avionics software is a safety-critical system of approximately 100K lines of Ada code.

Other recent work attempts to increase the level of formality and the predictability of the problem analysis process and its products. For example, Potts and his colleagues are developing process models and tools to support systematic requirements elicitation that include a formal structure for describing discussions about requirements [Potts 94]. Hsia and his colleagues, among others, are investigating formal approaches to the use of scenarios in eliciting and validating requirements [Hsia 94]. Recent work by Boehm and his colleagues [Boehm 94] seeks to address the accidental difficulties engendered by adversarial software procurement processes.

While none of the works mentioned can be considered a complete solution, it is clear that (1) the work is converging toward common assumptions and solutions, (2) the approaches all provide significantly improved capability to address both accidental and essential requirements difficulties, and (3) the solutions can be effectively applied in industry.

9. Conclusions

Requirements are intrinsically hard to do well. Beyond the need for discipline, there are a host of essential difficulties that attend both the understanding of requirements and their specification. Further, many of the difficulties in requirements will not yield to technical solution alone. Addressing all of the essential difficulties requires the application of technical solutions in the context of human factors such as the ability to manage complexity or communicate to diverse audiences. A requirements approach that does not account for both technical and human concerns can have only limited success. For developers seeking new methods, the lesson is caveat emptor. If someone tells you his method makes requirements easy, keep a hand on your wallet.

Nevertheless, difficulty is not impossibility and the inability to achieve perfection is not an excuse for surrender. While all of the approaches discussed have significant weaknesses, they all contribute to the attempt to make requirements analysis and specification a controlled, systematic, and effective process. Though there is no easy path, experience confirms that the use of *any* careful and systematic approach is preferable to an ad hoc and chaotic one. Further good news is that, if the requirements are done well, chances are much improved that the rest of the development will also go well. Unfortunately, ad hoc approaches remain the norm in much of the software industry.

A final observation is that the benefits of good requirements come at a cost. Such a difficult and exacting task cannot be done properly by personnel with inadequate experience, training, or resources. Providing the time and the means to do the job right is the task of responsible management. The time to commit the best and brightest is before, not after, disaster occurs. The monumental failures of a host of ambitious developments bear witness to the folly of doing otherwise.

10. Further Reading

Those seeking more depth on requirements methodologies than this tutorial can provide should read Alan Davis' book *Software Requirements: Objects, Functions, and States* [Davis 93]. In addition to a general discussion of issues in software requirements, Davis illustrates a number of problem analysis and specification techniques with a set of common examples and provides a comprehensive annotated bibliography.

For a better understanding of software requirements in the context of systems development, the reader is referred to the book of collected papers edited by Thayer and Dorfman, *System and Software Requirements Engineering* [Thayer 90]. This tutorial work contains in one volume both original papers and reprints from many of the authors discussed above. The companion volume, *Standards, Guidelines, and Examples on System and Software Requirements Engineering* [Dorfman 90] is a compendium of international and US government standards relating to system and software requirements and provides some illustrating examples.

For enjoyable reading as well as insightful commentary on requirements problems, methods, and a host of requirements-related issues, the reader is referred to Michael Jackson's recent book, *Software Requirements and Specifications: A Lexicon of Practice, Principles, and Prejudice.* [Jackson 95]

Acknowledgments

C. Colket at SPAWAR, E. Wald at ONR and A. Pyster at the Software Productivity Consortium supported the development of this report. The quality of this paper has been much improved thanks to thoughtful reviews by Paul Clements, Connie Heitmeyer, Jim Kirby, Bruce Labaw, Richard Morrison, and David Weiss.

References

[Alford 77]   Alford, M., "A Requirements Engineering Methodology for Real-Time Processing Requirements," *IEEE Trans. Software Eng.*, Vol. 3, No. 1, Jan. 1977, pp. 60–69.

[Alford 79]   Alford, M. and J. Lawson, "Software Requirements Engineering Methodology (Development)," *RADC-TR-79-168*, U.S. Air Force Rome Air Development Center, June 1979.

[Alspaugh 92]   Alspaugh, T. et al., *Software Requirements for the A-7E Aircraft*, NRL/FR/5530-92-9194, Naval Research Laboratory, Washington, D.C., 1992.

[Balin 94]   Balin, S., "Object-Oriented Requirements Analysis," in *Encyclopedia of Software Engineering*, J. Marciniak ed., John Wiley & Sons, New York, N.Y., 1994, pp. 740–756.

[Basili 81]   Basili, V. and D. Weiss, "Evaluation of a Software Requirements Document by Analysis of Change Data," *Proc. 5th Int'l Conf. Software Eng.*, IEEE CS Press, Los Alamitos, Calif., 1981, pp. 314–323.

[Boehm 81]   Boehm, B., *Software Engineering Economics*, Prentice-Hall, Englewood Cliffs, N.J., 1981.

[Boehm 94]   Boehm, B. et al., "Software Requirements as Negotiated Win Conditions," *Proc. 1st Int'l Conf. Requirements Eng.*, IEEE CS Press, Los Alamitos, Calif., 1994, pp. 74–83.

[Brooks 75]   Brooks, F., *The Mythical Man-Month*, Addison-Wesley, Reading, Mass., 1975.

[Brooks 87]   Brooks, F., "No Silver Bullet: Essence and Accidents of Software Engineering," *Computer*, Apr. 1987, pp. 10–19.

[CECOM 89]   *Software Methodology Catalog: Second Edition*, Technical report C01-091JB-0001-01, US Army Communications-Electronics Command, Fort Monmouth, N.J., Mar. 1989.

[Clements 95]   Clements, P., private communication, May 1995.

[Coad 90]   Coad, P. and E. Yourdon, *Object Oriented Analysis*, Prentice-Hall, Englewood Cliffs, N.J., 1990.

[Davis 77]   Davis, C. and C. Vick, "The Software Development System," *IEEE Trans. Software Eng.*, Vol. 3, No. 1, Jan. 1977, pp. 69–84.

[Davis 88]   Davis, A., "A Taxonomy for the Early Stages of the Software Development Life Cycle," *J. Systems and Software*, Sept. 1988, pp. 297–311.

[Davis 93]   Davis, A., *Software Requirements (Revised): Objects, Functions, and States*, Prentice-Hall, Englewood Cliffs, N.J., 1993.

[DeMarco 78]   DeMarco, T., *Structured Analysis and System Specification*, Prentice-Hall Englewood Cliffs, N.J., 1978.

[Dorfman 90]   Dorfman, M. and R. Thayer, eds., *Standards, Guidelines, and Examples on System and Software Requirements Engineering*, IEEE CS Press, Los Alamitos, Calif., 1990.

[Faulk 92]   Faulk, S. et al., "The Core Method for Real-Time Requirements," *IEEE Software*, Vol. 9, No. 5, Sept. 1992.

[Faulk 93]   Faulk, S. et al., *Consortium Requirements Engineering Guidebook*, Version 1.0, SPC-92060-CMC, Software Productivity Consortium, Herndon, Virginia, 1993.

[Faulk 94]   Faulk, S. et al., "Experience Applying the CoRE Method to the Lockheed C-130J," *Proc. 9th Ann. Conf. Computer Assurance*, IEEE Press, Piscataway, N.J., 1994, pp. 3–8.

[GAO 79]   US General Accounting Office, *Contracting for Computer Software Development—Serious Problems Require Management Attention to Avoid Wasting Additional Millions*, Report FGMSD-80-4, November 1979.

[GAO 92]   US General Accounting Office, *Mission Critical Systems: Defense Attempting to Address Major Software Challenges*, GAO/IMTEC-93-13, December 1992.

[Gane 79]   Gane, C. and T. Sarson, *Structured Systems Analysis*, Prentice-Hall, New Jersey, 1979.

[Hamilton 76]   Hamilton, M. and S. Zeldin, "Higher Order Software-A Methodology for Defining Software," *IEEE Trans. Software Eng.*, Vol. 2, No. 1, Jan. 1976, pp. 9–32.

[Harel 87]   Harel, D., "Statecharts: a Visual Formalism for Complex Systems," *Science of Computer Programming* 8, 1987, pp. 231–274.

[Hatley 87]   Hatley, D. and I. Pirbhai, *Strategies for Real-Time Specification*, Dorset House, New York, N.Y., 1987.

[Heitmeyer 95a]   Heitmeyer, C., B. Labaw, and D. Kiskis, "Consistency Checking of SCR-Style Requirements Specifications," *Proc. 2nd IEEE Int'l Symp. Requirements Eng.*, IEEE CS Press, Los Alamitos, Calif., 1995, pp. 56–63.

[Heitmeyer 95b]   Heitmeyer, C., R. Jeffords, and B. Labaw, *Tools for Analyzing SCR-Style Requirements Specifications: A Formal Foundation*, NRL Technical Report NRL-7499, U.S. Naval Research Laboratory, Washington, DC, 1995.

[Heninger 80]   Heninger, K., "Specifying Software Requirements for Complex Systems: New Techniques and Their Application," *IEEE Trans. Software Eng.*, Vol. 6, No. 1, Jan. 1980.

[Hester 81]   Hester, S., D. Parnas, and D. Utter, "Using Documentation as a Software Design Medium," *Bell System Technical J.*, Vol. 60, No. 8, Oct. 1981, pp. 1941–1977.

[Hsia 94]   Hsia, P. et al., "Formal Approach to Scenario Analysis," *IEEE Software*, Mar. 1994, pp. 33–41.

[Jackson 83]   Jackson, M., *System Development*, Prentice-Hall, Englewood Cliffs, N.J., 1983.

[Jackson 94]   Jackson, M., "Problems, Methods, and Specialization," *IEEE Software*, Nov. 1994, pp. 57–62.

[Jackson 95]   Jackson, M., *Software Requirements and Specifications: A Lexicon of Practice, Principles, and Prejudice*, ACM Press/Addison Wesley, Reading, Mass., 1995.

[Jaffe 91]   Jaffe, M. et al., "Software Requirements Analysis for Real-Time Process-Control Systems," *IEEE Trans. Software Eng.*, Vol. 17, No. 3, Mar. 1991, pp. 241–257.

[Leveson 94]   Leveson, N. et al., "Requirements Specification for Process-Control Systems," *IEEE Trans. Software Eng.*, Vol. 20, No. 9, Sept. 1994.

[Lutz 93]   Lutz, R., "Analyzing Software Requirements Errors in Safety-Critical Embedded Systems," *Proc. IEEE Int'l Symp. Requirements Eng.*, IEEE CS Press, Los Alamitos, Calif., 1993, pp. 126–133.

[Parnas 72]   Parnas, D., "On the Criteria to be Used in Decomposing Systems into Modules," *Comm. ACM*, Vol. 15, No. 12, Dec. 1972, pp. 1053–1058.

[Parnas 85a]   Parnas, D. and D. Weiss, "Active Design Reviews: Principles and Practices," *Proc. 8th Int'l Conf. Software Eng.*, IEEE CS Press, Los Alamitos, Calif., 1985.

[Parnas 85b]   Parnas, D. "Software Aspects of Strategic Defense Systems," *American Scientist*, Sept. 1985, pp. 432–440.

[Parnas 86]   Parnas, D. and P. Clements, "A Rational Design Process: How and Why to Fake It," *IEEE Trans. Software Eng.*, Vol. 12, No. 2, Feb. 1986, pp. 251–257.

[Parnas 89]   Parnas, D., *Education for Computing Professionals*, Technical Report 89-247, Department of Computing and Information Science, Queens University, Kingston, Ontario, 1989.

[Parnas 91]   Parnas, D. and J. Madey, *Functional Documentation for Computer Systems Engineering* (Version 2), CRL Report No. 237, McMaster University, Hamilton, Ontario, Canada, Sept. 1991.

[Potts 94]   Potts, C., K. Takahashi, and A. Anton, "Inquiry-Based Requirements Analysis," *IEEE Software*, Mar. 1994, pp. 21–32.

[Shlaer 88]   Shlaer, S. and S. Mellor, *Object-Oriented Systems Analysis: Modeling the World in Data*, Prentice-Hall, Englewood Cliffs, N.J., 1988.

[Ross 77]   Ross, D. and K. Schoman Jr., "Structured Analysis for Requirements Definitions," *IEEE Trans. Software Eng.*, Vol. 3, No. 1, Jan. 1977, pp. 6–15.

[Rumbaugh 91]   Rumbaugh, M. Blaha et al, *Object-Oriented Modeling and Design*, Prentice-Hall, Englewood Cliffs, N.J., 1991.

[Rushby 93]   Rushby, J., *Formal Methods and the Certification of Critical Systems*, CSL Technical Report SRI-CSL-93-07, SRI International, Menlo Park, Calif., Nov., 1993.

[Selic 94]   Selic, B., G. Gullekson, and P. Ward, *Real-Time Object-Oriented Modeling*, John Wiley & Sons, New York, N.Y., 1994.

[Svoboda 90]   Svoboda, C., "Structured Analysis," in *Tutorial: System and Software Requirements Engineering*, R. Thayer and M. Dorfman, eds., IEEE CS Press, Los Alamitos, Calif., 1990, pp. 218–237.

[Thayer 90]   Thayer, R. and M. Dorfman, eds., *Tutorial: System and Software Requirements Engineering*, IEEE CS Press, Los Alamitos, Calif., 1990.

[Ward 86]   Ward, P. and S. Mellor, *Structured Development for Real-Time Systems*, Vols. 1, 2, and 3, Prentice-Hall, Englewood Cliffs, N.J., 1986.

[Yourdon 89]   Yourdon, E., *Modern Structured Analysis*, Yourdon Press/Prentice-Hall, Englewood Cliffs, N.J., 1989.

[Zave 82]   Zave, P., "An Operational Approach to Requirements Specification for Embedded Systems," *IEEE Trans. Software Eng.*, Vol. 8, No. 3, May 1982, pp. 250–269.

Article presents an exception-oriented execution of a detailed plan.

Fundamentals of Project Management

BY WILLIAM B. MILLER

■ Project planning has essentially one purpose: establishing a foundation for execution of the plan and, therefore, successful completion of the project. The project plan is the game plan for the project. Other uses of the plan, such as communication, are important but secondary. Planning should be performed before work begins on project activities. It should include both general project planning and detailed planning for activities in the near future. Planning output should include:

— Definitions of project activities and required results.

— Estimates of work content of project activities, in terms of resources that could be used, such as mandays for people or processing hours for equipment.

— Activity schedules, with milestones and checkpoints for progress reviews.

— Specific assignments for personnel and other resources.

— Resource "loading" estimates (use of resources by time period) or budgets, for personnel, equipment, and other resources.

It is elementary that a plan should include this information. However, it has been my experience that many planners fail to include some of the information. Such a deficiency in plan is a harbinger of future problems.

Planning Responsibilities

Responsibilities for specific planning activities vary by project, but the fundamentals remain the same. They are:

1. The persons who are most knowledgeable about the project activities to be performed and the re-

sources to be used should provide most of the input to the plan. Frequently these persons are the individuals who will be performing or directly supervising the activities. In other cases, they may be support technicians, such as engineers, who are experts on the tasks to be performed.

2. Project management has final responsibility for the plan and should direct its preparation. The plan must reflect their perspective. Often the persons who are most knowledgeable about the activities and resources will have a forest-and-trees perspective problem, which may lead them to be too optimistic or pessimistic about the time and resources required to perform activities (a well-known problem in systems projects).

A good plan should be largely the product of the knowledgeable workers and supervisors, or support technicians, with as few modifications as requested by management. Extensive participation or no participation by management is a sign of trouble because the resulting plan will, respectively, be based on desires rather than facts, or fail to reflect the experience and insights of management.

The Planning Process

The planning process is the sequence of events that produces a project plan. In a pragmatic sense, any sequence of events is acceptable if the resulting plan is acceptable. However, there are certain steps in the process that will be effective for most projects; these steps are the fundamentals.

1. First, project management and key worker and supervisory personnel should be selected, and their planning responsibilities should be defined.

Reprinted with permission from *J. Systems Management*, Vol. 29, No. 11, Nov. 1978, pp. 22–29.

2. A general project plan, consisting of the planning output described earlier, should be developed. This general plan should be reasonable and feasible, but detailed analysis to support it is not necessary. The content and structure of the plan will be described further in the next section.

3. Approvals for the general plan should be obtained. There is no point in proceeding with detailed planning if the plan in general terms is not acceptable, for example with regard to completion dates or resource requirements.

4. A detailed project plan should be developed. This plan should be complete in all details. All inconsistencies, resource loading problems, and conflicts should be eliminated. An example of such a situation is an unmanageable number of checkpoints occurring close together in time, perhaps in one day. This and other aspects of the detailed plan will be discussed later.

5. The general project plan should be revised to be consistent with the detailed plan. The general plan should be a summary of the detailed plan.

6. Approval of the detailed and revised general plans should be obtained. The total project plan, made up of the detailed and general plans, should be published.

These steps are essential in most projects. The number of iterations of one or more of them that is required to develop an acceptable plan may vary. Skipping steps or doing them in a radically different sequence is a violation of fundamentals that at best will be an inefficient way of producing a plan.

Specifics of the Plan

The purpose of the planning phase is to produce a plan with the components described earlier: activities, expected results, work content, schedules, resource assignments, and resource loads (budgets). The specific information content of the components must facilitate execution of the plan. This requirement leads to the following fundamentals:

1. The project must be subdivided into "chewable bites," a number of manageable activities, each with its own tangible end product. The activities' end products may collectively be the project's end product, or they may be intermediate stages in the generation of the project end product.

Activity and output definitions normally occur early in the planning phase. It has been my experience that they are a good indicator of how smoothly the remainder of the project will go. People who understand the value of defining precisely what is to be accomplished accept the other controls easily. On the other hand, people who prefer fuzzy or nonexistent definitions of what has to be done also reject budgets, schedules and other controls.

2. Each activity must be scheduled. Scheduling involves estimating the work content of an activity (e.g. man-days) which may vary by the specific resource used, assigning activities to resources (e.g., persons, pieces of equipment), and determining when each activity should be performed in order to meet the overall project deadline.

There are many scheduling techniques (network methods, for example). In the context of fundamentals, the following guidelines regarding selection of and output from the scheduling method should be observed:
—The scheduling method should be only as complex as is appropriate for the project at hand.
—"Back scheduling" methods, which schedule activities based on start dates of subsequent activities. are generally preferable to "forward scheduling" methods, which schedule activities to be completed when resources are available so long as the overall project deadline is retained. "Back scheduling" preserves the proper sequence of activities and avoids rework problems that may arise from completing activities earlier than necessary (rework is a real-world, not a theoretical, problem with "forward scheduling"). "Forward scheduling" has application, however, when scheduling information, such as work content estimates, may be unreliable or when resource scheduling is a significant concern.
—In the scheduling output, elapsed times of activities (completion date less start date) should be minimized. Multiple parallel assignments for personnel and other resources should be avoided. "One thing at a time" is a good rule. Obviously, it cannot always be observed. However, one of the most frequent scheduling mistakes is the scheduling of several activities to occur simultaneously and use the same resources, on the assumption that by some kind of magic each activity will receive its correct share of resources and be completed on time.

WILLIAM B. MILLER

Mr. Miller is a management consultant in the San Francisco office of Touche Ross & Co. He is a frequent contributor to professional journals and has authored other articles on various aspects of systems design and EDP management. He holds the CDP, a B.S. in Engineering, and an M.S. in Computer Science.

3. The schedule should include status points after completion of each activity or consumption of a certain amount of resources. If an activity is complex or critical, or its output is intended to be a polished product, status points during the activity, to assess progress, should be scheduled. Status points ensure that completion occurs as scheduled, with satisfactory quality. Tangible output should be emphasized; dealing with "percent complete" or subjective measures of progress can be dangerous. Status reviews require effort from project workers and management. Time for the status points must be planned, and responsibilities assigned.

4. Responsibility for each activity and resource consumption objective should be clear. When many people are assigned to an item, one should be in charge. The plan should include time for this person's administrative duties.

5. Recovery time and resources should be provided in the schedule. On a complex project, nobody is smart enough to plan it correctly at the outset. On any project, things can go wrong, such as people becoming ill. New, unforeseen activities will crop up; they always do and not all of them can be deferred. Recovery time can be provided implicitly, for example by not scheduling weekend work or overtime. It can be provided explicitly by leaving slack (unallocated) time or resources that would otherwise be available (during the normal 40-hour week, for example).

A trick that is often used by experienced Project Managers is to plan all activities to consume fewer resources than estimated, for example planning all activities to use 85% of estimated resource requirements. The remaining 15% becomes available as recovery resources that can be applied with-

out exceeding the budget. This trick, of course, takes advantage of the fact that estimates are what their name states—estimates. Activity estimates will seldom be exactly accurate; they will be either high or low. In the absence of controls, the tendency is for only the low estimates and additional activities to be identified as the project progresses, causing budget overruns. On the activities where the estimates were high, work tends to expand to fill the budget. A good Project Manager will not allow that to happen and will bring such activities in under their budgets, at the 85% target or lower.

6. Resource "loading" or budgets—use of resources by time period—should be calculated for each resource employed on the project—people, equipment, money, etc. If the loading is inefficient, unrealistic, or does not meet project objectives, schedules and resource assignments should be adjusted in order to adjust the loading. When many resources are involved which are interchangeable except that activities' work contents depend on the specific resource used, this step may complicate planning because of many iterations of scheduling and loading calculations. The complexity is not a good reason for not performing the step. If it is not performed, the plan is sure to be deficient in some respect such as uneven equipment utilization or individuals scheduled for 60-hour weeks followed by 20-hour weeks.

The fundamentals apply to both general and detailed project planning. General planning should cover the life of the project at a macro level that is adequate for communication, resource commitments, upper management approvals, and integration with other projects. The general plan should include the same information as the detailed plan, but in summary form. Major activities, milestones and resource requirements should be specifically identified, but minor items should be lumped together.

The purpose of the detailed plan is control. The activities should be subdivided so far as is necessary to gain control. The fundamental rule is: an activity should be small enough that recovery will be easy if the activity is not completed as scheduled (which would be determined at the status point following the activity). A rule of thumb in many projects is that an activity should consume no more than 40 man-hours or 5 days elapsed time. Similarly, resource requirements should be subdivided, and status points for measurement of consumption should be scheduled such that excessive consumption would be identified while recovery was still possible. Planning and controlling at such a level of detail may not be popular with some people on the project. However, it is essential, and the situation is rare when controls can justifiably be abandoned in favor of goodwill.

The detailed plan should extend as far into the future as is feasible. One to three months probably is typical. Detailed planning should, therefore, be performed several times throughout the project, unless the project only covers a short time span for which the entire detailed plan can be developed at the beginning. In some cases, it may be a useful exercise to lay out the entire project in detail, but the purpose of such an exercise would be closer to the purpose of the general plan than to the purpose of the detailed plan. A detailed plan, against which progress will be measured rigorously, usually cannot be established more than a few weeks or months in advance of the activities to be performed.

A Project Manager without a plan is like a football team without a playbook, inventing plans during a game. However, I have seen some people try to operate that way. One company assigned a strategic planning project to a group of individuals from the planning function and gave them some general guidelines on what the plan should contain and who should have input to it. The planning person who managed the project did not put together a detailed plan and have it approved by the management who had given him his assignment. In fact, this individual appeared to believe that he was above such things as detailed planning, that they would have been a waste of his valuable time. His team produced a strategic plan that was good in many respects, but they overlooked a couple of matters that were important to corporate management, such as certain market analyses. The problems were corrected before the final plan was produced, but the project ended up requiring more money and time than had been budgeted.

Such failures have not been infrequent and will continue to be a problem so long as project situations exist. There is no evidence that projects are going to lose favor as a means of accomplishing business objectives. In fact, as Alvin Toffler predicted in *Future Shock*,[1] the project approach or "ad-hocracy" may continue to increase in popularity at the expense of traditional approaches that are ineffective in dealing quickly enough with new business problems arising at an ever-increasing rate. If business management is to cope with either today's projects or an increased volume of projects, as Toffler suggests, they simply must do better at using project management fundamentals such as thorough planning.

Planning Documentation

It should go without saying that the plan should be formally documented. However, a fundamental rule of documentation is that it should not be an end in itself, except as required for audit and archival purposes. Documentation is the basis for communication of the plan. It must be easy to understand. Charts and other visual aids are often appropriate. Frequently, the general plan and detailed plan should be separate documents because they communicate to different people.

For some kinds of projects, such as data processing projects, planning documentation may follow a standard format that reduces preparation time and is easily recognized by all parties involved. In other cases, the documentation may be unique and require explanation. Wherever possible, of course, proven documentation procedures should be used.

The documentation methodology should assist in developing the project plan. It should help in structuring the planning process. It may be an integral part of the planning. For example, with a network-structured plan, the development of the network and the plan may produce much of the documentation. If an automated system, such as a computerized scheduling system, provides planning assistance, adequate planning documentation may be normal output from the system.

Another fundamental is that the planning documentation should be useful in the execution phase of the project. Tracking project progress against anything other than the documented plan is inefficient and invites errors. This fundamental also provides a good cross-check on the content of the plan: anything that is to be measured during project execution should be spelled out in the plan, with anticipated results of the measurements. Conversely, there is no point in planning something if progress against the plan is not going to be measured. Planning and execution are opposite sides of the same coin.

Approval of the Plan

"Approval" should mean one thing: commitment. Approval of the plan should be obtained from two groups of people:
—The people who must accept the schedule and provide the required resources.
—The people who can cause the project to fail, by any means, fair or foul.
The two groups may or may not include the same persons.

The process of obtaining approvals should not be taken lightly. Clear, complete documentation of the plan is valuable. It is also important to remember that the people whose approval will be sought will not have lived closely with the planning process. The

[1]Alvin Toffler, *Future Shock*, Random House, Inc., 1970

persons presenting the plan must transmit on the receivers' wavelengths.

Sometimes approvals will not be immediately forthcoming. Depending on what the objections are to the plan, the options are to:

a. Modify the format and presentation to make the plan more understandable.
b. Apply more, fewer, or different resources to activities in order to change completion dates in the schedule.
c. Modify completion dates in order to affect resource usage (personnel, dollars, etc.).
d. Modify the scope of the project in order to affect completion dates or resource requirements.
e. Take a position that the plan as presented is necessary for successful completion of the project.

It is not possible to change one of the plan variables—activities and associated work content, schedules, and use of resources—without changing one or both of the others. (This does not imply that there are not several means of changing the components; for example, overtime may be an acceptable means for increasing resources in cases when hiring additional personnel may be unacceptable.) If such is possible, the plan has unnecessary slack in it. The only exception is an arbitrary management decision to eliminate recovery time from the schedule; this approach is rarely acceptable.

After the plan has been approved, it should be published with the approvals noted. The effect of the approval on the preparers of the plan and the individuals affected by the plan will be beneficial. In addition, the publication will usually have a positive effect on the persons who approved the plan, an effect that will tend to strengthen their commitments to it. It is difficult sometimes to know which effect is stronger or more important.

EXECUTION OF THE PLAN

Execution of the plan, of course, is what a project is all about. Control of the execution makes a project successful. Control is achieved by identifying and correcting things that are not proceeding according to the plan. Control actions include: monitoring progress of project activities, monitoring resource expenditures, monitoring overall project status, analysis of variances from plan, recovery of planning as required, and formal reporting of project status and recovery plans.

Control Responsibilities

In the final analysis, all control responsibilities rest with project management in the same way that the head coach and general manager bear overall responsibility for a football team's performance. On a day-to-day basis, responsibilities should be shared. The person (supervisor or worker) directly in charge of each activity or resource consumption objective in the plan should be responsible for monitoring progress, reporting status, and developing corrective action plans as required. If his (or her) part of the project gets into trouble, he has the first-line responsibility for getting it out of trouble.

Project management should be responsible for collecting status reports and corrective action plans. They should participate in the analysis of exceptions and recovery plans, and ensure that approved recovery plans are put into the formal control systems so that progress against the plans can be measured. They should prepare overall project reports and communicate project information to other management who need to be informed about the project.

The degree to which project management should participate in discussion of details is dependent upon the situation and the individuals involved. As far as I know, there is no valid guideline for such participation. There are good Project Managers who bore into many technical details, and there are equally good ones who rely totally on the process, the control system, and their administrative skills to attain their objectives.

Control Process

There are three steps in the control process, and these steps repeat throughout the life of a project.

1. Project status information—on activities and resource consumption—should be collected at points defined in the project plan. In addition, status information should be collected informally through a "grapevine" or "ear to the ground" process.

2. Recovery plans for exceptions to planned progress should be developed and approved by the responsible individuals.

3. The status reports and recovery plans should be published.

The repeating cycle of the three steps imposes order on the project. It creates a structure of the execution phase. A simple test of a project is whether a cycle of status determination, recovery planning and formal reporting has been established. If it has not, experience indicates that the project probably is not under control. If it has, the project may be under control, and you will have to look deeper, as described in the next section, to find out.

Guidelines for Status Reporting and Recovery Planning

Certain fundamental principles are applicable to the development of status reports and corrective action plans. Perhaps the most fundamental principle is that, for one reason or another, the project will not proceed as planned. Reasons normally include both faulty planning and faulty execution. This principle does not change the need for a plan, or course. Whether you are building a house or managing a project, you need a blueprint. The fact that the blueprint will prove to be inaccurate in some respects does not mean that you do not need it.

Given this fundamental principle and the objective of bringing the project in on schedule within budget, the remaining fundamentals are clear:

1. Identifying exceptions to plan as soon as possible after they occur is essential. Exception may involve resources or activities. They may involve either planned activities or resource usage, or totally new activities or resource requirements that were not foreseen during planning. The basic tool to identify exceptions should be the formal system, using status points in the plan. The status points, as you recall, were established at short enough intervals so that recovery would be possible if trouble were identified at the status points.

The facts of life are that the formal system will sometimes be slow or inaccurate, for example because of pressure to report satisfactory progress. You should establish some informal contacts, a "grapevine" that will pick up project scuttlebutt and the like. Much of the information obtained in such a fashion will be useless, but occasionally a grain of truth will emerge. In addition to being an adjunct to the formal system for status reporting purposes, this is virtually the only way to identify potential problems when project progress to date has not been affected.

2. The response to identified problems must be quick and effective. Recovery plans must be prepared, analyzed, and approved rapidly. Problem review sessions should not be allowed to end without a plan to fix the problem or a specific assignment in that direction. Decision matters, especially those affecting the overall project schedule or budget, should be surfaced immediately to the level of management that can make the required decisions.

Recovery planning usually includes making up activities that are behind schedule, adding new activities or resources, or reducing excessive resource consumption without changing activities' output. Sometimes activities must be redefined, however. A situation may develop in which accomplishing a planned activity will require far more resources than can be justified, and the proper action may be to eliminate the activity or reduce its scope. In such a case, the decision must be made quickly before more resources are wasted.

3. The response to problems should include procedures to reduce the chance of their recurrence or occurrence of other problems. Problems should be recorded on "Trouble Logs" and monitored until they are completely cleared up.

Each recovery plan should be challenged with the question: what is being done differently that will cause the recovery plan to succeed where the original plan failed? The reason for each problem should be determined and positive action taken to prevent it from happening again. The impact of a problem on other items in the plan should be determined in order to avoid a domino effect. This may be easy or difficult, depending on the project and the tools being used. For example, a network system can be very useful in such an analysis.

4. Recovery planning should be thorough. Timeliness is usually more important in recovery planning than it was in the original Planning phase, but the process should be the same. Sometimes quick-and-dirty recovery planning may be required in order to get the project turned around, but it does not replace the need for thorough replanning when the necessary time becomes available.

One company that I know of got themselves into trouble by not following these fundamentals on a Material Requirements Planning (MRP) project. MRP is a computerized production and inventory control technique. It works by "exploding" production schedules into time-phased requirements for constituent components and material by using computerized bills of material and predetermined decision rules for stocking and inventory replenishment. The project manager had schedules for some project activities but not for some other activities that required the same people. In addition, his approach to recovery planning consisted only of eliciting commitments from his supervisors that they would catch up somehow. During the execution of the project, some activities were not accomplished as planned and some new activities arose. In my experience, this is normal on MRP projects. The first mistake in reacting to the exceptions was the inadequate recovery planning that relied on supervisors' commitments and their subsequent whipcracking over their subordinates. Rational analyses of the problems would have been more useful. When the pressure techniques failed, as they often do, it was recognized that certain activities' schedules would not be met. Because other schedules and personnel assignments had not been made, however, it was impossible to determine the effect of the slippages on the overall project schedule. Needless to say, there was a great deal of unpleasantness over the project manager's position that he was not going to meet his schedule but that he did not know how much he would be late.

Documentation

Documentation from the planning phase is the foundation for controlling the execution phase. Documentation from the execution phase provides continuous verification that the project is under control as it proceeds towards its conclusion. Documentation is the scoreboard that tells you if your team is winning.

The execution documentation should be based on the planning documentation, for ease of communication and to ensure that all essential information has been included. On many projects, the format that was appropriate for display of planned events, activities, and resource consumption will be equally appropriate for display of the actual occurrences. Sometimes, both planned and actual data can be displayed on the same document. This approach not only improves communication and understanding, but also assists in reducing the administrative burden of documentation. Automated systems may also help to reduce the amount of "administrivia" if many or all reports can be automatically generated from a simple set of input data.

Summary documentation during the execution phase should also parallel the planning documentation. It should be based on the general (macro level) plan produced during the planning phase. Execution documentation at a level different from either the general or the detailed plan is difficult to understand because there is nothing to which it can be related.

Documentation of exception conditions should clearly describe the planned condition, the actual condition, analysis of the problem and its impact, and the corrective action required or initiated. At its lowest level, dealing with specific exceptions such documentation can be directly useful in reacting to the conditions and solving the problems, as well as in communicating the situation to interested persons. When summarized and compared to a summary of the project plan, the documentation of exceptions should be the key indicator of project status to project management and other management. The information to

be summarized should be based on the elements of the plan. For example, if specific resource consumption objectives were planned, exceptions to the plan might be summarized in absolute value, compared to planned objectives in terms of percentage overrun or underrun, and extrapolated to end-of-project status.

Project management should at all times have an emotional or subjective impression of the status of the project. If this impression is not the same as the impression conveyed by the formal status reports, then something is amiss, and an investigation is warranted. Formal systems cannot entirely replace "gut feeling."

Recovery planning generally should be documented in the same way as the original planning phase. Recovery plans may be integrated into the overall project plan, using different notation to distinguish the recovery plans from the original plans. Recovery plans should not simply overlay the original plans, because of the potential loss of knowledge that recovery plans were necessary, which could lead to a false sense of security. It is seldom wise to bury the fact that replanning was required. It is also not appropriate to skip the approval process on recovery plans. They should be subjected to the same kinds of review as the original plan, possibly with increased attention to timeliness. The review may be less extensive if fewer resources are involved than in the original plan and no overall project delay is anticipated. If significant resources are involved or if a delay in the overall project schedule is anticipated, the review should be thorough, of course.

Conclusion

I have described what I believe are the fundamentals of project management, the rules that must be followed to get something done. The rules are summarized in Exhibit I, a Project Management Checklist.

Discussion of specific kinds of projects is beyond the scope of this article. For this reason, I have not dealt with issues such as how to select a scheduling or budgeting technique for a project, how to estimate work content of activities, how to determine the specific activities and resources to be controlled, or how to report progress on activities and resource consumption.

Discussion of personnel and environmental considerations is also beyond my scope here. When implementing the fundamentals, of course, the characteristics of the environment and the individuals who are involved must be considered. A technique that works on one project may be unnecessary or unsuccessful on another project that is identical except for the individuals or the environment. **•jsm**

PROJECT MANAGEMENT CHECKLIST

I. **Project Planning**

   A.   Responsibilities

      1.   Project workers, supervisors and support technicians were heavily involved in the planning.
      2.   Project management directed preparation of the plan, provided their input to it, and accept responsibility for it.

   B.   Process

      1.   The General plan was approved prior to working on the Detailed plan.
      2.   The Detailed plan was prepared, analyzed for reasonableness and feasibility, and modified as required. The General plan was modified to be consistent with the Detailed plan.
      3.   The General and Detailed plans were formally approved and published.

   C.   Specifics of the Plan

      1.   Project activities and tangible output from each activity were defined.
      2.   Work content of each activity was estimated.
      3.   Each activity was scheduled and assigned to a resource; elapsed time of activities and multiple assignments to resources were minimized; responsibility for each item in the schedule is clear.
      4.   Status points were included for measurement of activities' progress and resource consumption.
      5.   Recovery time and resources were provided, either implicitly or explicitly.
      6.   The plan was adjusted to obtain efficient and effective use of resources.
      7.   The General plan covered all major items over the life of the project, and the Detailed plan covered all items in the near future.
      8.   Status points in the Detailed plan were established such that recovery would not be difficult if problems were identified at the status points.

   D.   Documentation

      1.   Wherever possible, proven documentation procedures were used.
      2.   All items (activities, resources) that were planned and are to be controlled during project execution were documented.

   E.   Approvals

      1.   Approvals of the plan were obtained from the persons who must support the plan or not oppose it in order for the project to be successful.

II. **Execution of the Plan**

   A.   Responsibilities

      1.   Project workers and supervisors have been monitoring progress, reporting status, and developing corrective action plans.
      2.   Project management has carried out their responsibilities for analysis and approval of status reports and recovery plans, and for communication with upper management and other persons who are outside of day-to-day project activities.

   B.   Process

      1.   A structured process of status reporting, recovery planning, and publication of project progress reports was implemented.

   C.   Implementation of Control Guidelines

      1.   Formal and informal systems were implemented to identify exceptions to plan soon after they occurred or before they occurred.
      2.   Response time to problems has been short; recovery plans have been prepared and approved quickly, and management has been available to make decisions.
      3.   The response to problems has included analyses of why they occurred and positive actions to ensure that they or similar problems will not occur in the future.
      4.   When problems have occurred, their impact on other items in the plan has been determined, and the other items have been replanned as required.
      5.   Recovery planning has been thorough, based on the Planning fundamentals.

   D.   Documentation

      1.   The documentation procedures were designed to be consistent with the Planning documentation and to make use of it wherever possible.
      2.   Detailed documentation of status, including exception conditions, has been developed and used in problem analysis and recovery planning. Summary documentation of project status and recovery plans has been prepared.
      3.   Recovery planning documentation has preserved visibility of the original plan and the variance of the recovery plan from it.

   E.   Approvals

      1.   Approvals have been obtained for all changes to the original plan; the approval process was the same as for the original plan, with the depth of the review reflecting the significance of the changes.

EXHIBIT I

Applying Corporate Software Development Policies

E.A. Goldberg

December 6, 1977
January 27, 1978

SEID SOFTWARE DEVELOPMENT POLICIES OBJECTIVES

- Provide Management Visibility
- Reduce Software Development Risks
- Identify and Work Problems Early
- Provide Compatibility with New Trends in DoD Software Acquisition

SOFTWARE DEVELOPMENT POLICY APPLICABILITY

- Applies to All New SEID Projects Developing Software
- Applies to Both Deliverable and Non-Deliverable Software
- Includes Formal Procedure for Requesting Deviations and Waivers
  – SEID General Manager Must Approve Deviations and Waivers for All Deliverable Software
  – Deviations Must Be Identified during Proposal Phase

WHAT'S NEW

- Deviations and Waivers Must Be Formally Approved
  – Conformance to Good Standards and Practices Is No Longer the Exception but the Rule
- Verification Required
  – Requirements Verification
  – Design Verification
- Test-Related Activities
  – Test All Requirements
  – Perform Off-Nominal Testing
  – Determine Readiness for Acceptance Testing
- New Planning Documentation
  – Software End-Product Acceptance Plan
  – Configuration Management Plan
  – Quality Assurance Plan

Reprinted with permission from *TRW, Defense and Space Group*, Dec. 1977. Copyright © 1977 by TRW.

SEID SOFTWARE POLICY HIERARCHY

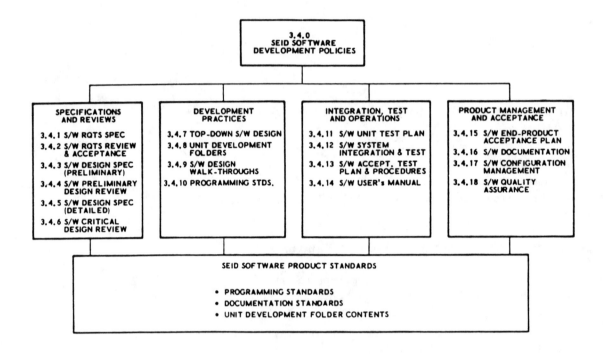

SEID POLICY OVER THE SOFTWARE LIFE CYCLE

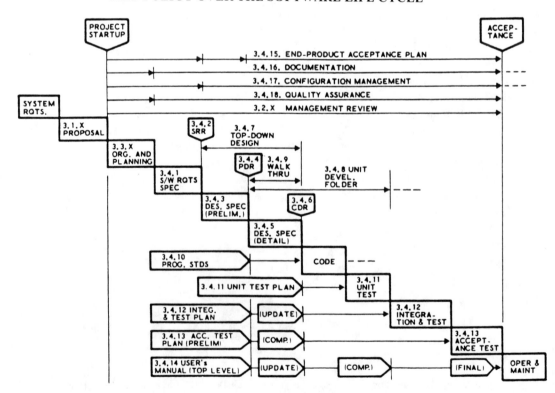

150

SPECIFICATIONS AND REVIEWS

SEID POLICY REQUIRES SOFTWARE PROJECTS TO

- Prepare Written Software Requirements Specification to Control Functional, Performance, and Interface Requirements
- Analyze and Evaluate Software Requirements Specification for Technical and Contractual Acceptability
- Conduct Software Requirements Review (SRR) to Achieve Written Customer Agreement on Software Requirements
- Prepare Software Preliminary Design Specification Which Establishes Design Baseline for Detailed Design of Software End Products
- Verify Preliminary Software Design and Demonstrate That Aggregate Data Processing Resource Budgets Are within Total Available Resources
- Conduct Preliminary Design Review
- Prepare Software Detailed Design Document from Which Code Will Be Produced
- Verify Detailed Software Design
- Conduct Critical Design Review to Obtain Commitment to an Acceptance Test Program and Commitment to Proceed into Coding Phase

POLICY 3.4.1
SOFTWARE REQUIREMENTS SPECIFICATION

> SIED Software Projects Shall Prepare a Software Requirements Specification to Control Functional, Performance, and Interface Requirements for Software End Products

This Policy
Requires
Project to

- Produce Software Requirements Specification Prior to Software Requirements Review in Format Specified by Contract or SEID Standards
- Obtain Written Customer Approval of this Specification as Basis for Computer Program and Data Base End Product Acceptance
- Obtain Written TRW and Customer Approval for All Subsequent Changes to Specification

POLICY 3.4.2
SOFTWARE REQUIREMENTS REVIEW AND ACCEPTANCE

SEID Software Projects Shall Conduct a Software Requirements Review (SRR) to Achieve Written Agreement with Customer on Provisions of Software Requirements Specification

---

This Policy Requires Project to

- Prepare For SRR by:
  - Analyzing and Evaluating Software Requirements Specification for Technical and Contractual Acceptability
  - Developing Response to Each Problem Identified in Analysis or in Customer Review Comments
- Conduct an SRR for TRW-Generated and Customer-Provided Requirements
  - Present Analysis Results; Describe Analysis Techniques
  - Address Issues and Problems
  - Document Agreements and Action Items and Obtain Project Manager and Customer Signature
  - Review Software End Product Acceptance Plan
- Obtain Policy Waiver if Customer Will Not Approve Updated Software Requirements Specification

REQUIRED ANALYSIS TO PREPARE FOR SRR

- Analyze Total Requirements Set for Completeness, Consistency, Testability, and Technical Feasibility from
  - Flow-Oriented Viewpoint
  - Functional Breakdown Viewpoint
- Analyze Each Individual Requirement to Verify
  - Mandatory Requirements Are Clearly Distinguished from Design Goals and Options
  - Compatibility with System-Level Objectives
  - Technical Feasibility
  - Testability
  - Completeness
- Analyze Total Requirements Set for Compatibility with Schedule, Funding, and Resources

POLICY 3.4.3
SOFTWARE DESIGN SPECIFICATION (PRELIMINARY)

> SEID Software Projects Shall Prepare a Preliminary Design Specification That Establishes the Design Baseline for Detailed Design of the Software End Products

This Policy
Requires
Project to

- Produce Preliminary Design Specification Prior to Preliminary Design Review in Format Specified by Contract or SEID Standards
- Demonstrate That Aggregate Data Processing Resource Budgets Are within Total Available Resources/Requirements
- Establish Preliminary Design Specifications as Design Baseline after Preliminary Design Review

POLICY 3.4.4
SOFTWARE PRELIMINARY DESIGN REVIEW

> SEID Software Projects Shall Perform Design and Planning Activities Required to Establish a Preliminary Software Design Baseline and to Proceed into Detailed Design and Development

This Policy
Requires
Project to

- Provide Reviewers with Specified Review Materials
- Prepare for Preliminary Design Review (PDR) by:
  - Verifying the Preliminary Software Design
  - Reviewing Implementation Plans and Project/Performer Commitments
  - Identifying Technical and Contractual Issues, Including Non-Satisfied Requirements
- Conduct PDR Which Addresses:
  - Design Overview, Identifying Software Structure, Design Rationale, Operation in System Environment, User Interface
  - Design Verification Results
  - Overview of Implementation and Test Plans
  - Technical and Contractual Issues
- Document and Obtain Customer and TRW Written Approval on Disposition of Identified Technical and Contractual Issues, Agreements and Action Items

REVIEW MATERIALS REQUIRED PRIOR TO PDR

- Preliminary Design Specification
- Approved Software Requirements Specification (Including Interface Specifications)
- Proposed Changes to Software Requirements Specification
- Preliminary Users Manual
- Preliminary Acceptance Test Plan
- Preliminary Performance Estimates

REQUIRED PRELIMINARY DESIGN VERIFICATION ACTIVITIES

- Verify:
  - Every Requirement Has Been Accounted for
  - Design Is Valid from Flow-Oriented and Functional Breakdown Points of View
  - Aggregate Design Budgets Satisfy Software Requirements Specification and Do Not Exceed Physical and Functional Limitations
- Substantiate Software Design and Algorithm Selection through Engineering Analysis
- Identify Design Approaches and Alternatives for High Risk Items

POLICY 3.4.5
SOFTWARE DESIGN SPECIFICATION (DETAILED)

SEID Software Projects Shall Update and Expand the Preliminary Design Specification into a Detailed Design (Build-To) Specification from Which the Code Will Be Produced

---

This Policy
Requires
Project to

- Produce Detailed Design Specification Prior to Critical Design Review in Format Specified by Contract or SEID Standards
- Adhere to Basic Control Structures Allowed in Structured Programming
- Update Detailed Design Specification after Integration Testing to Reflect As-Built Software

POLICY 3.4.6
SOFTWARE CRITICAL DESIGN REVIEW

SEID Software Projects Shall Conduct a Critical Design Review to Gain Concurrence in the Adequacy of the Detailed Software Design, and Obtain Commitment to Proceed into the Coding Phase and Commitment to an Acceptance Test Program

---

This Policy
Requires
Project to

- Provide Reviewers with Specified Review Materials
- Prepare for Critical Design Review (CDR) by
  - Verifying Detailed Software Design
  - Reviewing Detailed Implementation and Test Plans and Project/Performer Commitments
  - Identifying Critical Issues, Including Unsatisfied Requirements
- Conduct CDR Which Addresses
  - Design Overview Identifying Operation in System Environment; User Interface
  - Design Verification Results
  - Overview of Implementation and Test Plans
  - Technical and Contractual Issues
- Document and Obtain Customer and TRW Written Approval on Disposition of All Identified Critical Issues, Agreements, and Action Items

REVIEW MATERIALS REQUIRED FOR CDR

- Detailed Design Specification
- Current Software Requirements Specification (Including Interface Specifications)
- Proposed Changes to Software Requirements Specifications
- Updated or Current Acceptance Test Plan
- Design Evaluation or Trade Study Results
- Updated Performance Estimates

EXAMPLES OR PROJECT MANAGER'S DISCRETIONARY AREAS

- Documentation
  - Level of Detail and Size of Specifications
  - Number of Volumes and Relationship to Specific End Products
- Degree of Formality
  - Preliminary Design Baseline
  - Detail Design Baseline
  - Associated Change Control Procedures
- Use of Requirements Specification or Design Specification Languages
- Analysis Required for SRR, PDR, CDR
  - Could Be Full Scale System Simulation or Simple Hand Analysis
- SRR, PDR, CDR
  - Presentation Format and Material Used
  - Duration

SEID POLICY OVER THE SOFTWARE LIFE CYCLE

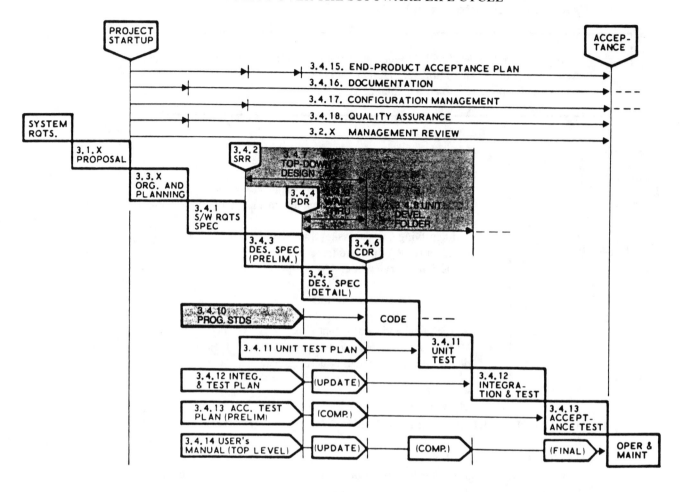

DEVELOPMENT PRACTICES

SEID Policy Requires Software Projects to

- Perform Software Design Using a Top-Down Approach
- Prepare and Maintain a Unit Development Folder (UDF) for Each Software Unit
- Conduct Design Walk-Throughs at Unit Level as Design of Each Unit Completed
- Use Programming Standards during Software Design, Code, and Maintenance Which Include:
  - Flowcharting Standards
  - Structured Programming Standards for All Higher Order Languages
  - Coding Standards
  - In-Line Commenting and Preface Text Standards

POLICY 3.4.7
TOP-DOWN SOFTWARE DESIGN

SEID Software Projects Shall Design Software Using a Top-Down Approach

---

This Policy
Requires
Project to

- Perform Design by Starting with Top-Level System Function, Proceeding through Downward Allocation, Evaluation, and Iteration
  − Initiate Design by Establishing Functional Design Hierarchy, Where Top-Level Is Over-All Software Mission
  − Break Down and Partition Software into Blocks for Successive Levels of Greater Functional Detail
  − Allocate and Map Requirements onto Design Hierarchy
  − Structure Lowest Level of Software Components So That Program Control Logic Can Implement All Input Output Paths
- Prototype Critical Lower Level Components When Appropriate

POLICY 3.4.8
UNIT DEVELOPMENT FOLDERS

SEID Software Projects Shall Prepare and Maintain a Unit Development Folder (UDF) for Each Software Unit

---

This Policy
Requires
Project to

- Establish UDF's within One Month after POR, Using Format Specified by Project or SEID Standards
- Periodically Review UDF's to Assess Technical Adequacy and Schedule Compliance
- Periodically Audit UDF's in Accordance with Quality Assurance Plan to Assess Compliance with Project Standards
- Maintain UDF's until As-Built Software Documentation Is Baselined

UNIT DEVELOPMENT FOLDER COVER SHEET

Program Name_____

Unit Name_____ Custodian_____

Routines Included_____

Section No.	Description	Due Date	Date Completed	Originator	Reviewer/Date
1	Requirements				
2	Design Prelim: Description "Code to" "As Built":				
3	Functional Capabilities List				
4	Unit Code				
5	Unit Test Plan				
6	Test Case Results				
7	Problem Reports				
8	Notes				
9	Reviewer's Comments				

POLICY 3.4.9
SOFTWARE DESIGN WALK-THROUGHS

> SEID Software Projects Shall Conduct Unit Design Walk-Throughs

This Policy Requires Project to

- Conduct Design Walk-Throughs at Unit Level as Design of Each Unit Is Completed
  - One or More Individuals Other Than Originator Must Review (Designer/Programmer/Tester Desirable)
  - Originator Presents Design in Presence of Reviewers
  - Scope Includes Checks for
    * Design Responsiveness to Requirements
    * Design Completeness and Consistency
    * Flow of Data
    * Testability
    * Error Recovery Procedures
    * Modularity
- Identify in Writing Problems Uncovered in Walk-Throughs

POLICY 3.4.10
PROGRAMMING STANDARDS

SEID Software Projects Shall Use Programming Standards during Software Design, Code, and Maintenance

---

This Policy
Requires
Project to

- Produce Project-Specific Programming Standards Document Prior to PDR Unless Programming Standards in "SEID Software Product Standards" Are Used
- Conduct Periodic Audits of Design Documentation and Code in Accordance with Quality Assurance Plan to Assess Compliance with Programming Standards
- Maintain Programming Standards Current during Software Design, Code, and Maintenance

SEID SOFTWARE PRODUCT STANDARDS

- Complements Software Development Policies by Providing
  - Outlines of Documents Required by Policies
  - Minimum Contents for Unit Development Folders
  - Specific Programming Standards
    * Flow Charts
    * Structured Programming
    * Preface Commentary
    * Coding
- Deviations
  - If Standards and Policy Affected, Policy Deviation Only
  - If Only Standards Affected, Standards Deviation Only
    * Approved by Project Manager and Project Review Authority

EXAMPLES OF PROJECT MANAGER'S DISCRETIONARY AREAS

- Design Walk Throughs
  - Selection of Reviewers
  - Duration of Review
- Problem/Corrective Action Disposition from Audits and Walk Throughs
- Top-Down Coding and Other Good Practices
- Level of Detail in UDF'S
  - Requirements
  - Detailed Design
  - Unit Test Plans
  - Unit Test Results
- Use of Software Design Languages

SEID POLICY OVER THE SOFTWARE LIFE CYCLE

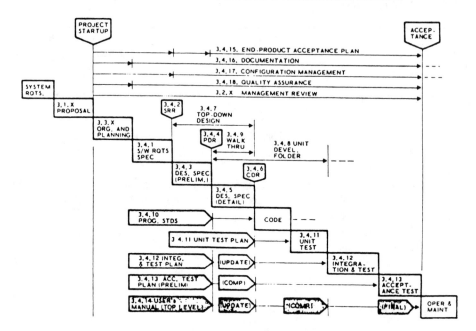

INTEGRATION, TEST, AND OPERATIONS

SEID Policy Requires Project to
- Prepare an Overall Unit Test Plan Defining Testing Standards for Unit-Level Testing
- Prepare Integration and Test Plans and Conduct Integration and Test Activities to
  – Integrate Software into Nominally Executing Production
  – Demonstrate Satisfaction of All Software Requirements
  – Demonstrate Software Operability over a Range of Conditions
- Establish Software Test Baseline
- Review Test Results and Readiness for Acceptance Tests
- Prepare Acceptance Test Plans (and or Operator-Oriented Software) and Achieve Written Agreement for Customer Acceptance
- Conduct Acceptance Test Program with Independent Test Organization
- Produce a User's Manual Containing Instructions for Operating the Software

POLICY 3.4.11
SOFTWARE UNIT TEST PLAN

SEID Software Projects Shall Prepare an Overall Unit Test Plan That Defines the Testing Standards for Unit-Level Testing

This Policy Requires Project to	• Produce Unit Test Plan in Format Specified by Contract or SEID Standards • Review and Approve Unit Test Plan Prior to CDR • Does Not Contain unit-Specific Test Cases—These Appear Only in UDF

160

POLICY 3.4.12
SOFTWARE SYSTEM INTEGRATION AND TEST

SEID Software Projects Shall Plan for and Conduct Software Integration and Test Activities to Be Accomplished Prior to Acceptance Testing Which
- Integrate Software Units into a Cohesive, Nominally Executing Product
- Demonstrate Satisfaction of All Software Requirements
- Demonstrate Software Operability over a Range of Operating Conditions

This Policy Requires Project to

- Produce Integration and Test Plans in Format Specified by Contract or SEID Standards
- Produce Plans within Two Months of PDR, Update Prior to CDR, and Update as Appropriate Prior to Test Initiation
- Prepare Test Activity Network Showing Integration and Test Strategy in Terms of Test Event and Schedule Interdependencies
- Design Tests to Exercise Software Throughout Anticipated Range of Operating Conditions
- Employ Discrepancy Reporting System after Software Test Baseline Is Established
- Review Test Planning and Preparation Activities Prior to Test Initiation
- Review Test Results and Readiness for Acceptance Testing after Test Completion

POLICY 3.4.13
SOFTWARE ACCEPTANCE TEST PLAN AND PROCEDURES

SEID Software Projects Shall Prepare an Acceptance Test Plan and Acceptance Test Procedures

This Policy Requires Project to

- Produce Preliminary Acceptance Test Plan for PDR and Complete Acceptance Test Plan for CDR
- Achieve Written Agreement with Customer That Execution of Defined Test Case in Manners Satisfying Acceptance Criteria, Will Result in Customer Acceptance
- Obtain Written Approval by TRW and Customer for All Changes to Approved Plan
- Produce Acceptance Test Procedures for Interactive or Operator-Oriented Software
- Ensure Acceptance Test Program Is Directed by an Independent Project Test Organization Not Reporting to Development Organization

161

POLICY 3.4.14
SOFTWARE USER'S MANUAL

SEID Software Projects Shall Produce a Software User's Manual Containing Instructions for Operating the Deliverable Software System

This Policy
Requires
Project to

- Produce Software User's Manual in Format Specified in Contract or SEID Standards
  - Provide Top-Level Operational Description and Specification of Man/Machine Interfaces in PDR Version
  - Update User's Manual for CDR
  - Produce Complete Preliminary User's Manual Prior to Software Integration, for Use and Validation during Testing
  - Deliver Final User's Manual When Software Delivered to Customer

EXAMPLES OF PROJECT MANAGER'S DISCRETIONARY AREAS

- Test Plans
  - Level Of Detail
  - Size
  - Number of Physical Volumes
- Degree of Formality
  - Change Control
  - Discrepancy Reporting System
  - When to Establish Test Baseline
- Specific Organization for Acceptance
  - Several Options Acceptable
- Use of Test Data Folders and Other Good Test Practices

SEID POLICY OVER THE SOFTWARE LIFE CYCLE

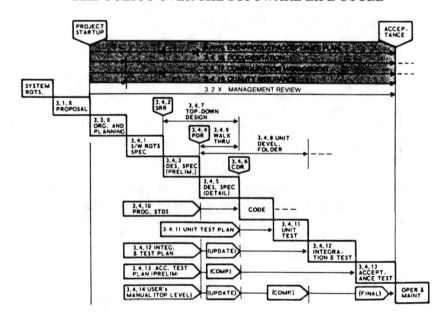

162

PRODUCT MANAGEMENT AND ACCEPTANCE

SEID Policy Requires Software Projects to

- Produce a Software End-Product Acceptance Plan Covering All End-Products and Services Called for by Contract
- Produce, at a Minimum, Mandatory Set of Documents Complying with Provisions of Contract and SEID Policy/Standards
- Prepare a Configuration Management Plan and Perform Configuration Management Functions Required to Establish a Series of Baseline and Control Changes to Establish Baselines
- Operate a Software Product Development Library
- Prepare a Quality Assurance Plan and Perform Quality Assurance Functions Appropriate to Contract and Product

POLICY 3.4.15
SOFTWARE END-PRODUCT ACCEPTANCE PLAN

> SEID Software Projects Shall Follow an Orderly Procedure, Governed by a Written Plan, to Prepare for and Achieve Customer Acceptance of All End-Products and Services Called for by Contact

This Policy
Requires
Project to

- Produce a Software End-Product Acceptance Plan
  - Review Draft at SRR
  - Obtain Project and Customer Approval before End of PDR
- Maintain a File of Acceptance-Related Data
- Track Progress toward Acceptance (Per Plan)
- Conduct an Acceptance Audit Near End of Contract Period

POLICY 3.4.16
SOFTWARE DOCUMENTATION

> SEID Software Projects Shall Plan and Produce a Set of Software Documents That Comply with the Contract and SEID Policies

This Policy
Requires
Project to

- Identify Project Document Set
  - Early in Project Planning (or Proposal)
  - Identify Title, Purpose, Schedule for Each Document
- Use Format from (in Order of Procedence)
  - Contract
  - SEID Software Product Standards
  - Project Specific Outline (Only When Contract/Standards Do Not Provide an Outline)
- Choose Document Size and Binding to Suit Project/Customer/User Needs

MANDATORY DOCUMENTS

• Software Requirements Specification	3.4.1	2.1
• Software Design Specification	3.4.3 and	2.5
• Software End-Product Acceptance Plan	3.4.15	2.2
• Software Unit Test Plan	3.4.11	2.6
• Software Integration and Test Plan	3.4.12	2.7
• Software Acceptance Test Plan	3.4.13	2.8
• Software User's Manual	3.4.14	2.9
• Software Configuration Management Plan	3.4.17	2.4
• Software Quality Assurance Plan	3.4.18	2.3

POLICY 3.4.17
SOFTWARE CONFIGURATION MANAGEMENT

> SEID Software Projects Shall Perform Configuration Management Functions Required to Establish a Series of Baselines and Control Changes to Them

This Policy
Requires
Project to

- Prepare a CM Plan, and Get It Approved, Prior to SRR, by
  - Project Manager
  - SEID PA Manager
- Follow Approved CM Procedures for Issuance, Pretention, Change Control, Packaging, Delivery
- Operate a Software Product Development Library

MINIMUM BASELINES

BASELINES	ESTABLISHED
Requirements	At SRR Close-Out
Design	At PDR Close-Out
Test	During Integration and Test
Product	At Software Acceptance

POLICY 3.4.18
SOFTWARE QUALITY ASSURANCE

SEID Software Projects Shall Plan and Perform Quality Assurance Functions Appropriate to Contract and Product

---

This Policy
Requires
Project to

- Prepare a QA Plan
- Get Plan Approved (within One Month of Project Startup) by
  - Project Manager
  - SEID PA Manager
- Identify Person/Organization That Will Perform Project QA Functions
- Provide for Periodic QA Audits
  - Relationship to Contract
  - Relationship to Policies and Standards

EXAMPLES OF PROJECT MANAGER'S DISCRETIONARY AREAS

- Document Size (Level of Detail) and Binding
  - Two-Page IOC May Suffice
  - Many Binding Options: Separate Volumes Versus Sections of a Comprehensive Project Plan
- CM Task Definition, Activity Level, and Detailed Procedures Subject to
  - Minimum Tasks Specified in Contract/Policies
  - Plan Approval by SEID PA Manager
- QA Task Definition, Activity Level, and Detailed Procedures, Subject to
  - Minimum Tasks Specified in Contract/Policies
  - Plan Approval by SEID PA Manager
- Degree of Formality of CM and QA Controls

CUSTOMER BENEFITS

We Can Now Guarantee Our Customers That They Will Get the Same Brand of Good Management Provided on Showcase Projects

C.W. Besserer-March 1977

- Customer Always Knows What He Is Getting
  - Requirements Are Documented and Baselined
  - End-Product Acceptance Plan Establishes What Will Be Delivered and When
  - Traceability Is Established from Requirements to Design to Test
  - Early Users' Manual Explain Man/Machine Interfaces

- Customer Can Now Expect Certain Minimum Standards of Testing
  - Requirements and Design Are Verified Prior to Associated Review Point
  - All Requirements Are Tested
  - Software Is Exercised over Range of Off-Nominal Operating Conditions
  - Early Acceptance Test Plan Establishes Acceptance Criteria
  - An Independent Project Test Organization Directs Acceptance Test

- Customer Achieves Assurance of Software Quality through Schedule Reviews
  - Customer Involvement in Reviews Encouraged
  - Formal Review Points at SRR, PDR, And CDR Establish Requirements and Design Baselines
  - Design Walk-Through Held to Catch Design Errors
  - Readiness Review for Acceptance Tests
  - Quality Assurance Audits Ensure Policies and Standards Being Followed (Review Requirements, Design, Documentation, Code, Testing, and Configuration Management)

- Customer Receives Set of Documentation Appropriate to Customer/User/Project Needs
  - If Customer Format Not Specified Format of SEID Product Standard Used
  - UDF's Minimize Documentation Costs by Providing a Timely Accessible Collection of All Data Pertaining to a Unit

- Customer Experiences Shorter Project Start-up Transients
  - Uniform Set of Policies and Standards Results in Ease of Personnel Transferability among Projects and in Minimal Personnel Retaining for New Projects
  - Universal Set of Programming Standards Avoids Need for Recreating Standards on Each New Project
  - Structured Programming and Top Down Design Results in More Uniform Software Development and Easier Software Maintainability

Inserting New Technologies into a Software Project

Edward Yourdon
Independent Management Consultant

A software development project is usually a part of an overall systems development project, whose purpose is to deliver new or improved functionality to a community of end users. The new system, with its highly visible "high tech" technology, is often a source of concern to some of the end users, who ask "How will this new technology affect me? Will it help me do my job better, or will it actually be a hindrance? Do I have any choice in using this new technology, or is it being forced on me from above?"

Ironically, participants in the software development project often ask the same questions of themselves as they build the system—for they often find that they themselves are required to use new and unfamiliar technology to build their system. Examples abound:

- New hardware, new terminals, inexpensive personal computers, and so on

- New programming languages (Ada, C, C++, Visual Basic, Delphi, and Java for instance)

- New database management systems, telecommunications systems, distributed systems, and client-server systems, among others

- New productivity tools (such as CASE, OOA, and OOD, visual tools, human-computer interface development tools)

- New project management methodologies

- New application areas (Internet, graphics, fly-by-wire aircraft systems, word processing, small-office and small-company applications, for example)

- New software paradigms (object-oriented development, formal methods, prototyping, reuse, viewpoints, SSADM)

Sometimes the new technology is a minor and insignificant part of the software development project. But when the new technology is a major component of the project—and especially when it is perceived as a critical component—a number of problems can occur. For instance, because the technology is new, the available in-house development staff usually needs training. This can present logistical and budgetary problems, as well as complicating the project schedule. As a result, some organizations avoid doing any training in the new technology; others will spend only enough money to train the project leader, who is then expected to pass the newly learned (and usually imperfectly learned) material—by word of mouth or by photocopying of course materials—to the rest of the project team. Only rarely does the organization invest the time and money to ensure that all of the project team members are properly trained to use the new technology.

Depending on the circumstances, there may be "political resistance" to the use of the new technology. Any of the following groups might object: the members of the project team; the project manager, or peers of the project manager; higher levels of management; members of the quality assurance department, members of the internal auditing department, members of the training department or DP standards department, and so on, and/or external auditors.

The reasons for such political resistance are myriad, and the reader can almost certainly supply his own list. Among the more common examples of resistance are the "not invented here" syndrome, the statement that "This is not the right time to try a new technology," and "We've always done things our own way, and it's always worked."

Furthermore, the new technology may be perceived as "the straw that breaks the camel's back." Some software projects have enough other problems (such as unrealistic schedules, uncooperative users, inexperienced management or staff) that the addition of a new, unfamiliar technology is "the last straw." The irony is that the new technology is often brought in in an attempt to solve those other project problems—for example, "There is no way we can develop all of this software in time using Pascal, so we'll bring in Visual Basic."

Worse, if the software development project is perceived as a failure, the new technology associated with the project may be blamed for the failure. Whether the blame is justified or not, it sometimes leads to a political decision (often accompanied by a great deal of emotion) to "throw the baby out with the bath water:"

to throw out the new technology and outlaw its use on subsequent projects.

And then, of course, there is the danger that the new technology doesn't work! For example, the project team might decide to use a fourth-generation programming language, only to discover later that it runs 10 times or 100 times less efficiently than the conventional third-generation languages; or the project team might use a new programmer workstation that doesn't work at all; or it might pick a database management system that has serious interface problems with the vendor's telecommunications system. Or it might fall victim to "vaporware:" new technology that looks promising but does not actually exist when the project team needs it.

But in my experience, project failures associated with new technology have more often been the result of "technology transfer" issues of the kind described above rather than failures in the technology itself. Technology is not perfect, to be sure; and the promises made by vendors of technology often exceed, by an order of magnitude, what can actually be delivered. But these failings of technology are overshadowed, time and again, by the failure of the project team and the project manager to properly assess and use the technology.

General Advice on New Technology

Sometimes the problem is not the new technology but inappropriate use of the new technology. The most common example of this is a desire on the part of the project team (or, sometimes, the project leader) to turn a development project into a research project in an attempt to experiment with and explore new technology. If the project team is far removed from the end user (geographically, politically, spiritually, and so on.) and if it does not understand the "bottom line" business objectives that led to the request for a new system in the first place, then it will be very easy for them to fall into this trap. And since the end user is not in a position to know whether new software development technology is necessary (he has enough trouble dealing with the technological impact of the new system), it is often up to the project manager to ensure that the project team does not fritter away its time and energy (and risk the success of the project) playing with technology for the sake of technology.

Another common problem is that of multiple new technologies being introduced simultaneously into a project—for example, a new programming language plus a new database management system plus a new project management methodology. In addition to exacerbating the problems that would have been experienced with any one new technology, there is another problem: incompatibility between the various new technologies. Sometimes the incompatibility is entirely technical in nature—the new programming language is incompatible with the new database management system, say, or the new programmer workstation is incompatible with the data dictionary that the rest of the organization uses—but more often, the incompatibility is one of terms, definitions, and semantics. For example, the terms and definitions associated with a new project management methodology (Microsoft Project, PSI's Guide to The Project Management Body of Knowledge, and so on) may be incompatible with the new software engineering approach—for example, with object-oriented analysis, visual developments, incremental and evolutionary processes, among others).

Finally, there is the problem of imposed technology—that is, the case where neither the project team nor the project manager has any desire to use a new technology, but is forced to do so by higher levels of management; outside or external standards; the organization's standards department; and/or the end user (who may have inherited the new technology from somewhere else).

Externally imposed technology (or anything else new that is externally imposed) is a real problem for the project manager: if it succeeds, the manager will get no credit; if it fails, the manager will get all of the blame. The most important thing for the project manager, in my experience, is to be sure that the entire project team presents a common, unified front to the rest of the organization. They can actively oppose the new technology; they can grudgingly accept it; they can announce an enthusiastic, "devil may care" attitude of adopting the new technology. But whatever they do, the project team (the individual programmers, analysts, and other team members) should be singing the same tune as the project manager. This requires a great deal of trust and communication between the project manager and the project team members; lacking that communication, such externally imposed new technology can act as a wedge that will drive the team apart from the manager.

Inserting New Technologies into a Software Project

From the comments above, one might conclude that it would be better not to use new technology in a software development project. But this is not realistic or practical, of course: There are a number of reasons—both good and bad—for implementing new technology. The trick is to incorporate new technology into the software development project without disrupting or threatening the success of the project. Having watched several software development projects go through this experience, I have found the following techniques to be of great help:

Make sure all interested parties know why the new technology is being used. It is important for the project manager to explain to subordinates, peers, and higher level managers why the new technology is being used; if appropriate, the project manager should also be prepared to explain the risks and the benefits of the new technology. Support from higher levels of management is also important: programmers and systems analysts will be reluctant to use a new technology if they sense that managers two or three levels above them are fundamentally disinterested in it or opposed to it.

Provide appropriate training before the project team uses the new technology. Though this suggestion should be an obvious one, I am constantly surprised by how often it is ignored. The project team is often given (a) no training, or (b) training six months before they have a chance to use the technology, or (c) training six months after they have begun using the new technology, or (d) superficial and inadequate training.

Try to use the new technology on a prototype or pilot project before using it on a "real" project. A pilot project in some other part of the software development organization can provide invaluable experience about the new technology; it can also provide one or more internal "consultants" who can offer assistance to the project team. If this is not possible (and it is usually beyond the control of the project manager to arrange such pilot projects), then the project manager should consider using the new technology to build a subset, or a prototype, of the overall system that the project team is working on. For example, a three-to-six-month miniproject could be formed to build a small piece of the overall system with the new technology. This would provide hands-on experience that would prove invaluable for the overall project, which might continue on for another two to three years. One of the advantages of this approach is that it allows the organization to develop its own customized "user's manual" to show all of the project members how to use the new technology. Sometimes this user's manual can take the form of a standard textbook or a set of training materials; more often, though, it will be an edited amalgam of several different textbooks, illustrated with examples that are pertinent to the organization.

Get outside technical assistance throughout the project. External consulting assistance may appear expensive, but it usually represents a very minor part of the overall project budget—and it is an incredibly cheap form of "insurance" when using new, complex technology that could threaten the success of the project. The consulting assistance can be provided by the new technology's vendor, if appropriate, or can be obtained from other outside organizations. In some cases, the consulting can be provided from other groups within the organization; however, my experience has been that such consulting is generally not successful if it is provided by the organization's training department or standards department. In any case, the technical support or consulting assistance should be budgeted explicitly so that it will not be considered a "luxury," to be discarded at the first available moment.

Give the project team a forum for voicing their concerns and problems. In almost every case, the project team will run into problems as they begin to use the technology. Even if the problems are not catastrophic, the project team will feel a certain amount of frustration and resentment—and if they are made to feel that their concerns are not legitimate, there is a significant danger that they will, to whatever extent possible, avoid using the new technology. (If the new technology is a new mainframe computer, they may not be able to avoid it at all, aside from the extreme action of quitting; but if the new technology is something "soft" like a new project management methodology or a new software engineering discipline, it may be very easy to stop using it.) Periodic "gripe" sessions—perhaps including the new technology's vendor, and with the consultants mentioned above—are a good way for the project team to let off steam, as well as a good way for the project manager to get an early warning of potentially serious problems.

Use common sense, on a case-by-case basis, to determine exceptions to the use of the new technology. A new technology may have been adopted on the assumption that it will be universally appropriate for the project—but as the real work of the project gets under way, it may become evident that the new technology isn't appropriate in certain areas. For example, the project team may have decided to use a new fourth-generation language for their software development work; it may be discovered midway through the project that a more conventional third-generation language—even (ugh!) assembly—is necessary for certain parts of the system where throughput and efficiency are important. Such decisions need to be made on a case-by-case basis, and they should be made by the project manager (who, in turn, may have to consult with outside auditors, higher levels of management, and so on) rather than by the software developers themselves.

Avoid paralysis. In the extreme case, the project team can become thoroughly overwhelmed by the new technology and gradually end up spending all of its time (a) trying to understand the new technology, (b) arguing about the merits of the new technology, or (c) trying to make it work. For example, a project team using structured analysis for the first time will sometimes experience "analysis paralysis," and the project manager will find that the entire team is spending all of its time arguing about whether or not they are correctly following the procedures of structured analysis that they have read in a textbook. The project manager must watch for this paralysis and force the team to move on—either by making hard, unilateral decisions on his or her own, or by making use of the consulting assistance described earlier to answer questions about the new technology.

Necessary Attributes of a Good Software Engineering Technology

An equally important concept in inserting new technologies into a software development project is the selection of the proper technology for the task at hand. Below is a list of "rules" that can be applied to selecting an appropriate technology:

- The technology is documented—The procedures for using the technology exist in a document or user's manual.

- The technology is repeatable—Each application of the technology is the same.

- The technology is teachable—Sufficient detailed procedures and examples exist to be able to instruct qualified people in its application.

- The technology is based on proven techniques—The technology implements proven fundamental procedures or other simpler technologies (for example, a new CASE tool may implement the Yourdon technique).

- The technology has been validated—The technology has been shown to work correctly on large numbers of applications.

- The technology is correct for the task at hand—The capabilities of the technology are appropriate for job to be done.

Summary

In summary, the most effective and economical way to implement a new technology into a software project is to

- ensure that all interested parties are aware as to why the new technology is being used,

- provide appropriate and timely training for the new technology,

- use the new technology on a "real" project (a real project should be an important but not critical software system or a subset of the current project),

- get outside technical assistance throughout the project on the technology being introduced,

- give the project team an outlet for their concerns and problems,

- use common sense to determine when to use, and when not to use, the new technology, and, finally,

- avoid technology paralysis (spending more time on the technology rather than the problem at hand).

A Final Thought

In any technological field, especially the field of computer software, it is easy to become overly enamored with technology issues. Those who develop software systems are quite accustomed to the cultural resistance that is shown by the end users for whom the system is built; software developers often complain that end users don't "appreciate" the elegance or sophistication of the system.

The irony is that this same group of software developers has its own cultural resistance to new technology. Over and over again, we have seen that the technology itself advances more quickly than the ability (or willingness) of the end user population (which in this case means software developers) to adapt to it.

It has been observed that it took the military community 75 years to change from the technology of muskets to the technology of rifles. A software development manager who is not sensitive to technology transfer problems runs the risk of experiencing the same kind of delay!

Fundamentals of Master Scheduling for the Project Manager

Kent A. Cori
Donohue & Associates, Inc.

The role of the project manager is to effectively schedule, allocate, use, and replace resources to achieve specified project goals. One of his or her primary project tasks is to schedule and budget the activities and resources (people, materials, and equipment) so that resources are available when needed, activities are completed in the correct order, and the project objective is reached in a cost effective and efficient manner. The project Master Schedule is one of the most formidable tools available to the project manager in performing his or her duties.

We will address the importance of planning to the project manager and survey the techniques that can be employed for scheduling a typical project. The role of the project manager, preparation of the project Master Schedule and project budget, scheduling and budgeting considerations and computer applications will be discussed. In addition, five popular scheduling techniques will be described and compared.

Functions Of The Project Manager

A project consists of a set of well defined, related tasks culminating in a major output and requiring an extensive period of time to complete. Projects may be unique, such as custom designing manufacturing machinery, or require outputs that are so large or time consuming that they have to be produced one at a time, such as construction of a highway interchange. Project management is the process of facilitating the performance of others to attain the project objective.

Project management can be categorized into four separate functional areas. These are planning, organizing, directing, and controlling.

These areas and the activities which comprise each are shown in Figure 1. Note that project management revolves on the hub of decision making which in turn revolves around information.

Preparing The Project Master Schedule

The major output of the planning process is the project Master Schedule. This is a graphic presentation of all project related activities necessary to produce required output. The project Master Schedule and the thought process behind it are the keys to a successful project. They allow the project manager to effectively coordinate and facilitate the efforts of the entire project team for the life of the project. This schedule is dynamic in that it will undoubtedly be modified as the project proceeds and unanticipated changes in scope, logic, or timing are required.

Without the Master Schedule, effective project control would be virtually impossible. Directing the project team would be extremely difficult if individual tasks have not been identified and the interrelationships among them defined. Control of the overall project is based on periodically monitoring progress and comparing the results to the Master Schedule. If the Master Schedule does not exist, it is impossible to accurately estimate project status. One of the project manager's primary administrative responsibilities is to complete the project within budget. Projects which are not completed within the time frame established by the Master Schedule almost invariably exceed planned costs.

Many project managers are reluctant to prepare a project plan. The most common complaint is that planning takes too much time and costs too much money. What these project managers do not realize is that because planning is a means of preventive action in that it requires anticipation of potential future difficulties, the long-term payoff is far greater than the short-term cost. Another objection is that it is too tedious. Planning is an iterative process requiring mental activity rather than action. This barrier is a result of the fact that most project managers perceive themselves as "doers," not "thinkers." Finally, ego affects the project

This article is reprinted from *Project Management Journal,* June 1985, with permission of the Project Management Institute, 130 South State Road, Upper Darby, PA 19082, a worldwide organization of advancing the state-of-the-art in project management.

Figure 1
Project Management Cycle

manager's attitude toward planning. Many feel that they can handle any eventuality and prefer to "shoot from the hip." Unfortunately, this adversely affects their overall performances which in turn reduces the effectiveness of their project teams.

For a schedule to be effective, it must possess several major characteristics. It must be:

- Understandable by those who must use it;
- Sufficiently detailed to provide a basis for measurement and control of project progress;
- Capable of highlighting critical tasks;
- Flexible, easily modified and updated;
- Based upon reliable time estimates;
- Conform to available resources; and
- Compatible with plans for other projects that share these same resources.

The project manager must be aware from the outset of the scheduling process that many factors must be considered in preparation of the project Master Schedule. Some of the major factors that may affect the project schedule are the project objectives, demands of other projects, resource requirements and constraints, and individual capabilities of team members. The range of competing factors is usually so extensive

that the whole process of planning must be regarded somewhat as an intuitive art. The job of the project manager is to replace intuition with scientific reasoning to as great a degree as possible. This is done by employing a number of different techniques in a logical sequence that is designed to eliminate one variable at a time.

Seven separate steps are necessary for the development of any project Master Schedule. These steps must always be undertaken in the proper sequence, although the amount of attention devoted to each and the methods used to complete each step are dependent upon the size, complexity, and duration of the project. The seven steps are:

1. Defining the project objectives.
2. Breaking down the work to be accomplished.
3. Sequencing the project activities.
4. Estimating the activity durations and costs.
5. Reconciling the project Master Schedule with project time constraints.
6. Reconciling the project Master Schedule with resource constraints.
7. Reviewing the schedule.

Defining Project Objectives

The primary responsibility of the project manager is to ensure that the end product meets the client's requirements; therefore, the first scheduling task of the project manager is to clarify project objectives by translating them into quantifiable terms. A project objective is a statement specifying the results to be achieved. These statements form the foundation for the entire planning process, including development of the Master Schedule.

The project objectives will be reviewed frequently throughout the project. They will be referred to at the onset of the project to identify the project team's responsibilities. During the project, they will be reviewed to identify changes that fall outside the original project scope. At the project's conclusion, they will be reviewed to help the project manager perform an objective postmortum review of the project.

A well defined project objective has several characteristics. The objective will be:

1. Attainable — The objective identifies a target which can be reasonably achieved given the project's time and resource constraints. If the objective is set too high, credibility is destroyed because the sense of shortfall is greater than the sense of accomplishment.

2. Definitive — It spells out in concrete terms what is to be achieved and to what degree. The results to be attained are clearly defined. Only those objectives related to project or organizational goals are included. Routine project activities must not be mistaken for objectives.
3. Quantifiable — It specifies a yardstick for completion which can be identified by all concerned, especially those responsible for its achievement. The establishment of measurable objectives is mandatory so that performance can be compared to a standard.
4. Specific Duration — It defines the time parameters within which the task is to be achieved. This is also necessary for evaluation of project progress.

Breaking Down The Work To Be Accomplished

Once well thought out project objectives are developed, the project manager can move on to producing a work breakdown structure (WBS) of activities to be performed. The WBS is nothing more or less than a checklist of the work that must be accomplished to meet the project objectives. A WBS is prepared through a very structured approach; general work is broken down into smaller, more specialized work. Major project work packages are first identified. The tasks necessary to produce these work packages can then be defined. These tasks can be further segmented into subtasks. Finally, the activities necessary for completion of these subtasks are listed.

The WBS lists the major project outputs and those departments or individuals primarily responsible for their completion. The WBS is a tool used by the project manager to become intimately familiar with the scope of the project.

This enhances his or her ability to monitor *all* the work in progress. This systematic approach also helps prevent the omission of critical tasks or activities. In any large project something will be forgotten; however, by using this approach the number of omissions will be greatly reduced. The WBS is also useful in developing budgets for each discipline or department.

Sequencing The Work Activities

It is obvious that production of the Master Schedule involves identifying the interrelationships among activities. This, in turn, influences the sequence in which they are to be accomplished.

For very simple projects, the use of milestones or a

Gantt chart is often sufficient. These charts provide a clear display of the time scale involved, but do not illustrate the interrelationships among the various activities. A Gantt chart is also very useful for estimating the relationship between work load and time. A relatively recent development in this area is full wall scheduling. Under this method, members of the project team all have input into the project Master Schedule.

Unfortunately, the use of milestones, a Gantt chart, or full wall scheduling as the only means for scheduling medium to large scale projects is usually not adequate. The interdependence among activities is a critical factor in the management of even a moderately complex project. In this instance, a precedence network analysis approach can be an extremely effective management tool. This approach utilizes a graphic technique to clearly illustrate activity interrelationships and sequence. The two best known techniques are CPM (Critical Path Method) and PERT (Program Evaluation and Review Technique). Precedence network scheduling techniques display a project in graphic form and relate its component activities in such a way as to focus attention on those which are crucial to the project's completion. Precedence networks can be drawn to a time scale to facilitate resource allocation and budgeting.

A more detailed discussion and comparison of the various scheduling techniques is presented later in this article.

Estimating Activity Durations And Costs

Once the individual activities have been defined and the sequence in which they are to occur has been identified, it is necessary to make an estimate of the amount of time that must elapse between the start and completion of each activity. These estimates are not based directly on the work content in man-hours, but solely upon the calendar time required to complete the activity. Such estimates are typically based on the experience of the scheduler with similar projects. Normal delays must be included.

The estimation of activity duration is related to the costs for that activity. It is usually more expensive to "crash" or complete an activity in an unusually short period of time. This directly affects project cost.

Neither overall project timing constraints nor resource limitations are directly considered at this stage. These will be considered in subsequent steps.

Reconciling The Master Schedule With Available Project Timing Constraints

This step has three main objectives:

1. To determine the anticipated duration of the entire project.
2. To identify those activities which play a critical part in contributing to the overall project duration. These are the activities that, together, form the critical path of a precedence network diagram.
3. To quantify the amount of float possessed by all noncritical activities.

The first of these objectives can be achieved by any of the major scheduling techniques. However, to achieve the remaining two objectives requires the use of some form of a precedence network analysis technique.

If this time analysis predicts a project duration longer than originally desired, it is necessary to review and perhaps revise the network. It may be possible to reduce some activity duration estimates, although this must never be done without a good reason. A more fruitful approach usually lies in examining the structure of the network itself, in rearranging it so that some activities can be started earlier in relation to others.

For all but the very simplest projects, the use of a computer is necessary to carry out the time analysis of the network and the subsequent resource allocation.

Reconciling The Master Schedule With Available Resources

Once the overall project time constraints are met, allocation of resources can be considered. If a firm happens to be short of work with a large reserve of resources waiting to be employed, then it would be theoretically possible to complete a project without worry about resource allocations at all. Each task or activity could simply be started as soon as possible, dependent only upon the sequencing restrictions defined in the network diagram. Resources scheduled on this unlimited basis form a load pattern called a resource aggregation.

These resource aggregation patterns are characteristically very uneven. They display sharp peaks and troughs in the day-to-day demand for each type of resource (equipment, materials, labor). This state of affairs is undesirable partly because the peaks are likely to exceed the quantity of resources available and also because an uneven usage of resources is typically uneconomical. Steps must be taken to smooth out the work load. This is the process of resource allocation or resource leveling. It is achieved by adjusting the scheduled starting dates for some noncritical activities which would otherwise occur during peak loading periods. The project manager endeavors to produce a smooth pattern of resource demand without delaying the completion of the project. This is done by revising the schedule within the network logic and project timing constraints already identified, and the amount of float possessed by each noncritical activity. If any activity has to be delayed beyond this calculated float, the project duration will be extended with consequences.

Projected costs must also be reconciled with the budget. It may be necessary to increase the duration of selected activities or eliminate them entirely to reduce costs in order to meet the budget.

Reviewing The Schedule

Once the schedule is complete, the project manager should audit it to determine whether it is realistic. Reasonable criteria should have been applied in the generation of activity budgets and durations. The completed network plan makes clear the effects of the factors influencing the scheduling and budgeting process. The effects of technical and management reviews, vacations, conflicts or resource constraints should be apparent, for example.

The project manager must remember that planning is an evolutionary process. The results of this audit may necessitate additional revisions to the schedule. The project manager should also review the assumptions that went into the development of the schedule. Times to complete activities are often based on the questionable assumption that a particular resource, such as a particular piece of equipment, will be available at a given point in time. Sometimes activity durations are based on greater-than-regular work week performance by some employees. This is always a dangerous assumption. Although this may be required as the project progresses, it is seldom reasonable to base a schedule on this assumption at the beginning of a project. In addition, the project manager should ensure that the necessary flexibility is available in the schedule to accommodate unanticipated project delays, such as inclement weather.

Survey Of Five Scheduling Techniques

As previously discussed, five of the major scheduling approaches are the milestone, Gantt, full wall scheduling, CPM, and PERT techniques. A detailed presentation of the mechanics for each of these scheduling techniques is beyond the scope of this article. Several authors (e.g., [2] [3] [4] [5] [7] [9]) have published detailed descriptions of the formats, conventions and procedures to be followed in preparing the various types of schedules. However, it is imperative that the project manager understand the purpose, advantages and disadvantages of each of these scheduling techniques; therefore, a general discussion and comparison of each follows.

The Milestone Chart

The milestone chart is the simplest scheduling method. This method is best applied to small projects being performed by only a few people because it does not exhibit the interrelationships among the activities. This approach has also been used to summarize complex schedules containing many tasks.

The advantages of the milestone chart are the ease and minimal cost of preparation. The disadvantage is that a milestone chart shows only completion dates. This may result in uncertainty over activity start dates and interrelationships for all but very simple projects. Comparing the actual completion dates with the target completion dates provides only a general indication of overall schedule status. This approach does not provide sufficient feedback to the project manager for control of even moderately complex projects.

The Gantt Chart

The Gantt or bar chart is frequently used for smaller projects (less than 25 activities) and overcomes some of the disadvantages of milestone charts. This type of schedule is perhaps the most widely used scheduling technique. Many people find it easier to understand a Gantt chart than a precedence network.

Although it is not possible to show the interdependence among activities on the Gantt chart, it is easier to show possible overlapping of activities than with either a CPM or PERT network. In many cases, CPM and PERT networks are translated directly onto a Gantt calendar chart. The Gantt chart can then be used to estimate resource and budget requirements versus time. This is done by identifying the amount of resources or budget needed per unit of time for each activity and calculating the total for all activities occurring during a specified time period.

Full Wall Scheduling

A technique known as "full wall scheduling" has been used successfully by several firms in recent years.

A large wall on which vertical lines are drawn five inches apart and horizontal lines spaced three inches apart is required. The spaces between each pair of vertical lines represent one work week. The horizontal lines serve to separate the members of the project team. This method generally works best for projects with more than 25 but fewer than 100 tasks, and with a project team of three to ten people.

The project manager first develops a preliminary milestone schedule and list of project tasks, identifying who is responsible for each task. Each task is written on two index cards. The first card is labeled "start" and the second card is labeled "finish." Each team member is then given the appropriate cards.

The entire project team is assembled in the room where the scheduling wall is located. Each person begins by tacking each card onto the wall under a week they select. As the scheduling proceeds, tasks may be divided into subtasks or better defined as required. Additional tasks not anticipated by the project manager are also added at this stage. The arrangement of the cards will be continually modified until all participants are satisfied that the necessary constraints and activity interrelationships have been addressed and the project schedule is attainable. The project manager then makes a record drawing of the full wall schedule and distributes it to the project team members.

The major advantage of the full wall scheduling procedure is the high degree of interaction that takes place during the scheduling meeting. Conflicts can be identified early, discussed and resolved. It also forces the project team members to make a firm commitment to the project manager on their assigned activities very early in the project.

A disadvantage of the full wall scheduling technique is that it requires all parties to meet for the scheduling activity. Firms with multiple offices may face logistics problems. Also, getting a large project team together for a relatively long period of time can be difficult. However, if the project manager thoroughly develops the task outline and milestone schedule prior to the meeting, and efficiently directs the proceedings during the scheduling meeting, the time required for the actual activity can be minimized.

A second major disadvantage of this method is that it does not clearly show the interrelationships of tasks or the critical path as do the precedence methods of scheduling, although these interrelationships must be identified in order to develop the schedule. Because changes that occur during the project often require revision of the original project Master Schedule, the project manager must rely on his or her memory to reconstruct the interrelationships. This is seldom feasible for medium to large size projects.

Precedence Networks

The most popular forms of the precedence network are the Critical Path Method (CPM), the Program Evaluation and Review Technique (PERT), and their variants. Scheduling by means of a precedence network is a dynamic process in which subdivisions, modifications, additions or deletions of activities may be made at any point in time. Initial development of the network requires that the project be thoroughly defined and thought out. The network diagram clearly and precisely communicates the plan of action to the project team and the client.

A project is most amenable to these techniques if:
- It has well defined activities.
- Activities may be started, stopped, and conducted separately within a given sequence.
- Activities interrelate with other activities.
- Activities are ordered in that they must follow each other in a given sequence.
- An activity, once started, must continue without interruption until completion.

The network is a graphic model portraying the sequential relationships between key events in a project and showing the plan of action. CPM and PERT identify the critical path, which is the longest sequence of connected activities through the network. This critical path serves as the basis for planning and controlling a project.

To expedite or "fast-track" a project, it is necessary only to speed up those activities on the critical path. Without knowledge of the critical path activities, the project manager would have to fast-track all activities, resulting in wasted resources. This approach also allows the project manager to identify those activities which are not critical. If unavoidable delays in the overall project occur, the project manager can delay these activities if desired to reduce unwarranted resource demand.

Because changes in the project scope and timing requirements typically occur as the project proceeds, the critical path identified at the outset of the project may not ultimately determine the overall project duration. Often, some activity that was not originally on the critical path is delayed to such an extent that the entire project is prolonged, creating a new critical path. The

project manager must continually monitor those activities which have a high delay potential and have very little float as well as those on the critical path. The more complicated the project, the more "near-critical" activities and paths will exist. The project manager must assess the impacts of significant project changes on these activities as well as those on the critical path to be assured that a new critical path has not been formed.

The differences between CPM and PERT are not fundamental, but merely one of viewpoint. The first basic difference is that CPM emphasizes activities while PERT is event oriented. On a CPM chart, events would not be symbolized, rather arrows representing each activity would connect to each other at nodes. In a PERT chart, events are specifically designated and emphasized by their placement in boxes. Arrows connecting the boxes have no specific identification. The advantage of a PERT event oriented chart is that the events can be considered milestones. These milestones can be spelled out in contracts or reports to facilitate managerial control.

The second major difference between the two techniques is the fact that PERT permits explicit treatment of probability for its time estimates while CPM does not. This distinction reflects PERT's origin and scheduling advanced development projects that are characterized by high degrees of uncertainty and CPM's origin in the scheduling of fairly routine plant maintenance activities. In general, CPM is used by construction and other industries where the project includes well defined activities with a low level of uncertainty. PERT is more likely to be used where research development and design form significant parts of the project resulting in relatively high levels of uncertainty.

The PERT technique acknowledges the effects of probability by including estimates of the minimum, most likely, and maximum periods of time required to complete an activity. The expected time for each activity is then calculated by taking an average of these three estimates. Some authors [3] [4] [6] [9] give the most likely time estimate a higher weight to reflect its greater probability of occurrence. However, the overall project duration is not significantly different using either approach.

Many managers have found that such efforts are not necessary and result in an overly complicated planning process. This often leads to reluctance to accept the basic idea of network planning, to the disadvantage of the project. Many project managers simply use the most likely time estimate for each activity duration. The decision whether to use CPM or PERT and whether to use a single or multiple activity duration estimates is most often based on personal preference.

Recently developed variations of the CPM and PERT techniques have allowed these approaches to be used for estimating, monitoring and controlling project resource requirements and costs. This is done by plotting the network on a time scale (x-axis) and inputting anticipated costs and resource requirements for each activity. This then enables projection of costs and resource needs for a specified time period without the intermediate step of translating the network into a bar chart format.

There are several rules of thumb to be used in developing either a CPM or PERT network:
1. The network should have a minimum of about 20 events. A Gantt chart is usually more appropriate for projects smaller than this.
2. Networks that are not computerized should usually be limited to those with fewer than 100 events; 300 events is a practical upper limit. Computerized networks of as many as 12,500 activities have been used on large construction projects although 1000 to 2000 is more common. Networks for non-construction types of projects are frequently much smaller. The project manager must realize that the greater the number of activities used in the network, the more difficult the network becomes to encompass and update.
3. Project characteristics that justify the use of a large number of descriptive activities or events are:
   • Very critical
   • High risk or uncertainty
   • Involvement of many people or organizations
   • Technical complexity
   • Activity at diverse geographic locations

Comparison Of The Five Scheduling Techniques

Each of the five scheduling techniques discussed has inherent strengths and weaknesses. These strengths and weaknesses are summarized in Table 1.

The type of scheduling technique to be used for a project should be selected on a case-by-case basis. Table 2 rates each of the techniques with regard to some of the more important selection criteria.

Computerization Of Scheduling Techniques

Small projects can be analyzed manually but the use of computer analysis offers many advantages for even moderately complex projects. The use of a computer permits not only the resource allocation of single projects, but also the simultaneous consideration of all activities from the total range of projects being handled within an entire firm, so that the computer schedules the firm's complete resources. Provided that the networks for all projects have been sensibly constructed, multi-project scheduling by computer tends to produce working schedules that remain valid for the life of each project, and need little or no revision as work proceeds.

Computer software packages are available which will plot the network, illustrate the critical path, identify the available float for each activity, project resource and budget requirements, and summarize the results in conveniently tabulated reports. These packages can handle any number of projects at one time, making them suitable for scheduling the firm's total operations. Many of these packages can be used for all three types of scheduling techniques.

Examples of currently available software packages that can handle projects with up to 5000 activities and yet still be run on microcomputers are: PMS-II by North American Mica, Inc.; PERTMASTER by Westminster Software, Inc.; CPM/PERT by Elite Software; and TRAC LINE by TRAC LINE Software, Inc. These packages typically cost $500-$1500. Several of these also include resource allocation subroutines.

There are also software packages that can handle extremely large projects that are suitable for large mainframe computers. These include: PAC I, II and III by AGS Management Systems, Inc.; PMC2 by M. Bryce & Associates, Inc.; and CRAM by Environmental Services, Incorporated. These systems can cost $10,000 or more.

Summary

The planning stage is a critical aspect of any project. During this stage, the project manager defines the project objectives, identifies the activities necessary to complete the project, estimates the level of resources and amount of time necessary to complete the project, and establishes the framework for management control of the project. The project Master Schedule is one of the major planning and control tools available to the project manager. In order to prepare an effective project Master Schedule, it is necessary to follow a structured approach. Several commonly accepted scheduling techniques are available to the project manager. Each has its inherent advantages and disadvantages. Each can be used singly or in conjunction with other scheduling techniques and each can be computerized. The information contained in this article should be sufficient to convince the project manager of the importance of preparing a project Master Schedule and provide the basis for selection and development of the most appropriate technique or techniques for his or her next project.

References

1. Badawy, M.K., *Developing Managerial Skills in Engineers and Scientists.* New York: Van Nostrand Reinhold Company, 1982.
2. Burstein, D. A System to Keep Projects on Budget, on Schedule. *Consulting Engineer,* July, 1983, 69-72.
3. Burstein, D., & Stasiowski, F., *Project Management for the Design Professional.* London: Architectural Press, Ltd., 1982.
4. Chase, R.B., & Aquilano, N.J. Production and Operations Management: A Life Cycle Approach. *Production and Operations Management: A Life Cycle Approach.* Homewood, IL: Richard D. Irwin, Inc., 1981.
5. Ivancevich, J.M., Donnelly, J.H. Jr., & Gibson, J.L. *Managing for Performance.* Plano, TX: Business Publications Inc., 1983.
6. Knutson, J.R. *How to be a Successful Project Manager.* Boston, MA: Education for Management, Inc., 1980.
7. Lock, D. (ed.) *Engineers Handbook of Management Techniques.* Epping, Essex, England: Gower Press, Limited, 1973.
8. O'Brien, J.J., & Zilly, R.G., *Contractor's Management Handbook.* New York, NY: McGraw-Hill Book Company, 1971.
9. Spiegle, E. *The Engineer as Manager.* Seattle, WA: Battelle, Inc., 1983.
10. Spirer, H.F., & Symons, G.E. *Successful Management of Civil Engineering Projects.* Larchmont, NY: MGI Management Institute, Inc., 1979.

Kent Cori, P.E., is the Public Works Engineering Department Manager for the consulting engineering firm of Donohue & Associates, Inc. at their Milwaukee, Wisconsin Division Office. Mr. Cori has his B.S. Civil and Environmental Engineering, University of Wisconsin, Madison and his M.B.A., University of Wisconsin, Whitewater.

* * *

Table 1
Comparison of Scheduling Techniques

MILESTONE TECHNIQUE

Criteria	Strengths	Weaknesses
Applicability	Only small errors in measurement are likely to occur if activity durations are short.	No explicit technique for depicting interrelationships.
Reliability	Simplicity of system affords some reliability.	Frequently unreliable because judgment of estimator may change over time. Numerous estimates in a large project, each with some unreliability, may lead to errors in judging status.
Implementation	Easiest of all systems because it is well understood.	Difficult to implement for the control of operations where time standards do not ordinarily exist and must be developed.
Simulation Capabilities	_____	No significant capability.

Criteria	Strengths	Weaknesses
Updating Status	Easy to update periodically. Not necessary to use computer.	
Flexibility	————————	Poor accommodation of frequent logic changes.
Cost	Data gathering, processing and display relatively inexpensive.	The chart tends to be inflexible. Program changes require new charts.

GANTT TECHNIQUE

Criteria	Strengths	Weaknesses
Applicability	Only small errors in measurement are likely to occur if activity durations are short.	No explicit technique for depicting interrelationships.
Reliability	Single duration estimate for each activity avoids errors due to over-complexity.	Frequently unreliable because judgment of estimator may change over time. Numerous estimates in a large project, each with some unreliability, may lead to errors in judging status.
Implementation	Easiest of all systems in some respects because it is well understood.	Quite difficult to implement for the control of operations where time standards do not ordinarily exist and must be developed.
Simulation Capabilities	————————	No significant capability.
Updating Status	Easy to update graphs periodically if no major program changes. Not necessary to use computer.	May have to redo graphs because of inability to update current charts.
Flexibility	Can also be used for estimating resource requirements.	If significant logic changes occur frequently, numerous charts must be completely reconstructed.
Cost	Data gathering and processing relatively inexpensive. Display can be inexpensive if existing graphs can be updated and if inexpensive materials are used.	The graph tends to be inflexible. Program changes require new graphs, which are time consuming and costly. Expensive display devices are frequently used.

FULL WALL TECHNIQUE

Criteria	Strengths	Weaknesses
Applicability	Accurately depicts work sequence.	No explicit representation of activity inter-relationships. Can not be easily computerized.

Reliability	Single duration estimate for each activity avoids errors due to over-complexity. Input from project team members often eliminates errors and problems at the outset.	Numerous estimates in a large project, each with some unreliability, may lead to significant errors in judging overall project status.
Implementation	Graphic display of work sequence and early discussion of project is desired by project managers. Easily explained and understood.	Time requirements and logistics problems are difficult to overcome.
Simulation Capabilities	————————	No significant capability.
Updating Status	Moderate capability. Activities are clearly identified and time estimates can be obtained as needed.	Usually requires redrawing schedule. Often difficult to update because activity interrelationships are not explicitly shown.
Flexibility	Schedule can be changed to reflect scope changes. Can be used to estimate resource requirements.	Schedules for even moderately complex projects become complicated.
Cost	Can reduce overall project costs through better planning and control.	More man-hours are required than in any other system; hence this approach is often the most costly.

CPM TECHNIQUE

Criteria	Strengths	Weaknesses
Applicability	Accurately depicts work sequence and interrelationships among activities.	No formula is provided to estimate probable time to completion; consequently, the technique is as valid as the estimator. The margin of error is generally less on projects with little uncertainty.
Reliability	Single duration estimate for each activity avoids errors due to over-complexity.	Numerous estimates in a large project, each with some unreliability, may lead to significant errors in judging overall project status.
Implementation	Graphic display of work sequence and activity interrelationships is desired by managers of complex projects.	Relatively difficult to explain to those unused to approach. Complexity of schedule may intimidate clients.
Simulation Capabilities	Excellent for simulating alternative plans if computerized, especially when coupled with time-cost-resource aspects.	Requires computer for all but very small projects.
Updating Status	Good capability. Activities are clearly identified and time estimates can be obtained as needed.	Schedules for even moderately complex projects require use of computer.

| Flexibility | Portions of the network can be easily changed to reflect scope changes if computerized. Can be used to estimate resource requirements if plotted on time scale. | Schedules for even moderately complex projects require use of computer. |
| Cost | Can reduce overall project costs significantly through better planning and control. | Considerable data are required to use CPM as both a planning and status reporting tool and a computer is almost invariably required. Therefore, the cost outlay can be fairly extensive. |

PERT TECHNIQUE

Criteria	Strengths	Weaknesses
Applicability	PERT, like CPM, is capable of depicting work sequence. The use of three time estimates should make it more accurate than any other technique.	Overly complex for small projects.
Reliability	Probabilistic duration estimates may be more accurate than single estimate.	Securing three duration estimates for each activity requires more information which could introduce additional error.
Implementation	Graphic display of sequence and event interrelationships is desired by managers of complex projects.	The complete PERT system is quite complex, and therefore, difficult to implement. May intimidate first time users and clients.
Simulation Capabilities	Excellent for simulating alternative plans if computerized, especially when coupled with time-cost-resource aspects.	Requires computer for all but very small projects.
Updating Status	Events are clearly identified and elapsed times can be obtained as needed.	Estimation of activity durations is quite time consuming, and calculation of expected times requires use of a computer.
Flexibility	As the project changes over time, the network and new time estimates can be readily adjusted to reflect changes. Can be used to estimate resource requirements if plotted on time scale.	Schedules for even moderately complex projects require use of computer.
Cost	Can reduce overall project costs significantly through better planning and control.	More data and more computation are required than in any other system; hence the system is very costly.

Table 2
Selecting a Scheduling Technique

Criteria	Milestone	Gantt	Full Wall	CPM	PERT
Activities versus Events Oriented	Event	Activity	Event	Activity	Event
Suitability for Large Projects	Poor	Poor	Fair	Excellent	Excellent
Suitability for Small Projects	Good	Good	Poor	Poor	Poor
Degree of Control	Very Low	Low	Moderate	High	Highest
Acceptance by Unsophisticated Users	Best	Excellent	Good	Fair	Poor
Ease of Assembly	Easiest	Easy	Hardest	Hard	Harder
Degree of Flexibility	Lowest	Low	Moderate	High	Highest
Ease of Manual Calculation	Easiest	Easy	Moderate	Hard	Hardest
Accuracy of Projections	Fair	Fair	High	Higher	Highest
Cost to Prepare and Maintain	Lowest	Low	Highest	High	Higher
Vague Project Scope	Poorest	Poor	Fair	Good	Excellent
Complex Project Logic	Poorest	Poor	Better	Excellent	Excellent
Critical Completion Date	Fair	Fair	Good	Good	Excellent
Frequent Progress Check Required	Good	Good	Good	Fair	Hard
Frequent Updating Required	Easiest	Easy	Hardest	Hard	Harder
Frequent Logic Changes Required	Poor	Poor	Poor	Fair	Fair
Appeal to Client	Good	Good	Excellent	Excellent	Excellent

Work Breakdown Structures

Richard E. Fairley
Colorado Technical University
Colorado Springs, CO 80907

Richard H. Thayer
California State University, Sacramento
Sacramento, CA 95819

1. Introduction

A work breakdown structure (WBS) is a method of representing, in a hierarchical manner, the parts of a process or product. It can be used for representing a process (for example, requirements analysis, design, coding, or testing), a product (for example, applications program, utility program, or system software), or both. The WBS is a major system engineering tool and is considered one of the best project management tools in existence today.

This paper presents an overview of the WBS, its various forms, the process of preparing a WBS, and an example of a WBS.

2. Definitions

There are three types of work breakdown structures:

1. *Process WBS:* A WBS that partitions a large process into smaller and smaller processes. Each process is eventually decomposed into tasks that can be assigned to individuals for accomplishment.

2. *Product WBS:* A WBS that partitions a large entity into its components. Each component and its interfaces are identified, resulting in a clearer identification of the larger system.

3. *Hybrid* WBS: A WBS that includes both process and product elements.

There are two methods for representing a WBS:

1. Figure 1 provides an example of a WBS represented as a tree-structured graph. A graphical WBS is a set of activities or product elements that illustrates the "is contained in" relationships between higher level activities and/or product elements and lower level activities and/or product elements. The lower level activities and/or product elements are contained in the upper level activities and/or product elements. An organizational chart is an example of a graphical WBS where the smaller organizational elements are contained in the larger ones.

2. Figure 2 illustrates the indented list form of a WBS, in which indentations are used to show the relationships between higher-level product elements and/or processes and lower level product elements and/or processes. The elements with the greater indentions are contained in the elements with the lesser indentations.

A decimal numbering system is used to systematically label the elements of a WBS. For example, the identifier "4.2.1" identifies the indicated element as the first element of the second element of the fourth element in the WBS. Three digits in the number "4.2.1" indicates that the element is on the third level of the WBS. The leading "0" used to identify the top-level node of a WBS is, by convention, omitted from subsequent numbers. The top-level node is counted as level zero of the WBS. Numeric labels are used on both the graphical and indented forms of a WBS.

3. Examples

Figures 3 and 4 are examples of process and product WBSs. For purposes of illustration only, the process WBS is shown as a graphical WBS; the product WBS is shown as an indented list. The two representation methods would be just as satisfactory if the illustration were reversed, that is, the process WBS was shown as an indented list and the product WBS was shown as a graphical WBS.

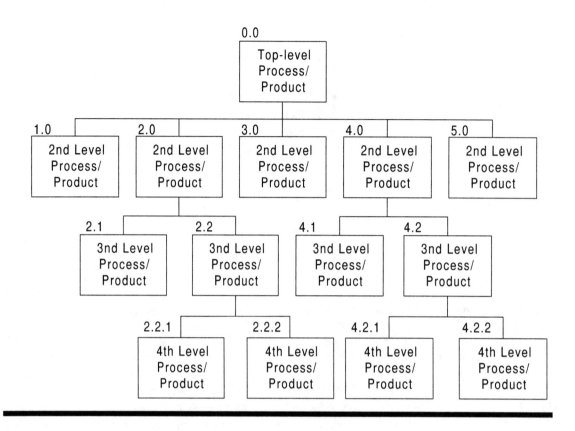

Figure 1. A hierarchical work breakdown structure (WBS).

0. Top-level process or product element (0th level)
    1. 1st level process or product element
    2. 1st level process or product element
        2.1 2nd level process or product element
        2.2 2nd level process or product element
            2.2.1 3rd level process or product element
            2.2.2 3rd level process or product element
    3. 1st level process or product element
    4. 1st level process or product element
        4.1 2nd level process or product element
        4.2 2nd level process or product element
            4.2.1 3rd level process or product element
            4.2.2 3rd level process or product element
    5. 1st level process or product element

Figure 2. Indented-list work breakdown structure (WBS).

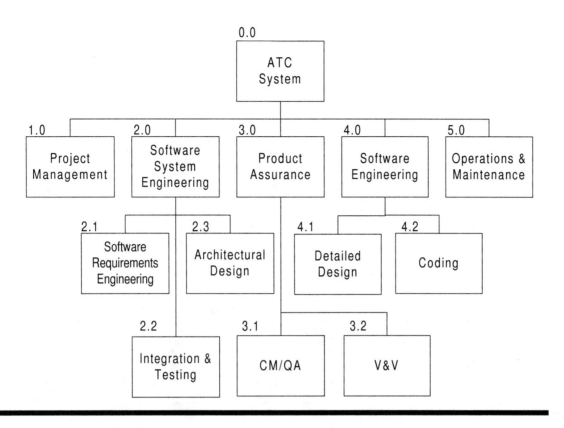

Figure 3. ATC work breakdown structure (process).

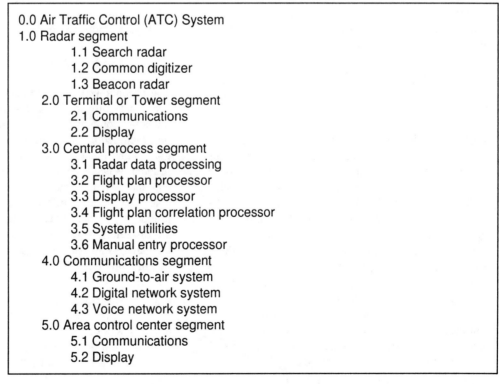

0.0 Air Traffic Control (ATC) System
1.0 Radar segment
     1.1 Search radar
     1.2 Common digitizer
     1.3 Beacon radar
2.0 Terminal or Tower segment
     2.1 Communications
     2.2 Display
3.0 Central process segment
     3.1 Radar data processing
     3.2 Flight plan processor
     3.3 Display processor
     3.4 Flight plan correlation processor
     3.5 System utilities
     3.6 Manual entry processor
4.0 Communications segment
     4.1 Ground-to-air system
     4.2 Digital network system
     4.3 Voice network system
5.0 Area control center segment
     5.1 Communications
     5.2 Display

Figure 4. ATC work breakdown structure (product).

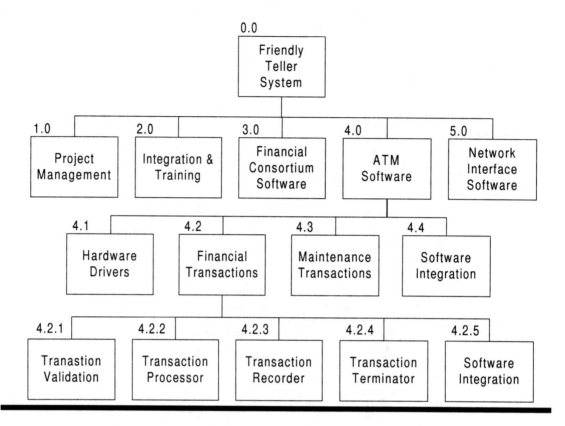

Figure 5. Example of a hybrid WBS.

Figure 5 illustrates a hybrid WBS that intermixes product and process elements. Note that elements 1.0, 2.0, 4.4, and 4.2.5 are process elements and the remainder are product elements.

4. Applications of the WBS

4.1 Process WBS

The process WBS is used by project managers to manage their software engineering projects. The WBS presents a "picture" of the activities that have to be accomplished to ensure a successful software project.

The top level of the WBS identifies the project by name. The second level of the WBS identifies the major work elements to be done, such as planning, organizing, requirements analysis, design, coding, testing, and so forth. The third level describes the more detailed activities that must be completed in order to accomplish the second-level activities.

The lowest-level process elements in a WBS represent tasks. A task is the smallest unit of management accountability for work assigned. These small units of management accountability are specified in "work packages." A work package is a task specification that is suitable for assignment to one or two persons for a

duration of one or two weeks (the one-to-two rule of WBS decomposition).

Figure 3 provides an example of a process WBS.

4.2 Product WBS

The product WBS is a primary tool of systems engineers and software engineers. A product WBS illustrates the components and interfaces of the product to be developed or produced and relates the elements of the product to each other and to the end product. The product WBS specifies the hardware, software, and data that together completely define a project deliverable. The top level of the product WBS identifies the product by name. Other elements of a product WBS are discrete, identifiable items of hardware, software, and data. Refer back to Figure 4 for a simple illustration of a product WBS.

4.3 Hybrid WBS

Many practitioners combine the product and process elements of a project into one WBS. Some design the WBS by beginning with process elements and interleaving product with process elements; others begin with product elements and interleave the processes;

others intermix products and processes on the same levels (see Figure 5 for an illustration of the latter approach). A process-product WBS begins with a process, alternates process and product elements, and terminates with the product elements. The rationale behind this approach is that processes produce products. Subproducts, in turn, require development processes. The terminal elements of this hybrid WBS are product components.

This approach is used by managers who first want to determine, and second, want to control project cost and schedule for each product element. Activities that cannot be attached to a particular product element, such as quality assurance and project management, are identified as stand-alone processes.

4.3 WBS Dictionary

Each element of a WBS is defined in a WBS dictionary. The elements are usually identified by their names and decimal numbers. Dictionary entries for process elements are work packages or pointers to work packages; entries for product elements are the requirements allocated to those elements or pointers to the requirements.

5. Developing a WBS

5.1 Rolling Wave

It is not always possible to develop the complete WBS down to the desired lowest levels at the beginning of a project. Normally, a "rolling wave" approach is used. The top levels of the WBS are developed down to the second or third level. Analysis is done to determine which processes or product will be done first. The corresponding top-level elements are then partitioned down to their lowest levels in only those areas that are needed in the near future (typically four to six weeks). All other elements are deferred. In other words, WBS elements are continuously being rolled into the future and decomposed when necessary (the "wave" rolls forward in time).

5.2 Steps in Developing the WBS

1. Determine the purpose of the WBS. For example, is it to identify the elements of a product? To determine the cost of the system? To determine the types of people needed? To assign work to individuals? And so forth.

2. Identify the top of the WBS. This is the name of the project for a process-oriented WBS and the name of the product for the product-oriented WBS.

3. Partition the WBS into its major components. A good rule of thumb is to keep the partitioning into 7 ± 2 elements.

4. Partition each of the major components into 7 ± 2 elements. And so forth.

5. Terminate the partitioning when the goal of the WBS is reached. For purposes of planning and estimation, the goal may be to decompose the WBS until all hidden complexities are exposed and experts can estimate time and cost for their parts. For purposes of assigning work to individuals, the goal may be to decompose the WBS until each lowest-level task is a work element for one to two people for one to two weeks.

6. Develop a WBS dictionary entry for each lowest-level element of the WBS.

7. Document the results.

5.3 Some Special Notes

1. There is some disagreement in the industry as to whether the top level of a WBS is level "zero" or level "one." (The former is illustrated in Figure 1.) Always ask for clarification when you are dealing with another individual or agency.

2. The second level of the WBS that has numbers like 1., 2., 3., …, n. have an implied leading "0". For example, the above numbers might read 0.1., 0.2., 0.3., …, 0.n.

3. A WBS is often measured by the number of levels in the WBS. The top level is sometimes counted as level zero and sometimes as level one; the convention in this paper is to count the top level as level zero. It is important to know the counting rule when there is a requirement to develop a WBS to a given number of levels. Figure 1 contains three levels.

4. Each level of the WBS should contain no more than 7 ± 2 elements. Any level containing more than 7 ± 2 should be partitioned into two or more levels.

6. Specifying Tasks in Software Project Work Packages

Each lowest-level work activity in a process WBS (generally known as a *task*) is specified in a work package A work package specification should specify the following for each task:

- Identifying number, name, and brief description of the task

- Estimated duration (schedule) of the task

- Resources need to accomplish the task (including numbers of individuals and required skills)

- Predecessor and successor tasks
- Work products to be produced
- Completion criteria for the task (including quality criteria for the work products)
- Risks associated with successful completion of the task.

As discussed above, not all tasks are identified at the beginning of a project. A rolling-wave approach is generally used. It is important to note that every work package must produce a tangible work product that is verified by objective acceptance criteria.

An example of a work package is provided in Figure 6. (Note: space is also provided to document legacy information after the work package is complete)

Activity number:	4.3.5
Activity name:	ARCH-SS-XYZ
Activity description:	Specify the architectural structure of subsystem XYZ
Estimated duration:	1 week
Resources needed:	**Personnel**: 2 senior telecomm designers
	Skill: Designers familiar with X25 protocol
	Tools: 1 Sun workstation running IDE;
	Travel: One 3-day design review in San Diego
Work products:	Architectural specification for SS-XYZ
	Test Plan for subsystem XYZ
Baselines?	Yes for both
Predecessors:	4.3.2
Successors:	4.3.6.1; 4.3.6.2
Completion criteria:	Sign-off for subsystem XYZ by chief architect
Risks:	Availability of senior designers

Implementation

Personnel assigned:_____

Starting date: _____ Completion date: _____

Costs (budgeted and actual): $_____ $_____

Legacy comments:

Figure 6. Example of a work package specification.[1]

[1] Fairley, R.E., *Software Project Management*, a professional seminar, Technology Exchange Company, an Addison-Wesley Company. Reading, Mass., 1990.

A collection of work packages can be analyzed for the following characteristics:

- Completeness

- Consistency

- Cost by task and by "roll-up" (Roll-up is defined as the aggregation of lower-level element values into a single higher-level element value)

- Duration by task and by roll-up

- Personnel by type, number, and need date

- Other resources by type, number, and need date

- Personnel and resource conflicts

- Activity networks

- Risk by task and by roll-up

7. Summary and Conclusion

A work breakdown structure is a hierarchical decomposition of a work process and/or a work product. Project managers use the process elements of a WBS to plan, organize, and track a project. System engineers use the product elements of a WBS to partition the product into components and interfaces. A WBS can be represented as a graphical tree structure or as an indented list. Systematic numbering of a WBS assists in relating the elements of the WBS to one another.

The WBS is a fundamental tool for specifying the components and interfaces of a software product and for planning and tracking the work activities of a software project. The lowest level process elements in a WBS are tasks; work packages are used to plan and track tasks. Usually, a task is a unit of work for one to two people for one to two weeks (the one-to-two rule). Decomposition of work activities to the task level is normally done in a rolling-wave manner.

Many project managers and system engineers use the WBS as the fundamental tool for planning and coordinating their work processes and work products. Integration of process and product elements in a single WBS clarifies the relationships among work processes and work products.

A Case Study

Development of a Work Breakdown Structure

This case study illustrates development of a process-oriented work breakdown structure for building the software component of an Automated Teller Machine. This WBS is the one the developer will use to build the system. Emphasis is placed on developing a detailed WBS for one component of the ATM software.

A process-oriented WBS must be consistent with the overall structure of the development organization. The Systems Branch of our company is organized as follows:

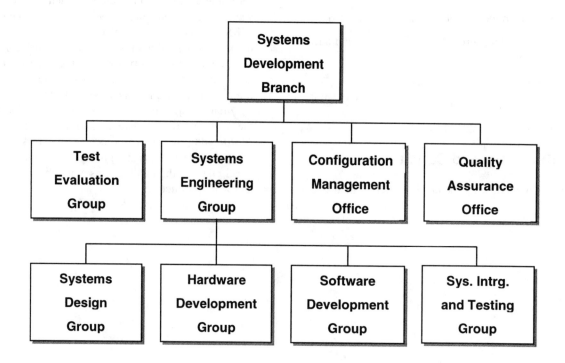

Existing elements of the organization are incorporated into the project WBS (System Engineering, Systems Integration and Testing, Configuration Management); additional elements (such as Technical Publications) must be provided by the project manager. The project structure is thus a combination of functional and project formats. The resulting top-level, process-oriented view of the software project is as follows:

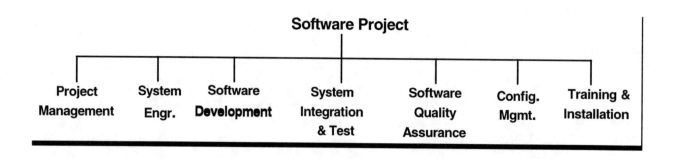

The ATM system structure, as determined by System Engineering, is as follows:

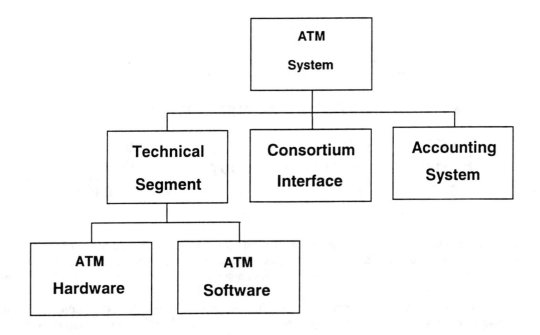

The ATM software has three major components: User Financial Transactions (FINAT), Hardware Drivers (ATMHD), and Maintenance Capability (MAINT). Development of these components could be organized by project phase (design—DES, code and unit test—CUT, component integration and test—CIT, and software integration and test—SIT) or by product component (FINAT, ATMHD, MAINT). The result WBS elements would have the following structures:

BY PROJECT PHASE

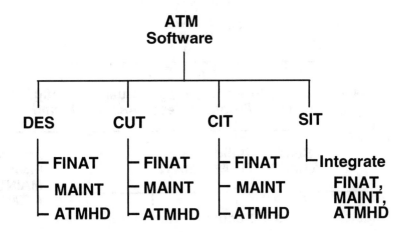

BY PRODUCT COMPONENT

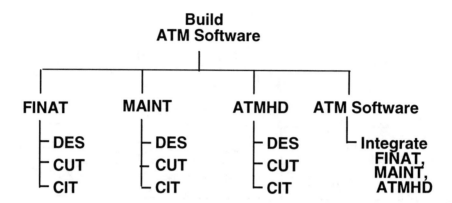

The project manager chooses to organize the WBS elements for the ATM software along product component lines because she wants all developers involved in all types of development activities (design, code, test), and because she wants to establish clean interfaces between software components, which will be inherent in the communication interfaces among developers.

The project manager might choose to organize the project along process lines if the organization was structured by functional groups having special expertise (design, code, test) that could be utilized to develop the software or if the project tracking and accounting software required the project to be organized in that way.

For purposes of this case study, only the Financial Transaction component of the ATM software will be further decomposed. Partitioning of the requirements for the Financial Transaction component results in four major components: Validator, Processor, Recorder, and Terminator. Each of these components must be designed, coded, and unit tested, and the subcomponent of each major component must be integrated and tested. Finally, the four major components must be integrated to form the Financial Transaction component of the system. This component would then be integrated with the other two system components (Hardware Drivers and Maintenance) to produce the ATM software system.

The partial WBS for the elements discussed in this case study is illustrated as follows:

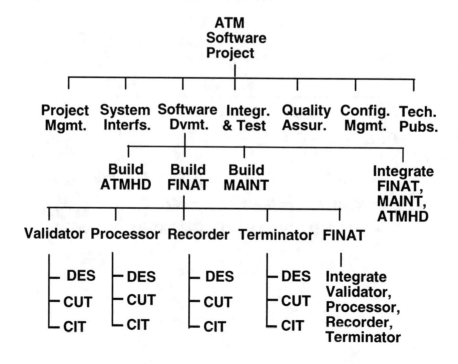

192

Observe that the resulting WBS is four levels deep; the fan-out at each level is seven or less. A software project WBS is usually in the range of four to seven levels deep, depending on the size and complexity of the product. Also note that the product components and interfaces (at all levels) are embedded in the WBS. Systematic numbering of the WBS has been omitted because of space limitations on the page; the numbers assigned to WBS elements are as follows:

WBS NUMBERING

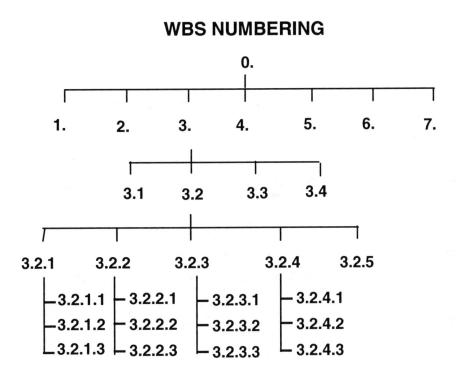

The level-four tasks are sufficiently decomposed so that individual tasks can be assigned to one or two individuals for one or two weeks. The work package for each task would contain information as illustrated in the work package for task 3.2.1.1 (detailed design of the Transaction Validator):

Information in the collection work packages is sufficient to determine the activity network for the FINAT component of the ATM software (including the critical path, which determines the overall schedule for the work), the staff requirements (including number of people, required skills, when needed, and for how long), other necessary resources, risk factors for the tasks, work products to be produced, and the completion criteria for the work products.

As stated previously, and illustrated in the case study, the work breakdown structure is a fundamental tool for specifying the design of a software product and for organizing, planning, and tracking a software project.

WORK PACKAGE SPECIFICATION	
Activity number:	3.2.1.1
Activity name:	DESIGN_TRANSACTION_VALIDATOR
Activity description:	Specify detailed design and test plan for Transaction Validator
Estimated duration:	1 week
Resources needed:	
— Personnel:	1 senior designer
— Skills:	Designer must be familiar with the ATM architectural design, UNIX, and IDE
—Tools:	One Sun workstation running IDE
—Travel:	None
Products:	Architectural specification for VALIDATOR
	Component test plan for VALIDATOR
Baselines:	VALIDATOR test plan
Predecessor Tasks:	2.3.2 - An approved architectural concept for the ATM software
Successor Tasks:	3.2.1.2 - code and unit test the VALIDATOR software
Risks:	Senior designer not identified
Completion criteria:	Sign-off by FINAT Software Architect

Software Risk Management

Richard H. Thayer
California State University, Sacramento
Sacramento, CA 95819-6021

Richard E. Fairley
Colorado Technical University
Colorado Springs, CO 80907-3896

Abstract

Risk management is an organized means of identifying risk factors (risk identification), developing and selecting risk handling options (risk analysis), and mitigating risk when they become problems (risk handling). The primary goal of risk management is to identify and respond to potential problems with sufficient lead time to avoid a crisis. It is important that a risk management strategy is established early in a software project and that risk is continually addressed throughout the system lifecycle. This paper defines and explains the various elements of risk management.

1. Introduction

A *project risk* is a potential problem that would be detrimental to a project's success should it materialize. The major components of risk are the probability that something undesirable might happen and the resulting consequences should the undesired event occur. For example, the project might overrun the schedule, resulting in delayed delivery of the product; exceed its budget, which would result in a cost overrun; or deliver an unsuitable product, which would result in customer and user dissatisfaction. Risk is present in some form and degree in most human activities. It is certainly present in software engineering projects.

Project risk is characterized by the following:

- Uncertainty is involved (0 < Probability < 1).

- A loss is associated with it (life, money, property, reputation, and so forth).

- It is manageable—in the sense that human action can be applied to change its form and degree.

Risk exposure is the product of probability and potential loss. A *problem* is a risk that has materialized. A problem arises when the undesired event has occurred and a potential loss is now real.

When we are dealing with risk in this general sense, it is not always easy to distinguish between single events, multiple events, continuous events, and interdependent events, or between cause and effect. In considering an undertaking, many risks may be identified. Systematic risk management requires that initial apprehensions be turned into specific root causes, and that the probabilities and potential losses be established. The specific outcome we wish to avoid must be explicitly stated in order to identify possible courses of action for risk reduction.

2. Risk Management versus Project Management

There is a basic difference between risk management and traditional project management. The goal of traditional project management is to control pervasive risks by using systematic procedures. In contrast, risk management is concerned with identifying and managing the unique aspects of a specific project that might prevent delivery of a suitable product, on time and within budget.

Software project management deals with problems generic to all software projects. Over time, methods of reducing generic and pervasive risks have become institutionalized in the tools and techniques used to develop software. For example, project planning, configuration management, and verification and validation are all proven risk reduction techniques. In this sense, traditional software engineering project management can be viewed as a systematic approach to controlling generic risk factors.

Therefore, the goal of traditional project management is to control generic and pervasive risks that might hinder development of a satisfactory product on time and within budget. Other examples (and their potential generic solutions) are:

- Costly late fixes (dealt with by early requirements and design verification)
- Error-prone products (dealt with by verification, validation, and incremental testing throughout the lifecycle)
- Uncontrolled development processes (dealt with by planning and control based on well-defined processes)
- Uncontrolled product (dealt with by configuration management and quality assurance)
- Poor communications (dealt with by documentation, reviews, and technical interchange meetings)

However, on its own, traditional project management is a recipe for "problem management" in that difficult decisions are addressed and actions taken only when problems arise. In this sense, *project management is reactive, whereas risk management is proactive.*

Risk management deals with potential problems unique to a specific software project. Risk management allows developers, managers, and customers to make informed decisions based on systematic assessment of what might go wrong, the associated probabilities, and the severity of the impacts. Risk management is also concerned with developing strategies and plans to abate the major risk factors, to resolve those risks that do become problems, and to continually reassess risk. Real risk management occurs when significant decision making, planning, resources, money, and effort are expended to reduce the probabilities and/or impacts of identified risk factors. The extent to which time and effort are invested in these processes determine whether risk management is being accomplished, over and above traditional project management.

Risk management is not synonymous with project management, nor is it a replacement for project management, nor is it something entirely separate. Rather, it is an explicit augmentation and extension of traditional project management, and is closely intertwined with the information-gathering and decision-making functions of project management. "When a project is successful, it is not because there were no problems but that the problems were overcome." [1] Risk management does not guarantee success, but has the primary goal of identifying and responding to potential problems with sufficient lead time to avoid crisis

situations, so that it becomes possible to conduct a project that meets its target goals.

3. Risk Identification

The first step in risk management is identification of project risk factors. Risks cannot be analyzed or handled until they are identified and described in an understandable way. *Risk identification is an organized, thorough approach to seeking out the real risks associated with a program.* It is *not* a process of trying to invent highly improbable scenarios of unlikely events in an effort to cover every conceivable possibility of outrageous fortune.

Some degree of risk always exists in the programmatic, technical, quality, logistics, production, and engineering areas. Programmatic risks include funding, schedule, contractual, and political risks. Technical risks may involve the risk of meeting a performance requirement or a safety or security requirement, and may also include risks in the feasibility of a design concept or the risks associated with using state-of-the-art hardware or software. Software quality risks include reliability, maintainability, operability, and trainability concerns. Understanding of risks in these and other areas evolves over time. Consequently, risk assessment must continue throughout all phases of a software project.

There are many methods for identifying risk. Any source of information that allows recognition of a potential problem can be used for risk identification. These include the following:

- Lifecycle cost and schedule analysis
- Requirements documents
- Prototyping and simulation models
- Lessons-learned files
- Trade studies and analyses
- Work breakdown structures (WBSs)
- Schedule networks

Five common, and interrelated, areas of risk for software projects are schedule, cost, requirements, quality, and operational risks. Identification of each is discussed in turn.

3.1 Schedule Risks

Techniques for identifying schedule risks include algorithmic scheduling models, critical path methods, and PERT analysis. Probabilistic techniques, such as PERT and Monte Carlo simulation, can provide ranges of probabilities for achieving various project milestones (including project completion) based on probabilistic values for the duration of the individual project tasks and the sequencing dependencies among those tasks.

The schedule network is a source for identifying potential risk. Nodes or junction points with a high degree of fan-in (see Figure 1, node 8) and those with a high degree of fan-out (see Figure 1, node 3) are potential high-risk areas.

A node with a high degree of fan-in has many tasks that must be completed before the milestone can be achieved. Thus, no subsequent tasks can be initiated until all tasks fanning into the node are completed; delay in any one will delay all subsequent tasks. Similarly, a node with a high degree of fan-out requires completion of all predecessor tasks before the (perhaps many) successor tasks can be initiated.

Activities (nodes) on the critical path also are potential areas of high risk. A slip in schedule for any activity on the critical path will result in a slip of the overall schedule. (See path ABGJKLM in Figure 1.) In addition, if all slack time is used along a noncritical path, any subsequent delays will delay the entire project.

3.2 Cost Risks

Techniques for identifying cost risks include use of algorithmic cost models and analysis of project as-

sumptions. [2] Monte Carlo simulation can provide statistical ranges of cost based on probability distributions for the cost drivers. Aggregating the costs and associated risk factors for each element of the work breakdown structure (WBS) can provide a detailed cost-risk analysis. [3]

Budgets are usually determined using effort (people × time) as the primary cost factor. However, as observed by Brooks [4], [5], people and time are not interchangeable. The nonlinear increase in cost with decreasing schedule may result in a very high risk that the project cannot be completed within the budget.

Other factors that influence cost and schedule risks are as follows:

- *Creeping requirements*—Project requirements slowly increase without a corresponding increase in the budget (or the schedule).

- *Schedule compression*—Brought about by pressures from marketing, upper management, and the customer, which results in a nonlinear increase in software costs. [2], [6]

- *Unreasonable budgets*—Budget estimates based on the price necessary to satisfy the market, upper management, and/or the customer rather than to satisfy the technical requirements.

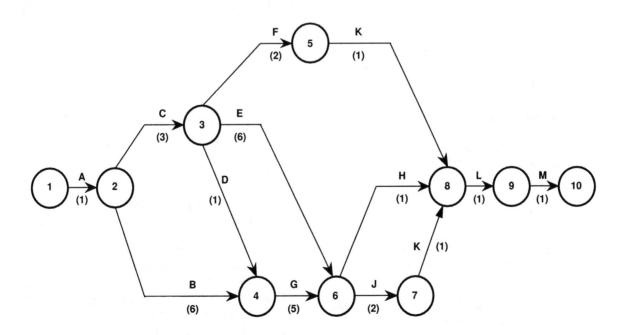

Letters = Activities; Numbers = Milestones; (x) = Activity duration

Figure 1. Activity network.

3.3 Requirements Risks

Many risk factors for software projects result from requirements that are inadequate in one or more of the following ways:

- *Incorrect requirements*—Requirements that do not correctly state user needs and customer expectations

- *Incomplete requirements*—Requirements that do not state desired product features or particular aspects of desired product features

- *Inconsistent requirements*—Requirements that conflict with other requirements in the same specification

- *Unclear requirements*—Requirements that have more than one semantic interpretation

- *Unverifiable requirements*—Requirements for which no finite process exists to verify that the product meets the requirements

- *Untraceable requirements*—Requirements for which there is no audit trail from requirements to tested code and back

- *Volatile requirements*—Requirements that are constantly changed; continual addition of new requirements

Any correction to the software requirements to correct the unexpected incomplete requirements, inconsistent requirements, unclear requirements, and so forth, will result in an unbudgeted increase in cost and schedule or decrease in desirable features.

3.4 Quality Risks

Many risk factors for software projects result from the delivery of unexpectedly poor software quality such as:

- *Unreliable*—The software does not perform its intended functions under specified conditions for stated periods of time

- *Unusable*—Unreasonable effort is required to use the software or to train software users

- *Unmaintainable*—Extraordinary effort is required to locate and fix errors in the software or to upgrade it for future use

- *Nonportable*—Extreme difficulty is encountered in converting the software for use in a different operating environment

- *Nonexpandable*—Software capability or performance cannot be increased by enhancing current functions or adding new functions/data

Any correction to the software product to correct the unexpected poor quality will result in an unbudgeted increase in cost and schedule or decrease in desirable features.

3.5 Operational Risks

By operational risk, we mean the risk that a project may produce a system that does not satisfy operational needs (that is, does not possess the functional, performance, or quality attributes the customers and users want and need). By operational risk, we do not mean the risk of hazard from a system in operation. Hazard is an intrinsic property or condition of a system that has the potential to cause an accident. Commonly used techniques for identifying operational risk include performance modeling, reliability modeling, and quality factor analysis.

4. Risk Analysis

Risk analysis requires an examination of identified risks to determine the probabilities of undesired events and the consequences associated with those events. The purpose of risk analysis is to discover the causes, effects, and magnitude of identified risks, and to develop and examine alternative options for managing the identified risks. Many tools, such as schedule network models and lifecycle cost models, can aid the analysis.

The product of risk analysis is a "watch list." This is a list of prioritized risk factors, consequences of those risks, and the indicators that signal the onset of a problem; that is, the event that indicates a potential problem has become a real problem. A typical watch list shows the trigger events or metrics (for example, externally supplied item delayed more than two weeks), the related areas of impact (for example, development schedule delayed), and, as they are developed, the risk handling actions to be taken to avoid or minimize the impact of a risk becoming a problem.

An often-used instance of a watch list is the "top-10" problem-tracking list. The project manager and the development staff periodically (we suggest weekly) assess the greatest technical and/or managerial risks and lists them in priority order. This list becomes the key in deciding where to focus managerial and technical effort (see Table 1 for an example). Note there do *not* have to be exactly 10 problems. Ten has

Table 1. Top-10 problem tracking list. [7]

This Week	Last week	Number of Weeks	Problem
1	1	3	Scoping requirements to fit schedule and budget
2	–	1	Errors in Ada compiler
3	3	3	Obtaining Sun workstations on time
4	7	2	Writing the SQA plan
5	4	2	Obtaining training on the Sun and Java
No longer on list			
–	6	–	Insufficient software engineers

been selected over the years as a reasonable number that can be tracked on a frequent basis by a skilled project manager.

The watch list is periodically reevaluated (weekly at the working level, monthly at the management and customer levels); items are added, modified, or deleted as appropriate.

5. Risk Handling

Risk handling is the third element in the risk management process. Risk handling includes techniques and methods developed to reduce and/or control risk. Risk management is incomplete if there are no provisions for handling the identified and quantified risk.

Techniques for handling risk fall into five categories:

- Risk avoidance
- Risk assumption
- Problem control (prevention)
- Risk transfer
- Knowledge acquisition

Risk handling methods are constrained only by the ingenuity and skills of the project manager and the project staff. While an explicit decision to ignore (or assume) a risk is a viable option, an implicit decision to do the same is not. A documented action with supporting rationale is required for all risk handling options.

See Table 2 for some non-software examples of risk handling techniques.

5.1   Risk Avoidance

Risk avoidance involves avoiding a high-risk approach

to software development by selecting a lower-risk approach. The statement, "I will not accept this risk; I will look for a less risky solution to the problem," reflects the intent of risk avoidance. Selecting a low-risk solution is not always appropriate; a higher risk solution may be deemed more appropriate because of increased design flexibility, potentially lower cost, or potentially early delivery of the product.

To avoid risk means to avoid the probability and/or consequences of an undesired event happening. Risk avoidance may be reflected, for example, in the choice of system architecture or in the selection of a level-3 subcontractor. [9] Not every risk can be avoided. It should be noted that avoiding risk in one area of a project might increase risk in another area.

5.2   Risk Assumption

Risk assumption involves a conscious decision to accept the consequences should an undesired event occur. It is typified by the statement, "I am aware of the risk, and I choose to accept this risk because of the potential benefits of this approach." Some amount of risk assumption is always present in software development programs. The project manager must determine the appropriate level of risk that can safely be assumed in each situation as it arises.

Risk assumption acknowledges the existence of risk and a decision to accept the consequences if problems occur. The process of identification, analysis, and selection of risk handling techniques allow the project manager to assume the "right" risks, such as those with low probability, low impact, or both. Those that are too risky to assume may be avoided by adopting lower risk approaches such as risk avoidance or risk control.

Table 2. Risk handling techniques. [8]

Risk	Avoidance	Assumption	Control	Transfer	Knowledge Acquisition
Vehicle and/or occupant injury in an auto accident while driving to work	Live close to work and walk Ride rapid-transit systems	Drive to work and hope for the best	Reduce speed limits Wear seat belts Strengthen side panels Go with a safe driver	Carry auto insurance Operate good emergency medical systems Sue the other driver	Determine safest automobiles through crash tests Determine safest route to work
Developing cataracts from microwave oven radiation	Use gas or electric ovens Don't cook food	Use microwave oven only when you are in hurry	Provide users with Faraday shielding Design ovens with door interlocks	Carry health insurance Provide free cornea transplants	Measure radiation for different ovens Evaluate good cooking practices
Getting shot by someone with a handgun	Eliminate handguns	Assume it will happen to the other guy	Stay away from high crime areas Be constantly vigilant Buy bullet-proof glass for car	Carry health insurance Operate good emergency medical systems Sue person who shot you	Determine areas to avoid Establish warning signs of impending danger
The hard disk on your computer will crash	Don't use a hard disk	Keep on using the disk and promise yourself to back it up tomorrow	Periodically back up the disk	Use a disk-recovery software utility	Determine frequently of failures for different hard disks

5.3   Risk Control

The statement, "I am aware of the risk, and I will develop options to reduce the potential of the problem occurring and to reduce its effect should the problem occur," typifies this approach. Risk control involves the continuous monitoring of project status and the development of other solutions if the risk becomes a problem. This often involves the use of reviews, verification and validation, development of fallback positions, and similar management actions. Risk control involves development of a risk reduction plan and tracking to that plan. This includes not only the traditional cost and schedule plans but also technical performance plans.

Risk control also involves continual measurement of project status and development of options and fallback positions to permit alternative, lower risk approaches should the problem occur (sometimes called

contingency plans). For example, developing alternative sources for commercial-off-the-shelf (COTS) software, parallel development of critical components (called *n-version* programming), or increasing the budget and/or personnel assigned if necessary.

5.4   Risk Transfer

Risk transfer involves transferring potential problems to other areas of responsibility. For example, transferring some data processing functions from the client to the server may mitigate risk of poor client performance in a client-server system. The risk of insufficient user training for a new system can be reduced by transferring those responsibilities to the customer. Care must be taken that transfer of a risk factor includes transfer of the responsibility for a successful outcome; transferring a difficult technical issue to a subcontractor does not eliminate the risk of product failure because failure of the subcontractor will result in failure of the overall product.

5.5   Knowledge Acquisition

While this is not a "true" risk handling technique, uncertainty can be reduced by obtaining additional information. Knowledge acquisition consists of gathering additional information to further assess risk and to develop new contingency plans. This is a continuous process that enables the participants to perform risk management with greater confidence. Knowledge acquisition techniques include:

- Prototyping
- Benchmarking
- Simulation and modeling
- Incremental development

6. Optimum Levels of Risk

Risk identification, analysis, and handling are not free; however, they can be cost-effective. Risk management is somewhat like buying insurance—if a potential problem does not occur, we can be subjected to criticism for having wasted time and money on problems that did not materialize. The question is thus, how much time and effort to spend on risk management?

One method of calculating the cost-effectiveness of risk management is to

- determine the probability of an undesired event,
- determine the cost of the loss if the risk becomes a problem, and
- compute the maximum amount that should be spent on risk management by using the following algorithm to compute risk exposure (RE):

RE = (probability of loss) × (amount of loss) = the amount of money that can be spent to mitigate the risk.

Another technique is to examine the risk leverage factor that would result from mitigating the risk. Risk Leverage (RL) is computed by the following algorithm:

RL = [(risk exposure before) − (risk exposure after)] / (cost of risk mitigation)

where "risk exposure before" is the risk exposure before risk mitigation and "risk exposure after" is the risk exposure after risk mitigation. Risk mitigation activities may reduce probability, potential loss, or both. Higher values of risk leverage indicate the better areas for investing in risk management.

7. Risk Monitoring

Risks identified and accepted in the risk identification and analysis phases should be monitored constantly. Particular attention should be paid to the "risk triggers," which are values of indicator metrics that have been identified to "sound the alarm" that a potential problem that either has or has a high probability of become a real problem.

One of the major traps of risk management is refusal to acknowledge that a risk has become a problem and the resulting need to implement a risk-handling plan. It is easy to say, "Let's look at this situation again next week and see if corrective action is still warranted." This approach, when carried on day after day, can result in a major problem in the months to come. As Fred Brooks said in his famous book, *The Mythical Man-Month*, "How does a project get to be a year late? ... One day at a time." [5]

8. Risk Management Program Planning

The risk management program plan should describe risk identification, risk analysis, and risk handling. The plan should describe the role of risk assessment in design reviews, technical performance monitoring, and change control processes. It should describe the methods of risk reduction, monitoring, and handling to be used for each assessed risk. The risk management program plan should require that a separate risk handling plan be prepared for each high-risk item, identify the timing for its development, citing originator and review responsibilities. The plan should also require that a risk reduction report be prepared for each item classified as medium or high risk. The risk management plan should contain, for each accepted risk, the following:

- Statement and assessment of the risk factor
- Probability of the risk becoming a problem
- Consequences and/or cost of the problem
- Alternatives considered with risk, cost, and schedule of each
- Recommended risk reduction/abatement method

- Impact statement for implementation (cost/schedule/technical)
- Responsible organization and personnel
- Risk indicator metrics to be tracked
- Risk trigger thresholds
- Criteria for closure of the problem (should it occur)
- Reviews and decision points
- Recommended backup developments and tests including cost and schedule

Planning for the management of risk makes ultimate sense in order to do the following:

- Eliminate risk wherever possible,
- Isolate and minimize risk,
- Develop alternate courses of action, and
- Establish time and money reserves to cover risks that are not known (the unknown unknowns)

The purpose of risk management planning is simply to focus organized, purposeful thought on the subject of eliminating, minimizing, or containing the effects of undesired events.

9. Summary and Conclusions

The risk factors for every software project should be identified, analyzed, and handled. Every project should have a risk management plan, and every manager should keep an up-to-date list of the project's top-10 project risks. Risk metrics should be collected, analyzed, and heeded; and preplanned risk handling activities should be implemented when the project metrics indicate that a risk has become a problem.

Acknowledgment

This paper is based on Chapter 15, "Risk Analysis and Management," from the *System Engineering Management Guide* [10] with additional information from *Risk Management: Concepts and Guidance*, [11] the paper by Richard E. Fairley [12] and the paper by Richard E. Fairley and Paul Rooks [13].

References

1. Rook, P., "Controlling Software Projects," *Software Engineering J.*, Jan. 1986, pp. 7–16.

2. Boehm, B.W., *Software Engineering Economics*, Prentice-Hall, Englewood Cliffs, NJ, 1981.

3. Fairley, R.E. and R.H. Thayer, "Work Breakdown Structure," *Software Engineering Project Management*, 2nd ed., R.H. Thayer, ed., IEEE Computer Society Press, Los Alamitos, Calif., 1997.

4. Brooks, F.P. Jr., *The Mythical Man-Month: Essays on Software Engineering*, Addison-Wesley, Reading, Mass., 1975.

5. Brooks, Frederick P., "The Mythical Man-Month," *Datamation*, Vol. 20, No. 12, Dec. 1974. Reprinted in *Software Engineering Project Management*, 2nd ed., R.H. Thayer, ed., IEEE Computer Society Press, Los Alamitos, Calif., 1997.

6. Gaffney, J.E., "How to Estimate Software Project Schedules," in *Software Engineering Project Management*, 2nd ed., R.H. Thayer, ed., IEEE Computer Society Press, Los Alamitos, Calif., 1997.

7. Boehm, B.W., *Tutorial on Software Risk Management*, IEEE Computer Society Press, Los Alamitos, Calif., 1989.

8. Modified from M. Granger Morgan, "Table 1: Risk-abatement strategies fall into four major categories: Choosing and managing technology-induced risk," *IEEE Spectrum*, Dec. 1981, p. 56.

9. Paulk, M.C., B. Curtis, M.B. Chrissis, and C.V. Weber, "Capability Maturity Model for Software in Software Engineering," *Software Engineering*, M. Dorfman and R.H. Thayer, eds., IEEE Computer Society Press, Los Alamitos, Calif., 1997. Reprinted in *Software Engineering Project Management*, 2nd ed., R.H. Thayer, ed., IEEE Computer Society Press, Los Alamitos, Calif., 1997.

10. *System Engineering Management Guide*, Defense Systems Management College, Superintendent of Documents, US Government Printing Office, Washington, DC, Jan. 1990.

11. *Risk Management: Concepts and Guidance*, Defense Systems Management College, Superintendent of Documents, US Government Printing Office, Washington, DC, Mar. 1989.

12. Fairley, R.E., "Risk Management for Software Projects," *IEEE Software*, Vol. 11, No. 3, May 1994.

13. Fairley, R.E., and P. Rook, "Risk Management for Software Development," in *Software Engineering*, M. Dorfman and R.H. Thayer, eds., IEEE Computer Society Press, Los Alamitos, Calif., 1997.

A Guide for Preparing Software Project Management Plans

John M. Glabas
California State Controller's Office
Sacramento, CA 95814

Richard E. Fairley
Colorado Technical University
Colorado Springs, CO 80907-3896

1. Introduction

This guide describes the structure and content of software project management plans (SPMP). It identifies those essential elements that should appear, and the optional elements that may appear, in all SPMPs. The guide is intended to assist a project manager, software engineer, or student in the selection, organization, and presentation of planning information needed by managers, customers, system engineers, software engineers, and members of a software project team.

This guide is primarily concerned with management plans for software products; however, it can be used to plan any project for developing or modifying systems that include computers, other hardware, software, people, and procedures. If the guide is used to prepare the plan for an entire system, the resulting plan should be called a *system* project management plan.

The guide is generic in nature; it can be applied to commercial software, scientific, or military software projects, both real-time and batch-oriented. Applicability of the guide is not restricted by the size, complexity, or criticality of the software product. The guide can be used to produce an SPMP for any segment of a product development life cycle. The SPMP may be used for part, or all of, the initial product development effort, a major product enhancement, or ongoing maintenance activities.

This document does not provide any guidance for development of customer requirements, nor does it recommend any particular product development strategy, design methodology, tool, or technique. However, this guide does require that the technical methods used on a project be specified in the SPMP for that project.

The remainder of this guide is organized as follows: Clause[1] 2 provides an introduction to the concepts and terminology of software project planning; Clause 3 provides an overview of software project management plans; Clause 4 presents a detailed description of the various components of a plan; and the Annex contains definitions of terms used throughout this document.

2. Concepts and Terminology of Software Project Planning

A *software project* encompasses all of the technical and managerial efforts required to deliver a product or set of products to a *customer*, which satisfies the terms of the *project agreement*. These project efforts must be planned, initiated, monitored, and controlled to ensure adherence to schedule, budget, and quality criteria. An informal discussion of this viewpoint follows. Precise definitions of the italicized terms used throughout this discussion are provided in the Annex.

A software project has a specific duration, consumes resources, and produces tangible work products. Some of the work products are delivered to the customer; these are the *project deliverables*. The customer is the individual or organization that specifies the product requirements and accepts delivery of the resulting project deliverables. The term "customer," as used here, is not meant to imply a financial transaction between the developer and the customer.

The project agreement is a document or set of documents that defines the scope, duration, cost, and

---

[1] The 1996 revision of the IEEE Style Manual specifies the use of "clause" and "annex" in place of "section" and "appendix," respectively.

deliverables for the project. A project agreement typically takes the form of a contract, a statement of work, a systems engineering specification, a user requirements specification, a business plan, or a project charter. Specifications for the project deliverables should include the exact items, quantities, delivery dates, and delivery locations required to satisfy the terms of the project agreement. The project deliverables may be self contained or they may be a part of a larger system.

From the manager's point of view, the various efforts required to complete a software project can be categorized as project *functions*, *activities*, and *tasks*. A task is the smallest unit of management accountability; it is thus the atomic unit of planning and tracking for a software project. Tasks have finite durations, consume resources, and produce tangible results. These results are typically a document or a code module that can be assessed according to some predetermined acceptance criteria.

The exact nature of the work to be done in completing the task is specified in a *work package*. The work package typically consists of a package name, a description of the work to be done, the preconditions for initiating the task, the estimated duration of the task, required resources (for example, numbers and types of personnel, machines, software, tools, travel, secretarial support), the work products to be produced, the acceptance criteria for the work products, the risks, the completion criteria for the task, and the successor tasks.

A task is successfully completed when the completion criteria for the task are satisfied; the completion criteria include, and may be identical to, the acceptance criteria for the work products produced by the task. A work product might be the *project plan*, a portion of the project plan, the functional requirements, a design document, a source code module, a set of test plans, the user's manual, meeting minutes, memos, schedules, the project budget, or anomaly reports.

The appropriate size for a task is somewhat problematic. During initial project planning, tasks are by necessity large units of work. Because tasks are the atomic units of measurement, planning, and control, large tasks must be decomposed to sizes that permit adequate monitoring of the project. It may be impossible to decompose these large tasks without thorough analysis and some preliminary design work on the product, but eventually each task must be decomposed so that a well-defined work assignment exists for each worker assigned to each task. On the other hand, a task should be large enough to avoid micromanagement of the project and to allow some autonomy on

the part of the task workers. A typical level of task decomposition is for a duration of one staff-week to one staff-month.

Related tasks are usually grouped into hierarchical sets of activities and functions. An activity is a major unit of work (for example, preliminary design and integration testing) that culminates in achievement of a major *project milestone*. A project function is an activity that spans the entire duration of the project (for example, configuration management, or quality assurance). Activities and functions can have subactivities and subfunctions; tasks are the lowest-level elements in the hierarchy. The grouping of related tasks into functions and activities imposes a hierarchical structure on a project that allows separation of concerns and provides a rationale for organizing the project team. The hierarchical relationships among activities, functions, and tasks are often depicted using a *work breakdown structure*.

In addition to hierarchical relations, activities (and associated tasks) also have precedence relations. Typically, an activity or task cannot be initiated until other activities have been completed, and a completed activity or task may be a precondition to the initiation of other work elements. Precedence relations can be depicted using precedence charts, PERT charts, and critical path charts.

Completed activities and tasks result in project milestones. A task should not have externally visible milestones, other than task completion; such a composite task should be treated as a project activity, and the original tasks should become the subtasks of the activity. The hierarchical and precedence relations among tasks must be planned, tracked, and reorganized as evolving circumstances may dictate.

A project milestone is a scheduled event used to measure progress (for example, successful preliminary design review or integration testing completed). Achievement of a milestone usually results in one or more *baselines*, which are work products that have been formally reviewed and accepted. Baselined work products are placed under change control and can be changed only through formal change control procedures. A baseline (for example, design document or test plan) often forms the basis for further work.

A *process model* for a software project depicts the relationship of the project functions, activities, and tasks to the milestones, baselines, reviews, and flow of work products. Examples of process models include the waterfall model, the spiral model, the incremental model, the evolutionary model, and the functional model. The process model for a software project must explicitly incorporate project initiation and project termination activities.

3. An Overview of Software Project Management Plans

The software project management plan (SPMP) is the controlling document for a software project. It specifies the technical and managerial approaches to be used in developing a software product or the software component of a larger product. Related plans for the project (for example, configuration management, quality assurance, verification and validation) are considered to be part of the SPMP and they must be incorporated, either directly or by reference, in the SPMP. The plan must specify the managerial and technical functions, activities, and tasks in sufficient detail to ensure that the resulting software product will satisfy the needs, software requirements, and contractual agreements of the project.

The SPMP is the companion document to the statement of customer requirements. In practice, development of the initial version and subsequent updates to these two documents must proceed in parallel, with iterations, trade-offs, and checks for consistency being made between the documents. Typically, portions of these documents, and sometimes the entire document, are incorporated into the project agreement.

An SPMP is the project manager's statement of understanding with the development organization and the project team members. The project agreement (which includes some or all of the SPMP) forms the statement of understanding between the project manager and the customer. Initial development and periodic updating of the SPMP is the manager's tool for establishing and maintaining communication with the customer, the development organization, and the project team members.

The format of the SPMP is presented in Table 1. The various clauses and subclauses of an SPMP should be ordered in the prescribed sequence; however, initial development and subsequent updating to the SPMP need not proceed in the indicated sequence. As indicated in Table 1, the essential elements of an SPMP are:

1. *Front matter*. This material includes the title page, a revision sheet that contains the history of updates to the SPMP, a preface that summarizes the scope and purpose of the SPMP, a table of contents, and lists of figures and tables.

2. *Overview*. A clause of the SPMP that specifies the scope of the SPMP, the purpose of the SPMP, the deliverables and the mecha-nisms for managing the evolution of the SPMP. The first clause of an SPMP shall always be "Overview."

3. *References*. A clause of the SPMP that specifies all documents and other sources of information referenced in the SPMP.

4. *Definitions*. A clause of the SPMP that specifies all definitions, acronyms, and abbreviations needed to properly interpret the SPMP.

5. *Project Organization*. A clause of the SPMP that specifies the process model for the project; describes the project organizational structure; identifies organizational boundaries and interfaces; and defines key responsibilities for the project.

6. *Managerial Process*. A clause of the SPMP that specifies the project management processes for the project. Items included within this clause shall be consistent with the statement of scope and shall include management objectives and priorities; project assumptions, dependencies, and constraints; the plans for project-integral processes; and the monitoring and controlling plans to be used.

7. *Technical Process*. A clause of the SPMP that specifies plans for managing the scope of the product; the technical methods, tools, and techniques used to deliver the specified product; and software documentation plans.

8. *Work Activity Plan*. A clause of the SPMP that specifies the project activities and their scope; identifies the dependency relationships among the activities, establishes schedules; provides the allocation of budget; states the resource requirements; and states quality assurance and risk considerations.

9. *Additional Components*. A clause of the SPMP that specifies certain other components that may be in this clause of the SPMP as annexes. Additional areas of importance on a particular project might include a training plan for product users, a system installation plan, or a product maintenance plan.

Annexes can be used to provide supporting details that would detract from the SPMP if included in the body.

An index of key terms and acronyms may be included in the SPMP when it is necessary or helpful to the reader.

Table 1. Outline of a software project management plan.

4. Detailed Description of Software Project Management Plans

This clause of the guide describes each of the essential elements in a software project management plan. This presentation follows the format presented in Table 1.

The front matter of an SPMP consists of the title page, revision sheet, preface, table of contents, and indexes for the figures and tables contained in the SPMP.

The title page should contain a title and a revision notice sufficient to uniquely identify the document. A separate revision sheet should contain the version number of the current document, the date of release, approval signature, a list of pages that have been changed in the current version of the plan, and a list of version numbers and dates of release for all previous versions of the SPMP.

The preface should indicate the SPMP's scope of activities, purpose, and intended audience.

The table of contents and the lists of figures and tables should provide the titles and page numbers for clause headings, subclause headings, and figures and tables.

4.1 Overview (Clause 1 of the SPMP)

This clause shall provide an overview of both the project and the product to be produced; the scope of both the project and the product; a list of project deliverables; and the evolution considerations for the SPMP.

4.1.1 Scope (Subclause 1.1 of the SPMP). This subclause shall define the scope of both the project and the product to be delivered.

The statement of project scope shall be specific in its identification of the activities that shall be performed in order to deliver a product, meeting stated requirements. These identified project activities shall be described in a manner that clarifies what activities will occur. As necessary, activities that will be specifically excluded from the project are to be clearly defined, as well.

The statement of product scope shall be specific in its description of the product to be produced. The identified product shall be described in a manner that clarifies what the product will, and as necessary, will not do. The scope should include statements describing the application of the product, including the relevant benefits, objectives, and goals. The statement of scope shall be consistent with similar statements in higher level documents, if they exist. The statement of scope shall not be construed as an official statement of project requirements.

4.1.2 Purpose (Subclause 1.2 of the SPMP). This subclause shall provide a brief statement of the business need to be satisfied by the project, with a concise summary of the project objectives. The purpose shall describe the relationship of this project to other projects, and as appropriate, how this project will be integrated with other projects or ongoing work processes. A reference to the official statement of product requirements shall be provided in this subclause of the SPMP. This statement of purpose shall not be construed as an official statement of product requirements.

4.1.3 Project Deliverables (Subclause 1.3 of the SPMP). This subclause shall list the work products that will be delivered to the customer, the delivery dates, delivery locations, and quantities required to satisfy the terms of the project agreement. This list of project deliverables shall not be construed as an official statement of project requirements.

4.1.4 Evolution of the SPMP (Subclause 1.4 of the SPMP). This subclause shall specify the plans for producing both scheduled and unscheduled updates to the SPMP. Methods of disseminating the updates shall be specified. This subclause shall also specify the mechanisms used to place the initial version of the SPMP under change control and to control subsequent changes to the SPMP.

4.2 References (Clause 2 of the SPMP)

This clause shall provide a complete list of all documents and other sources of information referenced in the SPMP. Each document should be identified by title, report number, date, author, and publishing organization. Other sources of information, such as electronic files, shall be identified in an unambiguous manner using identifiers such as date and version number. Any deviations from referenced standards or policies shall be identified and justifications shall be provided.

4.3 Definitions (Clause 3 of the SPMP)

This clause shall define, or provide references to the definition of all terms and acronyms required to properly interpret the SPMP. Each definition should be numbered as a subclause. Acronyms shall be included within the definitions clause.

4.4 Project Organization (Clause 4 of the SPMP)

This clause shall specify the process model for the project, describe the project organizational structure, identify organizational boundaries and interfaces, and define individual responsibilities for the project.

4.4.1 Process Model (Subclause 4.1 of the SPMP). This subclause shall define the relationships among major project functions and activities by specifying the timing of major milestones, baselines, reviews, work products, project deliverables, and sign-offs that span the project. The process model may be described using a combination of graphical and textual notations. The project process model shall include project initiation and project termination activities.

4.4.2 Organizational Structure (Subclause 4.2 of the SPMP). This subclause shall describe the internal management structure of the project. Graphical devices such as organizational charts or matrix diagrams may be used to depict the lines of authority, responsibility, and communication within the project.

4.4.3 Organizational Boundaries and Interfaces (Subclause 4.3 of the SPMP). This subclause shall describe the administrative and managerial boundaries between the project and each of the following entities: the parent organization, the customer organization, subcontracted organizations, or any other organizational entities that interact with the project. In addition, the administrative and managerial interfaces of the project-integral processes, such as configuration management, quality assurance, and verification and validation, shall be specified in this subclause.

4.4.4 Project Responsibilities (Subclause 4.4 of the SPMP). This subclause shall identify and state the nature of each major project function and activity, and identify the individuals who are responsible for those functions and activities. A matrix of functions and activities versus responsible individuals may be used to depict project responsibilities.

4.5 Managerial Process (Clause 5 of the SPMP)

This clause shall specify the project management processes for the project. This clause shall be consistent with the statement of scope and shall include management objectives and priorities; project assumptions, dependencies, and constraints; plans for project-integral processes; and the monitoring and controlling plans to be used.

4.5.1 Management Objectives or Priorities (Subclause 5.1 of the SPMP). This subclause shall describe the philosophy, goals, and priorities for management activities during the project. Topics to be specified may include, but are not limited to, the frequency and mechanisms of reporting to be used; the relative priorities among requirements, schedule, and budget of the project; risk management procedures to be followed; and a statement of intent to acquire, modify, or use existing software.

4.5.2 Assumptions, Dependencies, and Constraints (Subclause 5.2 of the SPMP). This subclause shall state the assumptions on which the project is based, the external events on which the project depends, and the constraints under which the project is to be conducted.

4.5.3 Integral Processes (Clause 5.3 of the SPMP). This subclause shall contain, either directly or by reference to another document, plans for the integral processes necessary for the successful completion of the software project. These processes may include, but are not limited to, configuration management, software quality assurance, and verification and validation. Plans for integral processes shall be developed to a level of detail consistent with the other clauses of the SPMP. The standards integral to the project, and the methods and resources required to assure compliance, should be specified. In particular, the responsibilities, resource requirements, schedules, and budgets for each process shall be specified. The nature and type of integral processes required will

vary from project to project; however, the absence of a software quality assurance, configuration management, or verification and validation plan shall be explicitly justified in software project management plans that do not include them.

4.5.4 Project Scope Management (Clause 5.4 of the SPMP). This subclause shall contain, either directly or by reference to another document, the plan for managing the scope of the project. The project scope specifies the project work processes that shall be completed in order to deliver a product. The Project Scope Management plan shall specify the methods by which the project scope will be measured against the management plans contained within the SPMP. The plan should include procedures for integrating scope changes into the SPMP. This plan should include the assessment of the probability of changes to the project scope, including the factors that may result in project scope change. The plan should include assessments of probable occurrences, frequency, duration, and the degree to which factors are likely to affect the scope. Since the project scope and the product scope (see 4.6.1) are interrelated, consideration should be given to how changes to project scope may affect the product scope, and conversely, how changes to the product scope may affect the scope of the project. This plan will indicate how causative factors and resulting changes should be identified and the method by which the changes will be documented, communicated, and controlled.

4.5.5 Schedule Management Plan (Clause 5.5 of the SPMP). This subclause shall contain, either directly or by reference to another document, the plan for ensuring that the project is completed on time. The plan should specify the documents that serve as inputs or that place constraints on the schedule. The plan should specify the tools or methodology that will be used to manage the schedule. The plan should include a description of factors most likely to result in schedule changes. The degree to which these known factors will potentially affect the schedule should be described. The plan will indicate how causative factors and resulting changes should be identified and the method by which the changes will be documented, communicated, and controlled.

4.5.6 Budget Management Plan (Clause 5.6 of the SPMP). This subclause shall contain, either directly or by reference to another document, the plan for ensuring that the project is completed within the established budget. The plan should specify the documents that serve as inputs or that place constraints on the budget. The plan should specify the tools or methodology that will be used to manage the budget. The plan should include a description of factors most likely to result in budget changes and, if known, when these factors are most likely to occur. The degree to which known factors could affect the budget should be described. This clause will describe the method to be used in responding to changes to the established budget, and the process for incorporating those changes into the SPMP. This plan will indicate how causative factors and resulting changes should be identified and the method by which the changes will be documented, communicated, and controlled.

4.5.7 Resource Management Plan (Clause 5.7 of the SPMP). This subclause shall specify, either directly or by reference to another document, the plan for managing the resources required for successful completion of the project. The plan should specify the methods used to estimate material, service, and human resource requirements. The plan should include, but not be limited to, estimates of the numbers and required skill levels of personnel required to complete the project; the numbers and required quality attributes of material resources, and the nature of service contracts. The plan should describe the point in the project when each resource will be required, the method for obtaining the resource, the duration of need, and operational integration or phase-out of the resource. Training requirements of human resources, and training associated with the use of a material resource, should be specified. Constraints to obtaining resources and potential conflicts that may result from shared resources shall be specified. This plan should include a description of factors most likely to result in resource requirement changes. The probable degree to which changes in resource requirements will affect the project should be described. This plan will indicate how changes to resource requirements will be identified and the method by which the changes will be documented, communicated, and controlled.

4.5.8 Quality Assurance Management Plan (Clause 5.8 of the SPMP). This subclause shall specify, either directly or by reference to another document, the plan for managing the quality of both the process and the project. The plan should specify the standards that are integral to the project and the methods and resources required to implement and ensure compliance with those standards. This plan should include a description of the factors most likely to result in changes to project quality. The degree to which changes to project quality will affect the project should be described. This plan will indicate how changes to project quality will be identified, and the method by which identified changes will be documented, communicated, and controlled.

4.5.9 Risk Management Plan (Subclause 5.9 of the SPMP). This subclause shall specify, either directly or by reference to another document, plans for managing the risk factors associated with the project.

This subclause shall describe the methods that will be used to identify risk factors, as well as evaluate the potential impact of the identified risks. The plan should also describe contingency planning and methods for implementing these contingency plans. The plan should include mechanisms for tracking the various risk factors, evaluating changes in the level of associated risk, and responses to those changes. Risk factors that should be considered include contractual risks, technological risks, risks due to size and complexity of the product, risks in personnel acquisition and retention, and risks in achieving customer acceptance of the product. The degree to which identified risks will affect the project should be described. This plan will indicate how changes resulting from identified risks will be identified and the method by which those changes will be documented, communicated, and controlled.

4.5.10 Resource Procurement Plan (Clause 5.10 of the SPMP). This subclause shall specify, either directly or by reference to another document, the plan for managing the project procurement process. This plan should include a description of the procurement process, including assignment of responsibility for all aspects of the process. The plan should include the process for obtaining tangible and intangible resources. The plan should specify the procurement process for both expendable and non-expendable materials. The plan should include, but not be limited to, equipment, estimates of computer time, computer hardware and software, service contracts, facilities, transportation, and training. The plan should describe the point in the project when each procurement effort will be required, the vendor and, as appropriate, the method of disposal after project close-out. Constraints to obtaining necessary materials and services shall be specified. This plan should include a description of factors most likely to result in the need for procurement changes. The probable degree to which such changes will affect the project should be described. This plan will indicate how changes in procurement needs will be identified and the method by which the changes will be documented, communicated, and controlled.

4.5.11 Communications Management Plan (Clause 5.11 of the SPMP). This subclause shall specify, either directly or by reference to another document, the plan for managing communications related to the project. This plan will define the reporting mechanisms, report formats, information flows, review and audit mechanisms, and other tools and techniques to be used in monitoring and controlling adherence to the SPMP. Project monitoring should occur at the activity level. The frequency and detail of communications related to project monitoring and control should be consistent with the project scope, criticality, risks, and visibility. The degree to which specific communication failures can affect the project should be described. This plan will indicate how changes resulting from communications failures will be identified and the method by which the changes will be documented, communicated, and controlled.

4.6 Technical Process (Clause 6 of the SPMP)

This clause shall specify, either directly or by reference to another document, plans for managing the scope of the product, the technical methods, tools, and techniques used to deliver the specified product, and software documentation plans.

4.6.1 Product Scope Management (Subclause 6.1 of the SPMP). This subclause shall contain, either directly or by reference to another document, the plan for managing the scope of the product. The plan shall be specific in the methods by which the project scope will be measured against the product requirements. This plan should include the assessment of the probability of changes to requirements and the resulting product scope. This plan should include the factors that may change the product scope. This plan should include an assessment of probable occurrences, frequency, duration, and the degree to which factors are likely to affect the scope. Since the project scope (see 4.5.4) and the product scope are interrelated, consideration should be given as to how changes to the scope of a product may impact the scope of the overall project. This plan will indicate how causative factors and resulting changes in requirements should be identified and the method by which the changes will be documented, communicated, and controlled.

4.6.2 Methods, Tools, and Techniques (Subclause 6.2 of the SPMP). This subclause shall specify, either directly or by reference to another document, plans that describe the computing system, development methodologies, team structures, programming language and other notations, tools, and techniques, to be used to specify, design, build, test, integrate, document, deliver, modify, and maintain the project deliverables. In addition, the technical standards, policies, and procedures governing development and/or modification of the work products and project deliverables shall be included.

4.6.3 Software Documentation Plan (Subclause 6.3 of the SPMP). This subclause shall specify, either directly or by reference to another document, plans that describe the documentation plan for the software project. The documentation plan shall specify the documentation requirements, and the milestones, baselines, reviews, and sign-offs for software docu-

mentation. The documentation plan may also contain a style guide, naming conventions, and documentation formats. The documentation plan shall provide a summary of the schedule and resource requirements for the documentation effort.

4.7 Work Activity Plan (Clause 7 of the SPMP)

This clause shall define the activities and their scope, identify the dependency relationships among the activities, establish schedules, provide the allocation of budget, state the resource requirements, and state quality assurance and risk considerations.

4.7.1 Activity Definitions and Scope (Subclause 7.1 of the SPMP). This subclause shall specify and define the activities to be completed in order to satisfy the project requirements. The scope of each activity will be clearly defined. Each activity shall be uniquely identified; identification may be based on a numbering scheme and/or descriptive titles. A diagram depicting the breakdown of activities into subactivities and tasks (a work breakdown structure) may be used to depict hierarchical relationships among activities. Sufficient detail should exist in the breakdown of work activities, allowing the exposure of hidden complexities. A detailed breakdown enhances the process of estimating required resources and schedules to complete the work activity. The level of detail sufficient to satisfy the requirements of this subclause should be commensurate with the complexity, criticality, and size of the project.

4.7.2 Activity Dependencies (Subclause 7.2 of the SPMP). This subclause shall specify the ordering among project activities and associated tasks to account for the dependency relationships among activities, and the dependency relationships of activities on external events. Techniques such as dependency lists and matrices, directed graphs, and critical path methods could be used to indicate activity dependencies.

4.7.3 Activity Scheduling (Subclause 7.3 of the SPMP). This subclause shall specify the schedule for the various activities, taking into account the precedence relationships and the required milestone dates. Schedules may be expressed in absolute calendar time or in increments relative to a key product or project milestone.

4.7.4 Activity Budget (Subclause 7.4 of the SPMP). This subclause shall specify the allocation of budget to the various activities and tasks. An earned value scheme may be used to allocate budget and to track expenditures.

4.7.5 Activity Resource Requirements (Subclause 7.5 of the SPMP). This subclause of the SPMP shall specify, as a function of time, estimates of the total resources required to complete the activity.

Numbers and types of personnel, computer time, support software, computer hardware, office and laboratory facilities, travel budget, and maintenance requirements for product activities and tasks are typical resources that should be specified. An earned-value scheme may be used to allocate resources and to track resource utilization.

4.8 Additional Components (Clause 8 of the SPMP)

Certain additional components may be required. These may be included by annexing additional materials to the SPMP. Additional items of importance on any particular project may include subcontractor management plans, security plans, independent verification and validation plans, training plans, hardware procurement plans, facility plans, installation plans, data conversion plans, system transition plans, or product maintenance plans.

Annexes

Annexes may be included, either directly or by reference, to provide supporting details that could detract from the SPMP if included in the body of the SPMP. This would include detailed personnel lists, details of cost estimates, detailed work breakdown structures, supplementary information that the audience may want to know, and a glossary of terms that is too large to be placed in the body of the SPMP.

Index

An index to the key terms and acronyms used throughout the SPMP is optional but recommended if it will improve the usability of the SPMP.

References

The following documents contain information that may be useful in preparing a software project management plan:

ANSI/IEEE Std. 610.12-1990, IEEE Standard Glossary of Software Engineering Terminology, IEEE, New York, 1990.

ANSI/IEEE Std. 730-1984, IEEE Standard for Software Quality Assurance Plans, IEEE, New York, 1984.

ANSI/IEEE Std. 828-1983, IEEE Standard for Software Configuration Management Plans, IEEE, New York, 1983.

ANSI/IEEE Std. 983-1986, Guide for Software Quality Assurance Planning, IEEE, New York, 1986.

ANSI/IEEE Std. 1012-1986, IEEE Standard for Software Verification and Validation Plans, IEEE, New York, 1986.

Annex A

Definitions

activity—A major unit of work to be completed in achieving the objectives of a software project. An activity has precise starting and ending dates, incorporates a set of tasks to be completed, consumes resources, and produces tangible results. An activity may contain other activities in a hierarchical manner. The lowest-level activities in the hierarchy must have task descendants. Dependencies often exist among activities. Completion of one activity or task may provide necessary preconditions for initiation of subsequent activities and tasks.

baseline—A work product that has been formally reviewed and agreed upon and that can be changed only through formal change control procedures. Baselines are frequently deliverables and often provide the basis for further work.

customer—An individual or organization that provides the product specifications and formally accepts the project deliverables. The customer may be internal or external to the parent organization of the project. A financial transaction between customer and developer is not necessarily an implied condition.

document—A data medium, electronic or paper, and the data recorded on it.

documentation—(1) A collection of documents on a given subject. (2) Any written or pictorial information describing, defining, specifying, reporting, or certifying activities, requirements, procedures, or results.

function—An activity or set of activities that spans the entire duration of a software project. Examples of project functions include project management, configuration management, quality assurance, and project cost accounting. Functions may be decomposed into subfunctions and activities.

milestone—A scheduled event that is used to measure progress. An individual project member or manager is identified and held accountable for achieving the milestone on time and within budget. Examples of major milestones include a customer or managerial sign-off, issuance of a specification, completion of system integration, and product delivery. Minor milestones might include baselining a software module or completing a chapter of the users' manual.

process model—A model of a software project that depicts the relationships of the project functions, activities, and tasks to the major milestones, baselines, reviews, work products, project deliverables, and sign-offs (both customer and managerial) that span the project. A process model must include project initiation and project termination activities. A software project may span only a segment of the software product life cycle; in this case, the process model spans a subinterval of the product life cycle.

project agreement—A document or set of documents agreed to by the developer and the customer that specifies the scope, objectives, assumptions, management interfaces, risks, staffing plan resource requirements, cost estimates, schedule, resource and budget allocations, project deliverables, and acceptance criteria for the project. Documents in a project agreement include some or all of the following: a contract, a statement of work, systems engineering specifications, user requirements specifications, functional specifications, a business plan, or a project charter.

project deliverables—The items to be delivered to the customer, including quantities, delivery dates, and delivery locations, as specified in the project agreement. The project deliverables may include some or all of, but are not limited to, the following: customer requirements, functional specifications, design specifications, design documentation, source code, object code, users' manuals, principles of operation, installation instructions, training aids, product development tools, and maintenance procedures. Project deliverables may be self-contained or may be part of a larger system.

review—A meeting at which a work product or set of work products is presented to project personnel, managers, users, customers, or other interested parties for comment or approval.

software product—Computer software, related documents, and documentation that are developed or modified for delivery to a customer.

software product life cycle—The set of all events and endeavors that occur within the birth-to-death cycle of a software product.

software project—The set of all activities, functions, and tasks, both technical and managerial, required to satisfy the terms and conditions of the project agreement. A software project has specific starting and ending dates, consumes resources, and has the goal of producing a product or set of products that satisfies the project requirements, as specified in the project agreement. A software project may be self-contained or may be part of a larger project. In some cases, a software project may span many years and consist of numerous subprojects, each being well defined and self contained and having project deliverables.

software project management—The process of planning, organizing, staffing, monitoring, and controlling a software project.

software project management plan (SPMP)—The controlling document for managing a software project. A software project management plan defines the technical and managerial functions, activities, and tasks necessary to satisfy the requirements of a software project, as defined in the project agreement.

task—The smallest unit of work subject to management accountability. A task must be small enough to allow adequate planning and tracking of the project, but large enough to avoid micromanagement. The specification of work to be accomplished to complete a task is documented in a work package. The typical work package size is from one staff-week to one staff-month. Related tasks are grouped to form activities.

work breakdown structure (WBS)—A deliverable-oriented, hierarchical ordering of project activity elements that organizes and defines the total scope of the project. Each descending level of the WBS represents decomposition into increasingly detailed definitions of project activities.

work package—A specification of the work to be accomplished to complete a project task. A work package specifies the objectives of the work, the staffing requirements, the expected duration, the resources to be used, the results to be produced, the acceptance criteria for the work products, the name of the responsible individual, and any special considerations for the work.

work product—Any code module, documentation, or other tangible item that results from working on a project function, activity, or task. Examples of work products include the project plan, functional requirements, design documents, source code, test plans, meeting minutes, schedules, budgets, and anomaly reports. Some subset of work products will form the set of project deliverables.

Chapter 5

Software Cost, Schedule, and Size

1. Chapter Introduction

One of the keys to a successful project is an accurate estimate of the expected effort to complete the software development and meet the expected completion date. Effort is normally displayed as a cost in monetary terms. Most (if not all) cost-estimation techniques are based on past experiences, either

- the personal experiences of the estimator, or

- quantitative data from past projects within the company environment.

The cost-estimation procedure then attempts to reflect a relationship between future cost and prior experience.

WELL CHARLES, DELAYING THE SCHEDULE AGAIN I SEE.

> *I have but one lamp by which my feet are guided and that is the lamp of experience; I know of no way of judging the future but by the past.*
>
> —Patrick Henry

1.1 Major Issues in Estimating Software Cost

There are many issues concerned with software cost estimates. Some of these are as follows:

- Companies and/or projects do not collect project cost data on past projects. This makes it difficult to use past projects as a basis for estimating future projects.
- Precision of estimate is far greater than its accuracy.
- Estimates are usually based on lines of code, which in itself is an estimate.
- Software cost estimates are hard to justify.
- Cost models are not perceived to be very reliable; therefore they are not used with any degree of regularity.
- Software cost estimates are convenient to reduce when developers want to lower their bid.

1.2 Why Are Software Estimations So Unreliable?

There are many reasons why software cost estimates are unreliable. Some of these are as follows:

- Lack of historical data from past projects on which to base estimates.
- First-of-a-kind system. Past history on similar projects does not exist.
- Lack of expertise by the estimator in making estimates.
- Things left out. There are often large pieces that just never get put on the list of things to do and are discovered later.

- Premature estimation. Estimates must be given before a proper understanding of the project is available or developed.
- Productive time is not 40 hours per week, yet many schedules are built as if it were.
- Failure to update estimates when the project or environment changes.
- Undue (unfounded) optimism on the part of the developers.

1.3 Cost (and Schedule) Estimation Techniques

Barry Boehm listed a number of cost estimates in his book on software engineering cost models [1].

- *Algorithmic models*—Algorithms for producing a software cost estimate (COCOMO is an example)
- *Rules of thumb*—Guidelines that have evolved over time
- *Expert judgment*—Consulting one or more experts (Delphi technique is an example)
- *Estimation by analogy*—Comparisons with completed projects
- *Design to cost*—Product is matched to the effort (cost) available
- *Price-to-win estimating*—Price believed to be necessary to win the job (not a cost estimate)
- *Top-down estimating*—Overall estimate derived from global properties (Intermediate COCOMO is an example)
- *Bottom-up estimating*—Each component is separately estimated and the results aggregated (WBS a useful tool)

> *"Just give me five people and one year, and I can develop the system for you."*
>
> —Reported by a software manager to the *Tutorial* author (long before a proper understanding of the problem existed).

In contrast, Winston Royce said [2]

> *"If you have done the project before use an* analogy*; if you haven't, use* COCOMO. *"*

2. Chapter Overview

The seven articles in this chapter are devoted to establishing the cost, schedule, and size of the software to be delivered. The first article, by Richard Stutzke, presents a thorough overview of state-of-the-art software cost estimation. The next article is a tutorial on cost estimation and the use of COCOMO. The next two articles are extracts from a report [3] from the Software Productivity Consortium, Herndon, VA. Another article, by Capers Jones, gives a means of providing rough estimates for software costs and schedules (but not recommended by Jones). The last article in the chapter is a new article on a new software cost model—COCOMO 2.0.

3. Article Descriptions

The Stutzke article surveys the current software cost models. Stutzke points out that managers want software delivered on schedule and within cost—a rarity in past software development projects. The article describes the difficulty in estimating accurate software costs—particularly before the project is well defined. Stutzke divides the software cost-estimation models into two methods: experience-based models and parameter-based models.

Starting with the 1960s and proceeding through the 1990s, Stutzke describes the various software cost models that have been developed. The author does not recommend one method over another. What he does state is that each software development organization must develop or adapt an appropriate cost model to suit their own environment. He also advocates that the developer use two models where the strength and weakness of each model complement each other—for example, use one parametric-based model and one (manual) approach based on experience.

The Constructive Cost Model (COCOMO) developed by Barry Boehm and documented in his reference book, *Software Engineering Economics*, [1] is the most-used software cost and schedule estimation model in the world today [4]. Deanna Legg, a graduate of the California State University, Sacramento, with an MS in computer science prepared a user manual on how to estimate software cost and schedule based on

COCOMO (by Boehm) for a project involving a State of California department. The manual provides sufficient information to enable a user to manually estimate the expected cost and schedule of a software project using COCOMO.

The next article is "How to Estimate Software System Size" a chapter from *The Software Measurement Guidebook* [3] produced by the Software Productivity Consortium by John Gaffney and Robert Cruickshank. The article discusses the impact of size on the cost and length of time required to develop a software system. This article provides methods for estimating software size and emphasizes the methods that can be applied early in the software development cycle. Estimating the size of a new software system is the key to estimating development costs, both in dollar terms and for labor and other resources required. The two principal types of measurements for software product size are these:

1. *Lines of code*: This is a number of source statements delivered at the completion of the software product.
2. *Function points*: This is a measure of the amount of functionality delivered by the software system.

Function-point estimating techniques, originally developed by Allan J. Albright and John Gaffney, were developed to *directly* estimate software costs from software requirements. The argument asserted that function points were directly related to the functionality of the system. Thus, function points were easier to compute at the beginning of the project than the traditional lines of code used in many software estimation tools to date.

However, function points are primarily used today for indirectly computing software costs. First, function points are computed, and then the function point count is used to estimate software size in terms of lines of code. The lines of code are then used to estimate software development cost with the more traditional software estimation techniques (for example, COCOMO).

To convert function point counts to lines of code, researchers like Capers Jones [5] analyzed numerous software products and determined a constant relationship between lines of code and function points. This constant, called a function point index (Fi), multiplies the function point to obtain the estimated lines of code. The equation is:

LOC = #FPs * Fi (Where Fi is language dependent)
Where:

Language	Fi
Assembler	320 LOC/FP
C	150
COBOL	105
FORTRAN	105
Pascal	91
Ada	71
PL/1	65
Prolog/LISP	64
Smalltalk	21
Spread sheet	6

It is interesting to note that Fi is also a measure of the "power" of the language.

The next article, "How to Estimate A Software Project Schedule," was also a chapter from the *Software Measurement Guidebook* produced for the Software Productivity Consortium by John Gaffney. The article points out that it is important to accurately estimate the time required to develop a software product and to be able to perform effort/schedule trade-offs.

This article provides answers to the following schedule-related questions:

- How long will the development take?

- What effect will changes in schedule have on the development effort?

- What is the staffing profile for the project over the project duration?

The fifth article is a very short monologue by Capers Jones entitled "By Popular Demand: Software Estimating Rules of Thumb." Jones is a particularly well-known individual in software engineering who specializes in the areas of software cost estimation and software scheduling. Apparently, he wrote this short article at the request of numerous personnel from industry yearning for a "quick and dirty" way of estimating software costs to be used with a pocket calculator. He said that he wrote this article reluctantly,

indicating that accurate software estimation is too complex for simple rules of thumb.

Jones wrote ten simple rules of thumb for estimating software sizes, software costs, and software schedules. Each is based on function-point estimates, rather than the more traditional lines of code. He also points out and emphasizes that simple rules of thumb, although they continue to be popular, are never accurate and should never be used in place of formal estimating methods. However, they are interesting to read.

The last article is a look into the future of software cost-estimating models, particularly the world's most popular model, COCOMO. This article, "Cost Models for Future Software Life Cycle Processes: COCOMO 2.0," was written by a number of people associated with the University of Southern California's Center for Software Engineering, which is directed by Barry Boehm. This new article by Boehm and colleagues summarizes research in deriving a new COCOMO 2.0 model tailored to new forms of software development, such as the following:

- Non-sequential and rapid development process models

- Re-use driven approaches involving commercial off-the-shelf (COTS) packages to include re-engineering, applications composition, and applications generations capabilities

- Object-oriented approaches supported by distributed middleware

- Software process maturity initiatives

The major new modeling capabilities of COCOMO 2.0 are a tailored family of software sizing models, involving object points, function points, and source lines of code. COCOMO 2.0 also involves non-linear models of software reuse and re-engineering, an exponent-driver approach for modeling relative software diseconomies of scale, and several modifications to the original COCOMO effort cost-drivers. This model will serve as a framework for an extensive current data collection analysis effort to further refine and calibrate the model's estimation capability.

References

1. Boehm, B.W., *Software Engineering Economics*, Prentice Hall, Englewood Cliffs, NJ, 1981.

2. Private conversation with the author in 1987 when Dr. Royce was director of the Lockheed Software Technology Center.

3. *Software Measurement Guidebook*, SPC-91060-CMC, Software Productivity Consortium Services Corporation, Herndon, VA, Dec. 1992.

4. The tutorial author has traveled to many of the major continents of the world, giving seminars to new and experienced software project managers, and invariably, COCOMO is the cost estimating technique in use (when any is used at all, of course).

5. Jones, C., "A New Look at Languages," *Computerworld*, Nov. 7, 1988, pp. 97.

Software Estimating Technology: A Survey[1]

Richard D. Stutzke

Science Applications International Corporation
6725 Odyssey Drive
Huntsville, AL 35806-3301
Voice: (205) 971-6624
Fax: (205) 971-6550
Internet: Richard.D.Stutzke@cpmx.saic.com

Introduction

Our world increasingly relies on software. There is a seemingly insatiable demand for more functionality, interfaces that are easier to use, faster response, and fewer defects. Developers must strive to achieve these objectives while simultaneously reducing development costs and cycle time. Above all, senior management wants software delivered on schedule and within cost, a rarity in past software development projects. Software Process Improvement (SPI), as advocated by the Software Engineering Institute (SEI), helps to achieve these objectives. Project planning and tracking are identified as two Key Process Areas in the SEI's Capability Maturity Model (CMM).

Software cost and schedule estimation supports the planning and tracking of software projects. Estimation is receiving renewed attention during the 1990s to cope with new ways of building software and to provide more accurate and dependable estimates of costs and schedules. This article discusses problems encountered in software estimation, surveys previous work in the field and describes current work, provides an approach to improve software estimation, and offers some predictions and advice concerning software estimation.

Description of the Problem

The estimator must estimate the effort (person-hours) and duration (calendar-days) for the project to enable managers to determine important business measures such as product costs, return on investment, and time to market. The estimation process is difficult for several reasons:

- Conflicting project goals

- Lack of a detailed product description

- Wide variation in effort needed to reuse code

- Emergence of new development processes, methods, and tools

The following paragraphs discuss each of these reasons.

The first reason is that projects often must satisfy conflicting goals. Projects to develop (or maintain) software must provide specified functionality within specified performance criteria, within a specified cost and/or schedule, and with some desired level of quality (typically defined as the absence of defects). Software engineering processes can be chosen to meet any one of these project goals. Usually, however, more than one goal must be satisfied by a particular project. These multiple constraints complicate the estimating process.

The second reason is that estimates are required before the product is well defined. Software functionality is very difficult to define, especially in the early stages of a project. The basis for the first good cost estimate is not usually available for totally new systems until the top-level design has been defined. (This design is an instance of the product's "software architecture".) This level of design is only defined at the Preliminary Design Review (PDR) in United States Department of Defense (DoD) contracts (and sometimes not even then, which leads to undesirable consequences). This milestone is reached after approximately 20 percent of the total effort and 40 percent of the total duration have been expended by the project staff. At this point in a project, typical accuracies for the estimated effort and duration are within 25 percent of the final project actuals. In general, the accuracy of

---

[1] This paper is an expanded and updated version of a paper that appeared in the May 1996 issue of the journal *CROSSTALK*. It contains more detail on some of the parametric models and additional information about some new models. The entire article has been reformatted to improve readability. Some minor corrections have been made as well.

estimates increases as a project proceeds since more information becomes available, for example, product structure, product size, and team productivity. Figure 1 illustrates this and is adapted from Boehm [1]. (Commercial software projects behave similarly.) To reduce costs (as well as to improve quality and reduce development times), some projects are employing predefined *domain-specific software architectures* (DSSAs). The development costs for such projects can be estimated more accurately than for projects that build a totally new product since more information about the product is available earlier. (The Advanced Research Projects Agency and the SEI, among others, are sponsoring work on DSSAs.) In general, however, the estimator must apply considerable skill to estimate project cost and schedule early in a project.

For modifications of existing code, more data are available earlier and so more accurate estimates are possible for this kind of project compared to totally new development. This is important since approxi-

mately half of all software maintenance work is really a response to changes in the original requirements and/or in the system's external environment (that is, mission, interfaces to other systems, and so forth) and involves modification of existing code. (The choice of the software architecture significantly influences modifiability and hence maintainability. Architecture-based reuse is another motivation for the work on DSSAs.)

The need to modify existing code is the third reason that software cost estimating is difficult. It is hard to identify and quantify the factors affecting the effort needed to incorporate existing code in a product. The code must be located, understood, modified, integrated, and tested. The costs for performing these activities depend on how the code is structured, on the programmer's knowledge of the code, as well as on other things. The modification of code is a subset of a broader activity called software reuse, which is faced with these same problems.

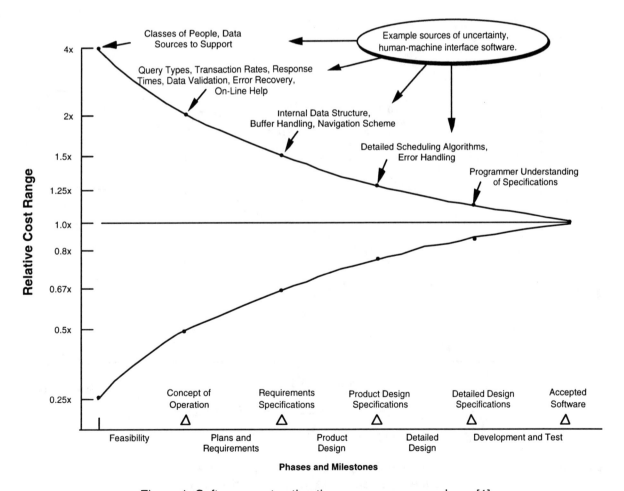

Figure 1. Software cost estimation accuracy versus phase.[1]

Various cost estimation models have been developed to qualify the economic costs of building and using reusable components. For example, Richard Selby [2] analyzed costs at NASA's Software Engineering Laboratory and found that there is a large increase in programmer effort as soon as a programmer has to "look inside" the component. The cost of reusing a component depends on its suitability for the intended application, its structure, and other factors. Figure 2 illustrates this effect by showing the cost to reuse software compared to the cost of developing totally new software as a function of the amount of existing code that must be modified to install the code in a new system. For example, modifications may be necessary to accommodate a new operating environment (such as porting from Berkeley Unix to DEC Ultrix).

Figure 2 is based on a model I developed using data from Richard Selby [2], Rainer Gerlich and Ulrich Denskat [3], and Barry Boehm and colleagues [4]. The two curves shown correspond to the best and worst cases for reuse on the basis of the factors mentioned above. These curves have several noteworthy features. First, the cost is not zero even if no code is modified. Second, the costs increase faster than linearly at first. Third, the cost of modifying all of the existing code is more expensive than developing the code from scratch. (Effort is wasted to understand, then discard the existing code before the new code is written. This effort is never expended if the decision is made to develop totally new code from the start.) As shown in the figure, for the worst case, the economic break-even point occurs when only 20 percent of the code is modified; reuse is not cost-effective above the break-even point. Such nonlinear behavior is not handled in existing cost models.

A fourth reason is that the way software is being built is changing. New development processes are emerging, and new ways are needed to estimate the costs and schedules for the new processes. These processes endeavor to provide higher quality software (that is, fewer defects), produce more modular and maintainable software, and/or deliver software (products and prototypes) to the end user faster.

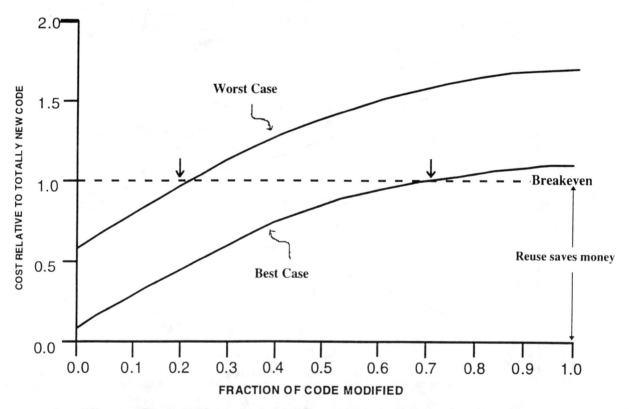

Figure 2. Reusing software is not always cost-effective.

To meet these and the other objectives (stated previously), developers are using combinations of prebuilt code components and labor-saving tools. For example, much programming is being put into the hands of the users themselves by providing macro definition capabilities in many products. These capabilities allow users to define sequences of frequently used commands.[2] A slightly more sophisticated approach is to allow domain experts to construct applications using special tools such as Fourth Generation Languages (4GLs) and application composition tools. Larger systems intended for specialized (one of a kind) applications are often built using commercial off-the-shelf (COTS) products to provide functionality in areas that are understood well enough to be standardized. Examples are graphical user interfaces (GUI) and relational database management systems (RDBMSs). The trend toward object-oriented languages and Ada supports this component-based software construction by making it easier to develop "plug compatible" components. Thus, code reuse is becoming an increasingly large factor in cost estimation. A good understanding of the cost factors associated with software reuse thus becomes even more important.

Lastly, some authors like Richard Selby [5] have proposed "measurement-driven development processes" wherein process activities are adapted during the course of a project based on measurements of process performance. Planning and costing such processes prior to the start of the project is impossible. (Controlling them will also be difficult.)

What Is An Estimate?

As a minimum, the estimator must compute the effort (cost) and duration (schedule) for the project's process activities; identify associated costs such as equipment, travel, and staff training; and state the rationale behind the calculations (including the input values used, assumptions, and so forth). Estimation is closely tied to the details of the product's requirements and design (primarily the software architecture) and the activities of the chosen development process. These must be well understood in order to produce accurate estimates.

It is also highly desirable for the estimator to indicate the confidence in the reported values via ranges

or standard deviations. The estimator should also try to state the assumptions and risks to highlight any areas of limited understanding relating to the requirements, product design, or development process.

Estimation Methods

There are two basic classes of estimation methods: experience-based estimation and parametric models. Each has weaknesses. Experience-based estimation may be flawed due to obsolescence of the historical data used or because the estimators' memories of past projects are flawed. Parametric models typically have a particular "perspective." Some clearly fit a military standard development process (such as that defined by DoD-Std-2167A). Other models fit commercial development procedures. Estimators must choose models suited to their project environment and ensure that these models are correctly calibrated to the project environment. In spite of their intrinsic weaknesses, both classes of methods have their uses.

Survey of Past Work

The formal study of software estimating technology did not begin until the 1960s, although some earlier work was done on models of research and development by Peter Norden [6]. This section gives a chronological summary of the work in the field.

The 1960s

In the 1960s, while at RCA, Frank Freiman developed the concept of parametric estimating, and this led to the development of the PRICE model for hardware. This was the first generally available computerized estimating tool. It was extended to handle software in the 1970s.

The 1970s

The 1970s was a very active period. During this decade, the need to accurately predict the costs and schedules for software development became increasingly important and so began to receive more attention. Larger and larger systems were being built and many past projects had been financial disasters. Frederick Brooks, while at IBM, described many of these problems in his book *The Mythical Man-Month* [7]. His book provides an entertaining but realistic account of the problems as perceived at that time.

During the 1970s, high-order languages, such as FORTRAN, ALGOL, JOVIAL, and Pascal, were

---

[2] There is an analogy here to the situation shortly after telephones were introduced in the United States. Someone predicted that soon the majority of the United States' population would have to be employed as telephone operators in order to handle the workload of connecting calls. Instead, technology changed and now everyone serves as their own operator, using direct dialing to connect nearly all of their calls.

coming into increasingly wider use but did not support reuse. Also, programming tools (other than compilers for the languages and simple text editors) were in very limited use. For these two reasons, systems were essentially built by hand from scratch. The cost models of this period thus emphasized new development.

During this period, many authors analyzed project data using statistical techniques in an attempt to identify the major factors contributing to software development costs. Significant factors were identified using correlation techniques and were then incorporated in models using regression techniques. (Regression is a statistical method for predicting values of one or more dependent variables from a collection of independent (predictor) variables. Basically, the model's coefficients are chosen to produce the "best possible" fit to actual, validated project data.) Unfortunately, in practice there is never enough data to define a model completely, nor are there any accepted "laws of software physics" that could constrain the form of the model's basic equations. As noted by Samuel Conte [8], researchers must thus resort to so-called "composite models" created using a combination of analytic equations, statistical data fitting, and expert judgment. Experts differ on which independent variables are significant and on the form of estimating equations, giving rise to diverse models. The coefficients of a particular model are determined using actual project data and regression techniques. Most estimating models are in fact composite models. Such models are one form of Cost Estimating Relation (CER).

The prototypical composite model is the COnstructive COst MOdel (COCOMO) developed by Barry W. Boehm in the late 1970s and described in his classic book *Software Engineering Economics* [1]. Various implementations of COCOMO continue to be widely used throughout the world. COCOMO provides formulas for estimating the total development effort and time. The "nominal" effort depends on the amount of software to be produced, measured in Delivered Source Instructions (essentially source lines of code without comments). The nominal effort is adjusted to account for the effects of 15 cost drivers, which describe attributes of the product, computer, personnel, and project. (The project attributes include the effects of modern methods and tools.) Estimators use five- or six-point Lickert scales to rate each cost driver attribute. These ratings are converted into quantitative values using tables. The quantitative values are multiplied to give the total Effort Adjustment Factor (EAF). (The range of effort adjustment, based on the ratio of the highest possible to lowest possible values of EAF, is 817.) The adjusted effort is then used to compute the development schedule. Finally,

additional tables are used to allocate the effort and development time by phase and by activity.[3]

COCOMO distinguishes three "development modes" that essentially correspond to the formality of the development process. For example, the "embedded" mode is used to estimate the development of large, complex systems such as those built to military specifications. Different coefficients are used in the effort and schedule equations for each mode. COCOMO also has three levels of detail. Basic COCOMO excludes the effects of the cost driver attributes. Intermediate COCOMO uses the EAF as just described. Detailed COCOMO uses quantitative cost driver values that are phase dependent. Intermediate COCOMO is the version most commonly used. COCOMO, like other composite models, also has ways to handle the reuse, modification, and maintenance of existing code.

The PRICE Software Cost Model (PRICE S), another software cost and schedule estimation model, was initially developed from 1975 through 1977 at RCA by Frank Freiman and Robert Park based on data from over 400 projects. Parametric models in the PRICE family were the first generally available, computerized cost estimation models. William Rapp programmed the models, among them PRICE S, to run on mainframe computers at RCA, making them available via a timesharing (dial-in) service.

The PRICE Software Cost Model is described in [9] and [10]. The model operates as follows. The "central equation" computes the nominal effort to perform the tasks in an ideal world. Then the nominal effort is adjusted to account for non-nominal factors such as interface complexity, personnel skill, tools, utilization of available target computer resources, and so on. The adjusted effort is then used to compute the nominal ("reference") schedule. Additional adjustments are made to obtain the final estimated schedule, as well as the final estimated effort (since compressing schedule and overlapping phases affect costs). There are approximately a dozen cost and schedule drivers used in the PRICE S model. The PRICE S calculations also handle the reuse/reengineering of code. Studies made in 1979, 1981, and 1984 found

---

[3] The names of the phases and activities are unfortunately nearly identical: analysis, design, code, test, and so on. The phases refer to the time when activities are performed. The problem is that activities span phases. For example, most of the effort for the Requirements Analysis activity is expended during the analysis phase, but some effort is also expended later to revise the requirements to reflect new knowledge obtained during the subsequent design and coding phases. This close correspondence of the phases and activities reflects the "Waterfall" development of the 1970s. Other estimating tools do this also. Unfortunately, the close similarity of the names can sometimes cause users to misinterpret the numbers computed by such models.

that PRICE S predicts costs within 8-15 percent of project actuals.

The PRICE S central equation computes effort based on the "volume" of the software to be produced. Volume is computed based on the amount of code to be produced (measured in source lines of code (SLOC) or function points), the programming language used (LANG), and the complexity of the application (APPL). The nominal effort is then computed by raising the volume to a power that is a function of the organization's productivity factor (PROFAC).[4] PROFAC is determined based on language type, application complexity, and platform type (described below) using a table. (The value of PROFAC can also be determined by calibration using the organization's own historical data; this is preferable.) The nominal effort is then adjusted to account for the effects of the various cost drivers. The platform (PLTFM) cost driver describes the formality in which the development must take place. For example, software intended for internal use is developed less formally than software for manned space vehicles. (COCOMO's modes (organic, semi-detached, embedded) plus its required reliability (RELY) cost driver accomplish a purpose similar to the PLTFM parameter in PRICE S.)

A shortcoming of these 1970s models is that the independent variables were often "result measures" such as the size in lines of code. Such values are readily measured but only after the project has been completed. It is very difficult to predict the values of such variables before the start of the project.[5] This means that many of the models, although based on statistical analyses of actual result data, were hard to use in practice since the values of the independent variables were hard to determine before the project team had analyzed the requirements and had prepared a fairly detailed design. Another shortcoming of such models is that they assume that software will be developed using the same process as was used previously. This assumption is becoming increasingly unrealistic because new processes, methods, and tools continue to be developed.

At the end of the 1970s, Allan Albrecht and John

Gaffney of IBM developed *function point analysis* (FPA) for estimating the size and development effort for management information systems [11], [12]. Components of a system are classified into five types according to specific rules. These types are inputs, outputs, inquiries, logical internal files, and external interface files. Each type has an assigned weight based on characteristics of the component. These weights are proportional to the development effort needed to construct components of that type. The estimator counts the number of components of each type, multiplies these counts by the corresponding weight, sums these products, and multiplies the sum by a factor to account for global system characteristics. The result is the "size" of the system measured in "function points." The estimator then uses the team's productivity (in function points/person-month) to compute the development effort.

Later in the 1970s, two authors endeavored to define models based on theoretical grounds. Lawrence H. Putnam [13] based his Software Lifecycle Model (SLIM) on the Norden-Rayleigh curve plus empirical results from 50 U.S. Army projects. Putnam's data indicate that the development staffing rises smoothly and drops sharply during acceptance testing. Putnam reports that the shape fits the first part of the Norden-Rayleigh curve and uses this fact to relate the area under the curve (which corresponds to the development effort) to the curve's parameters.

Putnam's other empirical results are expressed as two equations describing relations between the development effort and the schedule. The first equation, called the "software equation," states that development effort is proportional to the cube of the size and inversely proportional to the fourth power of the development time. The second equation, the "manpower buildup" equation, states that the effort is proportional to the cube of the development time. Solving these two coupled equations gives the basic predictive equations used in Quantitative Software Management's SLIM tool. The solution represents the minimum development time (maximum development effort) for the project. The SLIM tool uses other management constraints (for example, staffing caps and desired product reliability level) to define a bounded region of possible solutions representing minimum cost, minimum time, and so forth.

Putnam's manpower buildup equation has development time proportional to the cube root of the effort, while COCOMO's various development modes use an exponent ranging from 0.32 to 0.38. (The Jensen model, described later, also has development time proportional to the cube root of the effort.) For details see Kitchenham (published as Chapter 9 of Fenton [14]).

---

[4] Actually, effort is computed using separate equations for three phases: design, implementation (coding), and testing. The actual functions used to compute the volume, the exponent, and the adjustments for some of the cost drivers are proprietary and are not published.

[5] Some methods have been developed to help estimators estimate size. These methods rely on analogies to similar projects whose costs are recorded in a database, on averaging techniques to elicit the consensus of experts (Delphi, PERT) and combinations thereof. One such combination, developed by George Bozoki of Lockheed, uses sophisticated statistical techniques in conjunction with historical data. Bozoki's model is sold as the Software Sizing Model (SSM) by Galorath Associates.

Some authors, such as Conte [8], have criticized SLIM's modeling of the effort/schedule trade-off. Putnam's (and SLIM's) "software equation" implies that effort scales inversely as the fourth power of the development time, leading to severe cost increases for compressed schedules. Actually, Putnam's model limits the range of applicability of the fourth-power model relation using other constraints. Generally, development time computed by the Putnam model can range between some minimum development time and a time approximately 30 percent greater than this minimum time.

The second author attempting to define a model based on theoretical grounds was Maurice H. Halstead [15]. Halstead defined software size in terms of the number of operators and operands defined in the program and proposed relations to estimate the development time and effort. To obtain this size information before the start of a project was of course nearly impossible because a good understanding of the detailed design is not available until later. Subsequent work by S.D. Conte ([8], page 300) has shown that Halstead's relations are based on limited data and Halstead's model is no longer used for estimation purposes. (Don Coleman and colleagues [16] have recently reported some success in using it to predict the "maintainability" of software.)

Comparison of the Major Composite Models

It is instructive to compare the basic equations of the 1970s era composite models. First, look at the development effort. SLIM has development effort proportional to the size raised to the 1.29 power. Both COCOMO ("embedded" mode) and Jensen's Software Estimation Model (SEM), described in the next section, have development effort proportional to the size raised to the 1.20 power. The PRICE S model is more complex, and the full equations have not been published. One complication is that PRICE S computes the effort for three phases and then sums these values. The other models, in contrast, compute a total core effort and then allocate it to the phases. We can say, however, that the effort estimated by PRICE S appears to increase approximately linearly with the volume (which is equivalent to the size used by the other models) for a given value of the productivity factor (PROFAC). The slope of the line decreases with increasing values of PROFAC.

Most of these models have the nominal development time ("schedule") proportional to the cube root of the estimated development effort (which includes all of the adjustments for non-nominal conditions).

This is exactly true for the SLIM and SEM models. (For details, see Kitchenham, published as Chapter 9 of [14].) Intermediate COCOMO's various development modes use exponents ranging from 0.32 to 0.38. It is not so easy to make a clear statement for PRICE S since its schedule equations are complex, and not all details are published. PRICE S computes the nominal schedule as proportional to the volume raised to the 0.37 power. If we assume that the effort is proportional to the volume raised to a power of 1.1 or so, then the PRICE S model would have schedule proportional to effort raised to approximately the 0.34 power, and so PRICE S would appear to be consistent with the other models. (This is rather approximate, of course, since the PRICE S volume consists of size (in SLOC) multiplied by factors reflecting complexity and language. The other models use size directly.)

The COCOMO, SLIM, and SEM models all have effort proportional to the size raised to the 1.2 or 1.3 power, and development time proportional to the cube root of the effort. PRICE S has effort approximately proportional to the size raised 1.1 power, and development time is also approximately proportional to the cube root of the effort. The basic equations of these 1970s-era composite models are thus similar even though the models were developed independently. These similarities suggest that there may be some common "laws of software estimating," at least for the case of new software development. Because of these similarities, these models have comparable accuracies, generally predicting effort within 10-20 percent of project actuals for some appreciable fraction of the projects analyzed.

The 1980s

During the 1980s, work continued to improve and consolidate the best models. As PCs started to come into general use, many models were programmed. Several firms began selling computerized estimating tools. Following the publication of the COCOMO equations in 1981, several tools that implemented COCOMO appeared during the latter half of the 1980s.

The DoD introduced the Ada programming language in 1983 [American National Standards Institute (ANSI) and DoD-Std-1815A-1983] to reduce the costs of developing large systems. Certain features of Ada significantly impact development and maintenance costs, and so Barry Boehm and Walker Royce defined a revised model called Ada COCOMO [17]. This model also addressed the fact that systems were being built incrementally in an effort to handle the inevitable changes in requirements.

Robert C. Tausworthe [18] extended the work of

Boehm, Herd, Putnam, Walston and Felix, and Wolverton to develop a cost model for the National Aeronautics and Space Administration (NASA) Jet Propulsion Laboratory. Tausworthe's model was further extended by Donald Reifer to produce the PC-based SOFTCOST-R model, which is now sold by Resource Calculations Inc.

Randall W. Jensen [19] extended Putnam's work by eliminating some of the undesirable behavior of Putnam's SLIM. Putnam's SLIM equation has development effort proportional to size (measured in source lines of code) cubed divided by development time to the fourth power. Jensen asserted that development effort is proportional to the square of the size divided by the square of the development time. Both Jensen and Putnam apply the constraint that effort divided by the cube of the development time is less than some constant (which is chosen based on product and project parameters). Jensen's equations reduce to equations that are close to those of COCOMO's "embedded" mode but the effect of various cost drivers is handled quite differently. Daniel Galorath and co-workers continue to refine the Jensen model and market it as the Software Estimation Model (SEM), part of the System Evaluation and Estimation of Resources (SEER) tool set. SEER-SEM Version 4.5 was released in late 1996. (Jensen has recently proposed a new model, which is described in the next section.)

In 1984, Albrecht [20] published a major revision to the FPA method. These revisions sharpened the rules for rating the complexity of the software. The original version of FPA had a single empirically-derived weight for each type of component. The new method subdivided each type of component by complexity according to certain rules. Different weights are used for low, medium, and high complexity components. This revised method is the basis for the current standard as defined by the International Function Point Users Group (IFPUG).

FPA was extended by Capers Jones [21] to include the effect of computationally complex algorithms on development costs. His "Feature Point Method" counts FPA's five types plus a sixth type called algorithms. His method also eliminates the classification of the elements in terms of three levels of complexity; a single weight is used for each element type. Various PC-based tools implement these FPA-based methods, such as Function Point Workbench and Checkpoint from Software Productivity Research, and FPXpert and Estimacs from Computer Associates International.

Charles Symons [22] proposed another revision of FPA to achieve the following major goals: reduce the subjectivity in dealing with files, make the size independent of whether the system was implemented as a single system or a set of related subsystems, and change the emphasis of function points away from gauging the value to users to predicting development effort. His method, called Mark II Function Points, bases the computation of size (functionality) on "logical transactions." Each processing activity done by the system is analyzed in terms of the number of data items input, referenced, and output. These are counted and weighted to compute the "size" in function points.

The 1990s

Because of the increasing diversity of software development processes, the 1990s are seeing renewed attention on developing improved cost models. The SEI started a small initiative on software estimation improvement in 1994. Of more interest is an effort led by Barry Boehm, now at the University of Southern California, to revise and extend the COCOMO model which has served the industry well for so long (over 15 years).

The new version of COCOMO [4], called COCOMO 2.0, is still in development and will address the various types of development processes mentioned earlier. COCOMO 2.0 explicitly handles the availability of additional information in later stages of a project, the nonlinear costs of reusing software components, and the effects of several factors on the diseconomies of scale. (Some of these are the turnover rate of the staff, the geographic dispersion of the team, and the "maturity" of the development process as defined by the SEI.) The model also revises some coefficient values and eliminates discontinuities present in the old model (related to "development modes" and maintenance versus adaptation). Barry Boehm is leading a group of industrial and academic affiliates to review the revised set of COCOMO equations and to collect data to evaluate hypotheses to select the significant parameters for COCOMO 2.0. Boehm and his coworkers expect to provide the refined equations, representing an improved and calibrated cost model, in early 1997.

FPA has recently been extended to handle scientific and real-time systems by Scott Whitmire [23]. He acknowledges Tom DeMarco's statement [24] that all software has three dimensions: data, function, and control. Whitmire asserts that classical FPA addresses only the data dimension of a software program. His three-dimensional (3D) function point method provides a way to quantify characteristics of the other two dimensions. The 3D function point index (that is, the amount of functionality in the software) is computed in a way similar to that of classical FPA, with the addition of two new element types: transformations and transitions. The method is not yet rigorously validated.

In 1996, John Gaffney [25] reported that using only a subset of the elements of a function point count provides estimates of development effort that are as accurate as those produced using classical function points. His analysis showed that the development effort was highly correlated with just the counts of the inputs and outputs. (Gaffney actually evaluated six linear models and five nonlinear models.) Gaffney's "simplified function point estimation method" does not use the three levels of complexity (low, medium, high) for the elements that are part of the official IFPUG FPA method. (Capers Jones' Feature Points method, as mentioned previously, also does not use the three levels of complexity.)

COCOMO 2.0 [4] defines an object point estimation procedure for use in small projects which construct products by combining existing software components. This method is based on a procedure in Appendix B.3 of [26] and productivity data for 19 projects presented in [27]. The total size of the software is estimated in object points. Then a nominal productivity is determined based on two factors: developer experience and capability, and Integrated Computer-Aided Software Engineering (ICASE) tool maturity and capability. Dividing the size by the productivity gives the estimated effort. Object points are based on three elements: screens, reports, and components (assumed to be written in a third-generation language). The "objects" to be produced are identified and each is assigned a complexity rating of simple, medium, or difficult. These ratings depend on the number of screen views, report sections, and referenced data tables, as well as on the source of the data tables (client or server). Weights are assigned to each pairing of object type and complexity. Adding all of the weighted object instances gives the total object point count. This count is decreased by multiplying by one minus the fraction of reuse expected or planned (that is, 100 percent–Reuse percent). This method combines simplified elements (similar to Gaffney's method) and- complexity ratings of the elements (similar to FPA). It is considered to be part of the COCOMO 2.0 model and will no doubt evolve in the future.

Lastly, Randall Jensen has extended his original model [19] to explicitly handle the effects of management [28] on project costs and schedule. The new model, called SAGE (no acronym), considers factors such as the working environment (multiple development sites), team experience, and the degree of resource dedication. (The COCOMO 2.0 model also considers similar factors.) The SAGE model was first formulated in 1995 and handles new development. A new version that handles software maintenance is to be released in 1997.

An Approach to Improve Estimation

I recommend a four-pronged approach to improve software cost and schedule estimation within an organization. These prongs are technology, process, sponsorship, and infrastructure. Since people are the key, the last three of these prongs relate to helping people apply the best available practices. These actions will enable the organization to use the best-known software estimation practices to accurately cost and intelligently manage software projects during the remainder of the 1990s and into the next century.

Improving Estimating Technology

Since various efforts are underway to improve cost models, it is important to stay abreast of developments in the field via attendance at conferences and membership in professional societies. The primary professional societies for cost estimation include the International Society of Parametric Analysts (ISPA), the COCOMO User's Group, and the Society of Cost Estimating and Analysis (SCEA). A related organization is the IFPUG. Meetings and conferences include ISPA conferences, the annual COCOMO Conference, the annual European Software Cost Modeling Conference (ESCOM), and IFPUG conferences. These provide access to state-of-the-art information on cost estimation and models in the US and abroad. Lastly, books and journals provide another source of useful information. This information can be conveyed to the staff via the organization's Software Engineering Process Group (SEPG).

Defining the Process

No single estimating method is suited for every type of project and, moreover, each model has its own particular strengths and weaknesses. Each organization needs to define its own estimating process suited to its needs, using policies and assistance provided by the SEPG. The process defined by each particular organization is documented so it can be applied consistently, taught to others, reviewed for completeness and correctness, and improved. I advocate a documented estimating process using at least two methods with complementary strengths and weaknesses, coupled with independent reviews. For example, a parametric model and a manual method are typically used together.

Since there is much uncertainty about software size in the early stages of a project, I advocate regular review of progress, assumptions, and product requirements during a project to detect changes and violations of the assumptions underlying the estimate. Proactive risk management is a part of this review process as well. Additional reviews may be triggered when unexpected events occur, such as new or changed requirements.

When conditions change, estimates are revised. Since more data become available as a project unfolds, this means different cost models and CERs are often used in the later stages of a project. These give more accurate predictions, providing managers with the best possible information on expected costs as the project unfolds.

Obtaining Management Sponsorship

Managers must lead the way to improve software cost estimation practices, but managers are faced with many demands on their time and resources. Each organization, via its SEPG and its training program, can engender management support for improving software cost estimation in two ways. First, make managers aware of typical estimation problems and methods available to solve or, whenever possible, to avoid these problems. This is best done with a short course that provides an overview of software estimation.

Second, the organization's SEPG should define standard measures for software projects, and an integrated approach for collecting these metrics. The information collected should be useful to both the manager and the estimator. Managers use the information for day-to-day project management. Estimators use the data as inputs to CERs and to calibrate the estimation models. Another practical strategy is to have support organizations (such as Configuration Management, Quality Assurance, Finance and Accounting) collect and report many of the measures needed, thereby reducing the burden on the software engineers and their managers.

Providing the Infrastructure

The organization should establish an infrastructure to advocate and sustain efforts to improve software cost estimation techniques. The primary means used is the organization's SEPG. The CMM developed by the SEI can be used as the guide for this program. The SEPG is assisted by the organization's training department, which conducts a comprehensive management training program, and organizational policies relating to software development and project management.

The SEPG develops and maintains (under configuration control) the organization's defined process.

This document contains policies relating to software development and specifies requirements for processes acceptable to the organization and that comply with the criteria of the SEI's CMM. The defined processes are enacted via several sets of detailed procedures, each meeting the needs of particular business units within the organization. Of particular interest, in the present context, are procedures for metrics, cost estimation, project planning, and project tracking.

The SEPG (or related working groups) conducts activities that relate to improving software cost estimation practices. For example, a metrics working group would define metrics to track projects and gauge their progress and costs. As noted above, these standardized metrics are chosen to be useful to both cost estimators and project managers. Similarly, a tools working group would review available tools, including estimation and planning tools, to identify the "best of breed" for possible use by projects. The tools working group could also arrange licenses for selected tools, thereby making them available on a "try-before-buy" basis. A training working group would develop and deliver courses that teach managers and software engineers techniques to estimate and plan better.

Lastly, it may even be desirable to establish a "Software Estimation Assistance Team" (SEAT) to promote the adoption and effective use of improved cost estimation techniques within the organization. The SEAT would track the evolution of software cost estimation methods and models, identify the ones most useful for the organization's various business areas, and act as a technology transfer agent by revising training courses, updating portions of the organizational process definition, and mentoring projects that need help with software estimation. The SEAT would provide information and advice for proposals having large software content. SEAT members could also review cost estimates for proposals and projects.

Some Predictions

Developers of software estimation models continue to be challenged by the obstacle that no valid theoretical models of software development exist. There are no universal laws of "software physics" that can define constraints on and relationships between various independent variables characterizing the product and the project environment. Some approximate equations can be found, but these will surely change as computer technology advances. New software architectures, reusable components, development processes, and support tools will change the products and the project environment, and so new estimation models and techniques will continue to appear. For example,

COCOMO 2.0 will use "object points" as a size measure for early stages of a project.

Consequently, cost estimation will remain an experimental science for the foreseeable future. Estimators must rely on judgment and intuition to define heuristic rules and then validate these via analysis of actual project data. Once the significant factors have been isolated, simplified models can be defined and calibrated for use by the estimators. The resulting models can then be used in industry. This is what the COCOMO 2.0 project is doing.

Practical Advice

There are many parametric models for estimating software development cost and schedule. Prospective users of these models should realize that all models are approximations. To use models correctly, users should understand the assumptions and limitations of each model and should calibrate the model for their development organization. The estimates produced by a model should always be checked against one or more estimates produced using other methods. As the late Paul Rook observed, the real value of parametric models is to help estimators understand the interaction of the many factors affecting software development costs and schedule. The actual estimated values for the cost and schedule are of secondary importance. Some senior managers may disagree with this statement. I would answer that the estimated values are meaningless without an understanding of their accuracy and sensitivity to the uncertainties and risks associated with the project. Models help managers understand these risks and so lead to better decisions.

Each organization should endeavor to track the evolution and refinement of software estimation models in the literature and via conferences. It should also establish a means to identify and infuse proven techniques into active use throughout the organization. These actions will enable the organization to use the best known software estimation practices to accurately cost and intelligently manage software projects during the remainder of the 1990s and into the next century.

References

[1] Boehm, B.W., *Software Engineering Economics*, Prentice-Hall, Englewood Cliffs, N.J., 1981. Section 29.7 describes several models not discussed in this article, as well as the models developed by Herd, Putnam, Walston and Wolverton.

[2] Selby, R., "Empirically Analyzing Reuse in a Production Environment" in *Software Reuse: Emerging Technology*, W. Tracz, editor, IEEE CS Press, Los Alamitos, Calif., 1988, pp. 176–189.

[3] Gerlich, R. and U. Denskat, "A Cost Estimation Model for Maintenance and High Reuse," *Proc. EuroMan Software Cost Modeling Conference* (ESCOM 1994), 1994.

[4] Boehm, B.W., B. Clark, E. Horowitz, C. Westland, R. Madachy, and R. Selby, "Cost Models for Future Software Lifecycle Processes: COCOMO 2.0," *Annals of Software Engineering*, Vol. 1, 1995, pp. 57–94. An earlier description was presented in the tutorial "COCOMO, Ada COCOMO and COCOMO 2.0" by Barry Boehm in the *Proc. 9th Int'l COCOMO Estimation Meeting*, 1994.

[5] Selby, R., D. Schmidt, and J. Berney, "Metric-Driven Analysis and Feedback Systems for Enabling Empirically Guided Software Development," *Proc. 13th Int'l Conf. Software Engineering* (ICSE 13), IEEE CS Press, Los Alamitos, Calif., 1991, pp. 288–298.

[6] Norden, P.V., "Curve Fitting for a Model of Applied Research and Development Scheduling," *IBM J. Research and Development*, Vol. 2, No. 3, July 1958.

[7] Brooks, F.P., *The Mythical Man-Month*, Addison-Wesley, Reading, Mass., 1975. An updated and expanded edition was published in 1995.

[8] Conte, S.D., H.E. Dunsmore, and V.Y. Shen, *Software Engineering Metrics and Models*, Benjamin Cummings, Menlo Park, Calif., 1986.

[9] Park, R.E., *The Central Equations of the PRICE Software Cost Model*, Lockheed Martin PRICE Systems, Ste. 200, 700 East Gate Dr., Mt. Laurel, NJ 08054, 1988.

[10] Minkiewicz, A. and A. DeMarco, *The PRICE Software Model*, Lockheed Martin PRICE Systems, Ste. 200, 700 East Gate Dr., Mt. Laurel, NJ 08054, 1995.

[11] Albrecht, A.J., "Measuring Application Development Productivity," *Proc. Joint SHARE, GUIDE, and IBM Application Development Symp.*, Oct. 1979.

[12] Albrecht, A.J. and J.E. Gaftney, "Software Function, Source Lines of Code and Development Effort Prediction: A Software Science Validation," *IEEE Trans. Software Eng.*, Vol. 9, No. 2, Nov. 1983.

[13] Putnam, L.H., "A General Empirical Solution to the Macro Software Sizing and Estimating Problem," *IEEE Trans. Software Eng.* SE-4, July 1978, pp. 345–361.

[14] Fenton, N.E., "Software Metrics: A Rigorous Approach," Chapman & Hall, London, 1995.

[15] Halstead, M.H., *Elements of Software Science*, Elsevier, New York, 1977.

[16] Coleman, D., D. Ash, B. Lowther, and P. Oman, "Using Metrics to Evaluate Software System Maintainability," *Computer*, Aug. 1994, pp. 44–49.

[17] Boehm, B.W., and W. Royce, "Ada COCOMO and the Ada Process Model," *Proc. 3rd Int'l COCOMO Users Meeting*, Software Eng. Inst., Pittsburgh, Nov. 1987, plus refinements presented at the Fourth Int'l COCOMO Users Group Meeting held in Nov. l988.

[18] Tausworthe, R.C., *Deep Space Network Estimation Model*, Jet Propulsion Report 81-7, NASA Jet Propulsion Laboratory, Pasadena, Calif., 1981.

[19] Jensen, R.W., "A Comparison of the Jensen and COCOMO Estimation Models," *Proc. Int'l Soc. of Parametric Analysts*, Int'l Soc. of Parametric Analysts, PO Box 6402, Chesterfield, MO 63006-6402, 1984, pp. 96–106.

[20] Albrecht, A.J., *AD/M Productivity Measurement and Estimate Validation*, IBM Corporate Information Systems, IBM Corp., Purchase, N.Y., May 1984.

[21] Jones, C., *The SPR Feature Point Method*, Software Productivity Research, Inc., Software Productivity Research Inc., 1 New England Executive Park, Burlington, MA 01803, 1986.

[22] Symons, C., *Software Sizing and Estimating: Mark II FPA*, Wiley & Sons, New York, 1991.

[23] Whitmire, S.A., *3D Function Points: Scientific and Real-Time Extensions to Function Points*, Boeing Airplane Company report BCS-G3252, dated 1992. It was published in the *Proc. 1992 Pacific Northwest Quality Conference*. A more accessible reference by the same author is "An Introduction to 3D Function Points," *Software Development*, Apr. 1995, p. 43.

[24] DeMarco, T., *Controlling Software Projects*, Yourdon Press, Englewood Cliffs, N.J., 1982.

[25] Gaffney, J.E., Jr., "Software Cost Estimation Using Simplified Function Points," *Proc. 8th Ann. Software Technology Conf.*, 1996.

[26] Kauffman, R. and R. Kumar, *Modeling Estimation Expertise in Object Based ICASE Environments*, Stern School of Business report, New York Univ., Jan. 1993.

[27] Banker, R., R. Kauffman, and R. Kumar, "An Empirical Test of Object-Based Output Measurement Metrics on a Computer Aided Software Engineering (CASE) Environment," *J. Management Information Systems* (circa 1994).

[28] Jensen, R.W., "Management Impact on Software Cost and Schedule," *Crosstalk*, July 1996, pp. 6–10.

Synopsis of COCOMO

Deanna B. Legg
California State University, Sacramento
Sacramento, CA 95819-6061

1. Introduction

Constructive Cost Model (COCOMO) is a software cost estimation method that is based on a set of empirically derived equations. The equations incorporate a number of variables considered to be the major cost drivers of software development and maintenance. This paper summarizes Basic and Intermediate COCOMO as described in *Software Engineering Economics* by Barry W. Boehm, Prentice-Hall, Inc., Englewood Cliffs, N.J., 1981, and reprinted with their permission. For a more detailed and highly readable description of COCOMO and how to use it, refer to Boehm.

2. Life Cycle Phases and Activities

The different phases of COCOMO are based on the classical waterfall model of the software life cycle (Figure 1). The basic steps of the waterfall model are: System Feasibility, Software Plans and Requirements, Software Design, Programming, Integration and Test, Implementation, and Maintenance.

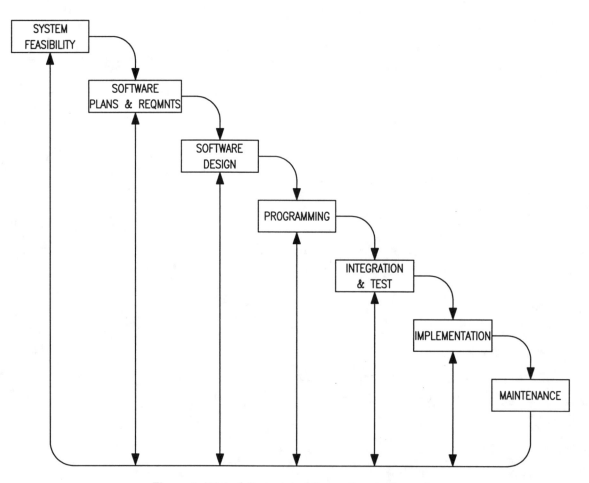

Figure 1. Waterfall model of the software life cycle.

The COCOMO model provides effort estimates for the development life cycle phases only (Software Design, Programming, and Integration and Test). The Plans and Requirements phase and the Maintenance phase are estimated as separate quantities. System Feasibility and Implementation are not included in the model.

The COCOMO estimate also shows how the effort for each phase is distributed between eight major project activities. The eight activities are defined in Table 1. The distribution of tasks by activity and phase is shown in Table 2.

3. Versions of COCOMO

There are three versions of COCOMO: Basic, Intermediate, and Detailed. Basic COCOMO is used mostly for rough, early estimates. Intermediate COCOMO, the most commonly used version, includes 15 different factors to account for the influence of various project attributes such as personnel capability, use of modern tools, hardware constraints, and so forth. The third version, Detailed COCOMO, accounts for the influence of the different factors on individual project phases. Detailed COCOMO is not used very often and will not be discussed here.

4. Definitions and Assumptions

Listed below are the major definitions and assumptions that form the basis of the COCOMO cost estimation model:

- The primary cost driver is the number of delivered source instructions (DSI). The term "delivered" is meant to exclude non-delivered support software. However, if the support software is developed with the same standards (reviews, test plans, documentation) as the delivered software, then the support software should be included. "Source, but excludes comments and unmodified utility software. instructions" includes all program instructions, data declarations, and job control language

- The development period covered by COCOMO cost estimates starts at the beginning of the software design phase and ends at the end of the integration and test phase.

- COCOMO cost estimates cover those and *only* those activities indicated in Table 3 (Software work breakdown: activities included). Activities that are *not* included are shown in Table 4.

Table 1. Activity definitions (Boehm, p.49).

Requirements Analysis	Determination, specification, review and update of software functional, performance, interface, and verification requirements.
Software Design	Determination, specification, review and update of hardware-software architecture, program design, and database design.
Programming	Detailed design, code, unit test and integration of individual computer program components. Includes programming personnel planning, tool acquisition, database development, component level documentation and intermediate level programming management.
Test Planning	Specification, review and update of software test and acceptance test plans. Acquisition of associated test drivers, test tools and test data.
Verification and Validation (V&V)	Performance of independent requirements validation, design V&V, software test, and acceptance test. Acquisition of requirements and design V&V tools.
Project Office Functions	Project level management functions. Includes project level planning and control, contract and subcontract management, and customer interface.
Configuration Management & Quality Assurance (CM/QA)	Configuration management includes software identification, change control, status accounting, operation of program support library, development and monitoring of end item acceptance plan. Quality assurance includes development and monitoring of project standards, and technical audits of software products and processes.
Manuals	Development and update of users' manuals, operators' manuals and maintenance manuals.

Table 2. Project tasks by activity and phase (Boehm, p.50).

ACTIVITY	PHASE			
	PLANS & REQUIREMENTS	SOFTWARE DESIGN	PROGRAMMING	INTEGRATION & TEST
Requirements Analysis	Analyze existing system, determine user needs, integrate, document, and iterate requirements.	Update requirements.	Update requirements.	Update requirements.
Software Design	Develop basic architecture, models, prototypes, risk analysis.	Develop software design, models, prototypes, risk analysis.	Update design.	Update design.
Programming	Top-level personnel and tools planning.	Personnel planning, acquire tools, utilities.	Detailed design, code and unit test, component documentation, integration planning.	Integrate software, update components.
Test Planning	Acceptance test requirements, top-level test plans.	Draft test plans, acquire test tools.	Detailed test plans, acquire test tools.	Detailed test plans, install test tools.
Verification & Validation	Validate requirements, acquire requirements, design V&V tools.	V&V software design, acquire design V&V tools.	V&V top portions of code, V&V design changes.	Perform software test, acceptance test, V&V design changes.
Project Office Functions	Project level management, project planning, contracts, liaison, etc.	Project level management, status monitoring, contracts, liaison, etc.	Project level management, status monitoring, contracts, liaison, etc.	Project level management, status monitoring, contracts, liaison, etc.
CM/QA	CM/QA plans, procedures, acceptance plans, identify CM/QA tools.	CM/QA of requirements, design; project standards, acquire CM/QA tools.	CM/QA of requirements, design; code, operate library.	CM/QA of requirements, design; code, operate library, monitor acceptance plan.
	Outline portions of users' manual.	Draft users', operators' manuals, outline maintenance manual.	Full draft users' and operators' manuals.	Final users', operators', and maintenance manuals.

Table 3. Software work breakdown: activities included in COCOMO (Boehm, p.52).

MANAGEMENT	SYSTEM ENGINEERING	PROGRAMMING	TEST & EVALUATION	DATA	IMPLEMENTATION	MAINTENANCE*
Cost/schedule/ performance mgmt.	Software Requirements update	Detailed design	Software test Plans Procedures Test Reports	Manuals	- - -	Software update
Contract mgmt.	Software product design Design Design V&V PDR Design update Design tools	Code & unit test	Acceptance test Plans Procedures Tests Reports			Corrective maintenance
Subcontract mgmt.		Integration				Adaptive maintenance
Customer interface	Configuration mgmt. Program support library		Test support Test beds Test tools Test data			Perfective maintenance
Branch office mgmt.						
Management reviews & audits	End item acceptance plan					
	Quality assurance Standards					
	------------ Software Requirements* Development Validation SRR Tools					

* These activities are estimated separately from the development cost estimate.

Table 4. Software work breakdown: activities not included in COCOMO (Boehm, p.52).

MANAGEMENT	SYSTEM ENGINEERING	PROGRAMMING	TEST & EVALUATION	DATA	IMPLEMENTATION	MAINTENANCE
- -	Feasibility studies	- -	- -	- -	Installation Plans Installation activities Test Report Conversion Plans Activities Programs Database Documents Test Reports Training	Database administration

- COCOMO estimates cover all direct charged labor on the project for the activities indicated on the software work breakdown (Table 3). Labor that is not direct charged, such as secretaries, computer operators, higher management, etc., is not included.

- A COCOMO person-month consists of 19 days (152 hours) of working time. This figure incorporates the average time off due to sick leave, holidays, and vacation.

- COCOMO estimates assume that the project will be managed well by both the developer and the customer.

- COCOMO estimates assume that the requirements specification does not significantly change after the plans and requirements phase.

- COCOMO should not be used for projects below 2000 DSI, since differences in personnel will tend to dominate all other effects.

5. Development Types

The COCOMO Models include three software development types: organic, semi-detached, and embedded. In the organic type, relatively small software teams develop familiar types of software in an in-house environment. Most of the personnel connected with the project have previous experience working with related or similar systems in the organization.

In the embedded type, the project may require new technology, unfamiliar algorithms, or an innovative new method of solving a problem. The most distinguishing feature of the embedded type is the need to operate within tight constraints.

Semi-detached is an intermediate stage between organic and embedded types. Intermediate can mean either an intermediate level of the project characteristics, or a mixture of organic and embedded type characteristics. Table 5 shows a summary of the organic, semi-detached, and embedded types of software development.

6. Basic COCOMO

Type	Effort	Schedule
Organic	$PM = 2.4\,(KDSI)^{1.05}$	$TD = 2.5\,(PM)^{0.38}$
Semi-Detached	$PM = 3.0\,(KDSI)^{1.12}$	$TD = 2.5\,(PM)^{0.35}$
Embedded	$PM = 3.6\,(KDSI)^{1.20}$	$TD = 2.5\,(PM)^{0.32}$

PM = person-month

KDSI = delivered source instructions, in thousands

TD = number of months estimated for software development

6.1   Example Basic COCOMO Calculation

Let us assume that a project is organic type and the estimated size is 128,000 lines of code. From the Basic equations, we can estimate the following:

Effort: $PM = 2.4\,(128)^{1.05}$ = 392 person-months
Productivity: 128,000 DSI / 392 PM   = 327 DSI/PM
Schedule: $TD = 2.5\,(392)^{0.38}$ = 24 months
Avg. Staffing: 392 PM / 24 months = 16 FSP

FSP = Full-time-equivalent staff personnel

7. Maintenance

Software maintenance is defined as the modification of existing software while leaving its primary functions intact. The definition does not include major redesign and redevelopment resulting in greater than 50 percent new code.

The COCOMO estimate for annual software maintenance is calculated in terms of the Annual Change Traffic (ACT). ACT is defined as the fraction of the software product's source instructions, which undergoes change during a typical year. The changes may be through addition or modification.

The COCOMO maintenance equations are

ACT   = (Added DSI + Modified DSI) / Total DSI
$(PM)_{AM}$ = $(ACT)(PM)_{DEV}$
$(FSP)_M$ = $(PM)_{AM}$ / 12

7.1   Example Maintenance Calculation

Consider an organic type project of 128 KDSI that has a development effort of 392 PM. The project had 8000 DSI added and 3400 DSI modified during its first year of maintenance.

ACT = (8000 + 3400) / 128000 = 0.09

The annual maintenance effort is

$(PM)_{AM}$ = (0.09)(392) = 35 PM

The number of FSP required to maintain the software is

$(FSP)_M$ = 35 / 12 = 3 FSP

8. Intermediate COCOMO

Intermediate COCOMO is a compatible extension to Basic COCOMO. Intermediate COCOMO provides a greater accuracy and level of detail which makes it

Table 5. Distinguishing features of software development types (Boehm, p.81).

FEATURE	ORGANIC TYPE	SEMI-DETACHED TYPE	EMBEDDED TYPE
Organizational understanding of software objectives	Thorough	Considerable	General
Experience in working with related software systems	Extensive	Considerable	Moderate
Need for software conformance with external interface specifications	Basic	Considerable	Full
Concurrent development of associated new hardware and operational procedures	Some	Moderate	Extensive
Need for innovative data processing architectures, algorithms	Minimal	Some	Considerable
Premium on early completion	Low	Medium	High
Software size range	<50 KDSI	<300 KDSI	All sizes
Examples	Batch data reduction, Scientific models Business models Familiar OS, compiler Simple inventory, production control	Most transaction processing systems New OS, DBMS Ambitious inventory, production control Simple command control	Large, complex transaction processing systems Ambitious, very large OS Avionics Ambitious command control

more suitable for cost estimation in the more detailed stages of software product definition.

8.1 Nominal Effort Estimation

Development Type		Nominal Effort Equation
Organic	$(PM)_{NOM}$	$= 3.2 \, (KDSI)^{1.05}$
Semi-detached	$(PM)_{NOM}$	$= 3.0 \, (KDSI)^{1.12}$
Embedded	$(PM)_{NOM}$	$= 2.8 \, (KDSI)^{1.20}$

Note that the Intermediate COCOMO exponents for the three software development types are the same as Basic COCOMO, but the coefficients are different. The Intermediate development schedule is determined using the Basic COCOMO schedule equations.

8.2 Cost Drivers

Intermediate COCOMO incorporates 15 predictor variables, called cost drivers, to account for software project cost variations that are not directly correlated to project size. These cost drivers are grouped into four categories: software product attributes, computer attributes, personnel attributes, and project attributes.

8.2.1 Software Attributes

RELY: Required Software Reliability—The software product's reliability is measured as a qualitative factor. The rating scale for RELY is as follows:

- Very Low—The effect of a software failure is merely the inconvenience for the developers to fix the problem.
- Low—The effect of a software failure is a low-level loss to users with relatively easy recovery.
- Nominal—The effect of a software failure is a moderate loss to users and recovery is difficult but can occur without serious damages.
- High—The effect of a software failure can be major financial loss or extreme human inconvenience.
- Very High—The effect of a software failure can be danger to human safety.

DATA: Data Base Size—The DATA ratings are defined by the following ratio:

- D/P = (Data base size in bytes)/(program size in DSI). Data base size is the amount of data to be assembled and stored in secondary storage by the time of software completion.

CPLX: Software Complexity—The ratings are specified as a function of the primary type of operations to be performed. (See Table 6, Module complexity rating versus type of module.)

8.2.2 Computer Attributes

TIME: Execution Time Constraint—The ratings are defined as the percentage of available execution time expected to be used by the software project and any other software running on the computer system.

STOR: Main Storage Constraint—The ratings are defined as the percentage of main storage expected to be used by the software project and any other software on the computer system.

VIRT: Virtual Machine Volatility—The virtual machine consists of the hardware and software that a given software system uses to perform its functions. The VIRT ratings are specified as the change frequency of the virtual machine. A major change significantly affects approximately 10 percent of routines under development. A minor change significantly affects approximately 1 percent of routines under development.

TURN: Computer Turnaround Time—The ratings are expressed in terms of the level of computer response time available.

8.2.3 Personnel Attributes

ACAP: Analyst Capability—The major attributes that should be considered in the rating are efficiency, thoroughness, effective communication, team cooperation, and analytical ability. The evaluation should be based on the capability of the analysts as a team rather than as individuals.

AEXP: Applications Experience—The ratings are based on the project team's level of experience with similar types of applications.

PCAP: Programmer Capability—The major attributes that should be considered in the rating are efficiency, thoroughness, effective communication, team cooperation, and programming ability. The evaluation should be based on capability, not experience. The rating should reflect the capability of the programmers as a team rather than as individuals.

VEXP: Virtual Machine Experience—The virtual machine consists of the hardware and software that a given software system uses to perform its functions. For this cost driver, the programming language is not considered part of the virtual machine. The ratings are specified as the project team's average level of experience with the virtual machine to be used.

Table 6. Module complexity rating versus type of module (Boehm, p.122).

Rating	Control Operations	Computational Operations	Device-dependent Operations	Data Management Operations
Very Low	Straight-line code with a few non-nested SP operators: DOs, CASEs, IF-THEN-ELSEs, simple predicates.	Evaluation of simple expressions: e.g., A=(B+C) * (D-E).	Simple read, write statements with simple formats.	Simple arrays in main memory.
Low	Straightforward nesting of SP operators. Mostly simple predicates.	Evaluation of moderate level expressions, e.g. D=SQRT (B**2.4*A*C).	No cognizance needed of particular processor or I/O device characteristics. I/O done at GET/PUT level. No cognizance of overlap.	Single file subsetting with no data structure changes, no edits, no intermediate files.
Nominal	Mostly simple nesting. Some intermodule control. Decision tables.	Use of standard math and statistical routines. Basic matrix/vector operations.	I/O processing includes device selection, status checking and error processing.	Multi-file input and single file output. Simple structural changes, simple edits.
High	Highly nested SP operators with many compound predicates. Queue and stack control. Considerable intermodule control.	Basic numerical analysis: multivariate interpolation, ordinary differential equations. Basic truncation, roundoff concerns.	Operations at physical I/O level (physical storage address translations, seeks, reads, etc.). Optimized I/O overlap.	Special purpose subroutines activated by data stream contents. Complex data restructuring at record level.
Very High	Reentrant and recursive coding. Fixed-parity interrupt handling.	Difficult but structured N.A.: near singular matrix equations, partial differential equations.	Routines for interrupt diagnosis, servicing, masking. Communication line handling.	A generalized, parameter driven file structuring routine. File building, command processing, search optimization.
Extra High	Multiple resource scheduling with dynamically changing priorities. Microcode level control.	Difficult and unstructured N.A.: highly accurate analysis of noisy, stochastic data.	Device timing-dependent coding, microprogrammed operations.	Highly coupled, dynamic relational structures. Natural language data management.

SP = Structured Programming, NA = Numerical Analysis

LEXP: Programming Language Experience—The ratings are specified as the project team's average level of experience with the programming language to be used.

8.2.4   Project Attributes

MODP: Use of Modern Programming Practices—The ratings are defined as the extent to which modern programming practices are used in developing software and the relative experience of the project team in using these practices. The specific practices included are these:

- Top-down requirements analysis and design
- Structured design notation
- Top-down incremental development
- Design and code walk-throughs or inspections
- Structured code
- Program librarian

TOOL: Use of Software Tools—The ratings are defined as the extent to which software tools are used in software development.

SCED: Schedule Constraint—The nominal schedule for a project is calculated with the basic COCOMO schedule equation using the adjusted effort estimate (PM)DEV. The ratings for the SCED cost driver are then defined as the percentage of schedule change with respect to the project's calculated nominal schedule.

- $(PM)_{DEV}$ is calculated by multiplying $(PM)_{NOM}$ by its effort adjustment factor (EAF) as described later in item 10 of Table 8 (Procedures for using the Component Level Estimation Form).

8.3   Adaptation Adjustment

A software development project may contain a significant amount of previously developed software, which has been adapted for use in the new project. The effects of incorporating adapted software are calculated with an equivalent number of delivered source instructions (EDSI). The EDSI value is used in place of the DSI value in the COCOMO equations.

An intermediate quantity, the adaptation adjustment factor (AAF) is calculated first.

AAF = 0.40(DM) + 0.30(CDM) + 0.30(IM)

DM = percent design modified

CDM = percent code modified

IM = percent of integration required for modified software

The equivalent delivered source instructions (EDSI) value is calculated with the following equation:

EDSI = (Adapted DSI)(AAF / 100)

8.4   Component Level Estimation Form

For early cost estimations, Intermediate COCOMO may be used as a macro model where the cost driver attributes are assumed to be applied uniformly across the entire software product. For more detailed and accurate cost estimation, Intermediate COCOMO may also be applied at the software component level. Boehm provides a standard form, the Component Level Estimation Form (CLEF), shown in Table 7, for organizing and recording software cost estimation information at the component level. The steps for calculating the values are given in Table 8 (Procedures for using the Component Level Estimation Form).

8.5   Adjusted Annual Maintenance

The Intermediate COCOMO effort multipliers can be applied to the maintenance phase. Most of the cost drivers are evaluated the same way for maintenance as they are for development. The exceptions are SCED, RELY, and MODP.

SCED is not used for the maintenance phase. Set this effort multiplier to 1.00 (nominal). RELY is determined from Table 11. MODP is determined from Table 12.

The adjusted annual maintenance effort equation is:

$$(PM)AM = (EAF)M(PM)NOM(ACT)$$

where (EAF)M is the effort adjustment factor. The (EAF)M is the product of all the maintenance effort multipliers.

The steps for calculating the adjusted annual maintenance effort are given in Table 13 (Procedures for using the CLEF for software maintenance cost estimation).

Table 7. Component Level Estimation Form (CLEF) (Boehm, p.147).

PROJECT: DEV. TYPE: ANALYST: DATE:

1	2	3	SOFTWARE						COMPUTER				PERSONNEL					PROJECT				19	20	21	22	23	24
			4	5	6	7	8	9	10	11	12	13	14	15	16	17	18										
Component	EDSI	AAF	RELY	DATA	CPLX	TIME	STOR	VIRT	TURN	ACAP	AEXP	PCAP	VEXP	LEXP	MODP	TOOL	SCED	EAF	(PM) NOM	(PM) DEV / (PM) AM	EDSI/ PM ACT	$K	$/ EDSI
1																							
2																							
3																							
4																							
5																							
6																							
7																							
8																							
9																							
10																							
11	Total EDSI																	Totals					
12	(PM)$_{NOM}$																	Schedule (months)					
13	(EDSI/PM)$_{NOM}$																						

Component Level Estimation Form (CLEF)

Table 8. Procedures for using the Component Level Estimation Form (CLEF) (Boehm, p.148).

1. Identify all of the software product's components in column 1.
2. Estimate the sizes in DSI of all the components. If the component is not being adapted from existing software, enter its size in column 2 (EDSI). If it is being adapted, compute its adaptation adjustment factor (AAF) by the equation given below, enter it in column 3, then compute the Equivalent DSI (EDSI) and enter it in column 2.
3. Add up the total EDSI for the software and enter it in row 11.
4. Use the appropriate nominal effort equation for the specified development type (given below) to estimate the nominal amount development effort $(PM)_{NOM}$ as a function of total EDSI and enter it in row 12.
5. Compute the nominal productivity $(EDSI/PM)_{NOM} = $ (total EDSI)/$(PM)_{NOM}$ and enter it in row 13.
6. For each component, compute $(PM)_{NOM} = EDSI/(EDSI/PM)_{NOM}$ and enter it in column 20.
7. Provide cost driver ratings (columns 4 to 18) for all components, using the rating scales in Table 9.
8. Enter the corresponding effort multipliers for all components in columns 4 to 18 using Table 10.
9. For each component (row), compute the effort adjustment factor (EAF) as the product of the effort multipliers in columns 4 to 18 and enter it in column 19.
10. Multiply $(PM)_{NOM}$ (column 20) for each component by its EAF to produce the adjusted estimate for $(PM)_{DEV}$, which is entered in column 21.
11. Add up the total adjusted man-month estimates for all components and enter that in row 11, column 21.
12. Use the appropriate basic development schedule equation for the specified development type (given below) to compute the number of months required for software development and enter it in row 12, column 21.
13. For each component and for the entire software, compute the estimated productivity $EDSI/PM = EDSI/(PM)_{DEV}$ and enter it in column 22.
14. Estimate the average manpower cost ($K/PM) for each component and enter it in column 23 (upper half).
15. Compute the dollar cost for each component $K = (PM)_{DEV}($K/PM)$ and enter it in column 23 (lower half).
16. Add up the total software development cost in $K and enter it in row 11, column 23.
17. For each component and for the entire software, compute the cost per instruction $/EDSI = (1000)($K)/EDSI$ and enter them in column 24.

ADAPTATION EQUATIONS:

$AAF = 0.4$ (Percent design modified) $+ 0.3$ (Percent code modified) $+ 0.3$ (Percent integration modified)

$EDSI = $ (Adapted DSI)(AAF)/100

EFFORT AND SCHEDULE EQUATIONS:

Development Type	Nominal Effort	Schedule
Organic	$(PM)_{NOM} = 3.2 (KEDSI)^{1.05}$	$TD = 2.5 (PM)_{DEV}^{0.38}$
Semi-detached	$(PM)_{NOM} = 3.0 (KEDSI)^{1.12}$	$TD = 2.5 (PM)_{DEV}^{0.35}$
Embedded	$(PM)_{NOM} = 2.8 (KEDSI)^{1.20}$	$TD = 2.5 (PM)_{DEV}^{0.32}$

241

Table 9. Software cost driver ratings (Boehm, p.119).

Cost Drivers	Rating: Very Low	Rating: Low	Rating: Nominal	Rating: High	Rating: Very High	Rating: Extra High
Software Attributes						
RELY	Effect: slight inconvenience	Low, easily recoverable losses	Moderate, recoverable losses	High financial loss	Risk to human life	
DATA		* D/P < 10	10 <= D/P < 100	100 <= D/P < 1000	D/P >= 1000	
CPLX	See Table 6	See Table 6	See Table 6	See Table 6	See Table 6	See Table 6
Computer Attributes						
TIME			<= 50% use of available execution time	70%	85%	95%
STOR			<= 50% use of available storage	70%	85%	95%
VIRT		Major change every 12 months, Minor: 1month	Major: 6 months Minor: 2 weeks	Major: 2 months Minor: 1 week	Major: 2 weeks Minor: 2 days	
TURN		Interactive	Average turnaround <4 hrs	4 - 12 hours	> 12 hours	
Personnel Attributes						
ACAP	15th percentile	35th percentile	55th percentile	75th percentile	90th percentile	
AEXP	<= 4 months	1 year	3 years	6 years	12 years	
PCAP	15th percentile	35th percentile	55th percentile	75th percentile	90th percentile	
VEXP	<= 1 month	4 months	1 year	3 years		
LEXP	<= 1 month experience	4 months	1 year	3 years		
Project Attributes						
MODP	No use	Beginning use	Some use	General use	Routine use	
TOOL	Basic microprocessor tools	Basic mini tools	Basic midi/maxi tools	Strong maxi programming, test tools	Add requirements, design, mgmt, doc. tools	
SCED	75% of nominal	85%	100%	130%	160%	

* D = Database size in bytes, P = Program size in DSI

Table 10. Software development effort multipliers (Boehm, p.118).

COST DRIVERS	Rating: Very Low	Rating: Low	Rating: Nominal	Rating: High	Rating: Very High	Rating: Extra High
SOFTWARE ATTRIBUTES						
RELY Required software reliability	.75	.88	1.00	1.15	1.40	
DATA Database size		.94	1.00	1.08	1.16	
CPLX Software complexity	.70	.85	1.00	1.15	1.30	1.65
COMPUTER ATTRIBUTES						
TIME Execution time constraint			1.00	1.11	1.30	1.66
STOR Main storage constraint			1.00	1.06	1.21	1.56
VIRT Virtual machine volatility		.87	1.00	1.15	1.30	
TURN Computer turnaround time		.87	1.00	1.07	1.15	
PERSONNEL ATTRIBUTES						
ACAP Analyst capability	1.46	1.19	1.00	.86	.71	
AEXP Applications experience	1.29	1.13	1.00	.91	.82	
PCAP Programmer capability	1.42	1.17	1.00	.86	.70	
VEXP Virtual machine experience	1.21	1.10	1.00	.90		
LEXP Program language experience	1.14	1.07	1.00	.95		
PROJECT ATTRIBUTES						
MODP Use of modern program practices	1.24	1.10	1.00	.91	0.82	
TOOL Use of software tools	1.24	1.10	1.00	.91	0.83	
SCED Required development schedule	1.23	1.08	1.00	1.04	1.10	

Table 11. *RELY* effort multipliers for software maintenance (Boehm, p. 129).

Very Low	Low	Nominal	High	Very High
1.35	1.15	1.00	0.98	1.10

Table 12. *MODP* effort multipliers for software maintenance (Boehm, p.130).

Software Size	Rating				
(KDSI)	Very Low	Low	Nominal	High	Very High
2	1.25	1.12	1.00	0.90	0.81
8	1.30	1.14	1.00	0.88	0.77
32	1.35	1.16	1.00	0.86	0.74
128	1.40	1.18	1.00	0.85	0.72
512	1.45	1.20	1.00	0.84	0.70

9. Calibrating the Constant Term

A given software development team may be able to develop a specially calibrated version of COCOMO that will be more accurate and easier to use. A more tailored version may be achieved by calibrating the nominal effort equations, by consolidating or eliminating redundant cost drivers, and by adding further cost drivers that may be significant for a particular software team.

The simplest and most stable way to calibrate COCOMO is to establish the most appropriate development type for the software team and then to use a least-squares approximation technique to calibrate the constant term. The software team must complete and collect data on several projects. The larger the number of projects, the more reliable the calibration will be.

The calibrated constant c, is calculated as follows:

$$c = \frac{\sum_{i=1}^{n} PM_i Q_i}{\sum_{i=1}^{n} Q_i^2}$$

where

$n =$ total number of completed projects

$I =$ each individual project

For organic type:

$Pm_i = 3.2 \, (KDSI)^{1.05} * EAF_i$

$Q_i = (KDSI_i)^{1.05} * EAF_i$

For semi-detached type:

$Pm_i = 3.0 \, (KDSI)^{1.12} * EAF_i$

$Q_i = (KDSI_i)^{1.12} * EAF_i$

For embedded type:

$Pm_i = 2.8 \, (KDSI)^{1.20} * EAF_i$

$Q_i = (KDSI_i)^{1.20} * EAF_i$

(Note: The numbers used in these equations should be the actual values for the completed projects, not the estimated values.)

10. Summary

The COCOMO cost estimation model is based on the classical waterfall model of the software life cycle. Basic COCOMO is used for early rough estimates. Intermediate COCOMO is used for more accurate estimates at the component level. Intermediate COCOMO incorporates 15 cost drivers to account for software project cost variations that are not directly related to project size. Estimates are made for the entire development process and for individual phases and activities. Software maintenance costs are estimated separately.

The COCOMO cost estimation model is more accurate when calibrated to the development environment. Detailed records of actual project data should be maintained to provide the historical database needed to calibrate any cost estimation model. The most reliable cost estimate will be achieved by using several complementary cost estimation techniques and by refining the resultant estimates.

Appendix: Abbreviations and Acronyms.

ACT   Annual Change Traffic
ADSI   Adapted Delivered Source Instructions
AEXP   Applications Experience
AM   Annual Maintenance
CDM   Percent Code Modified
CM   Configuration Management
COCOMO Constructive Cost Model
CPLX   Software Complexity
DATA   Database Size
DEV   Development
DM   Percent Design Modified
DSI   Delivered Source Instruction
EAF   Effort Adjustment Factor
EDSI   Equivalent Delivered Source Instructions
FSP   Full-Time Equivalent Software Personnel
IM   Percent Integration Modified
KDSI   Thousands of Delivered Source Instructions
LEXP   Language Experience
MODP Modern Programming Practices
NA   Numerical Analysis
NAM   Nominal Annual Maintenance
NOM   Nominal
PCAP   Programmer Capability
PDR   Product Design Review
PM   Person Months
QA   Quality Assurance
RELY   Required Software Reliability
SCED   Required Development Schedule
SP   Structured Programming
SRR   Software Requirements Review
STOR   Main Storage Restraint
TD   Development Schedule
TIME   Execution Time Restraint
TOOL   Use of Software Tools
TURN   Computer Turnaround Time
V&V   Verification and Validation
VEXP   Virtual Machine Experience
VIRT   Virtual Machine Volatility

How to Estimate Software System Size[1]

John E. Gaffney, Jr.[2]
Lockheed Martin
Rockville, MD 20850

Robert D. Cruickshank
Software Productivity Consortium
Herndon, VA 22070

1. Size Estimation

The effort, cost, and length of time required to develop software all depends on the size of the software products to be developed. This paper describes software product size.

1.1 The Importance of Size Estimation

Size estimation is an important activity in the quantitative management of software projects because most cost estimation algorithms use size estimates as an input, and the misestimation of size will lead to inaccurate cost estimates. Misestimation of software product size is probably a greater source of error in software cost estimates than misestimation of productivity or unit costs. The biggest difficulty in using the cost estimation algorithms available today is the problem of providing sound sizing estimates [Boehm 1983].

Software size estimation is also difficult because there is no fundamental size to accomplish a stated requirement. The size of the software component created to satisfy a requirement may depend on the software engineers assigned to the job [Boehm 1983]. The nature of this dependence is not readily discernible. Therefore, careful size estimation and the use of empirically based size estimation algorithms are of prime importance.

1.2 Size Estimation Activities

This paper is designed to help you answer the question, "How big will the system be?" It provides several methods for estimating software size, emphasizing those that you can apply early in the development cycle.

Estimating the size of a new software system is the key to estimating development cost, both in dollar terms and in the amount of labor and other resources required, since the size determines a large part of the cost of a software system. An accurate estimate of size is important because size is the basis for estimates of development costs for software. Errors in the estimate of a software system's size often exceed the estimation error for the amount of labor required for development and for productivity of its creation.

You should reestimate software product size throughout the development process. You should derive the initial estimate prior to the initiation of software development using your knowledge of the requirements. You can derive subsequent estimates during the development process based on increased knowledge about the software system as it evolves. You should derive this additional information from further elaboration and expansion of the requirements, the design, and other intermediate products, for example, documentation, of the process as you create them during development. The methodology presented here uses knowledge about what is to be built, that is, the requirements, as well as what has been designed and/or coded to date during the development process. However, the emphasis here is on the development of "front-end" estimates, those you make before you begin the actual development.

There are two principal types of measures of software product size:

- *The Amount of Code.* This is the number of source statements or number of source lines of code (SLOC), as discussed in [Boehm 1981, Stutzke 1997]. A SLOC count tends to

[1] Adapted from Chapter 7, SPC-91060-CMC, Version 02.01.00, Software Productivity Service Corporation, Herndon, VA, Aug. 1994. Reprinted in Software Management Consortium, *The Software Measurement Guidebook*, Int'l Thomson Computer Press, Boston, Mass., 1995.

[2] This paper was originally prepared while the author was with the Software Productivity Consortium.

vary with the language in which the software is written. That is, in general, a given system is expressible in fewer higher level language statements (for example, Ada) than are required for a lower level language (for example, assembly).

- *The Number of Function (or Feature) Points.* This is a measure of the amount of function provided by the software system, as defined in Section 5. It is independent of the language in which the system is written although the cost of development is not.

This section focuses on the estimation of code size in SLOC because it is the more general approach.

1.3 Size Estimation and the Development Cycle

This section is particularly concerned with estimating the size of a new software system very early in the development cycle, that is, in the proposal or conceptual and requirements analysis activities. At this very early point in the development cycle, there is usually very little detailed information available about the intended software system. You may not have assigned new and reused code to the planned functions. Later in the development cycle, when you have assigned new and reused code to functions, you can estimate the size of the functions to be represented by new code using other methods presented in this section. When you identify the functions to be implemented by reused code, you can count the reused code.

1.4 Size Estimation and Process Maturity Levels

Software organizations at process maturity levels 1 and 2 [Paulk et al. 1991] concentrate on using methods that require a minimum of experience data. An organization at levels 3 through 5 will use methods that emphasize the use of experience data to estimate size, incorporating lessons learned from results of the organization's process modifications and development experience.

Software size is the primary parametric input to most cost and schedule estimating algorithms, but the estimates of size used for these purposes are frequently based on guesses or anecdotal information. Inaccuracies in size estimates are the primary cause for inaccuracies in cost and schedule estimates. Even where you know your unit costs and where you have thoroughly analyzed your schedule constraints, the overall cost and schedule estimates for your software

development projects may lack precision because your size estimates were not derived using systematic methods.

Code size estimates should be based on the past experience of your own organization. This experience should be accessible in terms of the data available in a formal database. This database should contain the sizes of computer software configuration items (CSCIs), the number of major inputs and outputs, the code counts, and other such information. You should take considerable care in making a direct comparison between projects, that is, between the new project in question and a previous project as it appears in the experience database. You should make a careful analysis of both the similarities and differences of the functions in both projects before basing your size estimates on previous experience.

2. Size Estimation During the Development Cycle

This section shows you ways to estimate software product size throughout the development cycle.

2.1 Size Estimation by Development Activity

A software development organization that has a defined process (that is, the process of an organization at SEI process maturity level 3) should have accumulated enough data in its software experience database so that it can make reasonable estimates of size throughout the life cycle of the software. Your organization should use systematic methods for size estimation such as those presented in this section. The life cycle is composed of many activities, all of which you define and place under management control at process maturity level 3. It is not necessary to make size estimates as the product transitions from one development activity to another, but you should make size estimates at several milestones during development.

Monitor a software development project, with all of its associated software products, throughout the development cycle using a continuous measurement process. Make measurements such as estimates of product size in the conceptual and the requirements stages; at proposal time; at project initiation; and throughout design, coding, and testing. Considerable variation characterizes software product size estimates done early in the development cycle because so little detail about the software is available. Size estimates you make throughout the design, code, and test activities are subject to much less variation since you have based them primarily on code counts made during development. The increasing accuracy of size estimates characterizes the process of measurement and size estimation through the development cycle.

In general, when your software development project is in the system-level conceptual stage, you should use a technique such as function block counting (see Section 3) since you know very little else but the major functions included in the system. As the project moves from conception to proposal, techniques like I/O counting (see Section 6) come into play since you will have defined the main interfaces between the major functions. At proposal time, you can use function block and I/O techniques as cross-checks on each other to achieve a reasonable level of confidence that you made a suitable size estimate. At the design phase, you should count source lines of design (SLOD) statements and convert them to SLOC estimates by a SLOC-to-SLOD ratio derived from your organization's experience. As the project moves from design to coding and testing, use code counts to give very accurate estimates of final product cost. Finally, code growth becomes important during the testing activities. Section 7 presents size estimation methods applicable at all of these points in the development cycle.

2.2 Using Source Lines of Design to Estimate Software Size

During the conduct of the design activity, information in the form of SLOD counts are available if you use a design language. Preserve these SLOD counts in your software experience database. When the corresponding SLOC counts become available, compute a SLOC-to-SLOD ratio and preserve it. This ratio will aid you in converting SLOD to SLOC estimates for future projects. You can use an estimate for this ratio based on past project development experience or other information that may be available to you. Alternatively, you can compute function-point-to-SLOD ratios and use them for future estimates of the amount of design (in SLOD) that you will develop for a system of some given size in function points.

2.3 Size Estimation Steps

You should follow these steps in making size estimates:

- At the conceptual or requirements stages, compile the requirements for the system and its major parts, such as CSCI or a software product, whose size you wish to estimate.

- Get all of the data you can about the system you are to estimate (that is, functions to be

performed, counts of inputs and outputs, and so forth).

- Get as much detail as you can. Get the data for as many of the (likely) component functions or parts of the system as you can. Consult with those who have the most expert knowledge of the components or functions in which you are interested. Take advantage of the fact that an underestimate of the size of one component often cancels the overestimate of the size of another component.

- Make several estimates at each stage of development based on different types of data, then compare them. If they differ beyond 10 to 20 percent, reconsider your assumptions and try again. Repeat the process.

3. Function Block Counting

This section describes a method for estimating a software system's size based on the number of major software functions or subfunctions that you expect to compose the system. When you have very little information about the intended application system, you can make a rough estimate of the software system size using the counted or estimated number of CSCIs or computer software components (CSCs). This method has the advantage of requiring little information, so you can apply it very early in the development cycle. You can apply this method at the conceptualization or requirements stages when the size implication of a requirement is itself the input to a decision-making process, for example, the decision to include the function or to bid on a contract. The method has the disadvantage of not directly including the effect of other information that may be available about the application system.

You can count major functions and equate them to the number of CSCIs or the number of CSCs. You can also count major functions as function blocks in a system description document or in a system-level block diagram or flow chart. At the conception of the system (when you are planning the system at the top level), you should identify the major software functions and count them as function blocks. A function block corresponds to a CSCI; the next level of decomposition, major subfunctions, corresponds to a CSC.

You can apply the methods presented here at one or two levels of decomposition: at the CSCI or CSC level. Gaffney [1984] and Britcher and Gaffney [1985] demonstrated that, under the assumption that most systems have the same number of decomposition els, you can estimate the system's size as a function of the number of functional elements at any one level. Thus, you would not expect a larger system to have more (vertical) levels of decomposition than a smaller one. Instead, the larger system would have more units of code at each level: CSCI and CSC.

You can base your estimate of software system size on the number of CSCs or CSCIs that you expect to compose the system. Britcher and Gaffney [1985] present figures of 41.6 thousand lines of code (KSLOC) and 4.16 KSLOC, respectively, for the expected values of size for a CSCI and a CSC. Experience suggests that the size of a CSCI can vary rather substantially among systems or even within a given system. It is quite reasonable to expect a substantial variation since the estimation process uses little information about the actual system. Some data on the experience of an aerospace contractor showed that the standard deviation of the sizes of a CSCI averaged 27.5 percent of the expected value, $\sigma/E = 0.275$ (see Section 4). The values presented here are undoubtedly domain-dependent, and you should adapt these values to the domain or environment in question.

Your organization should collect data about the sizes of the CSCI and CSC and then develop average size figures to use in developing function block estimates as described here. However, if no such data is available, then you might use the figures of 41.6 KSLOC and 11.45 KSLOC (= 0.275 × 41.6), respectively, for the expected value and standard deviation of the size of each CSCI in the system whose size you wish to estimate. Then, based on the statistical concepts presented in Section 4, calculate the expected estimate of size in KSLOC and the estimated standard deviation of the size in KSLOC of the overall system using the equations:

$$E_{tot} = 41.6 \cdot N$$
$$\sigma_{tot} = 0.275 \cdot E_{tot}$$

where N is the number of CSCIs. Alternatively, you can multiply the number of CSCs by 4.16 KSLOC to produce an estimate of size. One of the estimates would be based on your estimate of the number of CSCIs, and the other estimate would be based on your estimate of the number of CSCs. You can use the two product size estimates as a cross-check on each other.

In summary, the steps of the function block method are as follows:

- Count or estimate the number of blocks at a given level of detail, that is, at the CSCI or CSC level, or both.

- Multiply the number of blocks by the expected value of the size for that type of block.

This is the expected size of the system overall.

- Compute the standard deviation of estimated system size.

- Compute the desired range of the system size for the probability levels desired per the method described in Section 4.

- Apply this method for both the count of CSCIs and for the count of CSCs, and pool the results. Do not apply this method when there are fewer than three function blocks.

4. Statistical Size Estimation

This section describes a systematic method for estimating the code size of a software system by estimating the ranges of size of the component elements such as CSCs and CSCIs that will compose it. This method enables you to make systematic estimates of the sizes of the software system's individual components that you are to develop. The method involves decomposing the system into a number of functions, considering each of them in turn, and then statistically operating on the data to obtain estimates of the overall size and the standard deviation of the estimate. This method enables you to reduce the effect of uncertainty in estimated sizes of the individual components and to obtain a better estimate of the overall system size. The source of the information for the size estimate typically is the sizes of components or units in similar jobs that your organization has done earlier, that is, software product sizes from your software experience database.

The method presented here systematizes the estimation-by-analogy approach based on your organization's experience. Such estimates are done by an individual or by pooling the educated guesses of a group of people. The method is described in Putnam [1978]. The steps in this process are as follows:

- Determine the functions that will compose the new system.

- Compile size data about any similar functions previously developed.

- Identify the differences between the similar functions and the new ones.

- For each component (i), function whose size you are to estimate, estimate three parameters:

—The lowest possible number of source statements (or function points or other size measure); a_i

—The highest possible number of source statements (or function points or other size measure); b_i

—The most likely number of source statements (or function points or other size measure); m_i

- Compute two numbers for the estimated size of each of the components, the expected value and the standard deviation. The formulas for calculating each of them are as follows:

—The equation for estimating the expected value of the number of source statements (or function points or other size measure) in the ith unit of code, E_i, is:

$$E_i = \frac{a_i + 4m_i + b_i}{6}$$

where a_i is the lowest possible number, b_i is the highest possible number, and m_i is the most likely number.

—The equation for estimating the standard deviation of the number of source statements (or function points or other size measure) in the ith unit of code, σ_i, is:

$$\sigma_i = \frac{(b_i - a_i)}{6}$$

- Tabulate the estimates for each of the components.

- Compute the expected value, E_{tot}, and the standard deviation, σ_{tot}, for the overall system.

$$E_{tot} = \sum_{i=1}^{n} E_i$$

$$\sigma_{tot} = \left(\sum_{i=1}^{n} \sigma_i^2 \right)^{1/2}$$

Table 1 is an example of a table that you can use when applying the method just described. It illustrates a case in which there are four units of software to be built.

You can approximate the uncertainty in the overall size of the system using the values just calculated for the overall expected value and standard deviation under the assumption that the size is normally distributed. You would expect this approximation to be more accurate for cases in which there are larger numbers of functions in the overall system. Some of the size uncertainty ranges are:

68 percent range: $E_{tot} \pm 1\ \sigma$: 45,135 to 57,883
99 percent range: $E_{tot} \pm 3\ \sigma$: 32,387 to 70,631

The 99 percent probability range is much wider than the 68 percent range. You can use the method described here to provide a range of size estimates for use in the calculation of cost risk as described in Section 5.

The method of calculating size uncertainty ranges just presented assumes that the estimate it produces is unbiased toward either overestimation or underestimation. However, some experience indicates that the "most likely" estimates are biased more toward the lower limit than the upper one. The sizes of actual software products tend more toward the upper limit [Boehm 1981]. This observation is in keeping with a common view that software estimators tend to underestimate the size of their products. Section 7 gives more detail on size growth.

Table 1. Size estimation table example.

Function	Smallest	Most Likely	Largest	Expected	Standard Deviation
A	5,830	8,962	17,750	9,905	1,987
B	9,375	14,625	28,000	15,979	3,104
C	6,300	13,700	36,250	16,225	4,992
D	5,875	8,975	14,625	9,400	1,458
Overall				$E_{tot} = 51,509$	$\sigma_{tot} = 6,374$

5. Function Points

This section describes the nature of the function point size measure and how to compute and apply it.

5.1. Definition of Function Points

The function point metric intends to measure the functionality of the software product in standard units, independent of the coding language. A function point is a measure of software functionality based on the counted or estimated number of "externals" (inputs, outputs, inquiries, and interfaces) of a system plus the estimated number of its internal files. This section briefly describes the nature of the function point measure and summarizes how you calculate it.

You calculate the function point metric by counting the number of each of the four types of system externals, plus the count of internal logical files. The statement of software system requirements often describes the externally visible behavior of the intended system. The function point measure relates directly to that view, as the counts of the four types of externals are measures from which it is calculated. Definitions of the five items that are counted (or estimated) in computing the function point measure are listed below.

- *External inputs.* Unique data and/or control inputs that enter the external boundary of the system that cause processing to take place. Specific examples include input files (data files, control files), input tables, input forms (documents, data entry sheets), input screens (data screens, functional screens), and input transactions (control discretes, interrupts, system messages, and error messages).

- *External outputs.* Unique data and/or control outputs that leave the external boundary of the system after processing has occurred. Specific examples include output files (data files, control files), output tables, output reports (printed and screen reports from a single interrupt, system messages, and error messages).

- *External inquiries.* Unique I/O queries that require an immediate response. Specific examples include prompts, interrupts, and calls.

- *External interfaces.* Unique files or programs that are passed across the external boundary of the system. Specific examples include common utilities (I/O routines, sorting algorithms), math libraries (library of matrix manipulation routines, library of coordinate conversion routines), program libraries (run-time libraries, package or generic libraries), shared databases, and shared files.

- *Internal files.* A logical grouping of data or control information stored internal to the system. Specific examples include databases, logical files, control files, and directories.

You estimate the complexity of each element of the five categories (for example, external input) as low, medium, or high. Then, you multiply each count by the appropriate weight shown in Table 2 and sum it to determine the "function count."

Table 2. Function count weights for complexity.

Description	Complexity Weights		
	Low	Medium	High
External Inputs	3	4	6
External Outputs	4	5	7
External Inquiries	3	4	6
External Interfaces	5	7	10
Internal Files	7	10	15

The next step in the calculation of function points is to determine the "value adjustment factor" by assessing the impact of 14 factors that affect the functional size of the system. These factors are:

1. Data communications
2. Distributed functions
3. Performance
4. Heavily used operational configuration
5. Transaction rate
6. Online data entry
7. Design for end-user efficiency
8. Online update (for logical internal files)
9. Complex processing
10. Reusability of system code
11. Installation ease
12. Operational ease
13. Multiple sites
14. Ease of change

These factors are evaluated on a scale that runs from 0 to 5 defined as 0—factor not present or has no influence, 1—insignificant influence, 2—moderate influence, 3—average influence, 4—significant influence, 5—strong influence.

After the 14 factors have been rated and summed, the total must be converted to a complexity adjustment multiplier by the following formula:

$$\text{Multiplier} = \text{Sum} \cdot 0.01 + 0.65$$

Finally, you calculate the function point count by multiplying the function count by the value adjustment multiplier. The result is the final adjusted function point totals. More information about function points, including rules for calculating them, is given in Albrecht [1979], Albrecht and Gaffney [1983], and Jones [1990 and 1991].

5.2 Example of Function Point Calculation

Jones [1991] gives an example of a low complexity application with 1 external input, 2 external outputs, 1 logical file, and no interfaces or inquiries. The calculation with the weights in Table 2 gives 18 unadjusted function points. Of the 14 influential factors, online data entry and online update are rated at 2, end-user efficiency and operational ease rated at 3, and all the other factors are rated at 0. The total of the influence factors is 10. When this sum is entered into the above value adjustment formula, a value adjustment multiplier of 0.75 is obtained. Therefore, there is (0.75)(18) = 13.5 total adjusted function points.

5.3 Applications of Function Points

Function points correlate well with software cost, as do lines of code for management information systems (MIS) software. However, you cannot assure that the unit cost per function point is independent of the language used to implement the software component. This uncertainty exists because the cost of development is a function of code size as well as the amount of functionality to be implemented [Gaffney 1986].

The function point size metric is consistent across languages and applications. When you know the SLOC-to-function point ratio for a particular language, you can use function points to estimate source code size in SLOC by multiplying that ratio by the number of function points. For example, Jones [1986] states that there are 106 COBOL statements per function point.

Experience with MIS and commercial software shows that, using function points, you can make an early estimate of size, generally quite successfully, for those classes of software. However, function point advocates typically use the counts of the five items cited above as the basis for calculating function points, as described above, and not as the basis for making an estimate of the count of source statements.

Jones [1991] presents a variant of function points called feature points. Feature points are based on counts of the five externals discussed in connection with function points plus a count of the number of algorithms. Jones [1991] has asserted the utility of this metric for various real-time and system applications.

5.4 Calculation of Physical Program Size

Even if you can calculate the function point number relatively consistently and accurately, it does not provide all of the information that you need to answer all your questions about the size of a software product. It is likely that you can estimate the physical implementation size of a program or major function, such as a CSCI, relatively easily from a KSLOC estimate. To do this, you should use data about the compiler's functioning, in particular the average expansion from SLOC to the number of object statements. Then, multiply this figure by the average size (in bytes) of an object statement, based on experience captured in the experience database. Unfortunately, this process is not likely to be done easily when function points are the measure of program size. This is because there is, in general, no fundamental (physical) program size to perform a given function. Indeed, Boehm [1983] reported on an experiment in which there was a several-fold variation in the sizes of the programs designed to meet the same functional objectives but with different optimizing criteria.

6. How to Estimate Software Size by Counting Externals

This section shows how to estimate the size of an aerospace software system in KSLOC using external measures of the intended system's requirements. Here, aerospace software can be characterized as real-time command-and-control embedded software. This method is of particular interest since the measures you use are counts that are often available very early in the development cycle. The method is a generalization of the function point method described in Section 5. The four external measures used here are defined in Section 5.

The method described here [Gaffney and Werling 1991] is based on the observation that the unweighted sum of the counts of the externals (the primitives from which you determine the function point value) correlates about as well with the source statement count as do function points. Since the calculation of function points involves a subjective estimation of some additional factors, including the appropriate weighting to apply to the counts of each of the primitives, use of the "raw" sum of the primitives could prove advantageous since it does not require making the additional subjective judgments implicit in the estimation of function points. Not doing the weighting and other processing of the raw counts is simpler and might result in a reduced degree of error in the source statement estimate and also the development labor estimate determined in part from it.

You can apply an empirical software size-estimating model, based on counts of the program externals defined here, to both embedded and business software systems. The estimates of the parameters of such a model are best developed by the organization intending to use it, based on data from the experience of that organization. However, if such data is not available, you can use either of the two estimating equations presented here, one for the case of three externals and the other for four externals.

The first estimating equation for estimating size from counts of externals is:

$$S = 13.94 + 0.034A$$

where S is the software system size in KSLOC and A is the sum of three program externals—inputs, outputs, and inquiries. The second estimating equation is:

$$S = 12.28 + 0.030E$$

where S is the software system size in KSLOC and E is the sum of all four program externals.

The estimation procedure is as follows:

- Collect counts of program externals and product size in KSLOC for projects in your software experience database.

- Develop an organization-specific estimating formula for estimating size from counts of externals. To derive such a formula, use the project data in the organization's software experience database to plot size (on the y-axis) against counts of externals (on the x-axis), and fit a line that seems to best represent the data. Although a visual fit can be made, it is preferable to use a linear regression fit, as described in Graybill [1961] and other standard texts.

- To estimate size for a new proposal, identify the number of program externals for each major program unit (CSCI or equivalent).

- Estimate size in KSLOC by using the formulas above or those derived from your experience data, and the appropriate counts of externals.

You can obtain the data for the estimating model and use it to develop an estimate of software size for your project at requirements time. This allows you to make a more accurate estimate of development costs earlier in the project. You can pool this estimate with size estimates developed using other techniques.

7. Software Product Size Growth

The size, however measured, of software products of all types tends to grow from the time you initiate development to the time you deliver the product. No matter how accurate the data used to make the initial estimate, and no matter how precise the method used to make the initial estimate, the delivered size will differ significantly in most cases from the initial estimate of size. This growth adds to the development cost and thus becomes an important consideration.

The proportion of code growth over the development cycle can be defined as:

$$Growth = \frac{(Delivered\_Size) - (Initial\_Estimate)}{(Initial\_Estimate)}$$

where size can be measured in SLOC, function points, and so forth.

Code growth occurs because you almost always tend to underestimate size at the conceptual, proposal, and requirements phases of the software project. You tend to be optimistic and may not know or fully understand the requirements, and both of these factors cause underestimation. Since this code growth can add to cost, staffing, and schedule problems, you must measure it to understand it.

Cruickshank [1985] gives some experience with code growth in aerospace software development. Table 3 summarizes this experience, based on 16 projects in the 200 to 400 KSLOC range.

For example, you would expect a software development effort scheduled to take 24 months from preliminary design through CSCI (functional test) to grow 19 percent from the original estimate. If the pre-design estimate is 320 SLOC, then the estimate of the delivered size is (320)(1.19) = 380.8 KSLOC.

You should make estimates of delivered size and code growth, and you should make plans to deal with the predicted growth. You should also establish a reserve account to fund the costs resulting from code growth.

8. Combining Estimates

You should develop several independent estimates of size, if possible. This can be done in terms of the method used and/or in terms of the people who develop the estimate using some particular method. Different methods of size estimation might use different information about the application. Hence, if the application of two different methods yields relatively close estimates, then you would tend to feel comfortable about them. However, if they differ considerably, this should be cause for you to examine why this is so. One reason could be that the assumptions underlying the two estimates are incompatible. You also might use several people to develop an estimate using a single method. For example, using the statistical size estimation procedure described in Section 4, different individuals might be responsible for developing the estimates of each of the functions (that is, A, B. ...0). Alternatively, several people might develop estimates of the size of each function. Then, the parameter values smallest, largest, and most likely (see Section 4) would be computed. This is an application of the well-known Delphi technique that is used to combine information from several experts in a field of knowledge. In summary, it is always better to have a number of independent estimates in terms of *both* people and method.

Another approach is to combine several estimates of size for an entire software product or for each of the functions that compose it. The approach is to combine several estimates by weighting them by your estimates of their probabilities of correctness. Of course, you should be sure that the sum of their probabilities is 1.0. Such a set of estimates might span the range from optimistic (it will be small!) to pessimistic (we do not understand the application!).

Now, we consider an example of this approach. Consider the hypothetical data in Table 4. Suppose you have three different size estimates and you associate each with a weight that is an estimate of the probability of correctness as follows:

Table 3. Code growth factors.

Development Time in Months (Design through CSCI Test)	Percent Growth Initiation to Delivery
12	11
24	19
36	32
48	55

Table 4. Sample software product size estimates.

KSLOC	Probability	Weighted Size
100	0.20	20
150	0.30	45
200	0.50	100

Then, your combined estimate is 165 KSLOC. Alternatively, you might use each of the size estimates, together with its probability weighting, to develop a cost risk [see SPC, Chapter 8, 1994].

9. Summary of Recommendations

General recommendations on size estimation are as follows:

- Estimate the size of every product (at least each CSCI) separately.
- Test the estimated size for compatibility with the schedule and estimated development effort.
- Make size/development effort trade-off studies for every product.
- Make sure that methods for size estimation, compatibility testing among size, effort, schedule, and trade-offs are part of your software standards.
- Track code growth during development.
- Develop and use an experience database for *your* organization to aid in size estimation.
- Form your estimate independently of market pressures.
- Help management establish the level of risk.
- Provide information to help management make informed decisions.
- Determine cost and schedule estimates based on the size estimate.
- Estimate size in several ways.
- Make size estimates throughout development.
- Base your estimates of size on *your organization's experience*, retained in its database.
- Relate code size to the size of other products of the software development process such as the amount of design. This technique facilitates making updates during the development process as you elaborate the requirements.
- Remember that a good estimate of size is *key* to a good estimate of cost.
- Realize that there are various ways to estimate size.
- Form your estimate based on *counting* available functions, input/output, and so on, of your project.
- Update your estimate throughout the development process.

References

[Albrecht 1979] Albrecht, A.J., "Measuring Application Development Productivity," *IBM Application Development Symp. Proc.*, 1979, GUIDE Int'l and SHARE Int'l, IBM Corporation, 1979, pp. 83–92.

[Albrecht and Gaffney 1983] Albrecht, A.J., and J.E. Gaffney, Jr., "Software Function, Source Lines of Code, Development Effort Prediction: A Software Science Validation," *IEEE Trans. Software Eng.*, Vol. SE-9, No. 6, Nov. 1983, pp. 639–648.

[Boehm 1981] Boehm, B.W., *Software Engineering Economics,* Prentice-Hall, Englewood Cliffs, N.J., 1981.

[Boehm 1983] Boehm, B.W., "Software Cost Estimation: Outstanding Research Issues," presented at *Workshop on Software Cost Engineering,* MITRE Corporation, Bedford, Mass., Sept. 1983.

[Britcher and Gaffney 1985] Britcher, R.N., and J.E. Gaffney, Jr., "Reliable Size Estimates for Software System Decomposed as State Machines," *Proc. COMPSAC 1985,* IEEE Computer Society Press, Los Alamitos, Calif., 1985, pp. 104–110.

[Cruickshank 1985] Cruickshank, R.D., "Cost Relationships in Simulator Software Development," presented at the *Summer Computer Simulation Conf.*, 1985.

[Gaffney 1984] Gaffney, J.E., Jr., "Estimation of Software Code Size Based on Quantitative Aspects of Function (With Application of Expert System Technology), *J. Parametrics*, Vol. 4, No. 3, 1984, pg. 23–34.

[Gaffney 1986] Gaffney, J.E., Jr., "The Impact on Software Development Costs of Using HOLs," *IEEE Trans. Software Eng.*, Vol. SE-12, No. 3, 1986, pp. 496–499.

[Gaffney and Werling 1991] Gaffney, J.E., Jr., and R. Werling, "A Model for Analysis of Scale Economics and Software Productivity," ANALYSIS_PROJECT_DATA-91008-N, Software Productivity Consortium, Herndon, VA, 1990.

[Graybill 1961] Graybill, F.A., *An Introduction to Linear Statistical Models,* Vol. I, McGraw-Hill, N.Y., 1961.

[Jones 1986] Jones, Capers, *Programming Productivity,* McGraw-Hill, NY, 1986.

[Jones 1990] Jones, Capers, *Cost Estimation for Software Development,* Addison-Wesley, Wokingham, England, 1990.

[Jones 1991] Jones, Capers, *Applied Software Measurement: Assuring Productivity and Quality*, McGraw-Hill, N.Y., 1991.

[Paulk et al. 1997] Paulk, M.C., B. Curtis, M.B. Chrissis, and C.V. Weber, "Capability Maturity Model for Software," in *Software Engineering,* M. Dorfman and R.H. Thayer, eds., IEEE Computer Society Press, Los Alamitos, Calif., 1997.

[Putnam 1978] Putnam, L.H., "A General Empirical Solution to the Macro Software Sizing and Estimating Problem," *IEEE Trans. Software Eng.*, Vol. SE-4, No. 4, 1978, pp. 345–361.

[SPC, Chapter 8, 1994] *Software Measurement Guidebook*, Chapter 8, SPC-91060-CMC, Version 02.01.00, Software Productivity Service Corporation, Herndon, VA, Aug. 1994. Reprinted in Software Management Consortium, *The Software Measurement Guidebook*, Int'l Thomson Computer Press, Boston, Mass., 1995.

[Stutzke 1997] Stutzke, R.D., "Software Estimating Technology: A Survey," in *Software Engineering Project Management*, 2nd ed., R.H. Thayer, ed., IEEE Computer Society Press, Los Alamitos, Calif., 1997.

How to Estimate Software Project Schedules[1]

John E. Gaffney, Jr.[2]
Lockheed Martin
Rockville, MD 20850

1. Schedule Estimation Overview

It is important to accurately estimate the time required to develop a software product and to be able to perform schedule/development effort trade-offs. It is also important to be able to create a staffing curve for the project development labor that you can use in project planning.

This section provides methods that help you answer the following schedule-related questions:

- How long will the development take?

- What effect will a shrinking development schedule have on the development effort from what has either been imposed or will be required?

- What is the staffing profile, (that is, what is the profile of effort per month) over the project duration?

To address these questions, this section presents guidance in methods that tell you how to do the following:

- Estimate a development schedule, given that you know (or have an estimate of) the size of your software product and how much effort it will take to develop it.

- Make a trade-off between the length of the development schedule and the effort required to develop the product.

- Determine whether a schedule given to you is compatible with the size of a proposed product and the required effort estimated for its development.

- Develop a spread of software development labor over the development time (schedule) that you have estimated.

- Estimate the potential impact on the software development schedule of incorporating re-used code into the new software product that you are developing.

When planning the development of a new software product, you can make trade-offs among cost, schedule, and size. For example, if you want a lower cost, then you must reduce the product size. Schedule (the period of time for software development) is a key consideration in planning for a software development project. You expect the effect of varying quality requirements to impact schedule and/or cost. Often, you can ensure higher quality software, in part, through more extensive testing. Sometimes this may increase the development effort and development time (schedule) over the time you would require for a software product that does not need to be of that quality level.

2. Estimating the Development Schedule

This section tells you how to estimate the length of time, t_d, required to develop a software product, given that you know (or have estimated) its size [Gaffney and Cruickshank 1997] and how much effort you will need to do so [SPC, Chapter 8, 1994], [Legg 1997], [Stutzke 1997]. To estimate t_d, use the formula:

$$t_d = \left(\frac{S}{C \cdot K^p} \right)^{1/q}$$

S is the software product size in source lines of code (SLOC) (excluding comments) or equivalent SLOC (ESLOC) when reused code is involved (see Section 3). C is the technology constant that numerically represents both the complexity of the software to

---

[1] An earlier version printed in SPC-91060-CMC, Version 02.01.00, Software Productivity Service Corporation, Herndon, VA, Aug. 1994. Reprinted in Software Management Consortium, *The Software Measurement Guidebook*, Int'l Thomson Computer Press, Boston, MA, 1995.

[2] This paper was originally prepared while the author was with the Software Productivity Consortium.

be developed and the sophistication of the development environment. The parameter C can be regarded as a generalized productivity measure since it includes the effects of project duration (schedule) and effort and size (together implying productivity). K is the development effort in labor years Finally, t_d is the development schedule (design through installation) in years. A set of values for the parameters p and q is $p = 0.6288$ and $q = 0.5355$ [SPC, Chapter 8, 1994]. It is desirable that you establish values based on your organization's experience.

You can also compute the schedule for other periods using this formula, but with the figures for K and C adjusted accordingly.

This equation is based on the software development equation discussed in [SPC, Chapter 8, 1994], and developed by Larry Putnam [Putnam 1978], which is

$$S = C \cdot K^p \cdot t_{d^q}$$

Now consider an example application of the equation for estimating t_d. Suppose that $C = 6{,}000$; $S = 300{,}000$; $K = 166.7$ labor years (equivalent to a development productivity of 150 SLOC/LM, where LM = labor months), $p = 0.6288$; and $q = 0.5555$. Solving for t_d and substituting the parameter values, you obtain:

$$t_d = \left(\frac{300{,}000}{6{,}000 \cdot 166.7^{0.6288}} \right)^{\frac{1.0}{0.5555}} = 3.5 \text{ years}$$

3. Schedule Impact of Reused Code

To examine the effect of code reuse on your (estimated) development schedule, determine the size in thousands ESLOC (KESLOC) of your software system using the equation

$$\text{KESLOC} = S_N + S_R \left(C_{VR}/C_{VN} \right)$$

where S_N is the amount (in KSLOC) of new code in the application system, and S_R is the amount (in KSLOC) of reused code in the application system. C_{VN} is the unit cost (LM/KSLOC or LH/SLOC, where LH = labor hours) of new code in your application system; C_{VR} is the unit cost of reused code in your application system.

To relate the lengths of the development schedule for a case in which the system consists of all-new code to one that consists, in part, of reused code, let

K_N = The effort (labor years) to develop an application system composed of all-new code.

K_R = The effort to develop an application system consisting of both new and reused code.

P = The relative productivity enhancement to be found in developing the system when reuse is involved as compared with the case in which it is not.

t_{dn} = The development schedule (months or years) for an application system of size S KSLOC composed of all-new code.

t_{dr} = The development schedule for an application system of size S KESLOC composed of both new and reused code.

R = The proportion of code reuse = $S_R/(S_N + S_R)$.

Gaffney and Durek [1991] give a formula that relates the schedule for developing a software system implemented with all-new code to one required if the software system is implemented with a combination of new and reused code:

$$\frac{t_{dr}}{t_{dn}} = P^{\frac{(p-1)}{q}}$$

where

$$\frac{K_R}{K_N} = \frac{1}{P} = \frac{C_{VN} \cdot (1 - R) + C_{VR} \cdot R}{C_{VN}} = 1 + R \cdot \left(\frac{C_{VR}}{C_{VN}} - 1 \right)$$

You may use the relation for K_R/K_N for various parametric "what-if" analyses to estimate the possible effect of various amounts of code reuse on the development schedule.

As an example, let $C_{VN} = 5.0$ LM/KSLOC, $C_{VR} = 0.375$ LM/KSLOC, and $R = 0.9$. Then $1/P = 0.1675$ and $P = 5.97$. Using the values of $p = 0.6288$ and $q = 0.5555$ given in Section 2,

$$\frac{t_{dr}}{t_{dn}} = P^{\frac{(p-1)}{q}} = P^{-0.6682} = 0.30$$

The schedule to develop the software product containing new and reused code is only 30 percent as long as that to develop the same product with all-new code.

Figure 1 shows the relative schedule reduction versus the relative productivity enhancement for two sets of values for the parameters p and q. The top curve uses the parameter values developed by Putnam [1978] of $p = .3333$ and $q = 1.3333$. The bottom curve uses more recent parameter values developed by Gaffney [1983] of $p = 0.6288$ and $q = .5555$. The thin shaded area between the curves shows that $p^{(p-1)}/q$ is relatively insensitive to a fairly wide range of p and q; therefore, it is a fairly robust estimator of t_{dr}/t_{dn}.

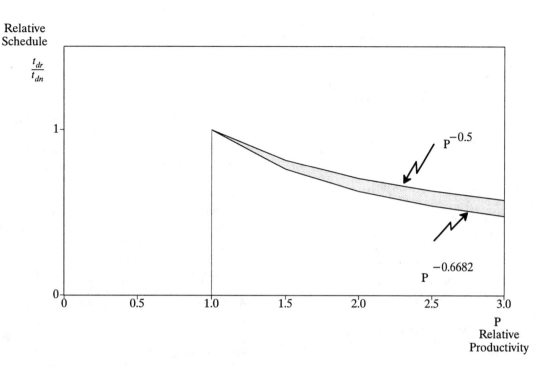

Figure 1. Schedule reduction versus productivity enhancement.

4. Schedule/Development Effort Trade-off

Suppose that you used the software development equation of Section 2 to estimate that the "ideal" length of the schedule for your software product is t_0. This is based on a size estimate of S ESLOC and on a development labor effort estimate of K_0 labor years with a technology constant of C. Now, suppose that you want to compute the amount of labor years required if you were to reduce the schedule from t_0 to t_1 (a figure that may have been imposed on you). The labor years required will increase to K_1, which is calculated using the equation

$$K_1 = K_0 \cdot \left(\frac{t_0}{t_1} \right)^{q/p} = K_0 \cdot \left(\frac{t_0}{t_1} \right)^{0.8834}$$

This equation is a schedule/development effort trade-off equation and is derived from the software development equation given above. A word of caution. Use this equation *only* to estimate the effect of schedule compression on your development effort.

As an example, suppose there was a 20 percent schedule reduction. Then $t_0/t_1 = 1/.8 = 1.25$. Suppose the originally estimated effort was $K_0 = 50$ labor years. Then the effort for the case in which the schedule was reduced by 20 percent would be $K_1 = 60.9$ labor years or an increase of 22 percent. This calcula-

tion illustrates the effect of schedule compression on development effort that you can expect.

Make schedule/development effort trade-off studies for all software development projects and products. Trade-off methods should be part of your organization's software standards. There are obviously limitations in the proportionate amount that the development schedule can be reduced. For example, if t_1 were to take the value of 0.1, that is, a 90 percent reduction in the development schedule, the increase in effort would be about 7.6 times the original effort. But experience shows that no increase could overcome this drastic schedule reduction to produce a product. A very large amount of effort applied to software development in a very short time interval is not feasible.

5. Schedule/Effort/Size Compatibility

You should determine whether the figures (estimates or objectives) for schedule, size, and effort for your project are compatible. The customer may impose the length of time for development, or you may perceive a need to quickly get a new product out into the marketplace. Independent of such considerations, you may develop a size estimate of your intended software product and an estimate of the productivity with which it is likely to have been developed and thence an estimate of the development labor required. It is important to determine if these estimates for size (S), effort (K), and development period (t_d) are mutually compatible. You can determine their compatibility by using a test based on an application of the software development equation. First, you estimate the value of the technology constant C implied by the values of S, K, and t_d that you have been given or otherwise determined. You calculate C from the equation

$$C = \left(\frac{S}{t_d^{0.5555} \cdot K^{0.6288}} \right)$$

On the basis of the value calculated for C, for this example, you can determine whether a given schedule is compatible with the size and effort (and hence, productivity) proposed for the project by using the process shown in Figure 2. That is, you compare the C that you have calculated (estimated for the project) with the C's for compatible complete projects, based on your organization's experience.

6. Software Development Labor Profiles

This section provides an equation that you can use to create an overall spread of labor months of development labor over the schedule of length t_d months. The equation is based on the Rayleigh [Norden 1958 and 1970] distribution. Putnam [1978] built on Norden's [1958 and 1970] work and showed that a Rayleigh curve represents, to a reasonable degree of approximation, the application of labor resources to the creation of a software product. The equation presented

here is a variant of the Putnam [1978] representation. The method does not take into consideration the individual activities that constitute the development project you are planning nor does it take into consideration the nature of the technology your organization uses for the project in question.

You will probably need to do some adjusting and modify the spread that the procedure provides. However, the procedure does give you a first approximation. Obviously, the relatively simple staffing model presented here cannot reflect the effects various factors could have on your selection of a staffing profile appropriate to your particular software development situation. You should also think about your project's activities in detail when doing labor resource spreading. View the staffing profile estimate developed with the method demonstrated here as only a first estimate. Clearly, it is preferable for you to develop a staffing profile based on your organization's experience. That experience might cause a different emphasis, such as greater front-loading, than the profile estimate based on the Rayleigh model.

You might use a two-step process to develop a staffing profile. First, make an estimate based on the Rayleigh model. Next, look at the spread the Rayleigh model provides and decide if it looks reasonable, based on whatever experience your organization has. Your evaluation of the profile may lead you to modify it, perhaps adding more effort (that is, a faster build-up) to the initial portion of the spread. Several modification cycles may be required, depending on your expectations.

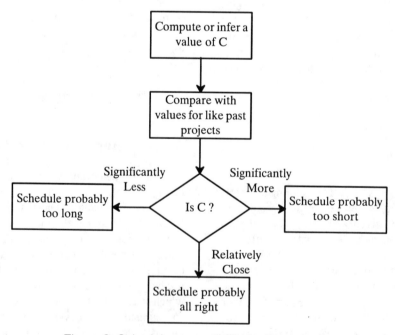

Figure 2. Schedule compatibility testing process.

260

Two variants of the Rayleigh staffing profile model are presented in this section. The first, the basic model, employs two parameters, K and t_d. The expanded model uses three parameters, those from the basic model plus an additional one, X. X corresponds to the ratio of the peak staffing level to the staffing level at the time of delivery, t_d (see Table 1).

6.1   Basic Rayleigh Model

The "instantaneous" or density form of the Rayleigh distribution is as follows:

$$y(t) = \frac{E}{t_p^2} \cdot t \cdot e^{-\frac{t^2}{2t_p^2}}$$

The cumulative form is as follows:

$$Y(t) = E \cdot \left(1 - e^{-\frac{t^2}{2t_p^2}} \right)$$

Note that t is the time, E is the total area under the curve to infinity, and $Y(t)$ is the area under the curve to time t. Since your software development project will not run to infinity, this model has to be adjusted to represent a practical staffing profile. You replace E by K/X, where K is the total labor expended from $t = 0$ to $t = t_d$, the time of delivery, and X is a factor, the determination of which is described later in this section. Note that $Y(t_d) = K$. Also note that the parameter t_p in the Rayleigh model is the location of the peak of the instantaneous curve $y(t)$.

6.2   Practical, Discrete Rayleigh Model

Your software project staffing will be done in terms of discrete intervals of time (months in the examples shown here; the method applies to weeks or other convenient intervals as well, however). Consequently, we now indicate the nature of the more practical discrete model that you should use and illustrate its application with an example.

The instantaneous form of the staffing curve is given by

$$y(t) = \frac{K/X}{t_p^2} \cdot t \cdot e^{-\frac{t^2}{2t_p^2}}$$

The cumulative form of the staffing curve is given by

$$Y(t) = \frac{K}{X} \cdot \left(1 - e^{-\frac{t^2}{2t_p^2}} \right)$$

You should use the discrete form of this method to develop your (initial estimate of the) staffing profile. It gives you the effort, $F(t)$, for each one-month interval in the t_d months that compose your software development period. Note that t extends from time equal to $t-1$ to time equal to t. $F(t)$ is given by the equation

$$F(t) = Y(t) - Y(t-1) = \frac{K}{X} \cdot \left(e^{-\frac{(t-1)^2}{2t_p^2}} - e^{-\frac{t^2}{2t_p^2}} \right)$$

where K is the total development effort equal to $K(t_d)$ as explained above. Note that $K = XE$, where E is the area under the curve from 0 to infinity. Note that t is the interval or month number and that there are $N = t_d/12$ one-month intervals in a development period of t_d months.

Table 1. Relative staffing levels and schedules.

X	R= y(t_d)/y(t_p)	r= t_d/t_p
0.6754	0.8029	1.5000
0.8647	0.4463	2.0000
0.9561	0.1810	2.5000
0.9802	0.0916	2.8000
0.9889	0.0549	3.0000
0.9990	0.0061	3.7169

Now, we consider how you should select the value of X that you should use. You can fix the ratio of $y(t_d)$, the approximate staffing level at the end of the development process, relative to the approximate peak staffing level, $y(t_p)$. This ratio is the definition of the parameter R. X is fixed by selecting a value of R. This selection also establishes the ratio, $r = t_d/t_p$, the number of schedule months relative to the month in which the peak staffing occurs. Table 1 shows some values for R, r, and X. Section 6.3 shows you how to compute the values of these parameters.

If you do not want to select a value for X, you can use $X = 0.999$ to obtain a first-pass staffing profile estimate.

6.3 Formulas Relating X, r, t_d, and t_p

Recognize that

$$X = 1 - e^{\frac{-t_d^2}{2t_p^2}}$$

and that

$$r = t_d/t_p$$

Thus, you can write

$$X = 1 - e^{-\frac{t^2}{2}}$$

Therefore, $r = (-2 \cdot LN(1 - X))^{1/2}$, where LN means the natural logarithm. Note the minus sign. This is okay. The expression $LN(1 - X)$ will be negative because $1 - X$ is less than 1.

Also, $t_p = (-t_d^2/(2 \cdot LN(1 - X))$. You can calculate values for $R = y(t_d)/y(t_p)$ by substituting into the expression given earlier for $y(t)$ the instantaneous Rayleigh staffing profile.

6.4 Procedure for Calculating Staffing Profile

You should use the following steps to calculate the values of a Rayleigh staffing profile estimate:

- Select the value of t_d, the number of months of development schedule. Determine this figure using the methodology presented earlier in this section.

- Calculate the value of X based on the value of r, the approximate ratio of the staffing level at the peak of the staffing profile relative to that upon delivery. You can use your organizational experience, expert opinion, or detailed planning for the project, as the basis for your selection of r, and hence X.

- Calculate the value of t_p, the number of months into development at which the peak staffing is estimated to occur. Use the formula given above to do so. Round to the nearest number of whole months.

- Select the value of K, the number of LM effort required to develop the software. Use the methodology presented in [SPC, Chapter 8, 1994] to do so.

- Calculate $Y(t)$, for all integer values of t from $t = 1$ to $t = t_d$.

$$Y(t) = \frac{K}{X} \cdot \left(1 - e^{-\frac{t^2}{2t_p^2}} \right)$$

- Calculate the month-by-month values of the staffing profile $F(t)$, for all integer values of t from $t = 1$ to $t = t_d$.

6.5 An Example of Rayleigh Staffing Profiles

Now, we apply the methodology described above to the development of two alternative staffing profiles for a software development project. The two profiles differ with respect to the value of R, and hence, of X used. The first profile, Case A, reflects a situation in which there is relatively early peaking and build-down during the development period. The second, Case B, represents the situation in which the staffing level is not reduced to such a great degree after the peak, which also occurs later in the development period. Case B may reflect a less mature development organization.

The example development project has been estimated to require 1,000 LM of effort and to require 20 months for completion. Table 2 presents the values of R that were selected, and the values of r, and so on, that correspond to them.

The staffing profiles for Cases A and B are provided in Figures 3 and 4.

Table 2. Example values of R, and so on.

Case	R	r	$t_p = t_d/r$	X	K/X	$1/(2 \cdot t_p^2)$
A	0.0549	3.00	6.667	0.9889	1011.22	0.0112
B	0.4463	2.00	10.00	0.8647	1156.47	0.0050

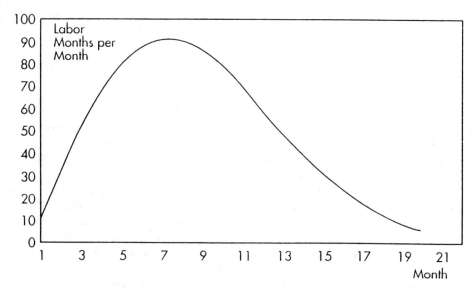

Figure 3. Case A, labor months per month.

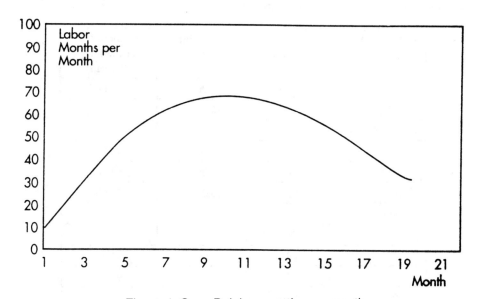

Figure 4. Case B, labor months per month.

263

7. Estimates of Possible Schedule Values and Risk

Now, you develop an estimate of the amount of (calendar) time, or the schedule, required to perform the development that you have just costed. As you can recall from [SPC, Chapter 8, 1994], there is a COCOMO schedule model that relates cost or effort in labor months (LM) and schedule in months. The model equation is of the form

$$T = aC^b$$

where T is the schedule in months, C is the cost in LM, and a and b are empirical constants.

Ideally, you have data about past projects in your database that you can use to calculate values for the constants a and b based on the experience of your organization. Assume, for the present example, that you do not have such data. Therefore, you will use the values in COCOMO. You will note a value of 2.5 for a and three alternative values for b: 0.32, 0.35, and 0.38. These values are quite close. Use a value of 0.33. It is a good engineering approximation and allows you to recognize that schedule essentially varies as the 1/3 power of cost, thus facilitating estimating the effect of cost changes on schedule. Thus, you decide to estimate the length of the development schedule, T (in months), as a function of the cost in LM, using the equation

$$T = 2.5(LM)^{0.33}$$

Now, you calculate the values of schedule corresponding to the values of cost you have determined. The cost values, the corresponding schedule values, and their individual and cumulative probabilities are presented in Table 3.

You can combine the set of schedule estimates shown in Table 3 to produce a weighted average, or "expected value," of the schedule of your product in a manner similar to what was done for cost. The weighted average schedule is 19.9 months (= (15.79 × 0.08) + (15.93 × 0.10) + ...). If you are asked for *the* (one or your best) estimate of the schedule, or period of time, expected to be required to develop the new software product, this is the value you should cite.

Determine the estimated schedule corresponding to a 20 percent risk, using interpolation as in the case of cost risk estimation. Applying this method to the values in the table, you estimate the 20 percent schedule risk point to be 21.67 months. Because schedule varies only as the third power of cost, you would expect (and can observe from the table) that the schedule uncertainty range is considerably smaller than the cost values from Table 3. Similar to the situation with costs, this cumulative plot can be used to help you to answer questions such as, "What risk do I assume if I adopt a development schedule of 21.7 months?" Figure 5 is a plot of the cumulative distribution of the possible schedule.

Table 3. Example linear distribution of costs and schedule.

Cost (LM)	Schedule (Months)	Probability (Percent)	Cumulative Probability (Percent)
266.41	15.79	8.00	8.00
273.80	15.93	10.00	18.00
410.70	18.21	2.00	20.00
501.19	19.45	20.00	40.00
515.10	19.63	25.00	65.00
687.23	21.59	10.00	75.00
706.30	21.78	12.50	87.50
772.65	22.44	5.00	92.50
973.00	24.21	2.00	94.50
1,000.00	24.43	2.50	97.00
1,059.45	24.90	2.50	99.50
1,500.00	27.93	0.50	100.00

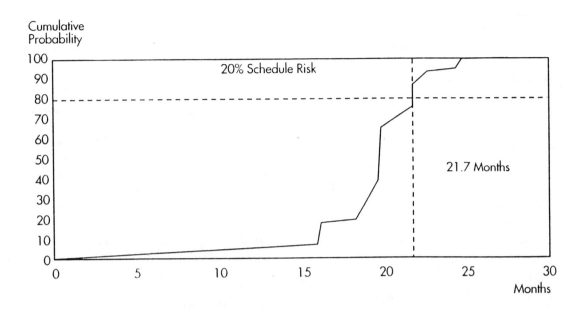

Figure 5. Cumulative distribution of schedule and schedule risk.

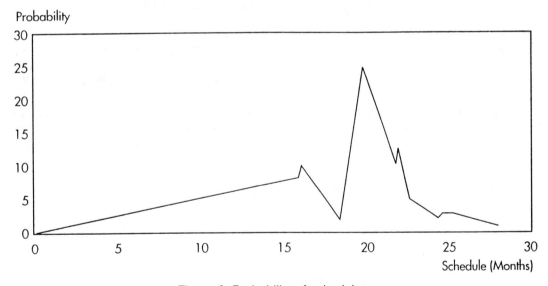

Figure 6. Probability of schedule.

Also, analogous to what was suggested that you do with cost data, you might find it useful to plot the schedule values that you have estimated and their associated probabilities. That is, you plot the data "Schedule" and the "Probability (Percent)" columns of Table 3. You thus produce the "probability density function" for the estimated possible values of schedule for your software development project. This is done in Figure 6. You will observe that this plot looks roughly like a normal probability density function.

This suggests that, in some instances, you might find it useful to approximate the probability density function of the estimated possible periods of time (schedule values) for a software development project as a normal distribution.

8. Summary of Recommendations

The recommendations on schedule estimation presented in this section are as follows:

- Estimate the schedule for every product.
- Recognize that methods for schedule estimation, compatibility testing, and trade-offs should be part of your software standards.
- Test the estimated schedule for compatibility with the size and estimated development effort.
- Generate a labor profile for every software product.
- Make schedule/development effort trade-off studies for every product.
- Track schedule growth during development.
- Develop and use an experience database to aid in schedule estimation.
- Relate schedule, effort, and size.
- Do trade-off studies between schedule and effort.
- Reuse code, if possible, to reduce the schedule.
- Test for compatibility of schedule, effort, and size.
- Use a Rayleigh distribution to develop an initial estimate of the overall software product development staffing profile.

References

[Gaffney and Cruickshank 1997] Gaffney, R.E., Jr., and R.D. Cruickshank, "How to Estimate Software Size," in *Software Engineering Project Management*, 2nd ed., R.H. Thayer, ed., IEEE Computer Society Press, Los Alamitos, Calif., 1997.

[Gaffney and Durek 1991] Gaffney, J.E., Jr., and T.A. Durek, "Software Reuse—Key to Enhanced Productivity; Some Quality Models," *The Economics of Information Systems and Software*, R. Veryard, ed., Butterworth Heineman, Oxford, England, 1991.

[Legg 1997], Legg, D.B., "How to estimate software costs using COCOMO," in *Software Engineering Project Management*, 2nd ed., R.H. Thayer, ed., IEEE Computer Society Press, Los Alamitos, Calif., 1997.

[Nordon 1958] Nordon, P.V., "Curve Fitting for a Model of Applied Research and Development Schedule," *IBM J. Research & Development,* Vol. 2, No. 3, July 1958, pp. 232–248.

[Nordon 1970] Nordon, P.V., "Using Tools for Project Management," *The Management of Production*, M.K. Starr, ed., Penguin Books, Baltimore, MD, 1970, pp. 71–101.

[Putnam 1978] Putnam, L.H., "A General Empirical Solution to the Macro Software Sizing and Estimating Problem," *IEEE Trans. Software Eng.*, Vol. SE-4, No. 4, 1978, pp. 345–361.

[SPC, Chapter 8, 1994] *Software Measurement Guidebook*, Chapter 8, SPC-91060-CMC, Version 02.01.00, Software Productivity Service Corporation, Herndon, VA, Aug. 1994. Reprinted in Software Management Consortium, *The Software Measurement Guidebook*, Int'l Thomson Computer Press, Boston, Mass., 1995.

[Stutzke 1997] Stutzke, R.D., "Software Estimating Technology: A Survey," in *Software Engineering Project Management*, 2nd ed., R.H. Thayer, ed., IEEE Computer Society Press, Los Alamitos, Calif., 1997.

Capers Jones, Software Productivity Research Inc., 1 New England Executive Park, Burlington, MA 01803-5005; phone (617) 273-0140; fax (617) 273-5176; Internet capers@xanadu.spr.com; CompuServe 75430,231

By popular demand:

Software estimating rules of thumb

Capers Jones
Software Productivity Research

Accurate software estimating is too difficult for simple rules of thumb. Yet in spite of their inadequacy—and the availability of more than 50 commercial software-estimating tools—simple rules of thumb remain the most common estimating approach.

Many companies develop and market software cost and quality estimating tools. Including my own firm's two proprietary tools, there are at least 50 commercial software-estimating tools on the market in the United States, and the worldwide total exceeds 75. Most of these tools are far superior to manual estimating methods in both ease of use and repeatability, and many are also more accurate.

In a comparative study of 50 manual estimates and 50 estimates produced by tools, I found two significant results. Manual estimates were wrong more than 75 percent of the time, and the errors were almost always on the side of excessive optimism—that is, they significantly underestimated both schedules and costs. Automated estimating tools came far closer to matching historical data, and errors tended toward conservatism—that is, they predicted slightly higher costs and longer schedules. This is the "fail safe" mode of software estimation.

Of course, even automated estimating tools give optimistic results if users exaggerate staff experience, understate application complexity, minimize paperwork and quality control, and ignore learning curves. These are common failures with manual estimates, and they can be carried over to automated estimates.

> **E**ven automated estimating tools give optimistic results if users exaggerate staff experience, understate application complexity, minimize paperwork and quality control, and ignore learning curves.

Why bother?

In spite of the plentiful availability of commercial software-estimating tools, I continue to receive e-mail and phone messages requesting simple rules of thumb that can be used with pocket calculators. So, in response, here are 10 simple rules of thumb covering various aspects of software development and maintenance.

These rules are based on function points and encompass software sizing algorithms, schedule algorithms, quality algorithms, and other interesting topics. The rules assume the version 3.0 function-point counting rules published by the International Function Point Users Group (IFPUG). Adjustments will be needed for the British Mark II function-point rules or the newer version 4.0 IFPUG rules.

Before proceeding, I must issue strong cautions:

- Simple rules of thumb are not accurate; the following rules are known to have a high margin of error.
- Simple rules of thumb should not be used for contracts, bids, or other serious business purposes.
- The best that can be said about simple rules of thumb is that they are easy to use and can provide a "sanity check" of estimates produced by other, more rigorous methods.

Sizing rules of thumb

Predicting the size of deliverables is the usual starting point for software cost estimating. The function-point metric has transformed sizing from a very difficult task to one that is easy and reasonably accurate.

Source code. Now that thousands of software projects have been measured using both function points and lines of code (LOC), we have empirical ratios for converting LOC data into function points and vice versa. The following rule is based on "logical statements" rather than "physical lines." The physical-line metric has such wide and random variations from language to language and programmer to programmer that it is not suited for sizing and estimating.

> Rule 1: One function point = 100 logical source code statements.

The ratio of noncommentary logical source-code statements to function points ranges from more than 300 statements per function point for basic assembly languages to less than 20 for object-oriented languages and many program generators. Since procedural languages such as C, Cobol, Fortran, and Pascal are close to the 100-to-1 mark, that value can serve as a rough conversion factor.

This rule has a high margin of error and needs significant adjustment when dealing with object-oriented programming languages, application generators, or applications with substantial reusable code.

Reprinted from *Computer*, Vol. 29, No. 3, Mar. 1996, pp. 116–118.

Paper deliverables. Software is a paper-intensive industry. More than 50 kinds of documents can be created for large software projects. For many large systems—especially large military projects—paperwork costs far more than source code. The following rule of thumb encompasses the sum of the pages that will be created in requirements, specifications, plans, user manuals, and other business-related software documents.

> Rule 2: Raising the number of function points to the 1.15 power predicts approximate page counts for paper documents associated with software projects.

A simple corollary rule, multiply pages by 400, predicts the approximate number of English words the pages contain.

Paperwork is such a major element of software costs and schedules that it cannot be ignored. Indeed, one of the major problems with the LOC metric was its tendency to conceal both the volume of paper deliverables and the high cost of software paperwork.

Creeping requirements. Dealing with new and changing requirements after completion of the initial requirements phase poses one of the software world's most severe problems. The function-point metric is extremely useful in measuring the rate at which requirements creep. In fact, "cost per function point" is now appearing in software contracts and outsourcing agreements. For contract purposes, cost per function point is used with a sliding scale that becomes more expensive for features added later in the development cycle.

> Rule 3: Creeping user requirements will grow at an average rate of 1 percent per month over the entire development schedule.

This rule means that for a two-year project, the functionality at delivery will be about 24 percent larger than when the requirements were first collected. For a three-year project, the delivered functionality will be about 36 percent larger.

Test cases. The function-point metric is extremely useful for test-case sizing, since the structure of function-point analysis closely parallels the items that need to be validated by testing. Commercial software-estimating tools can predict the number of test cases for more than a dozen discrete forms of testing. This simple rule of thumb encompasses the sum of all test cases.

> Rule 4: Raising the number of function points to the 1.2 power predicts the approximate number of test cases created.

A simple corollary can predict the number of times each test case will be run or executed during development: Assume that each test case will be executed about four times during software development.

Defect potentials. An application's defect potential is the sum of bugs or errors in four major deliverables—requirements, design, coding, user-documentation—plus bad fixes or secondary errors introduced in fixing a prior error.

Because the cost and effort of finding and fixing bugs is usually the largest identifiable software cost element, ignoring defects can throw off estimates, schedules, and costs by massive amounts.

> Rule 5: Raising the number of function points to the 1.25 power predicts the approximate defect potential for new software projects.

A corollary can predict the defect potential for enhancements. In this case, the rule applies to the size of the enhancement rather than the base being updated: Raising the number of function points to the 1.27 power predicts the approximate defect potential for enhancement software projects.

A higher power is used in the enhancement rule because latent defects, lurking in the base product, will be encountered during enhancement.

Defect removal efficiency. The defect potential is the life-cycle total of errors that must be eliminated. The defect potential will be reduced between 85 percent (approximate industry norm) and 99 percent ("best in class" result) prior to delivery. Thus, the number of delivered defects is only a small fraction of the overall defect potential.

An interesting rule can size the number of defects found and approximate the defect removal efficiency of various reviews, inspections, and tests:

> Rule 6: Each software review, inspection, or test step will find and remove 30 percent of the bugs that are present.

> **D**ealing with new and changing requirements after completion of the initial requirements phase poses one of the software world's most severe problems.

This rule implies six to 12 consecutive defect-removal operations to achieve high quality levels. This is why major software producers normally use multistage design reviews and code inspections, and various levels of testing from unit test through system test.

Rules for schedules, resources, and costs

Once the various deliverables have been quantified, the next stage is to predict schedules, resources, and costs.

Software schedules. Schedule estimation is a high-priority topic among clients, project managers, and software executives. Rule 7 calculates the approximate interval from the start of requirements until the first delivery to a client:

> Rule 7: Raising the number of function points to the 0.4 power predicts the approximate development schedule in calendar months.

This generic rule needs to be adjusted between civilian and military projects, since military software usually takes more time. For enhancements, the rule applies to the size of the enhancement, not of the base application.

Software staffing. The next rule of thumb concerns the people needed to build the application. Rule 8 is based on the concept of assignment scope, or the amount of work that will normally be one person's responsibility. The rule includes software developers, quality assurance personnel, testers, technical writers, database administrators, and project managers.

Rule 8: Dividing the number of function points by 150 predicts the approximate number of personnel required for the application.

A corollary estimates personnel needed to maintain the project:

Rule 9: Dividing the number of function points by 500 predicts the approximate number of maintenance personnel required to keep the application updated.

This rule implies that one person can perform minor updates and keep about 500 function points of software operational. (Another interesting maintenance rule of thumb is: Raising the function point total to the 0.25 power yields the approximate number of years the application will stay in use.)

Software development effort. The last rule of thumb is a hybrid rule that combines rules 7 and 8:

Rule 10: Multiply software development schedules by number of personnel to predict the approximate number of staff months of effort.

For example, assume you are concerned with a project of 1,000 function points in size. Using rule 7, or raising 1,000 function points to the 0.4 power, indicates a schedule of about 16 calendar months. Using rule 8, or dividing 1,000 function points by 150, indicates a staff of about 6.6 full-time personnel. Multiplying 16 calendar months by 6.6 personnel indicates a total of about 106 staff months to build this particular project. (Incidentally, another common but rough rule of thumb defines a staff month as 22 working days with six productive hours each day, or 132 work hours per month.)

> **S**imple rules of thumb continue to be popular, but they are never accurate and are not a substitute for formal estimating methods.

SIMPLE RULES OF THUMB continue to be popular, but they are never accurate and are not a substitute for formal estimating methods. I presented them primarily as examples of the project-management information now possible with function-point metrics. There are at least another dozen rules of thumb for predicting annual software enhancements, optimal enhancement size, and software growth rates during maintenance.

I hope the obvious limitations of these simplistic rules will motivate readers to explore more accurate and powerful methods.

Cost models for future software life cycle processes: COCOMO 2.0

Barry Boehm[†], Bradford Clark, Ellis Horowitz and Chris Westland

USC Center for Software Engineering, University of Southern California, Los Angeles, CA 90089-0781, USA

Ray Madachy

USC Center for Software Engineering and Litton Data Systems

Richard Selby

UC Irvine and Amadeus Software Research

Current software cost estimation models, such as the 1981 Constructive Cost Model (COCOMO) for software cost estimation and its 1987 Ada COCOMO update, have been experiencing increasing difficulties in estimating the costs of software developed to new life cycle processes and capabilities. These include non-sequential and rapid-development process models; reuse-driven approaches involving commercial off-the-shelf (COTS) packages, re-engineering, applications composition, and applications generation capabilities; object-oriented approaches supported by distributed middleware; and software process maturity initiatives. This paper summarizes research in deriving a baseline COCOMO 2.0 model tailored to these new forms of software development, including rationale for the model decisions. The major new modeling capabilities of COCOMO 2.0 are a tailorable family of software sizing models, involving Object Points, Function Points, and Source Lines of Code; nonlinear models for software reuse and re-engineering; an exponent-driver approach for modeling relative software diseconomies of scale; and several additions, deletions and updates to previous COCOMO effort-multiplier cost drivers. This model is serving as a framework for an extensive current data collection and analysis effort to further refine and calibrate the model's estimation capabilities.

1. INTRODUCTION

1.1 Motivation

"We are becoming a software company" is an increasingly-repeated phrase in organizations as diverse as finance, transportation, aerospace, electronics, and manufacturing firms. Competitive advantage is increasingly dependent on the development of smart, tailorable products and services, and on the ability to develop and adapt these products and services more rapidly than competitors' adaptation times.

[†]E-mail: boehm@sunset.usc.edu

Reprinted with permission from *Annals of Software Engineering*, Vol. 1, 1995, pp. 57–94.

Dramatic reductions in computer hardware platform costs, and the prevalence of commodity software solutions have indirectly put downward pressure on systems development costs. This situation makes cost-benefit calculations even more important in selecting the correct components for construction and life cycle evolution of a system, and in convincing skeptical financial management of the business case for software investments. It also highlights the need for concurrent product and process determination, and for the ability to conduct trade-off analyses among software and system life cycle costs, cycle times, functions, performance, and qualities.

Concurrently, a new generation of software processes and products is changing the way organizations develop software. These new approaches – evolutionary, risk-driven, and collaborative software processes; fourth generation languages and application generators; commercial off-the-shelf (COTS) and reuse-driven software approaches; fast-track software development approaches; software process maturity initiatives – lead to significant benefits in terms of improved software quality and reduced software cost, risk, and cycle time.

However, although some of the existing software cost models have initiatives addressing aspects of these issues, these new approaches have not to date been strongly matched by complementary new models for estimating software costs and schedules. This makes it difficult for organizations to conduct effective planning, analysis, and control of projects using the new approaches.

These concerns have led the authors to formulate a new version of the Constructive Cost Model (COCOMO) for software effort, cost, and schedule estimation. The original COCOMO [Boehm 1981] and its specialized Ada COCOMO successor [Boehm and Royce 1989] were reasonably well-matched to the classes of software project that they modeled: largely custom, built-to-specification software [Miyazaki and Mori 1985; Goudy 1987]. Although Ada COCOMO added a capability for estimating the costs and schedules for incremental software development, COCOMO encountered increasing difficulty in estimating the costs of business software [Kemerer 1987; Ruhl and Gunn 1991], of object-oriented software [Pfleeger 1991], of software created via spiral or evolutionary development models, or of software developed largely via commercial off-the-shelf (COTS) applications-composition capabilities.

1.2 COCOMO 2.0 Objectives

The initial definition of COCOMO 2.0 and its rationale are described in this paper. The definition will be refined as additional data are collected and analyzed. The primary objectives of the COCOMO 2.0 effort are:

- To develop a software cost and schedule estimation model tuned to the life cycle practices of the 1990's and 2000's.

- To develop software cost database and tool support capabilities for continuous model improvement.

- To provide a quantitative analytic framework, and a set of tools and techniques for evaluating the effects of software technology improvements on software life cycle costs and schedules.

These objectives support the primary needs expressed by software cost estimation users in a recent Software Engineering Institute survey [Park *et al.* 1994]. In priority order, these needs were for support of project planning and scheduling, project staffing, estimates-to-complete, project preparation, replanning and rescheduling, project tracking, contract negotiation, proposal evaluation, resource leveling, concept exploration, design evaluation, and bid/no-bid decisions. For each of these needs, COCOMO 2.0 will provide more up-to-date support than its COCOMO and Ada COCOMO predecessors.

1.3 Topics Addressed

Section 2 describes the future software marketplace model being used to guide the development of COCOMO 2.0. Section 3 presents the overall COCOMO 2.0 strategy and its rationale. Section 4 summarizes the COCOMO 2.0 software sizing approach, involving a tailorable mix of Object Points, Function Points, and Source Lines of Code, with new adjustment models for reuse and re-engineering. Section 5 discusses the new exponent-driver approach to modeling relative project diseconomies of scale, replacing the previous COCOMO development modes. Section 6 summarizes the revisions to the COCOMO effort-multiplier cost drivers, including a number of additions, deletions, and updates. Section 7 presents the resulting conclusions based on COCOMO 2.0's current state.

2. FUTURE SOFTWARE PRACTICES MARKETPLACE MODEL

Figure 1 summarizes the model of the future software practices marketplace that we are using to guide the development of COCOMO 2.0. It includes a large upper "end-user programming" sector with roughly 55 million practitioners in the U.S. by the year

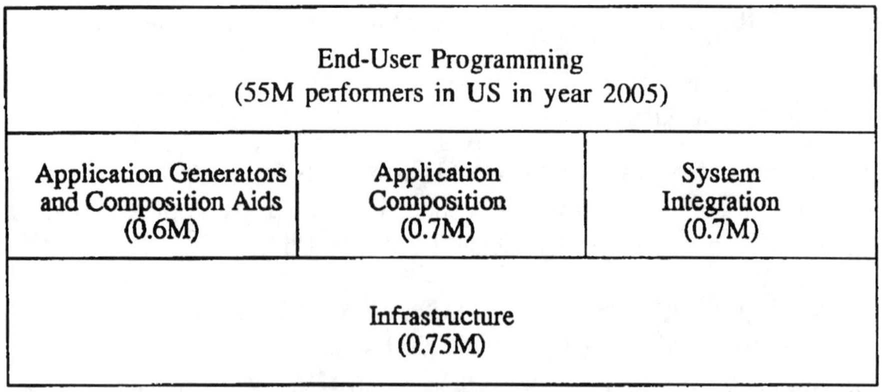

End-User Programming (55M performers in US in year 2005)		
Application Generators and Composition Aids (0.6M)	Application Composition (0.7M)	System Integration (0.7M)
Infrastructure (0.75M)		

Figure 1. Future software practices marketplace model.

2005; a lower "infrastructure" sector with roughly 0.75 million practitioners; and three intermediate sectors, involving the development of application generators and composition aids (0.6 million practitioners), the development of systems by applications composition (0.7 million), and system integration of large-scale and/or embedded software systems (0.7 million).[1]

End-User Programming will be driven by increasing computer literacy and competitive pressures for rapid, flexible, and user-driven information processing solutions. These trends will push the software marketplace toward having users develop most information processing applications themselves via application generators. Some example application generators are spreadsheets, extended query systems, and simple, specialized planning or inventory systems. They enable users to determine their desired information processing application via domain-familiar options, parameters, or simple rules. Every enterprise from Fortune 100 companies to small businesses and the U.S. Department of Defense will be involved in this sector.

Typical *Infrastructure* sector products will be in the areas of operating systems, database management systems, user interface management systems, and networking systems. Increasingly, the Infrastructure sector will address "middleware" solutions for such generic problems as distributed processing and transaction processing. Representative firms in the Infrastructure sector are Microsoft, NeXT, Oracle, Sybase, Novell, and the major computer vendors.

In contrast to end-user programmers, who will generally know a good deal about their applications domain and relatively little about computer science, the infrastructure developers will generally know a good deal about computer science and relatively little about applications. Their product lines will have many reusable components, but the pace of technology (new processor, memory, communications, display, and multimedia technology) will require them to build many components and capabilities from scratch.

Performers in the three *intermediate sectors* in figure 1 will need to know a good deal about computer science-intensive Infrastructure software and also one or more application domains. Creating this talent pool is a major national challenge.

---

[1] These figures are judgement-based extensions of the Bureau of Labor Statistics moderate-growth labor distribution scenario for the year 2005 [CSTB 1993; Silvestri and Likaseiwicz 1991]. The 55 million End-User programming figure was obtained by applying judgement-based extrapolations of the 1989 Bureau of the Census data on computer usage fractions by occupation [Kominski 1991] to generate end-user programming fractions by occupation category. These were then applied to the 2005 occupation-category populations (e.g. 10% of the 25M people in "Service Occupations"; 40% of the 17M people in "Marketing and Sales Occupations"). The 2005 total of 2.75M software practitioners was obtained by applying a factor of 1.6 to the number of people traditionally identified as "Systems Analysts and Computer Scientists" (0.829M in 2005) and "Computer Programmers" (0.882M). The expansion factor of 1.6 to cover software personnel with other job titles is based on the results of a 1983 survey on this topic [Boehm 1983]. The 2005 distribution of the 2.75M software developers is a judgement-based extrapolation of current trends.

The *Application Generators* sector will create largely prepackaged capabilities for user programming. Typical firms operating in this sector are Microsoft, Lotus, Novell, Borland, and vendors of computer-aided planning, engineering, manufacturing, and financial analysis systems. Their product lines will have many reusable components, but will also require a good deal of new-capability development from scratch. *Application Composition Aids* will be developed both by the above firms and by software product-line investments of firms in the Application Composition sector.

The *Application Composition* sector deals with applications which are too diversified to be handled by prepackaged solutions, but which are sufficiently simple to be rapidly composable from interoperable components. Typical components will be graphic user interface (GUI) builders, database or object managers, middleware for distributed processing or transaction processing, hypermedia handlers, smart data finders, and domain-specific components such as financial, medical, or industrial process control packages.

Most large firms will have groups to compose such applications, but a great many specialized software firms will provide composed applications on contract. These range from large, versatile firms such as Andersen Consulting and EDS, to small firms specializing in such speciality areas as decision support or transaction processing, or in such application domains as finance or manufacturing.

The *System Integration* sector deals with large-scale, highly embedded, or unprecedented systems. Portions of these systems can be developed with Application Composition capabilities, but their demands generally require a significant amount of up-front systems engineering and custom software development. Aerospace firms operate within this sector, as do major system integration firms such as EDS and Andersen Consulting, large firms developing software-intensive products and services (telecommunications, automotive, financial, and electronic products firms), and firms developing large-scale corporate information systems of manufacturing support systems.

3. COCOMO 2.0 STRATEGY AND RATIONALE

The four main elements of the COCOMO 2.0 strategy are:

- Preserve the openness of the original COCOMO.
- Key the structure of COCOMO 2.0 to the future software marketplace sectors described above.
- Key the inputs and outputs of the COCOMO 2.0 submodels to the level of information available.
- Enable the COCOMO 2.0 submodels to be tailored to a project's particular process strategy.

COCOMO 2.0 follows the openness principles used in the original COCOMO. Thus, all of its relationships and algorithms will be publicly available. Also, all of its interfaces are designed to be public, well-defined, and parametrized, so that complementary preprocessors (analogy, case-based, or other size estimation models), post-processors (project planning and control tools, project dynamics models, risk analyzers), and higher level packages (project management packages, product negotiation aids) can be combined straightforwardly with COCOMO 2.0.

To support the software marketplace sectors above, COCOMO 2.0 provides a family of increasingly detailed software cost estimation models, each tuned to the sectors' needs and type of information available to support software cost estimation.

3.1 COCOMO 2.0 Models for the Software Marketplace Sectors

The User Programming sector does not need a COCOMO 2.0 model. Its applications are typically developed in hours to days, so a simple activity-based estimate will generally be sufficient.

The COCOMO 2.0 model for the Application Composition sector is based on Object Points. Object Points are a count of the screens, reports and third-generation language modules developed in the application, each weighted by a three-level (simple, medium, difficult) complexity factor [Banker *et al.* 1994; Kauffman and Kumar 1993]. This is commensurate with the level of information generally known about an Application Composition product during its planning stages, and the corresponding level of accuracy needed for its software estimates (such applications are generally developed by a small team in a few weeks to months).

The COCOMO 2.0 capability for estimation of *Application Generator, System Integration,* or *Infrastructure* developments is based on a tailorable mix of the Application Composition model (for early prototype efforts) and two increasingly detailed estimation models for subsequent portions of the life cycle.

3.2 COCOMO 2.0 Model Rationale and Elaboration

The rationale for providing this tailorable mix of models rests on three primary premises.

First, unlike the initial COCOMO situation in the late 1970's, in which there was a single, preferred software life cycle model (the waterfall model), current and future software projects will be tailoring their processes to their particular process drivers. These process drivers include COTS or reusable software availability; degree of understanding of architectures and requirements; market window or other schedule constraints; and required reliability (see [Boehm 1989, pp. 436–437] for an example of such tailoring guidelines).

Second, the granularity of the software cost estimation model used needs to be consistent with the granularity of the information available to support software cost estimation. In the early stages of a software project, very little may be known about the size of the product to be developed, the nature of the target platform, the nature of the personnel to be involved in the project, or the detailed specifics of the process to be used.

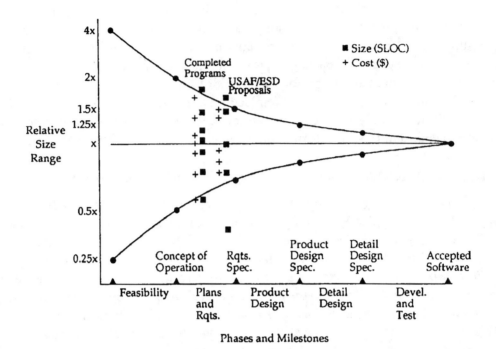

Figure 2. Software costing and sizing accuracy versus phase.

Figure 2, extended from [Boehm 1981, p. 311], indicates the effect of project uncertainties on the accuracy of software size and cost estimates. In the very early stages, one may not know the specific nature of the product to be developed to better than a factor of 4. As the life cycle proceeds, and product decisions are made, the nature of the products and its consequent size are better known, and the nature of the process and its consequent cost drivers are better known. The earlier "completed programs" size and effort data points in figure 2 are the actual sizes and efforts of seven software products built to a partially-defined specification [Boehm *et al.* 1984].[2] The later "USAF/ESD proposals" data points are from five proposals submitted to the U.S. Air Force Electronic Systems Division in response to a fairly thorough specification [Devenny 1976].

Third, given the situation in premises 1 and 2, COCOMO 2.0 enables projects to furnish coarse-grained cost driver information in the early project stages, and increasingly fine-grained information in later stages. Consequently, COCOMO 2.0 does not produce point estimates of software cost and effort, but rather range estimates tied to the degree of definition of the estimation inputs. The uncertainty ranges in figure 2 are used as starting points for these estimation ranges.

---

[2] These seven projects implemented the same algorithmic version of the Intermediate COCOMO cost model, but with the use of different interpretations of the other product specifications: produce a "friendly user interface" with a "single-user file system".

With respect to *process strategy*, Application Generator, System Integration, and Infrastructure software projects will involve a mix of three major process models. The appropriate sequencing of these models will depend on the project's marketplace drivers and degree of product understanding.

The *Early Prototyping* stage involves prototyping efforts to resolve potential high-risk issues such as user interfaces, software/system interaction, performance, or technology maturity. The costs of this type of effort are best estimated by the Application Composition model.

The *Early Design* stage involves exploration of alternative software/system architectures and concepts of operation. At this stage, not enough is generally known to support fine-grain cost estimation. The corresponding COCOMO 2.0 capability involves the use of function points and a small number of additional cost drivers.

The *Post-Architecture* stage involves the actual development and maintenance of a software product. This stage proceeds most cost-effectively if a software life-cycle architecture has been developed; validated with respect to the system's mission, concept of operation, and risk; and established as the framework for the product. The corresponding COCOMO 2.0 model has about the same granularity as the previous COCOMO and Ada COCOMO models. It uses source instructions and/or function points for sizing, with modifiers for reuse and software breakage; a set of seventeen multiplicative cost drivers; and a set of five factors determining the project's scaling exponent. These factors replace the development modes (Organic, Semidetached, or Embedded) in the original COCOMO model, and refine the four exponent-scaling factors in Ada COCOMO.

To summarize, COCOMO 2.0 provides the following three-model series for estimation of Application Generator, System Integration, and Infrastructure software projects:

1. The earliest phases or spiral cycles will generally involve prototyping, using Application Composition capabilities. The COCOMO 2.0 Application Composition model supports these phases, and any other prototyping activities occurring later in the life cycle.

2. The next phases or spiral cycles will generally involve exploration of architectural alternatives or incremental development strategies. To support these activities, COCOMO 2.0 provides an early estimation model. This uses function points for sizing, and a coarse-grained set of seven cost drivers (e.g. two cost drivers for Personnel Capability and Personnel Experience in place of the six current Post-Architecture model cost drivers covering various aspects of personnel capability, continuity and experience). Again, this level of detail is consistent with the general level of information available and the general level of estimation accuracy needed at this stage.

3. Once the project is ready to develop and sustain a fielded system, it should have a life-cycle architecture, which provides more accurate information on cost driver

inputs and enables more accurate cost estimates. To support this stage of development COCOMO 2.0 provides a model whose granularity is roughly equivalent to the current COCOMO and Ada COCOMO models. It can use either source lines of code or function points for a sizing parameter, a refinement of the COCOMO development modes as a scaling factor, and seventeen multiplicative cost drivers.

The above should be considered as current working hypotheses about the most effective forms for COCOMO 2.0. They will be subject to revision based on subsequent data analysis. Data analysis should also enable the further calibration of the relationships between object points, function points, and source lines of code for various languages and composition systems, enabling flexibility in the choice of sizing parameters.

3.3 Other Major Differences Between COCOMO and COCOMO 2.0

The tailorable mix of models and variable-granularity cost model inputs and outputs are not the only differences between the original COCOMO and COCOMO 2.0. The other major differences involve size-related effects involving reuse and re-engineering, changes in scaling effects, and changes in cost drivers. These are summarized in table 1, and elaborated in sections 4, 5, and 6. Explanations of the acronyms and abbreviations in table 1 are provided in section 9.

4.   COST FACTORS: SIZING

This section provides the definitions and rationale for the three sizing quantities used in COCOMO 2.0: Object Points, Unadjusted Function Points, and Source Lines of Code. It then discusses the COCOMO 2.0 size-related parameters used in dealing with software reuse, re-engineering, conversion, and maintenance.

4.1   Application Composition: Object Points

Object Point estimation is a relatively new software sizing approach, but it is well-matched to the practices in the Application Composition sector. It is also a good match to associated prototyping efforts based on the use of a rapid-composition Integrated Computer Aided Software Environment (ICASE) providing graphic user interface builders, software development tools, and large, composable infrastructure and application components. In these areas, it has compared well to Function Point estimation on a nontrivial (but still limited) set of applications.

The comparative study [Banker *et al.* 1994] of Object Point versus Function Point estimation analyzed a sample of nineteen investment banking software projects from a single organization, developed using ICASE application composition capabilities, and ranging from 4.7 to 71.9 person−months of effort. The study found that the Object Points approach explained 73% of the variance (R^2) in person−months adjusted for reuse, as compared to 76% for Function Points.

Table 1

Comparison of COCOMO, Ada COCOMO, and COCOMO 2.0.

	COCOMO	Ada COCOMO	COCOMO 2.0: Stage 1	COCOMO 2.0: Stage 2	COCOMO 2.0: Stage 3
Size	Delivered Source Instructions (DSI) or Source Lines Of Code (SLOC)	DSI or SLOC	Object Points	Function Points (FP) and Language	FP and Language or SLOC
Reuse	Equivalent SLOC = Linear $f(DM, CM, IM)$	Equivalent SLOC = Linear $f(DM, CM, IM)$	Implicit in model	% unmodified reuse: SR % modified reuse: nonlinear $f(AA, SU, DM, CM, IM)$	Equivalent SLOC = nonlinear $f(AA, SU, DM, CM, IM)$
Breakage	Requirements Volatility rating (RVOL)	RVOL rating	Implicit in model	Breakage %: BRAK	BRAK
Maintenance	Annual Change Traffic (ACT) = %added + %modified	ACT	Object Point Reuse Model	Reuse model	Reuse model
Scale (b) in $MM_{NOM} = a(Size)^b$	Organic: 1.05 Semidetached: 1.12 Embedded 1.20	Embedded: 1.04–1.24 depending on the degree of: • early risk elimination • solid architecture • stable requirements • Ada process maturity	1.0	1.01–1.26 depending on the degree of: • precedentedness • conformity • early architecture, risk resolution • team cohesion • process maturity (SEI)	1.01–1.26 depending on the degree of: • precedentedness • conformity • early architecture, risk resolution • team cohesion • process maturity (SEI)
Product cost drivers	RELY, DATA, CPLX	RELY*, DATA, CPLX*, RUSE	None	RCPX*†, RUSE*†	RELY, DATA, DOCU*†, CPLX†, RUSE†
Platform cost drivers	TIME, STOR, VIRT, TURN	TIME, STOR, VMVH, VMVT, TURN	None	Platform difficulty: PDIF*†	TIME, STOR, PVOL(=VIRT)
Personnel cost drivers	ACAP, AEXP, PCAP, VEXP, LEXP	ACAP*, AEXP, PCAP*, VEXP, LEXP*	None	Personnel capability and experience: PERS*†, PREX*†	ACAP*, AEXP†, PCAP*, PEXP*†, LTEX*†, PCON*†
Project cost drivers	MODP, TOOL, SCED	MODP*, TOOL*, SCED, SECU	None	SCED, FCIL*†	TOOL*†, SCED, SITE*†

* Different multipliers.
† Different rating scale.

279

A subsequent statistically designed experiment [Kauffman and Kumar 1993] involved four experienced project managers using Object Points and Function Points to estimate the effort required on two completed projects (3.5 and 6 actual person–months), based on project descriptions of the type available at the beginning of such projects. The experiment found that Object Points and Function Points produced comparably accurate results (slightly more accurate with Object Points, but not statistically significant). From a usage standpoint, the average time to produce an Object Point estimate was about 47% of the corresponding average time for Function Point estimates. Also, the managers considered the Object Point method easier to use (both of these results were statistically significant).

Thus, although these results are not yet broadly based, their match to Applications Composition software development appears promising enough to justify selecting Object Points as the starting point for the COCOMO 2.0 Application Composition estimation model.

4.1.1 COCOMO 2.0 Object Point Estimation Procedure

Figure 3 presents the baseline COCOMO 2.0 Object Point procedure for estimating the effort involved in Application Composition and prototyping projects. It is a synthesis of the procedure in Appendix B.3 of [Kauffman and Kumar 1993] and the productivity data from the nineteen project data points in [Banker et al. 1994].

Definitions of terms in figure 3 are as follows:

- *NOP*: New Object Points (Object Point count adjusted for reuse).

- *srvr*: number of server (mainframe or equivalent) data tables used in conjunction with the SCREEN or REPORT.

- *clnt*: number of client (personal workstation) data tables used in conjunction with the SCREEN or REPORT.

- *%reuse*: the percentage of screens, reports, and 3GL modules reused from previous applications, pro-rated by degree of reuse.

The productivity rates in figure 3 are based on an analysis of the year-1 and year-2 project data in [Banker et al. 1994]. In year-1, the CASE tool was itself under construction and the developers were new to its use. The average productivity of 7 NOP/person–month in the twelve year-1 projects is associated with the Low levels of developer and ICASE maturity and capability in figure 3. In the seven year-2 projects, both the CASE tool and the developer's capabilities were considerably more mature. The average productivity was 25 NOP/person–month, corresponding with the High levels of developer and ICASE maturity in figure 3.

As another definitional point, note that the use of the term "object" in "Object Points" defines screens, reports, and 3GL modules as objects. This may or may not have any relationship to other definitions of "objects", such as those possessing

Step 1: Assess Object-Counts: estimate the number of screens, reports, and 3GL components that will comprise this application. Assume the standard definitions of these objects in your ICASE environment.

Step 2: Classify each object instance into simple, medium and difficult complexity levels depending on values of characteristic dimensions. Use the following scheme:

For Screens				For Reports			
Number of Views contained	# and source of data tables			Number of Sections contained	# and source of data tables		
	Total < 4 (< 2 srvr < 3 clnt)	Total < 8 (2/3 srvr 3-5 clnt)	Total 8+ (> 3 srvr > 5 clnt)		Total < 4 (< 2 srvr < 3 clnt)	Total < 8 (2/3 srvr 3-5 clnt)	Total 8+ (> 3 srvr > 5 clnt)
< 3	simple	simple	medium	0 or 1	simple	simple	medium
3 - 7	simple	medium	difficult	2 or 3	simple	medium	difficult
> 8	medium	difficult	difficult	4 +	medium	difficult	difficult

Step 3: Weigh the number in each cell using the following scheme. The weights reflect the relative effort required to implement an instance of that complexity level.:

Object Type	Complexity-Weight		
	Simple	Medium	Difficult
Screen	1	2	3
Report	2	5	8
3GL Component			10

Step 4: Determine Object-Points: add all the weighted object instances to get one number, the Object-Point count.

Step 5: Estimate percentage of reuse you expect to be achieved in this project. Compute the New Object Points to be developed, $NOP = (Object\text{-}Points)(100 - \%reuse)/100$.

Step 6: Determine a productivity rate, $PROD = NOP$ / person-month, from the following scheme

Developers' experience and capability	Very Low	Low	Nominal	High	Very High
ICASE maturity and capability	Very Low	Low	Nominal	High	Very High
PROD	4	7	13	25	50

Step 7: Compute the estimated person-months: $PM = NOP$ / $PROD$.

Figure 3. Baseline object point estimation procedure.

features such as class affiliation, inheritance, encapsulation, message passing, and so forth. Counting rules for "objects" of that nature, when used in languages such as C++, will be discussed under "source lines of code" in the next section.

4.2. Applications Development

As described in section 3.2, the COCOMO 2.0 model uses function points as the basis for measuring size for the Early Design stage, and function points and/or SLOC for Post-Architecture stage sizing. For comparable size measurement across COCOMO 2.0 participants contributing size data and users furnishing size estimates to the model, standard counting rules are necessary. A consistent definition for size within projects as a prerequisite for project planning and control, and a consistent definition across projects is a prerequisite for process improvement [Park 1992].

The COCOMO 2.0 model has adopted counting rules that have been formulated by wide-community participation or standardization efforts. The source lines of code metrics are based on the Software Engineering Institute source statement definition checklist [Park 1992]. The function point metrics are based on the International Function Point User Group (IFPUG) Guidelines [IFPUG 1994].

4.2.1 Lines of Code Counting Rules

In COCOMO 2.0, the logical source statement has been chosen as the standard line of code. Defining a line of code is difficult due to conceptual differences involved in accounting for executable statements and data declarations in different languages. The goal is to measure the amount of intellectual work put into program development, but difficulties arise when trying to define consistent measures across different languages. To minimize these problems, the Software Engineering Institute (SEI) definition checklist for a logical source statement is used in defining the line of code measure. The Software Engineering Institute has developed this checklist as part of a system of definition checklists, report forms and supplemental forms to support measurement definitions [Park 1992; Goethert et al. 1992].

Figure 4 shows a portion of the definition checklist as it is being applied to support the development of the COCOMO 2.0 model. Each checkmark in the "Includes" column identifies a particular statement type or attribute included in the definition, and vice versa for the "Excludes" column. Other sections in the definition clarify attributes for usage, delivery, functionality, replications and development status. There are also clarifications for language specific statements for ADA, C, C++, CMS-2, COBOL, FORTRAN, JOVIAL and PASCAL.

Some changes were made to the line-of-code definition that depart from the default definitions provided in [Park 1992]. These changes eliminate categories of software which are generally small sources of project effort. Not included in the definition are commercial off-the-shelf software (COTS), government furnished software (GFS), other products, language support libraries, and operating systems, or other commercial libraries. Code generated with source code generators is not included, though measurements will be taken with and without generated code to support analysis.

The "COCOMO 2.0 line-of-code definition" is calculated directly by the Amadeus automated metrics collection tool [Amadeus 1994; Selby et al. 1991], which is being used to ensure uniformly collected data in the COCOMO 2.0 data collection and analysis project. We have developed a set of Amadeus measurement templates that

Definition Checklist for Source Statements Counts

Definition name: <u>Logical Source Statements</u> Date: _____

<u>(basic definition)</u> Originator: <u>COCOMO 2.0</u>

Measurement unit:	Physical source lines				
	Logical source statements	✔			

Statement type	Definition ✔	Data Array ☐		Includes	Excludes
When a line or statement contains more than one type, classify it as the type with the highest precedence.					
1 Executable	Order of precedence →		1	✔	
2 Nonexecutable					
3 Declarations			2	✔	
4 Compiler directives			3	✔	
5 Comments					
6 On their own lines			4		✔
7 On lines with source code			5		✔
8 Banners and nonblank spacers			6		✔
9 Blank (empty) comments			7		✔
10 Blank lines			8		✔
11					
12					

How produced	Definition ✔	Data array ☐	Includes	Excludes
1 Programmed			✔	
2 Generated with source code generators				✔
3 Converted with automated translators			✔	
4 Copied or reused without change			✔	
5 Modified			✔	
6 Removed				✔
7				
8				

Origin	Definition ✔	Data array ☐	Includes	Excludes
1 New work: no prior existence			✔	
2 Prior work: taken or adapted from				
3 A previous version, build, or release			✔	
4 Commercial, off-the-shelf software (COTS), other than libraries				✔
5 Government furnished software (GFS), other than reuse libraries				✔
6 Another product				✔
7 A vendor-supplied language support library (unmodified)				✔
8 A vendor-supplied operating system or utility (unmodified)				✔
9 A local or modified language support library or operating system				✔
10 Other commercial library				✔
11 A reuse library (software designed for reuse)			✔	
12 Other software component or library			✔	
13				
14				

Figure 4. Definition checklist.

support the COCOMO 2.0 data definitions for use by the organizations collecting data, in order to facilitate standard definitions and consistent data across participating sites.

To support further data analysis, Amadeus will automatically collect additional measures including total source lines, comments, executable statements, declarations, structure, component interfaces, nesting, and others. The tool will provide various size measures, including some of the object sizing metrics in [Chidamber and Kemerer 1994], and the COCOMO sizing formulation will adapt as further data is collected and analyzed.

4.2.2 Function Point Counting Rules

The function point cost estimation approach is based on the amount of functionality in a software project and a set of individual project factors [Behrens 1983; Kunkler 1985; IFPUG 1994]. Function points are useful estimators since they are based on information that is available early in the project life cycle. A brief summary of function points and their calculation in support of COCOMO 2.0 is as follows.

4.2.2.1 Function Point Introduction

Function points measure a software project by quantifying the information processing functionality associated with major external data or control input, output, or file types. Five user function types should be identified, as defined in table 2.

Table 2

User function types.

External Input (Inputs)	Count each unique user data or user control input type that (i) enters the external boundary of the software system being measured and (ii) adds or changes data in a logical internal file.
External Output (Outputs)	Count each unique user data or control output type that leaves the external boundary of the software system being measured.
Internal Logical File (Files)	Count each major logical group of user data or control information in the software system as a logical internal file type. Include each logical file (e.g. each logical group of data) that is generated, used, or maintained by the software system.
External Interface Files (Interfaces)	Files passed or shared between software systems should be counted as external interface file types within each system
External Inquiry (Queries)	Count each unique input-output combination, where an input causes and generates an immediate output, as an external inquiry type.

Each instance of these function types is then classified by complexity level. The complexity levels determine a set of weights, which are applied to their corresponding function counts to determine the Unadjusted Function Points quantity. This is the Function Point sizing metric used by COCOMO 2.0. The usual Function Point procedure involves assessing the degree of influence (DI) of fourteen application characteristics on the software project determined according to a rating scale of 0.0 to 0.05 for each characteristic. The fourteen ratings are added together, and then added to a base level of 0.65 to produce a general characteristic adjustment factor that ranges from 0.65 to 1.35.

Each of these fourteen characteristics, such as distributed functions, performance, and reusability, thus have a maximum of 5% contribution to estimated effort. This is significantly inconsistent with COCOMO experience; thus, COCOMO 2.0 uses Unadjusted Function Points for sizing, and applies its reuse factors, cost driver effort multipliers, and exponent scale factors to this sizing quantity. The COCOMO 2.0 procedure for determining Unadjusted Function Points is shown in figure 5.

4.3   Reuse and Re-engineering

4.3.1 Nonlinear Reuse Effects

The COCOMO 2.0 treatment of software reuse and re-engineering differs significantly from that of the original COCOMO in that it uses a nonlinear estimation model. In the original COCOMO reuse model, the cost of reusing software is basically a linear function of the extent that the reused software needs to be modified. This involves estimating the amount of software to be adapted, ASLOC, and three degree-of-modification parameters: DM, the percentage of design modification; CM, the percentage of code modification; and IM, the percentage of the original integration effort required for integrating the reused software.

These are used to determine an equivalent number of new instructions to be used as the COCOMO size parameter:

$$ESLOC = ASLOC \times \frac{(0.4 \times DM + 0.3 \times CM + 0.3 \times IM)}{100}. \tag{1}$$

Thus, if the software is used without modification, its additional size contribution will be zero. Otherwise, its additional size contribution will be a linear function of DM, CM, and IM.

However, the analysis in [Selby 1988] of reuse costs across nearly 3000 reused modules in the NASA Software Engineering Laboratory indicates that the reuse cost function is nonlinear in two significant ways (see figure 6):

• It does not go through the origin. There is generally a cost of about 5% for assessing, selecting, and assimilating the reusable component.

Step 1:   Determine function counts by type. The unadjusted function counts should be counted by a lead technical person based on information in the software requirements and design documents. The number of each of the five user function types should be counted (Internal Logical File[*] (ILF), External Interface File (EIF), External Input (EI), External Output (EO), and External Inquiry (EQ)).

Step 2:   Determine complexity-level function counts. Classify each function count into Low, Average and High complexity levels depending on the number of data element types contained and the number of file types referenced. Use the following scheme:

For ILF and EIF				For EO and EQ				For EI			
Record Elements	Data Elements			File Types	Data Elements			File Types	Data Elements		
	1 - 19	20 - 50	51+		1 - 5	6 - 19	20+		1 - 4	5 - 15	16+
1	Low	Low	Avg	0 or 1	Low	Low	Avg	0 or 1	Low	Low	Avg
2 - 5	Low	Avg	High	2 - 3	Low	Avg	High	2 - 3	Low	Avg	High
6+	Avg	High	High	4+	Avg	High	High	3+	Avg	High	High

Step 3:   Apply complexity weights. Weight the number in each cell using the following scheme. The weights reflect the relative value of the function to the user.

Function Type	Complexity-Weight		
	Low	Average	High
Internal Logical Files	7	10	15
External Interface Files	5	7	10
External Inputs	3	4	6
External Outputs	4	5	7
External Inquiries	3	4	6

Step 4:   Compute Unadjusted Function Points. Add all the weighted functions counts to get one number, the Unadjusted Function Points.

---

[*] Note: The word *file* refers to a logically related group of data and not the physical implementation of those groups of data

Figure 5. Function count procedure.

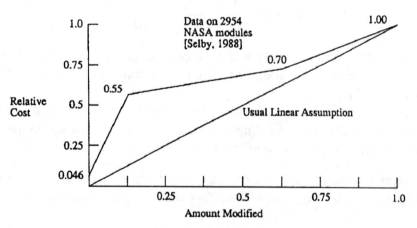

Figure 6. Nonlinear reuse effects.

- Small modifications generate disproportionately large costs. This is primarily due to two factors: the cost of understanding the software to be modified, and the relative cost of interface checking.

A COCOMO 2.0 reuse model which accommodates these nonlinearities is presented below.

4.3.2 COCOMO 2.0 Reuse Model

The paper by Parikh and Zvegintzov [1983] contains data indicating that 47% of the effort in software maintenance involves understanding the software to be modified. Thus, as soon as one goes from unmodified (black-box) reuse to modified-software (white-box) reuse, one encounters this software understanding penalty. Also, Gerlich and Denskat [1994] show that, if one modifies k out of m software modules, the number N of modules interface checks required is $N = k * (m - k) + k * (k - 1)/2$.

Figure 7 shows this relation between the number of modules modified k and the resulting number of module interface checks required.

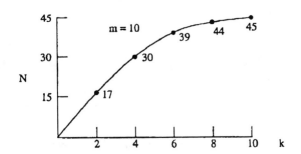

Figure 7. Number of module interface checks
versus fraction modified.

The shape of this curve is similar for other values of m. It indicates that there are nonlinear effects involved in the module interface checking which occurs during the design, code, integration, and test of modified software.

The size of both the software understanding penalty and the module interface checking penalty can be reduced by good software structuring. Modular, hierarchical structuring can reduce the number of interfaces which need checking [Gerlich and Denskat 1994], and software which is well structured, explained, and related to its mission will be easier to understand. COCOMO 2.0 reflects this in its allocation of estimated effort for modifying reusable software. The COCOMO 2.0 reuse equation for equivalent new software to be developed is:

$$ESLOC = ASLOC \times \frac{(AA + SU + 0.4 \times DM + 0.3 \times CM + 0.3 \times IM)}{100}. \qquad (2)$$

Table 3

Rating scale for software understanding increment SU.

	Very low	Low	Nominal	High	Very high
Structure	Very low cohesion, high coupling, spaghetti code.	Moderately low cohesion, high coupling.	Reasonably well-structured; some weak areas.	High cohesion, low coupling.	Strong modularity, information hiding in data/control structures.
Application clarity	No match between program and application world-views.	Some correlation between program and application.	Moderate correlation between program and application.	Good correlation between program and application.	Clear match between program and application world-views.
Self-descriptiveness	Obscure code: documentation missing, obscure or obsolete.	Some code commentary and headers; some useful documentation.	Moderate level of code commentary, headers, documentation.	Good code commentary and headers; useful documentation; some weak areas.	Self-descriptive code; documentation up to date, well-organized, with design rationale.
SU increment to AAF	50	40	30	20	10

Table 4

Rating scale for Assessement and Assimilation increment (AA).

AA increment	Level of AA effort
0	None
2	Basic module search and documentation
4	Some module Test and Evaluation (T&E), documentation
6	Considerable module T&E, documentation
8	Extensive module T&E, documentation

The software understanding increment SU is obtained from table 3. As indicated in table 3, if the software is rated very high on structure, application clarity, and self-descriptiveness, the software understanding and interface checking penalty is only 10%. If the software is rated very low on these factors, the penalty is 50%.

The other nonlinear reuse increment deals with the degree of assessment and assimilation needed to determine whether a fully-reused software module is appropriate to the application, and to integrate its description into the overall product description. Table 4 provides the rating scale and values for the Assessment and Assimilation increment AA. For software conversion, this factor extends the Conversion Planning Increment in [Boehm 1981, p. 558].

4.3.3 Re-engineering and Conversion Cost Estimation

The COCOMO 2.0 reuse model needs additional refinement to estimate the costs of software re-engineering and conversion. The major difference in re-engineering and conversion is the efficiency of automated tools for software restructuring. These can lead to very high values for the percentage of code modified (CM in the COCOMO 2.0 reuse model), but with very little corresponding effort. For example, in the NIST re-engineering case study [Ruhl and Gunn 1991], 80% of the code (13,131 COBOL source statements) was re-engineered by automatic translation, and the actual re-engineering effort, 35 person–months, was a factor of 4 lower than the COCOMO estimate of 152 person–months.

The COCOMO 2.0 re-engineering and conversion estimation approach involves estimation of an additional parameter, AT, the percentage of the code that is re-engineered by automatic translation. Based on an analysis of the project data above, an effort estimator for automated translation is 2400 source statements/person–month; the normal COCOMO 2.0 reuse model is used for the remainder of the re-engineered software.

The NIST case study also provides useful guidance on estimating the AT factor, which is a strong function of the difference between the boundary conditions (e.g. use of COTS packages, change from batch to interactive operation) of the old code and the re-engineered code. The NIST data on percentage of automated translation (from an original batch processing application without COTS utilities) are given in table 5.

Table 5

Variation in percentage of automated re-engineering
[Ruhl and Gunn 1991].

Re-engineering target	AT (% automated translation)
Batch processing	96%
Batch with SORT	90%
Batch with DBMS	88%
Batch, SORT, DBMS	82%
Interactive	50%

4.4 Breakage

COCOMO 2.0 replaces the COCOMO Requirements Volatility effort multiplier and the Ada COCOMO Requirements Volatility exponent driver by a breakage percentage, BRAK, used to adjust the effective size of the product. Consider a project which delivers 100,000 instructions but discards the equivalent of an additional 20,000 instructions. This project would have a BRAK value of 20, which would be used to adjust its effective size to 120,000 instructions for COCOMO 2.0 estimation. The BRAK factor is not used in the Application Composition model, where a certain degree of product iteration is expected, and included in the data calibration.

4.5   Application Maintenance

The original COCOMO used Annual Change Traffic (ACT), the percentage of code modified and added to the software product per year, as the primary measure for sizing a software maintenance activity. This has caused some difficulties, primarily the restriction to annual increment and a set of inconsistencies with the reuse model. COCOMO 2.0 remedies these difficulties by applying the reuse model to maintenance as well.

5.   COST FACTORS: SCALING

5.1.   Modeling Software Economies and Diseconomies of Scale

Software cost estimation models often have an exponential factor to account for the relative economies or diseconomies of scale encountered as a software project increases its size. This factor is generally represented as the exponent B in the equation:

$$Effort = A \times (Size)^B. \tag{3}$$

If $B < 1.0$, the project exhibits economies of scale. If the product's size is doubled, the project effort is less than doubled. The project's productivity increases as the product size is increased. Some project economies of scale can be achieved via project-specific tools (e.g. simulations, testbeds), but in general these are difficult to achieve. For small projects, fixed startup costs such as tool tailoring and setup of standards and administrative reports are often a source of economies of scale.

If $B = 1.0$, the economies and diseconomies of scale are in balance. This linear model is often used for cost estimation of small projects. It is used for the COCOMO 2.0 Application Composition model.

If $B > 1.0$, the project exhibits diseconomies of scale. This is generally due to two main factors: growth of interpersonnel communications overhead and growth of large-system integration overhead. Larger projects will have more personnel, and thus more interpersonnel communications paths consuming overhead. Integrating a small product as part of a larger product requires not only the effort to develop the small product, but also the additional overhead effort to design, maintain, integrate, and test its interfaces with the remainder of the product.

See [Banker *et al.* 1994a] for a further discussion of software economies and diseconomies of scale.

The COCOMO 2.0 value for the coefficient A in equation (3), provisionally set at 3.0. Initial calibration of COCOMO 2.0 to the original COCOMO project database [Boehm 1981, pp. 496–497], indicates that this is a reasonable starting point.

5.2 COCOMO and Ada COCOMO Scaling Approaches

The data analysis on the original COCOMO indicated that its projects exhibited net diseconomies of scale. The projects factored into three classes or modes of software development (Organic, Semidetached, and Embedded), whose exponents B were 1.05, 1.12, and 1.20, respectively. The distinguishing factors of these modes were basically environmental: Embedded-mode projects were more unprecedented, requiring more communications overhead and complex integration; and less flexible, requiring more communications overhead and extra effort to resolve issues within tight schedule, budget, interface, and performance constraints.

The scaling model in Ada COCOMO continued to exhibit diseconomies of scale, but recognized that a good deal of the diseconomy could be reduced via management controllables. Communications overhead and integration overhead could be reduced significantly by early risk and error elimination; by using thorough, validated architectural specifications; and by stabilizing requirements. These practices were combined into an Ada process model [Boehm and Royce 1989; Royce 1990]. The project's use of these practices, and an Ada process model experience or maturity factor, were used in Ada COCOMO to determine the scale factor B.

Ada COCOMO applied this approach to only one of the COCOMO development modes, the Embedded mode. Rather than a single exponent $B = 1.20$ for this mode, Ada COCOMO enabled B to vary from 1.04 to 1.24, depending on the project's progress in reducing diseconomies of scale via early risk elimination, solid architecture, stable requirements, and Ada process maturity.

5.3 COCOMO 2.0 Scaling Approach

COCOMO 2.0 combines the COCOMO and Ada COCOMO scaling approaches into a single rating-driven model. It is similar to that of Ada COCOMO in having additive factors applied to a base exponent B. It includes the Ada COCOMO factors, but combines the architecture and risk factors into a single factor, and replaces the Ada process maturity factor with a Software Engineering Institute (SEI) process maturity factor (the exact form of this factor is still being worked out with the SEI). The scaling model also adds two factors, precedentedness and flexibility, to account for the mode effects in the original COCOMO, and adds a Team Cohesiveness factor to account for the diseconomy-of-scale effects on software projects whose developers, customers, and users have difficulty in synchronizing their efforts. It does not include the Ada COCOMO Requirements Volatility factor, which is now covered by increasing the effective product size via the Breakage factor.

Table 6 provides the rating levels for the COCOMO 2.0 scale factors. A project's numerical ratings W_i are summed across all of the factors, and used to determine a scale exponent B via the following formula:

$$B = 1.01 + 0.01 \sum W_i. \tag{4}$$

Table 6

Rating scheme for the COCOMO 2.0 scale factors.

Scale factors (W_i)	Very low (5)	Low (4)	Nominal (3)	High (2)	Very high (1)	Extra high (0)
Precedentedness	thoroughly unprecedented	largely unprecedented	somewhat unprecedented	generally familiar	largely familiar	thoroughly familiar
Development flexibility	rigorous	occasional relaxation	some relaxation	general conformity	some conformity	general goals
Architecture/ risk resolution*	little (20%)	some (40%)	often (60%)	generally (75%)	mostly (90%)	full (100%)
Team cohesion	very difficult interactions	some difficult interactions	basically cooperative interactions	largely cooperative	highly cooperative	seamless interactions
Process maturity†	5 minus weighted average of "Yes" answers to CMM Maturity Questionnaire					

* % significant module interfaces specified, % significant risks eliminated.

† The form of the Process Maturity scale is being resolved in coordination with the SEI. The intent is to produce a process maturity rating as a weighted average of the project's percentage compliance levels to the 18 Key Process Areas in Version 1.1 of the Capability Maturity Model-based [Paulk et al. 1993] rather than to use the previous 1-to-5 maturity levels. The weights to be applied to the Key Process Areas are still being determined.

Thus, a 100 KSLOC project with Extra High (0) ratings for all factors will have $W_i = 0$, $B = 1.01$, and a relative effort $E = 100^{1.01} = 105$ *PM*. A project with Very Low (5) ratings for all factors with have $W_i = 25$, $B = 1.26$, and a relative effort $E = 331$ *PM*. This represents a large variation, but the increase involved in a one-unit change in one of the factors is only about 4.7%. Thus, this approach avoids the 40% swings involved in choosing a development mode for a 100 KSLOC product in the original COCOMO.

6. COST FACTORS: EFFORT-MULTIPLIER COST DRIVERS

COCOMO 2.0 continues the COCOMO and Ada COCOMO practice of using a set of effort multipliers to adjust the nominal person–month estimate obtained from the project's size and exponent drivers:

$$PM_{adjusted} = PM_{nominal} \times \left(\prod_i EM_i \right). \tag{5}$$

The primary selection and definition criteria for COCOMO 2.0 effort-multiplier cost drivers were:

- Continuity. Unless there has been a strong rationale otherwise, the COCOMO 2.0 baseline rating scales and effort multipliers are consistent with those in COCOMO and Ada COCOMO.
- Parsimony. Effort-multiplier cost drivers are included in the COCOMO 2.0 baseline model only if there has been a strong rationale that they would independently explain a significant source of project effort or productivity variation.

Table 1 summarized the COCOMO 2.0 effort-multiplier cost drivers by the four categories of Product, Platform, Personnel, and Project Factors. The superscripts following the cost driver names indicated the differences between the COCOMO 2.0 cost drivers and their counterparts in COCOMO and Ada COCOMO:

blank – No difference in rating scales or effort multipliers.
*   – Same rating scales, different effort multipliers.
†   – Different rating scales, different effort multipliers.

Table 7 provides the COCOMO 2.0 effort-multiplier rating scales. The following subsections elaborate on the treatment of these effort-multiplier cost drivers, and discuss those which have been dropped in COCOMO 2.0.

6.1 Product Factors

6.1.1 RELY – Required Software Reliability

COCOMO 2.0 retains the original COCOMO RELY rating scales and effort multipliers. Ada COCOMO contained a lower set of effort-multiplier values for the higher RELY levels, based on a rationale that Ada's strong typing, tasking, exceptions, and other features eliminated significant classes of potential defects. Given the absence of strong evidence of a general effort-multiplier trend in this direction, the COCOMO 2.0 baseline RELY multipliers have not been changed from the original COCOMO, in consonance with the continuity criterion above.

6.1.2 DATA – Data Base Size

As with RELY, there has been no strong evidence of a need for change of the DATA ratings and effort multipliers. They remain the same in COCOMO 2.0 under the continuity criterion.

6.1.3 CPLX – Product Complexity

Table 8 provides the new COCOMO 2.0 CPLX rating scale. It has been updated to reflect several changes in computer and software technology and applications. These include an additional rating scale for User Interface Management Operations, effects of distributed and parallel processing, and advances in data/object base technology and middleware technology.

Ada COCOMO contained a lower set of effort-multiplier values for the higher CPLX levels, based on a rationale that its models for tasking, exceptions, encapsulation, etc., made many previously complex issues easier to deal with. However, the rating scale revisions in table 8 introduce additional high-complexity areas such as parallelization, distributed hard real-time control, and virtual reality, which are not particularly simplified by Ada or other programming language constructs. Overall, it appears that the growth in desired product complexity keeps pace with the growth in technology. Thus, the COCOMO 2.0 baseline CPLX multipliers have not been changed from the original COCOMO, in consonance with the continuity criterion.

6.1.4 RUSE – Required Reusability

Ada COCOMO added this cost driver to account for the additional effort needed to construct components intended for reuse on the current or futute projects. It had four rating levels and multipliers ranging from 1.0 to 1.5. Subsequent experience indicated that both the rating levels and range of effort multipliers needed to be expanded. For example, AT&T has experienced a cost esculation factor of 2.25 in developing software for broad-based reuse. In reconciling recent experience with the previous Ada COCOMO data, it appeared that broad-based reuse required a High or Very High level of Required Reliability, which brought the effective Ada COCOMO reuse-multiplier range up to $(1.5)(1.4) = 2.10$. The baseline RUSE COCOMO 2.0 effort multipliers have a productivity range of 1.75, yielding a combined RUSE-RELY productivity range of $(1.75)(1.4) = 2.45$.

Table 7

Effort-multiplier cost driver ratings for the post-architecture model.

	Very low	Low	Nominal	High	Very high	Extra high
RELY	slight inconvenience	low, easily recoverable losses	moderate, easily recoverable losses	high financial loss	risk to human life	
DATA		DB bytes/Pgm SLOC < 10	$10 \leq D/P < 100$	$100 \leq D/P < 1000$	$D/P \geq 1000$	
CPLX			see table 8			
RUSE		none	across project	across program	across product line	across multiple product lines
DOCU	Many life-cycle needs uncovered	Some life-cycle needs uncovered	Right-sized to life-cycle needs	Excessive for life-cycle needs	Very excessive for life-cycle needs	
TIME			≤50% use of available execution time	70%	85%	95%
STOR			≤50% use of available storage	70%	85%	95%
PVOL		major change every 12 mo.; minor change every 1 mo.	major: 6 mo.; minor: 2 wk.	major: 2 mo.; minor: 1 wk.	major: 2 wk.; minor: 2 days	

	Very low	Low	Nominal	High	Very high	Extra high
ACAP	15th percentile	35th percentile	55th percentile	75th percentile	90th percentile	
PCAP	15th percentile	35th percentile	55th percentile	75th percentile	90th percentile	
PCON	48%/year	24%/year	12%/year	6%/year	3%/year	
AEXP	≤2 months	6 months	1 year	3 years	6 years	
PEXP	≤2 months	6 months	1 year	3 years	6 years	
LTEX	≤2 months	6 months	1 year	3 years	6 years	
TOOL	edit, code, debug	simple, frontend backend CASE, little integration	basic life cyle tools, moderately integrated	strong, mature life cycle tools, moderately integrated	strong, mature, proactive life cycle tools, well integrated with processes, methods, reuse	
SITE: Collocation	International	Multi-city and Multi-company	Multi-city or Multi-company	Same city or metro. area	Same building or complex	Fully collocated
SITE: Communications	Some phone, mail	Individual phone, FAX	Narrowband email	Wideband elect. comm.	Wideband elect. comm. occasional video conf.	Interaction multimedia
SCED	75% of nominal	85%	100%	130%	160%	

296

Table 8

Module complexity ratings versus type of module.

	Very low	Low	Nominal	High	Very high	Extra high
Control operations	Straight-line code with a few non-nested structured programming operators: DOs, CASEs, IFTHEN-ELSEs. Simple module composition via procedure calls or simple scripts.	Straightforward nesting of structured programming operators. Mostly simple predicates.	Mostly simple nesting. Some intermodule control. Decision tables. Simple call-backs or message passing, including middleware-supported distributed processing.	Highly nested structured programming operators with many compound predicates. Queue and stack control. Homogeneous, distributed processing. Single processor soft real-time control.	Reentrant and recursive coding. Fixed-priority interrupt handling. Task synchronization, complex callbacks, heterogenous distributed hard real-time control.	Multiple resource scheduling with dynamically changing priorities. Microcode-level control. Distributed hard real-time control.
Computational operations	Evaluation of simple expressions: e.g, $A = B + C * (D - E)$.	Evaluation of moderate-level expressions: e.g. $D = SQRT(B**2 - 4 * A * C)$.	Use of standard math and statistical routines. Basic matrix/vector operations.	Basic numerical analysis: multivariate interpolation, ordinary differential equations. Basic truncation, roundoff concerns.	Difficult but structured numerical analysis: near-singular matrix equations, partial differential equations. Simple parallelization.	Difficult and unstructured numerical analysis: highly accurate analysis of noisy, stochastic data. Complex parallelization.
Device-dependent operations	Simple read, write statements with simple formats.	No cognizance needed of particular processor or I/O device characteristics. I/O done at GET/PUT level.	I/O processing includes device selection, status checking and error processing.	Operations at physical I/O level (physical storage address translations; seeks, reads, etc.). Optimized I/O overlap.	Routines for interrupt diagnosis, servicing, masking. Communication line handling. Performance-intensive embedded systems.	Device timing-dependent coding, micro-programmed operations. Performance-critical embedded systems.
Data management operations	Simple arrays in main memory. Simple COTS-DB queries, updates.	Single file subsetting with no data structure changes, no edits, no intermediate files. Moderately complex COTS-DB queries, updates.	Multi-file input and single-file output. Simple structural changes, simple edits. Complex COTS-DB queries, updates.	Simple triggers activated by data stream contents. Complex data restructuring.	Distributed database coordination. Complex triggers. Search optimization.	Highly coupled, dynamic relational and object structures. Natural language data managment.
User interface management operations	Simple input forms, report generators.	Use of simple graphic user interface (GUI) builders.	Simple use of widget set.	Widget set development and extension. Simple voice I/O, multimedia.	Moderately complex, 2D/3D, dynamic graphics, multimedia.	Complex multimedia, virtual reality.

6.1.5 DOCU – Documentation Match to Life-cycle Needs

Several software cost models have a cost driver for the level of required documentation. In COCOMO 2.0, the rating scale for the DOCU cost driver is evaluated in terms of the suitability of the project's documentation to its life-cycle needs. The rating scale goes from Very Low (many life-cycle needs uncovered) to Very High (very excessive for life-cycle needs). The baseline productivity range for DOCU is 1.38.

6.2 Platform Factors

The platform refers to the target-machine complex of hardware and infrastructure software (previously called the virtual machine). The factors have been revised to reflect this as described in this section. Some additional platform factors were considered, such as distribution, paralellism, embeddedness, and real-time operation, but these considerations have been accommodated by the expansion on the Product Complexity rating scales in table 8.

6.2.1 TIME – Execution Time Constraint
STOR – Main Storage Constraint

Given the remarkable increase in available processor execution time and main storage, one can question whether these constraint variables are still relevant. However, many applications continue to expand to consume whatever resources are available, making these cost drivers still relevant. Following the continuity criterion, the rating scales and multipliers are not changed in COCOMO 2.0, since there has been no strong evidence of need for changing them.

6.2.2 PVOL – Platform Volatility

This variable was called Virtual Machine Volatility (VIRT) in COCOMO. In Ada COCOMO, it was split into Host Volatility and Target Volatility drivers to reflect the Ada host–target software development approach prevalent at the time. The current trend appears to be toward distributed software development, with relatively stable hosts and less well-defined boundaries between hosts and targets. Thus, following the Parsimony criterion, COCOMO 2.0 is returning to a single Platform Volatility driver. Following the continuity guideline, its rating scale and effort multipliers are not changed from the original COCOMO VIRT counterpart. "Platform" has the same definition as did "Virtual Machine": the complex of hardware and software (OS, DBMS, etc.) the software product calls on to perform its task.

6.2.3 TURN – Computer Turnaround Time

Computer turnaround time was a significant cost driver during the initial COCOMO calibration period in the 1970's, since many software developers were still primarily supported by batch-processing computers. Currently, most software developers are supported by interactive workstations, and the trend is toward interactive support for all software developers. As a result, the TURN cost driver has lost most of its significance, and is dropped in COCOMO 2.0.

6.3 Personnel Factors

6.3.1 ACAP – Analyst Capability
PCAP – Programmer Capability

Both COCOMO and Ada COCOMO had combined productivity ranges (the ratios of highest to lowest effort multipliers) of somewhat over a factor of 4, reflecting the strong influence of personnel capability on software productivity. In the original COCOMO, the individual productivity ranges were roughly equal, 2.06 for ACAP and 2.03 for PCAP. In Ada COCOMO, the Ada Process Model was organized around a small number of good analysts producing a definitive specification to be implemented by generally less-capable programmers. This led to a higher productivity range, 2.57 for ACAP as compared to 1.62 for PCAP.

Current trends continue to emphasize the importance of highly capable analysts. However, the increasing role of complex COTS packages, and the significant productivity leverage associated with programmers' ability to deal with these COTS packages, indicates a trend toward higher importance of programmer capability as well.

For these reasons, the COCOMO 2.0 baseline effort multipliers for ACAP and PCAP maintain the same composite productivity range, but provide an intermediate position with respect to the relative productivity ranges of ACAP and PCAP. The resulting baseline COCOMO 2.0 effort multipliers have productivity ranges of 2.24 for ACAP and 1.85 for PCAP.

6.3.2 AEXP – Application Experience
PEXP – Platform Experience
LTEX – Language and Tool Experience

COCOMO 2.0 makes three primary changes in these three personnel experience cost drivers:

- Transforming them to a common rating scale, to avoid some previous confusion.

- Broadening the productivity influence of PEXP, recognizing the importance of understanding the use of more powerful platforms, including more graphic user interface, database, networking, and distributed middleware capabilities.

- Extending the previous Language Experience cost driver to include experience with software tools and methods.

The resulting baseline COCOMO 2.0 effort multipliers for these cost drivers have the following comparative effect on previous COCOMO productivity ranges:

- AEXP: 1.54 in COCOMO 2.0 versus 1.57 in COCOMO and Ada COCOMO;
- PEXP: 1.58 in COCOMO 2.0 versus 1.34 in COCOMO and Ada COCOMO (VEXP);
- LTEX: 1.51 in COCOMO 2.0 versus 1.20 in COCOMO and 1.47 in Ada COCOMO (LEXP).

6.3.3 PCON – Personnel Continuity

The original COCOMO data collection and analysis included a potential PCON cost driver, but the analysis results were inconclusive and the cost driver was not included [Boehm 1981, pp. 486–487]. The COCOMO 2.0 rating scale for PCON is in terms of the project's annual personnel turnover: from 3% to 48%. The corresponding baseline productivity range is 1.52.

6.4 Project Factors

6.4.1 MODP – Use of Modern Programming Practices

The definition of "modern programming practices" has evolved into a broader "mature software engineering practices" term exemplified by the Software Engineering Institute Capability Maturity Model [Paulk *et al.* 1993] and comparable models such as ISO 9000-3 and SPICE. The cost estimation effects of this broader set of practices are addressed in COCOMO 2.0 via the Process Maturity exponent driver. As a result, the MODP effort-multiplier cost driver has been dropped.

6.4.2 TOOL – Use of Software Tools

Software tools have improved significantly since the 1970's projects used to calibrate COCOMO. Ada COCOMO added two rating levels to address late 1980's and expected 1990's tool capabilities. Since then, the number of projects with COCOMO TOOL ratings of Very Low and Low have become scarce. Therefore, COCOMO 2.0 has shifted the TOOL scale to eliminate the original Very Low and Low levels and to use an updated interpretation of the upper five Ada COCOMO rating levels as the TOOL scale. The elimination of two rating levels between Ada COCOMO and COCOMO 2.0 reduced the productivity range from 2.00 to 1.61.

6.4.3 SITE – Multisite Development

Given the increasing frequency of multisite developments, and indications from COCOMO users and from other cost models that multisite development effects are significant, the SITE cost driver has been added in COCOMO 2.0. Determining its cost driver rating involves the assessment and averaging of two factors: site collocation (from fully collocated to international distribution) and communication support (from surface mail and some phone access to full interactive multimedia). The corresponding baseline productivity range is 1.57.

6.4.4 SCED – Required Development Schedule

Given that there has been no strong evidence of a need to change the SCED ratings and effort multipliers, they remain the same in the baseline COCOMO 2.0 under the continuity criterion.

6.4.5 SECU – Classified Security Application

Ada COCOMO included a SECU cost driver which applied an effort multiplier of 1.10 of a project-required classified security procedures. Using the parsimony criterion, since most projects do not need to deal with this, we have dropped it from COCOMO 2.0.

7. ADDITIONAL COCOMO 2.0 CAPABILITIES

This section covers the remainder of the initial COCOMO 2.0 capabilities: Early Design and Post-Architecture estimation models using Function Points; schedule estimation, and output estimate ranges. Further COCOMO 2.0 capabilities, such as the effects of reuse and applications composition on phase and activity distribution of effort and schedule, will be covered in future papers.

7.1 Early Design and Post-Architecture Function Point Estimation

Once one has estimated a product's Unadjusted Function Points, using the procedure in section 4.2.2 and figure 5, one needs to account for the product's level of implementation language (assembly, higher-order language, fourth-generation languages, etc.) in order to assess the relative conciseness of implementation per function point. COCOMO 2.0 does this for both Early Design and Post-Architecture models by using tables such as those generated by Software Productivity Research [SPR 1993] to translate Unadjusted Function Points into equivalent SLOC.

For Post-Architecture, the calculations then proceed in the same way as with SLOC. In fact, one can implement COCOMO 2.0 to enable some components to be sized using function points, and others (which function points may not describe well, such as real-time or scientific computations) in SLOC.

For Early Design function point estimation, conversion to equivalent SLOC and application of the scaling factors in section 5 are handled in the same way as for Post-Architecture. In Early Design, however, a reduced set of effort-multiplier cost drivers is used. These are obtained by combining the Post-Architecture cost drivers as shown in table 9.

Table 9

Early design and post-architecture cost drivers.

Early design cost driver	Counterpart combined post-arch. cost driver
RCPX	RELY, DATA, CPLX, DOCU
RUSE	RUSE
PDIF	TIME, STOR, PVOL
PERS	ACAP, PCAP, PCON
PREX	AEXP, PEXP, LTEX
FCIL	TOOL, SITE
SCED	SCED

The resulting seven cost drivers are easier to estimate in early stages of software development than the seventeen Post-Architecture cost drivers. However, their larger productivity ranges (up to 5.45 for PERS and 5.21 for RCPX) stimulate more variability in their resulting estimates. This situation is addressed by assigning a higher standard deviation to Early Design (versus Post-Architecture) estimates; see section 7.3.

7.2 Development Schedule Estimates

The initial version of COCOMO 2.0 provides a simple schedule estimation capability similar to those in COCOMO and Ada COCOMO. The initial baseline schedule equation for all three COCOMO 2.0 models is:

$$TDEV = [3.0 \times (PM)^{(0.33 + 0.2 \times (B - 1.01))}] \times \frac{SCEDPercentage}{100}, \qquad (6)$$

where *TDEV* is the calendar time in months from the determination of its requirements baseline to the completion of an acceptance activity certifying that the product satisfies its requirements. PM is the estimated person–months excluding the SCED effort multiplier, and *SCEDPercentage* is the schedule compression/expansion percentage in the SCED cost driver rating table, table 7.

Future versions of COCOMO 2.0 will have a more extensive schedule estimation model, reflecting the different classes of process model a project can use; the effects of reusable and COTS software; and the effects of application composition capabilities.

7.3 Output Ranges

A number of COCOMO users have expressed a preference for estimate ranges rather than point estimates as COCOMO outputs. The three models of COCOMO 2.0 enable the estimation of likely ranges of output estimates, using the costing and sizing accuracy relationships in section 3.2, figure 2. Once the most likely effort estimate E is calculated from the chosen model (Application Composition, Early Design, or Post-Architecture), a set of optimistic and pessimistic estimates, representing roughly one standard deviation around the most likely estimate, are calculated as follows:

Model	Optimistic estimate	Pessimistic estimate
Application Composition	0.50 E	2.0 E
Early Design	0.67 E	1.5 E
Post-Architecture	0.80 E	1.25 E

The effort range values can be used in the schedule equation (equation (6)) to determine schedule range values.

8.   CONCLUSIONS

Software development trends towards reuse, re-engineering, commercial off-the-shelf (COTS) packages, object orientation, application composition capabilities, non-sequential process models, rapid development approaches, and distributed middleware capabilities require new approaches to software estimation.

The wide variety of current and future software processes, and the variability of information available to support software cost estimation, require a family of models to achieve effective cost estimates.

The baseline COCOMO 2.0 family of software cost estimation models presented here provides a tailorable cost estimation capability well matched to the major current and likely future software process trends.

The baseline COCOMO 2.0 model effectively addresses its objectives of openness, parsimony, and continuity from previous COCOMO models. It is currently serving as the framework for an extensive data collection and analysis effort to further refine and calibrate its estimation capabilities. Initial calibration of COCOMO 2.0 to the previous COCOMO database indicates that its estimation accuracy is comparable to that of the original COCOMO model for this sample.

ACRONYMS AND ABBREVIATIONS

3GL	Third Generation Language
AA	Percentage of reuse effort due to assessment and assimilation
ACAP	Analyst Capability
ACT	Annual Change Traffic
ASLOC	Adapted Source Lines Of Code
AEXP	Applications Experience

AT	Automated Translation
BRAK	Breakage
CASE	Computer Aided Software Engineering
CM	Percentage of code modified during reuse
CMM	Capability Maturity Model
COCOMO	Constructive Cost Model
COTS	Commercial Off-The-Shelf
CPLX	Product Complexity
CSTB	Computer Science and Telecommunications Board
DATA	Database Size
DBMS	Database Management System
DI	Degree of Influence
DM	Percentage of design modified during reuse
DOCU	Documentation match to life-cycle needs
EDS	Electronic Data Systems
ESLOC	Equivalent Source Lines Of Code
FCIL	Facilities
FP	Function Points
GFS	Government Furnished Software
GUI	Graphical User Interface
ICASE	Integrated Computer Aided Software Environment
IM	Percentage of integration redone during reuse
KSLOC	Thousands of Source Lines Of Code
LEXP	Programming Language Experience
LTEX	Language and Tool Experience
MODP	Modern Programming Practices
NIST	National Institute of Standards and Technology
NOP	New Object Points
OS	Operating System
PCAP	Programming Capability
PCON	Personnel Continuity
PDIF	Platform Difficulty
PERS	Personnel Capability
PEXP	Platform Experience
PL	Product Line
PM	Person Month
PREX	Personnel Experience
PROD	Productivity rate
PVOL	Platform Volatility

RCPX	Product Reliability and Complexity
RELY	Required Software Reliability
RUSE	Required Reusability
RVOL	Requirements Volatility
SCED	Required Development Schedule
SECU	Classified Security Application
SEI	Software Engineering Institute
SITE	Multi-site operation
SLOC	Source Lines Of Code
STOR	Main Storage Constraint
T&E	Test and Evaluation
SU	Percentage of reuse effort due to software understanding
TIME	Execution Time Constraint
TOOL	Use of Software Tools
TURN	Computer Turnaround Time
USAF/ESD	U.S. Air Force Electronic Systems Division
VEXP	Virtual Machine Experience
VIRT	Virtual Machine Volatility
VMVH	Virtual Machine Volatility: Host
VMVT	Virtual Machine Volatility: Target

ACKNOWLEDGEMENTS

This work has been supported both financially and technically by the COCOMO 2.0 Program Affiliates: Aerospace, AT&T Bell Laboratories, Bellcore, DISA, EDS, E-Systems, Hewlett–Packard, Hughes, IDA, IDE, JPL, Litton Data Systems, Lockheed, Loral, MDAC, Motorola, Northrop, Rational, Rockwell, SAIC, SEI, SPC, TASC, Teledyne, TI, TRW, USAF Rome Laboratory, US Army Research Laboratory, Xerox.

REFERENCES

Amadeus (1994), *Amadeus Measurement System User's Guide*, Version 2.3a, Amadeus Software Research, Inc., Irvine, CA.

Banker, R., R. Kauffman, and R. Kumar (1994), "An Empirical Test of Object-Based Output Measurement Metrics in a Computer Aided Software Engineering (CASE) Environment", *Journal of Management Information Systems*, to appear.

Banker, R., H. Chang, and C. Kemerer (1994a), "Evidence on Economics of Scale in Software Development", *Information and Software Technology*, to appear.

Behrens, C. (1983), "Measuring the Productivity of Computer Systems Development Activities with Function Points", *IEEE Transactions on Software Engineering*, November.

Boehm, B. (1981), *Software Engineering Economics*, Prentice–Hall.

Boehm, B. (1983), "The Hardware/Software Cost Ratio: Is It a Myth?" *Computer 16*, 3, pp. 78–80.

Boehm, B. (1985), "COCOMO: Answering the Most Frequent Questions", In *Proceedings, First COCOMO Users' Group Meeting*, Wang Institute, Tyngsboro, MA.

Boehm, B. (1989), *Software Risk Management*, IEEE Computer Society Press, Los Alamitos, CA.

Boehm, B., T. Gray, and T. Seewaldt (1984), "Prototyping vs. Specifying: A Multi-Project Experiment", *IEEE Transactions on Software Engineering*, May, 133–145.

Boehm, B., and W. Royce (1989), "Ada COCOMO and the Ada Process Model", *Proceedings, Fifth COCOMO Users' Group Meeting*, Software Engineering Institute, Pittsburgh, PA.

Chidamber, S., and C. Kemerer (1994), "A Metrics Suite for Object Oriented Design", *IEEE Transactions on Software Engineering*, to appear.

Computer Science and Telecommunications Board (CSTB) National Research Council (1993), *Computing Professionals: Changing Needs for the 1990's*, National Academy Press, Washington, DC.

Devenny, T. (1976), "An Exploratory Study of Software Cost Estimating at the Electronic Systems Division", Thesis No. GSM/SM/765-4, Air Force Institute of Technology, Dayton, OH.

Gerlich, R., and U. Denskat (1994), "A Cost Estimation Model for Maintenance and High Reuse", *Proceedings, ESCOM 1994*, Ivrea, Italy.

Goethert, W., E. Bailey, and M. Busby (1992), "Software Effort and Schedule Measurement: A Framework for Counting Staff Hours and Reporting Schedule Information", CMU/SEI-92-TR-21, Software Engineering Institute, Pittsburgh, PA.

Goudy, R. (1987), "COCOMO-Based Personnel Requirements Model", *Proceedings, Third COCOMO Users' Group Meeting*, Software Engineering Institute, Pittsburgh, PA.

IFPUG (1994), *IFPUG Function Point Counting Practices: Manual Release 4.0*, International Function Point Users' Group, Westerville, OH.

Kauffman, R. and R. Kumar (1993), "Modeling Estimation Expertise in Object Based ICASE Environments", Stern School of Business Report, New York University.

Kemerer, C. (1987), "An Empirical Validation of Software Cost Estimation Models", *Communications of the ACM*, 416–429.

Kominski, R. (1991), *Computer Use in the United States: 1989*, Current Population Reports, Series P-23, No. 171, U.S. Bureau of the Census, Washington, DC.

Kunkler, J. (1983), "A Cooperative Industry Study on Software Development/Maintenance Productivity", Xerox Corporation, Xerox Square – XRX2 52A, Rochester, NY 14644, Third Report.

Miyazaki, Y. and K. Mori (1985), "COCOMO Evaluation and Tailoring", *Proceedings, ICSE 8*, IEEE–ACM–BCS, London, pp. 292–299.

Parikh, G. and N. Zvegintzov (1983), "The World of Software Maintenance", *Tutorial on Software Maintenance*, IEEE Computer Society Press, pp. 1–3.

Park, R. (1992), "Software Size Measurement: A Framework for Counting Source Statements", CMU/SEI-92-TR-20, Software Engineering Institute, Pittsburgh, PA.

Park, R., W. Goethert, and J. Webb (1994), "Software Cost and Schedule Estimating: A Process Improvement Initiative", CMU/SEI-94-TR-03, Software Engineering Institute, Pittsburgh, PA.

Paulk, M., B. Curtis, M. Chrissis, and C. Weber (1993), Capability Maturity Model for Software, Version 1.1", CMU/SEI-93-TR-24, Software Engineering Institute, Pittsburgh, PA.

Pfleeger, S. (1991), "Model of Software Effort and Productivity", *Information and Software Technology 33*, 3, 224–231.

Royce, W. (1990), "TRW's Ada Process Model for Incremental Development of Large Software Systems, *Proceedings, ICSE 12*, Nice, France.

Ruhl, M. and M. Gunn (1991), "Software Reengineering: A Case Study and Lessons Learned", NIST Special Publication 500-193, Washington, DC.

Selby, R. (1988), "Empirically Analyzing Software Reuse in a Production Environment", In *Software Reuse: Emerging Technology*, W. Tracz, Ed., IEEE Computer Society Press, pp. 176–189.

Selby, R., A Porter, D. Schmidt, and J. Berney (1991), "Metric-Driven Analysis and Feedback Systems for Enabling Empirically Guided Software Development", *Proceedings of the Thirteenth International Conference on Software Engineering (ICSE 13)*, Austin, TX, pp. 288–298.

Silvestri, G. and J. Lukasiewicz (1991), "Occupational Employment Projections", *Monthly Labor Review 114*, 11, 64–94.

SPR (1993), "Checkpoint User's Guide for the Evaluator", Software Productivity Research, Inc., Burlington, MA.

Chapter 6

Organizing a Software Engineering Project

1. Chapter Introduction

Organizing a software engineering project is defined as all the management activities that result in the design of a formal structure of software engineering tasks and relationships between these tasks. Organizing involves determining and itemizing the activities required to achieve the objects of the software development project, arranging these activities into logical groups, and determining the relationships within and between the groups. It also involves assignment of each group of activity to an organizational entity and the delegation of responsibility and authority to the organizational entity to execute the assignment.

Organizing a software engineering project can be partitioned into six general management activities (see Table 6.1). Each activity in the table is followed by its definition or an amplifying description.

OKAY CHARLES, YOU'RE IT! GO SEE WHAT'S IN THE PIT.

Table 6.1. Organizing activities for software projects.

Activity	Definition or Explanation
Identify and group project function, activities and tasks	Define, size, and categorize the work to be done.
Select organizational structures	Select appropriate structures to accomplish the project and to monitor, control, communicate, and coordinate.
Create organizational positions	Establish title, job descriptions, and job relationships for each project role.
Establish position qualifications	Define qualifications for persons to fill each position.
Define responsibilities and authority	Define responsibilities for each organizational position and the authority to be granted for fulfillment of those responsibilities.
Document organizational decisions	Document titles, positions, job descriptions, responsibilities, authorities, relationships, and position qualifications.

2. Chapter Overview

The three articles in this chapter discuss the various aspects of organizing a software engineering project. The activities listed in Table 6.1 were used as an outline for the purpose of identifying quality articles related to organizing activities. All articles here deal with identifying general software-engineering tasks and the organizational structures necessary to accomplish them.

The three articles by Robert Youker, Stuckenbruck, and Mantei provide criteria for selecting the appropriate organizational structures for the software product and process. Youker outlines the three major organizational structures used by software development projects. Stuckenbruck indicates the need for top management to give a clear project charter (document) for the matrix organization in defining responsibilities and authority for the project manager as well as the role of the functional departments. Mantei's article identifies three different types of software engineering teams along with the appropriate positional responsibilities and authority.

3. Article Descriptions

The first article is a well-known article from the *Project Management Quarterly* by Robert Youker, "Organizational Alternatives for Project Management." This paper, although written in 1977, still provides the best description of the three most important project organizational structures—function, project, and matrix.

This paper stipulates that there are really only two project organizations, project and functional, and that

the various degrees of mixing of these two techniques are what we call a "matrix" organization (see Figure 6 in Youker's paper). The author also discusses how to make matrix organizational structures work. (The *Project Management Quarterly* (now called *Project Management Journal*) is a publication of the Project Management Institute.

Stuckenbruck's article definitively describes the application of the matrix organization to a project. He sometimes refers to the matrix organization as the "two-boss" organization and defines it as a "multidisciplinary team whose members are drawn from various line or functional units of the hierarchical organization." Stuckenbruck also lists eight advantages and 10 disadvantages of using the matrix organization. He points out that the matrix approach is frequently a readily available scapegoat for other organizational problems, such as poor planning and inadequate control. The author devotes considerable time discussing how to make the matrix organization successfully work. Stuckenbruck believes there is a need to achieve a balance of power between the matrix and functional organizations.

The article by Stuckenbruck was also published by the Project Management Institute. Individuals interested in finding out more about the Institute can contact them at 130 South State Road, Upper Darby, PA 19082.

Mantei's article is a modern-day classic, written as a master's project when Mantei was at the University of Michigan. The article analyzes and discusses the various programming team structures and the effect these structures have on programming tasks. The teams' structures that are analyzed include the chief programmer teams, the egoless programming team, and the controlled-decentralized team. (The controlled-decentralized team structure is more frequently called the hierarchical or project team structure.) This article also describes seven salient properties of programming tasks and compares the performance of each team structure against these properties.

Organization alternatives for project managers

There is no one perfect organizational structure for managing projects and similar temporary organizations. But you can—and should—assess the feasibility of the various alternatives.

ROBERT YOUKER

Economic Development Institute
World Bank

Robert Youker *is a lecturer in EDI's Industry and Public Utilities Courses Division and director of the Agri-Industry Course. Formerly president of Planalog Management Systems, a managing consulting firm, Mr. Youker has also acted as deputy director of the Division of Private and International Organizations of the Peace Corps.*

This article is adapted from Project Management Quarterly, *Vol. VIII, No. 1, by permission of Project Management Institute, P.O. Box 43, Drexel Hill, Pennsylvania 19026.*

IN THE PAST TEN YEARS interest has grown in techniques and approaches for management of temporary projects (in contrast to ongoing operations). There has been an explosion of literature dealing with these techniques and strategies, and more recently, we have seen the beginnings of organized academic research on various aspects of project management.

However, in discussions and in the literature we still seem to be confused about the exact meaning of some terms. This is particularly true in the area of alternative approaches for the management of projects.

Functional organizations

The most prevalent organizational structure in the world today is the basic hierarchical structure (Figure 1). This is the standard pyramid with top management at the top of the chart and middle and lower management spreading out down the pyramid. The organization is usually broken down into different functional units, such as engineering, research, accounting, and administration.

The hierarchical structure was originally based on such management theories as specialization, line and staff relations, authority and responsibility, and span of control. According to the doctrine of specialization, the major functional subunits are staffed by such disciplines as engineering and accounting. It is considered easier to manage specialists if they are grouped together and if the department head has training and experience in that particular discipline.

The strength of the functional organization is in its centralization of similar resources. For example, the engineering department provides a secure and comfortable organizational arrangement with well-defined career paths for a young engineer. Mutual support is provided by physical proximity.

The functional organization also has a number of weaknesses. When it is involved in multiple projects, conflicts invariably arise over the relative priorities of these projects in the competition for resources. Also, the functional department based on a technical specialty often places more emphasis on its own specialty than on the goals of the project. Lack of moti-

This article is reprinted from *Project Management Quarterly,* Vol. VIII, No. 1, March 1977, with permission of the Project Management Institute, 130 South State Road, Upper Darby, PA 19082, a worldwide organization of advancing the state-of-the-art in project management.

Figure 1
Functional Organization

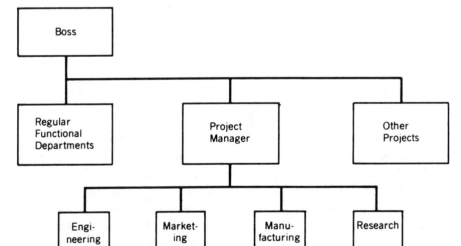

Boss

VP — Engineering — X

VP — Finance — X

VP — X — Research

VP — Marketing — X

VP — Manufacturing — X

Figure 2
Projectized Organization

Boss

Regular Functional Departments

Project Manager

Other Projects

Engineering

Marketing

Manufacturing

Research

---

vation and inertia are other problems.

However, many companies use the functional organization for their project work as well as their standard operations. The world is a complicated place. In addition to discipline and function, other nuclei for organizational structures include products, technologies, customers, and geographic location.

Project organizations

The opposite of the hierarchical, functional organization is the single-purpose project or vertical organization. In a projectized organization, all the resources necessary to attain a specific objective are separated from the regular functional structure and set up as a self-contained unit headed by a project manager. The project manager is given considerable authority over the project and may acquire resources from either inside or outside the overall organization. All personnel on the project are under the direct authority of the project manager for the duration of the project.

In effect, a large organization sets up a smaller, temporary, special-purpose structure with a specific objective. It is interesting to note that the internal structure of the project organization is functional, that is, that the project team is divided into various functional areas (Figure 2).

Note that the term here is "project organization," not "project management." You can manage projects with all three types of organizational structure. The advantages of the project organization come from the singleness of purpose and the unity of command. An esprit de corps is developed through the clear understanding of, and focus on, the single objective. Informal communication is effective in a close-knit team, and the project manager has all the necessary resources under his direct control.

The project organization, however, is not a perfect solution to all project management problems, as some have suggested. Setting up a new, highly visible temporary structure upsets the regular organization. Facilities are duplicated and resources are used inefficiently. Another serious problem is the question of job security upon termination of the temporary project. Personnel often lose their "home" in the functional structure while they are off working on a project.

The functional, hierarchical organization is organized around technical inputs, such as engineering and marketing. The project organization is a single-purpose structure organized around project outputs, such as a new dam or a new product. Both of these are unidimensional structures in a multidimensional world. The problem in each is to get a proper balance between the long-term objective of functional departments in building technical expertise and the short-term objectives of the project.

Matrix organizations

The matrix organization is a multidimensional structure that tries to maximize the strengths and minimize the weaknesses of both the project and the functional structures. It combines the standard vertical hierarchical structure with a superimposed lateral or horizontal structure of a project coordinator (Figure 3).

The major benefits of the matrix organization are the balancing of ob-

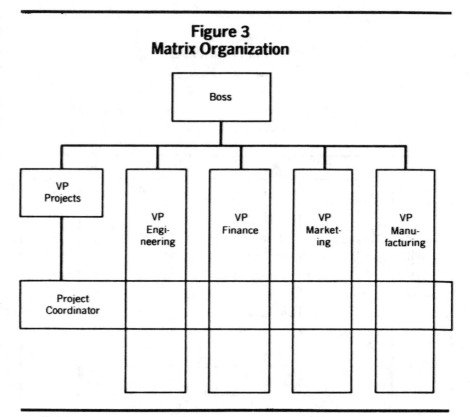

Figure 3
Matrix Organization

jectives, the coordination across functional department lines, and the visibility of the project objectives through the project coordinator's office. The major disadvantage is that the man in the middle is working for two bosses. Vertically, he reports to his functional department head. Horizontally, he reports to the project coordinator or project manager. In a conflict situation he can be caught in the middle.

The project manager often feels that he has little authority with regard to the functional departments. On the other hand, the functional department head often feels that the project coordinator is interfering in his territory.

The solution to this problem is to define the roles, responsibility, and authority of each of the actors clearly. The project coordinator specifies

what is to be done and the functional department is responsible for how it is done (Figure 4).

Criteria for selecting an organizational structure

In the field of management, zealots like to say that their particular model is best. Neophytes want a simple and unambiguous answer. Experienced and thoughtful observers, however, know that no one particular approach is perfect for all situations. The current vogue in management literature is the contingency model. This theory states that the best solution is contingent upon the key factors in the environment in which the solution will have to operate.

The same is true for the choice of an organizational structure. What we need, then, is a list of key factors that

Figure 4
Matrix Organization Relationship
of Project Management to Functional Management

The Manager of Projects is Responsible for:

1. Directing and evaluating project manager activity.
2. Planning, proposing, and implementing project management policy.
3. Assuring project compliance with commitments.

Functional Managers are Responsible for:

1. Accomplishing work package tasks on schedule and within budget.
2. Providing functional policy and procedural guidance.
3. Providing adequately skilled staff.
4. Maintaining technical excellence.

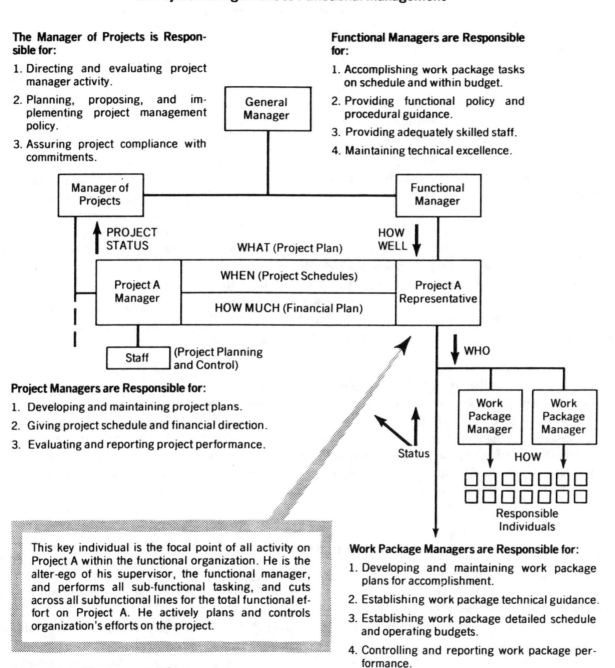

Project Managers are Responsible for:

1. Developing and maintaining project plans.
2. Giving project schedule and financial direction.
3. Evaluating and reporting project performance.

This key individual is the focal point of all activity on Project A within the functional organization. He is the alter-ego of his supervisor, the functional manager, and performs all sub-functional tasking, and cuts across all subfunctional lines for the total functional effort on Project A. He actively plans and controls organization's efforts on the project.

Work Package Managers are Responsible for:

1. Developing and maintaining work package plans for accomplishment.
2. Establishing work package technical guidance.
3. Establishing work package detailed schedule and operating budgets.
4. Controlling and reporting work package performance.

Adapted from **Management: A Systems Approach,**
by Cleland and King, McGraw-Hill Book Co., 1972, p. 347.

Figure 5
Criteria for Organization Design Decisions

	Functional	Favors Matrix	Project
Uncertainty	Low	High	High
Technology	Standard	Complicated	New
Complexity	Low	Medium	High
Duration	Short	Medium	Long
Size	Small	Medium	Large
Importance	Low	Medium	High
Customer	Diverse	Medium	One
Interdependency (Within)	Low	Medium	High
Interdependency (Between)	High	Medium	Low
Time Criticality	Low	Medium	High
Resource Criticality	Depends	Depends	Depends
Differentiation	Low	High	Medium

will help us to choose the right organizational structure for the given conditions on a specific project with a given organization and a particular environment. A set of such factors is listed in Figure 5.

For example, an organization developing many new but small projects with standard technology would most likely find a functional structure best. On the other hand, a company with a long, large, complex, and important project should favor the project organizational structure. A firm in the pharmaceutical business with many complicated technologies would probably go to a matrix structure.

It is possible to use all three structures in the same company on different projects. All three structures might also be used on the same project at different levels—for example, an overall matrix structure for the project with a functional substructure in engineering and a project organization in another functional subarea.

Before we can make a final choice, however, we must consider the following additional factors:

1. What is the relationship between organizational design, the skills of the project manager, and the project planning and reporting system?

2. Are there ways we can improve coordination and commitment in the functional structure without moving to a project or matrix structure?

3. What variations exist in the matrix structure and what are the advantages of each variation?

Project managers and organizational design

It is not possible to decide on the organizational design without also deciding whom to select as the project manager and what kind of design you want for the planning and reporting systems. These decisions are closely interrelated. For example, a successful project organization requires a project manager with the broad skills of a general manager. He must combine technical knowledge of the subject matter with management abilities before he can lead the entire project team. It makes no sense to select a project organization form if such a project manager is not available.

The planning and reporting system in a project organization can be fairly simple because the team is in close proximity. The opposite is true in the management of projects through a functional organization. Information in the form of plans, schedules, budgets, and reports is the key medium for integrating a functional organization. Therefore, a more sophisticated planning and reporting system is required in a functional organization than in a project organization.

Improving lateral communications in the functional structure

Organizations typically turn to a project organization or a matrix organization because the normal functional structure has failed on a series of projects. It is not necessary, however, to "throw the baby out with the bath water." Before giving up on the functional organization, analyze the real problems and see if steps can be taken short of reorganization. Some results of a reorganization may be favorable, but other unintended but logical consequences are certain to be unfavorable.

Methods of lateral or horizontal communication need to be developed across functional department boundaries. Alternative approaches for lateral communication include:

1. Such procedures as plans, budgets, schedules, and review meetings.

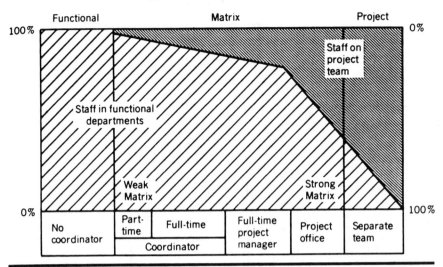

Figure 6
Organizational Continuum

2. Direct contact between managers.

3. Informal liaison roles.

4. Teams.

These are integrating mechanisms short of the establishment of a matrix organization. They help to break down the barriers that seem to separate different disciplines, departments, and geographic locations.

Weak to strong matrix—a continuum

The three major organizational forms—functional, matrix, and project—may be presented as a continuum ranging from functional at one end to project at the other end (Figure 6). The matrix form falls in between and includes a wide variety of structures, from a weak matrix near functional to a strong matrix near project. The continuum in Figure 6 is based on the percentage of personnel who work in their own functional department versus the percentage of personnel who are full-time members of the project team. Note that in a functional or-

ganization the project team has no personnel of its own. The dividing line between functional and matrix is the point at which an individual is appointed with part-time responsibility for coordination across functional department lines.

The bottom line of Figure 6 shows that a weak matrix has a part-time coordinator. The matrix gets stronger as you move from full-time coordinator to full-time project manager and finally to a project office that includes such personnel as systems engineers, cost analysts, and schedule analysts. The difference between a coordinator and a manager is the difference between mere integration and actual decision-making.

On the far right we have the project organization. Ordinarily, there is a clear distinction between a strong matrix in which most of the work is still being performed in the functional departments and a project organization in which the majority of the personnel are on the project team.

It is rare for a project organization

to have all the personnel on its team. Usually some functions, such as accounting or maintenance, would still be performed by the functional structure.

Some persons have taken issue with the use of the term "strong matrix." They say that a strong matrix comes from an even balance of power between the functional departments and the project office. That may be true in some instances, but not always. Strong and weak are not used in the sense of good and bad. Rather, they refer to the relative size and power of the integrative function in the matrix.

Measuring authority: Functional vs. project staff

Another way to differentiate between a strong matrix and a weak matrix is to analyze the relative degree of power between the functional departments and the project staff. We could construct another continuum with function on the left and project on the right. For a given project we would decide where the power rests on the continuum for decisions over project objectives, budgets, cost control, quality, time schedule, resources, personnel selection, and liaison with top management. On any given project the power will be strongly functional for some factors and strongly project for others. However, a profile line can be drawn from top to bottom that would indicate whether the trend is to the left (weak) or to the right (strong).

Making matrix management work

Matrix management is a controversial concept. Some people have had bad experiences operating in a matrix. Others have had a great deal of success. It does require careful definition of authority and responsibility as well as strenuous efforts toward coordination and diplomacy. The matrix is basically a balance of power between the goals of the functional structure and of a specific project.

Overloaded functional departments

One key problem with matrix organizations is that they tend to overload the functional departments with work. If a functional department makes a commitment to work more man-hours on projects than it has available, conflicts over priorities between projects are inevitable. This problem can be alleviated, if not solved, by better planning.

A matrix organization will not work effectively unless a matrix strategic plan setting priorities on objectives and a matrix budget allocating resources also exist. For example, in Figure 7, the project manager for Project A will add horizontally across functional departments to get his total budget. In a similar manner, the vice-president of manufacturing must add vertically across all the projects for which he has committed funds and resources as well as his strictly departmental efforts. The matrix budget must add up to 100 percent in both directions. The usual picture is that the functional departments are overcommitted and show required man-hours of perhaps 120 percent of actual man-hours available. When this happens, politics and disappointment become inevitable.

The golden rule in matrix management states, "He who has the gold

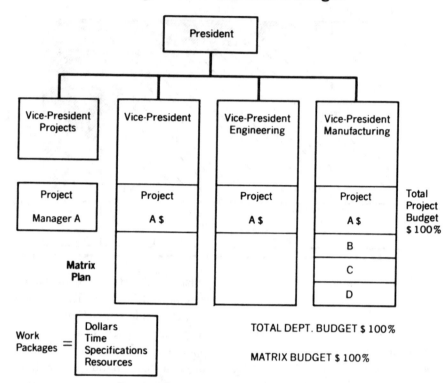

**Figure 7
Matrix Organization and Matrix Budget**

makes the rules." If a project manager does not control the budget, he can only beg for handouts from the functional departments. A matrix budget assigns resources to the project manager for purchases from the functional departments. Making up such a budget takes careful work during long-range and annual planning. Regular updating of the matrix plan and budget are also necessary.

Survival techniques in the matrix

A common picture of the project coordinator in a matrix organization is of a frustrated diplomat struggling to cajole the functional departments into performing the work on schedule and within budget. His po-

sition is difficult, but the following approaches can help:

1. It is important to have a charter from top management defining responsibilities and authority for the project manager as well as the role of the functional departments.

2. The project coordinator or manager must anticipate conflicts in the matrix. Conflict is inevitable with dual authority, but it can be constructively channeled.

3. Since conflict is inevitable, it is important to take positive steps to develop teamwork. Regular lunches or social gatherings help to foster a team spirit. In recent years, the behavioral sciences have developed a number of specific techniques for alleviating or using conflict effectively.

Training programs for matrix managers should include experiences with such techniques.

4. The project coordinator's main power comes from the approved objectives, plans, and budgets for the project. Use these documents to hold departments to their commitments.

5. It is vital that the functional department heads be committed to the plans and schedules for the project as well as the lower-level task leaders. Functional managers should review and sign off on these documents.

6. It is usually best to avoid direct conflict with the functional department heads. The matrix manager should use his boss when a situation threatens to get out of hand.

7. It is important to remember that the project coordinator is concerned with "what" is to be done, not "how." Use a management-by-objectives approach and do not supervise the functional departments (Figure 4) too closely.

8. Many of the problems of matrix management flow from the uncertainty inherent in the project environment. By definition, a project is, to some extent, a "new" effort. Careful and continuous planning can help reduce uncertainty.

No one perfect organizational structure for managing projects exists. The functional, the project, and the different matrix structures all have strengths and weaknesses. The final choice should come after weighing various factors in the nature of the task, the needs of the organization, and the environment of the project. The functional structure will work for many projects in many or-

ganizations, especially if lateral communications can be improved through integrating mechanisms and procedures short of hiring a matrix coordinator.

When a matrix approach is chosen, the entire organization must put a good deal of effort into it to make it work. In particular, the project coordinator or project manager in the matrix must be carefully chosen and

trained. His interpersonal skills are more important than his technical knowledge.

In many situations, a project organization may appear to be the simplest solution from the viewpoint of the project manager. However, the functional managers or top management may not find it to be the best long-range or most strategic decision. ●

The Matrix Organization

LINN C. STUCKENBRUCK
University of Southern California

Ed. note: The Southern California Chapter of the Project Management Institute has been working on a book project for approximately one year. The title of the book will be The Implementation of Project Management, *and it has been designed as an aid to the newly appointed project manager, who says, "Now what do I do?" The project plan is to have the book ready for sale at the 1979 International Seminar/Symposium at Atlanta. The following paper is a representative chapter from the book.*

What Is A Matrix Organization?

A matrix organization is defined as one in which there is dual or multiple managerial accountability and responsibility. However, the term matrix means quite different things to different people and in different industries (1)(5). In a matrix there are usually two chains of command, one along functional lines and the other along project, product, or client lines. Other chains of command such as geographic location are also possible.

The matrix organizational form may vary from one in which the project manager holds a very strong managerial position to one in which he plays only a coordinating role. To illustrate the organizational principles, a matrix will be considered first in which there is a balance of power between the project and functional managers. It must be recognized that such a balanced situation, considered by some authorities to be ideal, probably seldom occurs in practice.

The Two-Boss Matrix

In a balanced matrix organization various people in the organization have two bosses (figure 1). This represents an abandonment of the age-old management concept, "Thou shalt have but one boss above thee." None of the reporting relationships shown in figure 1 are dotted-line relationships. Solid- and dotted-line relationships have various interpretations depending upon local management custom. However, solid lines normally connect managers with their direct subordinates, the man above being the boss. Dotted lines are usually used to indicate staff relationships or reporting relationships of lesser importance. The project manager in the matrix organization is not a staff man nor does he normally have less authority than the functional managers reporting on the same level. Neither can the relationships shown in figure 1 be simply described by such terms as "he reports to the functional manager only for technical direction," or "he reports to the project office for budgetary and schedule control." Such descriptions are inadequate to describe how the matrix organization really works because in reality, not just on paper, the project personnel do have two bosses.

Implicit in the definition of the matrix organization is the recognition that the project is temporary whereas the functional departments are more permanent. Although all organizations are temporary in that they are con-

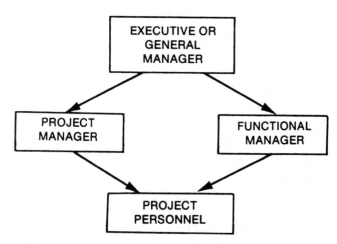

Figure 1: The basic unit of the matrix organization.

This article is reprinted from *A Decade of Project Management,* 1981, with permission of the Project Management Institute, 130 South State Road, Upper Darby, PA 19082, a worldwide organization of advancing the state-of-the-art in project management.

stantly changing, the matrix is designed to be temporary and a particular organizational structure lasts only for the finite life of the project.

Why the Matrix?

The matrix developed as a natural evolution of organizational structures in answer to a very definite real-world need. The need was for an organizational form capable of managing the recent very large and very complex programs, projects, and problems, and for managing limited resources. The conventional hierarchical management organization could not cope with the added complexity and the enormous amount of information that had to be processed, and conventional management theory was of little help in solving these new and unique problems.

Most management theorists predicted that the lack of any clear-cut single line of responsibility and authority would result in managerial ineffectiveness. There is no evidence to indicate that multiple authority and role conflict lead to ineffectiveness (16).

The primary reason for adopting the matrix in a large organization can be pinpointed in the fact that functions and skills are fragmented throughout the organizational structure. Individual functional departments have great difficulty in solving very large problems because of a failure to view the total system and a tendency to sub-optimize or solve the problem within their particular discipline. According to an old aerospace cliche, "An engineer attacks *every* problem as if it had an engineering solution." How few of today's big civil and social problems have purely technical solutions?

Since it was found to be impractical to fragment the problem and have the various functional organizations work only on their portion of the problem, "microcompanies" were formed (21). This represented the development of the pure project organization. It was very rapidly realized that this alternative was not only very unwieldly but had many disadvantages with respect to efficient functional operations. The matrix was the next logical development.

Growth of the Matrix

As problems and projects have become more complex, the inadequacy of the hierarchical organizational structure became apparent. At the same time, the necessity for designing the organization around the task to be performed was realized. Fortunately, varied but more complex organizational alternatives have become available. The present management philosophy is that there is no "one best way" for all projects to organize. Rather there

are many alternatives from which to select a specific project. Among these alternatives are various forms of the matrix.

A formalized matrix form of organization was first developed and documented in the United States aerospace industry where it evolved during the growth of the large, complex projects of the 1950s and 1960s. If a project was very large, it usually became a pure project organization in which all of the functions and resources necessary to accomplish the objectives of the project were put in a single hierarchical organization. This alternative worked very well if the project or program was very large, and if the government customer was similarly organized, and if the customer not only insisted on such an organization but was willing to pay for its added expense.

However, the aerospace industry found that it had many more projects which were not particularly large, but were exceedingly complex, and therefore not conveniently handled within a single discipline. Today, it is rare to find a real-world problem that is unidisciplinary. In addition, top management still felt a strong need to have a single source of information and a single point of responsibility for each project or program. Some form of project management was obviously needed, and not being willing to bear the expense of making each project a little empire of its own, the matrix was a natural evolution in management thinking. The term "matrix" began to be applied to organizations at this time, and as indicated by Davis and Lawrence, "It probably seemed like a fitting term for mathematically trained engineers in that industry to apply to the gridlike structure that was evolving . . . " (10).

The Matrix Organization

It has been recognized that the matrix organizational structure has applications far beyond that of project (program or product) management (12). However, in this discussion the matrix will only be considered from the viewpoint of its most highly developed application — that of project management.

The term "matrix project organization" refers to a multidisciplinary team whose members are drawn from various line or functional units of the heirarchical organization. The organization so developed is temporary in nature, since it is built around the project or specific task to be done rather than on organizational functions. The matrix is thus built up as a team of personnel drawn from both the project and the functional or disciplinary organizations. In other words a project organization is superimposed on the conventional functional hierarchical organization.

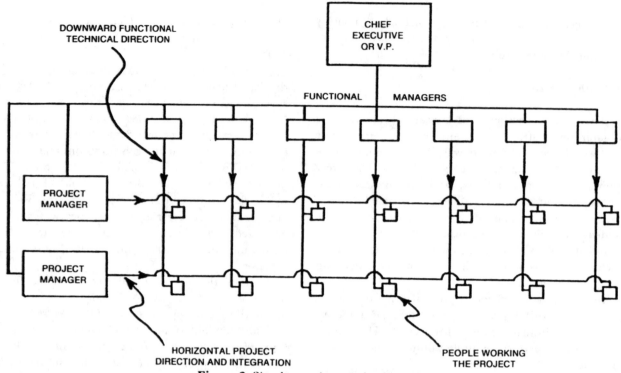

CHIEF
EXECUTIVE
OR V.P.

FUNCTIONAL   MANAGERS

PROJECT
MANAGER

PROJECT
MANAGER

HORIZONTAL PROJECT
DIRECTION AND INTEGRATION

PEOPLE WORKING
THE PROJECT

Figure 2. Simple matrix organization

The matrix in its simplest form is shown diagramatically in figure 2, indicating how the matrix received its name.

The matrix shown in figure 2 represents a general organizational structure. To be more specific, engineering, research, product and construction matrix organizations are shown in figures 3, 4, 5, and 6 respectively.

The matrix is thus a multi-dimensional structure that tries to maximize the strengths and minimize the weaknesses of both the project and the functional structures (25).

Does the Matrix Work?

No specific organizational form can be guaranteed to work at all times, or to improve productive output. However, it can be said that some organizational forms have a better chance of working than others, particularly if they are designed to meet the needs of project work. As previously indicated, the matrix meets a number of well-defined needs. The principal need is for an organizational structure that can handle the great complexity of a multidisciplinary effort.

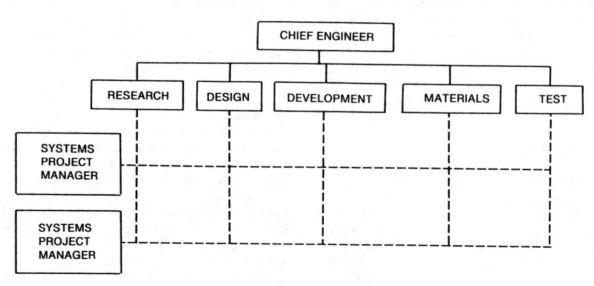

CHIEF ENGINEER

RESEARCH | DESIGN | DEVELOPMENT | MATERIALS | TEST

SYSTEMS
PROJECT
MANAGER

SYSTEMS
PROJECT
MANAGER

Figure 3. An engineering matrix organization

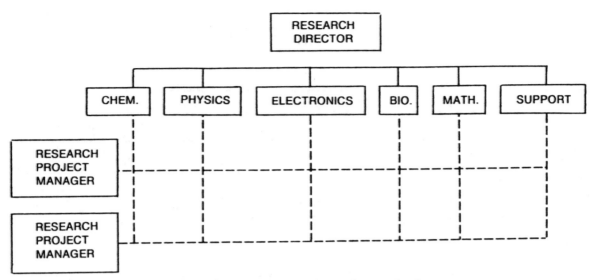

Figure 4. A research matrix organization

If the multidisciplinary need is really there, and if project management is necessary, then the matrix is a viable organizational solution. However, the matrix is a complex organizational form and will not automatically work. The number of things that can go wrong is endless, but the most usual reason for failure of the matrix results from either foot-dragging or downright sabotage on the part of functional management and even by lower level supervision. As indicated in the previous discussion of project management, it is necessary to assure that the matrix will work by thoroughly selling the concept to top management and to all involved functional management. If everyone involved in the matrix is "a believer," and every effort is expended to make it work, the matrix will work and will result in outstanding project accomplish-

ment. As indicated previously, if only takes one uncooperative disciplinary manager dragging his feet to make the whole project fail. However, active, enthusiastic, and aggressive support by top management will counteract even the most recalcitrant functional manager.

Advantages of the Matrix

The matrix organization has many advantages which far outweigh its principal disadvantage of complexity. Among the more universally accepted advantages of the matrix which go beyond the advantages of project management in general are the following (2)(22):

- *Project Objectives Clear* — Project objectives will not only be highly visible through the project office, but

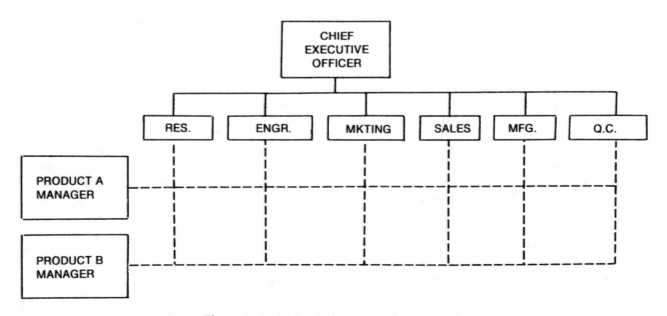

Figure 5. A product industry matrix organization

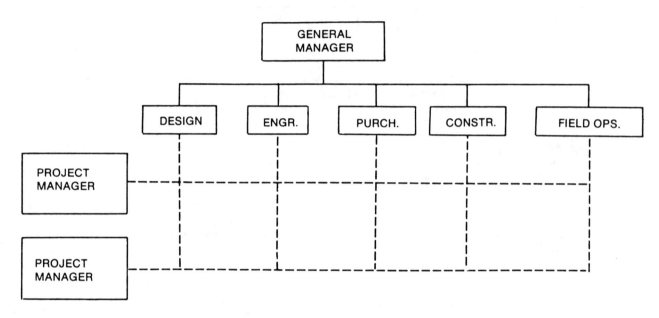

Figure 6. A construction industry matrix organization

will also be balanced with the objectives of the functional organization.

• *Project Integration* — There is a clear and workable mechanism for achieving project integration of subsystems and work packages across functional departmental lines. Coordination across functional lines can easily be achieved.

• *Efficient Use of Resources* — The maximum efficient utilization can be made of scarce company resources. It is the most efficient use of manpower since personnel can be used only part-time if desired, and can be shared between projects. It is the most efficient use of facilities, machinery, equipment, and other resources since these resources can be shared between or among projects. Allocation of scarce resources can be negotiated between project and functional management, or corporate priorities may be established. The matrix is therefore less expensive than an equivalent pure project organization.

• *Information Flow* — Information dissemination should be very effective since there is provision for both horizontal and vertical flow. Horizontal flow provides for project systems information to flow from functional unit to functional unit. Vertical flow provides for detailed disciplinary information to flow from project to project, and to various levels of management. Information of use to other projects is not locked up within a single project.

• *Retention of Disciplinary Teams* — Teams of functional experts and specialists are kept together even though

projects come and go. Therefore technology and know-how is not lost when a project is completed. Specialists like to work with other specialists in the same discipline, and they will be better able to continually exchange ideas and information. As a result, when teams of functional specialists work together, a synergistic effect occurs, resulting in increased innovation and productive output, even though individually they may be working on different projects.

• *High Morale* — Morale problems occur less frequently since the worker in the matrix responds first to the morale-building experience of working on a successful project resulting in visible achievements. This will be true whether the achievement is a ballistic missile, an aircraft, a power plant, or the introduction of a new soap into the marketplace. Secondly, worker morale is normally higher when they can work with their fellow specialists. Thirdly, by retaining his functional "home," the specialist may have a clearer career progression up the functional ladder. On the other hand, if he finds that his talents and interests are multidisciplinary, he can set his career objectives toward the project office.

• *Development of Project Managers* — The matrix is an excellent training ground for prospective project managers since promising candidates can easily be spotted in the multidisciplinary project environment. A common occurrence would be the transfer of a person who had demonstrated the ability to work across functional departmental lines to the project office as an assistant project manager. His career progression would then be to project manager, which is an excellent path leading to top management.

- *Project Shutdown* — In a matrix organization project termination is not the traumatic and painful event that it can be in a pure project organization. It is not uncommon for a large aerospace or construction project to have several thousand people working in a pure project organization. What do you do with several thousand people when the project is completed? Large layoffs are almost unavoidable since only a relatively few people can be relocated unless major buildups in another project are occurring. Matrix projects are normally smaller with fewer people overall involved. In addition, the people are spread across a whole functional organization and each department has only a few people to relocate.

Problems of the Matrix

The matrix organization does have some disadvantages and problems, but they need not be considered insurmountable. Knowing what problems may occur is "half the battle" in overcoming them. The following disadvantages are inherent in the matrix organization:

- *Two Bosses* — The major disadvantage is that the personnel on the project are working for two bosses. In any type of conflict situation a person could easily become "the man in the middle." Further problems of conflict can be caused by project personnel playing one boss against the other.
- *Complexity* — The matrix organization is inherently more complex than either a functional or a pure project organization, since it is the superimposition of one on the other. This complexity shows itself in the following problems:
  - *Difficulties in Monitoring and Controlling* — Complexity results from the number of managers and personnel involved and from the number of people that must be kept informed. Fortunately, modern computer techniques have helped to keep this problem under control, but basically it's still a "people" problem.
  - *Complex Information Flow* — This is a problem only because there are so many people and organizational units involved. Both the project and functional managers must be certain that they have touched bases with each other for any major decisions in their areas of responsibility.
  - *Fast Reaction Difficult* — The project manager is sometimes faced with a problem of achieving fast reaction times, primarily since there are so many people to be consulted. The project manager in

the matrix usually does not have strong vested authority, therefore considerable negotiation is necessary. Project management was primarily conceived to prevent this problem, but it can be a problem if the management system keeps the project manager from making any decisions without consultation with functional and top management. If the matrix is working, the problem won't occur.
  - *Conflicting Guidance* — The more complex organization with two lines of authority always increases the possibility of conflicting instructions and guidance.
- *Priorities* — A matrix organization with a number of projects faces real problems with project priorities and resource allocation. Each project manager will obviously consider his project to have the highest priority. Similarly, each functional manager will consider that the allocation of resources and priorities within his department is his own business. As a result, the decisions involving project priorities and often the allocation of resources must be made at a high level. This often puts an undue and unwelcome load on the top executive officer in the matrix. This problem has led to the use of a manager of projects, or a super project manager in some organizations. His principal functions would be to consult with higher levels of management to assure equitable allocation of resources and to periodically reassess project priorities. This effort can be extremely valuable in reducing conflict and anxiety within the matrix.
- *Management Goals* — There is a constant, although often unperceived, struggle in balancing the goals and objectives of project and functional management. A strong project manager may place undue emphasis on time and cost constraints, while a functional manager may concentrate on technical excellence at the expense of schedules. Top management must assure that a careful balance of the goals of both project and functional management is maintained.
- *Potential for Conflict* — As discussed in a later section of this chapter, whenever there are two project managers competing for resources, there is potential for conflict. This conflict may evidence itself primarily as a struggle for power. However, it also may evidence itself by backbiting, foot-dragging and project sabotage. Conflict and competition may also be constructive as an aid to achieving high performance; however, it cannot be allowed to degenerate to personal antagonism and discord. In project work conflict is inevitable; keeping it constructive is the

problem in matrix management.

- *Effects of Conflict on Management* — Since conflict and stress are inherent in the matrix organization, considerable attention must be given to the individuals who will function as both project and functional managers. Individuals vary greatly in their ability to function effectively under stress. Conflict, particularly the role conflict typical of the two-boss situation, can produce stress, anxiety, and reduced job satisfaction. Considerable attention must be directed toward assuring that prospective managers have a high tolerance for conflict situations.

Davis and Lawrence have discussed the problems of the matrix which they term matrix pathologies (11). They list and discuss the following problems: power struggles, anarchy, groupitis, collapse during economic crunch, excessive overhead, decision strangulation, sinking, layering, and navel gazing. They indicate that many of these difficulties occur in more conventional organizations, but that the matrix seems somewhat more vulnerable to these particular ailments.

They indicate that power struggles are inevitable in a matrix because it is different from the traditionally structured hierarchy. In the matrix, power struggles are a logical derivative of the ambiguity and shared power that has been built purposefully into the design. Corporations will find it exceedingly difficult to prevent power struggles from developing, but they must prevent them from reaching destructive lengths.

Anarchy is defined as a company quite literally coming apart at the seams during a period of stress. As the authors admit, this is an unlikely occurrence, and the more explicit the organizational agreements are the less likely it is to occur.

Groupitis refers to confusing matrix behavior with group decision making. The matrix does not require that all business decisions be hammered out in group meetings. Group decision making should be done as often as necessary, and as little as possible.

Collapse during economic crunch refers to the frequently noted fact that matrix organizations seem to blossom during periods of rapid growth and prosperity, and to be buffeted and/or cast away during periods of economic decline. It seems natural that during periods of crisis, top management thinks that the organization needs a firmer hand and reinstitutes the authoritarian structure. "There is no more time for organizational toys and tinkering. The matrix is done in." Thus the matrix is the readily available scapegoat for other organizational problems such as poor planning and inadequate control.

One of the concerns of organizations first encountering the matrix is that it is too costly since it appears, on the surface, to double up on management by adding another

chain of command. It is true that initially overhead costs do rise, but as the matrix matures, these overhead costs decrease and productivity gains appear.

It is suggested that moving into a matrix can lead to the strangulation of the decision process. "Will all bold initiatives be watered down by too many cooks?" Three possible situations can arise: (1) the necessity for constant clearing of all issues with the functional managers, (2) escalation of conflict caused by constant referral of problems up the dual chain of command, and (3) some managers feel that every decision must be a crisp, unilateral decision, therefore they will be very uncomfortable and ineffective in a matrix organization.

Sinking refers to the observation that there seems to be some difficulty in keeping the matrix viable at the corporate or institutional level, and a corresponding tendency for it to sink down to lower levels in the organization where it survives and thrives. This phenomena may be indicative of top management not understanding the matrix or the matrix may just be finding its proper place.

Layering is defined as a phenomena in which matrices within matrices are found. By itself, layering may not be a problem, but it sometimes creates more problems than it solves because the unnecessary complexity may be more of a burden than it is worth.

Navel gazing refers to the tendency to become absorbed in the organization's internal relations at the expense of the world outside the organization, particularly to clients. This concentration on the internal workings of the organization is most likely to occur in the early phases of a matrix when new behaviors have to be learned.

Making the Matrix Work

After examining the disadvantages and problems of working in a matrix organization, one may view the problems as insurmountable. How then does a company get this complex organizational form to function? Its successful operation, like that of any management organization, depends almost entirely on actions and activities of the various people involved. First, top management must give real and immediate support to the matrix, including a clear project charter. This charter should state the purpose of the project and spell out the responsibilities and authority of the project manager. In addition it should indicate to the fullest extent possible his relationships with the functional managers involved in the project.

Functional management must modify much of their managerial thinking and their usual operational procedures and activities in order to make the matrix work.

This may mean a considerable change in the way they determine their priorities. It may be a considerable shock to functional management to find that their priorities must change, and that the project comes first. Project management must realize that they get their job accomplished primarily through the process of negotiation, and that they should become negotiation experts. If all major decisions are made with the concurrence of the involved functional managers, the project manager finds himself in a very strong position in insisting that the decision be carried out and that the desired goals be accomplished. In addition, the project personnel must be able to adapt to the two-boss situation which can be a traumatic experience when first encountered.

Who Is the Real Boss?

Whenever the two-boss situation is encountered, the logical question that can be asked is: who is the real boss? Theoretically it should be possible to divide the authority and responsibility more or less equally between the project and functional managers. However, there is no agreement among the experts as to whether a balance of power is necessary or even desirable.

Even if there is a balance of power, the question of who is the real boss may depend on other factors. For instance, the line or discipline manager is usually perceived as the real boss by the employees in a matrix organization. This is a natural situation since the discipline manager represents "home base" — the disciplinary home to which the employee returns after the project is completed. In addition, the disciplinary manager normally carries the most weight when it comes to performance evaluations and promotions. However, there are usually some employees who relate so strongly to the overall project, that they perceive the project manager to be the real boss. So perhaps there is no one real boss, rather there is a continually shifting balance of power (29).

Balance of Power

At the heart of the operation of the matrix is the balance of power. Theoretically, it should be possible to divide the authority and responsibility more or less equally between the project and functional managers, however to do so is difficult and seldom occurs. It has been attempted to clearly delineate the authority and responsibilities of both project and functional management so as to assure a balance of power. Such a delineation has been presented by one management author (7) who has divided the responsibilities as shown in table 1.

Table 1. Delineation of Responsibilities

Project Manager's Responsibilities
1. What is to be done?
2. When will the task be done?
3. Why will the task be done?
4. How much money is available to do the task?
5. How well has the total project been done?

Functional Manager's Responsibilities
1. How will the task be done?
2. Where will the task be done?
3. Who will do the task?
4. How well has the functional input been integrated into the project?

Another way of stating the roles is: the project manager is responsible for the overall integration of the total project system and the functional manager is responsible for technical direction in his discipline.

The so-called responsibility chart has been proposed as a useful device in defining jurisdictional areas of management (17)(20). A simplified example of a responsibility chart is show in table 2. Such a chart is probably more meaningful than organization charts or job descriptions, particularly is it is filled in during a meeting of all concerned managers resulting in agreement on the job responsibilities. This process results in potential conflicts being confronted early, before specific problems arise.

Table 2. Example of a Responsibility Chart
Source: Ref. 17, p. 171.

Actors \ Decisions	Laboratory Manager	General Manager	Project Manager	Marketing Manager	Controller
Change in Budget					
Allocate Manpower					
Change in Design Specification					
Change in Schedule					

R = Responsible
A = Approve
C = Consult
I = Inform

Certainly such a delineation indicates where the major responsibilities lie, but it cannot guarantee a balance of power. In fact, there are many reasons why it is almost impossible to have a truly "equal" balance of power between functional and project management. Not the least of these reasons is the fact that we are dealing with people, and all people, including managers, are different. Managers have differing personalities and differing management styles. Some management styles depend on the persuasive abilities of the manager while others depend on or tend to fall back on strong support from top management. In addition, power is a fluctuating and constantly changing condition that cannot be static even if one so desired (23).

The breakdown of responsibilities shown in table 1 and table 2, although useful in planning and decision making, is highly simplistic. What conscientious, knowledgeable project manager would not get personally involved in "how will the task be done?" His project schedule and "when will the task be done?" responsibilities do not allow him the luxury of sitting back and waiting for functional management to make every technical decision. He must ensure that technical decisions are made on schedule. He then must review the key technical decisions and challenge them if necessary. As project integrator, he has the overriding responsibility for evaluating *every* key project decision to determine how it interfaces with the other project tasks, and with his schedule and budget. The project manager therefore must get involved and influence every project action and as a last resort he always has appeal rights or veto power — for the good of the project. The project manager even gets involved in "who will do the task?" After all, the highest achievers and most innovative personnel in the discipline organizations will be highly sought after, and the project managers will seek to obtain only the very best people for their projects.

On the other hand, what good functional manager will not get deeply involved in the details of "what, when and for how much money?" He has a strong personal interest in these details since his organization has to perform the tasks spelled out in the project schedules and budgets. He must assure that the task is realistically priced and technically feasible. The responsibilities listed in table 1 can therefore only be used as indicators as to where the major responsibilities lie.

Since the project, program or product is usually a very important part of a company's activities, the project manager is a *very* important person. He is the one who puts the company in a position where it can make more profit, or lose money.

Therefore, in terms of the balance of power, it would seem that the project manager would always have the scale of power tipped in his direction, particularly with the firm support of top management. Not necessarily so!

In fact, not usually so, at least in a matrix organization. In a pure project organization, there is no question as to who holds the power. But in a matrix organization the functional manager has powerful forces on his side. As previously pointed out, the functional manager is normally perceived by project personnel to be the real boss. This is often inevitable since functional management is part of the unchanging ladder in the management hierarchy and is therefore perceived to be "permanent" by the employees. After all, the functional organization represents "home-base" to which project personnel expect to return after the completion of the project.

Very strong top-management support for the project manager is necessary to get the matrix to work, and even very strong support will not guarantee project success. However, the matrix will not work without it. The project manager must get the job done by every means at his disposal even though he may not be perceived as the real boss. He can always appeal to higher authority, however such actions must be kept to a minimum or top management may view the project manager as ineffective.

The Project/Functional Interface

The secret of the successfully functioning matrix can thus be seen to be not just a pure balance of power, but more a function of the type of interface relationships between the project and individual functional managers. Every project decision and action must be negotiated across this interface. This interface is a natural conflict situation since many of the goals and objectives of project and functional management are different. Depending on the personality and dedication of the respective managers, this interface relationship can be one of smooth-working cooperation or bitter conflict. A domineering personality or power play is not the answer. The overpowering manager may win the local skirmish, but usually manages sooner or later to alienate everyone working on the project. Cooperation and negotiation are the keys to successful decision making across the project/functional interface. Arbitrary and one-sided decisions by either the project or functional manager can only lead to or intensify the potential for conflict. Unfortunately for the project manager, he can accomplish little by himself, and must depend on the cooperation and support of the functional managers. That old definition of successful management — "one who gets things done by working through others" — is essential for successful project management in the matrix organization.

The project manager in a matrix organization has two very important interfaces — with top management and with functional management. A good working relationship with and ready access to top management is essential for resolving big problems and removing obstacles. A good working relationship with functional management will ensure that most problems are resolved at their level and will not have to go to top management. The conventional matrix model (figure 1) does not adequately emphasize these most important relationships. Obviously, neither the project manager nor the functional managers can sit in their offices and give orders. The various managers must be communicating with each other on at least a daily basis, and usually more often. Therefore a more adequate organizational model is shown in figure 7, which shows the managerial relationships as double-ended arrows, indicating that the relationships are two-way streets. Consultation, cooperation, and constant support are particularly necessary on the part of the project and functional managers. These are very important relationships, keys to the success of any matrix organization, and must be carefully nurtured and actively promoted by top management and by both project and functional management.

The difficulties that occur at the project/functional interface are emphasized if the salient differences between the role of the project manager and the traditional functional manager are analyzed. Such an analysis has been made by Cleland (7) and indicated that

"while these differences are possibly more theoretical than actual, differences do exist, and they affect the manager's modus operandi and philosophy." Both project and functional management must work to achieve activity harmony in spite of these conflicting objectives and roles. The matrix organization actually is a method of deliberately utilizing conflict to get a better job done. The project team must be more concerned with solving the problem rather than with *who* solves it. Teamwork and problem solving must be emphasized rather than role definition.

Achieving a Balance of Power

Achieving a balance of power between project and functional management may in many cases be a desirable goal. Certainly it should be a way of minimizing potential power struggles and unnecessary conflicts. There is no certain way to assure that there is a balance of power, and it is probably seldom really achieved. However, it can be approached by assuming that the project manager has the full support of top management and that he reports at a high enough level in the management hierarchy.

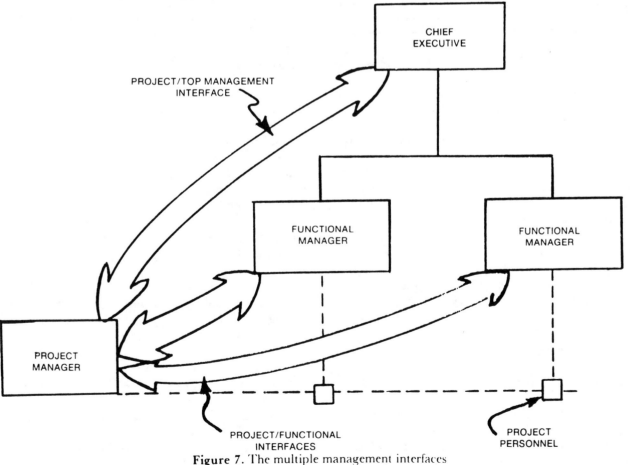

Figure 7. The multiple management interfaces

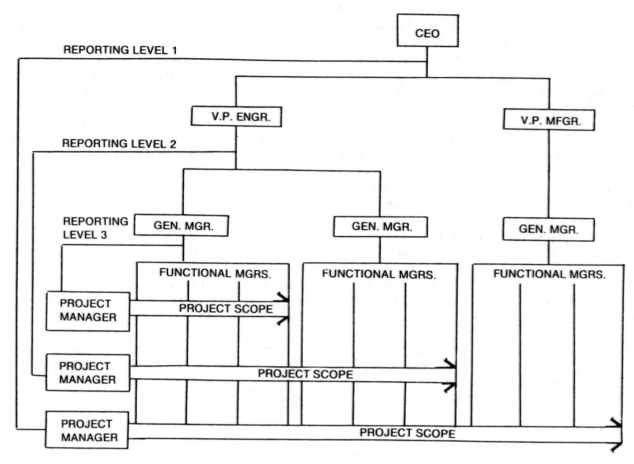

Figure 8. Project management reporting levels

How High Should Project Management Report?

It is not just a question of balance of power, but does the project manager have sufficient clout to be effective? For the most part, the project manager's clout is a direct function of the level at which he reports in the hierarchical organization. If he is to be effective, the project manager must be on at least an equal level with the highest level of functional management that he must deal with. As indicated in figure 8, there can be a considerable difference in reporting level depending whether the project is confined to a single department or spreads across the entire company's activities. This optimum reporting level will change during the life of a project as the effort progresses from basic research to the manufacture of a product.

Strong vs. Weak Matrix

In many situations it may not be desirable to have a balance of power. For instance, a project may be so important to the company, or the budget and schedule so tight that top management feels that the project manager must be in a very strong position. Or perhaps the project manager feels that he must tilt the organizational balance of power in his favor to obtain better project performance. For instance, construction management has found from experience that a strong project office is often necessary to achieve good project performance (3). On the other hand, top management may feel that functional management needs more backing. In either case, the balance of power can be tilted in either direction by changing any one or any combination of the following three factors:

- *The administrative relationship.* — The levels at which the project and involved functional managers report, and the backing which they receive from top management.
- *The physical relationship.* — The physical distances between the various people involved in the project
- *The time spent on the project.* — The amount of time spent on the project by the respective managers

These three factors can be used to describe whether the matrix is strong or weak. The strong matrix is one in which the balance of power is definitely on the side of project management. This can be shown by the model in

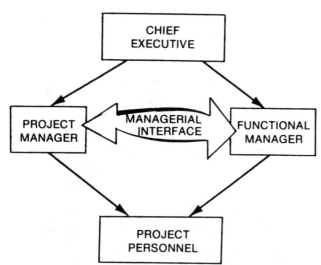

Figure 9. The balance of power in a strong matrix

figure 9. A weak matrix has been described by project managers as one in which the balance of power tilts decisively in the direction of line or functional management. Many organizations have thus, for various reasons including the inability to make the two-boss system work, modified the matrix by shifting the balance of power. Galbraith has described the managerial alternatives as a continuum ranging from pure project to functional (figure 10) (13)(17). The matrix falls in the middle of the continuum, and can range from very weak to very strong depending on the relative balance of power.

It is easy to see how the administrative relationships can be used to create a strong matrix. The higher the project manager reports in the hierarchical organization, and the more visible support he gets from top management, the more likely it is that the matrix will be strong. The physical relationship would involve actually split-

ting the project personnel away from their physical reporting relationship with their functional managers. One approach would be to put the entire project team together in the same room, away from their functional bosses. This would seem to be very desirable on the part of most project managers, but would have some disadvantages in regard to utilization of functional facilities and interaction with other functional personnel. The approach of putting all the project personnel together has been described as a tight matrix, whereas the situation of widely-separated project personnel has been described as a loose matrix.

The organizational alternatives have also been described in terms of the percentage of the organizational personnel who are full-time members of the project team (25). In this manner, the various organizational structures can be described as a continuum where the three organizational forms (functional, project, and matrix) are a continuum ranging from functional on one end and pure project on the other (figure 3, chapter 4). In a functional organization, there is no one on the project team, and in a pure project organization, essentially everybody is on the project team. The matrix falls in between, and includes a variety of organizational alternatives ranging from a weak to a strong matrix. A weak matrix is described as having only a part-time coordinator whereas a strong matrix has a project office containing such project functions as systems engineering, cost analysis, scheduling, and planning.

Summary

The matrix organizational structure has had a great influence on project management. The matrix evolved to fill a need for an organization capable of dealing with great project size and complexity. The result was increased organizational complexity. However, it has greatly added to the versatility and effectiveness of project management. The matrix has permitted project management to be effective not only for very large projects but small projects as well, and has been extremely valuable for solving multidisciplinary problems.

The matrix organizational form is only desirable if there is a real need for its added complexity. Not only is it not for everyone, but it cannot be guaranteed to work. It will only work if the entire organization, from top management to the project personnel, are thoroughly "sold" on the matrix concept. There are many reasons why the matrix will not work, but failure to lay the groundwork and fully prepare the organization is the principle reason for failure. The matrix will function and result in very improved project productivity if top

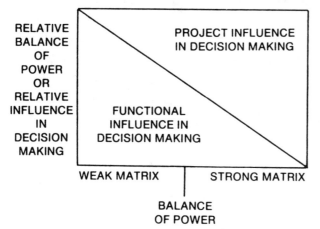

Figure 10. The balance of power in weak and strong matrices

management gives its unwavering support and if functional management and the project personnel accept the matrix as a "way of life" which can only be of great advantage to the company in improving output and profit.

REFERENCES

1. Archibald, Russell D., *Managing High-Technology Programs and Projects*. New York: John Wiley & Sons, 1976, pp. 14–15.
2. Blake, Stewart P., *Managing for Responsive Research and Development*. San Francisco: W. H. Freeman and Co., 1978, p. 176.
3. Caspe, Marc S., "An Overview of Project Management and Project Management Services," *Project Management Quarterly* VII: 4, December 1976, pp. 30–39.
4. Cleland, David I. and William R. King, *Systems, Organizations, Analysis, Management: A Book of Readings*. New York: McGraw-Hill Book Company, 1969, pp. 281–290.
5. Cleland, David I. and William R. King, *Management: A Systems Approach*. New York: McGraw-Hill Book Company, 1972, pp. 337–362.
6. Cleland, David I. and William R. King, *Systems Analysis and Project Management*, Second Edition. New York: McGraw-Hill Book Company, 1975, pp. 183–202.
7. Cleland, David I. and William R. King, *Systems Analysis*, p. 237.
8. Cleland, David I., "Understanding Project Authority," *Business Horizons* Spring 1966, p. 231.
9. Davis, Stanley M. "Two Models of Organization: Unity of Command versus Balance of Power," *Sloan Management Review* Fall 1974, pp. 29–40.
10. Davis, Stanley M. and Paul R. Lawrence, *Matrix*. Reading, Mass.: Addison-Wesley Publishing Company, 1977, p. 3.
11. Davis, Stanley M. and Paul R. Lawrence, *Matrix*, pp. 129–144.
12. Davis, Stanley M. and Paul R. Lawrence, *Matrix*, pp. 155–192.
13. Galbraith, Jay R., "Matrix Organization Designs," *Business Horizons* February 1971, pp. 29–40.
14. Galbraith, Jay R., ed., *Matrix Organizations: Organization Design for High Technology*. Cambridge, Mass.: MIT Press, 1971.
15. Galbraith, Jay R., *Designing Complex Organizations*. Reading, Mass.: Addison-Wesley Publishing Company, 1974.
16. Galbraith, Jay R., *Organizational Design*. Reading, Mass.: Addison-Wesley Publishing Company, 1977, p. 167.
17. Galbraith, Jay R., *Organizational Design*, p. 171.
18. Grinnell, Sherman K. and Howard P. Apple, "When Two Bosses Are Better Than One," *Machine Design* January 9, 1975, pp. 84–87.
19. Mee, John F., "Ideational Items: Matrix Organization," *Business Horizons* Summer 1964, pp. 70–72. (Reprinted in Cleland and King, *Systems, Organizations, Analysis, Management: A Book of Readings*, pp. 23–25.)
20. Melcher, R., "Roles and Relationships: Clarifying the Manager's Job," *Personnel* May–June 1967. (Reprinted in Caspe, "An Overview of Project Management and Project Management Services," pp. 365–371.)
21. Miller, J. Wade, Jr. and Robert J. Wolf, "The 'Micro-Company,'" *Personnel* July–August 1968, pp. 35–42.
22. Middleton, C. J., "How to Set Up a Project Organization," *Harvard Business Review* March–April 1967, pp. 73–82.
23. Sayles, Leonard R., "Matrix Management: The Structure with a Future," *Organizational Dynamics* Autumn 1976, pp. 2–17.
24. Tytler, Kathryn, "Making Matrix Management Work — And When And Why It's Worth The Effort," *Training* October 1975, pp. 78–82.
25. Youker, Robert B., "Organizational Alternatives for Project Management," *Project Management Quarterly* VIII: 1, March 1977, pp. 18–24. (Reprinted in *Management Review*, November 1967, pp. 46–52.)

The Effect of Programming Team Structures on Programming Tasks

Marilyn Mantei
The University of Michigan

1. Introduction

Two philosophies for organizing programming teams have achieved a moderate amount of popularity, if not utilization, in the data processing field. These are the egoless programming team proposed by Weinberg [28] and the chief programmer team proposed by Mills [18] and implemented by Baker [1]. In Weinberg's structure, the decision-making authority is diffused throughout project membership; in Baker's team, it belongs to the chief programmer. Communication exchanges are decentralized in Weinberg's team and centralized in the chief programmer organization. Neither structure is totally

SUMMARY: The literature recognizes two group structures for managing programming projects: Baker's chief programmer team and Weinberg's egoless team. Although each structure's success in project management can be demonstrated, this success is clearly dependent on the type of programming task undertaken. Here, for the purposes of comparison, a third project organization which lies between the other two in its communication patterns and dissemination of decision-making authority is presented. Recommendations are given for selecting one of the three team organizations depending on the task to be performed.

decentralized, democratic, centralized, or autocratic, but both Weinberg and Baker present arguments on why their methods will lead to superior project performance. Baker's project succeeds with a specific, difficult, and highly structured task. Weinberg's recommendations have no specific task in mind.

Research conducted in small group dynamics [7, 23, 27] suggests that a decision to use either team structure is not clear-cut and that there are strong task dependencies associated with each group's performance. The next two sections an-

alyze Weinberg and Baker's organizations. In Section 4, a third, commonly encountered team organization is presented for the purposes of comparison. The fifth section conducts this comparison, recommending which of the three structures should be selected for a given property of a programming task.

2. An Analysis of Weinberg's Team Structure

Weinberg is a promoter of the egoless programming concept. His teams are groups of ten or fewer

Key words and phrases: chief programmer team, project management, software engineering, group dynamics, programming team structures
CR Categories: 3.50, 4.6
Author's address: M. Mantei, Graduate School of Business Administration, The University of Michigan, Ann Arbor, MI 48109.
© 1981 ACM 0001-0782/81/0300-0106 75¢.

"The Effect of Programming Team Structures on Programming Tasks" by M. Mantei from *Communications of the ACM*, Vol. 24, No. 3, Mar. 1981, pp. 106–113. Copyright © Association for Computing Machinery, Inc. 1981. Reprinted by permission.

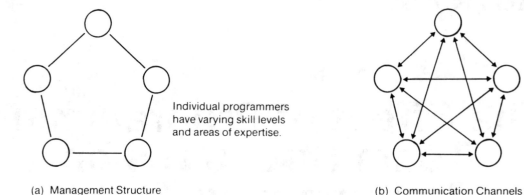

(a) Management Structure

Individual programmers have varying skill levels and areas of expertise.

(b) Communication Channels

Fig. 1. Egoless Team Structure. Authority is dispersed and communication linkages decentralized.

programmers who exchange their code with other team members for error examination. In addition to code exchanges, goals are set by group consensus. Group leadership is a rotating function, becoming the responsibility of the individual with the abilities that are currently needed. Figure 1(a) illustrates the basic management structure of an egoless team; Figure 1(b) shows the communication exchanges that occur within this structure. The team proposed by Weinberg is acknowledged to be mythical in light of today's organization practices, but Weinberg feels that it is the appropriate organization for the best qualitative and quantitative code generation. Using the factors of amount of code produced, of time to produce code, and of error freeness to gauge programming performance, some task-related problems occur with Weinberg's team structure.

Bavelas [3] and Leavitt [14], in their experiments on centralized and decentralized group problem-solving behavior, found that decentralized groups take more time and generate twice as many communications as centralized groups. This suggests that a Weinberg group would function well in long-term continuing projects without time constraints (such as program maintenance). It would not, however, adequately perform a rush programming project.

A second weakness of Wein-

berg's proposal is the *risky shift phenomena* [5]. Groups engage in riskier behavior than individuals, both because of the dispersion of failure and the high value associated with risk taking in Western culture. In the case of a group programming team, decisions to attempt riskier solutions to a software problem or to establish high risk deadlines would be more easily made. In a software project with a tight deadline or a crucial customer, a group decision might cause the project to fail.

The democratic team structure works best when the problem is difficult. When the problem is simple, performance is better in an autocratic highly structured group [12]. Ironically, democratic groups attempt to become more autocratic as task difficulty increases. In the decentralized group, the additional communication which aided in solving the difficult problem is superfluous; it interferes with the simple problem solution. Tasks such as report generation and payroll programming fall into the category of simple tasks—for these, a Weinberg group is least efficient.

The decentralized group is lauded for its open communication channels. They allow the dissemination of programming information to all participants via informal channels. By virtue of code exchanges and open communication, Weinberg concludes that the product will be

superior. March and Simon [16] point out that hierarchical structures are built to limit the flow of information, because of the human mind's limited processing capabilities. In the decentralized groups, as investigated by Bavelas, although twice as many communications were exchanged as in centralized groups, the groups often failed to finish their task. Similarly, individuals within a nonstructured programming group may be unable to organize project information effectively and many suffer from information overload. The structure and limited flow associated with hierarchical control may be assets to information assimilation.

Decentralized groups exhibit greater conformity than centralized groups [11]; they enforce a uniformity of behavior and punish deviations from the norm [20]. This is good if it results in quality documentation and coding practices, but it may hurt experimental software development or the production of novel ideas.

Despite the pressure to conform and an apparent lack of information organization, decentralized groups exhibit the greatest job satisfaction [23]. For long projects hurt by high turnover rates, job satisfaction is a major concern. Job satisfaction is also important for healthy relationships with the public or a customer—if indeed this is a necessary element of the programming project.

In summary, Weinberg's decentralized democratic group does not perform well in tasks with time constraints, simple solutions, large information exchange requirements, or unusual approaches. A difficult task of considerable duration which demands personal interaction with the customer is optimal for a Weinberg team.

3. An Analysis of Baker's Team Structure

Baker describes the use of a highly structured programming team to develop a complex on-line information retrieval system for the New York Times Data Bank; the team is a three-person unit. It consists of a *chief programmer*, who manages a *senior level programmer* and a *program librarian*. Additional programmers and analysts are added to the team on a temporary basis to meet specific project needs. Figure 2(a) illustrates the structure of the chief programmer team; the communication channels are shown in Figure 2(b).

The chief programmer manages all technical aspects of the project, reporting horizontally to a project manager who performs the administrative work. Program design and assignment are initiated at the top level of the team. Communication occurs

through a programming library system, which contains up-to-date information on all code developed. The program librarian maintains the library and performs clerical support for the project. Rigid program standards are upheld by the chief programmer.

The Baker team is a centralized autocratic structure in which problem solutions and goal decisions are made at the top level. The task which the team undertakes is well-defined, but large and complex. Definite time constraints exist. Baker concludes that this compact highly structured team led to the successful completion of the project and that it has general applicability.

Several weaknesses exist in Baker's argument. Shaw [21] finds that a centralized communication network is more vulnerable to saturation at the top level. Information from all lower modes in this structure flows upward to the parent mode. Baker's team was intentionally small and worked with a highly structured system for managing project information; both these factors were critical to the success of the project. A third, equally important factor was the team leader's ability to handle project communication. This ability is closely related to the leader's software expertise. A less experienced leader or a more complex problem might have changed the project's success, even with staffing constraints and information management. Yourdon [29] points out that

the effective chief programmer is a rare individual and indicates that most so-called chief programmer teams are headed by someone who is unlikely to adequately handle the communication complexity.

Centralized groups exhibit low morale [3]; this, in turn, leads to dissatisfaction and poor group cohesiveness. Members of highly cohesive groups communicate with each other to a greater extent than members of groups with low cohesion [15]. With a clearly defined problem that is split into distinct modules, this lack of communication will have little impact, but an ill-defined problem with many interfaces would suffer in a chief programmer team environment. The two software modules (the interface systems) on this project which might have served as indicators of this communication condition are, as a matter of fact, developed as a joint effort between the chief programmer and another team member.

Communication in a status hierarchy tends to be directed upward; its content is more positive than that of any communication directed downward [27]. In a tricky, difficult programming task, this favorable one-way flow of communication denies the group leader access to a better solution or, at least, an indication of problems in the current solution. Decentralized groups generate more and better solutions to problems than individuals working alone [25]—such as a chief programmer. The major basis for the success

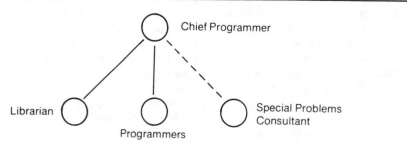

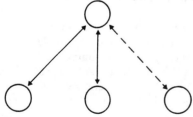

(a) Management Structure   (b) Communication Channels

Fig. 2. Chief Programmer Team Structure. Authority is vested in the chief programmer and communication is centralized to this individual.

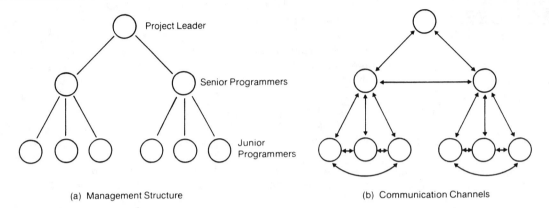

(a) Management Structure   (b) Communication Channels

Fig. 3. Controlled Decentralized Team Structure. Authority is vested in the project leader and senior programmers, but communication at each level of the management hierarchy is decentralized.

of the New York Times Data Bank project was the team's ability to meet the delivery date. A centralized structure completes tasks more quickly than any decentralized form of control [14], but perhaps a more creative solution might have resulted from a different approach. Proponents of good software management stress concern for the software life cycle [8, 9, 13]. This implies that consideration be given not only to project completion schedules but to the software's usability, cost to the customer, and modifiability.

In summary, communication exists to a much lesser degree in centralized groups and is directed toward the manager. Both difficult tasks requiring multiple inputs for solution and unstructured tasks requiring substantial cooperation fare poorly in this kind of communication environment. Group morale and, thus, goal motivation are low in such a hierarchical structure. A simple, well-structured programming task with rigid completion deadlines and little individual interface with the client is perfect for the chief programmer team.

4. An Analysis of a Controlled Decentralized Team Structure

In practice, programming team structures vary considerably. Most take on some form of organization that draws from both Weinberg's egoless team and Baker's chief programmer team. A third, frequently used organization which we will call the controlled decentralized (CD) team is described in this section.

The controlled decentralized team has a project leader who governs a group of senior programmers. Each senior programmer, in turn, manages a group of junior programmers. Figure 3(a) illustrates the organization of this group; Figure 3(b) indicates the flow of communication that takes place in this type of group structure.

Metzger [17] describes this organization as a reasonable management approach. He makes two recommendations: First, he suggests that intermediate levels of management are preferable to requiring all senior programmers to report to the project leader and, second, he recommends that the programming groups be partitioned not according to code module assigned, but in terms of the type of role played in the project, e.g., test, maintenance, etc. Shneiderman [24] lists this structure as the most probable type of project organization. Like Yourdon [29], he suggests that the individual subgroups in the project participate in structured walkthroughs and code exchanges in the manner of Weinberg's egoless teams.

The CD team possesses control over the goal selection and decision-making aspects of the Baker team and the decentralized communication aspects of the Weinberg team. Setting project goals and dividing work among the groups are the tasks of the project leader. More detailed control over the project's functions is assigned to the senior programmers. Within each programming subgroup, the organization is decentralized. Problem solving is a group activity as is checking for code errors. Each group leader serves as the sole recipient or gatekeeper of project information for the subgroup and acts as a liaison with the leaders of the other groups. The communication and control problems of the egoless and chief programmer teams do not disappear in a CD structure but occur in the subgroups of the controlled decentralized team that correspond to the Weinberg and Baker teams: Thus, the properties of the subtask allocated to any of the subgroups interact, in a similar fashion, with the subgroup structure.

The decentralized subgroups of the CD team work poorly with highly structured or simple tasks. Group solutions are best directed at difficult problems. Much of the creative and difficult part of programming is planning the design and partitioning the work. In the CD struc-

COMPUTING PRACTICES

ture this work is completed by the project leader. The senior programmers then take on their portion of the task and develop a group solution. Ironically, when the task is most difficult, the team structure is least effective. A poll of programming managers and academics indicated that the area they believed needed the most attention in software engineering was the planning and design stage [26], the work carried out by the CD team project leader.

With small problems, the CD team is unnecessary since its very structure presumes the existence of a larger project. As Brooks [6] points out, even though adding individuals to a project increases the communication problems and, thus, the effectiveness of the project's members, it is still necessary to have large teams for those programming tasks which are so large they could not be accomplished in a reasonable length of time by a few programmers.

Although control over projects is exercised from above, the group problem-solving approach at lower levels will take longer, and projects will be more likely to fall behind in meeting deadlines. The structure of the CD team would tend to centralize the egoless programming subgroups. Because of the senior programmer's gatekeeper role, he or she would emerge as an informal leader in group sessions. This, in turn, would lower individual satisfaction with the project and generate the ensuing problems of a high job turnover rate and group socialization difficulties. Because of this strong tendency toward centralization, shorter projects are best for the CD structure.

A controlled decentralized team is an effective error-purge mechanism. The code walkthroughs and group input at the code generation level will filter out many errors. Code generated in this fashion is more reliable than code coming from a chief programmer team operation.

Programming tasks that are not easily subdivided suffer in a CD team. Note in Figure 3(b) that communication between groups occurs at the senior programmer level. Projects requiring micro-decision communication about code interfaces cannot expect this communication to be conveyed effectively through a liaison person functioning at a macro level in the project.

In summary, the controlled decentralized team will work best for large projects which are reasonably straightforward and short-lived. Such teams can be expected to produce highly reliable code but not necessarily on time or in a friendly manner. They are ill-suited for long-term researchlike projects.

Team Structure and Programming Task Relationships

This section describes seven salient properties of programming tasks and compares the performance of each team structure discussed in relationship to these task properties. The relevant properties are:

(1) *Difficulty.* The program required to solve the problem can be complex, consisting of many decision points and data interfaces, or it may be a simple decision tree. Distributed processing systems and projects with severe core or rapid response time constraints fall into the *difficult* category. Much of the scientific programming would come under the *simple* category heading.

(2) *Size.* Programs may range from ten to hundreds of thousands of lines of code for any given project.

(3) *Duration.* The lifetime of the programming team varies. Maintenance teams have a long lifetime; one-shot project teams have a short lifetime.

(4) *Modularity.* If a task can be completely compartmentalized into subtasks, it is highly modular. Most programming problems can be split into subtasks, but the amount of communication required between the subtasks determines their modularity rating. A tape system for payroll reports is a highly modular task.

A data management system for the same purpose has a low degree of modularity.

(5) *Reliability.* Some tasks such as patient monitoring systems have severe failure penalties, while other tasks, such as natural language processing experiments, need not be as reliable, although working programs are always desirable. The reliability measure depends on the social, financial, and psychological requirements of the task.

(6) *Time.* How much time is required for task completion? Is the time adequate or is there time pressure? The penalty for not meeting a deadline strongly affects this measure.

(7) *Sociability.* Some programming tasks require considerable communication with the user or with other technical personnel, such as engineers or mathematicians, while other tasks involve interaction with the team alone. Computer center consulting groups that develop user aids have higher sociability requirements than groups programming their own set of software tools.

Throughout this paper, the labels egoless programming team and chief programmer team have prevailed. For the purposes of comparison, these terms have been changed to names reflecting the decision-making authority and communication structure of the teams. The three teams are:

1. Democratic Decentralized (DD). This group is like Weinberg's proposed team; it has no leaders, but appoints task coordinators for short durations. Decisions on problem solutions and goal direction are made by group consensus. Communication among members is horizontal.

2. Controlled Decentralized (CD). The CD group has a leader who coordinates tasks. Secondary management positions exist below that of the leader. Problem solving remains a group activity but partitioning the problem among groups is a task of the leader. Communication is decentralized in the subgroups and centralized along the control hierarchy.

Table 1. Recommended Team Structures for Programming Task Features.

Group Structures	Programming Task Characteristics													
	Difficulty		Size		Duration		Modularity		Reliability		Time Required		Sociability	
	High	Low	Large	Small	Short	Long	High	Low	High	Low	Strict	Lax	High	Low
Democratic Decentralized	X			X		X		X	X			X	X	
Controlled Decentralized		X	X		X		X		X			X		X
Controlled Centralized		X	X		X		X			X	X			X

3. Controlled Centralized (CC). This group is like Baker's team. Both problem solving and goal directions are generated by the team leader. Communication is vertical along the path of control.

The expected interaction of each of these team structures with the factors governing program tasks can be drawn from experimental research on small group dynamics. To assess performance quality, team structures are assumed to be evaluated on the quality of generated code and the time in which the code generation was completed.

Table I lists recommended group structures for each task variable. Under the category *task difficulty*, simple problems are best performed by a centralized structure which completes tasks faster. Decentralization works best for difficult problems. Groups are found to generate more and better solutions than individuals. Unfortunately, the CD team is centralized precisely where the problem is difficult. The DD team is the best solution for difficult problems. For simpler programming tasks, a CC or CD structure is recommended.

As programming tasks increase in size, the amount of cooperation required among group members increases. Group performance is negatively correlated with the cooperation requirements of a task. As tasks become *very large*, the DD group is no longer viable because of its cooperation requirements. CC and CD groups can be effectively regrouped into smaller structures to handle the task. When the task size requires a smaller number of programmers, the DD group performs better because of its high level of communication. For *very small* tasks, the CC group is best because it does not require the additional communication of democratic groups; but then, a group is unnecessary. An individual will do.

The duration of the task interacts with group morale. Short tasks may not require high group morale, whereas long tasks will suffer from high personnel turnover if morale is low. DD groups have high morale and high job satisfaction. This should be the preferred group structure for ongoing tasks. The CC and CD groups are effective for short-term tasks.

If task modularity is low, the DD group performs best because of its higher volume of communication. Cooperative (read DD) groups have higher orderliness scores than competitive (read CC) groups [10]. This orderliness is essential for maintaining the interfaces of a low modularity task. Nondirective leadership has been found to be most effective when a task has a high multiplicity of solutions. Directive leadership is best for tasks with low multiplicity solution choices [22]. A DD group can be characterized as having nondirective leadership, CC and CD groups as having directive leadership. High modularity tasks have a low multiplicity of solutions, and thus the CD and CC groups can be expected to exhibit the best performance given such tasks.

CC and CD groups perform well when confronted with high reliability requirement problems. Decentralized groups have been found to make less errors and produce better solutions to problems. A CC group is more error-prone and probably should never be used for projects in which relatively simple errors can result in disaster.

A decentralized group takes longer to complete a problem than a centralized group. If tasks have severe time constraints, a CC team is best. When time is not crucial, the low motivation of CC groups can interfere with task completion. Therefore, the more democratic groups are preferred, with the DD structure being the best choice.

If a task requires high sociability, the DD team structure is best. Groups learn faster than individuals (such as the team leaders of CC groups). Therefore, a DD group would understand a user's interface problem in a shorter period of time. DD groups are higher in social interaction and morale than CD or CC groups. These traits will enhance their social relationships with the task contacts.

6. Conclusion

Many programming task features interact with each other, e.g., a large project is often a difficult one. Group structures that are effective for one aspect of a task may be totally wrong for another. In selecting a team structure, it is important to use a decision-making algorithm to prioritize, weight, or combine the crucial task variables.

Little experimental work on programming team and task interaction has been carried out. Basili and Reiter [2] found relationships between the size of a programming group and several software metrics. They also

COMPUTING PRACTICES

found cost differential behavior arising from the software development approach taken, with structured techniques being notably cheaper. Only one programming task was performed by the experimental groups. Weinberg's suggestions on group organization are anecdotal and Baker's conclusions are confounded by the team personnel and the programming methods selected.

Most of the research on group problem-solving behavior was conducted in a laboratory setting with students and tasks of short duration. A problem exists in trying to apply these conclusions to the external work environment. In particular, programming tasks generally involve an entirely different time span than laboratory experiments. Becker [4] scathingly criticizes these "cage" experiments. Rogers [19] suggests substituting network analysis field work to understand the effects of group structures.

None of these task/structure recommendations have been tested in a software development environment. Despite all these shortcomings, the application of a body of research on group dynamics to the organization of personnel on a programming project is a step forward from the hit-and-miss guessing that is the current state of the art.

References

1. Baker. F.T. Chief programmer team management of production programming. *IBM Syst. J. 1* (1972), 57–73. Baker presents a case history of a program project management organization, the chief programmer team. This compact management strategy coupled with top-down program development methods achieves above average success in terms of productivity and error-free code.

2. Basili, V.R., and Reiter, R.W., Jr. The investigation of human factors in software development. *Comptr. 12*, 12 (Dec. 1979), 21–38. This paper examines the impact of a programming team's size and program development approach, disciplined or ad hoc, on the software product. The disciplined method resulted in major savings in development efficiency and smaller groups built larger code modules.

3. Bavelas. A. Communication patterns in task-oriented groups. *J. Acoustical Soc. America 22* (1950), 725–730. Bavelas describes an experiment in which the communication structures of a circle, wheel, and chain were imposed on small groups by the physical arrangement of cubicles and message slots. Each structure was then measured for its problem-solving efficiency.

4. Becker, H. Vitalizing sociological theory. *Amer. Sociological Rev. 19* (1954), 377–388. Becker refers to the small group laboratory studies as "cage studies" and recommends their use by sociological theorists only for an awareness of such studies' limiting conditions.

5. Bem. D.J., Wallace. M.A., and Kogen. N. Group decision making under risk of adversive consequences. *J. Personality and Social Psychol. 1* (1965), 453–460. This paper demonstrates, in a context of adversive consequences (loss of money, induced nausea, etc.), that unanimous group decisions concerning matters of risk shift toward greater risk-taking than individual decisions. Moreover, the authors provide evidence that the underlying process for the risky shift is a diffusion of the responsibility among group members.

6. Brooks, F.P., Jr. *The Mythical Man-Month: Essays on Software Engineering*. Addison-Wesley. Reading. Mass., 1975. This work is a lyrical, enjoyable, and sage discussion of the problems and pitfalls that beset a mammoth software project—developing the IBM 360 operating system.

7. Cartwright, D., and Zander. D., Eds. *Group Dynamics: Research and Theory*. 3rd edition. Harper and Row. N.Y., 1968. This serves as an excellent compendium of the spurt of group dynamics research activity in the late 1950s which laid the groundwork for what we know about group behavior today.

8. Cave. W.C., and Salisbury. A.B. Controlling the software life cycle—The project management task. *IEEE Trans. Soft. Engr. SE-4*, 4 (July 1978), 326–334. This paper describes project management methods for controlling the life cycle of large software systems distributed to multiple users. It emphasizes responding to user satisfaction and user requirements and suggests methods to establish and maintain control in an extended dynamic environment.

9. De Roze, B.C., and Nyman, T.H. The software life cycle—A management and technological challenge in the department of defense. *IEEE Trans. Soft. Engr. SE-4*, 4 (July 1978), 309–318. De Roze and Nyman describe the software life cycle management policy and practices that have been established by the Department of Defense for improving the software development process.

10. Deutsch. M. The effects of cooperation and competition upon group process. *Human Relations 2* (1949), 129–152, 199–231. Deutsch describes an experiment which establishes two forms of group relationships, cooperative and competitive. Besides better communication, increased orderliness and higher productivity result when the cooperative group relationship exists.

11. Goldberg, S.C. Influence and leadership as a function of group structure. *J. Abnormal and Social Psychol. 51* (1955), 119–122. The experiment described in this paper compares

group influence on group members in three organization structures: a star, a fork, and a chain. Individuals holding central positions were influenced less than other group members.

12. Guetzkow, H., and Simon, H.A. The impact of certain communication nets upon organization and performance in task-oriented groups. *Mgmt. Sci. 1* (1955), 233–250. The authors establish three communication structures: all-channel, wheel, and circle; they then examine their effect on solving a relatively simple communication problem. The restrictions of the wheel organization aided the solution process, whereas those of the circle hindered it. The lack of restrictions in the all-channel case also hurt the solution process.

13. Jensen, R.W., and Tonies, C.C., Eds. *Software Engineering*. Prentice-Hall, Englewood Cliffs, N.J., 1979. Here, several breakdowns of what constitutes a software life cycle are presented. The authors indicate that if the customer-use phase is included in this breakdown, the time spent on the code development constitutes a relatively small portion of the project.

14. Leavitt, H.J. Some effects of certain communication patterns on group performance. *J. Abnormal and Social Psychol. 46* (1951), 38–50. Leavitt compares problem-solving effectiveness in both wheel and circle communication structures. The wheel structure was faster but the circle structure accounted for fewer errors.

15. Lott, A.J., and Lott, B.E. Group cohesiveness, communication level, and conformity. *J. Abnormal and Social Psychol. 62* (1961), 408–412. This paper describes an experiment in which groups were scored on cohesiveness and then tallied for the amount of communication generated in a discussion session. Highly cohesive groups communicated more.

16. March, J.G., and Simon, H.A. *Organizations*. Wiley, New York, 1958. March and Simon focus on the members of formal organizations as rational men. From this, they point out that the basic features of organizational structure and function derive from characteristics of the human problem-solving process and rational choice.

17. Metzger, P.W. *Managing a Programming Project*. Prentice-Hall, Englewood Cliffs, N.J., 1973. Metzger suggests a project organization constrained in terms of the types of tasks that are undertaken in the development of a software system. He goes on to describe how these tasks should be managed via this hierarchical arrangement.

18. Mills, H.D. Chief programmer teams: Principles and procedures. IBM Rep. FSC 71-5108, IBM Fed. Syst. Div., Gaithersburg, Md., 1971. Mills suggests that the large team approach to programming projects could eventually be replaced by smaller, tightly organized and functionally specialized teams led by a chief programmer.

19. Rogers, E.M., and Agarwala-Rogers, R. *Communication in Organizations*. Free Press, N.Y., 1976. The basic research on group structures in small group network communication is summarized and critiqued in a thoroughly readable manner.

20. Schachter, S. Deviation, rejection and communication. *J. Abnormal and Social Psy-*

chol. 46 (1951), 190–207. This article describes an experiment in which three group members were paid to respectively 1) deviate from, 2) follow, and 3) change over to the group position taken on an issue. Groups with high cohesiveness scores produced greater rejection only of the deviant individual.

21. Shaw, M.E. Some effects of unequal distribution of information upon group performance in various communication nets. *J. Abnormal and Social Psychol. 49* (1954), 547–553. In this paper, the amount of independence and, thus, individual satisfaction are examined in various group structures. Low centralization in groups led to member satisfaction.

22. Shaw, M.E., and Blum, J.M. Effects of leadership styles upon performance as a function of task structure. *J. Personality and Social Psychol. 3* (1966), 238–242. Shaw and Blum describe an experiment in which they manipulated the leadership of two groups to be nondirective or directive. Given three tasks of varying solution multiplicity, directive leadership performed best with low multiplicity tasks.

23. Shaw, M.E. *Group Dynamics: The Psychology of Small Group Behavior.* McGraw-Hill, N.Y., 1971.

24. Shneiderman, B. *Software Psychology.* Winthrop, Cambridge, Mass., 1980. Shneiderman discusses the good and bad points of the Weinberg and Baker teams and a third conventional team. He notes that an egoless team may be difficult to maintain and a competent chief programmer hard to find, concluding that the currently existing conventional organization has strong chances for successful projects—especially with a competent manager.

25. Taylor, D.W., and Faust, W.L. Twenty questions: Efficiency of problem solving as a function of the size of the group. *J. Experimental Psychol. 44* (1952), 360–363. Taylor compares individual problem-solving to group problem-solving in a game of 20 questions. Even after several days of practice, groups of two and four individuals asked less questions to discover an answer than sole participants.

26. Thayer, R.H., Pyster, A., and Wood, R.C. The challenge of software engineering project management. *Comptr. 13*, 8 (Aug. 1980), 51–59. The three authors report on a survey of software project management experts who were asked to indicate the most important issues facing software engineering. The structure of programming projects was rated as unimportant; planning received the highest ratings.

27. Thibaut, J.W., and Kelley, H.H. *The Social Psychology of Groups.* Wiley, N.Y., 1959. The second section of this book presents a general theory for group formation and group dynamics—in particular, the status systems within groups, conformity requirements, group goal setting behaviors, and the roles played by individuals within the group. In all, not light reading for the nonsociologist.

28. Weinberg, G. *The Psychology of Computer Programming.* Van Nostrand Reinhold, N.Y., 1971. Weinberg provides homilies, advice, and some wisdom about the psychological considerations of the programming process. It is here that he suggests the egoless approach to programming and discusses its potential advantages—Weinberg is short on supportive research, but the book is fun to read.

29. Yourdon, E. *Managing the Structured Technique.* Prentice-Hall, Englewood Cliffs, N.J., 1976. Yourdon discusses the chief programmer team and Weinberg's egoless debugging techniques in a complete scenario for project management. He labels the chief programmer team impractical because of the dearth of true chief programmers.

Chapter 7

Staffing a Software Engineering Project

1. Chapter Introduction

Staffing a software engineering project is defined as all the management activities that involve manning and keeping manned the positions that were established by the organizational structure. This includes selecting candidates for positions, training or otherwise developing both candidates and incumbents to accomplish their tasks effectively, appraising and compensating the incumbents, and terminating the incumbent when the organizational structure position or incumbent is no longer needed.

Staffing for a software engineering project can be partitioned into eight general management activities (see Table 7.1). Each activity in the table is followed by its definition or an amplifying description.

SO... HAVE YOU HAD MUCH EXPERIENCE CATCHING BUGS?

Table 7.1. Staffing activities for software projects.

Activity	Definition or Explanation
Fill organizational positions	Select, recruit, or promote qualified people for each project position.
Assimilate newly assigned personnel	Orient and familiarize new people with the organization, facilities, and tasks to be done on the project.
Educate or train personnel	Make up deficiencies in meeting position qualifications through training and education.
Provide for general development	Improve knowledge, attitudes, and skills of project personnel.
Evaluate and appraise personnel	Record and analyze the quantity and quality of project work as the basis for personnel evaluations. Set performance goals and appraise personnel periodically.
Compensate	Provide wages, bonuses, benefits, or other financial remuneration commensurate with project responsibilities and performance.
Terminate assignments	Transfer or separate project personnel as necessary.
Document staffing decisions	Record staffing plans, training, and training plans, appraisal records, and compensation recommendations.

2. Chapter Overview

The six articles of Chapter 7 address the correct staffing and training for a software engineering project. The management activities listed in Table 7.1 were used as an outline for identifying articles on staffing activities.

The article by Robert A. Zawacki discusses the function of recruiting to fill organizational positions. The article by G.E. Bryan provides a statistical look at software personnel and defines their differences. Kathryn Bartol and David Martin first point out that software personnel turnover is unavoidable, and secondly, computer personnel terminate their jobs for a variety of reasons. Marie Moneysmith deals with annual performance evaluations and appraisals. Al Davis tells a short story illustrating the trials of a new project manager forced to fire one of his engineers.

3. Article Descriptions

Zawacki's article is interestingly entitled "How to Pick Eagles;" that is, how to go about picking promising recruits for the task of software development. The author feels that the interview and selection process should be geared to match a person's growth needs to the scope of the position. He points out that if an interviewer selects only high-quality personnel when all the positions are not high quality, some of the software engineers hired will end up with low job satisfaction and, more importantly, low levels of productivity.

Zawacki lists those items that appear to influence an interviewer in the selection process. He also discusses the reasons for these biases. Zawacki provides an interview guideline for those interested in selecting the best applicant for the job position.

The second article, by Bryan, reports on an effort to gather data measuring individual programmer performance in a stable work group over a 12-year period. The work group was responsible for developing and supporting a single operating system consisting of 4.2 million lines of code, associated programming products, communication systems, and databases. Analysis of the data shows a wide variation in productivity between individuals and groups. Eight percent of the total work was performed by a single programmer out of a workforce of nearly 200. A top 27 percent of programmers did 78 percent of the work. The reason for including this article is to demonstrate to project managers that the proper or improper selection (staffing) of software engineers or programmers for a particular project can cause a very large variation in software productivity.

For interested readers, the article by H. Sackman, W.R. Erikson, and E.E. Grant, entitled "Exploratory Experimental Studies Comparing Online and Offline Programming Performance," published in the first edition of this tutorial, is also on programming productivity. The experimental results of this article include the often-quoted statistic, "The capabilities of individual programmers can vary as much as 26 to 1" [1].

The third article, by Bartol and Martin, addresses the management problems associated with turnover of the data processing staff. The authors indicate that all turnovers are not detrimental. A change in staff can offer bases for new ideas and a way to get rid of unsuitable people. The responsibility of staff termination and retention lies with management.

The fourth article, with the unusual title of "I'm OK—and You're Not," is a short, two-page article by Moneysmith addressing the problem of evaluating employees. Moneysmith makes several good points concerning the right and wrong way to evaluate an employee.

Once you have evaluated your employees, it may be necessary to eliminate the obviously poor performers and malcontents. The last article, by Davis (also the author of an article on lifecycle models for this tutorial), is a short article on his experiences as a new project manager. He accounts two experiences he had when circumstances forced him to fire someone (both, from his account, deserved firing). He provides some insight into how to do it properly and summarizes with the statements that

- firing someone is very painful, and

- no matter how many people are "behind you" when you make a painful decision, you are all alone once you implement it.

Reference

1. Sackman, H., W.R. Erikson, and E.E. Grant, "Exploratory Experimental Studies Comparing On-line and Off-line Programming Performance," *Comm. ACM*, Vol. 11, No. 1, Jan. 1968, pp. 3–11. Reprinted in *Tutorial: Software Engineering Project Management*, R.H. Thayer, ed., IEEE Computer Society Press, Washington, DC, 1988.

Here's a brief guide to interviewing and selecting the best candidate for the job.

HOW TO PICK EAGLES

by Robert A. Zawacki

While speaking recently at an Amdahl users group, I was asked the following question: "Have you ever published anything on how to select the right people for dp jobs?" I had just finished reading Ken Follett's best-selling book, *On Wings of Eagles* (William Morrow and Co. Inc., New York, 1983), and was fascinated by the author's frequent descriptions of how Electronic Data Systems selected "eagles," or promising recruits. This made me reflect on what I knew about interviewing and selecting the right dp person for the job.

What is your objective during the selection process? I assume it is to match people with dp jobs. I recommend a review of the following framework before beginning the selection process.

The objective during the selection process is to match a person's growth need strength (*GNS*) with a job's scope task or motivating potential score (*MPS*). *GNS* is an individual's need to grow, to develop beyond the present point, to be stretched and challenged by the job. The scope of the job can range from high to low. A high-scope task in dp is development, while a low-scope task is mounting tapes in operations. During the interview, the interviewer is attempting to select high-*GNS* people for high scope jobs (see cell 1 in Fig. 1) and conversely to select lower *GNS* people for lower-scope jobs (cell 4, Fig. 1).

During the interview, the interviewer is attempting to match people and jobs and to minimize the mismatches in cells 2 and 3 (also Fig. 1).

An interviewer who selects only high-*GNS* people may end up with a flock of eagles who are assigned to jobs that are lower in scope because high-scope jobs are scarce. This mismatch soon results in lower job satisfaction and productivity once the learning phase is over.

All available research indicates that the ability of a dp manager to predict how a future employee will perform, based upon a one-hour interview, is very low. Yet most managers have great confidence in their predictive ability based upon impressions formed in a brief interview. An industrial psychologist, Abraham K. Korman, in his book, *Industrial and Organizational Psychology* (Prentice-Hall, Englewood Cliffs, N.J., 1971), summarizes what influences a manager's judgment in the selection situation:

- Interviewers tend to develop a stereotype of a good candidate and then seem to match applicants with stereotypes.
- Biases are established early in the interview.
- During an interview in which the applicant is accepted, the interviewer talks more and in a more favorable tone than in an interview in which the applicant is rejected.
- Interviewers are influenced more by unfavorable than by favorable information.
- Seeing negative candidates before positive candidates will result in a greater number of favorable acceptances than the other way around.
- There are reliable and consistent individual differences among interviewers in their perceptions of the applicants they see as acceptable.
- Factual written data seem to be more important than physical appearance in determining judgments; this increases with the interviewing experience.

In *Applied Psychology in Personnel Management* (Reston Publishing Co., Reston, Va., 1982), Wayne F. Cascio updated Korman's summary with these additional conclusions:

- Early impressions are crystallized after a mean interview time of only four minutes.
- The ability of a candidate to respond concisely, to answer questions fully, to state personal opinions when relevant, and to keep to the subject at hand appears to be crucial to obtaining a favorable employment decision.
- Interviewers benefit very little from day-to-day interviewing experience.
- An interviewer who begins an interview with an unfavorable expectancy may tend to give an applicant less credit for past accomplishments and ultimately may be more likely to decide that the applicant is unacceptable.
- Interviews must be structured.

SO WHY THE VARIANCE?

Why is there a discrepancy between a manager's belief about his or her predictive ability and the research results? There appear to be two main reasons for this mismatch of effectiveness. First, interviewees tend to give sociably desirable answers to the interviewer. Assume a systems analyst desperately wants a job at the Hartford Insurance Group because her husband was recently transferred to Hartford. She can prepare for the interview by studying the company's financial reports, familiarize herself with its products, equipment, and even talk to other systems analysts at the company. In a one-hour interview, the odds are in her favor that she will get the job.

Second, the interviewer's biases are formed by a poor research methodology. In the example above, assume the interviewer interviews five people for the systems analysis job—a high-scope job. After interviewing each candidate, the interviewer selects the person who was rated the highest. This person joins the company and is an above-average employee for the next two or three years. The interviewer's impressions about his predictive ability are reinforced because he sees the positive results of his interview. What the interviewer does not know is how the other four would have performed. They may even be superior to the person hired.

There are three types of interviews: structured or patterned, nondirective, and problem interviews. In the problem interview, a project or situation is given to the applicant. A group interview where job-related questions are asked is an exmple of this type of interview. The major shortcoming of the problem interview is that it can be perceived by the applicant as a stress interview. When an interview is perceived as stressful, a programmer (who has employment options), may say, "If that is the way they treat their people, who would want to work there?"

The major shortcoming of the nondirective interview is that some dp managers believe they have an innate talent for selecting good people and they "wing it" during the interview. Being able to talk a good game does not necessarily ensure success with an interview. All applicants must be asked the same questions for comparisons to be valid. Because of the shortcomings of other methods, we therefore recommend the patterned or structured interview.

Patterned interview guidelines.

1. Preparing for the interview.

   a. Arrange for a comfortable physical environment.

   b. Get away from the telephone and interruptions.

   c. Clear your mind and review these guidelines.

   d. Write down four or five open-ended questions that will help you evaluate a candidate's growth potential, strengths, and other attributes.

   e. Review the position description and determine the scope of the job (*MPS*). Determine the cell in Fig. 1 that you are attempting to fill through the interview.

   f. Review the candidate's résumé.

2. Structuring the interview.

   a. Use multiple interviewers; this increases the predictive validity.

   b. Keep short notes.

   c. Ask each candidate the same core questions.

3. Conducting the interview.

   a. The opening minutes of the interview are critical because both candidate and interviewer are forming impressions.

   b. Greet the candidate in a friendly manner.

   c. Establish rapport and trust by discussing a common point of interest. Determine this from the candidate's résumé.

   d. Be aware of your facial expressions. Talk in a relaxed manner and attempt to smile.

   e. Try to conduct the interview face-to-face. Do not have a desk or table between yourself and the candidate.

   f. Start with a broad general question to relax the applicant. Then proceed to more specific questions.

   g. Ask open-ended questions that permit the applicant to do at least 50% of the talking. For example, a poor question would be "Did you graduate from college?" A better way to word it would be, "Please tell me about your college courses and experiences."

   h. Give positive strokes to the candidate when possible: "You completed a very complex and innovative project while working at *xyz* Corp."

   i. Use pauses to your advantage to keep the applicant talking.

   j. Bring the interview to a polite close. Observe time limits and gently remind the candidate that you are out of time.

   k. End the interview by telling the candidate the time schedule for hiring and when and who will get back to her.

   l. Escort the candidate to the next interviewer and thank him for his time and interest.

4. After the Interview.

   a. Record the interview while answers to questions and impressions are fresh in your mind.

   b. Schedule a meeting with other interviewers to compare and discuss all candidates.

   c. Send a follow-up letter to the selected candidate and to any unsuccessful candidates. I recommend a personal letter from a dp manager rather than a general letter from a personnel specialist. How the unsuccessful candidates are "cooled out" is critical. Beside considerations of common decency, it must be remembered rejected applicants may be a source for future employment needs, and a company's image is affected by how candidates are treated.

While the personal interview has low predictive validity, most dp managers still want to meet and see candidates rather than leaving that process to personnel. By following these guidelines, the accuracy of the interview process can be improved. That, in turn, will contribute to the overall effectiveness of the dp department.

Robert A. Zawacki is a principal in the consulting firm, Couger/Zawacki and Associates, Colorado Springs, where he has been studying and consulting on the human side of dp for the past nine years. His most recent book is *Supervisory Management*, Harper & Row, New York, 1984.

FIG. 1

LEVEL OF CONGRUENCE RESULTING FROM DEGREE OF MATCH BETWEEN GNS AND TASK SCOPE

HIGH SCOPE

NATURE OF THE TASK

LOW SCOPE

HIGH-SCOPE TASK—MPS
HIGH-GNS INDIVIDUAL
LEVEL OF CONGRUENCE: HIGH
CELL 1

HIGH-SCOPE TASK—MPS
LOW-GNS INDIVIDUAL
LEVEL OF CONGRUENCE: LOW
CELL 2

CELL 3
LOW-SCOPE TASK—MPS
HIGH-GNS INDIVIDUAL
LEVEL OF CONGRUENCE: LOW

CELL 4
LOW-SCOPE TASK—MPS
LOW-GNS INDIVIDUAL
LEVEL OF CONGRUENCE: HIGH

HIGH GNS

LOW GNS

NATURE OF THE INDIVIDUAL

Not All Programmers Are Created Equal

G. Edward Bryan
GEB Software Technology
581 Paseo Miramar
Pacific Palisades, CA 90272
310-454-9461
edbryan@alumni.caltech.edu

Abstract - Data measuring individual
programmer performance was gathered over
a 12-year period in a stable work group
responsible for developing and supporting a
single 4.2-million-line operating system and
associated program products, communication
systems, and databases. Analysis shows a
wide variation in productivity from best- to
poorest-performing individuals and groups.
Eight percent of the work result was done
by a single programmer out of a workforce
of almost 200. A variation of 200:1
separated the top programmer from the
poorest performers. The top 27% of
programmers did 78% of the work.

The programming environment was
stable and uniform over the time period:
education, training, general ability level,
work environment, development tools, and
methodology were all the same or similar.
The development lab was remote and largely
isolated from outside distractions and
influences. Programmers typically were
concurrently responsible for both
maintenance and development of new
functions, usually for the same code module.
The average productivity of the group is
several times higher than industry averages
and this fact is demonstrably not caused by
documentation being excessive or code
verbose; both were efficient in comparison
to similar systems.

The wide variation in productivity is
due to individual ability. Training, tools,
methodology, and education, while
important, cannot make up for individual
ability. To get an accurate project plan the
range of variation in individual productivity
must be taken into account. A project can
only be on time and on budget if the widely
varying abilities of the staff are taken into
account. A project may be properly staffed
by one person, 2 people, or 20 people
depending on individual ability.

INTRODUCTION

No one will be surprised that some
programmers are better than others,[1] but
there are few hard measurements of this
variability in long-term, very large projects.
We have long known that planning cannot
be done using average productivity rates,
and that we must include individual
capabilities if we are to make good forecasts
for project completion. The data presented
here confirms and quantifies variation in
ability among programmers.

This paper describes data gathered
over a 12-year span of time during which
the CP-6 system was both being maintained
and simultaneously enhanced and extended
while being rapidly installed at customer
sites. The data used for this study is that

recorded by STARLOG, a database in which all problem reports were registered and in which all the progress toward a solution was recorded. This database covers the entire CP-6 program product set and the full set of time from general release in December 1979 until the present day. This study uses the portion of the data covering March 1980 through February 1992: 12 full years. There were never more than 70 programmers on the CP-6 project. The effort began with a total staff of 60 people, peaked at 150 (including some hardware engineers), and added projects besides CP-6 as the staff declined to 15 by the end of 1992. The database, however, records nearly 200 individuals who worked on the project over the 12 years. The data is complete and comprehensive — every problem in the delivered product during that period of time was recorded, both those discovered by customers and those discovered at the development center where the released product ran in production to carry out both new product development and current product support. The database also includes problems reported before customer release — those discovered during alpha and beta testing — although these are separately identified and not included in this analysis, which is limited to problems reported for the released product.

The CP-6 Product

In order to establish the scope of the project — to establish that the project is a large complex one requiring significant skill, design, and coordination efforts — the following paragraphs describe the product scope, its development history, and its size.

CP-6 includes a host operating system (and a second, nearly identical OS for the communications machine), communications software (TCP/IP, X.400, X.25, HASP, sync and async), a full set of compilers (C, FORTRAN, COBOL, PL-6, APL, BASIC, RPG, PASCAL, TeX, etc.), networked and SQL relational databases, and a full set of end-user and operations support utilities. The operating system includes compatible timesharing, batch, and transaction processing modes. Additions in recent years have been adaptation for DPS8000 and DPS90 systems (Bull mainframe computers), newer disks and other peripherals, a UNIX-compatible C compiler, and OSI and TCP/IP communications via connected UNIX-based systems, which gives CP-6 a strong connection to open systems. In all, over 60 program products are included in the set.

Development History

In July 1975, when Xerox suddenly announced its exit from the computer business, Honeywell (later bought by Bull) agreed to take on support of Xerox's computer users; in July 1976 it established the Los Angeles Development Center (LADC) to create a new operating system, language compilers, database facilities, and other associated software to provide a growth path for the 150 CP-V systems then running on Xerox hardware under CP-V, Xerox's operating system for its Sigma line of computers. The new system, named CP-6, was to be a replacement for CP-V, even though it was to run on incompatible hardware (36bit data replaced 32bit, ASCII coding replaced EBCDIC). It was to have the look and feel of CP-V and thus satisfy CP-V users even though both data and programs needed conversion. Most languages were upgraded to the latest standards, and many problems that users had experienced with CP-V were eliminated. Users were pleased: It was CP-V with all the bad things removed and many improvements added. As a completely new development, CP-6 adopted a new high-level system programming language, PL-6, and a modern development methodology was used throughout. The developers felt that they had the unique opportunity to "do it right". The first beta test was at Carleton University in July 1979; four general-release systems were installed in December 1979. There was a build-up of installed systems in the early and mid-eighties to a peak of over 90 systems worldwide. The system was placed in maintenance status in late 1987. In 1993 there remained just under 50 systems in Europe, Canada, and the United States.

Product Size

Ninety-eight percent of the system is implemented in the PL/1-like high-level language PL-6. PL-6 is designed exclusively as a system programming language. It has no formatted I/O, and its I/O is via direct calls on the CP-6 OS. The system and program products have 3.6 million source lines of PL-6, and there are 1.1 million additional lines of software tools and utilities (including 600,000 lines in the "X account," made available to customers). These programs contribute to the development process: they include reusable software and tools for development, documentation, integration, testing, distribution, and management. They are equivalent to the C library of UNIX systems. The more than 2 million lines of test cases and regression tests produced also contribute to system quality. The initial software factory of cross-compilers, assemblers, debuggers, and hardware simulators on CP-V included 500,000 source lines. All of these lines of code were at developed at LADC with the exception of

200,000 lines of purchased test cases and COBOL, SORT, and MERGE, which were developed separately at Honeywell's Phoenix facility.

This size, while large as software projects go, is not large as modern operating systems go, nor is it large compared to OSs of the same era. Rather it is small. Thus it is not possible that the productivity is achieved by writing long and inefficient code. Commentary lines averaged about 25% of total lines in the system and program products and are included in the line counts above.

Problem Reporting Database, STARLOG

Problem reporting, problem analysis, and delivery of fixes are automated by means of an on-line system that connects customers and their computers to LADC's computers and the programmers responsible for fixing them. Customers use an international communication network to enter problems (STARs) directly into the STARLOG database, adding information or providing test cases at the request of programmers pursuing a solution. STARs are visible to all customers for information, access to work-arounds, and final fixes. Often, several customers contribute information to help solve a single problem. Problems are automatically assigned to the programmer responsible for the area of the error, but may be reassigned to a different person as the cause of the problem becomes clearer. The database records the time and date of each step in the fix process, including the final disposition type. E-mail interfaces send mail to programmers when STARs arrive in their area of responsibility and when test cases or test results have arrived from the customer. Managers and programmers are notified when high-severity problems are entered. Tools and communication lines provide direct access to customer computers for analysis or for transmitting analytical information to the LADC machine. Fixes are prepared and tested on the LADC support machine and transmitted electronically to each customer's machine weekly. The system is totally software. On the figure are marked the times of subsequent maintenance and product enhancement releases, which account for many of the peaks in problem reporting.[2]

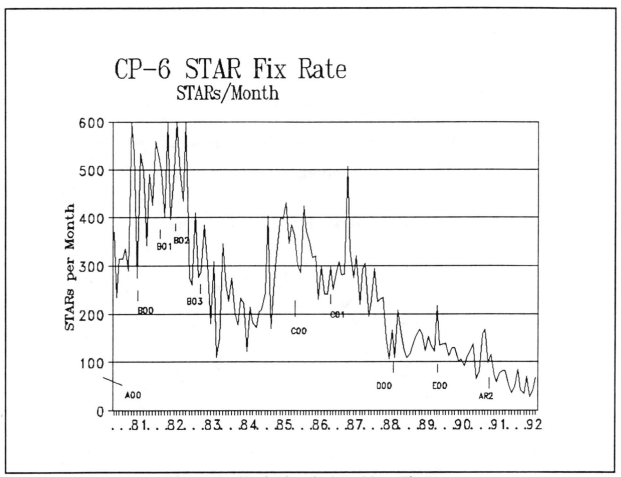

Figure 1 CP-6 Historical Problem Fix Rate

paperless — all CP-6 problem reports and solutions are electronic. Problems have been fixed in the customer's computer in as little as 10 minutes from the time the problem is reported. Figure 1 shows the problem fix rate over the 12 years of this study. It is clear that the system had a high initial problem rate, as is common for

Productivity and Quality

LADC programmers achieved a code production rate of 1,000 high-level source lines of net delivered product code per programmer man-month (6,000 assembler equivalent lines per man-month). The fully

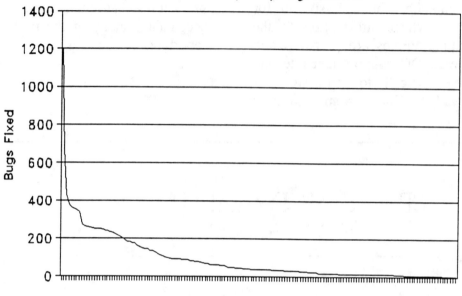

Software Errors Fixed
Number Fixed per programmer

156 Programmers in Rank order of Fixes

Figure 2 Software Bugs Fixed by Programmer

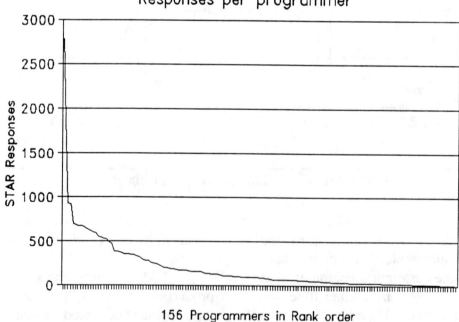

Total STARs Responded
Responses per programmer

156 Programmers in Rank order

Figure 3 Total STARs Answered by Each Programmer

burdened cost per net line of code developed over the project life is $10 per line in 1992 dollars. The quality rate achieved is one software error per 387 lines of product code delivered to customers (2.7 errors per 1,000 lines of source code), counting all errors in the 12 years under study.[3] Thus the average productivity and quality of LADC programmers is much greater than industry averages.

In terms of function points the size of CP-6 is 20,000 for the first release, growing to 60,000 in its 1992 release. For projects of this size Jones[4] records industry productivity rates of about one function point per person-month. For both the first release and the entire project CP-6 programmers produced 7 function points per person-month.

Programming Environment

The environment in which the work was carried out was relatively constant: All programmers used the same development tool set and the same development methodology, although both the tool set and the methodology evolved during the project. For example, after 1978 maintenance and development was carried out using the system itself, which had a strong positive effect on the bug discovery and fix rate. All programmers had approximately the same education and experience level: BS or MS in computer science or equivalent experience. Often programmers came from a college or university that used CP-V, CP-6's predecessor. A core group of about 40 programmers had development experience with the prior product, CP-V. They were located in a development laboratory dedicated to CP-6 development, remote from the distracting influence of the rest of the corporation. LADC was devoted exclusively to CP-6, except for short periods

in 1985, 1987, and 1988 when non-CP-6 projects used less than a total of 10 person-years.

ANALYSIS OF PROGRAMMER PRODUCTIVITY

Some programmers are *lots* better than others. Although this principal result of the current study is well known, the extent to which it is true is not well quantified. CP-6's STARLOG database contains data which makes it possible to analyze the form and extent of the differences in programmer productivity. Several metrics display these differences. The first is total STARS closed by each programmer working on CP-6. There are two general categories of STARS: 1) actual program errors, bugs, for which STARLOG reports the details of problem solution, and 2) responses to queries which are answered with information, including reporting of duplicate problems. Figures 2 and 3 display, respectively, the number of bugs fixed by the top 156 programmers responding to STARS — data for the 36 programmers fixing fewer than 5 problems are not shown — and the total STAR responses, both informational responses as well as fixes. Over time the number of STARs reporting unique software bugs has been about half of total STARs reported.

A comparison the two charts shows that their form is nearly identical. Individuals change position in the hierarchy, but the general shape remains constant. One staff position that makes a difference in an individual's position in the hierarchy is that of STARLORD, the person who has the responsibility for reading and doing an initial review of each arriving STAR, answering if possible. Many problem reports are a matter of misunderstanding or need for more information. The

Fixes per Man Year

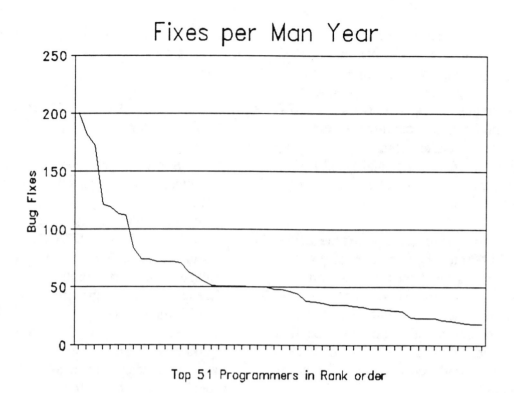

Figure 4 Software Bug Fixing Rate by the Top 51 Programmers

Software Bugs Fixed per Man Year

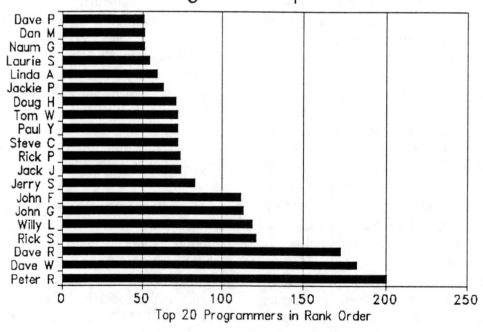

Figure 5 Fix Productivity Rate by the Top 20 Programmers

STARLORD can often answer these questions immediately. Also, STARLORDs can often identify duplicate problem reports,closing them with a "duplicate" response.

Productivity

Of course, not everyone worked on the project for the full 12 years, nor did everyone spend full time in problem-fixing support tasks. Most of the lower-performing programmers worked on the project for only a short time. Also, the best programmers carried responsibilities for both development and support — all of the top 27 programmers in productivity carried both responsibilities. In Figures 4 and 5 the data has been adjusted to account for years on the job and proportion of development responsibility — when they would not have been working on support. The person-year numbers are "gross," not "net," figures: They have not been adjusted to reflect work time devoted to sickness, vacation, holidays, meetings, training, and other non-product-related work time. Gross manpower for the 12-year period is about 320 person-years; net, as recorded in the corporate manpower tracking system, is 217 person-years, although this figure probably does not reflect all of the overtime actually incurred. Again, these charts show the highly skewed

form, with a few programmers delivering the large majority of the results. By extension and experience at the time, it is believed that these same programmers are as good at development work as they are at support work.

Overall productivity results in terms of total fixes corresponding to Figures 1 and 2 are shown in Figure 6.

The remarkable skew in the productivity curve is shown in the table. The 192 programmers are divided into three groups: 1) the single programmer who fixed more than 1,000 bugs, 2) those fixing between 100 and 1,000 bugs, and 3) those who fixed fewer. The top programmer fixed a remarkable 8% of all problems. The combined group closing more than 100 STARs, 23% of programmers, accomplished 74% of the work.

The 51 top-performing programmers in terms of STAR fixes per person-year of effort are further analyzed in Figure 7.

These programmers, as a group, fixed 11,151 bugs, or 78% of the total. Their average productivity is 58 STARs/PY. The top programmer did not, as you might think, fix only easy problems. Quite the contrary: He fixed problems in difficult system and communications areas. He also

Range	# Progrs	% Progrs	# Fixes	Fixes/Progr	% Fixes
< 100 fixes	146	77%	3791	26	26%
100-1000	42	22%	9,483	225	66%
>1000	1	0.5%	1,203	1,203	8%
Total	192		14,477	75	

Figure 6   Overall Total Fixes

Range	Number	Avg PY	Average Fixes/PY	# Fixed	% Fixed	%Fixed/ Programmer
Top programmer	1	6	201	1,203	8.3%	8.3%
Programmers 2-6	5	1.5	142	1,082	7.5%	1.5%
Programmers 7-16	10	3.8	75	3,046	21.0%	2.1%
Programmers 17-51	35	4.6	36	5,820	40.2%	1.2%

Figure 7   Fixes Per Person-Year

ranged widely throughout the system software, fixing problems in areas where he was neither the author of the code nor otherwise had special knowledge. Programmers in the second group are mostly programmers who worked on the system for only a few years. Their productivity was high, but it was not sustained over a long period and thus they did not close the number of STARs that would be consistent with their high productivity rates. They worked during the early years of the system's introduction, when bug rates were very high. They worked in their areas of expertise, a factor that contributed to the high fix rates. Some of them wrote shaky code, but fixed the problems quickly when they occurred, probably an indication of inadequate unit test. Some programmers on occasion combined two or more related fixes under a single STAR and thus made their fix rate lower, but this effect is not thought to be large. Fixes per person-year is a quite crude measure of productivity, since the difficulty (and thus the time required) for fixing a STAR has a very wide range — from a few minutes to many months. However, the relative performance of programmers correctly shows the wide range of ability, since most were faced with the same range of problem difficulty.

CONCLUSIONS

Some programmers are better than others by an exceptionally wide margin. The best-producing people can be 20 or more times better than the low-end group. A factor of more than 100:1 may separate programmers at the ends of the spectrum. This happens in groups of programmers working on the same project, operating in the same environment, using the same tools and development methods, with the same training, and with the same education and experience level. Planning projects accurately requires taking this exceptionally wide variation into account. Accurate planning must assess and take into account the abilities of the individuals assigned to the project. When a single individual can carry out the work of an entire department, that skill cannot be ignored if accurate project plans are to be laid and carried out.

1. Studies of the variation in programmers' productivity have shown variations as high as 25:1. Among them are Sackman, Erikson and Grant 1968, Curtis 1981, Mills 1983, Boehm 1984, 1987, and 1988, DeMarco and Lister 1985, Curtis et al. 1986, Valett and McGarry 1989.

2. Analysis of the STARLOG database is reported in Fielding, Roy T., Selby, Richard W., and Bryan, G. Edward, "An Empirical Microanalysis of Software Failure Data from a 12-Year Software Maintenance Process," in publication, November 1992.

3. Bryan, G. Edward, "CP-6: Quality and Productivity Measures in the 15-Year Life Cycle of an Operating System," *Software Quality Journal 2, 129-144,* June 1993.

4. Jones, Capers, *Applied Software Measurement*, McGraw-Hill, 1991

Managing the Consequences of DP Turnover: A Human Resources Planning Perspective

Kathryn M. Bartol
University of Maryland

David C. Martin
American University

Abstract

This paper argues that there are both positive and negative consequences associated with turnover in the data processing field. In order to maximize the positive consequences, data processing managers must analyze employees in terms of a quality-replaceability matrix. This matrix helps to determine what further managerial actions are necessary in order to have appropriate human resources to meet the data processing needs of the organization.

Consequences of Turnover

Effectively managing turnover requires a consideration of both the negative and positive consequences of turnover. Only after weighing the pros and cons of turnover, can managers effectively manage their human resources.

Negative Consequences

Negative consequences generally receive the most attention when considering the effects of turnover. We outline some of the major negative consequences of turnover applicable to the data processing function.

- Major Project Disruption. The loss of key personnel during software development can seriously delay and even permanently impair important projects. During the systems design phase, for example, the resignation of heavily involved personnel may result in significant losses of vital undocumented information and necessitate the recollection of data related to systems parameters and requirements (Lasden, 1980). During the programming, testing, and implementation phases, losses of key personnel can over-burden other project participants, cause the project to fall behind schedule, lead to schedule and cost overruns, and increase the probability of errors in the final system.

- Other Performance Related Disruptions. Major performance disruptions can also occur with the loss of important personnel who are working in areas other than major systems development. For example, the loss of personnel who perform maintenance on complex systems may cause delays in implementing needed changes. Furthermore, inexperienced replacements may unwittingly make changes that lead to serious output errors which may or may not be recognized immediately. Similar arguments can be made for the potential disruptive effects of resignations in other areas such as management or systems programming.

- Loss of Strategic Opportunities. Turnover of critical personnel can sometimes cause organizations to postpone or cancel projects which can enhance their position relative to competitors and/or increase profits (Mobley, 1982). For example, a turnover-caused postponement of a project to link a major parts supplier with its customers may enable a competitor to make market inroads (Barrel and Konsynski, 1983).

- Recruitment and Selection Costs. Although the monetary costs associated with recruitment and selection are widely recognized, there has been little systematic research documenting actual costs. Recruitment involves such costs as advertising, employment agency fees, travel costs associated with campus visits or recruitment at computer related associations, entertainment costs for prospective recruits, administrative costs, and even bounty payments to present employees for recommending new prospects (Cherlin, 1981; McLaughlin, 1979; Sloane, 1983). Selection involves such costs as reference checks, interviewing, testing, further travel and entertainment costs for prospective employees, and related administrative costs (Mobley, 1979).

- Training and Development Costs. Even if the individual possesses the needed technical skills, there is a learning curve involved until the individual becomes familiar with the organization. McLaughlin (1979) notes that it frequently takes six to eighteen months for a new recruit in the data processing field to reach a reasonable productivity level. Without even considering the salary being paid to the new recruit, initial training costs can involve orientation, the time of a trainer, and disruptions of productivity among others as they try to orient the newcomer. Based on an informal survey, Acker (1981) estimates that the cost of recruiting, relocating, and the first three months of training is likely to run in the range of $6,000 to $10,000 per new hire. However, this figure appears to be rather conservative if one considers the true costs of replacing a good performer with experience in the organization.

- Decline in Morale. Personnel leaving an organization can frequently cause morale problems, particularly if the person is perceived as leaving due to poor conditions. Remaining employees may view the person leaving as getting ahead and they themselves may be induced to think about searching for a new organization. In addition, the loss of a key person on a project and the ensuing work difficulties may discourage those who remain. Finally, an individual leaving may have serious detrimental effects on a cohesive work group, at least in the short run (Stew, 1980).

Positive Consequences

Not all consequences of turnover are negative. Increasingly the positive aspects of turnover are being studied by researchers (e.g., Mobley, 1982; Dalton, Todor, and Krackhardt, 1982). There are several potentially positive consequences of turnover that are particularly applicable to the data processing field.

- Increased Performance. One positive possibility is that relatively poor performers will leave and be replaced by better performers (Muchinsky and Morrow, 1980). Where this occurs, there can be a net gain in productivity, especially in the long run.

- Salary and Benefit Cost Savings. Higher levels of turnover normally produce a work force with less longevity. A relatively junior work force is much less costly to the organization in the form of regular pay, overtime pay, FICA, costs, pensions, and length of vacations. Dalton and Todor (1982) suggest that considerable cost savings can be realized by accepting a higher turnover rate in an organization and that the savings could be maximized by hiring new people who have the requisite skills to replace more senior employees who are at the top of the pay scale. In many situations in the data processing area, however, the loss of valuable experience can outweigh cost savings.

- Innovation and Adaptability. New employees frequently bring with them technological expertise and experience gained elsewhere. This infusion of new knowledge and ideas is important in helping an organization remain innovative. Turnover can also help facilitate changes in staffing patterns to reflect new needs. For example, many data processing organizations now require individuals with advanced technical knowledge in data communications. The increasing availability of software packages could also change the necessary configurations of talent needed in the future. Thus turnover can enable organizations to adapt more quickly to changing environments.

- Increased Internal Mobility. Particularly when more senior employees leave, the turnover opens up promotional possibilities for high performing, lower level staff (Stew, 1980). These opportunities may be crucial for retaining newer promising employees. LaBelle, Shaw, and Hellenack (1980) have argued for the importance of career ladders and promotional possibilities in the data processing field.
- Increased Morale. When poor performers or individuals who tend to create destructive conflict leave, the result can be increased morale. For example, the removal of an individual who misses deadlines, does inferior work, and delays projects can be a boost to others on the project and make those who are performing well feel more equitably treated. Bartol (1983) found that individuals who viewed their organizations as rewarding professional behavior were less likely to turnover. Turnover of individuals who do not engage in professional behaviors may help to enhance perceptions that the organization does indeed value high quality work.

- Decrease in Other Withdrawal Behaviors. Mobley (1982) has noted that individuals who are unhappy with a particular organization may not leave the organization, but may engage in other forms of withdrawal such as absenteeism, poor quality work, and even sabotage. Sabotage is a particularly difficult problem for the data processing field, because the damage which can be done by an individual employee through programming changes and security breaches is greater than with most jobs. It frequently is better if disgruntled employees leave an organization before withdrawal behaviors become acute.

Quality-Replacement Matrix

Negative and positive consequences of turnover are normally viewed in terms of their cumulative effects on an organization. e.g., high turnover is costly or low turnover does not provide enough new ideas, fresh views, and stimulation. Yet, when one considers actually managing turnover, the perspective must shift to turnover as an individual phenomenon. Decisions concerning whether or not an individual remains with an organization are usually a product of the forces to remain versus the forces to leave as they impact on a particular person (Vroom, 1964). Thus, turnover must be managed as it applies to individuals and their specific situations.

The goal of the organization is to retain those individuals who are high quality employees in terms of job skills and particularly those who are difficult to replace (Dalton, Todor, and Krackhardt, 1982). Similarly, those employees of inferior quality who are easily replaced should be terminated as soon as possible. Organizations, therefore, normally give unusual weight to the quality and replaceability of an individual when assessing an individual's net worth to the organization. These factors are paramount when considering those issues which normally lead to retaining a person in the organization, e.g., pay recognition, job autonomy, training, and participation in decision making.

The prime outcomes of the quality and replaceability issues as they relate to turnover are indicated in Figure 1. All employees in an organization can be classified into one of the four categories shown.

Replaceability

	Difficult	Easy
High	I Dysfunctional Turnover	II Functionality Depends on Costs
Low	IV Short Run Dysfunctional/Long Run Functional	III Functional Turnover

Quality (Potential)

Figure 1. The Quality-Replaceability Matrix

Figure 1 suggests that high quality employees are assets to the organization and that, if they are difficult to replace, turnover among this group (Category I) is very dysfunctional for the organization. A systems analyst who does high quality work and also is familiar with the organization is an example of an individual who would fall into Category I. On the other hand, those high quality employees who are relatively easy to replace (Category II) may or may not become costly turnovers to the organization. An example of an individual in Category II would be a high quality keypunch operator. In some cases it could be cost effective from an economic, psychological, and organizational health standpoint to replace an individual from this group. In other instances, costs associated with the turnover of an individual in this group may be prohibitive, even though replacements are readily available. Thus organizations have some choice when dealing with individuals in this category and their actions should be dictated by the costs associated with the decision. However, serious consideration should be given to the quality of performance rendered by the person. It is possible that an individual in this group (Category II) who performs well may become even more valuable with a small investment in training. Even though the final decision concerning what the organization would do to preclude or induce turnover is one of choice, it is likely that for people in this group (Category II) the organization will take actions which would result in the person remaining.

However, in contrast to this group of employees, those who are regarded as low quality and difficult to replace Category IV) also represent a choice for the organization. A maintenance programmer who is slow and frequently makes errors before finally making necessary changes may know a system very well and, therefore, be difficult to replace in the short run. Because such individuals are difficult to replace, it may be some time before a new person hired can adequately perform the job. This could result in some short term problems for the organization. Yet if a suitable replacement is eventually selected, the losses associated with the turnover may be attenuated over time and the long term result could be quite positive. This type of scenario is usually both time and resource dependent. Yet because individuals in Category IV are low quality employees, even though they are difficult to replace, the organization should view them as being there by the choice of the organization and as individuals that may be terminated or leave at some future time.

The last group of individuals indicated in Figure 1 is that which includes the low quality employees who are easily replaced. An example here would be a programmer who has not kept up technically and who accomplishes very little on the job. This is the group (Category III) which most organizations want to terminate as soon as possible. Departures of Category III individuals will improve the efficiency and overall health of the organization. This is functional turnover--it is the proper releasing or terminating of individuals who do not meet the norms of the organization. It is normally good both for the organization and the individual, at least in the long run. However, some firms have policies which permit termination only in the most severe situations.

Thus effective management of the turnover process is an extremely critical function. Data processing managers who wish to be staffed adequately for future challenges and opportunities must devote considerable attention to managing turnover.

Turnover Management Process

There are several basic steps involved in managing turnover. Each of these steps is outlined below.

Categorizing Employees

Employees must be evaluated in view of their potential value to the organization. Many issues must be considered when making such an evaluation. These include not only levels of current performance, but also the degree to which they could master the necessary skills required to perform their current jobs, their demonstrated capabilities and desires to assume additional responsibility, their abilities to work with others, their abilities to manage, and ultimately their abilities to extend the organizational image to the desired audience. Based on these and other considerations germane to the specific organization, employees should be evaluated and subsequently assigned to one of the categories (retain, choose likely to retain, choose likely to release, and release the employee) indicated in Figure 2.

Determining Personnel Actions to be Accomplished

Subsequent to determining the category into which employees fall, personnel actions appropriate for that group of individuals should be initiated. These should be of assistance to both the individual and the organization as both should benefit from this review. The goal of these actions should be to manage the careers of employees in such a manner as to make them so valuable to the organization that they are regarded as a Category I (retain) employee. Where they are not now performing satisfactorily and apparently will not perform to the standards of the organization, they should become candidates for Category III (release). Typically the personnel actions which should be considered for employees in each of the respective quadrants are as follows (See Figure 2):

- Category I (Retain). These are the organization's most valued employees. They must be challenged and supported, as their contributions are essential to the success of the organization. They should be trained to the maximum extent possible, not only in a technical area, but also in the broader aspects of operating the organization, to include management training when appropriate. These employees should be prepared for positions of increasing responsibility, assuming they desire to be promoted in the organization.

Replaceability

	Difficult	Easy
High	I Retain	II Choose - Likely To Retain
Low	IV Choose - Likely to Release	III Release

Quality (Potential)

Figure 2. Personnel Management Objectives for Each Category Or Employee

360

Bartol and Martin (1982) have argued that the quality of personnel will become even more important in the future than in the past because the role of data processing is changing. Data processing personnel need to be more heavily involved in helping to develop and implement data processing related aspects of an organization's strategic plan. To increasingly fulfill this role in the future will require not only technical skills, but also greater knowledge of the business of the organization.

Where possible, jobs for individuals in Category I should be enriched to include additional functions (Couger and Zawacki, 1980). Job enrichment normally includes the assignment of planning and budgetary control to the individual while focusing on the total responsibility for a given function (e.g., an entire system). The group of individuals may also be rotated between jobs to gain additional skills, experience, and exposure to other facets of the organization (Wallace & Szilagyi, 1982). Special efforts must be made to retain this group of individuals, to include adequate compensation, recognition of work, sponsorship of work initiatives, participation in appropriate decision making sessions, and encouragement to expand their functions.

- Category II (Choose, Likely to Retain). This group of individuals includes some of the most dependable employees in the organization. They have demonstrated that they can perform satisfactorily. They are people who have potential with the organization, yet are currently lacking or have not yet indicated that they have certain skills which would make them valuable assets to the organization. The organization can help employees in this group. Skill training can be provided, individuals can be rotated to other jobs to gain experience and insight, there can be some participation in the decision making which concerns their specific work, and they can be given projects which include a high degree of personal identity for them. However, the primary orientation of the career development actions for this group must be on technical and business skill acquisition and recognition through such means as promotions, which are contingent on becoming totally proficient in a given area. In those areas where there are an abundance of people qualified to perform a specific job, the primary emphasis for increasing the value of the person to the firm should be on learning and perfecting skills which are concerned with the next higher level of job which is normally a function which integrates several skills.

- Category III (Release the Employee). This group of individuals does not fit the norms of the organization. For any number of reasons (e.g., poor performance, absenteeism, lack of motivation, the person does possess adequate skills but does not have the motivation required to reach the minimum level of proficiency expected of a person in a particular job), the members of this group have not succeeded and are not expected to be able to meet the requirements of the organization. They should not receive additional training or be recipients of any other nonrequired organizational benefits. Depending on the specific individual circumstances, they should be given as much consideration as possible in assisting them find employment. However, the involuntary separation policy of some organization may preclude immediate dismissal of an individual except for extremely serious acts or omissions. Many factors, such as longevity, quality of performance during their careers with the organization, stress of the function, and circumstances under which the act was committed or omitted, are considered prior to arriving at a decision concerning the fate of the employee. However, in those cases where it is beneficial that the employee be separated but organizational policy precludes such action, the employee should probably be managed in a manner similar to those in Category IV.

- Category IV (Choose-Like to Release). These employees constitute a work force composed of questionable worth to the organization. They are characterized as being generally unreliable, undependable, requiring an unusual amount of supervision, and of marginal efficiency. Yet their output contributes to the overall production of the organization. Normally there would be a short term decrease in the firm's ability to meet its obligations if a person from this group left the organization. Yet the current prognosis for members of this group is that they will eventually leave the organization or the organization will choose to release them. Thus in a sense, they are in a state of movement toward either voluntary or involuntary separation. Organizations must decide whether or not these individuals could be trained and subsequently become the type of employee that should be retained (Category I). Perhaps a skill or behavioral training course could assist in reorienting the individual toward a more rewarding career both for him/herself and the organization. This should be the goal of the organization whenever possible. The actions by the organization must be very carefully considered as training is costly and must be viewed by individuals as a medium by which they could become valuable assets. Training, in those cases, should not be perceived as a reward for previous actions, but instead as a means of salvaging employees who otherwise may become turnover statistics. Where an organization's policy is to "retain and retrain" wherever possible (versus terminating the employee), training should be given to individuals who are viewed as belonging in Category III. The goal here would be eventual reclassification to Category II or I.

Planning Individual Career Development Actions

Specific actions, such as training, job rotation, promotion, or termination should be arranged for the individuals concerned, whenever possible, and included in the organizational budget. Planned action is particularly important because in many cases job opportunities will depend on vacancies which in most organizations are fairly predictable. Yet most replacement actions include some form of training which must arranged and funded. Thus, these significant individual actions must be programmed into the overall annual personnel management program and deliberately executed in order to provide the skills required by the organization at the time they are needed.

Developing Replacement Tables

In order to ensure that qualified people are available when required, specific actions must be taken by the organization to prepare them to perform specific jobs. This can be accomplished using several strategies. One of the most prevalent strategies used by organizations today is that of preparing a replacement table. This table lists each significant, normally highly skilled or supervisory, function, as well as the incumbent and the person who could be expected to replace the incumbent. The state of preparedness of the identified replacement is also indicated as well as actions which are to be taken to increase the ability of this individual to do the job. Replacement charts force supervisors to identify that training and experience necessary for individuals who are to prepared to assume certain positions. As such, these tables play a key role in the career development of many members of the organization.

Conducting Periodic Reviews

Both organizations and individuals change. Thus an individual may have been classified into a given category, but after a period of time following the completion of training, job rotation or other means of career enhancement, or even perhaps some unsatisfactory performance, the individual should be reevaluated. In some situations, a segment of the work force may improve significantly during a period of time and all members therein may be reclassified depending on their contribution to the group effort. However, the necessity for a periodic reevaluation is clear if the system is to be responsive to the needs of the organization. The timing of the reevaluation is a function of the character of the work environment and the demands of the individuals in the work force. Extremely dynamic work environments and highly complex jobs usually dictate more frequent evaluations, perhaps every ninety to one hundred and eighty days. Whereas more stable environments and well defined jobs are normally reevaluated less frequently, perhaps once a year. The reevaluation process then becomes the first step in succeeding personnel actions affecting the individual. Thus career development actions are planned, programmed and executed based on updated evaluations of employees.

Summary

There are both positive and negative consequences associated with turnover. In order to maximize the positive consequences, management must be proactive in ensuring that the proper personnel actions are planned, funded, and implemented. Only through the use of an effective turnover management process will data processing functions have the appropriate human resources to meet the needs of their organizations. Without such human resources, the tremendous potential for strategic utilization of computers will be lost to many organizations.

References

Acker, S.R., "Turning Around Turnover," *Data Management*, Mar. 1981, pp. 44–56.

Barrett, S. and Konsynski, B., "Inter-Organization Information Sharing Systems," *Management Information Systems Quarterly*, Dec. 1982, Special Issue, pp. 93–105.

Bartol, K.M., "Turnover Among DP Personnel: A Casual Analysis," *Comm. ACM*, in press.

Bartol, K.M. and Martin, D.C., "Managing Information Systems Personnel: A Review of Literature and Managerial Implications," *Management Information Systems Quarterly*, Dec. 1982, Special Issue, pp. 49–70.

Cherlin, M., "The toll of Turnover," *Datamation*, Vol. 27, No. 4, 1981, pp. 209–212.

Dalton, D.R., and Todor, W.D., "Turnover: A Lucrative Hard Dollar Phenomenon," *Academy of Management Review*, Vol. 7, 1982, pp. 212–218.

Gray, S.B., "1981 DP Salary Survey," *Datamation*, Vol. 28, No. 11, 1982, pp. 114–123.

LaBelle, C.D., Shaw K., and Hellenack, L.J., "Solving the Turnover Problem," *Datamation*, Vol. 26, No. 4, 1980, pp. 144–148.

Lasden, M., "Recycling Displaced Dissastisfied Pros," *Computer Decisions*, Vol. 12, No. 1, 1980, pp. 36–48.

McLaughlin, R.A., "The Old Bugagoo, Turnover," *Datamation*, Vol. 25, No. 11, 1979, pp. 97–101.

Mobley, W.H., "Some Unanswered Questions in Turnover and Withdrawal Research," *Academy of Management Review*, Vol. 7, 1981, pp. 111–116.

Mobley, W.H., *Employee Turnover: Causes, Consequences, and Control*, Addison-Wesley Publishing Co., Reading, Mass., 1982.

Muchinsky, P.M. and Morrow, P.C.A., "Multi-Disciplinary Model of Voluntary Turnover," *J. Vocational Behavior*, Vol. 17, 1980, pp. 263–290.

Sloane, A.A., *Personnel—Managing Human Resources*, Prentice Hall, Inc., Englewood Cliffs, N.J., 1983.

Staw, B.M., "The Consequences of Turnover," *J. Occupational Behaviour*, Vol. 1, 1980, pp. 253–273.

Steers, R.M. and Mowday, R.T., "Employee Turnover and the Post Decision Accomodation Process," in B. M. Staw and L. L. Cummings, Eds., *Research in Organizational Behavior*, JAI Press, Greenwich, Conn., 1981.

Vroom, V.H., *Work and Motivation*, Wiley, New York, N.Y., 1964.

Wallace, M.J. and Szilagyi, A.D., *Managing Behavior in Organizations*, Scott Foresman and Company, Glenview, Ill., 1982.

Willoughby, T.C., "Computing Personnel Turnover: A Review of the Literature," *Computer Personnel*, Autumn, Vol. 7, 1977, pp. 11–13.

I'm OK—and You're Not

*The annual performance review is a harrowing
experience for both the employee and the boss.*

BY MARIE MONEYSMITH

It doesn't matter which side of the desk you're sitting on: Employee evaluations can cause even the most stouthearted to shrink from the encounter. For the employee under review it's an understandably tense experience—something akin to awaiting a tax audit. Much less considered, but equally acute, is the anxiety level of the executive delivering the verdict.

"It's very seldom that I run into a manager who says she enjoys giving reviews," says Myrt W. Webb, a Los Angeles-based performance management consultant with 30 years' experience. "That's basically because the review is so negatively oriented. It's a confrontational kind of thing, a punishment, and a negative reinforcer."

A perfect example of this is the experience of Kaye B., a public relations director, who still recalls the first review she ever gave. "The employee was a woman who had an abrasive personality when she was in a *good* mood," she explains. "She'd been in the department longer than I had and was older, too. I was so intimidated by the thought of confronting her with any criticism that I put the review off for three months, knowing that it held up her raise. By the time I faced her, she was furious: She told me I was incompetent and unfit to be a director. We spent an hour shooting the criticism back and forth. If I knew then what I know now, I would have caught her off guard by talking about some of her good points instead of launching into a full-scale attack."

The negative nature of the review is complicated by the fact that what seems like a simple enough task is really a highly sensitive undertaking. "Most people have no training at all in

Marie Moneysmith last wrote for
SAVVY *about job boredom (February 1984).*

evaluation, and they don't feel comfortable with it," explains Charles Leo, a Sherman Oaks, California-based seminar leader and a specialist in performance evaluation systems. "Consequently, they avoid the review. They may not do it and say they did. Or they may not confront unsatisfactory behavior at all and say only good things—which doesn't help anyone."

"As it is usually done, the performance review probably does more harm than good," adds Webb. "One study found that 84 percent of the performance reviews examined had resulted in an ego-deflating experience for the employee, the reviewer or both."

Fortunately, this situation can be improved. Here are some suggestions:

Make employee evaluations an ongoing process. First and foremost, an employer should never accumulate a list of things done wrong during the year and then dump it on the employee during the review. Instead, practice giving reviews on a day-to-day basis. "Get used to telling your employees they're doing something inappropriate *when* they're doing it, not six months later," Leo advises. "The review should be a formal recap of what you've already discussed with the employee."

Evaluate behavior, not personality: Karen K., a marketing executive with a major food distributor, still remembers the review she had seven years ago, when she was criticized for not being more ambitious. "I was so flabbergasted, I couldn't even respond," she recalls. "Not one word was said about my performance, which, as it turned out, was fine. The entire review was based on my supervisor's idea that I was too complacent."

"The biggest problem managers have is a tendency to identify an employee by what she *is* instead of what she *does*," explains Webb. "Employees are afraid of being told they lack initiative, because that's perceived as a character flaw, and it's frightening. But if you point out to them that they only fulfilled 80 percent of the sales quota, they can accept that and deal with it."

An excellent tool that helps in this area is an agreed-upon description of what is expected from the employee. "Everyone needs to know from day one what constitutes an acceptable job, and also what is considered above-acceptable work," explains Cathy Kachur, faculty member of the University of California at San Diego, San Diego State, and National University business extension schools. "Without those standards you can't evaluate effectively."

Be candid. Granted, it's not easy to look someone in the eye and tell her where she needs to improve. But doing anything less shortchanges your employee *and* you. "It's a disservice to lie to the person or to shade the truth and then write something else behind her back," says Leo. "Never lead someone to think she's doing a perfect job when she's not."

Lynn F., a traffic manager in an ad agency, recalls a traumatic dismissal from a job where she had received a favorable review only weeks before.

"My supervisor said everything was fine, and three weeks later I was fired. It made me extremely wary of being told I was doing well," she says. "I was like Chicken Little for the next few years. No matter what I was accomplishing I kept expecting the sky to fall."

One tactic that helps in being candid is to avoid accusatory language. Statements like "You're not being very professional about following through on projects" are hard to accept. But when the same basic idea is restated as "Let's talk about why that report fell through the cracks and what we can do about it," it becomes more palatable.

Be specific. There's nothing worse than telling someone she needs to improve without explaining precisely what, how, and why. Criticizing someone for being slow is not an effective way to evaluate behavior. But pointing out to an employee that she regularly misses important weekly deadlines and then helping her to look at the causes of that lateness and what can be done about them is. "Discuss the implications and consequences of what the person is doing," says Leo. "Let her know right where she stands if the behavior is improved, and if it's not, what the outcome might be."

Critique and compliment. Praise is one the most powerful motivators there is. The person under review should be reminded of her strengths as well as of her weaknesses. "It is crucial that you concentrate on the things the person has done well, because they're what you want more of," Webb stresses. "The more you focus on those things, the more the employee will tend to bring those about."

Again, specifics are in order. Instead of "You're doing fine," let employees know that they have an exceptional ability to handle customers or a talent for taking charge in difficult situations.

Don't be afraid of dialogue. One common mistake when it comes to evaluations is using the "get it over with" approach. "The manager calls the employee in, reads a laundry list of areas to work on, and announces that the meeting is over," says Leo. "As a result, the employee is left reeling. You must give meetings like this enough time for a decent dialogue between the two of you. And minimize interruptions, because it puts someone off if you're taking phone calls. You should be there for the person, to solicit and to listen to her responses." For the same reason, you should hold the review in territory where you feel comfortable (your office or a conference room), not in a restaurant or in the employee's office, where you're likely to become distracted from the purpose of the review.

A couple of other points: Try turning the tables occasionally. "Every so often, check in with your employees," suggests Leo. "Ask them what you are doing as a manager that helps them— and what you're doing that doesn't. But don't do it during the review or right afterward, because it looks like you're being apologetic or condescending."

If the traditional review is something you're having a hard time dealing with right now, Webb offers another tactic. "Let the employee score herself on how she honestly feels she has performed over the last six months or so. Then the two of you can discuss the scorecard.

"The first time managers do this," Webb continues, "they are afraid the employees will judge themselves excellent in every category. But the surprising thing is that most people are far more critical of their behavior than someone else would be. It sounds dubious, but this method has been used for some time now, and it turns out that the premise is valid. Managers report that they don't mind doing performance reviews with this system."

Finally, come to terms with the fact that an evaluation is a difficult process and you may never feel completely comfortable doing it. The important thing is that it gets results. Jeannette F. has been a supervisor in a large accounting firm for twelve years and has completed dozens of reviews. "My palms don't sweat as much, and my voice doesn't crack like it did the first time," she says. "That's because I've seen people respond to realistic, constructive, fair criticism, and become better employees. And I know now that even though it can be uncomfortable, in the long run, everyone benefits from an honest evaluation."

MANAGER

How to get people and technology to work together.

Al Davis, Editor

TRIAL BY FIRING: SAGA OF A ROOKIE MANAGER

I have managed small and large software organizations for twelve years. I have managed groups as large as 140 professionals. Although I have been in many stressful circumstances, one of my most emotional episodes occurred when I first became a manager in 1978. This is the story of my first management experience. I hope you can learn from my mistakes.

— Al Davis

I JOINED THE INDUSTRIAL WORLD for the first time in 1977. As a member of the technical staff, I was expected to work individually doing innovative software engineering. My employer, a large telecommunications research laboratory, expected me to do research, publish the results, and generally "carry the flag" at public forums.

One year after I joined the company, my department manager resigned. Upper management decided, in its infinite wisdom, to fill the vacant position with the "best technical person" in the department. (A mistake made by so many companies: They assume great technical contributors are great leaders as well.) The director, Richard (not his real name, of course), entered my office. He told me Thomas had resigned, and the company believed I was the right person to fill his shoes.

OFFER I COULDN'T REFUSE. I told Richard I was a computer specialist and had neither training nor interest in management. Richard explained the "facts" to me:

♦ I would be letting down the company if I did not accept.

♦ My career would be greatly enhanced if I had management credentials.

♦ I could make a lot more money in management.

♦ Richard would personally guide me through the job.

How could I refuse? I accepted the job. I would be a "one-of-the-guys" manager. I would not let being a manager interfere with the trust and friendship I had developed with my col-

leagues (now my employees). I was in for a rude awakening.

Richard coached me through a wide variety of challenges during those first few months. Although I was actually enjoying the job, it was obvious that some members of the department had decided to change their relationship with me. They expressed growing suspicion of my motives and growing resentment that I had been promoted instead of them. Whether this attitude resulted from their own perceptions or my altered behavior, I will never know.

FIRING LINE. In addition to many little problems, I had two large ones. First, there was George. A member of the technical staff, George regularly arrived at 10 or so in the morning and often left by three or four in the afternoon. When he was at work, he acted belligerently, refusing to attend review meetings. His work was late and of poor quality.

Then there was the recruitment problem. The department was trying to grow rapidly. We were interviewing two to three candidates a week and making numerous offers, but everyone was turning us down. I could not figure out what was wrong.

One day, Richard called me into his office. He said he had become aware of both problems from anonymous sources. (I *had* discussed my woes with a few peers and with the people in personnel, but I had not yet approached Richard.) He asked me what I thought we should do. I had no idea. He had ideas. Richard wanted me to fire George immediately. Also, he had heard a rumor that another member of my technical staff, Bob, was bad-mouthing me and the department to prospective employees — that's why everyone was turning us down. Richard asked me to verify this information.

At this stage in my management career, I knew very little about management. I did not know about coaching. I did not know about my obligation to do everything in my power to understand my employees and to help them overcome any barriers that prevented them from excelling. Without such knowledge, I was

> **MY VERY FIRST MANAGEMENT EXPERIENCE WAS A RUDE AWAKENING.**

Editors: Alan Davis
University of Colorado
1867 Austin Bluffs Pkwy., Suite 200
Colorado Springs, CO 80933-7150
adavis@vivaldi.uccs.edu

Winston Royce
TRW
1 Federal Systems Park Dr.
STC 7165U
Fairfax, VA 22030
(703) 803-5025/6
fax: (703) 803-5108

a pawn of my boss. He told me to fire George, so I prepared to fire George.

Richard spent the next two days with me, role-playing the firing. He taught me to say the words, "You are fired," in a way that left no room for mis-understanding. He taught me to tell the employee to leave at once and come back, supervised, on the weekend to pick up all personal belongings. (I guess this was to prevent him from "polluting" other employees.) He taught me to always fire an employee on the ground floor of the building. (I guess this was just in case the employee decided to jump out — or throw me out — the window.)

I planned to fire George at 4:00 p.m. At 3:00 p.m., he walked into my office and resigned. I still do not know if he had seen the writing on the wall, if there had been a leak, if he had planned all along to quit and his performance was

LOOKING BACK, I REALIZE HOW LITTLE I KNEW.

suffering because his heart was no longer in the job, or if it was just a coincidence. In any case, I felt fairly proud that problem number one had been solved.

LONELY AT THE TOP. With Bob, I decided to take a direct approach. I called him into my office, having not yet learned that communication is easier when meeting with employees in their offices. I asked him, "Do you know why none of our prospective new hires has accepted our offers?"

He responded without hesitation: "Of course! Why would anybody possibly want to work here? This place is awful." I asked him if he knew how the candidates learned of this. Once again he responded quickly, "Oh, I tell them. You don't want me to lie to them, do you?" I tried to explain to him that the state of the department and my managerial competence were matters of opinion, but my words fell on deaf ears. He made it clear that he felt it was his responsibility to tell everybody. For the next couple of days, news of my meeting with Bob spread. Many of the other employees dropped by to tell me how appalled they were by Bob's actions. They all told me I needed to fire Bob or the department would never grow.

I went to Richard and explained the situation. His answer was predictable. To Richard, surgery was always the preferred cure. Once again, he role-played with me for two days. I learned my lines. I memorized my responses to all possible comments Bob might make. Humanity, tenderness, caring, and thoughtfulness were not considered. We rehearsed a hard-hearted, brainless severing of the relationship.

I planned to fire Bob at 4:00 p.m. (on the first floor!). At 3:00 p.m., I stared at my door, expecting him to enter and resign. Silence. For one very long hour, I stared at the door, the floor, the walls. The only visitor was another employee, who dropped in to tell me that Bob was in the hallway bragging about how he was going to make me fail as a manager. That added

to my resolve.

Four o'clock came. I called Bob into the office and played my role exactly as rehearsed. I told him he was fired. I told him to leave the premises at once. It did not feel real. I was but an actor in a play. I felt a mile of insulation surrounding me, insulating me from Bob and this dreadful task.

But Bob didn't leave at once. Instead, he went to the department's other employees and told them he had been fired. Within the hour, a parade of employees began that was to continue for the next few days. They all said something like, "How dare you fire Bob?" I did not sleep for many weeks. I kept seeing Bob, his wife, his kids. I tortured myself with guilt about what I had done to this family.

I learned two very important lessons that day:

♦ Firing somebody is very painful.

♦ No matter how many people are "behind you" when you make a painful decision, you are all alone once you implement it.

EPILOGUE. Looking back, I realize how little I knew about management then. I now know that your most important resource as a manager is people. You have a responsibility to know them, understand them, respect them, and coach and train them so each of them can reach their full potential. You have a responsibility to work around problems, to predict and prevent them, to be proactive, and to "carry the water" (sometimes literally by fetching refreshments when your employees are working long hours). In short, good managers serve their employees, not the reverse.

Quality management requires you to maintain a fine balance between "representing your people" to your company and "representing your company" to your people. Just like every aspect of management style, you must vary your actions and words for each situation, deciding carefully based on the emotions, politics, and facts of the situation. Always listen to others' opinions before taking action. Above all, be as objective as possible, honest, and ethical. Be what you expect others to be — nothing less. ♦

Chapter 8

Directing a Software Engineering Project

1. Chapter Introduction

Directing a software engineering project is defined as all the management activities that deal with guiding and motivating employees to follow the specified plan. Once employees are trained and oriented, the manager has a continuing responsibility for monitoring their assignments, guiding them toward improved performance, and motivating them to perform to the best of their abilities.

Directing a software engineering project can be partitioned into nine general management activities (see Table 8.1). Each activity in the table is followed by its definition or an amplifying description.

REMEMBER! A GOOD LEADER CAN RESPOND TO ANY EMERGENCY.

Table 8.1. Directing activities for software projects.

Activity	Definition or Explanation
Provide leadership	Create an environment in which project members can accomplish their assignments with enthusiasm and confidence.
Build teams	Provide a work environment in which project personnel can work together toward common project goals. Set performance goals for teams as well as for individuals.
Facilitate communication	Ensure a free flow of correct information among project members.
Coordinate activities	Combine project activities into effective and efficient arrangements.
Supervise personnel	Provide day-to-day instructions, guidance, and discipline to help project members fulfill their assigned duties.
Motivate personnel	Provide a work environment in which project personnel can satisfy their psychological needs.
Delegate authority	Allow project personnel to make decisions and expend resources within the limitations and constraints of their roles.
Resolve conflicts	Encourage constructive differences of opinion and help resolve the resulting conflicts.
Manage changes	Stimulate creativity and innovation in achieving project goals.
Document directing decisions	Document decisions involving delegation of authority, communication and coordination, conflict resolution, and change management.

2. Chapter Overview

This chapter contains five short articles on directing and motivating. The activities listed in Table 8.1 were used as an outline for identifying articles on directing activities.

The article by Richard E. Boyatzis discusses leadership through the use of power. The article by Eugene Raudsepp is an excellent treatment of one of the most effective management tools: the delegation of authority. Gary Powell and Barry Posner propose that the most powerful motivating forces are excitement and commitment, and Ken Whitaker and Jac Fitz-enz discuss what motivates managers and data processors.

The final document, by John Adams and Nicki Kirchof from the Project Management Institute, provides an overview of conflict management for project managers.

3. Article Descriptions

The initial article, by Boyatzis, describes leadership and the effective use of power. Power is defined as the ability of one person to influence another. This article discusses the various types of power and power bases. It states that managers and leaders have the ability and authority to influence others. Along with this authority comes the responsibility to be more aware of this power and to use it effectively. Boyatzis believes that there are five important attributes that determine the quality of an individual's leadership ability.

Raudsepp's article, "Delegate Your Way to Success," elaborates on one of the most valuable tools in the manager's toolbox: *the ability to delegate authority and resources to another individual in order to accomplish the objectives of the organization.* The author defines delegation of authority as the passing on, by one person to another, of the accountability for a given task. He reports that "a manager who delegates with intelligence and consistent follow-up can accomplish far more than the manager who hugs to his (or her) bosom the tasks his subordinates should be doing." He also provides a list of reasons as to why managers do not delegate authority and demonstrates how that can be avoided.

The third article, by Powell and Posner, discusses

the use of staff excitement and commitment as keys to project success. The article begins with an interesting scenario in which a typical pre-employment interview is conducted to determine if the applicant being interviewed would be right for the given project. The manager must make the project goals the goals of the worker. The article describes five lessons and corresponding payoffs the project manager could employ to motivate people to become more excited and committed to a project.

The fourth article, by Whitaker on "Motivating and Keeping Software Developers," is a brand-new article published just in time to make this edition. Whitaker discusses what motivates software developers and what does not. He establishes some interesting rules for motivating software developers (he also reminds us that everybody who contributes to the delivery of a software product is a software developer, not just software engineers or programmers). He establishes the following "rules" for successfully motivating and keeping software project team members:

- Define the product delivery process and clear roles for the developers.

- Use rewards, not incentives, to motivate the developers.

- Set goals and career plans for the software developers on a regular basis.

- Compensate (pay) in accordance with the job market in order to keep them.

The sixth and last article, by Adams and Kirchof, is the first chapter from a monograph, Conflict Management for Project Managers, published by the Project Management Institute. This short overview states that conflicts will exist in all project environments, particularly a matrix project organization. As the authors state, "Severe conflict is the rule in projects where participants are 'loaned' to the project and thus must report to two bosses, namely their functional managers for evaluation and career development, and the matrix project manager for task assignment and work direction." Because conflict is natural, it must be managed and used to benefit both the project and the organization. (The complete monograph can be obtained from the Project Management Institute, 130 South State Road, Upper Darby, PA 19086.)

Leadership: The Effective Use of Power

Richard E. Boyatzis[1]

Introduction

Managers and leaders of all kinds are in positions of relatively high ability to influence other people. With this ability comes a responsibility to use power effectively and to be more aware of the process of influencing others.

Pause and think about what words and images come to mind in connection with the idea of power—words like *dictator* or *force*, images like *war* or *riots*, i.e., words and images with bad connotations. But power is not bad. If you can separate the use of power from the goals of power, you can see that the goals may be "good" or "bad," but the exercise is neither. Yet, the use of power can be judged; it can be found to be effective or ineffective. When people react to power as something "bad," they are usually saying either that the use of power was ineffective, or that the goals of power were questionable. In this paper we are concerned with the effectiveness of power, specifically power in a work-organization setting.

There are five key dimensions which determine the quality of an individual's leadership ability. An effective leader is one who can:

1. Make other people feel strong, help them to feel that they have the ability to influence their future and their environment;

2. build others' trust in the leader;

3. structure cooperative relationships rather than competitive relationships;

4. resolve conflicts by mutual confrontation of issues rather than by avoidance or forcing a particular solution, and

5. stimulate and promote goal-oriented thinking and behavior.

Power is the ability of one person to influence another. You can, for instance, give a person advice, offer him a job, or threaten to reduce his salary; however, a more subtle concept of influence than this is involved in that person's *reaction to you.* "Influence" occurs when he respects you, likes you, or desires to be like you and thereby opens the door to some control over him. Two psychologists, John French and Bertram Raven, have identified five types of power: reward power, coercive power, identification power, expert power, and legitimate power. When you influence someone, you are using one or more of these types of power. Before we turn to a discussion of the expression of leadership ability in the five ways we just mentioned, let us look briefly at the sources of power.

Reward Power

Reward power is based on one person's perception of another's ability to reward him. It increases in direct proportion to the amount of rewards a person sees another as controlling. Within an organizational setting, giving someone a raise or bonus, promoting him to a job with more responsibility, expanding his budget—these are highly visible uses of reward power to influence a person to do a better job for the organization; stopping by someone's work place just to say good morning is a more indirect use and, again, depends on his perception of your ability to provide whatever he considers as a tangible reward.

Coercive Power

Coercive power is based on one person's perception of another's ability to punish him. The strength of coercive power is proportional—not necessarily to the ability to punish but to the degree to which he perceives ability to punish. Where perception of this ability is faulty, some tension is likely until his perception and reality are in closer accord. A reprimand for not submitting a report on time, scorn for mistakes, denying a raise or promotion—these are examples of coercive power used to force performance of job activities closer to the stated standards. Let us add that withholding a promised reward or a standard reward of some sort is also a use of coercive power.

Expert Power

The total "amount" of knowledge is being increased by new technologies and communication advances; at least as important as this growth pattern in the *content* is the growth trends in our *awareness* of the complexities in our social and physical environments. As populations increase, new forms of relationships (and more of them) come into being so that men are more interdependent and at the same time are (or should be) more willing to deal with change and ambiguity. In this kind of situation (our situation, right now, 1970's) the traditional recourse to hierarchical authority can be dysfunctional and the recourse to expert authority, whether formally recognized in an organization structure or not, can pay off.

1. Richard E. Boyatzis is Director of Organizational Development for McBer and Company. Originally published in *Management of Personal Quarterly*, Bureau of Industrial Relations, University of Michigan, 1971. Reprinted with the author's permission.

Boyatzis, R.E. (1971)– "Leadership: The Effective Use of Power," from *Management of Personnel Quarterly*, Vol. 10, No. 3.

Expert power is based, then, in one person's perception that another's expertise, knowledge and approach can offer him a payoff he can't achieve another way.

Identification Power

Identification power follows from one's perception of similarity between himself and another, or his desire to be like another. The Horatio Alger stories (or Mickey Rooney's Andy Hardy series) influenced American youth to work hard; the ability of these models to influence youth was based on identification power: many youths had the same economically poor childhood, possibly even touched also with temptations to break the law. Executives who are respected and well liked derive their power from many sources—but their identification power should not be underplayed; many people are willing to be influenced by people whom they feel are friends and can be trusted at a personal level.

Legitimate Power

Legitimate power stems from three sources: shared value, acceptance of social structure, or the sanction of a legitimizing agent. In a manufacturing company, a foreman assigns work to line workers. They do the work because they accept the management structure of the company which makes it legitimate for the foreman to assign work. When a person influences another, he is using one or more of these types of power. Let us now examine what effects each of these types of power, when used by a leader, or manager, has on his subordinates.

Making People Feel Strong

An effective leader makes other people feel strong. He helps them to gain an ability to influence their future and their environment. When a person feels strong, he enjoys his work, feels personally involved, and is motivated to continue and improve work. This is because a person who feels strong is more aware of his surroundings; he feels that he is able to direct his life and wants to gain as much information about life potentials as possible. An ineffective leader makes other people feel weak. When a person feels weak, he is not in control of his fate; he works to the extent that others tell him to work. He feels no sense of pride in his occupational accomplishments.

In working with several plant facilities of a large manufacturing company, I found one plant director who made the managers working in his plant feel strong and another director who made his managers feel weak. The director of plant A felt that he had to know what was happening in all parts of the plant at all times. He insisted on having all managers file weekly reports of operations. Decisions concerning personnel and changes in operating procedures had to have his approval. Any problems were supposed to be brought to his attention immediately. The director of plant B had monthly

staff meetings with the managers in his plant. He asked them to take part in setting the production goals for their units. He wanted them to obtain his approval only for major changes in operating procedures, and gave them most of the responsibility for their units. He told them to feel free to ask for his help on any matters.

The managers working for the director of plant A did what they were told because the director used reward and coercive power to influence them. He used his source of legitimate power as a reminder to the managers that he could punish them if they did not follow his instructions. He treated them as if they were weak, and they felt weak in their organization.

The managers working for the director of plant B had control over what they did. They eagerly accepted responsibility for their activities. The director of plant B based most of his influence on expert power, (an expert in administration and their type of manufacturing). He asked the managers to see him as a resource for help. By collectively setting goals with the managers and maintaining a warm, friendly attitude, the director was able to base his influence on identification power rather than depending on the reward and coercive power that was a part of his position. The managers in his plant felt strong and enjoyed their work. The production records of the two plants were similar, while the level of job satisfaction of the employees was different. Plant A had a high rate of turnover at the managerial level. There was a sense of urgency in the organization which caused tension. The director imposed an attitude of "Hurry up and do the work, or else" in the plant. The managers in plant B were satisfied with their work. They felt a personal challenge that resulted in their working diligently and creatively. They had a tendency to treat their subordinates in the same honest and friendly manner as the director treated them.

For a manager to base his influence primarily on his ability to reward or punish an employee, he must create a climate in which he maintains control of evaluations and the dispensation of rewards. The workers are dependent on the manager for all recognition of accomplishment or quality work; this makes people feel powerless. Managers who explain how they judge quality work to their subordinates and enter evaluation discussion sessions with their employees are helping their subordinates to feel responsible for their own work. Their influence becomes based on shared values of quality work and self appraisal, or their expertise in evaluating the work, at the same time their subordinates feel strong.

Building Trust in the Leader

An effective leader makes his subordinates feel that they are part of the organization and share an involvement in the company's operations. If they have concern for each other as human beings and trust each other, they can work more efficiently for the group because it *needs* their contribution, and because they don't have to waste time worrying about what others are going to do to them.

The manager of a research and development department of an electronics company was not concerned with building trust. He held regular staff meetings for the members of the department during which they discussed their work and periodically he would meet with each project group to discuss their progress. The engineers accomplished their assignments, but with little creativity in their solutions to problems. Interviewing several of the engineers made it apparent that they were reluctant to come up with new ideas because they felt that the manager would take the credit with top management. They felt he handled assignments in a purely political manner. When asked what they thought his major occupational goal was, they responded bitterly "To get ahead in this company."

The manager *was* fighting a political battle with other departments of the company for funding. He wanted to expand the research staff (pay higher salaries) and attempt several new projects. In dealing with his subordinates, he tried to show his concern for the quality of their work and their job satisfaction, but something was missing. The engineers responded to the manager's requests only because of his ability to punish or reward them. Although he believed it was important to be an effective manager, he had not based his influence on types of power that would inspire trust. The engineers did not feel a part of the company and were not aware of the goals of the research department, and therefore, suspected the manager of using the group for his own needs. What could he have done to build the necessary trust in him and commitment to the company? Had he clarified the goals of the department and explained how he thought the group could contribute to the goals of the company, the engineers could have seen how his actions related to their common goals, not just his personal goals. By sharing the proceedings of the corporate management meetings he attended, he could have highlighted for the engineers the obstacles the department was facing. Being more open generally than he was would have led to an increase in trust. The manager's ability to influence his subordinates would have been based on identification and expert power rather than reward and coercive power: identification power because the engineers would have felt that he was concerned about them as individuals, expert power because by communicating to them the intricacies of being a manager, he would allow them to see that he had special abilities as an administrator.

Cooperating to Achieve Common Goals

An effective leader structures the relationships among his subordinates so that they cooperate to achieve the shared goals of the department, and so that they cooperate with other departments to achieve the company's goal. When a competition is created, ostensibly one party wins and one party loses. But even the winner loses, if he loses the trust or respect of those he was competing with. An effective manager will have his subordinates working with each other to accomplish their own objectives. People working together are more able to accomplish their personal goals than when operating alone.

An executive who structures a competition between managers to build an incentive runs a high risk. By structuring the situation so that one wins and others lose, one manager's incentive to work has increased slightly (at least during the competition, it might slack by the time that he is enjoying the fruits of winning) and the others lose incentive. The results may represent an aggregate loss of incentive.

A manager's influence is based in part on his legitimate power in the organization. If he tends to structure competitive relationships within his department, his subordinates will be dependent on him for rewards (winning) and punishment (losing); if he structures cooperative relationships, his subordinates will be less dependent on him (if at all) for the rewards of cooperating, and he will be able to establish his influence on more effective bases—the bases of identification power and expert power.

Confronting Conflicts Instead of Running Away

An effective leader handles conflict by confronting it with his subordinates. He does not avoid the issues by denying the problem exists, by forcing his solution without consulting the other individuals involved, or by smoothing over the problem ("It isn't too bad; we'll get it licked"). He knows he cannot solve a problem by running away from it.

One morning, the president of XYZ, inc. received a call from his vice president of marketing who said that production had not fulfilled its commitment to meet a deadline for the promotion of a new product, and that the V.P. for production had admitted that the commodity would not be ready for another two months. The president asked him to be in his office at one o'clock that afternoon; they could settle the issue at that time. He also called the V.P. of production and all other vice presidents that might be involved and asked them to attend. The meeting started with heated words between the vice presidents each blaming someone else for the delay. The president quieted everyone to say that there were two goals for the meeting: first, they had to decide what would happen now in terms of maintaining good client relationships; second, they would discover what actions caused the delay and correct procedures so that it would not occur a second time. He stressed the fact that they were at the meeting to correct errors, not to affix blame and punish someone for a mistake.

The questions concerning what to do next were quickly settled. As the discussions about what caused the delay began, each person moved to the edge of his seat, ready to defend his past actions. The president asked for a historical rundown of the development of the new product and the production schedule. As each point was made, the president was careful to check to see if there was a challenge to the information. If someone disagreed, he asked the group to arrive at a consensus as to what really happened. Although the meeting took three hours, the vice presidents began to work together. By mutually confronting differences of perception as to what had occurred, they arrived at an accurate picture of the incidents leading to the delay. Some of the problems which contributed to the delay were intentional expressions of disapproval for other vice presidents. Once these disagreements were faced openly, they could understand each other's position and come to agreement.

The president, in this case, based his initial ability to influence the vice presidents on his expert power as an administrator, although he also utilized his legitimate power as the executive of the company to call the meeting. Once the meeting began, he moved beyond a reliance on legitimate power to influence the process of the meeting by emphasizing that the purpose of meeting was to correct the situation and by not affixing blame or punishing people—in other words, he eliminated the expectation of his use of reward or coercive power in the meeting to leave the way open for his expert authority to hold sway.

Coaching Goal-Oriented Behavior

An effective leader/manager helps his subordinates by cooperating to set meaningful goals. People work more diligently and efficiently when they have a verbalized description, not just some vague "understanding" or generalized expectations of where they are going. When a person sets a goal, he starts to think of his means, how he intends to achieve that goal. When a manager sets goals unilaterally for his subordinates, he is taking responsibility for their actions, he is basing his influence on reward and coercive power. He must allow his subordinates to participate in setting their goals so they can feel responsible for actions, and he thereby shows a trust in their capabilities and a concern for hearing

their opinions and ideas. His ability to influence his subordinates is then based on legitimate power to some extent and on identification power to a greater extent.

Where Do You Stand?

Feeling powerless is a major cause of tension in organizations, for it hinders organizational performance. The ineffective use of power leaves people with the feeling that one person or a small group of people run their lives. This paper has examined five characteristics which facilitate the effective use of power.

If these ideas sound interesting (even if you do not totally agree with them), you may want to examine how your subordinates perceive your exercice of influence and your behavior on the five characteristics discussed. In talking to them, listen for statements or concerns they might have about gaining power or keeping power they now have. Are they defensive about work decisions they have made when you ask about them? Do they make decisions without checking with you? Do they come to you with new ideas? Do they ask for your opinion on their failures as well as their successes? Do they feel that they have some control over seeing their performance goals? Do they feel that their part of the organization is in a state of continual conflict with another part of the organization?

Asking you subordinates how they feel about your exercise of influence may lead to some rewarding discussion. It certainly will be an effective use of power.

DELEGATE YOUR WAY TO SUCCESS

by Eugene Raudsepp

Reprinted from *Computer Decisions*, March 1981, pp. 157–164.

Most managers accept the premise that the best way to get their work done is to make optimum use of subordinates. Yet most managers admit, when pressed, that they don't delegate as much as they should.

The problem is probably more emotional than procedural. Effective delegation is, admittedly, one of the most difficult managerial tasks. It depends on the finely woven inter-relationship between the manager,

subordinates, and top management. It depends on the type of company and its goals. It also depends heavily on trust and confidence. But the biggest problem is that many managers, as they climb the executive ladder, continue to feel that if they want a job done right, they have to do it themselves.

A manager who delegates with intelligence and consistent follow-up can accomplish far more than the manager who hugs to his (or her)

bosom the tasks his subordinates should be doing. The manager should devote most of his time and energies to planning, supervising, and delegating. That way, he'll contribute more than he might even from a superlative job on tasks that

The author is president of Princeton Creative Research, Inc., Princeton, NJ, and is author of the books Creative Growth Games *and* More Creative Growth Games.

his subordinates might not do quite as well. Inadequate delegation limits a manager's effectiveness because he gets bogged down in detail. Carried to its logical extreme, nondelegation can bring operations almost to a standstill.

When a manager delegates successfully, he changes his role from a performer to a trainer, motivator, and evaluator. Through delegation, he develops initiative and self-starting ability in his subordinates. He broadens them on their jobs, increases production, and improves morale. Most employees strive to live up to what is expected of them. They are willing and eager to face challenges, knowing that they are expected to deliver.

What is delegation?

Delegation is simply the passing on, by one person to another, of responsibility for a given task. But effective delegation involves a great deal more.

Delegation is not the abdication of responsibility; it is a continuing process. The manager should always be available to give advice and assistance when needed. He should make sure that needed resources are available, check performance at agreed-upon dates, and generally remain involved as advisor, leader, and sharer of responsibility. He should keep checks and controls on every task he delegates. The degree and kind of control varies, of course, with each subordinate. Some subordinates resent overcontrol and do a good job without frequent checking. Others need the security of formalized periodic reports on their assignments. Either way, there's no excuse for suddenly discovering that a subordinate is not handling his assignment properly.

Effective delegation requires patience and an initial investment of time. "I could have done the job myself twice over for all the time I spent explaining the work to him," is a frequently voiced excuse for not delegating. This may be true, especially with new subordinates. But the time expended is bound to pay off

According to author Eugene Raudsepp, it is important for managers to instruct subordinates to accomplish certain results, rather than to perform certain activities.

in the long run.

Delegation should not be viewed as an opportunity to get rid of unpleasant jobs or those in which the manager is not proficient. Also, it's a mistake to delegate too many meaningless or "make-work" jobs, especially during slack periods. This is a transparent maneuver—one that could lead the subordinate to look on all future delegated tasks as unimportant.

Helps employees develop

Ideally, delegation should help a subordinate develop not only his skills but also his judgment. He must understand what kinds of decisions he has the authority to make. If his authority to make decisions is too restricted, he will infer a lack of confidence in his ability to handle responsibility. If a subordinate is to be held accountable, he or she must have responsibility and authority with a minimum of interference. Effective delegation includes the right to make decisions and mistakes.

Delegation requires meticulous planning, particularly if complex or difficult projects are involved. It entails establishing priorities, setting objectives, and deciding how the project should be accomplished and

by whom, how long it should take, and how well it should be done. This type of planning isn't easy, and some managers tend to avoid it.

There are dozens of reasons why managers do not delegate. Those given here are the most common—but they can be avoided.

Lack of confidence in subordinates. Fearing unsatisfactory results, a manager may reason that a subordinate's judgment might be faulty, or that he will not follow through on his chores. He may feel that the subordinate is too young to command the respect and cooperation of older workers.

Such a manager feels that he must keep track of every detail to get a job done right. He may be a perfectionist who sets high personal standards of performance. He is often tempted to perform a job himself, feeling that he can do the work better and more quickly than his subordinates. Such an attitude must be shunned unless the lack of confidence in a subordinate is based on past experience.

Lack of self-confidence. Many managers, especially those recently promoted or hired, feel insecure in their jobs and in their relationship with their superiors, peers, and subordinates. They may feel overwhelmed by their new duties and responsibilities. As a result, they regress to the pleasant and familiar security and routine of the work they did before they became managers.

Poor definition of duties. A manager must have a clear understanding of his responsibilities and authority. Obviously, he can delegate only those responsibilities that have been assigned to him. If he is unsure of the nature of his own job, he can hardly be expected to delegate properly.

Aversion to risk-taking. Delegation involves making calculated risks. Even with clear communication and instructions, proper controls, and trained subordinates, something will eventually go wrong.

Fear of subordinates as competitors. This frequently leads to open and excessive criticism of a subordinate's work, thwarting or playing down his achievements, pitting him against another subordinate to put him in a bad light, ignoring or side-tracking his suggestions and ideas, and concealing his talent or misusing it in low-skill jobs.

An inflated self-image. Some managers believe that they are the pivot upon which all their department's operations turn. This type of manager, as a rule, checks on all details himself. He makes all the decisions, and considers his way of doing things the only right one. He goes to great pains to hire people who reinforce his image of himself. To protect his "kingpin" posture, he makes certain, through selective communication, that only he gets the big picture of what is going on.

The effect that the "indispensable" manager has on his subordinates can be devastating. He fosters only dependence. Whatever self-confidence and individuality his subordinates may have had are soon obliterated; they become automatons who follow only directions and never initiate ideas of their own. Eventually, stronger subordinates become restive. They realize that their growth potential is severely stunted and that the only wise course of action is to resign and go on to someplace where they can grow.

Equating action with productivity. A manager may be hyperactive. Such a person is often afraid that delegation might leave him with nothing to do. Quite commonly, a hyperactive manager complains constantly about overwork, and subordinates have a difficult time getting to see him.

Fear of appearing lazy. Delegation might be construed, by both superiors and subordinates, as trying to avoid working. This can be a sensitive point. A manager, particularly a new one, or one who is unsure of his own talents, can also feel that it is a sign of weakness to need subordinates' help to keep up with workloads.

Poor example. A common reason a manager does not delegate is that his superior did not delegate. The reasoning is "If my boss got to where he is with his style of leadership, why shouldn't I copy him?"

Many young or newly promoted managers who have been held back by their own superiors in the past do not delegate because they want to keep the reins in their own hands, as a protective device.

Analyzing subordinates

A prime requisite for effective delegation is a comprehensive inventory of subordinates' capabilities: skills, qualifications, experience, special talents, interests, motivations, attitude, potential, and limitations.

Such analyses, which should include meetings with subordinates to get their own estimation of their abilities and aspirations, enables the manager to decide to which subordinates he can delegate immediately, and which need further coaching and experience.

Here are a few facts to make delegation easier for all concerned:
● Be sure you and your supervisor agree on what your job is. Take all the initiative you can without encroaching on others' rights. A narrow definition of your job restricts you.

● Be sure your subordinates understand what you expect them to do. The simplest way to delegate is to tell your subordinates what authority you reserve for yourself. It may help to list matters you want discussed with you before any action is taken.
● Prepare written policies your subordinates can use to guide their decisions. A soundly conceived and clearly understood set of policies lets subordinates make decisions and take action with confidence.
● Be humble enough to admit that someone else may be able to do the job as well as you can.

● Make as many subordinates as possible directly responsible to you.

This will help you communicate, make decisions, take action, and exercise control.
● Make subordinates responsible for accomplishing results rather than activities. Once the expected results are spelled out, the subordinate should be able to choose methods he will use in accomplishing them.
● Reward those who get things done. Subordinates will accept responsibility and actively participate in accomplishing objectives only if they feel that rewards go to those who perform. The rewards for being right must always be greater than the penalties for being wrong.
● Distinguish between rush jobs and the less immediate but more important things you have to do; spend more time on the important tasks than the trivial ones.

Self-questioning can ease the decision of what and how much to delegate:
● How important is the decision? Are the stakes so high that a mistake cannot be tolerated? If so, the matter probably cannot be delegated successfully.
● Even though you are more competent than your subordinate, are you as close to the problem? Is your decision more apt to be right?
● Does your failure to delegate mean that you are not giving adequate attention to other more important parts of your job?
● Does your failure to delegate mean you are not developing your subordinates? Are they capable of being developed? If not, can they be transferred or replaced?
● What do top managers really expect of you? Are they measuring you principally by results, so that your decisions must be right? Do they really expect you to develop people?

The art of delegation is a difficult one to learn, but it's a vital management skill. If you do it right, you'll improve employees' morale, get more work done, and ease the burden on yourself.   □

How Much Is Enough?

You can get a good idea of whether you are delegating as much as you should by answering the following questions. The more "Yes" answers you give, the more likely it is that you're not delegating enough.

- Do you often work overtime?
- Do you take work home evenings and on weekends?
- Is your pile of unfinished work increasing?
- Do you find that daily operations are so time-consuming that you have little time left over for planning and other important matters?
- Do you feel you have to have close control of every detail to have the job done right?
- Do you frequently find yourself bogged down, trying to cope with the morass of small details?
- Do you frequently have to postpone long-range projects?
- Are you harassed by frequent unexpected emergencies in your department?
- Is a good part of your working day spent on tasks your subordinates could do?
- Do you lack confidence and respect for your subordinates' abilities to shoulder more responsibilities?
- Do you understand what your responsibilities and authority are?
- Do you find yourself irritable and complaining when the work of your group doesn't live up to expectations?
- Do you find that your subordinates never show any initiative?
- Are friction and low morale characteristic of your work group?
- Do your subordinates defer all decisions on problems to you?
- Are policies to guide your subordinates in making decisions ambiguous?
- Do you instruct your subordinates to perform certain activities, rather than to accomplish certain results?
- Have subordinates stopped coming to you to present their ideas?
- Do operations slow down considerably when you are away from your job?
- Do you feel that you're abdicating your role as a manager if you have to ask your subordinates' assistance in order to complete your projects?
- After delegating a project, do you breathe down the subordinate's neck?
- Do you believe that your status and the salary you earn automatically mean that you have to be overworked?

Excitement And Commitment: Keys To Project Success

Gary N. Powell
University of Connecticut
Barry Z. Posner
University of Santa Clara

In *The Soul of a New Machine,* the Pulitzer Prize-winning account of the design of a new computer by a special project group at Data General, Tracy Kidder describes the rituals which the company used to get people excited and committed to the project. Almost every member of the project team passed through the initiation rite called "signing up." By signing up for the project, a person agreed to do whatever was necessary for the project to succeed. This could mean forsaking of family, friends, hobbies, and all vestiges of a non-work life until the project was completed. (When, of course, a new round of getting people signed up would be started again for the next project.)

The reasons behind the signing-up ritual for the company are simple. When workers have made this kind of commitment to a project, they are no longer coerced to work on it. Instead, they have volunteered.

Signing up began with the hiring of new recruits for the project. (Old hands who had been through the signing up process before were dealt with differently.) Applications were reviewed for indications that the applicant may or may not be inclined to sign up. For example, one man who listed "family life" as his main avocation was judged to be giving a sign that he may not be willing to sign up and was turned away. When an application provoked initially favorable reactions, the applicant was invited for an interview.

The following passage describes how Carl Alsing, one of the project managers, would conduct a typical interview. Alsing's thoughts during the interview are in parentheses.

Alsing would ask the young engineer, "What do you want to do?"

Exactly what the candidate said—whether he (most applicants were male) was interested in one aspect of computers or another—didn't matter. Indeed, Alsing didn't care if a recruit showed no special fondness for computers; and the fact that

an engineer had one of his own and liked to play with it did not argue for him.

If the recruit seemed to say in reply, "Well, I'm just out of grad school and I'm looking at a lot of possibilities and I'm not sure what field I want to get into yet," then Alsing would usually find a polite way to abbreviate the interview. But if the recruit said, for instance, "I'm really interested in computer design," then Alsing would prod. The ideal interview would proceed in the following fashion.

"What interests you about that?"

"I want to build one," says the recruit.

(That's what I want to hear,' thinks Alsing. "Now I want to find out if he means it.")

"What makes you think you can build a major computer?" asks Alsing.

"Hey," says the recruit, "no offense, but I've used some of the machines you guys have built. I think I can do a better job."

("West and I have a story that we tell about Eagle machine. But I want to hear this guy tell me part of that story first. If he does, if there's some fire in his eyes—I say 'in his eyes', because I don't know where it is, if it's there, it's there—but if he's a little cocky and I think we probably want this person, then I tell him our story.")

"Well," says Alsing, "we're building this machine that's way out in front in technology. We're gonna design all new hardware and tools." ("I'm trying to give him a sense of 'Hey, you've finally found in a big company a place where people are really doing the next thing.'") "Do you like the sound of that?" asks Alsing.

"Oh, yeah," says the recruit.

("Now I tell him the bad news.")

"It's gonna be tough," says Alsing. "If we hired you, you'd be working with a bunch of cyn-

This article is reprinted from *Project Management Journal,* December 1984, with permission of the Project Management Institute, 130 South State Road, Upper Darby, PA 19082, a worldwide organization of advancing the state-of-the-art in project management.

ics and egotists and it'd be hard to keep up with them."

"That doesn't scare me," says the recruit.

"There's a lot of fast people in this group," Alsing goes on. "it's gonna be a real hard job with a lot of long hours. And I mean long hours."

"No," says the recruit, in words more or less like these. "That's what I want to do, get in on the ground floor of a new architecture. I want to do a big machine. I want to be where the action is."

"Well," says Alsing, pulling a long face. "We can only let in the best of this year's graduates. We've already let in some awfully fast people. We'll have to let you know."

("We tell him that we only let in the best. Then we let him in.") [6]

Data General went to great lengths to get an unusually high degree of commitment to the computer design project, and for the most part they succeeded. You will not always get this kind of commitment to a project, and furthermore you may not need it to as great an extent. However, you will need to make sure that your project team is *behind* the project, all working in the same direction to achieve the project's goals rather than *in front of* the project, acting as a roadblock to progress. For this to be accomplished, people need a lot more than goals and objectives laid out before them and being told what to do. They need to feel like they are participating in an exciting venture, guided by a *shared vision* of how their joint efforts will make them successful.

The Shared Vision as a Key to Excellence

McKinsey & Company, a management consulting firm, recently conducted a study of American companies which were judged to be excellent in performance. In their best-selling report of the study, *In Search of Excellence,* Thomas Peters and Robert Waterman, Jr. found eight basic practices to be characteristic of successfully managed companies. In consulting the practice which might be most important, they said:

Let us suppose that we were asked for one all-purpose bit of advice for management, the truth that we were able to distill from the excellent companies research. We might be tempted to reply, "Figure out your value system. Decide what your company *stands for* [9]."

Excellent companies have clearly articulated beliefs about how they intend to run their businesses, which lead to a shared vision among employees that adherence to these beliefs will bring them success. For Caterpillar Tractor, the core belief is "24-hour parts service anywhere in the world," reflecting a high commitment to the prompt meeting of customer needs. At DuPont, the credo "better things for better living through chemistry" demonstrates a belief that product innovation is most important. The slogan "IBM means service" expresses the high customer service orientation of that company [5]. These phrases may sound like instant cliches, suitable for hanging on office walls or bulletin boards but not much else. Yet, to the contrary, they act as powerful motivating devices for thousands of employees in these companies as expressions for core beliefs.

Project managers can also promote shared visions among project team members. At Data General, the shared vision was to design a state-of-the-art computer. For a new sports-oriented cable television channel, the shared vision among program planners could be to broadcast a majority of the games of local teams ("The *best* coverage of local sports is on CABL"); to cover an eclectic range of sports such as on ABC-TV's Wide World of Sports, which pursued this vision with great success for many years ("See *all* the sports on CABL"); or to achieve excellence in technical coverage of sports ("Sports are *better* on CABL").

All of the above alternatives are plausible goals for the project teams involved. However, we have not yet identified what turns ordinary goals into shared visions which contribute to the success of the project. In other words, we need to address the question:

How can employees be stimulated to identify with project goals to the extent that they expend extra effort to achieve the goals?

This question can be answered in two ways. One way is to describe what project managers can do to promote the forming of shared visions. (The signing up ritual of Data General provides us an initial clue as to what may work.) The other way is to describe what people are looking for in their jobs that leads them to commit themselves to project goals. Since every management strategy ultimately is based on understanding of people, let us first examine why people do what they do on the job, or what motivates their work-related behavior. Then we will discuss how project managers can put this knowledge to use.

Why People Do What They Do

Management theories which attempt to explain why

people do what they do have gone through several stages of evolution. Before the twentieth century, there was no collection of thought called "management theory" at all. Nonetheless, management took place and people occasionally wrote down their thoughts about how to get others to go along with their wishes. For example, the Italian statesman Machiavelli wrote in *The Prince,* published in 1532, on whether it was better for a prince to be loved or feared:

> The reply is, that one ought to be both feared and loved, but as it is difficult for the two to go together, it is much safer to be feared than loved. Men have less scruple in offending one who makes himself loved than one who makes himself feared; for love is held by a chain of obligation which, men being selfish, is broken whenever it serves their purpose; but fear is maintained by a dread of punishment which never fails [7].

Not surprisingly, the term Machiavellianism has been handed down over the years to refer to political opportunism and denial of the relevance of morality in political affairs.

One of the first people to write explicitly about management was Frederick Taylor, who argued that management should be made into an exact science. Taylor was the grandfather of the time and motion study approach to management. He argued that, for management to be doing its job, work should be broken down into discrete, highly programmed segments which could be performed repetitively without variation by different workers. Max Weber complemented Taylor's theories by advocating that bureaucracy, or management by set rules and procedures, was the best form of organization. Thus the Taylor-Weber "rational" school of thought, which prevailed from about 1900 to 1930, was primarily concerned with rules about such issues as division of labor and optimum spans of control (numbers of people who should be working for a given manager). If they were speaking to today's project managers, Taylor and Weber would stress the establishment of distinct tasks for project team members, with assigned times and specified procedures by which the efforts of team members would be coordinated. The same would apply for managerial jobs if there were more than one project being managed.

An important challenge to this approach made by Elton Mayo ushered in the next stage of management thought. Mayo started out in the Taylor tradition by conducting experiments on the effects of various workplace characteristics on worker productivity at a Western Electric plant in Hawthorne, New Jersey. When the lighting was turned up for one experimental group of workers, productivity went up also. When the lighting was turned back down so that the effects of other factors could be tested, productivity went up again! Mayo concluded that the amount of attention paid to employees was an important influence on worker productivity [10]. The Hawthorne experiments prompted what was called the "human relations" school of thought, which prevailed from about 1930 to 1960. Speaking to project managers, Mayo would emphasize the establishment of open communications between themselves and project team members, so that employees would feel that management was concerned for them and cared that their needs were met.

In the early 1950's, Abraham Maslow extended the human relations approach to a "human potential" movement. Maslow proposed a hierarchy of human needs, ranging from the "lower order" needs of food, shelter, and economic security through "middle order" needs for social relationships and ego satisfaction up to the pinnacle of self-actualization needs, which could only be satisfied when all other needs were satisfied first. To Maslow, the healthy person was one who was operating at the top of the hierarchy—creative, autonomous, and virtually independent of others [8]. (Douglas McGregor's "Theory X versus Theory Y" promoted essentially the same view of human potential.)

Maslow's theory was basically self-oriented, in that it seemed to propose that people can best be self-fulfilled when they stand alone, rather than when they work in conjunction with others. As such, although it was developed two decades earlier, it provided perfect justification for what Tom Wolfe called the "me decade" of the 1970's. Daniel Yankelovich, in his early 1980's study of American attitudes and values over several decades, questioned this orientation. He identified the desire in people to *identify with* and *commit themselves* to something more than just satisfaction of their own needs. According to Yankelovich, individuals today are looking for something to believe in which is larger than themselves and which embraces other people besides themselves [12]. His exhortation to project managers would be to provide the opportunity for individuals to satisfy these needs by promoting visions of success and fulfillment which require coordinated effort and can be shared with other people.

We have reviewed several theorists' views of why people do what they do. The rational approach of Taylor and Weber stressed employees' presumed desires for predictability in their jobs and being told what to do. It basically regarded workers as similar to industrial machinery, with assigned tasks that were designed and regulated by others. The human relations approach of Mayo emphasized individuals' desires for being on the receiving end of managerial attention, satisfying their needs for social interaction and ego gratification. The human potential approach of Maslow regarded these previous approaches as addressing lower order and middle order needs, respectively; once these needs were satisfied, individuals were expected to pursue the higher order need of self-fulfillment or self-actualization. Maslow's theory focused on the "self" aspect of self-fulfillment. What can be called the "fulfillment with others" approach of Yankelovich focused on the needs for individuals to share in an experience of commitment with other people.

As you have probably noticed, the progression in these theories has been towards the shared visions approach which McKinsey & Company found characteristic of excellent American companies. Little mention is made in the rational or human relations approaches of the satisfaction and excitement which can come from visions of organizational success which are shared with other employees. However, Yankelovich incorporates elements of both of these approaches. He suggests that employees need guidance in coordinating their efforts, but that they also need to be encouraged to identify with a shared vision of how success can be achieved.

Now that we have a better understanding of the needs which motivate today's workers, let us look at what project managers can do to meet these needs.

Using People's Intelligence

The personal computer business was a major growth industry in the early 1980's. More than 150 competitors were fighting to carve out a niche for themselves in the rapidly changing market where demand was doubling every year. Technological advances which improved the state of the art and enabled computers to be assembled at lower costs were commonplace. IBM was a late-comer to the personal computer business, belatedly introducing its entry in August, 1981, at a time when Tandy (Radio Shack) and Apple Computer, Inc. were fighting for the market lead. Only two years later, *Business Week* announced that the battle for market supremacy was over and that the winner was IBM. The company once known solely for its large main-frame computers had taken over 26% of the annual market for personal computers in 1983 and was expected to

account for half of the world market in 1985 [3].

Texas Instruments (TI) had pioneered the home computer market four years previously and was focusing on the market for smaller, non-business oriented computers in 1983. However, its home computer operation lost a stunning $183 million in the second quarter of 1983, causing TI to report its first quarterly loss ever. Whereas, on April 21, 1983, the president of TI had predicted that 1983 would be a significantly *better* year than 1982, a June 10 news release predicted that 1983 would be a significantly *poorer* year for the company than 1982 [4].

What caused these differences in fortunes for the two companies? A large part of the answer lies in how project teams were created and managed. IBM set up the task force responsible for what was to become the company's personal computer (PC) as an independent business unit, not subject to the same rules which required most of its product design teams to account for their every move. As one of the PC designers put it, "If you're going to compete with five men in a garage, you have to do something different." What IBM did differently was to grant the team considerable autonomy to make its own decisions, as if it was a small business in itself rather than submerged in a larger company. As a result, some of the decisions made were contrary to IBM's traditional practices. For example, instead of using IBM-manufactured circuitry, the PC used a microprocessor made by another manufacturer as its heart. Upon granting the project team full responsibility for the design of the computer, IBM was delighted to find that a highly successful product which challenged the conventional company wisdom emerged.

At Texas Instruments, project management was a different story altogether. The company had been considered excellent according to McKinsey & Company's criteria. Peters and Waterman reported in *In Search of Excellence* that, according to TI Chairman Mark Shepherd, Jr., TI had a "fluid, project-oriented environment." However, in 1983, *Business Week* found that TI was operating more by a top-down, autocratic approach to decision-making than by placing responsibility in autonomous project teams. Project managers were demoralized when their proposals for product development, capital expenditures, and marketing strategy were consistently overruled at higher levels. Hence, the company was slow to recognize and respond to changes in the minicomputer market, suffered significant losses and eventually abandoned the market entirely.

What was the difference between the IBM and the TI approaches to the computer business? The major difference was that IBM was granting its project teams the freedom to make full use of people's intelligence. Project teams had relatively few constraints placed on the decisions they could make. They did not have *complete* latitude—for example, the team given the task to design a personal computer would not have lasted very long if it decided instead to design a new main-frame computer which could compete directly with IBM's existing product line. Instead, the team was given a fairly broad goal to be achieved (design a personal computer) with little further direction as to how to achieve it. In contrast, TI was *not* making full use of the intelligence of project team members. The company was setting performance goals to be achieved but was giving people little freedom to decide how they would go about achieving the goals. The end results of these two opposite approaches were high performance and morale at IBM, and low performance and morale at TI.

Many other examples can be cited to demonstrate that, to be successful, companies and project teams are organizing their efforts to make use of people's intelligence. The recent emphasis on quality circles, which has been borrowed from Japanese management, stems from the recognition that employees on the line often have good ideas about how to improve productivity which managers do not have. At higher levels, General Motors has been totally revamping the way it develops new cars, by centering experimental operations on "companies within a company" with the power to coordinate new car projects from design to marketing; this approach is replacing the older, design by committee approach in which responsibilities were divided among five divisions [2]. Even American Telephone & Telegraph Co., which recently underwent the divestiture of its 22 Bell operating companies, is recognizing the need to have more autonomous project groups to compete in the rapidly changing telecommunications industry.

In short, project teams achieve the best results when people have the chance to contribute their own ideas to the project and, when possible, responsibility for making important decisions based on their jobs. These conditions give project team members the opportunity to experience the fulfillment in their ideas with others which Yankelovich identified as a critical motivator for today's workers.

Of course, these conditions do not *guarantee* project success. When project team members are given the chance to use their collective intelligence, they may misread the market they are trying to penetrate, underestimate the demands of the task they are trying to accomplish, or commit any of a host of other possible errors which subtract from the success of the project. However, if project team members appear to have the necessary skills, aptitudes, and experience to make intelligent decisions, they are best motivated, and their talents are best taken advantage of, when they are given the chance to rise or fall based on their own decisions and efforts.

Rewarding Positive Behavior

So far, we have argued that considerable autonomy and responsibility should be granted to project teams and distributed among project team members in order to get best results. We have not yet said anything, though, about how project managers should respond to employees' performance, good or bad, as the project is being completed. For this, we need to introduce another critical aspect of getting people excited and committed—the rewarding of positive behavior.

B.F. Skinner observed that positive reinforcement of behavior, or the provision of rewards for jobs well done, contributes to the behavior being repeated. On the other hand, negative reinforcement of behavior, or the threat of punishment for jobs poorly done, discourages the behavior but does not necessarily contribute to someone's engaging in the desired behavior [11]. For example, criticizing telephone directory assistance operators when their average times per customer call are high could encourage operators to cut off requests for information prematurely rather than to be more efficient in their conveying of the necessary information.

Some companies have taken the notion of rewarding positive behavior and expanded it into elaborate systems of rites, rituals, and ceremonies. Mary Kay Cosmetics conducts "seminars" for salespeople at its Dallas headquarters which are actually reward-giving extravaganzas. On different awards nights, employees identified as heroes parade across the stage in bright red jackets to tell stories about how they achieved success in the Mary Kay traditions. Gifts of cars, diamonds, mink coats, etc., are given to top salespeople. The culmination of the extravaganza comes with the crowning of Queens (supersaleswomen) in each product category.

Another company presents plaques called "Attaboys" to reward outstanding individual performance. When an "Attaboy" is to be presented, the worker's manager rings a bell and all employees in the area drop whatever they are doing to witness the presentation of the plaque. When someone has received five "Attaboys," they are eligible for a "Gotcha" which is personally signed by the head of the company's U.S. operations [5]. In the same vein, the Los Angeles Dodgers baseball team instituted a "Mr. Potato Head" award during its 1983 season which was given to the best performer after every ballgame. The award lightened the clubhouse atmosphere as well as rewarded good performance and was seen to contribute to the team's winning of its division that year.

Such ceremonies border on the silly side, for sure. However, they provide the opportunity for people to laugh at themselves, which is always healthy. More importantly, they provide rewards for positive behavior which, as Skinner noted, almost always increase the probability that similar behavior will occur in the future.

Some people make the mistake of assuming that the only kind of reward employees will respond to is monetary. Although increased salary or bonuses certainly are appreciated, people's need for and liking of rewards extends much further. Verbal recognition of performance in front of one's peers, and visible manifestations of awards such as certificates, plaques, and other tangible gifts also serve as powerful rewards for people. They also provide a way of encouraging *shared* visions of success far more than individual monetary rewards. Project managers who are always looking for ways of rewarding positive behavior, thereby helping employees to share some of the psychological benefits of seeing themselves as winners, will contribute in an important way to the success of their projects.

When to Start

It is desirable that the building of commitment to the project take place as soon as possible. In the case of new recruits to be assigned to the project, this means at the time of hiring. (Recall how the signing up ritual was incorporated by Data General into its employment interviews for new computer engineers.) For people who already are employees, this means early in the planning stage of the project. The intelligence of project teams can be utilized best if their ideas are included in the plans for the project as well as the project's execution. Hence, the members of IBM's personal computer product development team were basi-

cally told to go and design a personal computer, while being left to develop whatever plans they needed for their work by themselves.

If employees are excited and committed to the project at its onset, they will be primed to give their utmost to the project throughout its duration. Then the job for the project manager becomes not to coerce employees into performing, but instead to act as a facilitator helping them in their efforts to produce a high quality output for the project on or in advance of schedule. Efforts to build a sense of commitment to the project among project team members in its early stages will most certainly pay off in the long run.

Lessons for the Project Manager

The lessons (and payoffs) for the project manager in getting people excited and committed are many:

1. *Create exciting possibilities* by giving project managers the BIG picture and by promoting the meaningfulness of their efforts. People need to know, at the onset, not only *what* they are trying to accomplish but for *whom* and *why*. To do otherwise is to foster the alienation and apathy of "it's just another job" or, to borrow from Gertrude Stein, "a job is like a job is like a job is like a job." Remember the ancient Greek tale of Sisyphus, who was condemned to spend eternity pushing a boulder up the mountainside. Upon arriving at the top, the boulder tumbled down the mountainside and Sisyphus began his lonely task again.

2. *Inspiring the shared vision* results from creating exciting possibilities. As Wayne Rosing, the design engineer on Apple's LISA project, put it, "It was a dream. And the dream was the major force behind all our efforts." Inspiration is fostered by the project manager's clarity of focus *and* perspective. The schedule, however important it is, is only the means to an end—the end must be worthy of our efforts. Or as Don Quixote Qidte, the man of LaMancha, told his project team, "It's a quest...to follow a dream." When there are shared goals the project team members are likely to be highly committed, loyal, productive, willing to put in long hours, and less hassled and tense.

3. *Increase visibility* of the project team's efforts. Part of the magic behind scheduling documents is that they are public and make visible the member's commitment. They also provide information about critical interdependencies, without which there is little incentive to cooperate or feel a shared sense of

responsibility and fate. Visibility may be the force which holds most major religions together as congregants are asked to "believe." Project managers need to "get religion" for their team by making visible and public the project team members' efforts for one another.

4. *Empower participants* to be effective by utilizing their intelligence and natural drive. After all, do you really know any healthy person who tries to be ineffective (even though at times even the best of us will fail)? Empowering others requires giving them the resources and authority necessary to make things happen. Many successful project managers discover that this does not result in a zero-sum game. On the contrary, as one senior project manager exclaimed, "Since I've started giving it [power] away, I've never had so much authority." This premise has been well tested: Effective managers find that empowering others — sharing their power and responsibility — results in more committed and responsible subordinates. Putting power in the hands of others is like investing money in a savings account: It is guaranteed to pay interest.

5. *Spread the Attaboys around* is another successful investment strategy for project managers. In our seminars we have never heard project team members say they were "thanked enough" by their managers. Among the many purposes that milestones serve should be marking time for celebration! Whether it is one hop at a time, like for Don Bennett, the first amputee to climb (hop) to the top of Mt. Rainer (14,400 feet high) or Neil Armstrong's "one small step for a man, one giant step for mankind," the result is the same: People want to be effective, people want to be noticed, and they want to be appreciated. One key characteristic of the excellent companies research is their respect for the individual and their almost childlike exuberance for hoopla around accomplishment. In the words of the *One Minute Manager*, "Find something they're doing right, and praise it right away."[1] Spreading the good word about the accomplishments of your project team members is likely to increase their visibility and to enhance their own power and reputation. Some of the credit will inevitably find its way back to their project manager and his/her ability to get people excited and committed.

There is an irony in all of this, however. Project managers who understand these lessons and adroitly apply these principles are not likely to remain very long as managers of their current projects if they work in a hierarchical organization. Instead, they are likely to be promoted to project manager positions with even larger responsibilities. Excitement and commitment, keys to *project* success, are also keys to *project manager* success!

References

1. Blanchard, K. & Johnson, S. *The One Minute Manager.* New York: Morrow, 1982.
2. GM Overhauls the Way New Cars Take Shape. *Business Week,* September 19, 1983, 114Q-114R.
3. How the PC Project Changed the Way IBM Thinks. *Business Week,* October 3, 1983, 86, 90.
4. Texas Instruments Cleans Up Its Act. *Business Week,* September 19, 1983, 56-61.
5. Deal, T.E. & Kennedy, A.A. *Corporate Cultures: The Rites and Rituals of Corporate Life.* Reading, MA: Addison-Wesley, 1982.
6. Kidder, T. *The Soul of a New Machine.* New York: Avon Books, 1981, 65-66.
7. Machiavelli, N. *The Prince.* New York: New American Library, 1952, 90.
8. Maslow, A.A. *Motivation and Personality.* New York: Harper & Row, 1954.
9. Peters,T.J. & Waterman, R.H., Jr. *In Search of Excellence: Lessons from America's Best-Run Companies.* New York: Harper & Row, 1982, 278.
10. Roethlisberger, F.J. & Dickson, W.J. *Management and the Worker.* Cambridge, MA: Harvard University Press, 1939.
11. Skinner, B.F. *Beyond Freedom and Dignity.* New York: Knopf, 1971.
12. Yankelovich, D. *New Rules: Searching for Self-Fulfillment in a World Turned Upside Down.* New York: Random House, 1981.

Dr. Gary N. Powell is an Associate Professor of Management and Organization at the University of Connecticut. He has published over 30 articles in professional journals and made over 50 presentations at professional meetings. In addition to project management, Dr. Powell's current research interests include leadership, power, recruitment, organizational change, and women and men in management.

Dr. Barry Z. Posner is an Associate Professor of Management at the Graduate Schools of Business and Administration, University of Santa Clara. He has published over 40 articles in a variety of professional journals, has recently completed two books for the American Management Association, and has planned and participated in management development programs for several major organizations. In addition to project management, Dr. Posner's training programs include leadership, motivation, group dynamics, conflict management, team building, and communications.

***

Motivating and Keeping Software Developers

Ken Whitaker, USDATA Corp.

The focus of the new Management column is to address the needs of those of us responsible for managing or leading computing professionals. The first column is about motivating and rewarding software developers. The author has survived the wars of managing the development of numerous shrinkwrapped software products. Over the past 24 years, he has led teams at Data General, Software Publishing Corp., and A.C. Nielsen. He wrote Managing Software Maniacs, *Wiley, 1994 and is a frequent speaker at software development conferences.*

—Mark Haas

So you're a software-development manager who must keep the "herd" motivated, yet somehow also release a product on schedule. If that's not enough, you must remind yourself, your team, and especially product management about the importance of quality.

First and foremost, you need to keep your folks motivated. This is especially difficult in a competitive job market that emphasizes high salaries and multiple opportunities for each software developer.

Two important issues you need to handle are

- making certain that developers understand their roles, and
- keeping developers happy, using either rewards or incentives.

CLEAR ROLES AND RESPONSIBILITIES

A software-development team always executes better when it uses a process—as long as everyone is accountable and everyone understands each milestone requirement. If handled properly, schedule leadership can be a motivator rather than a threat to creativity. This applies to startups as well as established software organizations.

Anyone can wing software development. But if everyone works under hacker rules, your folks will be doing rework throughout the project, no matter how talented they are. Hacker rules include

- Working without an agreement with marketing on the product concept.
- Working without agreed-upon schedules.
- Getting no customer feedback until the product is almost done.
- Having no agreement on a *pro forma*, the product line's profit-and-loss analysis.

Each milestone must have a certain degree of implied quality measurement. In addition, each milestone should

- be easy to understand,
- validate major achievements,
- provide value to the organization so that everyone knows their role, and
- help determine if a project is on schedule.

Milestones require a goal, a deliverable, and a definition of the most-important role for each organization that is a part of the product team. Typical product-team organizations include engineering, testing, documentation, sales, production, product management, and customer support. They should also include quality expectations, which management uses as a barometer to help determine a project's

> **It's especially difficult to keep your folks motivated in a competitive environment**

status. As long as everyone involved is objective about evaluating the quality issues needed to attain the next milestone, the project team will keep on track toward a successful project delivery.

For example, say the goal of the beta milestone is "technical completeness." In this case, the engineer's role might be, "Hand off the code to the testing group." One quality metric, for the user interface, might be "Every menu should bring up the expected dialog box or action without any crashes."

As long as the team agrees that every organization's goal has been fulfilled and that the necessary quality metric is met, the alpha milestone has been achieved.

Whatever you do, don't fall into the trap of reducing testing time to regain a release schedule. And don't redefine a milestone goal to accommodate a product deficiency. You'll only pay for these decisions later!

REWARDS VERSUS INCENTIVES

How many times have you heard these

Reprinted from *Computer*, Vol. 30, No. 1, Jan. 1997, pp. 126–128.

two lines from upper management, sales, or marketing: "Couldn't we release the software project (commonly known as "the Pig") sooner if your programmers put in more hours?" Or, "Let's dangle cash to motivate the engineers to deliver three months earlier!"

Motivating developers is a difficult skill to master. The motivational techniques you use will depend mostly on your company's culture. Now, "culture" is a word I despise. Why? Because a culture can take on a life of its own that defies reason, especially in software-development groups. Ultimately, culture becomes an excuse to justify any company, customer, or management decision.

Nevertheless, your motivational techniques should consider the effect of your company's culture and values. If you choose the right techniques, they can have dramatic impact long after the release of your current product. If your company is very aggressive (a couple come to mind) and the goal is to get products out at any cost, then by all means offer cash incentives. But be prepared to pay the consequences.

Most of us are in the software business because we like the technical challenge. This applies to writers, testers, and software engineers (*all* of whom I consider to be software developers). But we all need to make a living, and it is difficult to pass up money and other bonuses. You also expect that the more you learn and the more success you achieve, the more compensation you'll get. Unless it is for a start-up opportunity, a software developer will not typically go from one company to another for *less* money. And even with startups, the opportunity to get "lots of money" down the road is the incentive to take a pay cut.

Consider what motivates other organizations in your company: Salespeople are motivated by closing the sale, attaining quotas, being recognized, and making more money. Marketing professionals have a similar motivation: If the products they are managing are successful, sales will do well and the company will grow, and so will their wallets. The folks in finance are anxious for any reduction in expenses or increase in revenues, to save face with the board of directors and stockholders.

Deciding whether to use rewards or incentives is a key management challenge that most software organizations have to face. I find that this issue comes up about once every six months, like clockwork. A reward is typically some bonus associated with some accomplishment. Usually, the recipient is not expecting a reward. An incentive is typically some bonus associated with a future goal or milestone. The recipient normally has advanced expectations of the opportunity for an incentive. Don't make the mistake of publicly presenting recognition. I'm constantly amazed at how effective a *private* award is regarded by the employee and how ineffective a *public* award can be to the individual and the team.

Developers should be rewarded after they have accomplished some goal. Although a project has many milestones, there is nothing like delivering a quality product that satisfies customer requirements on or ahead of schedule. Let's look at an example.

The wrong way

Not too long ago, a famous software company announced that each developer and a guest would be awarded a vacation in Hawaii upon product delivery. The catch? The product, which was already late to market, had to be completed by a much-publicized date. Some spouses started shopping for resortwear. Morale was high. Music was blasting down the halls and source code was flying everywhere at all hours of the night.

As weeks became months, the desired delivery date came and went. The software product was not completed on time. What was senior management to do? What would you do as the development leader?

Development and marketing management assumed that maybe the original dates were not realistic. So they drew another line in the sand and told the team that Hawaii was still on, but the new date *must* be made. No expense was spared: cots and pizza were brought in! No music was allowed; it was now viewed as distracting. The longer developers worked, the more teamwork and quality programming went out the window. In fact, team meetings became so unruly that the beta milestone was somehow achieved three times!

The second release date was not met. Executive management became furious. Stockholders had lost patience and the board of directors was convinced that the product would never be released. This time, management mandated that a third scheduled release date had to be met and that all incentives were withdrawn. The company was suffering major losses and, frankly, the developers were paid enough and were expected to deliver.

Can you guess what happened? Yep, the best developers left the company, betrayed by what they considered to be ridiculous management and unrealistic goals. The remaining team members were so burned out, they practically had to start the project over to attempt to build the product right because the developers had taken so

> **Deciding whether to use rewards or incentives is a key management challenge that most software organizations have to face.**

many shortcuts to achieve the scheduled milestones.

The product was finally released 18 months later.

The right way

Another company, also faced with an important deadline, prioritized the product features and built a product that had only the *must-have* features. Once the alpha milestone (the barely limping milestone) was achieved, the best developers (two engineers, one tester, and one writer) received private rewards and a personalized letter from the president of the company. You see, these four were the technical stars, and their excitement could encourage the rest of the team. At the beta milestone (the functionally complete milestone), several other developers received similar rewards, including one of the engineers that received an award at alpha.

An unusual by-product of the second company's approach was that the developers actually added a few features that were in the *nice-to-have* category, a pleasant surprise for marketing.

Software development includes several disciplines. Don't make the mistake of taking care of only the engineers when the testers probably went through as much hell releasing a quality product. If you depend on teamwork in your organization to deliver products, the best way to destroy teamwork is by rewarding only a portion of the team.

Last but not least, realize that timing is crucial when issuing rewards. Don't wait a couple of months after a major accomplishment before you reward someone for that accomplishment. A key technique to reduce project risk is to reward key developers early in a product cycle—even as early as the alpha milestone.

GOAL SETTING AND CAREER PLANNING

It's not enough to motivate software developers when they work on high-profile, neat projects. There are some other critical success factors that can be more important to keep a developer over the long term.

If your company has a "strategy of the day," you run the risk of training developers to see the future only in terms of the next project, not as the fulfillment of an overall strategy. Most software companies are extremely weak at strategic planning. In the disturbing movie, *Miller's Crossing*, one bad guy was asked to "terminate" another bad guy. "I can't do it without a plan," he protested. "There's *got* to be a reason."

What is your career plan? In other words, if a developer in your group is not clear on what their goals are and what it takes to get to the next step, you are vulnerable to losing that developer. Presenting a career plan can be done in three easy steps:

1. Compare the developers' current job descriptions with the next higher one.
2. List and analyze the developers' strengths and weaknesses in their current job. This is good practice for preparing their annual performance appraisal.
3. Prepare a set of actions, their intended results, and how success will be measured for each. This helps set realistic expectations so that the next job level does not appear to be unattainable and the criteria for achieving it unmea-

surable. If you are not clear in your communication, your motivational meeting could turn into a demotivational meeting.

Do you feel it's not worth the effort to deal with any form of career planning? If so, you would do well to consider who does do a tremendous job of career planning: In one five-minute phone call, a recruiter can do this job for you.

COMPENSATION

Last, but not least, you need to constantly check that you are compensating people appropriately. Do annual salary surveys, and adjust salaries accordingly. I can assure you that during the past 12 months, the market value for software developers has skyrocketed. If you fail to recognize and react to market trends, you will lose key developers. This surge in compensation is not just in key metropolitan cities—it is nationwide.

If yours is a public company, consider awarding stock. Some companies restrict the distribution of stock to reward only a chosen few. Then they try to motivate all employees by reminding them how important stockholder equity is. How do developers feel, when they look in their pocket and realize that they don't have any way to get that equity other than buying stock on the open market?

Management usually reacts to a wave of departing developers rather than proactively doing the right things to make certain that developers don't even think about leaving. Do the right thing now.

To motivate and keep developers:

- Define a product delivery process and clear roles.
- Reward—don't use incentives.
- Set goals and make career plans on a regular basis.
- Compensate to keep people. ❖

Ken Whitaker is a certified leader of software lunatics at USDATA, a leading producer of SCADA/MMI graphics in Richardson, Texas. Contact him at kwhitaker @usdata.com.

He spends his time conversing with a big black box.

WHO IS THE DP PROFESSIONAL?

by Jac Fitz-enz

The average programmer is excessively independent—sometimes to a point of mild paranoia. He is often eccentric, slightly neurotic, and he borders upon a limited schizophrenia.

D.H. Brandon

Statements such as this one by D.H. Brandon, president of Brandon Consulting Group, Inc. of New York City, and a long time lecturer on data processing management topics, have served to stimulate investigations into the nature of the data processing professional.

A legend has developed around the mysterious creature who inhabits a large, air-conditioned room and spends his time conversing with a big, black box. Some people claim he is a genius, too bright for the common person to comprehend. Others say he is a recluse who is only capable of communicating with a box. Most accounts of his personality and behavior are inferences built on top of speculations. Solid data concerning his nature is hard to find.

Many managers and researchers have formed the opinion that programmers, as an occupational group, are rather unusual individuals compared with people who select other careers. They supposedly are willing to work in isolation, wish to avoid interaction and possible confrontation with others including direct supervisors, prefer minimal structure and routine, and are motivated primarily by achievement rather than external rewards, status, or approval of others.

In the data processing environment, so much happens so fast that training data processing personnel to be better managers usually takes a priority far behind technological concerns. If we will but find the time to teach our managers something about why people behave as they do, to train them in better communication methods and to show

them how to structure work so that personal drives can be unshackled, we could obtain an increase in productivity far surpassing what the latest piece of hardware or software can give us.

We conducted research in a dozen companies in the western United States during the latter part of 1977 to attempt to find out something about the dp pro's motivation to work and his desires for communicating with the organization that employs him. Data was gathered using a survey questionnaire designed and pretested for the specific project. Some 1,500 subjects in several industries, occupations, and job levels responded to the questionnaire.

Any study of motivation must proceed from the premise that motivation is an inherent trait. We talk about motivating employees. This is not possible. In reality, all a manager can do is provide a setting which allows an individual to satisfy his internal drives. As we reviewed our data it became apparent that this is a personality truism.

During the 1960s, Fred Herzberg directed a motivational research project which lead to his now popular two-factor theory of motivation. It claims that basic motivational elements can be split into two categories labeled "hygienes" or "dissatisfiers" and "motivators" or "satisfiers." Herzberg identified eleven hygienes: Salary, Possibility for Growth, Interpersonal Relations with Subordinates, Status, Interpersonal Relations with Superiors, Interpersonal Relations with Peers, Technical Supervision, Company Policy and Procedures, Working Conditions, Noninterference with Personal Life, and Job Security. These, he said, are aspects of the job which must be maintained at an essentially positive level before motivation can flourish.

His motivators or satisfiers number five: Achievement, Recognition, the Work Itself, Responsibility, and Advancement.

Herzberg's theory has been widely publicized. Because it is currently the most widely referenced theory in industrial training, we chose to correlate our findings with his.

Table 1 is a comparison of Herzberg's rankings with those of our subjects.

There are similarities and differences. Responsibility, which ranked fourth in the Herzberg results, dropped to seventh in our study. When we cut the data by Job Level, a reason for the shift surfaced.

Fig. 1 presents a cross section of the responses from programmer/analysts, project leaders, and managers.

While managers ranked Responsibility first and project leaders (PL's) ranked it fourth, programmer/analysts (P/A's) ranked it ninth. For the P/A's, Responsibility fell far below what are normally considered lower level hygiene factors. Even Personal Life topped Responsibility. This finding brought up some tantalizing questions.

If P/A's do not want the responsibility that goes with their work, it may suggest that they are copping out. Does it mean that they are approaching their jobs from a purely self-centered direction? Does it mean that they do not want to be accountable for their results? Of the first five Herzberg factors, four can be viewed as essentially ego-centered. Responsibility is the only factor Herzberg found to have an organizational orientation. Achievement, Recognition, Advancement, and the content of the Work Itself all supply the individual with personal satisfaction. Although having necessary responsibility to carry out the job is also ego-reinforcing, it has the corresponding element of obligation to the organization. Did the respondents rank it low because they took it as a given? Probably not. If that were so, it would follow that PL's and managers who rose from a programmer level should also take it for granted.

Men chose work itself as the greatest motivator. Women chose it fifth.

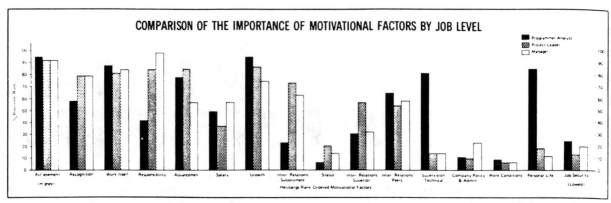

Fig. 1. Rankings of motivational factors are compared for programmer/analysts, project leaders, and managers.

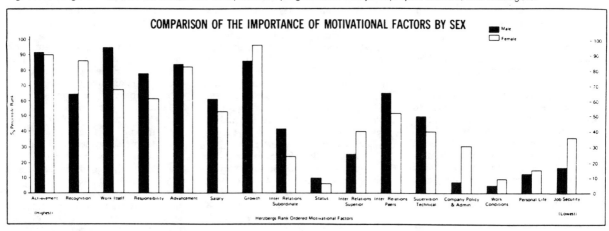

Fig. 2. The rankings of motivational factors are compared by sex.

RANK ORDER COMPARISON OF FIRST LEVEL FACTORS

Herzberg Results	Study Results
1. Achievement	1. Achievement
2. Recognition	2. Possibility for growth
3. Work itself	3. Work itself
4. Responsibility	4. Recognition
5. Advancement	5. Advancement
6. Salary	6. Supervision, technical
7. Possibility for growth	7. Responsibility
8. Interpersonal relations, subordinate	8. Interpersonal relations, peers
9. Status	9. Interpersonal relations, subordinate
10. Interpersonal relations, superior	10. Salary
11. Interpersonal relations, peers	11. Personal life
12. Supervision, technical	12. Interpersonal relations, superior
13. Company policy & admin.	13. Job security
14. Working conditions	14. Status
15. Personal life	15. Company policy & admin.
16. Job security	16. Working conditions

Table 1. Results of the 1960s Fred Herzberg study are compared with those of the author's study.

GENERATION GAP Subsequent to the survey, follow-up interviews were held with a number of programmers to elicit a reason for this difference. The interviews were not very illuminating. No seemingly sensible alternatives to the self-centered theory were given. As a result, we are stuck with one of two speculations. First, indeed the generation gap does exist. Today's younger workers may not value Responsibility the same way that Herzberg's subjects in the 1960s did. The second possibility is equally provocative. There may be something in the way the programmer's job is structured that robs him of a sense of responsibility and hence a desire for it. If that is the case, dp managers have a major problem on their hands. At this time, the finding leaves us perplexed and calls for further investigation.

When the data was subdivided by sex, as shown in Fig. 2, other peculiarities appeared.

Men chose the Work Itself as the greatest motivator and placed it in the 93rd percentile. Women chose it fifth in the 68th percentile. Conversely, the women placed Recognition third in the

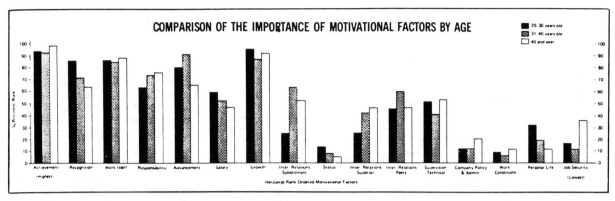

Fig. 3. The rankings of motivational factors are compared by age.

86th percentile; while men ranked it seventh in the 65th percentile.

Finally, the age breakdown in Fig. 3 brings out an interesting point. As age increased, the importance of Salary decreased almost in a straight line from 59th to 52nd to 46th percentile, and from seventh to ninth to eleventh in rank order. This result supports another popular conception of human motivation. Abraham Maslow proposed a theory in the '50s which placed needs in a hierarchy from basic survival through safety, social, and ego needs, to complete human fulfillment which he labeled self-actualization. He claimed that as one level of need is satisfied it is supplanted by a higher level need. In this case, as individuals aged and presumably made more money, thus satisfying survival and safety needs, salary became less motivating while need for personal growth and interpersonal relationships strengthened.

There are a number of other interesting variances overall from Herzberg's theory. The more we dissect the data, the more we can see that while there are basic similarities in the motivational patterns of people, individual differences do pertain. It is apparent that, to some degree, dp professionals have motivational drives which do not fully correspond to other occupational groups. The implication for management is that in order to have motivated employees, supervisors must understand and bear with individual needs. The monolithic notion that "people are all alike" simply is not supportable.

We also surveyed our subjects' attitudes toward organizational communication. We asked them to rank order, in terms of importance to them, organizational topics in which they were most interested. We also asked them to choose for each topic the source which they most and least preferred to have deliver the information. Table 2 shows the rank order of interest by job level, sex, and age.

Without exception, Job Performance and Career Opportunity information have been ranked first and second, well above all other topics. Personnel programs, such as salary and benefit information, usually rank third, closely followed by Company Profit performance and Changes in the work or organization of the unit. The remaining topics are of considerably less interest.

In this instance, overall changes ranked third, slightly ahead of Personnel information. Our guess is that since most dp departments are rapidly growing and changing organizations, this topic is of unusually high interest. In more stable units such as Accounting or Purchasing, change is not as prevalent. Profit information dropped from fourth to fifth in the ranking, and the degree of interest dropped off quite sharply.

Given the above, we would expect that the greatest effort would be being made to communicate information on performance and opportunity. Yet all evidence shows undeniably that organizations do their poorest jobs on these topics. A review of the literature over the past 20 years consistently shows cor-

PERSONAL INTEREST OPTIONS

Rank ordered	Job Level		Sex		Age		
	Percentile Rank		Percentile Rank		Percentile Rank		
Interests	Programmer/ Analyst	Project Leader	Manager	Male	Female	20-30	31-40	40+
1. Current job performance	90	85	92	92	99	95	90	92
2. Future career opportunities	87	89	82	89	94	92	86	78
3. Changes in organization & activities of dept.	63	63	62	62	71	66	57	61
4. Changes in personnel policies	55	53	45	44	46	49	50	61
5. Corporate profit performance	29	26	47	23	24	19	42	37
6. Company operating policies and procedures	24	37	21	15	22	31	29	23
7. General company activities	7	5	6	1	10	9	5	6

Table 2. Personal interest options are ranked by job level, sex, and age group.

We should spend more time helping supervisors become good communicators.

MOST PREFERRED COMMUNICATIONS SOURCE

Source options: A Immediate Supervisor (one level up)
B Senior DP Executive
C Senior Executive outside of DP
D Senior Staff Specialist

Topic	Job Level			Sex		Age		
	Programmer/ Analyst	Project Leader	Manager	Male	Female	20-30	31-40	40+
1. Current job performance	A	A	A	A	A	A	A	A
2. Future career opportunities	B	B	A	B	A	B	B	A
3. Changes in organization & activities of dept.	A	A	A	A	A	A	A	A
4. Changes in personnel policies	A	A	A	A	A	A	A	C
5. Corporate profit performance	C	C	C	C	C	C	C	C
6. Company operating policies and procedures	C	B	A	A	B	A	B	C
7. General company activities	A	A	A	A	A	A	A	A

Table 3. Most-preferred communications sources are ranked by job level, sex, and age group.

porate failure in coming up with a satisfactory performance appraisal system. Career counseling programs have received slightly less attention and no more success. The greatest gains in improving employee attitudes and morale are probably to be found in concentrating our efforts to effectively communicate this information.

The data on communication sources displayed in Table 3 is equally clear-cut.

ON THE SPOT The supervisor is unquestionably the person on the spot. Our early research was based on the assumption that while the immediate supervisor would be looked to for performance evaluation, other sources would be preferred for other topics. This was not and is not the case. Most often the supervisor appears as the most preferred source. Never is he chosen as the least preferred. On four to six topics out of seven, the supervisor is chosen first. The supervisor is better known, usually more trusted, and more capable of translating and interpreting for the subordinate the probable effect of most information.

Other research has shown that a supervisor has a great deal of influence on the general morale of his subordinates. More than any other individual, and more than other such potent forces as the company itself, the supervisor is the critical element. Hence, it is obvious we should spend more time helping supervisors become good communicators. They are important in both positive and negative situations. First, they are the most sought after communicators when it comes to telling the company story. Second, they can be the deciding force when there is individual or group discomfort.

Again, the opportunity is before us. We can achieve the greatest gains by training supervisors at all levels to communicate better. Conversely, we have the most to lose by continuing to ignore the current deficiency.

Charles Andrew, speaking at a recent conference of Production and Inventory Control Specialists, said:
"Successful implementation of an edp system has to start with a valid, realistic management theory—a balancing of the operations orientation with some practical thoughts from the behavioralists."

Gerald Weinberg, in his book on the application of psychology to computer programming, goes even further by noting that personality is displayed in everything we do or say. In particular he asserts, it is reflected in programming efforts. Weinberg believes that the personality of the programmer is observable in the manner in which he approaches the task and the product that results from his labor.

Our study attempted to determine some of the needs and communications desires of people in the business of data processing. When applied at this particular point in the rapid evolution of information processing, we feel it has particular significance.

The study has shown that while data processing professionals display some idiosyncracies, they have much in common with other people. A basic knowledge of human behavior can help us perceive and cope with the attitudes, interest, needs, and values of our employees. We must keep in mind that no matter how sophisticated our technology becomes, we will always have to rely on human beings to design, build, sell, install, service, and use it. Efficient and effective performance of these tasks is directly dependent on our ability to understand and manage these people. ✿

JAC FITZ-ENZ

Dr. Fitz-enz is director of industrial relations for Four-Phase Systems, Inc. in Cupertino, California. Prior to this he was vice president of organization development for Imperial Bank, in Los Angeles. He has published articles on personnel, training, and psychological subjects and has consulted with a variety of organizations. Dr. Fitz-enz received his Ph.D. in communications and industrial relations from the Univ. of Southern California, M.A. from San Francisco State, and B.A. from Notre Dame.

Conflict Management for Project Managers

by John R. Adams
Nicki S. Kirchof

Department of Management
School of Business
Western Carolina University
Cullowhee, North Carolina 28723

Published By:

PROJECT MANAGEMENT INSTITUTE
Drexel Hill, Pennsylvania 19026

First Printing: Oct. 1982
Second Printing: Feb. 1986

This article is reprinted from *Conflict Management for Project Managers* with permission of the Project Management Institute, 130
South State Road, Upper Darby, PA 19082, a worldwide organization of advancing the state-of-the-art in project management.

PREFACE

The project manager, by the nature of the work, must understand at least the rudiments of a wide variety of specialized fields if the project is to be successfully completed. Efforts to control the project to achieve specified cost, schedule, and performance targets, for example, lead the project manager deeply into the development of management information systems. An understanding of the engineering specialities which underlie the project is widely publicized as a requirement for an effective project manager. Contract management and negotiation skills are other fields in which the project manager must perform as the project progresses through its life cycle. Perhaps an even more critical skill requirement lies in the area of conflict management.

In most cases, those who become project managers begin their careers in one or more of the technical specialities which underlie the particular project of which they are in charge. Typically, because of their excellent performance of the technical work in their speciality, they are promoted into the ranks of project management. In general, their technical skill can be assumed. For a major project, however, the new job also requires consummate skill in managing human interrelationships in a highly conflict-prone environment. Conflicts *will* exist in all project environments. Severe conflict is the rule in projects where participants are "loaned" to the project and thus must report to two bosses, namely their functional manager for evaluation and career development, and the project manager for task assignment and work direction. In such conflict-prone situations, a failure on the part of the project manager to recognize and carefully manage the details of the conflict situation can easily lead to a total collapse of the project team.

Conflict is natural to all human organizations and can lead to many beneficial results for both the project and the project manager. To achieve these results, the project manager must be able to recognize and categorize the conflict situation, and then select from among the several strategies available — the conflict management approach that will resolve the issue with favorable results for the project. The purposes of this monograph are to (1) review the concepts of conflict and conflict management as they apply in the project environment; (2) summarize the conflict management methods available to the project manager and indicate the situations in which each might be most appropriately used; and (3) integrate these two purposes into an analysis of two-party conflict, indicating the probable results of a conflict situation between two parties when each uses varying modes of conflict management. Throughout the monograph, materials are carefully selected to be of value to the project manager from the viewpoint of the project manager.

The project manager, both the neophyte and the scarred veteran of many project wars, will find this monograph a useful summary and an excellent primer for conflict management. It is not intended that this monograph be an exhaustive or comprehensive coverage of conflict management theory. Rather, it is a selective presentation of the essentials of conflict management which are typically needed and used in the project management environment. The monograph is designed to be concise yet readable, usable either as an initial introduction or as a refresher in this field for the project manager. A periodic review of this monograph is likely to make us all more effective project managers.

CONFLICT IN
ORGANIZATIONS

One of the primary, underlying reasons conflict exists in organizations today is the tremendous amount of change that has occurred in the workplace in recent years. In order to survive in today's environment, organizations need to adapt rapidly to change. "The Industrial Revolution was characterized by the development of the factory system of production,"[1] which led to the division of labor and our modern, large-scale bureaucracy. Production systems were established to produce goods in the "most efficient" manner, and a change in that system was allowed only after extensive testing proved that the new method provided important and measurable improvements in efficiency. In this environment, change occurred very slowly. Organizations were highly structured and roles were clearly defined. In the past thirty years, however, there has been a revolution in popular concepts of organization which has led to the development of new organizational structures. This revolution has occurred primarily as a response to a rapidly changing environment which demanded dynamic organizations that could adapt to change. Some factors which have led to this "dynamic" environment are technological advances, new concepts of education, increased leisure time, and major societal concerns over environmental and energy issues.[2] Because of automation and other technological changes, new types of managerial occupations have developed along with changes in supervisor/subordinate relationships (Ritzer, 1977). The revolution in education has led to an abundance of educated people and positive implications for the professionals, but negative implications for the semi-skilled worker. Increased leisure time is an outgrowth of technological advances and the increase in the percentage of educated people. These changes lead to conflict as people disagree on how organizations should adapt and as they see the results of that adaptation benefiting or hurting their status and prospects.

Another basic cause of conflict which stems from the change that now seems to constantly surround organizations is the incongruence of goals and objectives of the organization's employees. Typically, the organization's goals and objectives are formulated by top management along with the purposes, values, and missions pursued by the organization. Employees have to abide by these goals and objectives to remain loyal to and employed by the firm. However, the firm's goals and objectives may differ markedly from the individual employee's personal goals and objectives, a situation which can cause extensive conflicts. Fifty years ago, the classical management organization, as shown in Figure 1, was found to be satisfactory for control of the organization's activities.[3] Conflicts were at a minimum, since employees were able to set and pursue long-range objectives consistent with those of the organization.[4]

The increased rate of change demanded a more dynamic organization. Projects and project terms were developed to deal with, manage, and create change. The goals of individuals and organizations became even more incongruent as the projectized organizational structure evolved (Figure 2). The organization structure became even more complex. Project managers and functional managers competed for authority. "Because the individual

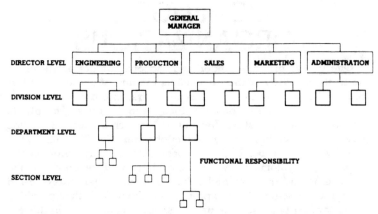

Figure 1. The Traditional Management Structure

Source: Harold Kerzner, *Project Management: A Systems Approach to Planning Scheduling and Controlling*. New York: Van Nostrand Reinhold Company, 1979, p. 42.

performing the work is now caught in a web of authority relationships, additional conflicts came about because functional managers were forced to share their authority with the project manager".[5] Therefore, inconsistent goals between supervisors and subordinates, as well as between individuals and organizations, existed in the projectized environment also, but for different reasons than those of the traditional organization.

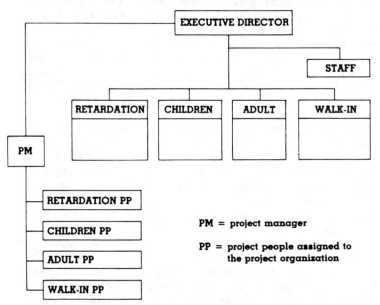

Figure 2. Projectized Form of Organization

Source: John R. Adams, Stephen C. Barndt and Martin D. Martin, *Managing by Project Management*, Dayton, Ohio, Universal Technology Corporation , 1979, p. 45.

These factors of change and incongruent goals evident in the individual/organization and the supervisor/subordinate relationships found within the project lead to high levels of conflict. Thus, the project organization is a major center of conflict. As Butler states:

> . . . the conflict specifically associated with project management may be classified into two broad, partly overlapping categories: (a) conflict associated with change; and (b) conflict associated with the concentration of professionals of diverse disciplines in a more or less autonomous group effort which has limited life.[6]

Therefore, conflict readily exists in a traditional organization and is even more evident in projects. Conflict is inevitable in organizations " . . . because they have limited means with which to satisfy the divergent interests of their various publics."[7] Conflict needs to be effectively managed, especially in a project environment, because of the imminent time, cost, and performance constraints imposed on the project effort. The primary responsibility for conflict management in the project lies with the project manager. If the project is to be successful, the project manager must cope with conflict and develop profitable resolutions.

Conflict management is a critical issue for the project manager, for uncontrolled conflict can literally tear the project apart. The purpose of this monograph is to provide the theoretical and practical understanding of conflict and its management needed to enable the project manager to successfully deal with the project's conflict problems. A view of conflict management with an emphasis on the project manager's role is developed. First, the theory of conflict management is reviewed. Second, conflict as it applies specifically in project organizations is analyzed and reviewed. Third, the relationship between the project manager and conflict management is examined. The role of the project manager is then reviewed in relation to power, the five modes of conflict resolution, and the project manager's ability to influence people toward less destructive conflict. Finally, an approach to conflict resolution for the project manager is provided.

THEORY OF CONFLICT MANAGEMENT

Conflict is generally defined as "a clash between hostile or opposing elements or ideas."[8] As applied to human behavior, it is a disagreement between individuals which can vary from a mild disagreement to a win/lose, emotion-packed confrontation. There are two basic, but opposing, views of conflict, the traditional and the modern (see Figure 3). The traditional view sees conflict as being primarily negative. In this view, conflict is caused by troublemakers; it is bad; and it should be avoided. The manager who views conflict in this way avoids admitting that it exists, keeps it under cover, and tries to suppress it. The contemporary view sees conflict in a more positive light. According to this view, conflict is inevitable. It is a natural result of change and is frequently beneficial to the manager if properly managed. In particular, an atmosphere of tension, and hence conflict, is essential in any organization committed to developing or working with new ideas, for innovation is simply the process of bringing together differing ideas and perspectives into a new and different synthesis. This latter view is much more realistic in modern organizations. In today's environment, conflict is inevitable because of the various competing unit objectives, personal goals, uses for resources, and

TRADITIONAL VIEW	CONTEMPORARY VIEW
• Caused by Trouble-Makers	• Inevitable between Humans
• Bad	• Often Beneficial
• Should be Avoided	• Natural Result of Change
• Must be Suppressed	• Can and Should Be Managed

Figure 3. What Is Conflict?

divergent viewpoints that exist and must be integrated toward the organization's objectives. It is how the individual manager views and deals with conflict that makes it constructive or destructive for the organization. From the author's perspective, the primary aim is to manage conflict constructively to achieve the organization's goals. In order to do this, it is necessary to understand the conditions leading to conflict, the potential results of conflict, and the various methods of dealing with conflict in an organizational setting.

In his book, *Interpersonal Conflict Resolution*, Alan C. Filley develops nine conditions which predispose an organization toward conflict (see Table 1).[9]

Table 1
Antecedent Conditions Leading to Conflict

1. Ambiguous Jurisdictions
2. Conflict of Interest
3. Communication Barriers
4. Dependence on One Party
5. Differentiation in Organization
6. Association of the Parties
7. Need for Consensus
8. Behavior Regulations
9. Unresolved Prior Conflicts

These antecedent conditions for conflict do not exist separately in any organization. It is the extent to which they exist in combination which creates the conditions for conflict. All of them may exist within a single organization at one time. As stated earlier, conflict is a disagreement among individuals. These antecedent conditions simply set the stage for personal disagreement.

The first antecedent condition is called "ambiguous jurisdictions." This situation occurs when two or more parties have related responsibilities, but their work boundaries and role definitions are unclear. This type of occurrence can be found frequently in both the projectized and the matrix organizational structures because both use the "two-boss concept." "Conflict of interest," the second condition leading to conflict, exists when two or more parties want to achieve different or inconsistent goals and desires relative to each other from their association with the organization. For example, the engineer may wish to build his reputation by association with a unique and advanced design, while the manager may be more concerned with completing the job on schedule and at low cost using a standard design. "Communication barriers" is the third condition of conflict. Communication difficulties create misunderstandings and inhibit their resolution by blocking efforts to explain the needs, viewpoints, and actions of those involved in the organization. When there is a "dependence on one party," there tends to be a situation of conflict because one person is dependent on the other to provide needed resources. "Differentiation in organization" exists when different sub-units of the organization are responsible for different tasks. This exists in all organizations. However, in modern organizations dealing with today's complex technologies, there tends to be large numbers of both horizontal and vertical divisions of tasks, creating many specialized groups with their own languages, acronyms, goals, and perspectives. "Association of the parties" is the sixth condition leading to conflict. When people *must* associate together and make joint decisions, conflicts can occur. This situation is especially prevalent when different technical groups have to work together with a variety of management groups. In this case, there may be little of the common ground needed for agreement found in the association. The "need for consensus" follows closely "association of the parties" as a condition leading to conflict. These two conditions are very similar in that, again, people *must* work together. But, when a need for consensus exists, people *must* willingly agree among themselves. There is no decision maker available able or willing to select among several alternatives and enforce the selected solution. When several people from different backgrounds, having different goals, must freely agree on a course of action, the conflict generated can be extremely protracted and difficult to manage. The eighth condition leading to conflict is called "behavior regulations." When the individual's behavior must be regulated closely, as in situations involving high levels of safety and security concerns, high levels of conflict frequently exist as individuals resist the tight boundaries placed on their actions. Their views of what is necessary may differ markedly from that of the organization, and the regulation of activities may inhibit the ease of accomplishing work. As a result, high levels of frustration may exist leading to extensive conflict. Finally, "unresolved prior conflicts" tend to build up and create an atmosphere of tension, which can lead to still more and more intense conflicts. In many cases, the longer conflicts last without a satisfactory resolution being developed, the more severe they become. The use of raw power to "settle" conflicts may also generate more intense conflict at a later time. If one party is unwilling to resolve a conflict, those people involved are likely to generate more difficulties until they may become totally unable to work together. Thus, a failure to manage and deal with conflicts largely guarantees that the manager's job will become more difficult in the future.

These nine antecedent conditions of conflict exist in every organization at all times to a greater or lesser extent. They tend to be more apparent in the project and matrix forms of organization because these organizational structures are frequently used to create change using modern, advanced technology in highly complex and uncertain situations. When these conditions are found, it is up to the project manager to avoid potential destructive results of conflict by controlling and channeling it into areas that can prove beneficial to the project.

Destructive conflict can be highly detrimental to the organization and can significantly alter its productivity. It can drastically hamper the decision making process, making it long, complex, and difficult. Conflict can also cause the formation of competing coalitions within the organization, thus reducing employee commitment to the organizational goals. In essence, destructive conflict can lead to a number of devisive, frustrating distractions which degrade the effort normally applied toward organizational goals.

In order to avoid these destructive consequences, the manager must channel the conflict in such a way that it is either resolved or used for constructive purposes. There are a number of positive results to be derived from conflict. One of these is the "diffusion of more serious conflict."[10] Games, for example, can be used to control the attitudes of people. Games provide a competitive situation which has entertainment value and can provide tension release to the parties involved.[11] Such conflict processes, which have acceptable resolution procedures already established, can function as preventive measures against more destructive outcomes. Similarly, systems which provide for participation by the members of an organization in decision making, while positively associated with the number of minor disputes between parties, are negatively associated with the number of major incidents which occur between members of the organization (Corwin, 1969).[12] Therefore, closeness among organization members is a means of channeling aggressive behavior and tends to result in disagreements which, in turn, reduce the likelihood of major fights and disruptions. Another positive value of conflict is the "stimulation of a search for new facts or resolutions."[13] When two parties who respect each other are involved in a disagreement, the process can sometimes lead to a clarification of facts. Conflict can also stimulate the search for new methods or solutions. "When parties are in conflict about which of two alternatives to accept, their disagreement may stimulate a search for another solution mutually acceptable to both."[14] In both cases, the conflict needs to be managed to keep attention on the facts of the situation and to keep the emotional content low.

An "increase in group cohesion and performance"[15] is another potential value of conflict. Conflict situations between two or more groups are likely to increase both the cohesiveness and the performance of the groups in question. In this situation, however, the effects of conflict must be divided into two periods: during the conflict itself, and after a winner and loser have been determined. During the conflict, there is extremely high loyalty to the group associated with willingness to conform to group attitudes and ideas. Little effort is made to understand the opponent, and the opponent's position is evaluated negatively. The level of effort allocated to the group effort is increased. Therefore, in this sense, competition is valuable as a stimulus to work groups. However, when conflicts end, the situation changes. The leader of the winning group gains status. This person's influence tends to continue and be extended. The leader of the losing group, however, loses status and tends to be blamed for the loss. The group atmosphere also changes. There exists a high level of tension, a desire to avoid problems, an intense desire to do better, and highly competitive feelings in the losing group. These factors decrease in the winning group and are replaced by a feeling of accomplishment and satisfaction.[16] The losing group will tend to try harder next time and the winning group will tend to relax. Therefore, during the conflict, there is an increase in group cohesion and performance in both groups. These attitudes can decrease in both groups once the conflict is resolved, but they decrease for different reasons. "The measure of power or ability"[17] is the fourth value of conflict. Conflict can provide a fairly accurate method of measurement. Through conflictive situations, the relative power between two parties may be identified. "Coercion, control, and suppression requires clear superiority of power of one party over another, whereas problem solving requires an equalization of power among the parties.[18] Suppression of one party by another can therefore be avoided by creating an approximately equal power balance, and this approach usually leads to the use of problem solving methods to resolve disagreements.

The potential results of conflict described above demonstrate that the results of conflict are not necessarily all bad. In fact, conflict is neither good nor bad but can have both positive and negative results for the organization. It really depends on the atmosphere created by the manager as he manages the conflict situations in his organization. Destructive results of conflict, however, need to be avoided by careful and detailed conflict management.

From a management perspective, there are five distinct methods for dealing with conflict (see Figure 4). The project manager must carefully select the appropriate mode for handling conflict within his organization so that an atmosphere conducive to constructive results is developed. The five modes, smoothing, withdrawing, compromise, forcing, and problem solving, are defined and viewed in light of their general effectiveness in this section.[19] Later, they are analyzed and reviewed in depth in relation to the project manager's role. *Smoothing* is defined as "deemphasizing differences and emphasizing commonalities over conflictual issues."[20] Smoothing keeps the atmosphere friendly; but if used too frequently or as the main or only method of dealing with conflict, the conflicts will never be faced. *Withdrawal* can be defined as "retreating from actual or potential disagreements and conflict situations."[21] This method is appropriate only in certain situations, for example, when a "cooling off" period is needed to gain perspective on the conflict situation. Both smoothing and withdrawal are delaying, ignoring tactics which will not resolve the conflict but will temporarily slow the situation down. Note that, if the conflict is not dealt with and resolved in the long run, future conflict will be more severe and intense. *Compromising,* "considering various issues, bargaining, and searching for solutions which attempt to bring some degree of satisfaction to the conflicting parties,"[22] is a situation where neither party can win, but each may get some degree of satisfaction out of the situation. A compromise *does* hurt; both parties must give up something that is important to them, but compromise *does* usually provide some acceptable form of a resolution. Forcing and problem solving also provide resolutions. *Forcing* is "exerting one's viewpoint at the potential expense of another party, characterized by a win-lose situation.[23] That is, one party wins while the other loses. Forcing can increase conflicts later as antagonisms build up among the parties involved. It should therefore generally be used by the project manager as a last resort. *Problem solving* (or confrontation) is a mode where the disagreement is addressed directly. It is a process where conflict is treated as a problem. That is, the problem is defined, information is collected, alternatives are developed and analyzed, and the most appropriate alternative is selected in a typical problem solving technique. This method is considered theoretically to be the best way of dealing with conflict because both parties can be fully satisfied if they can work together to find a solution that meets both of their needs. It is a time-consuming process, however, and it requires that both parties desire to solve the problem and are willing to work together toward a mutually agreeable solution. If a solution is needed quickly or immediately, however, the problem solving approach simply cannot work.

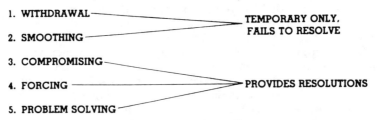

1. WITHDRAWAL ——————————— TEMPORARY ONLY,
2. SMOOTHING ——————————— FAILS TO RESOLVE
3. COMPROMISING —
4. FORCING ——————————— PROVIDES RESOLUTIONS
5. PROBLEM SOLVING —

PROJECT MANAGER MUST CAREFULLY SELECT THE APPROPRIATE MODE.

Figure 4. Five Conflict Management Modes

Of the five basic modes, some are more conducive to certain situations than others. Problem solving is considered the "best" mode since it can lead to innovative results capable of satisfying all parties. It does not work in all situations, however, especially when time is critical. Smoothing and withdrawing are delaying actions which cannot resolve the issue. Forcing provides a rapid solution but may make the conflict more intense in the long run. Compromise provides a resolution but rarely satisfies anyone. So, again, it is up to the project manager to identify the type and source of the conflict, evaluate the situation objectively, and select one of the conflict handling modes to solve the issue. In other words, the project manager must *manage* the conflict situation.

There are other methods the project manager can use in handling conflict. These differ from the five modes of conflict in that they relate more specifically to personal styles of handling conflict. Filley identifies these five styles of handling conflict as:

> high concern for personal goals and low concern for relationships (win-lose); low concern for personal goals and high concern for relationships (yield-lose); low concern for personal goals and low concern for relationships (lose, leave); moderate concern for personal goals and moderate concern for relationships (compromise style); and high concern for personal goals and high concern for relationships (integrative style).[24]

These essentially "one party" styles of conflict resolution can be related to the five modes as seen in Figure 5. With these relationships in mind, an examination of these personal styles follows. The win-lose style is the "tough battler" who seeks to meet his goals at all costs.[25] The yield-lose style is the friendly helper, "who overvalues maintenance of relationships with others and undervalues achievement of his own goals."[26] The lose-leave style person sees conflict as "a hopeless, useless, and punishing experience."[27] The compromise style person will try to find a position where each side can end up with something. Finally, the integrative style person seeks to satisfy his own goals as well as the goals of others.[28] He is the problem solver. Like the five modes reviewed earlier, the problem solving and compromise-oriented styles (integrative and compromise) are the most successful styles. The win-lose style, yield-lose style, and lose-leave styles would not be effective because of their extremes. The compromise style and integrative style must be evident in a successful project organization. The first three styles (win-lose, yield-lose, lose-leave) would ultimately lead to project failure, while the last two (compromise, integrative) would lead to project success.

In summary, conflict is inevitable in an organization and is usually considered to be a disagreement among two or more parties. The results can be good or bad for the organization, depending upon how the manager manages the conflict. The antecedent conditions for conflict provide a guideline for managers to follow in predicting the type and intensity of conflict likely to exist in the organization. Destructive conflict can be very detrimental to the organization, and it is the manager's responsibility to control and channel the conflict process for constructive results. The five methods of dealing with conflict and their general effectiveness give project managers some tools with which to manage conflict in their project environments.

		Concern for	
		Personal Goals	Relationships
Force	Win-lose	High	Low
Smooth	Yield-lose	Low	High
Withdraw	Lose-leave	Low	Low
Compromise	Compromise	Medium	Medium
Problem Solver	Integrative	High	High

Figure 5. Styles of Conflict Resolution

FOOTNOTES

1. George Ritzer, *Working: Conflict and Change*. Englewood Cliffs, N.J.: Prentice-Hall, Inc., 1977, p. 8.
2. Ibid., p. 40.
3. Harold Kerzner, *Project Management: A Systems Approach to Planning Scheduling and Controlling*. New York: Van Nostrand Reinhold Company, 1979, p. 42.
4. Ibid., p. 42.
5. Ibid., p. 48.
6. Arthur G. Butler Jr., "Project Management: A Study in Organizational Conflict," *Academy of Management Journal*. March 1973, p. 89.

7. Ibid., p. 86.
8. David B. Guralink, editor, *Webster's New World Dictionary.* Cleveland: William Collins and World Publishing Co., Inc., 1947, p. 298.
9. Alan C. Filley, *Interpersonal Conflict Resolution.* Glenview, Illinois: Scott, Foresman and Company, 1975, p. 4.
10. Ibid.
11. Ibid.
12. Ibid., p. 5.
13. Ibid.
14. Ibid.
15. Ibid., p. 6.
16. Ibid., p. 7.
17. Ibid.
18. Ibid.
19. See R.R. Blake and J.S. Mouton, *The Managerial Grid.* Houston: Gulf Publishing Company, 1964 and application by Hans J. Thamhain and David L. Wilemon, "Conflict Management in Project Life Cycles," *Sloan Management Review*, Vol. 16, No. 3, Spring 1973, pp. 31-50.
20. Hans J. Thamhain and David L. Wilemon, "Conflict Management in Project-Oriented Work Environments," *Proceedings of the Sixth Annual Seminar/Symposium.* Drexel Hill, Pennsylvania: Proceedings of the PMI, 1974, p. 3.
21. Ibid., p. 87.
22. Ibid.
23. Ibid.
24. Filley, p. 51.
25. Ibid.
26. Ibid.
27. Ibid., p. 52.
28. Ibid.

Chapter 9

Controlling a Software Engineering Project

1. Chapter Introduction

Controlling a software engineering project is defined as all the management activities that ensure that actual work advances according to plan. It measures performance against goals and plans, reveals when and where deviation exists, and helps to ensure accomplishment of plans by implementing corrective action.

Controlling a software engineering project can be partitioned into six general management activities (see Table 9.1). Each activity in the table is followed by its definition or an amplifying description.

OUR PLAN CALLS FOR US TO TURN RIGHT AT THE NEXT MILESTONE.

Table 9.1. Controlling activities for software projects.

Activity	Definition or Explanation
Develop standards of performance	Set goals that will be achieved when tasks are correctly accomplished.
Establish monitoring and reporting systems	Determine necessary data, who will receive it, when they will receive it, and what they will do with it to control the project.
Measure and analyze results	Compare achievements with standards, goals, and plans.
Initiate corrective actions	Bring requirements, plans, and actual project status into conformance.
Reward and discipline	Praise, remunerate, and discipline project personnel as appropriate.
Document controlling methods	Document the standards of performance, monitoring, and control systems, and reward and discipline mechanisms.

2. Chapter Overview

The five articles in this chapter all have to do with controlling a software engineering project. The activities listed in Table 9.1 were used as an outline for identifying articles on controlling activities. Chapter 10 continues the discussion on controlling with a look at software metrics and visibility of progress.

Patricia Hurst begins the discussion with the three "threads of control:" work definition, work measurement, and work monitoring. Andrew Ferrentino has written a short article on the problems of controlling a software engineering project when cost and schedule estimates are based on estimating the lines of deliverable code.

Hans Thamhain and David Wilemon, in another article from the Project Management Institute, discuss methods of controlling a project according to the plan that was established at the beginning of the project. The article written by Robert Dunn discusses software quality assurance and quality assurance techniques. The last article, by Ed Bersoff, defines configuration management. Configuration management keeps track of the various artifacts developed during the lifetime of a software project through identifying, controlling, auditing, and status accounting the various software development products.

3. Article Descriptions

As Hurst says in her article, there are three key elements required to obtain control of software projects in an organization: work definition, work measurement, and work monitoring. The goals of this article are to present a set of basic techniques for work defi-

nition, measurement, and monitoring and to show how they interrelate to provide "the threads of project control." The basic techniques include the software development process model, work-category and work-package work breakdown structures, binary reporting, and earned value tracking. The last three items are especially noteworthy.

The Ferrentino article concerns both the difficulties in estimating the correct cost and schedule for a software development project and the difficulties in delivering a system on time and within cost. The article questions the current approach in determining project status by comparing the number of lines of code completed to the number of lines of code estimated. He points out that an incompatibility exists when the original estimate was made using "lines of code" as an independent variable for estimating costs, but it is software functionality that is delivered (not lines of code). Ferrentino believes that "we can't make good estimates but we can make estimates good." He also argues that a combination of good software engineering and project management practices will enable us to deliver a software engineering project on time and within cost.

The next article, "Criteria for Controlling Projects According to Plan," by Thamhain and Wilemon, reports on a study that investigated practices of project managers. This study provides insight into the major issues of managing a project as reported by project managers. The article addresses the causes of schedule slips and budget overruns and provides criteria for effective project management and control. The projects reported on were primarily commercial applications.

Dunn's article provides a management perspective on Software Quality Assurance (frequently referred to as SQA). Dunn emphasizes that "...the quality of the software is expected to derive from the quality of the process used to develop or maintain software, and SQA is largely a matter of ensuring that a good process is in place, followed, and continuously improved." Dunn also lists a number of SQA tools that can be used by management to monitor and control the application and effectiveness of SQA.

In the last article, Ed Bersoff defines configuration management as:

> The discipline of identifying the configuration of a system at discrete points in time for the purpose of systematically controlling changes to the configuration and maintaining the integrity and traceability of the configuration throughout the system life cycle.

Configuration management keeps track of the various artifacts developed during the lifetime of a software project through identifying, controlling, auditing, and status accounting the various software development products.

Bersoff reminds us that controlling code is not enough; we must also control the documentation that enables us to use and operate the code. This article also provides a lengthy description of the program support library (PSL) function. Bersoff discusses the major problems involved in deciding how to properly manage the software configuration: too much control is cumbersome, but too little control invites disaster.

Software Project Management: Threads of Control

Patricia W. Hurst

Fastrak Training, Inc.
Columbia, MD

Abstract

At the heart of software process improvement efforts is control of the development environment through effective project management. The term "control" implies two important aspects. First, it means to meet schedule, costs and quality expectations for a specific project. Secondly, it means to do this consistently from project to project. The focus of this paper is on laying the foundations for control with respect to schedule and cost expectations. There are three keystone elements required to obtain control of software projects in an organization: work definition, work measurement, and work monitoring. The goals of this paper are to present a set of basic techniques for work definition, measurement, and monitoring and to show how they interrelate to provide "the threads of project control." The basic techniques include the software development process model, work-category and work-package work breakdown structures, binary reporting and earned-value tracking. A hypothetical project is used for illustration.

INTRODUCTION

Much has been written about the value of various aids and techniques available to the project manager for controlling a software development project. Such aids and techniques are of increasing interest to today's practitioners who are striving to improve their particular development environment. The motivation is for competitive advantage in one form or the other, whether it be to secure a higher rating according to the Software Engineering Institute's (SEI) Capability Maturity Model, to satisfy ISO 9000 requirements, to better predict and reduce internal development costs and schedules, or to outperform a competitor.

At the heart of such improvement efforts is *control* of the development environment through effective project management. The term "control" implies two important aspects. First, it means to meet schedule, cost, and quality expectations for a specific project. Secondly, as Juran [6] and others have noted, it means to do this consistently from project to project. To be in control of a development environment means then to be able to set expectations for each project and to consistently meet those expectations. The focus of this paper is on laying the foundations for control with respect to schedule and cost expectations.

The key question for the project manager and the development organization as a whole is, "How can control be obtained?" Over a decade ago in 1982, Demarco [3] began his book *Controlling Software Projects* with the now frequently quoted statement, "You can't control what you can't measure." Only by quantifying the work to be done can we set expectations for cost and schedule (and quality), determine whether those expectations are met, and evaluate consistency of meeting expectations for multiple projects. A corollary to this statement is, "You can't measure what you can't define." The work itself must be defined and used consistently if measurements are going to be useful. Furthermore, to ensure that for a particular project the work is being performed as defined within the parameters expected presents the need for monitoring the work at each step along the way. Thus, there are three keystone elements required to obtain control of software projects in an organization: work definition, work measurement, and work monitoring.

The goals of this paper are to present a set of basic techniques for work definition, measurement, and monitoring and to show how they interrelate to provide

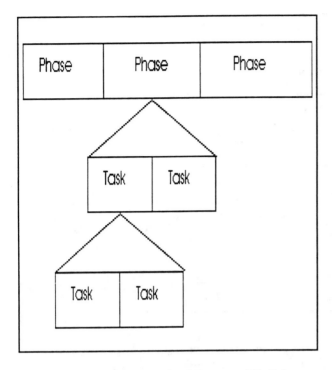

Figure 1. Hierarchical Process Model

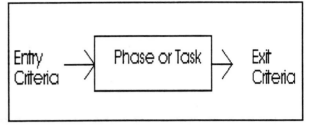

Figure 2. Phase or Task Entry/Exit Criteria

"the threads of project control." The basic techniques include the software development process model, work-package and work-category work breakdown structures, binary reporting, and earned-value tracking. A hypothetical project is used for illustration of techniques presented.

SOFTWARE DEVELOPMENT PROCESS MODEL

A software development process model defines the work required to produce a software product. It typically is shown as a hierarchical decomposition with "phases" of work shown at the highest level and "tasks" shown at lower levels as shown in Figure 1. It reflects the activities, methods, and practices that are to be used by a specific development team or by teams within an organization. It should include ALL of the development work that is planned. This should include not only the obvious tasks such as design, programming and testing, but also all other resource-consuming tasks such as client and inter-disciplinary reviews, prototyping, anticipated user feedback, and anticipated rework points.

The process model is an example of the "divide-and-conquer" strategy used to break a large or complex task into smaller, well-defined units so that focus can be placed on one manageable portion of the problem at

a time. Several high-level process models — such as the Waterfall, Spiral, and Evolutionary models — have been proposed and used by practitioners to provide a general strategy and approach to planning project phases/tasks at a high level of abstraction. Whether one of these models is used for overall strategy or whether another model is used, decomposition should be to the level at which the project manager will define the work to be eventually assigned to an individual(s), to schedule the work defined, and to monitor the work scheduled.

The hallmark of a well-defined process model is the clear definition of each task (and phase), from the highest level down to the most detailed level. Each task, as shown in Figure 2, should have the following:

- **Entry Criteria**

   These include tangible work products, such as documents or code, from previous tasks which must be completed and available in order for this task to be accomplished.

- **Exit Criteria**

   These include tangible work products produced as a result of the task being performed. Also included is evidence of any quality control procedures, such as peer inspection certification, which should be performed on the work products produced.

Also included in the definition of a task are the activities, methods, procedures, standards and constraints to be adhered to or followed.

A process model for a hypothetical project is shown in Figure 3. Software implementation is divided into increments. At the beginning of each increment, except for the first, time is allowed for "reworking" the design of the previous phase(s). Such a rework point is required for object-oriented projects which are iterative in nature

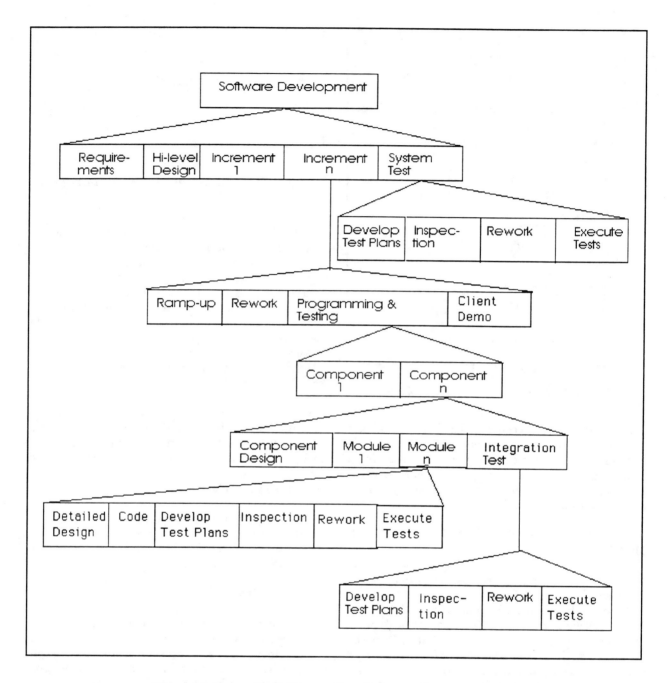

Figure 3. Example Software Development Process Model

as described by Pittman [7]. It is useful for other design methodologies as well. Ramp-up time is also included to accommodate the need for programmer "relaxation and reflection" after a pressurized schedule for the previous increment. The detailed tasks for building a software component are also defined. For example, the use of "code inspection" as a quality control procedure at the module level (the lowest subroutine or function level) is shown.

From the example given, it is important to note that tasks such as rework and ramp-up time can only be planned for if a thorough understanding of the work required is obtained. Defining, using and continually refining a process model based on past experiences is a key to developing control over a software development environment.

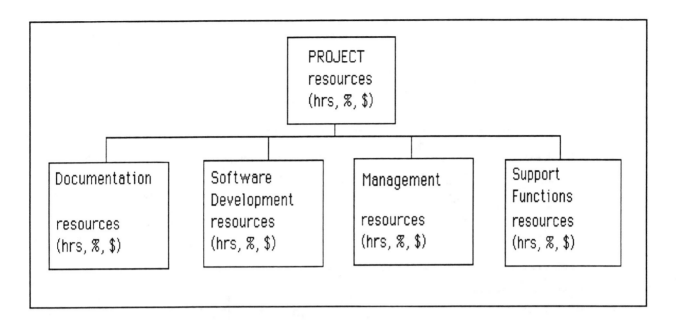

Figure 4. Top-Level Work Breakdown Structure

Such a process model provides a "template" to be used for specific projects. The number of actual increments and components, for example, may depend on the application or system size and required delivery schedule. But each time a higher-level task is to be performed, such as component development as shown in the example, the same lower-level process tasks as defined by the template will be applied. The process model for a particular project should reflect accurately and realistically how the project manager plans to proceed with the work at hand.

Because of the nature of software development projects, one specific process model rarely is adequate for all projects. Tailoring is often required. Simple examples may include excluding ramp-up time, inserting client review points, or adding peer inspections to a particular difficult step in design. Such variations are accommodated by adopting a broader and more general process model for an organization which is tailored for specific projects. Humphrey [5] defines this as a software process architecture — a framework within which project-specific processes are defined.

An organization may also have a need for several software process architectures which may in turn be tailored for specific projects. This may occur for a variety of reasons such as different methodologies and platforms being used, varying client-imposed procedures, and varying degrees of inter-disciplinary interactions.

WORK BREAKDOWN STRUCTURES

A work breakdown structure (WBS) also addresses the need of defining, and additionally measuring, the work for a particular project or for projects within an organization. This technique is typically used to present a view of the project from a broad vantage point. It subdivides the entire project — not just the software production portion — into tasks that are defined and that consume resources. Projects involve a variety of other activities in addition to the production of the software described by the software development process model. For the example project, a top-level WBS is shown in Figure 4. It shows the additional tasks of documentation, management, and support functions. Such tasks have their own process models, which can be defined similarly to that of software development. Staff resources are allocated to the defined tasks for a project and can be expressed in staff-hours, as percentages of the total, or in dollars. Other types of resources, such as travel budgets or memory usage, could also be allocated as appropriate for a project.

There are two useful views of a project which the WBS technique can provide: the work-package WBS and the work-category WBS. Both view the same project tasks and resource consumption, but the two views present this information in different ways and for different purposes.

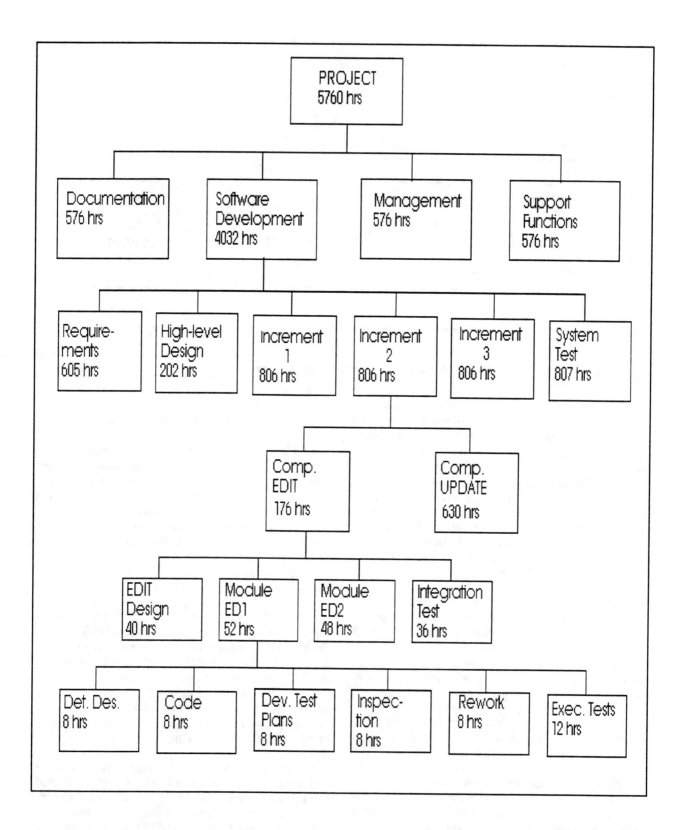

Figure 5. Example Work-Package Work Breakdown Structure

WORK-PACKAGE WBS

The work-package WBS views the project information as specific and unique tasks, or "work packages," to be performed during the project. A work package can be estimated, has entry/exit criteria, is assignable to an individual(s), can be scheduled, and can be monitored. Since this view shows the specific tasks to be performed, there is an interleaving of software architectural components — the actual coded pieces to be developed — with the processes defined by the software development process model templates.

Figure 5 shows a work-package WBS for the example project. The software-development portion is an implementation of the process model. Following design, the software is developed in three increments followed by a system test. Increment 2 is decomposed into development of two components, EDIT and UPDATE. EDIT is decomposed into two modules, ED1 and ED2, which are further decomposed into the lowest-level tasks as defined by the process model.

This WBS view is the primary tool for estimating, scheduling and monitoring the work-packages for a specific project. At the beginning of a project, the level of decomposition is shallow, but as the project progresses, each level can be decomposed further as the software components and modules are defined. The top two levels can be used for initial sizing and preliminary scheduling. At the end of requirements, the increments can be loosely defined giving a more detailed schedule. At the end of hi-level design, the increments become more firmly defined and the components are defined allowing a more detailed schedule. Following component design, the modules are defined and thus can be scheduled.

The work-package WBS is a primary aid for effective project planning and provides the basis for later monitoring of progress. It is used for defining the work tasks to be performed, estimating resources required for each task, scheduling the tasks, and assigning the tasks to individuals. It enhances communication between the project manager and team members by making expectations for each task clear through the exit criteria for each task. As tasks are completed, the actual resources consumed can be used to evaluate consistency with original estimates. The actuals can also be used to develop and update a historical data base which can in turn be used for the planning of future projects. The historical data base can be expressed as the work-category WBS discussed in the next section of this paper.

In summary, the work-package WBS is useful for:

- Estimating project work
- Scheduling the work
- Monitoring the work
- Evaluating consistency by comparing estimates to actuals
- Providing input for a historical data base

WORK-CATEGORY WBS

The work-category WBS views the project information as specific and unique types or "categories" of work. It defines the categories of tasks represented in the software development process model and the additional tasks.

Figure 6 shows a work-category WBS for the example project. Software development accounts for 70% of the total project effort and documentation, management, and support functions each account for 10%. The distribution of project effort by the top-level categories is shown in Figure 7.

In Figure 6, the staff-hours allocated to each category of work and the percentage relative to the staff-hours for the total project are shown. For example, design consumes 17% of the total project resources. The design work is composed of several different types — the hi-level design, the design of each system component, and the detailed design of each low-level module. These various types of design work are spread throughout the project as reflected in the work-package WBS. The total of all the design work taken together is 17% of the total project effort. The decomposition of the design work is shown at the next level in the figure. The hi-level design effort consumes 3% of the total project effort; component design consumes 5%; and detailed design consumes 9%. Similarly, 9% of the total effort is allocated to inspections which occur at several points during the project.

The example shows one possible grouping of categories of work. This is arbitrary and depends on how the project or organization chooses to organize their defined tasks.

At project initiation, the work-category WBS can be used for estimating the project resource requirements using a "top-down" approach. Here, the project is sized, an overall estimate of resources is determined based on the top 1-3 levels, and the estimated resources are allocated to the various categories based on percentages. These estimates would then be used by

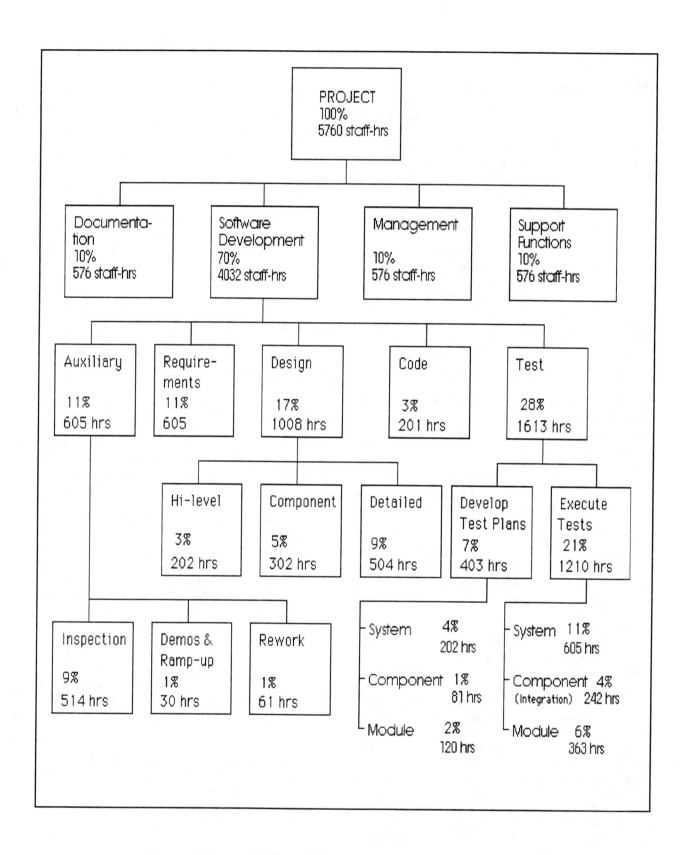

Figure 6. Example Work-Category Work Breakdown Structure

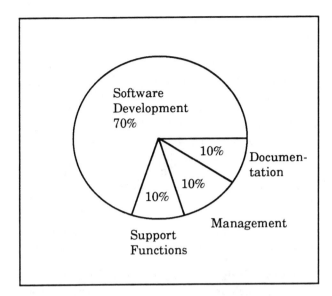

Figure 7. Distribution of Project Effort by Work Categories

the project manager to allocate resources for each of the work packages defined in the work-package WBS for a project.

This type of WBS is the basis for a historical data base for an organization. At project completion, the percentages can be updated to reflect reality and subsequently used as historical data for estimating future projects. Through the use of historical data, for example, Bell Northern Research [8] routinely allocates 15-25% of project effort to code inspections.

This view of project resource consumption can also be used to evaluate consistency between projects and to determine what tasks are large consumers of resources and are, thus, candidates for process improvement. In the example project, testing is the most costly category of work consuming 28% of the total effort (40% of the software development effort). This indicates that more effective testing could reduce the testing effort required and yield substantial savings. While the hypothetical example project shows a small 1% of effort being consumed by rework, a typical industry organization may find that 30% or more of their time is being consumed by rework. This would indicate that improvement of software engineering practices to reduce rework could yield substantial savings. The use of historical data derived from the work-category WBS can provide an organization with a powerful tool for improving their development practices.

In summary, the work-category WBS is useful for:

- Estimating and allocating project work by category
- Evaluating consistency by comparing estimates to actuals
- Providing a historical data base
- Identifying candidate tasks for process improvement

RELATIONSHIP BETWEEN THE WBS AND THE PROCESS MODEL

There is a direct relationship between the software development process model and the software development portions of the two WBS views presented. The process model provides the templates that define how the work will be performed on the project to the required level of detail. The two WBS views instantiate the model for a particular project by showing how the model will be implemented. The work-package WBS provides definition for all assignable and scheduleable tasks for developing the software. The work-category WBS provides a summary of the types or categories of work to be performed and the overall allocation of resources to the different categories.

BINARY REPORTING

Once an agreed-upon development plan and schedule is in place, performance against it should be monitored. Almost two decades ago, in his classic book *The Mythical Man Month* [2], Brooks answered the difficult question of, "How does a project get to be a year late?" His answer was: "One day at a time." Implicit to this answer is a challenge — to know when the project is one day late, a week late, or two weeks late so that corrective action can be taken to bring the project back within the target schedule range. It is easier to correct a deviation of a few days or weeks than it is months or (gasp!) years. This challenge of yesterday remains the challenge for today.

The hurdle to overcome is having concrete evidence of work performed instead of just knowing how much effort has been spent. When tasks assignments are too large, spanning several weeks or months, progress is typically reported in terms of effort spent against the scheduled or budgeted amount. The false assumption is that the work is progressing as planned. This leads to the well-known "90% complete syndrome" where a task previously assumed to be on track remains at the 90% complete level for weeks while the panicked developer scurries to complete all of the work products demanded. This hurdle is overcome by lower-level decomposition of tasks with well-defined and tangible exit criteria.

Thus, a well-defined process model with small granularity of tasks for software development, document preparation, and other project tasks provides the foundation to overcome this syndrome and meet the challenge identified by Brooks. Zells [12] calls such small tasks "inch pebbles." Fairley [4] suggests a time-span duration of one to two weeks as a "rule of thumb" for sizing tasks. Ward [11] suggests at least one task due for completion each week for an individual and under no circumstances should a team member ever have more than two weeks between task completion dates. A good guideline for a task is between 4-80 staff-hours of effort. This implies that the process model used should define tasks to this level of detail. The ability to define and schedule small units of work will best provide for close monitoring and control over project progress.

By scheduling small tasks with well-defined and tangible exit criteria, "binary" reporting of task completion can be effectively used. Binary reporting means that the task is in one of only two states; it is either complete or incomplete. Partial credit for effort spent is not given. This gives the project manager concrete information on progress made as opposed to how much effort has been consumed.

EARNED-VALUE TRACKING

Using the concept of binary reporting, the earned-value technique of project tracking is straight-forward and very effective for monitoring progress on small or large projects. Developed by the U. S. Air Force in 1978, the technique assigns an earned value (EV) to each task completed. This value is the amount of budgeted or estimated resource units, such as staff-hours, planned for consumption during task performance. The actual expenditure is also reported for each task. Thus, the earned value for a task can be compared to the actual expenditure. As the project progresses, expenditures can be compared to overall earned value to date to determine how well the project is progressing with respect to the resource budget.

Figure 8 illustrates earned-value reporting for Increment 2 in the example project. All of the tasks for this increment have been scheduled and as of the report date indicated, some of the work has been completed. The component EDIT is composed of a component design task, development of two modules (ED1 and ED2), and an integration test. The module development work has been decomposed according to the process model presented earlier and the individual tasks have been scheduled. For the component UPDATE, only the overall schedule date is shown. The

details would be similar to those for EDIT since the same process model would be used.

A closer look at module ED1 reveals that the detailed design task has been completed. The estimated or budgeted effort was 8 staff-hours; thus, the earned value (EV) is also 8 staff-hours. However, the actual effort spent was 12 staff-hours. This task has "overrun" the budgeted amount of effort. The tasks of coding, developing test plans, and rework have also exceeded the budgeted amounts. The time actually used for inspection of this module was slightly less than planned for.

For the EDIT tasks completed to date, the actual staff-hours spent (139) exceeds the planned or budgeted amount (120). This is also true for all of the tasks completed for this increment (188 actual versus 157 planned). Such detailed reporting allows the project manager to detect small deviations which may become cumulative, as Brooks noted, and to take early corrective action.

Figure 9 illustrates earned-value reporting at the project level and provides a summary for all high-level work-packages. For Documentation, the total effort planned for is 576 hours. Of this total, 300 hours of planned work have been completed to date— the earned value. However, the actual number of hours spent is 350. On the amount of documentation work completed to date, the effort spent is 17% more than was budgeted. Those 50 hours will have to be made up somewhere. Although some of the other items, such as management and support, have required less effort than budgeted to date, the overall project has exceeded the budget by 5% to date (2808 actual hours versus 2670 budgeted hours). If the work continues to exceed the budgets planned for, it seems doubtful that the staff-hours planned for will be sufficient.

A further look at the documentation item shows that 52% of the work has been completed but 61% of the total budget for this item has been consumed. Thus, this item has consumed an unplanned 9% of the total budget to date. For the total project, the overrun is 3%.

Figure 10 illustrates a graph of actual versus budgeted effort (earned value) for work completed to date in the example project. Early in the project, the actual effort required was less than the budgeted effort. As the project progressed, however, the actuals began to exceed the amount budgeted. If this trend continues, the project will continue to exceed its budget.

Earned-Value (EV) Detailed Report

Report Date: January 25

	Plan Start	Plan End	Actual End	Budget (hrs)	EV (hrs)	Actual (hrs)
INCREMENT 2	1/1	3/31		806	157	188 (Total)
Ramp-up	1/1	1/5	1/5	7	7	7
Rework	1/1	1/5	1/5	30	30	42
Component EDIT	1/8	2/12		176	120	139 (Sub-total)
Design	1/8	1/12	1/12	40	40	39
Module ED1						
Det. Design	1/15	1/19	1/19	8	8	12
Code	1/15	1/19	1/19	8	8	11
Dev. Test Plans	1/15	1/19	1/19	8	8	12
Inspection	1/22	1/24	1/19	8	8	7
Rework	1/22	1/24	1/25	8	8	16
Execute Tests	1/25	1/29		12		
Module ED2						
Det. Design	1/15	1/19	1/19	8	8	8
Code	1/15	1/19	1/19	8	8	6
Dev. Test Plans	1/15	1/19	1/19	8	8	8
Inspection	1/22	1/24	1/24	8	8	8
Rework	1/22	1/24	1/24	8	8	12
Execute Tests	1/25	1/29	--	8	0	0
Integration Test	2/1	2/12	--	36	0	0
Component UPDATE	2/1	3/31	--	630	0	0

Figure 8. Earned-Value Reporting for Increment 2 for the Example Project

Given this information, the next step for the project manager is to take corrective action. Some options include making personnel more effective, improving methods or procedures reflected in the process model, reducing the scope of work to be performed, increasing the project budget, or cancelling the project. Such information is critical in order for a project manager to take early corrective action and regain control while still feasible.

The earned-value technique also provides for additional information, such as monitoring the amount of work scheduled to be completed at a given point in time versus the amount of scheduled work actually completed. A discussion of such additional uses can be found in Boehm [1].

The use of binary reporting and the earned-value technique can be effective aids for alerting a project

Earned-Value (EV) Summary Report

Report Date: January 25

	To Date			Total Budget	Percent of Total Budget		
	EV	Actual	Actual-EV EV		To-date EV	To-date Actual	Difference
	hrs	hrs	%	hrs	%	%	%
DOCUMENTATION	300	350	17	576	52	61	9
MANAGEMENT	250	240	- 4	576	43	42	-1
SUPPORT	350	325	- 7	576	61	56	- 5
REQUIREMENTS	605	545	-10	605	100	90	-10
HI-LEVEL DESIGN	202	240	19	202	100	119	19
INCREMENT 1	806	920	14	806	100	114	14
INCREMENT 2	157	188	20	806	19	23	4
INCREMENT 3	0	—	—	806	0	—	—
SYSTEM TESTING	0	—	—	807	0	—	—
TOTAL	2670	2808	5	5760	46	49	3

Figure 9. Earned-Value Reporting at the Project Level for the Example Project

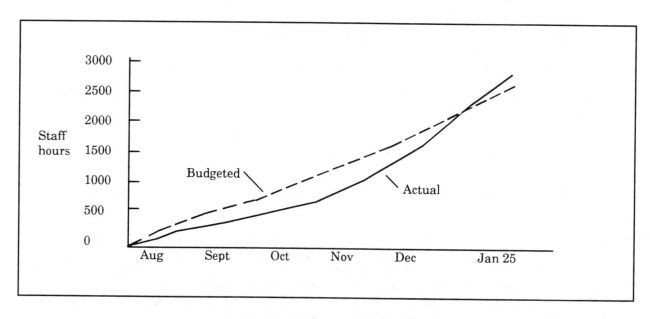

Figure 10. Cummulative Actual Versus Budgeted Staff-Hours to Date

manager as to discrepancies in the planned versus actual performance of a team. With reporting on a weekly basis, the project manager has concrete knowledge of actual progress or the lack thereof. This allows for corrective action to be taken in a timely fashion to ensure expectations are met if possible. This also allows for replanning of expectations such as project scope or schedule in a timely fashion.

In addition to monitoring an on-going project, the earned-value technique provides the organization with an historical data base of project performance. This actual performance data provides the effort allocation percentages shown in the work-category WBS. As noted earlier, such historical data can be used to ensure consistency across projects and to guide process improvement efforts.

SUMMARY AND CONCLUSION

For the past several years there has been an increasing awareness in the software development community that "business as usual" has become unacceptable if the demands for larger, more complex systems are to be produced with often decreasing delivery cycles. Several years ago, Yourdon [10] spoke to this issue when he began a series of articles on "The Decline and Fall of the American Programmer" with the rash prediction that "the American programmer is about to go the way of the dinosaur and the dodo bird." He was speaking of international competition and was urging the American software developers to recognize the need for more control and improvement of their development environments. Although this need is being recognized by organizations in increasing numbers, many are struggling with laying the foundations for realizing these goals.

The set of basic project-management techniques presented in this paper provides a project manager or an organization with the capability to lay the foundations for obtaining control over their development environment. They address three keystone elements required to obtain the firm foundations required — work definition, work measurement, and work monitoring. The techniques include the following:

- **Software Development Process Model**

  This model provides a template for all projects tasks. Such a model may be adopted for an organization with tailoring for specific projects.

- **Work-Package WBS**

  This WBS provides a view of all project tasks which are to be assigned to individuals, scheduled, and monitored. It includes tasks defined by the software development process model and additional tasks as well.

- **Work-Category WBS**

  This WBS provides a view of all project tasks by category. It includes tasks defined by the software development process model and additional tasks such as document preparation. It provides a historical data base of project performance and is useful for top-level project estimating and for identifying areas which could be improved with high pay-back.

- **Binary Reporting**

  This reporting technique defines when work on a scheduled task has been completed by accepting only one of two states, complete or incomplete. It requires well-defined exit criteria for each task and is most useful when tasks are small, such as between 4-80 staff-hours of effort.

- **Earned-Value Tracking**

  When combined with binary reporting of task completion, this technique allows a project manager to determine how well the project is progressing with respect to the resources budgeted. It provides actual performance data needed to update the remaining plans for a project. Thus, it provides early-alert indicators of possible problems for a project manager and it contributes to an historical data base for future estimating and process improvement.

The effective use of these techniques are interrelated and together provide the threads of control for a specific project as well as multiple organizational projects over time. Each views a project from different vantage points and each makes a unique contribution. The first critical step in project control is a realistic and completely defined software development process model. The remaining techniques build upon it. When defined to a small granularity of tasks, the process model is the key to effective use of the other management techniques.

These techniques provide a project manager or an organization with the tools necessary to control a current project as well as projects over time. For a current project, they provide for project planning and for accomplishing the first step of Brooks' challenge— knowing when a project is "a day late." They also provide the foundations for project replanning to meet the next step — taking corrective action. The use of these techniques provides the foundation for organizational control and improvement necessary to meet the project-management challenges of the future.

REFERENCES

[1]   Boehm, B., *Software Engineering Economics*, Englewood Cliffs, NJ: Prentice-Hall, 1981.

[2]   Brooks, F. Jr., *The Mythical Man Month*, Reading, MA: Addison-Wesley, 1975.

[3]   DeMarco, T., *Controlling Software Projects*, New York: Yourdon Press, 1982.

[4]   Fairley, R. E., *Software Project Management*, Reading, MA: Technology Exchange Co., 1990.

[5]   Humphrey, W., *Managing the Software Process*, Reading, MA: Addison-Wesley, 1989.

[6]   Juran, J., "Managing for World-Class Quality," *pmNETwork*, April 1992, pp. 5-8.

[7]   Pittman, M. "Lessons Learned In Managing Object-Oriented Development," *IEEE Software*, January 1993, pp. 43-53

[8]   Russell, G., "Experience with Inspection in Ultralarge-Scale Developments," *IEEE Software*, January 1992, pp. 25-31.

[9]   Tausworthe, R., "The Work Breakdown Structure in Software Project Management," *Journal of Systems and Software*, Vol. 1, 1980, pp. 181-186.

[10]   "The Decline and Fall of the American Programmer: From a Series of Articles by Ed Yourdon," *Deadline Newsletter*, April 1989, pp. 8-13.

[11]   Ward, J., "Productivity through Project Management: Controlling the Project Variables," *Information Systems Management*, Winter 1994, pp. 16-21.

[12]   Zells, L., *Managing Software Projects*, Wellesley, MA: QED Information Sciences, 1990.

ABOUT THE AUTHOR

PATRICIA W. HURST is a senior lecturer/instructor with Fastrak Training, Inc. in Columbia, MD. Her seminars and workshops include software engineering topics such as quality assurance, project management, process modeling and risk management. She has authored articles for leading publications and is the author of *Software Quality Assurance: Control, Metrics and Testing*, a course published by Technology Exchange Company, Reading, MA. She is past Editor and Publisher of *Deadline Newsletter*, a bimonthly publication of abstracts from leading journals and other publications of interest to the software-engineering community.

Despite claims to the contrary, no accurate method exists to predict time and manpower needed to develop a software system.

MAKING SOFTWARE DEVELOPMENT ESTIMATES "GOOD"

by Andrew B. Ferrentino

A software system was estimated to require 30,000 lines of source code and an 18-month development period. Six weeks before the scheduled delivery date, it was reported to be progressing according to plan. Two weeks before the scheduled delivery, project management reported that the estimated size of the system had been revised to over 100,000 lines of code. Delivery would be delayed at least one year. Sound familiar?

There are many reasons for such a disaster. One reason, possibly characteristic of most such projects, is the manner of interpretation and use of estimation by the project management. The problem begins with the failure to recognize the difference between estimation parameters, such as system size (measured in lines of source code), and the product of the development process, namely the system itself. When this distinction is lost, development progress is measured in terms of lines of code generated rather than the more concrete notion of functions fully implemented. Project progress, then, is measured as:

$$\frac{L_G}{L_E} \times 100\%$$

where L_G is lines of source code generated to date and L_E is total lines of source code originally estimated.

Applying this progress measure in the context of the horror story cited above, the following analysis might plausibly explain what happened. Six weeks before scheduled delivery, the number of lines of source code was 29,000, thus

$$\frac{L_G}{L_E} \times 100\% = \frac{29,000}{30,000} = 97\%$$

Project management may then have concluded that they were right on schedule even though many of the programmers on the project knew that, based on real progress, the end was nowhere in sight. The real progress is measured on the basis of the implemented, tested and documented functions, irrespective of the original estimate of system size.

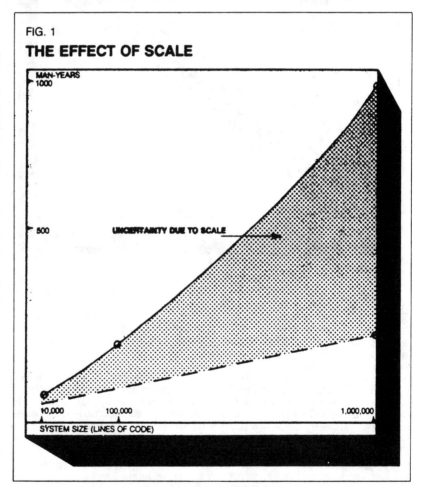

FIG. 1

THE EFFECT OF SCALE

MAN-YEARS
1000

500

UNCERTAINTY DUE TO SCALE

10,000   100,000   1,000,000

SYSTEM SIZE (LINES OF CODE)

If we could accurately predict the size of the system at the start of the project, lines of code generated would be an accurate measure of project progress. However:

1. Accurate estimation is not attainable in the current state of software engineering.

2. Some of the management pitfalls ensue from assuming that accurate estimation is possible.

3. There is a management approach to software development that can increase our success rate.

In essence, estimation is an educated guess at the time and manpower needed to develop a system. Although this guess can be quantified through analysis or statistics, it is still a guess. Despite claims to the contrary, there is no method to accurately predict the time and manpower needed to develop a software system. The parameters we use to compute our estimates, e.g., system scale, error removal, programmer productivity, and requirements stability vary enormously.

Reprinted with permission from *DATAMATION Magazine*, Sept. 1981, pp. 179–182.
Copyright © by Cahners Publishing, Reed Elsevier Inc.

Cost of error removal can vary widely, from as little as 5% to 10% to as much as 50% to 60% of total development cost.

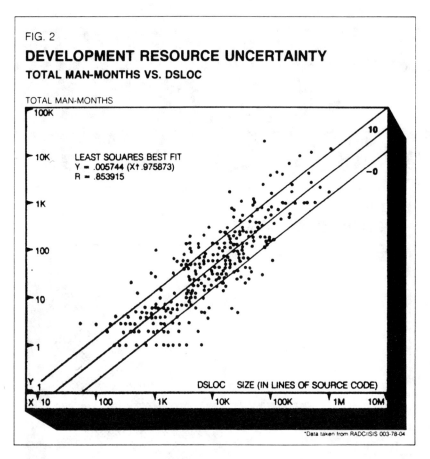

FIG. 2

DEVELOPMENT RESOURCE UNCERTAINTY
TOTAL MAN-MONTHS VS. DSLOC

TOTAL MAN-MONTHS

LEAST SQUARES BEST FIT
$Y = .005744 (X \uparrow .975873)$
$R = .853915$

DSLOC   SIZE (IN LINES OF SOURCE CODE)

*Data taken from RADC/ISIS 003-78-04

EFFECTS OF SCALE

As the size of a system increases, the resources required to develop the system do not increase linearly. Rather, they may increase exponentially, as shown in Fig. 1. The more people required to do the job, the greater the required interaction. The number of possible interactions increases in a squared relation with the number of people, i.e., with N people, there are $(N^2 - N)/2$ possible interactions. To manage these interactions, personnel must be increased.

If it were possible to eliminate the added interactions, the number of people required might increase only linearly with system size. The use of good design principles, such as decomposition, can result in designs where small task groups can independently develop parts of the system. The design of the system, then, and the degree to which the organization can be structured to mirror the design decomposition, can result in substantial resource savings. The cross-hatched area of Fig. 1, represents the variability associated with system scale.

The cost of error removal can vary widely. Error removal costs can be as little as 5% to 10% or as much as 50% to 60% of the total development cost. One factor determining the cost of error removal is the degree to which system testing is used. If system testing is the sole means of error removal the cost will be high, as most errors are introduced early in the development process and the cost of removing an error increases the longer it remains undetected.

The most difficult aspect is individual programmer variability. Many controlled experiments have tried to gauge this variable, and although the quantitative results differ, they are all consistent in demonstrating great variation from one individual to another. Below are typical ranges of variation from a representative sampling of programmers working on identical problems:

CODING TIME	25:1
ERROR REMOVAL TIME	26:1
Size (lines of code)	5:1

Despite this tremendous variation we tend to treat one programmer like another in estimating resources. To get the most productivity from a group, individual strengths must be identified and matched to the work. Because this is impractical for most projects, average productivity figures must be used in estimation. This introduces a large margin of uncertainty

If the requirements for a software system are well defined at the start of the development cycle and remain fixed throughout, the development resources should be much smaller than if the requirements are ill-defined or continually changing. Unfortunately, the latter is usually a fact of life. Good techniques for managing change are required if development costs are to be minimized.

One downfall of development projects is management that thinks requirements can be fixed at the start and kept constant. We had the unfortunate experience of being part of a project on which several million dollars were expended but which never progressed beyond the requirements phase. In this case, the customer was not willing to proceed with design until the "complete" requirements were specified. Because of the complexity of the problem, this was impractical and led to the failure of the project. With large systems (especially pioneers) requirements can rarely be fixed at the start. There is a continual learning process that causes change.

Requirements widely affect the development resources. If the development project team cannot effectively manage changing requirements, resource utilization will be unpredictable.

Fig. 2 shows actual development project statistics indicative of variability.* For 100,000 lines of code systems, note that the development resources vary from approximately 100 to 10,000 man-months—two orders of magnitude. It is difficult to assert that accurate estimation of development resources is plausible in the face of this data. In fact, we can do better than the range shown because the data represents projects of varying characteristics. When these characteristics are taken into account, then a statistically valid range can be derived for similar projects. But this is possible only in a *statistical* sense, i.e., when dealing with averages. When focusing on a specific project anything can happen, including complete failure.

HINDSIGHT ESTIMATE

The size of a system may have been estimated to be 80,000 lines of code but the completed system contained 175,000 lines of code. Was the original estimate no good? In hindsight one can say what the "correct" estimate should have been, but this is another way of saying that one can make an accurate estimate. The following anecdote shows that even in hindsight there is no correct estimate.

A system development job was bid and won for a fixed price of $250,000. After contract award the winning company learned that the next lowest bid was $1.2 million. An audit was immediately called and the professional audit team reported that indeed the system would cost over $1 million to develop.

Because optimizing programmer productivity is often impractical, average productivity figures must be used in estimation.

"Terrific references, but I'll give it to you straight—being an advanced systems technologist does not qualify you to be a second baseman."

©DATAMATION

To salvage the effort, a small, experienced team was assigned to the job. It endeavored to use all the best software engineering practices and management controls to develop a good design, control change, and reduce the impact of error. The system was developed for $300,000.

Now, in hindsight, which was the correct estimate: $250,000, $300,000 or $1.2 million? If the audit had never been performed but the team still managed to do it for $300,000, would the project have been considered a success? Or could the job have been done for $100,000? Or was it really a success after all?

None of the above statements are "correct," for a different team using different techniques may have performed the job for $1.5 million. The same team with the same techniques may have done the job for $600,000 if it had made a bad design decision requiring later correction. We can't make good estimates, but we can make estimates good.

It is imperative, then, to manage development projects in order to make estimates good. To accomplish this, a combination of management and software engineering techniques must be brought to bear, such as:
● Well-defined milestones: specification complete, coding complete, unit test complete, etc. must be used as the means to measure software development progress against budget expended.
● The concept of software development in increments (or releases) of increasing functions will provide a framework for controlling the impact of changing requirements.
● The application of advanced designed techniques such as information hiding and abstract machine hierarchies give rise to good designs.
● Verification techniques such as formal walkthroughs and informal proof techniques help to identify errors soon after they are introduced.   ✱

Andrew B. Ferrentino, vice president of Lesko/Fox Associates, Washington, D.C. management consultants, has had over 15 years' experience in the analysis, design, implementation, and management of communications/computer-based systems.

CARTOON BY SIDNEY HARRIS

Criteria For Controlling Projects According To Plan[1]

Hans J. Thamhain
Worcester Polytechnic Institute

David L. Wilemon
Syracuse University

Introduction

Few project managers would argue the need for controlling their projects according to established plans. The challenge is to apply the available tools and techniques effectively. That is, to manage the effort by leading the multifunctional personnel toward the agreed-on objectives within the given time and resource constraints. Even the most experienced practitioners often find it difficult to control programs in spite of apparent detail in the plan, personnel involvement, and even commitment. As summarized in Table 1, effective program management is a function of properly defining the work, budgets and schedules and then monitoring progress. Equally importantly, it is related to the ability to keep personnel involved and interested in the work, obtain and refuel commitment from the team as well as from upper management, and to resolve some of the enormous complexities on the technical, human and organizational side.

Responding to this interest, a field study was initiated to investigate the practices of project managers regarding their project control experiences. Specifically, the study investigates:

1. Type of project control problems experienced by project managers.
2. Project management practices and performance.
3. Criteria for effective project control.

Method Of Investigation

Data were collected over a period of three years from a sample of over 400 project leaders in predominantly technical undertakings, such as electronics, petrochemical, construction, and pharmaceutical projects. The

Table 1
Challenges of Managing Projects According to Plan

Rank	Challenge	Frequency (Mentioned by % of PM's)
1	Coping with End-Date Driven Schedules	85%
2	Coping with Resource Limitations	83%
3	Communicating Effectively among Task Groups	80%
4	Gaining Commitment from Team Members	74%
5	Establishing Measurable Milestones	70%
6	Coping with Changes	60%
7	Working Out Project Plan Agreement with Team	57%
8	Gaining Commitment from Management	45%
9	Dealing with Conflict	42%
10	Managing Vendors and Subcontractors	38%
11	Other Challenges	35%

[1]This article was previously published in the *1985 Proceedings of the Project Management Institute,* 16th Annual Seminar/Symposium, Denver, Colorado.

This article is reprinted from *Project Management Journal,* June 1986, with permission of the Project Management Institute, 130 South State Road, Upper Darby, PA 19082, a worldwide organization of advancing the state-of-the-art in project management.

data were collected mostly by questionnaires from attendees of project management workshops and seminars, as well as during in-plant consulting work conducted by the authors. Selectively, questionnaires were followed up by personal interviews. All data were checked for relevant sourcing to assure that the people who filled in the questionnaire had the minimum project leadership qualifications we established. These included: Two years of experience in managing multi-disciplinary projects, leading a minimum of three other project professionals, and being formally accountable for final results.

Table 2
Potential Problems* (Subtle Reasons) Leading to Schedule Slips and Budget Overruns

01 Difficulty of Defining Work in Sufficient Detail
02 Little Involvement of Project Personnel During Planning
03 Problems with Organizing and Building Project Team
04 No Firm Agreement to Project Plan by Functional Management
05 No Clear Charter for Key Project Personnel
06 Insufficiently Defined Project Team Organization
07 No Clear Role/Responsibility Definition for P-Personnel
08 Rush into Project Kick-off
09 Project Perceived as Not Important or Exciting
10 No Contingency Provisions
11 Inability to Measure True Project Performance
12 Poor Communications with Upper Management
13 Poor Communications with Customer or Sponsor
14 Poor Understanding of Organizational Interfaces
15 Difficulty in Working across Functional Lines
16 No Ties between Project Performance and Reward System
17 Poor Project Leadership
18 Weak Assistance and Help from Upper Management
19 Project Leader Not Involved with Team
20 Ignorant of Early Warning Signals and Feedback
21 Poor Ability to Manage Conflict
22 Credibility Problems with Task Leaders
23 Difficulties in Assessing Risks
24 Insensitivity to Organizational Culture/Value System
25 Insufficient Formal Procedural Project Guidelines
26 Apathy or Indifference by Project Team or Management
27 No Mutual Trust among Team Members
28 Too Much Unresolved/Dysfunctional Conflict
29 Power Struggles
30 Too Much Reliance on Established Cost Accounting System

*The tabulated potential problems represent summaries of data compiled during interviews with project personnel and management.

Sample Characteristics

The final qualifying sample included 304 project leaders from 183 technical projects. Each leader had an average of 5.2 years of project management experience. As shown by the sigma/standard deviation[2] the sample data are distributed widely:

Number of Project Leaders in Sample 304
Number of Projects in Sample 183
Number of Project Leaders
    per Project . . . . .1.66 ($\sigma = 1$)
Project Size (Average) . . . . $850K ($\sigma = 310K$)
Project Duration (Average) . . . 12 Months ($\sigma = 4$)
Multidisciplinary Nature
    (Average) . . . . 8 Team Members ($\sigma = 5$)
Project Management
    Experience/PM . . . . 5.2 Years ($\sigma = 2.5$)
Number of Previous Projects/PM . . . 6 ($\sigma = 4.5$)

Data were collected in three specific modes: (1) Open ended questions leading to a broad set of data, such as condensed in Table 2, and used for broad classifications and further, more detailed investigations; (2) Specific questions, requested to be answered on a tested five-point scale, such as shown in Figure 1. The scores enabled subsequent data ranking and correlation analysis; and (3) Interviews leading to a discussion of the previous findings and further qualitative investigations into the practices and experiences of project managers and their superiors.

All associations were measured by utilizing Kendall's Tau rank-order correlation. The agreement between project managers and their superiors on the reason for project control problems was tested by using the non-parametric Kruskal-Wallis one-way analysis of variance by ranks, setting the null-hypothesis for agreement at various confidence levels depending on the strength of the agreement or disagreement as specified in the write-up.

Discussion Of Results

The results of this study are being presented in four parts. First, the reasons for poor project control are analyzed as they relate to budget overruns and schedule slips. Second, the less tangible criteria for these control problems are discussed. This part shows that many of the reasons blamed for poor project perform-

---

[2]The distribution of the sample data is skewed. The sigma/standard deviation listed in parentheses corresponds to the positive side only.

Rank by General Managers	Rank by Project Managers	Reason or Problem	Rarely 1 — Sometimes 2 — Often 3 — Most Likely 4 — Always 5	Agreement Between GM & PM
1	10	Insufficient Front-End Planning	GM / PM	Disagree
2	3	Unrealistic Project Plan		Strongly Agree
3	8	Project Scope Underestimated		Disagree
4	1	Customer/Management Changes		Disagree
5	14	Insufficient Contingency Planning		Disagree
6	13	Inability to Track Progress	GM / PM	Disagree
7	5	Inablity to Detect Problems Early		Agree
8	9	Insufficient Number of Checkpoints		Agree
9	4	Staffing Problems		Disagree
10	2	Technical Complexities		Disagree
11	6	Priority Shifts		Disagree
12	10	No Commitment by Personnel to Plan		Agree
13	12	Uncooperative Support Groups		Agree
14	7	Sinking Team Spirit		Disagree
15	15	Unqualified Project Personnel		Agree

Directly Observed Reasons for Schedule Slips and Budget Overruns
Figure 1

ance, such as insufficient front-end planning and underestimating the complexities and scope, are really rooted in some less obvious organizational, managerial, and interpersonal problems. Third, the relationship between project performance and project management problems is discussed, and fourth, the criteria for effective project controls are summarized.

The Reasons for Poor Project Control

Figure 1 summarizes an investigation into 15 problem areas regarding their effects on poor project performance. Specifically, project managers and their superiors (such as senior functional managers and general managers) indicate on a five-point scale their perception of how frequently certain problems are responsible for schedule slips and budget overruns. The data indicate that project leaders perceive these problem areas in a somewhat different order than their superiors.

While *project leaders* most frequently blame the following reasons as being responsible for poor project performance:
1. Customer and Management Changes
2. Technical Complexities
3. Unrealistic Project Plans
4. Staffing Problems
5. Inability to Detect Problems Early,
senior management ranks these reasons somewhat differently:
1. Insufficient Front-End Planning
2. Unrealistic Project Plans
3. Underestimated Project Scope
4. Customer and Management Changes
5. Insufficient Contingency Planning

On balance, the data supports the findings of subsequent interviews that project leaders are more concerned with external influences such as changes, complexities, staffing, and priorities while senior managers focus more on what should and can be done to avoid problems.

In fact, the differences between project leaders' and senior/superior management's perceptions were measured statistically by using a Kruskal-Wallis analysis of variance by ranks, based on the following test statistics:

Strong Agreement: If acceptable at > 99% confidence

Agreement: If acceptable at > 90% confidence

Weak Agreement: If acceptable at > 80% confidence

Disagreement: If rejected at 80% confidence

Project leaders disagree with their superiors on the ranking of importance for all but six reasons. What this means is that while both groups of management actually agree on the basic reasons behind schedule slips and budget overruns, they attach different weights. The practical implication of this finding is that senior management expects proper project planning, organizing, and tracking from project leaders. They further believe that the "external" criteria, such as customer changes and project complexities, impact project performance only if the project had not been defined properly and sound management practices were ignored. On the other side, management's view that some of the subtle problems, such as sinking team spirit, priority shifts, and staffing, are of lesser importance might point to a potential problem area. Management might be less sensitive to these struggles, get less involved, and provide less assistance in solving these problems.

Less Obvious and Less Visible
Reasons for Poor Performance

Managers at all levels have long lists of "real" reasons why the problems identified in Figure 1 occur. They point out, for instance, that while insufficient front-end planning eventually got the project into trouble, the real culprits are much less obvious and visible. These subtle reasons, summarized in Table 2, strike a common theme. They relate strongly to organizational, managerial, and human aspects. In fact, the most frequently mentioned reasons for poor project performance can be classified in five categories:

1. Problems with organizing project team
2. Weak project leadership
3. Communication problems
4. Conflict and confusion
5. Insufficient upper management involvement

Most of the problems in Table 2 relate to the manager's ability to foster a work environment conducive to multidisciplinary teamwork, rich on professionally stimulating and interesting activities, involvement, and mutual trust. The ability to foster such a high-performance project environment requires sophisticated skills in leadership, technical, interpersonal, and administrative areas. To be effective, project managers must consider all facets of the job. They must consider the task, the people, the tools, and the organization. The days of the manager who gets by with technical expertise or pure administrative skills alone, are gone. Today the project manager must relate socially as well as technically. He or she must understand the culture and value system of the organization. Research[3] and experience show that effective project management is directly related to the level of proficiency at which these skills are mastered. This is also reflected in the 30 potential problems of our study (See Table 2) and the rank order correlations summarized in Table 3. As indicated by the correlation figure of $\tau = +.45$, the stronger managers felt about the reasons in Figure 1, the stronger they also felt about the problems in Table 2 as reasons for poor project performance. This correlation is statistically significant at a confidence level of 99% and supports the conclusion that both sets of problem areas are related and require similar skills for effective management.

Management Practice and Project Performance

Managers appear very confident in citing actual and potential problems. These managers are sure in their own mind that these problems, summarized in Figure 1 and Table 2, are indeed related to poor project performance. However, no such conclusion could be drawn without additional data and the specific statistical test shown in Table 3. As indicated by the strongly negative correlations between project performance and (1) potential problems ($\tau = -.55$) and (2) actual problems ($\tau = -.40$), the presence of either problem will indeed result in lower performance. Specifically, the stronger and more frequently project managers experience these problems, the lower was the manager judged by supe-

---

[3]For a detailed discussion of skill requirements of project managers and their impact on project performance see H. J. Thamhain & D. L. Wilemon, "Skill Requirements of Project Managers," *Convention Record, IEEE Joint Engineering Management Conference,* October 1978, and H. J. Thamhain, "Developing Engineering Management Skills" in *Management of R & D and Engineering,* North Holland Publishing Company, 1986.

Potential Problems vs. Actual	Correlation of (1) Potential Problems (Table 2) and (2) Directly Observed Reasons for Budget and Schedule Slips (Figure 1)	τ = −.45 **
Potential Problems vs. Performance	Correlation of (1) Potential Problems Leading for Budget and Schedule Slips (Table 2) and (2) Project Performance (Top Management Judgment)	τ = −.55 **
Actual Problems vs. Performance	Correlation of (1) Directly Observed Reasons for Budget and Schedule Slips (Figure 1) and (2) Project Performance	τ = −.40 **

All Tau values are   **99% Confidence Level (p = .01)
Kendall Tau
Rank-Order Correlation

Correlation of Project Management
Practices to Performance
Table 3

rior managers regarding overall on-time and on-budget performance.

Furthermore, it is interesting to note that the more subtle, potential problems correlate most strongly to poor performance ($\tau = -.55$). In fact, special insight has been gained by analyzing the association of each problem to project performance separately. Taken together, it shows that the following problems seem to be some of the most crucial *barriers* to high project performance:

- Team organization and staffing problems
- Work perceived not important, challenging, having growth potential
- Little team and management involvement during planning
- Conflict, confusion, power struggle
- Lacking commitment by team and management
- Poor project definition
- Difficulty in understanding and working across organizational interfaces
- Weak project leadership
- Measurability problems
- Changes, contingencies, and priority problems
- Poor communications, management involvement and support

To be effective, project leaders must not only recognize the potential barriers to performance, but also know where in the lifecycle of the project they most likely occur. The effective project leader takes preventive actions early in the project lifecycle and fosters a work environment that is conducive to active participation, interesting work, good communications, management involvement, and low conflict.

Criteria For Effective Project Control

The results presented so far focused on the reasons for poor project performance. That is, what went wrong and why were analyzed. This section concentrates on the lessons learned from the study and extensive interviews investigating the forces driving high project performance. Accordingly, this section summarizes the criteria which seem to be important for controlling projects according to plan. The write-up follows a recommendations format and flows with the project through its lifecycle wherever possible.

1. *Detailed Project Planning.* Develop a detailed project plan, involving all key personnel, defining the specific work to be performed, the timing, the resources, and the responsibilities.
2. *Break the overall program into phases and subsystems.* Use Work Breakdown Structure (WBS) as a planning tool.
3. *Results and Deliverables.* Define the program objectives and requirements in terms of specifications, schedule, resources and deliverable items for the total program and its subsystems.
4. *Measurable Milestones.* Define measurable milestones and checkpoints throughout the program. Measurability can be enhanced by defining specific results, deliverables, technical performance measures against schedule and budget.
5. *Commitment.* Obtain commitment from all key personnel regarding the program plan, its measures and results. This commitment can be enhanced and maintained by involving the team members early in the project planning, including the definition of results, measurable milestones, schedules and budgets. It is through this involvement that the team members gain a detailed understanding of the work to be performed, develop professional interests in the project and desires to succeed, and eventually make a firm commitment toward the specific task and the overall project objectives.
6. *Intra-Program Involvement.* Assure that the in-

terfacing project teams, such as engineering and manufacturing, work together, not only during the task transfer, but during the total life of the project. Such interphase involvement is necessary to assure effective implementation of the developments and to simply assure "doability" and responsiveness to the realities of the various functions supporting the project. It is enhanced by clearly defining the results/deliverables for each interphase point, agreed upon by both parties. In addition, a simple sign-off procedure, which defines who has to sign off on what items, is useful in establishing clear checkpoints for completion and to enhance involvement and cooperation of the interphasing team members.

7. *Project Tracking.* Define and implement a proper project tracking system which captures and processes project performance data conveniently summarized for reviews and management actions.

8. *Measurability.* Assure accurate measurements of project performance data, especially technical progress against schedule and budget.

9. *Regular Reviews.* Projects should be reviewed regularly, both on a work package (subsystem) level and total project level.

10. *Signing-On.* The process of "signing-on" project personnel during the initial phases of the project or each task seem to be very important to proper understanding of the project objectives, the specific tasks, and personal commitment. The sign-on process that is so well described in Tracy Kidders' book, *The Soul of a New Machine,* is greatly facilitated by sitting down with each team member and discussing the specific assignments, overall project objectives, as well as professional interests and support needs.

11. *Interesting Work.* The project leader should try to accommodate the professional interests and desires of supporting personnel when negotiating their tasks. Project effectiveness depends on the manager's ability to provide professionally stimulating and interesting work. This leads to increased project involvement, better communications, lower conflict, and stronger commitment. This is an environment where people work toward established objectives in a self-enforcing mode requiring a minimum of managerial controls. Although the scope of a project may be

fixed, the project manager usually has a degree of flexibility in allocating task assignments among various contributors.

12. *Communication.* Good communication is essential for effective project work. It is the responsibility of the task leaders and ultimately the project manager to provide the appropriate communication tools, techniques, and systems. These tools are not only the status meetings, reviews, schedules, and reporting systems, but also the objective statements, specifications, list of deliverables, the sign-off procedure and critical path analysis. It is up to the project leaders to orchestrate the various tools and systems, and to use them effectively.

13. *Leadership.* Assure proper program direction and leadership throughout the project lifecycle. This includes project definition, team organization, task coordination, problem identification and a search for solutions.

14. *Minimize Threats.* Project managers must foster a work environment that is low on personal conflict, power struggles, surprises, and unrealistic demands. An atmosphere of mutual trust is necessary for project personnel to communicate problems and concerns candidly and at an early point in time.

15. *Design a Personnel Appraisal and Reward System.* This should be consistent with the responsibilities of the people.

16. *Assure Continuous Senior Management Involvement, Endorsement, and Support of the Project.* This will surround the project with a priority image, enhance its visibility, and refuel overall commitment to the project and its objectives.

17. *Personal Drive.* Project managers can influence the climate of the work environment by their own actions. Concern for project team members, ability to integrate personal goals and needs of project personnel with project goals, and ability to create personal enthusiasm for the project itself can foster a climate of high motivation, work involvement, open communication, and ultimately high project performance.

A Final Note

Managing engineering programs toward established performance, schedule, and cost targets requires more than just another plan. It requires the total commitment of the performing organization plus the involvement and help of the sponsor/customer community. Successful program managers stress the importance of carefully designing the project planning and control system as well as the structural and authority relationships. All are critical to the implementation of an effective project control system. Other organizational issues, such as management style, personnel appraisals and compensation, and intraproject communication, must be carefully considered to make the system self-forcing; that is, project personnel throughout the organization must feel that participation in the project is desirable regarding the fulfillment of their professional needs and wants. Furthermore, project personnel must be convinced that management involvement is helpful in their work. Personnel must be convinced that identifying the true project status and communicating potential problems early will provide them with more assistance to problem solving, more cross-functional support, and in the end will lead to project success and the desired recognition for their accomplishments.

In summary, effective control of engineering programs or projects involves the ability to:

- Work out a detailed project plan, involving all key personnel
- Reach agreement on the plan among the project team members and the customer/sponsor
- Obtain commitment from the project team members
- Obtain commitment from management
- Define measurable milestones
- Attract and hold quality people
- Establish a controlling authority for each work package
- Detect problems early

References

1. Adams, J. R., & Barndt, S. E. Behavioral Implications of the Project Life Cycle. Chapter 12 in *Project Management Handbook*. New York: Van Nostrand Reinhold, 1983.
2. Archibald, Russel C. Planning the Project. In *Managing High-Technology Programs and Projects*. New York: Wiley, 1976.
3. Casher, J. D. How to Control Project Risks and Effectively Reduce the Chance of Failure. *Management Review,* June, 1984.
4. Delaney, W. A. Management by Phases. *Advanced Management Journal,* Winter, 1984.
5. King, W. R., & Cleland, D. I. Life Cycle Management. Chapter 11 in *Project Management Handbook*. New York: Van Nostrand Reinhold, 1983.
6. McDounough, E. F., & Kinnunen, R. M. Management Control of a New Product Development Project. *IEEE Transactions on Engineering Management,* February, 1984.
7. Pessemier, E. A. *Product Management*. New York: Wiley, 1982.
8. Spirer, H. F. Phasing out the Project. Chapter 13 in *Project Management Handbook*. New York: Van Nostrand Reinhold, 1983.
9. Stuckenbruck, L. C. Interface Management. Chapter 20 in *Matrix Management Systems Handbook*. New York: Van Nostrand Reinhold, 1984.
10. Thamhain, H. J. *Engineering Program Management*. New York: Wiley, 1984.
11. Thamhain, H. J., & Wilemon, D. L. Project Performance Measurement, The Keystone to Engineering Project Control. *Project Management Quarterly,* January, 1982.
12. Thamhain, H. J., & Wilemon, D. L. Conflict Management in Project Lifecycles. *Sloan Management Review,* Summer, 1975.
13. Tuminello, J. A Case Study of Information/Know-How Transfer. *IEEE Engineering Management Review,* June, 1984.
14. Urban, G. L., & Hauser, J. R. *Design and Marketing of New Products*. New York: Prentice Hall, 1980.
15. U.S. Air Force. *Systems Management - System Program Office Manual,* AFSCM 375-3, Washington, DC, 1964.

Dr. Hans J. Thamhain is an Associate Professor at the Management Department, Worcester Polytechnic Institute. Dr. David Wilemon is a Professor of Marketing Management at the School of Management, Syracuse University.

* * *

Software Quality Assurance: A Management Perspective

Robert H. Dunn
Systems for Quality Software
Easton, CT 06612

To many, quality assurance brings to mind the industrial quality-control model, wherein statistical analysis of measurements made at various production control points are used to prevent out-of-tolerance operations. To others, quality assurance means monitoring the adequacy and timeliness of responses to customer service complaints. Still others view quality assurance strictly in terms of process audits.

Software quality assurance (SQA) is none of these. It may borrow a bit from statistical quality control, may use measurements and analysis, and may rely on certain auditing procedures, but—except when used simply as a synonym for "testing"—SQA most closely follows the model of total quality management (TQM). That is, the quality of software is expected to derive from the quality of the process used to develop or maintain software, and SQA is largely a matter of ensuring that a good process is in place, followed, and continuously improved. The process, of course, includes all phases of testing, but testing is scarcely the only interest of SQA.

A proper process for development and maintenance encompasses management methods, technology, and personnel qualifications. Although involved in the entire process, SQA focuses on

- continuous improvement of the process through audits that attempt to determine where the process breaks down and through analysis of measurements of the process itself;
- defect prevention (feasible task definitions, traceability of requirements to verification steps, early defect detection, and the like);
- analysis of the product, including its effect on users; and
- testing of the final product (validation of the solution).

Note that concern for products is not inimical with emphasis on process. The proof, as always, lies in the pudding.

SQA arose in response to specific classes of problems confronting management. It is possible for a programming shop to experience only one of the classes, but two or more is the rule since the classes are interrelated. They are all familiar:

- Project out of control—uncertain progress and status, unreliable cost estimates, unreliable estimates of completion
- Poor performance—frequent crashes, results not necessarily repeatable, excessive use of such resources as time and memory
- Difficult maintenance—software overly complex, operational code no longer traceable to specific source code or data files and build lists
- Difficulty of use—customers or other users find software does not quite match their expectations or abilities or the environment in which the software is used

We don't have to look far to see why these four classes of problems are intertwined. Unreliable software may result from premature curtailment of testing caused by delayed progress during earlier stages of development. A program that runs too slowly may result from a botched maintenance job caused by the programmers' inability to understand the code they modified. In turn, the confusing code may result from a rushed design traceable to extensive delays in developing a requirements model. Customers may find a product unusable simply because training or user documentation didn't quite match the final product because of a constantly changing requirements model.

What is uncommon is to find problems in performance, maintenance, or use in a product whose development or maintenance was at all times attended by a high degree of project control. From a philosophical point of view, it would seem that project control should be the prime concern of SQA. From a practical point of view, the thought is of little consequence. The devil is in the details, and SQA succeeds by placing emphasis on the suitability of the process, defect prevention activities, analysis, and preparation and support for testing. Project control follows more or less automatically. Figure 1 lists the ways SQA attends to the details.

The elements of Figure 1 are self-evident to software managers. Not so for some of the techniques used in SQA that derive from the quality control community. Accordingly, we'll turn to these now.

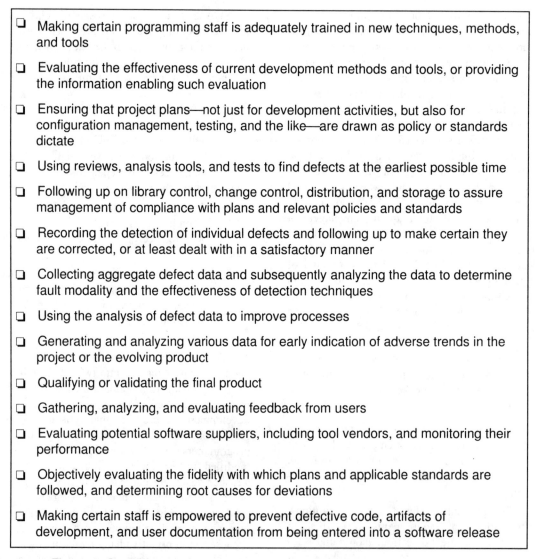

❏ Making certain programming staff is adequately trained in new techniques, methods, and tools

❏ Evaluating the effectiveness of current development methods and tools, or providing the information enabling such evaluation

❏ Ensuring that project plans—not just for development activities, but also for configuration management, testing, and the like—are drawn as policy or standards dictate

❏ Using reviews, analysis tools, and tests to find defects at the earliest possible time

❏ Following up on library control, change control, distribution, and storage to assure management of compliance with plans and relevant policies and standards

❏ Recording the detection of individual defects and following up to make certain they are corrected, or at least dealt with in a satisfactory manner

❏ Collecting aggregate defect data and subsequently analyzing the data to determine fault modality and the effectiveness of detection techniques

❏ Using the analysis of defect data to improve processes

❏ Generating and analyzing various data for early indication of adverse trends in the project or the evolving product

❏ Qualifying or validating the final product

❏ Gathering, analyzing, and evaluating feedback from users

❏ Evaluating potential software suppliers, including tool vendors, and monitoring their performance

❏ Objectively evaluating the fidelity with which plans and applicable standards are followed, and determining root causes for deviations

❏ Making certain staff is empowered to prevent defective code, artifacts of development, and user documentation from being entered into a software release

Figure 1. Constituents of a software quality assurance program.

The Techniques of Software Quality Assurance

Audits

Quality control has always relied on audits to confirm compliance with agreed-upon procedures. Audits used in SQA apply to both the product and the process used in producing the software. Among audits often performed we find the following:

- Build lists, to make certain that only approved items were link-edited

- Change control documents, to make certain they cover actual changes made in controlled code and, conversely, to make certain that approved changes were implemented

- Minutes of reviews, audited to find out if they actually occurred and if discrepancies were properly logged

- Master files of logged process discrepancies and product defects, audited to ensure closure of problems

- Test logs, audited for correct procedure and the logging of results

- User manuals, examined to ensure compliance with format standards and with the actual feature set contained in the release

- Project plans, to make certain they are complete, mutually consistent, and in conformance with approved development or maintenance standards

- Files of user problems, to ensure their intelligible logging, that action assignments were made, and that closure is eventually made

In theory, any objective person can perform an audit, at least if audit standards are available. In practice, many programming shops hire software quality engineers (SQE) for the purpose. This not only provides the necessary objectivity, but it also avoids the necessity of diverting other staff from essential development tasks. As we shall see, once on board, an SQE can serve other important roles as well.

Trend Data

SQA uses another common quality control tool, the detection and analysis of process variables that attach to quality and process control. The classic tool is the control chart (Deming 1982). Here, one plots variation of a product or process and compares the plot between constant limits. If the color of tennis balls rolling off the line starts to deviate from the upper and lower spectral limits, adjustments in the flow of dye need to be made. Now, software management has few statistically distributed variables to deal with, so such canonical control charts are seldom used in SQA. One such chart in use relates to the detection of bugs in a given defect removal operation (for example, integration testing). If the number of detected errors exceeds some upper limit—established on the basis of experience—we know that either the code is too buggy, or that preceding defect removal operations were sloppily performed.

A common control chart having only an upper bound is the curve of completed items versus time, wherein the bound is the total number of items scheduled. For example, we might chart the number of features resolved in code, or the number of code units submitted to the integration test team, or the number of successful test completions. In each of these, the upper bound is obvious. In a project in trouble, the curve often looks like that of Figure 2 [Marciniak 1994, p. 949].

A chart with only a lower bound, applicable to later phases of testing, is that of test failures versus time. The failure rate should decrease with time, and, indeed, management often decides that testing may not conclude until the rate has reached some predetermined level. Less frequently, failure rate data have been applied to one of several software reliability growth models to predict when the failure rate will reach a given level, estimate the number of bugs currently in the system, and so forth. One can trace these models back to the hardware reliability models in common use by the quality community. The models are based on the premise that failures can be described by a probability distribution (Musa et al. 1990). In the material world, reliability models deal with systems of vast numbers of identical parts that in response to external stress fail according to well-behaved statistical patterns. In the software world, the failures we see are not caused by external influences on software but by a non-homogeneous set of defects in the software. Where used, reliability growth models have served as a tool to help anticipate the future, not the basis for go/no-go decisions.

As a final example, we have the chart of known bugs in a system from release to release; alternatively, to account for the customary growth of a system, the fault density from release to release. Ideally, we want to see the number or density decrease as the system evolves. If it increases, especially if the fault density increases, management knows to look into maintenance practices, and quite possibly configuration control as well.

435

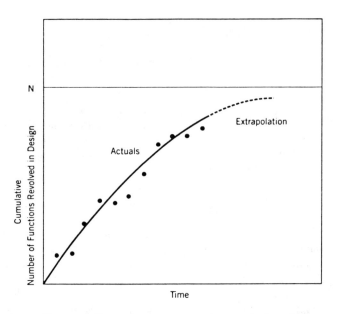

Figure 2. The 95 percent syndrome during design.

Direct Measurements of Software Products and Service

Apart from trend charts, product measurements (a mainstay of traditional quality control) enter into SQA as well. The most common non-structural measurement is the actual number of faults in a released product. It is no secret that reported faults—whether found in testing or by users—are classified into such categories as *fix now, analyze for impact, schedule for release x.x, fix if we ever get a chance* (and we know we'll not). Management needs to know the number in each category, both for the sake of the product and as an indicator of how well the development or maintenance process is working.

While we can conceive of other "measures of goodness," such as the time to fix a bug (a measure of maintainability), none are now common in SQA. Staff at Boeing Aerospace Company have proposed a number of quality indexes based on ratios. Example: "portability" is the ratio of the "effort to transport" to the "effort to develop" (Bowen 1985). Although several such ratios have intuitive appeal, they have not come into standard use because of the difficulty in acquiring the necessary data. However, one can calculate the ratio of the total time spent in fixing bugs to the time spent in developing new features, or similar measures that reflect the current state of a system.

Such data, like the chart of known bugs from release to release, may provide evidence of poor maintainability.

The most popular measures of software structure are size and complexity. Size, in terms of lines of source code or the number of statements, is found in such metrics as labor-months per KLOC and faults per KLOC. It may also be useful to compare programmer efficiency, if one can get comparable-size numbers from competitive products. The size of a program load may also be important. If one's competitors require four megabytes of PC memory, and we need only one megabyte, we have a selling point. Accordingly, comparing these measures with those of competitive products tells a bit about how well we're doing at directing development to user needs.

Many CASE tools provide measures of complexity, of which the McCabe graph-theoretic calculation for logic flow is the most popular (McCabe 1976). There are other measures, as well, and typically one uses whatever one's tools provide. Logic flow does not provide the full story on complexity—certainly module coupling and local naming and partitioning of data enter into complexity—but at least we can put a number on it.

Where service enters into the use of software, management needs to know how well the users are getting the service they need. This is particularly pertinent if the product is used in a competitive marketplace, but the satisfaction of in-house users is also a measure of how well the information systems (IS) organization does its job. Depending on the character of the product and the service that attaches, one might measure the percentage of calls for assistance that are handled by the person answering the phone, the time before anyone comes on line, the number of calls (an indirect measure of the usefulness of documentation or online help), and the like. And, of course, one cannot ignore the standard quality control technique of soliciting direct user feedback. Like product data, service data needs to be analyzed, with summary reports prepared for whoever can take action. This is another likely job for an SQE.

Failure Analysis

Indispensable to reliability engineering, the technique of failure analysis has a role to play in software as well. Analysts look for common failure modes, correlation of failure with operating conditions, and other clues to finding the source of failures when such failures do not easily lend themselves to diagnosis. Analysis of failures extends also to their root cause, a matter that may take considerable effort. Are deficient requirements models contributing a disproportionate share of problems? Do the designers need to better understand the operational environment? Are designs hurried through with scanty reviews? Such root-cause analysis, though often compromised by unavoidable

subjectivity, is essential to continuous improvement of the process.

Process Cause and Effect

Like the root-cause analysis of software failures, more general analyses attempt to find weak areas in the software process. Whether triggered by failures or by other observations, analysis is often tackled not by a single person but by a team. SQEs, if on staff, are well equipped by disposition to lead such teams. One of the techniques favored by an SQE is to organize a team effort about an Ishikawa cause-and-effect, or *fishbone*, diagram. Ishikawa based his scheme on five main objectives or control points: man, machine, material, method, and measurement. In discussion, each is found to derive from other factors. Ishikawa's objectives need to be adapted for software. For maintenance cost, we might replace man with staff, machine with software development environment, and material by product definition as in Figure 3 (Marciniak 1994, p. 953). For reducing the cost of failures, we might consider four main control points: caliber of staff, effectiveness of technology, effectiveness of tools, and maintainability (Dunn and Ullman 1994, pp. 241-245).

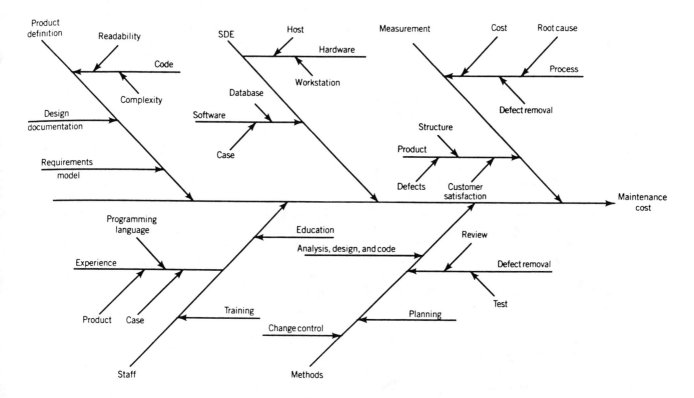

Figure 3. Process cause and effect.

437

Pareto Anaysis

In 1906 the economist Vilfredo Pareto published a treatise on skewed distributions of wealth among population groups. He discovered that 80 percent of the wealth was controlled by 20 percent of the people. The quality expert J.M. Juran seized on Pareto's work to describe the method of separating the "vital few" from the "trivial many." (Juran 1964, p. 49) If the quality of a product mostly derives from only a few of many processes required to produce it, these few should be where one concentrates failure analysis and improvement efforts. A noted study (Endres 1975) of 422 distinct modules in a large software system revealed that 15 percent of the faults could be attributed to three modules, 24 percent to 42 modules, and so on. Plainly, a project to improve the product should start with the three conspicuous troublemakers, then move on to the next 42.

Quality engineers use Pareto analysis for other applications as well. In 1989, in conjunction with a study to determine how to improve the quality of service to users of an overloaded data processing system, the author and an associate performed an (unpublished) analysis of the usage of an application program library. Of 170 programs used during one month, 10 accounted for 76 percent of all computer resource consumption. Obviously, the 10 were the first ones earmarked for streamlining.

Efficacy of Defect Removal

We perform reviews or inspections of requirements models, designs, and code. We perform static analysis of code and sometimes design. We test code in various ways. How good are any of these at finding faults? The earlier a fault can be found, the less it costs to fix (by far). So we want to know how effective each of these fault detection processes is. Consider that during unit test 5 bugs are found. During subsequent testing, another 4 bugs are found in the subject code unit. The first six months after release, one more bug is found. Of 10 bugs that could have been caught at unit test (assuming that none was an interface bug), only half actually were. For the subject code, the efficacy of defect removal (EOR) was 50 percent. In itself, this is unimportant. But for all the code of the system, indeed for all the systems developed or maintained using the same process, a 50 percent EOR is sad news.

In general, the EOR for a given defect removal process is formed by taking the ratio of the number of faults actually found to the number that theoretically could have been found, and multiplying by 100. (Dunn 1984, pp. 19–20) It's a good metric for improving the process. EOR doesn't derive directly from traditional quality control, but it relates to analyses of the process that starts with source inspection, incoming inspection, subassembly inspection, and so on until final equipment test.

Task Exit/Entrance Criteria

Making certain that a task isn't considered complete until it is truly complete is critical to project control. A requirements model, for example, should not be used as the basis for design until it has met all the standards established for requirements models, notwithstanding a few "to be determined" items (the closure of which will be tracked). Where we run into trouble is when we have an excessive number of TBDs, when the model has not been run past the customer—perhaps demonstrated in an executable prototype, where its review is given scant attention and no one assigned closure of the few problem areas that came up, where some of the information is passed on in formats unfamiliar to the staff who will implement the model.

To minimize the effect of "stuff thrown over the wall," management lists specific criteria that must be met before a task is signed off. Spot audits correlate sign-off sheets with the actual artifacts of completed tasks.

Similarly, tasks should not be started until the people who will implement them have a solid foundation to build on. We are all familiar with designers, driven by a schedule that called for them to start implementing a requirements model, who were forced to substitute guesses for the facts that would have been found in a proper definition of the problem. Not only does rework result, the design itself may incorporate material salvaged from guesswork badly spliced with material generated after the requirements were finally made clear. This all-too-common occurrence is compounded by plans that make staff available for a task by some given date. If the staff do not start on the task when they are supposed to, their time is wasted. In some cases management would do better to put together a few hastily improvised training sessions than to start a task prematurely. In any case, task entrance criteria should be established before work is begun. The diversity in life cycle definitions and programming paradigms currently in use make it impossible to give examples of entrance criteria. However, we can say that all have in common the thought that they include whatever is intended to be available to the people who will begin a new activity.

Other Aspects of SQA

Plainly, one doesn't place an order for CASE unless one is certain the tools will add to the process or solve specific problems. So improvement is a given, at least with regard to intent. The quality aspects deal with getting CASE from the best toolmakers and getting the best of the tools after they are delivered. Some software suppliers live up to their promises of support, some don't. We need to keep track of complaints from our staff that arose with products bought earlier from a vendor. We need to remind purchasing to check on the financial stability of suppliers. We need to have all this information available in easily interpreted form when we select a supplier.

Major tool acquisitions need to be carefully introduced. Use on pilot projects, training, staff feedback, and measurements of productivity and quality all enter into the evaluation of new tools. This, too, is part of quality management.

Test Control

As noted earlier, the term software quality assurance has been used simply as another way of saying "testing," especially testing of the final product. Here, we use SQA in a very different sense, one in which the connection between SQA and testing is the same as that between SQA and other programming activities—SQA's contribution to the quality of the process.

Planning

Software testing has three main objectives:

- Determining that code performs as it is expected to

- Exposing as many faults as possible

- Determining the extent to which the code is suitable for the application

The first of these implies demonstrating all the features or functions defined in the requirements model. Predetermined test data, in contrast to random data, largely drive these tests. For a new release of existing software, we also require execution of regression tests of the complete system—that is, the repetition of tests used for the last release. SQA often relies on elaborate schemes to trace functional requirements to the tests that will demonstrate functional performance.

Exposure of faults implies testing not only the functionality of software but also exercising its structure. In coverage-based testing, random input may be used to augment predetermined data, although without knowing what the correct output should be, such tests

often accomplish little in the absence of faults that cause system crashes.

Suitability is the stuff of beta testing, but also of in-house tests that explore the system's reliability and its envelope of performance (for example, what is the server's delay in responding to client requests, given different numbers of clients simultaneously online). Thorough test planning explores not only the full input space of a system but its output domain as well.

We might note that beta testing is directed not only to an operational system but also to any support—training, user documentation, hot-line support—it requires. Much of the value of beta testing will be lost in the absence of a system for tracking and correlating all problems. With regard to released code, it's worth observing that this is one place where all the input data are random. However, we need not be concerned about having an oracle to tell us if the operations are successful. Users know.

Quality assurance programs attempt to make certain that the three objectives are addressed, as appropriate, at all the levels of testing that are planned. Plainly, suitability is of less importance at the lowest level of tests than finding bugs, but to the extent that each objective can be realized, one designs test cases specific to the objective.

Following the Plans

Audits, covered earlier, are the primary means of seeing that tests are conducted in accordance with plans. Audits seek to confirm that all intended test cases were executed, that deviations from expected results were logged and if not fixed on the spot were assigned to solvers, and that results, required for comparisons with later tests, were properly archived. Spot audits also confirm the collection of data that test tools do not capture automatically. Such data as the time between test failures and the tabulation of code elements given quick fixes are among the measurements essential to a sustained quality program. SQEs generally act as the auditors.

Configuration Control

In most programming milieux, once code goes under project control—that is, once it is out of the hands of the programmer who wrote and in most cases gave it its first tests—a certain formality attaches to any changes to the code. At the very least, the identification of the latest edition is entered into build lists. At the other extreme, no change may be made without authorization. This is certainly the case for changes made in response to revisions to the requirements model.

Modern build systems coupled to library control tools provide the audit trails that, it would seem, are all that are needed to ensure configuration control. However, the tools can only report the constituency of a build and the authenticity of its source. They cannot confirm the anticipated constituency. That is, a test series may be run without the latest (and authorized) version of a module simply because it wasn't entered into the library and its edition code wasn't updated in the build script. This can easily happen when a current release is being fixed at the same time the next release is being evaluated. Management relies on assiduous monitoring, perhaps by SQEs, to avoid this and similar ambiguities.

Test Exit Approval

This is nothing more than a special case of the task exit criteria discussed earlier. However, since quality assurance has historically been associated with assessing the goodness of a product, it is worth noting that an SQA program entails confirmation that all testing tasks were completed, or at least that deviations were noted, approved, and tracked for closure. Typical items one might find on "check-off lists" include the following:

- Achieving the planned percentage of structural coverage
- Fault rate asymptotic to a predetermined level
- Satisfactory results from all tests, although "satisfactory" may involve judgment
- Results from the file of regression test scripts identical to earlier ones
- The availability of all measurements
- Agreement by user or customer agents that the tests were satisfactory
- Acceptable performance measurements

Validating operation with other software systems or special-purpose hardware entails criteria having to do with composite behavior. Here, we can expect to find items dealing with the test of all interface modes, tolerance to failures of interfacing hardware or software, and the like.

Some Final Thoughts

So far, we have been concerned with software development and maintenance in an orderly, managed environment. However, in all too many programming environments we have unstable requirements and unrealistic objectives. Management remote from programming (let's call it upper management) requires a new release of software with a long list of new features—all in two months. And every week the programming staff learns that one or another member of upper management, in response to user or marketplace pressure, redefines a function or adds a completely new one. Just as vexing is the moving target often implied by concurrent hardware/software design.

This is a difficult environment in which to follow an orderly sequence of design verification, defect detection, and thorough testing. All too often, shortcuts are taken, test strategies are compromised to concentrate on getting out any fatal bugs to the exclusion of lesser ones, and testing of a completely integrated system ends when the calendar says it must, regardless of results. The very content of the system is uncertain, owing to the abandonment of strict library control during integration testing, which can only lead to more costly maintenance of the system and increasing numbers of latent bugs.

In short, software quality assurance cannot exist without management commitment. We can have programming staffs of the highest caliber, the latest and best integrated programming tools, dedicated software quality engineers, and bad software. Something will be produced—it always is—but it won't exhibit quality. A chaotic environment is inimical to the concept of software quality assurance. In such an environment, the first step toward software quality assurance is to make order out of chaos.

References

Bowen, T., G. Wigli, and J. Tsai, *Specification of Software Quality Attributes*, RADC Report TR-85-37, Rome Air Development Center, Griffiss AFB, N.Y., Feb. 1985.

Deming, W.E., *Quality, Productivity, and Competitive Position*, MIT Press, Cambridge, Mass., 1982.

Dunn, R., *Software Defect Removal*, McGraw-Hill, New York, N.Y., 1984.

Dunn, R. and R. Ullman, *TQM for Computer Software*, 2nd ed., McGraw-Hill, New York, N.Y., 1994.

Endres, A., "An Analysis of Errors and Their Causes in System Programs," *IEEE Trans. Software Eng.*, SE-1, Jan. 1975, pp. 140–149.

Juran, J.M., *Managerial Breakthrough*, McGraw-Hill, New York, N.Y., 1964.

Marciniak, J.J., *Encyclopedia of Software Engineering*, John Wiley & Sons, New York., N.Y., 1994.

McCabe T., "A Complexity Measure," *IEEE Trans. Software Eng. SE-2*, Dec. 1976, pp. 308–320.

Musa, J., A. Iannino, and K. Okumoto, *Software Reliability*, McGraw-Hill, New York, N.Y., 1990.

Elements of Software Configuration Management

EDWARD H. BERSOFF, SENIOR MEMBER, IEEE

Abstract—Software configuration management (SCM) is one of the disciplines of the 1980's which grew in response to the many failures of the software industry throughout the 1970's. Over the last ten years, computers have been applied to the solution of so many complex problems that our ability to manage these applications has all too frequently failed. This has resulted in the development of a series of "new" disciplines intended to help control the software process.

This paper will focus on the discipline of SCM by first placing it in its proper context with respect to the rest of the software development process, as well as to the goals of that process. It will examine the constituent components of SCM, dwelling at some length on one of those components, configuration control. It will conclude with a look at what the 1980's might have in store.

Index Terms—Configuration management, management, product assurance, software.

INTRODUCTION

SOFTWARE configuration management (SCM) is one of the disciplines of the 1980's which grew in response to the many failures of our industry throughout the 1970's. Over the last ten years, computers have been applied to the solution of so many complex problems that our ability to manage these applications in the "traditional" way has all too frequently failed. Of course, tradition in the software business began only 30 years ago or less, but even new habits are difficult to break. In the 1970's we learned the hard way that the tasks involved in managing a software project were not linearly dependent on the number of lines of code produced. The relationship was, in fact, highly exponential. As the decade closed, we looked back on our failures [1], [2] trying to understand what went wrong and how we could correct it. We began to dissect the software development process [3], [4] and to define techniques by which it could be effectively managed [5]-[8]. This self-examination by some of the most talented and experienced members of the software community led to the development of a series of "new" disciplines intended to help control the software process.

While this paper will focus on the particular discipline of SCM, we will first place it in its proper context with respect to the rest of the software development process, as well as to the goals of that process. We will examine the constituent components of SCM, dwelling at some length on one of those components, configuration control. Once we have woven our way through all the trees, we will once again stand back and take a brief look at the forest and see what the 1980's might have in store.

Manuscript received April 15, 1982; revised December 1, 1982 and October 18, 1983.

The author is with BTG, Inc., 1945 Gallows Rd., Vienna, VA 22180.

SCM IN CONTEXT

It has been said that if you do not know where you are going, any road will get you there. In order to properly understand the role that SCM plays in the software development process, we must first understand what the goal of that process is, i.e., where we are going. For now, and perhaps for some time to come, software developers are people, people who respond to the needs of another set of people creating computer programs designed to satisfy those needs. These computer programs are the tangible output of a thought process—the conversion of a thought process into a product. The goal of the software developer is, or should be, the construction of a product which closely matches the real needs of the set of people for whom the software is developed. We call this goal the achievement of "product integrity." More formally stated, product integrity (depicted in Fig. 1) is defined to be the intrinsic set of attributes that characterize a product [9]:

- that fulfills user functional needs;
- that can easily and completely be traced through its life cycle;
- that meets specified performance criteria;
- whose cost expectations are met;
- whose delivery expectations are met.

The above definition is pragmatically based. It demands that product integrity be a measure of the satisfaction of the real needs and expectations of the software user. It places the burden for achieving the software goal, product integrity, squarely on the shoulders of the developer, for it is he alone who is in control of the development process. While, as we shall see, the user can establish safeguards and checkpoints to gain visibility into the development process, the prime responsibility for software success is the developer's. So our goal is now clear; we want to build software which exhibits all the characteristics of product integrity. Let us make sure that we all understand, however, what this thing called software really is. We have learned in recent times that equating the terms "software" and "computer programs" improperly restricts our view of software. Software is much more. A definition which can be used to focus the discussion in this paper is that software is information that is:

- structured with logical and functional properties;
- created and maintained in various forms and representations during the life cycle;
- tailored for machine processing in its fully developed state.

So by our definition, software is not simply a set of computer programs, but includes the documentation required to define, develop, and maintain these programs. While this notion is not very new, it still frequently escapes the software

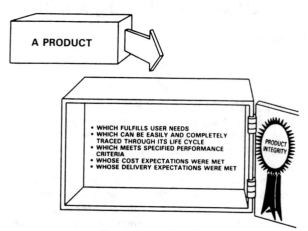

Fig. 1. Product integrity.

development manager who assumes that controlling a software product is the same as controlling computer code.

Now that we more fully appreciate what we are after, i.e., to build a software product with integrity, let us look at the one road which might get us there. We have, until now, used the term "developer" to characterize the organizational unit responsible for converting the software idea into a software product. But developers are, in reality, a complex set of interacting organizational entities. When undertaking a software project, most developers structure themselves into three basic discipline sets which include:

- project management,
- development, and
- product assurance.

Project management disciplines are both inwardly and outwardly directed. They support general management's need to see what is going on in a project and to ensure that the parent or host organization consistently develops products with integrity. At the same time, these disciplines look inside a project in support of the assignment, allocation, and control of all project resources. In that capacity, project management determines the relative allocation of resources to the set of development and product assurance disciplines. It is management's prerogative to specify the extent to which a given discipline will be applied to a given project. Historically, management has often been handicapped when it came to deciding how much of the product assurance disciplines were required. This was a result of both inexperience and organizational immaturity.

The development disciplines represent those traditionally applied to a software project. They include:

- analysis,
- design,
- engineering,
- production (coding),
- test (unit/subsystem),
- installation,
- documentation,
- training, and
- maintenance.

In the broadest sense, these are the disciplines required to take a system concept from its beginning through the development life cycle. It takes a well-structured, rigorous technical approach to system development, along with the right mix of development disciplines to attain product integrity, especially for software. The concept of an ordered, procedurally disciplined approach to system development is fundamental to product integrity. Such an approach provides successive development plateaus, each of which is an identifiable measure of progress which forms a part of the total foundation supporting the final product. Going sequentially from one baseline (plateau) to another with high probability of success, necessitates the use of the right development disciplines at precisely the right time.

The product assurance disciplines which are used by project management to gain visibility into the development process include:

- configuration management,
- quality assurance,
- validation and verification, and
- test and evaluation.

Proper employment of these product assurance disciplines by the project manager is basic to the success of a project since they provide the technical checks and balances over the product being developed. Fig. 2 represents the relationship among the management, development, and product assurance disciplines. Let us look at each of the product assurance disciplines briefly, in turn, before we explore the details of SCM.

Configuration management (CM) is the discipline of identifying the configuration of a system at discrete points in time for the purpose of systematically controlling changes to the configuration and maintaining the integrity and traceability of the configuration throughout the system life cycle. Software configuration management (SCM) is simply configuration management tailored to systems, or portions of systems, that are comprised predominantly of software. Thus, SCM does not differ substantially from the CM of hardware-oriented systems, which is generally well understood and effectively practiced. However, attempts to implement SCM have often failed because the particulars of SCM do not follow by direct analogy from the particulars of hardware CM and because SCM is a less mature discipline than that of hardware CM. We will return to this subject shortly.

Quality assurance (QA) as a discipline is commonly invoked throughout government and industry organizations with reasonable standardization when applied to systems comprised only of hardware. But there is enormous variation in thinking and practice when the QA discipline is invoked for a software development or for a system containing software components. QA has a long history, and much like CM, it has been largely developed and practiced on hardware projects. It is therefore mature, in that sense, as a discipline. Like CM, however, it is relatively immature when applied to software development. We define QA as consisting of the procedures, techniques, and tools applied by professionals to insure that a product meets or exceeds prespecified standards during a product's development cycle; and without specific prescribed standards, QA entails insuring that a product meets or

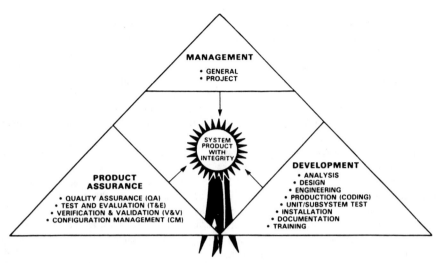

Fig. 2. The discipline triangle.

exceeds a minimum industrial and/or commercially acceptable level of excellence.

The QA discipline has not been uniformly treated, practiced or invoked relative to software development. First, very few organizations have software design and development standards that compare in any way with hardware standards for detail and completeness. Second, it takes a high level of software expertise to assess whether a software product meets prescribed standards. Third, few buyer organizations have provided for or have developed the capability to impose and then monitor software QA endeavors on seller organizations. Finally, few organizations have been concerned over precisely defining the difference between QA and other product assurance disciplines, CM often being subservient to QA or vice versa in a given development organization. Our definition of software given earlier suggests still another reason for the software QA discipline being in the same state as SCM so far as its universal application within the user, buyer, and seller communities. Software, as a form of information, cannot be standardized; only structures for defining/documenting software can be standardized. It follows that software development techniques can only be meaningfully standardized in relation to information structures, not information content.

The third of the four product assurance disciplines is validation and verification (V&V). Unlike CM and QA, V&V has come into being expressly for the purpose of coping with software and its development. Unlike QA, which prinicipally deals with the problem of a product's adherence to pre-established standards, V&V deals with the issue of how well software fulfills functional and performance requirements and the assurance that specified requirements are indeed stated and interpreted correctly. The verification part of V&V assures that a product meets its prescribed goals as defined through baseline documentation. That is, verification is a discipline imposed to ascertain that a product is what it was intended to be relative to its preceding baseline. The validation part of V&V, by contrast, is levied as a discipline to assure that a product not only meets the objectives specified through baseline documentation, but in addition, does the right job.

Stated another way, the validation discipline is invoked to insure that the end-user gets the right product. A buyer or seller may have misinterpreted user requirements or, perhaps, requirements have changed, or the user gets to know more about what he needs, or early specifications of requirements were wrong or incomplete or in a state of flux. The validation process serves to assure that such problems do not persist among the user, buyer, and seller. To enhance objectivity, it is often desirable to have an independent organization, from outside the developing organization, perform the V&V function.

The fourth of the product assurance disciplines is test and evaluation (T&E), perhaps the discipline most understood, and yet paradoxically, least practiced with uniformity. T&E is defined as the discipline imposed outside the development project organization to independently assess whether a product fulfills objectives. T&E does this through the execution of a set of test plans and procedures. Specifically in support of the end user, T&E entails evaluating product performance .in a live or near-live environment. Frequently, particularly within the miliatry arena, T&E is a major undertaking involving one or more systems which are to operate together, but which have been individually developed and accepted as stand-alone items. Some organizations formally turn over T&E responsibility to a group outside the development project organization after the product reaches a certain stage of development, their philosophy being that developers cannot be objective to the point of fully testing/evaluating what they have produced.

The definitions given for CM, QA, V&V, and T&E suggest some overlap in required skills and functions to be performed in order to invoke these disciplines collectively for product assurance purposes. Depending on many factors, the actual overlap may be significant or little. In fact, there are those who would argue that V&V and T&E are but subset functions of QA. But the contesting argument is that V&V and T&E have come into being as separate disciplines because conventional QA methods and techniques have failed to do an adequate job with respect to providing product assurance, particularly for computer-centered systems with software components. Management must be concerned with minimizing the application of excessive and redundant resources to address the overlap of these disciplines. What is important is that all the functions defined above are performed, not what they are called or who carries them out.

THE ELEMENTS OF SCM

When the need for the discipline of configuration management finally achieved widespread recognition within the software engineering community, the question arose as to how closely the software CM discipline ought to parallel the extant hardware practice of configuration management. Early SCM authors and practitioners [10] wisely chose the path of commonality with the hardware world, at least at the highest level. Of course, hardware engineering is different from software engineering, but broad similarities do exist and terms applied to one segment of the engineering community can easily be applied to another, even if the specific meanings of those terms differ significantly in detail. For that reason, the elements of SCM were chosen to be the same as those for hardware CM. As for hardware, the four components of SCM are:

- identification,
- control,
- auditing, and
- status accounting.

Let us examine each one in turn.

Software Configuration Identification: Effective management of the development of a system requires careful definition of its baseline components; changes to these components also need to be defined since these changes, together with the baselines, specify the system evolution. A system baseline is like a snapshot of the aggregate of system components as they exist at a given point in time; updates to this baseline are like frames in a movie strip of the system life cycle. The role of software configuration identification in the SCM process is to provide labels for these snapshots and the movie strip.

A baseline can be characterized by two labels. One label identifies the baseline itself, while the second label identifies an update to a particular baseline. An update to a baseline represents a baseline plus a set of changes that have been incorporated into it. Each of the baselines established during a software system's life cycle controls subsequent system development. At the time it is first established a software baseline embodies the actual software in its most recent state. When changes are made to the most recently established baseline, then, from the viewpoint of the software configuration manager, this baseline and these changes embody the actual software in its most recent state (although, from the viewpoint of the software developer, the actual software may be in a more advanced state).

The most elementary entity in the software configuration identification labeling mechanism is the software configuration item (SCI). Viewed from an SCM perspective, a software baseline appears as a set of SCI's. The SCI's within a baseline are related to one another via a tree-like hierarchy. As the software system evolves through its life cycle, the number of branches in this hierarchy generally increases; the first baseline may consist of no more than one SCI. The lowest level SCI's in the tree hierarchy may still be under development and not yet under SCM control. These entities are termed design objects or computer program components (see Fig. 3). Each baseline and each member in the associated family of updates will exist in one or more forms, such as a design document, source code on a disk, or executing object code.

In performing the identification function, the software configuration manager is, in effect, taking snapshots of the SCI's. Each baseline and its associated updates collectively represents the evolution of the software during each of its life cycle stages. These stages are staggered with respect to one another. Thus, the collection of life cycle stages looks like a collection of staggered and overlapping sequences of snapshots of SCI trees. Let us now imagine that this collection of snapshot sequences is threaded, in chronological order, onto a strip of movie film as in Fig. 4. Let us further imagine that the strip of movie film is run through a projector. Then we would see a history of the evolution of the software. Consequently, the identification of baselines and updates provides an explicit documentation trail linking all stages of the software life cycle. With the aid of this documentation trail, the software developer can assess the integrity of his product, and the software buyer can assess the integrity of the product he is paying for.

Software Configuration Control: The evolution of a software system is, in the language of SCM, the development of baselines and the incorporation of a series of changes into the baselines. In addition to these changes that explicitly affect existing baselines, there are changes that occur during early stages of the system life cycle that may affect baselines that do not yet exist. For example, some time before software coding begins (i.e., some time prior to the establishment of a design baseline), a contract may be modified to include a software warranty provision such as: system downtime due to software failures shall not exceed 30 minutes per day. This warranty provision will generally affect subsequent baselines but in a manner that cannot be explicitly determined *a priori*. One role of software configuration control is to provide the administrative mechanism for precipitating, preparing, evaluating, and approving or disapproving all change proposals throughout the system life cycle.

We have said that software, for configuration management purposes, is a collection of SCI's that are related to one another in a well-defined way. In early baselines and their associated updates, SCI's are specification documents (one or more volumes of text for each baseline or associated update); in later baselines and their associated updates, each SCI may manifest itself in any or all of the various software representations. Software configuration control focuses on managing changes to SCI's (existing or to be developed) in all of their representations. This process involves three basic ingredients.

1) Documentation (such as administrative forms and supporting technical and administrative material) for formally precipitating and defining a proposed change to a software system.

2) An organizational body for formally evaluating and

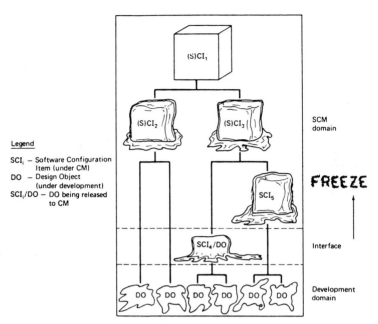

Fig. 3. The development/SCM interface.

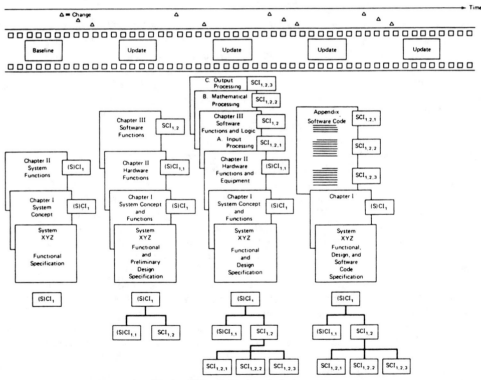

Fig. 4. SCI evolution in a single document.

approving or disapproving a proposed change to a software system (the Configuration Control Board).

3) Procedures for controlling changes to a software system.

The Engineering Change Proposal (ECP), a major control document, contains information such as a description of the proposed change, identification of the originating organization, rationale for the change, identification of affected baselines and SCI's (if appropriate), and specification of cost and schedule impacts. ECP's are reviewed and coordinated by the CCB, which is typically a body representing all organizational units which have a vested interest in proposed changes.

Fig. 5 depicts the software configuration control process.

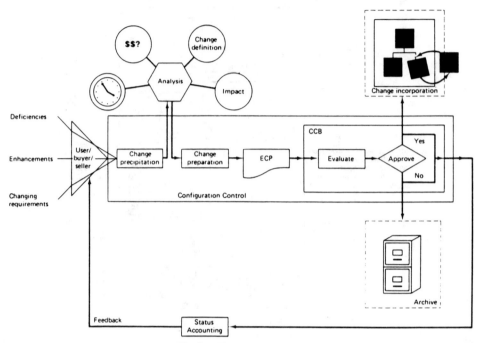

Fig. 5. The control process.

As the figure suggests, change incorporation is not an SCM function, but monitoring the change implementation process resulting in change incorporation is. Fig. 5 also emphasizes that the analysis that may be required to prepare an ECP is also outside the SCM purview. Note also from the figure how ECP's not approved by the CCB are not simply discarded but are archived for possible future reference.

Many automated tools support the control process. The major ones aid in controlling software change once the coding stage has been reached, and are generically referred to as program support libraries (PSL's). The level of support provided by PSL's, however, varies greatly. As a minimum, a PSL should provide a centralized and readily available repository for authoritative versions of each component of a software system. It should contain the data necessary for the orderly development and control of each SCI. Automation of other functions, such as library access control, software and document version maintenance, change recording, and document reconstruction, greatly enhance both the control and maintenance processes. These capabilities are currently available in systems such as SOFTOOL's change and configuration control environment (CCC).

A PSL supports a developmental approach in which project personnel work on a common visible product rather than on independent components. In those PSL's which include access controls, project personnel can be separately assigned read/write access to each software document/component, from programs to lines of code. Thus, all project personnel are assured ready access to the critical interface information necessary for effective software development. At the same time, modifications to various software components, whether sanctioned baselines or modules under development, can be closely controlled.

Under the PSL concept, the programmer operates under a well-defined set of parameters and exercises a narrower span of detailed control. This minimizes the need for explicit communication between analysts and programmers and makes the inclusion of new project personnel less traumatic since interface requirements are well documented. It also minimizes the preparation effort for technical audits.

Responsibility for maintenance of the PSL data varies depending on the level of automation provided. For those systems which provide only a repository for data, a secretary/librarian is usually responsible for maintaining the notebooks which will contain the data developed and used by project personnel and for maintenance of the PSL archives. More advanced PSL systems provide real time, on-line access to data and programs and automatically create the records necessary to fully trace the history of the development. In either case the PSL provides standardization of project recordkeeping, ensures that system documentation corresponds to the current system configuration, and guarantees the existence of adequate documentation of previous versions.

A PSL should support three main activities: code development, software management, and configuration control. Support to the development process includes support to design, coding, testing, documentation, and program maintenance along with associated database schema and subschema. A PSL provides this support through:

- storage and maintenance of software documentation and code,
- support to program compilation/testing,
- support for the generation of program/system documentation.

Support to the management of the software development process involves the storage and output of programming data such as:

- collection and automatic reporting of management data related to program development,

446

- control over the integrity and security of the data in the PSL,
- separation of the clerical activity related to the programming process.

PSL's provide support to the configuration control process through:

- access and change authorization control for all data in the library,
- control of software code releases,
- automatic program and document reconstruction,
- automatic change tracking and reporting,
- assurance of the consistency between documentation, code, and listings.

A PSL has four major components: internal libraries in machine-readable form, external libraries in hardcopy form, computer procedures, and office procedures. The components of a PSL system are interlocked to establish an exact correspondence between the internal units of code and external versions (such as listings) of the developing systems. This continuous correspondence is the characteristic of a PSL that guarantees ongoing visibility and identification of the developing system.

Different PSL implementations exist for various system environments with the specifics of the implementation dependent upon the hardware, software, user, and operating environment. The fundamental correspondence between the internal and external libraries in each environment, however, is established by the PSL librarian and computer procedures. The office procedures are specified in a project CM Plan so that the format of the external libraries is standard across software projects, and internal and external libraries are easily maintainable.

Newer PSL systems minimize the need for both office and computer procedures through the implementation of extensive management functionality. This functionality provides significant flexibility in controlling the access to data and allocating change authority, while providing a variety of status reporting capabilities. The availability of management information, such as a list of all the software structures changed to solve a particular Software Trouble Report or the details on the latest changes to a particular software document, provides a means for the control function to effectively operate without burdening the development team with cumbersome procedures and administrative paperwork. Current efforts in PSL refinement/ development are aimed at linking support of the development environment with that of the configuration control environment. The goal of such systems is to provide an integrated environment where control and management information is generated automatically as a part of a fully supported design and development process.

Software Configuration Auditing: Software configuration auditing provides the mechanism for determining the degree to which the current state of the software system mirrors the software system pictured in baseline and requirements documentation. It also provides the mechanism for formally establishing a baseline. A baseline in its formative stages (for example, a draft specification document that appears prior to the existence of the functional baseline) is referred to as a "to-be-established" baseline; the final state of the auditing process

conducted on a to-be-established baseline is a sanctioned baseline. The same may be said about baseline updates.

Software configuration auditing serves two purposes, configuration verification and configuration validation. Verification ensures that what is intended for each software configuration item as specified in one baseline or update is actually achieved in the succeeding baseline or update; validation ensures that the SCI configuration solves the right problem (i.e., that customer needs are satisfied). Software configuration auditing is applied to each baseline (and corresponding update) in its to-be-established state. An auditing process common to all baselines is the determination that an SCI structure exists and that its contents are based on all available information.

Software auditing is intended to increase software visibility and to establish traceability throughout the life cycle of the software product. Of course, this visibility and traceability are not achieved without cost. Software auditing costs time and money. But the judicious investment of time and money, particularly in the early stages of a project, pays dividends in the latter stages. These dividends include the avoidance of costly retrofits resulting from problems such as the sudden appearance of new requirements and the discovery of major design flaws. Conversely, failing to perform auditing, or constraining it to the later stages of the software life cycle, can jeopardize successful software development. Often in such cases, by the time discrepancies are discovered (if they are), the software cannot be easily or economically modified to rectify the discrepancies. The result is often a dissatisfied customer, large cost overruns, slipped schedules, or cancelled projects.

Software auditing makes visible to management the current status of the software in the life cycle product audited. It also reveals whether the project requirements are being satisfied and whether the intent of the preceding baseline has been fulfilled. With this visibility, project management can evaluate the integrity of the software product being developed, resolve issues that may have been raised by the audit, and correct defects in the development process. The visibility afforded by the software audit also provides a basis for the establishment of the audited life cycle product as a new baseline.

Software auditing provides traceability between a software life cycle product and the requirements for that product. Thus, as life cycle products are audited and baselines established, every requirement is traced successively from baseline to baseline. Disconnects are also made visible during the establishment of traceability. These disconnects include requirements not satisfied in the audited product and extraneous features observed in the product (i.e., features for which no stated requirement exists).

With the different point of view made possible by the visibility and traceability achieved in the software audit, management can make better decisions and exercise more incisive control over the software development process. The result of a software audit may be the establishment of a baseline, the redirection of project tasking, or an adjustment of applied project resources.

The responsibility for a successful software development project is shared by the buyer, seller, and user. Software auditing uniquely benefits each of these project participants. Appropriate auditing by each party provides checks and balances over the development effort. The scope and depth of the audits undertaken by the three parties may vary greatly. However, the purposes of these differing forms of software audit remain the same: to provide visibility and to establish traceability of the software life cycle products. An excellent overview of the software audit process, from which some of the above discussion has been extracted, appears in [11].

Software Configuration Status Accounting: A decision to make a change is generally followed by a time delay before the change is actually made, and changes to baselines generally occur over a protracted period of time before they are incorporated into baselines as updates. A mechanism is therefore needed for maintaining a record of how the system has evolved and where the system is at any time relative to what appears in published baseline documentation and written agreements. Software configuration status accounting provides this mechanism. Status accounting is the administrative tracking and reporting of all software items formally identified and controlled. It also involves the maintenance of records to support software configuration auditing. Thus, software configuration status accounting records the activity associated with the other three SCM functions and therefore provides the means by which the history of the software system life cycle can be traced.

Although administrative in nature, status accounting is a function that increases in complexity as the system life cycle progresses because of the multiple software representations that emerge with later baselines. This complexity generally results in large amounts of data to be recorded and reported. In particular, the scope of software configuration status accounting encompasses the recording and reporting of:

1) the time at which each representation of a baseline and update came into being;

2) the time at which each software configuration item came into being;

3) descriptive information about each SCI;

4) engineering change proposal status (approved, disapproved, awaiting action);

5) descriptive information about each ECP;

6) change status;

7) descriptive information about each change;

8) status of technical and administrative documentation associated with a baseline or update (such as a plan prescribing tests to be performed on a baseline for updating purposes);

9) deficiencies in a to-be-established baseline uncovered during a configuration audit.

Software configuration status accounting, because of its large data input and output requirements, is generally supported in part by automated processes such as the PSL described earlier. Data are collected and organized for input to a computer and reports giving the status of entities are compiled and generated by the computer.

The Management Dilemma

As we mentioned at the beginning of this paper, SCM and many of the other product assurance disciplines grew up in the 1970's in response to software failure. The new disciplines were designed to achieve visibility into the soft-

ware engineering process and thereby exercise some measure of control over that process. Students of mathematical control theory are taught early in their studies a simple example of the control process. Consider being confronted with a cup of hot coffee, filled to the top, which you are expected to carry from the kitchen counter to the kitchen table. It is easily verified that if you watch the cup as you carry it, you are likely to spill more coffee than if you were to keep your head turned away from the cup. The problem with looking at the cup is one of overcompensation. As you observe slight deviations from the straight-and-level, you adjust, but often you adjust too much. To compensate for that overadjustment, you tend to overadjust again, with the result being hot coffee on your floor.

This little diversion from our main topic of SCM has an obvious moral. There is a fundamental propensity on the part of the practitioners of the product assurance disciplines to overadjust, to overcompensate for the failures of the development disciplines. There is one sure way to eliminate failure completely from the software development process, and that is to stop it completely. The software project manager must learn how to apply his resources intelligently. He must achieve visibility and control, but he must not so encumber the developer so as to bring progress to a virtual halt. The product assurers have a virtuous perspective. They strive for perfection and point out when and where perfection has not been achieved. We seem to have a binary attitude about software; it is either correct or it is not. That is perhaps true, but we cannot expect anyone to deliver perfect software in any reasonable time period or for a reasonable sum of money. What we need to develop is software that is good enough. Some of the controls that we have placed on the developer have the deleterious effect of increasing costs and expanding schedules rather than shrinking them.

The dilemma to management is real. We must have the visibility and control that the product assurance disciplines have the capacity to provide. But we must be careful not to overcompensate and overcontrol. This is the fine line which will distinguish the successful software managers of the 1980's from the rest of the software engineering community.

Acknowledgment

The author wishes to acknowledge the contribution of B. J. Gregor to the preparation and critique of the final manuscript.

References

[1] "Contracting for computer software development—Serious problems require management attention to avoid wasting additional millions," General Accounting Office, Rep. FGMSD 80-4, Nov. 9, 1979.

[2] D. M. Weiss, "The MUDD report: A case study of Navy software development practices," Naval Res. Lab., Rep. 7909, May 21, 1975.

[3] B. W. Boehm, "Software engineering," *IEEE Trans. Comput.*, vol. C-25, pp. 1226–1241, Dec. 1976.

[4] *Proc. IEEE* (Special Issue on Software Engineering), vol. 68, Sept. 1980.

[5] E. Bersoff, V. Henderson, and S. Siegel, "Attaining software product integrity," *Tutorial: Software Configuration Management*, W. Bryan, C. Chadbourne, and S. Siegel, Eds., Los Alamitos, CA, IEEE Comput. Soc., Cat. EHO-169-3, 1981.

[6] B. W. Boehm *et al.*, *Characteristics of Software Quality*, TRW Series of Software Technology, vol. 1. New York: North-Holland, 1978.

[7] T. A. Thayer, *et al.*, *Software Reliability*, TRW Series of Software Technology, vol. 2. New York: North-Holland, 1978.

[8] D. J. Reifer, Ed., *Tutorial: Automated Tools for Software Eng.*, Los Alamitos, CA, IEEE Comput. Soc., Cat. EHO-169-3, 1979.

[9] E. Bersoff, V. Henderson, and S. Siegel, *Software Configuration Management*. Englewood Cliffs, NJ: Prentice-Hall, 1980.

[10] ——, "Software configuration management: A tutorial," *Computer*, vol. 12, pp. 6–14, Jan. 1979.

[11] W. Bryan, S. Siegel, and G. Whiteleather, "Auditing throughout the software life cycle: A primer," *Computer*, vol. 15, pp. 56–67, Mar. 1982.

[12] "Software configuration management," Naval Elec. Syst. Command, Software Management Guidebooks, vol. 2, undated.

Chapter 10

Software Metrics and Visibility of Progress

1. Chapter Introduction

The project manager is responsible for establishing the methods of monitoring the software project and reporting project status. Monitoring and reporting systems must be defined so that the project manager can determine project status and visibility of progress. Metrics are necessary to provide accurate status and reporting systems. The project manager needs reports on project progress and product quality to ensure that everything is advancing according to plan. The type, frequency, originator, and recipient of project reports must be specified. Status reporting metrics, which pro-

vide visibility of progress, not merely resources used or time passed, must be implemented.

A metric is a measure of the degree to which a process or product possesses a given attribute. Besides process and product metrics, other definitions of types of metrics are as follows:

- *Software quality metric*—A quantitative measure of the degree to which software possesses a given attribute that affects its quality. Examples are reliability, maintainability, and portability.

ACCORDING TO THESE ANCIENT WRITINGS, WE ARE **98** PERCENT FINISHED

451

- *Software quantity metric*—A quantitative measure of some physical attribute of software. Examples are lines of code, function points, and pages of documentation.
- *Management metric*—A management indicator that can be used to measure management activities such as budget spent, value earned, costs overrun, and schedule delays.

1.1 Software Engineering Metrics

An important set of metrics for software management was developed by the MITRE Corporation for the US Air Force Electronic System Division (now Electronic Systems Center) [1]. These ten metrics are considered by many to be the best set of management metrics available today. They are

- Software size metric
- Software volatility metric
- Design complexity metric
- Design progress metric
- Testing progress metric
- Software personnel metric
- Computer resources utilization metric
- Schedule progress metric
- Computer Software Unit (CSU) development progress metric
- Incremental-release content metric

See also the paper in this chapter by Herman Schultz.

1.2 Management Metrics

A set of management metrics was published by the US Air Force Systems Command (now part of the Air Force Material Command) in 1986 [2]. This set included the following:

- Computer resource utilization
- Software development manpower
- Requirements definition and stability
- Software progress (development and test)
- Cost and schedule deviations
- Software development tools

1.3 Software Engineering Institute Metrics

Measurement has been an integral part of the Software Engineering Institute's process improvement project since the beginning. The first set of guidelines published by this project [3] included 10 metrics at process maturity level 2:

- Planned versus actual staffing profiles
- Software size versus time
- Statistics on software code and test errors
- Actual versus planned units designed
- Actual versus planned units completing unit testing
- Actual versus planned units integrated
- Target computer memory utilization
- Target computer throughput utilization
- Target computer I/O channel utilization
- Software build/release content

With the publication in 1993 of the Software Engineering Institute's Capability Maturity Model for Software [4], measurements became one of the "common features" that are part of every key process area. See also the article by Mark Paulk, Bill Curtis, Mary Beth Chrissis, and Charles Weber in this tutorial.

2. Article Descriptions

The first article, "Software Peer Reviews," by David Wheeler, Bill Brykczynski, and Reginald Meeson, Jr., all from the Institute for Defense Analyses, covers two important peer reviews—inspections and walkthroughs. Inspections are considered by many to be one of the most valuable software engineering techniques available today for discovering and eventually eliminating software errors. Walkthroughs are a less rigorous way of discovering errors in software, but are perhaps easier and cheaper to implement.

The establishment of the older walkthrough technology is generally credited to Gerald Weinberg. In his book, The Psychology of Computer Programming [5], Weinberg established an organizational structure call an "egoless programming team" [see article by Marilyn Mantei in this tutorial]. In the concept of an egoless team, the software product was "owned" by the team as a whole rather than parts of it being "owned" by individuals. Part of the egoless team's procedures was to hold an "egoless programming review" in which the programmer "walked through his/her code in front of his/her team members (peers)." Managers did not attend an egoless review because an egoless programming team did not have a full-time manager. The "egoless review" was the forerunner of the walkthrough, as we know it today.

Michael Fagan of IBM developed inspections in 1975 and published his findings in 1976 [6]. Fagan did not believe that the walkthrough was rigorous enough. He felt that the failure to record the results of the review allowed many errors to "slip through the crack." IBM strongly supported Fagan's development and in the late 1970s required all IBM software development organizations worldwide to use Fagan's inspection system. In 1977, Fagan was given an award of $30,000 by IBM for his contribution to the corporation. This was one of the largest awards ever given, at that time, to an individual.

It should be pointed out that many companies and organizations call walkthroughs "inspections" and others call inspections "walkthroughs."

Additional information about the inspection process can be found in Wheeler, Brykczynski, and Meeson, *Software Inspection: An Industry Best Practice*, IEEE Computer Society Press, Los Alamitos, Calif., 1996.

The article by L. Bernstein on "Software Project Management Audits" shows how project audits can be used to uncover project strengths and weaknesses. This article presents a very clear view of the benefits and drawbacks of a project audit. The focus of an audit is on schedule analysis, project management tools, and the issues of working relationships. Bernstein explains what to do and what not to do in an audit.

Audits are instituted as needed (not regularly scheduled). Audits should only be initiated when there is an actual or potential failure. The article also presents a list of "things to look for" in conducting an audit and explains the who, when, where, how, and why an audit is brought forth. The article's author, an experienced auditor, says the most important tool the audit team can use is "nondirective listening." Finally, an audit interview questionnaire is provided in an appendix.

"The Unit Development Folder (UDF): A Ten-Year Perspective," by Frank Ingrassia, who originated the UDF, is an update of his landmark article on UDFs [7] for this tutorial's first edition. The UDF concept is still one of the most widely used software engineering management control techniques in today's environment. This updated article incorporates the changes in how the UDF is used since it was first introduced in 1977. Note: The unit development folder is sometime called a software development file/folder or a software engineering notebook.

The last article (actually part of a short technical report) is one of the best-known articles on software metrics in the current literature. Herman Schultz, for the MITRE Corporation, reported on a set of 10 metrics for managing a software project [1]. He used actual data from the Electronic Systems Division (ESD), which was then part of the Air Force System Command, to show the validity of the metrics.

The original report was written for US Government (read: military) program managers that had contracted with industry to develop their software system. The article's "government program manager" can be regarded as the developer's customer or buyer, the software developer's senior managers, or the software project manager.

Shultz's original report was shortened for this tutorial, highlighting just the five important management metrics plus a short tutorial on analyzing metrics. Readers should make every effort to read the original report.

References

1. Schultz, H.P., *Software Management Metrics*, ESD TR-88-001, prepared by The MITRE Corporation for the US Air Force, Electronic Systems Division, Hanscom AFB, Bedford, Mass., 1988.

2. *Air Force Systems Command Software Management Indicators: Management Insight*, AFSC Pamphlet 800-43, HQ AFSC, Andrews AFB, Washington, D.C., 1986.

3. Humphrey, W.S., and W.L. Sweet, *A Method for Assessing the Software Development Capability of Contractors"* CMU/SEI-87-TR-23, Software Engineering Institute, Carnegie Mellon University, Pittsburgh, P.A., 1987.

4. Paulk, M.C., B. Curtis, M.B. Chrissis, and C.V. Weber, *Key Practices of the Capability Maturity Model, Version 1.1,"* CMU/SEI-93-TR-25, Software Engineering Institute, Carnegie Mellon University, Pittsburgh, P.A., 1993.

5. Weinberg, G.M., *The Psychology of Computer Programming*, Van Nostrand Reinhold, New York, N.Y., 1971.

6. Fagan, M.E., "Design and Code Inspections to Reduce Errors in Program Development," *IBM Systems J.*, Vol. 15, No. 3, 1976, pp. 182–211.

7. Ingrassia, F.S., *The Unit Development Folder (UDF): An Effective Management Tool for Software Development*, TRW Technical Report TRW-SS-76-11, 1976.

Software Peer Reviews

David A. Wheeler
Bill Brykczynski
Reginald N. Meeson, Jr.
Institute for Defense Analyses
Alexandria, VA
dwheeler, bryk, rmeeson @ida.org

1. Introduction

Peer reviews are a method used in many different contexts to scrutinize the quality of written work and provide feedback to the author(s) on necessary corrections and improvements. Reviews can significantly improve resulting products. Conference and journal articles, for example, are typically reviewed by other authors and researchers. Software peer reviews apply similar techniques to software work products (for example, requirements, designs, code, and test plans). This paper provides a survey of peer review processes used in software development.

One process, discussed in detail in Section 2, is called *software inspection* or *inspection*. This is one of the most formal software peer review processes. This method prescribes a specific set of steps to be followed, assigns specific responsibilities to each participant, and focuses on defect detection. The inspection process includes detailed data collection on the effort invested in reviews and the number and kinds of defects detected. This data provides the strongest evidence available for the efficacy of peer reviews.

Another process is called the walkthrough. Walkthroughs are probably the most common form of software peer review. They cover a continuum of review processes ranging from highly structured "almost-inspections" to informational presentations about the product. The focus and objectives of walkthroughs are often different from those of inspections. Walkthroughs are described in detail in Section 3.

Software development typically involves many additional types of reviews. Section 4 presents a taxonomy that shows how inspections, walkthroughs, and many of these other processes are related. In Section 5 we return to the discussion of the benefits and costs of peer reviews. Section 6 summarizes the main points presented.

> ## Definition
> A software peer review is a process in which a software product (for example, requirements document, design, code module, or test plan) is examined by peers of the product's author(s). Peers are equals of the product's author(s) and have no undue influence over the author(s)' careers or pay scales. This examination may have one or more goals (for example, detecting faults or identifying improvements), may permit technical leads to participate, and may have other rules depending on the specific review process.

2. Software Inspection

Software inspection is an industry-proven process for improving software product quality and reducing development time and cost. Inspections can identify up to 80 percent of all software defects, and can do so early during software development [Fagan 1976a, Myers 1988, Weller 1993]. When inspections are combined with normal testing practices, defects in fielded software can be reduced by a factor of 10 [Russell 1991]. Inspections increase productivity and reduce costs and delivery time by decreasing the amount of rework typically experienced in software development. Inspections are used by many software industry leaders to gain the competitive advantages of better products that are produced more quickly and at lower cost.

Inspections were devised originally by Michael Fagan in the early 1970s at IBM's Kingston, New York facility [Fagan 1976a]. Fagan experimented with numerous techniques and variations of processes to identify software defects and improve product quality. His experiments resulted in an optimized process called the *software inspection process* that many software development organizations have applied with similar effectiveness.

This section provides a detailed description of the inspection process, data collected during the inspection process, and guidelines for implementing the process.

2.1 Inspection Process

Inspections are detailed reviews of work in progress. Small groups of co-workers (usually four or five) study work products independently and then meet to examine the work in detail. Work products are small but complete chunks of work on the order of 200 to 250 lines of code. Requirements, designs, and other work products are inspected in similar sized chunks. Work products are considered work in progress until the inspection and any necessary corrections are completed. Inspectors typically spend one to four hours reviewing the work product and related information before an inspection, depending on their familiarity with the material.

Inspections follow fairly rigidly defined rules, which are described below. One rule, for example, is that inspection meetings are limited to a maximum of two hours. Although there are variations in inspection practices, deviations from these rules generally tend to reduce inspection effectiveness. Terminology also differs among inspection users. We have adopted the inspection process and terminology defined in the IEEE Standard for Software Reviews and Audits, IEEE Std 1028 [IEEE 1989]. The process is outlined in Figure 1.

There are six principal steps in the software inspection process: planning, overview, preparation, examination, rework, and follow-up.

1. *Planning.* When a developer or author completes a work product, an inspection team is formed and a moderator is designated. The moderator ensures that the work product satisfies the inspection entry criteria (for example, code may be required to compile without error). Roles are assigned to inspection team members, copies of the work product and related materials are distributed, and an examination meeting is scheduled. Related materials may include, for example, requirements and design documentation.

2. *Overview.* If inspectors are not already familiar with the development project, an overview presentation may be needed. This is an optional step. One overview presentation can easily provide enough background and context to cover a number of inspections.

3. *Preparation.* Inspectors prepare individually for the examination meeting by thoroughly studying the work product and related materials. Checklists are used to help detect common defects. The IEEE standard suggests 1.5 hours per inspector as a nominal preparation time. More time may be needed if inspectors are not already familiar with the project and related work.

4. *Examination.* The examination is the meeting where the inspectors review the work product together. Many people refer to this meeting as "the inspection." Before beginning the meeting, the moderator ensures that all the inspectors are sufficiently prepared. The person designated as the reader paraphrases the work product while everyone else reads along, looking for defects. No time is spent during the examination discussing how defects occurred or how to correct them. Only the work product is under scrutiny, not the author. All defects detected are classified and recorded. Examinations are generally limited to a maximum of two hours in length. Inspectors tire after two hours and their abilities to identify defects decrease dramatically [Fagan 1976a]. At the end of the meeting the team determines if the product is to be accepted as is, reworked with the moderator verifying the results, or reworked and then re-inspected.

5. *Rework.* The author corrects all identified defects following the examination meeting.

6. *Follow-Up.* The author's corrections are checked by the moderator. If the moderator is satisfied, the inspection is officially completed and the work product is typically placed under configuration control.

Additional steps and variations to the process have been suggested. One suggestion is to spend some time analyzing the causes of defects. It is often possible to trace the cause of systematically recurring defects to a correctable problem elsewhere in the development process. This analysis need not be conducted for every inspection. It is really part of a large software development process improvement activity. Another suggestion is to hold an optional "third hour" meeting following the examination where corrections and general improvements may be discussed [Gilb 1987]. This may be productive, but remember that examinations are limited to two hours because inspectors tire.

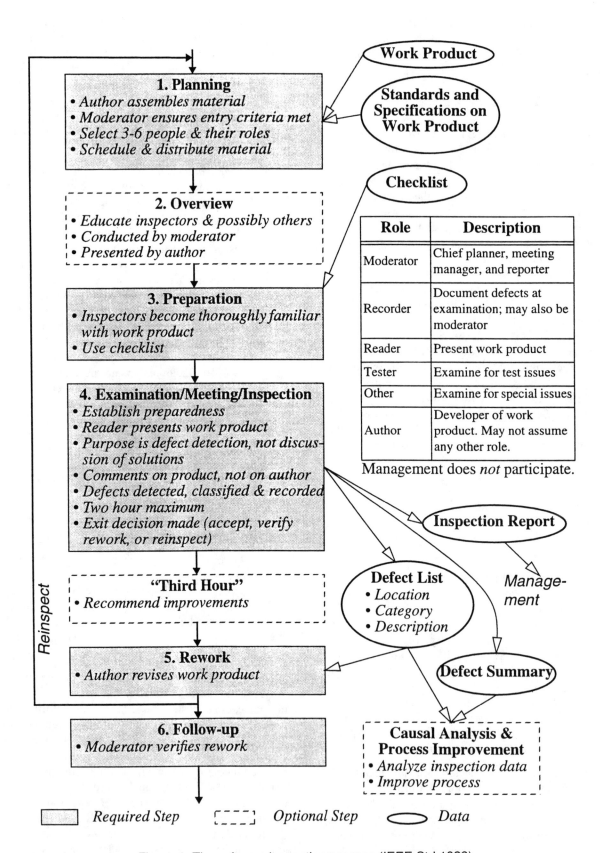

Figure 1. The software inspection process (IEEE Std 1028).

Inspection teams are formed from small groups of co-workers. The IEEE standard suggests three to six people. Teams of four or five are common in practice. Team members include the author of the work product being inspected and co-workers who are developing related work products or who have similar interests in assuring the quality of the work at hand.

Successful inspection meetings (examinations) require several roles to be filled. In addition to the author, these roles include a moderator, who runs the inspection meeting; a reader, who paraphrases the work product during the examination; and a recorder or scribe, who records the location and brief descriptions of all defects discovered. The author may not fill any of these other roles. In particular, the author is not allowed to be the moderator or the reader.

Skilled moderators are essential to successful examinations. Moderators must ensure the team's preparedness, pace the progress of the examination, and keep it focused on finding defects. Being a moderator is not a full-time job. Like all the other reviewers, a moderator is a peer of the author. Moderators need more inspection experience and training than the other inspection roles.

Managers should not participate in inspections. Experience shows that when managers participate, inspections tend to identify only superficial defects. By identifying only superficial defects, inspectors appear to be finding respectable numbers of defects and authors are not embarrassed by having serious flaws in their work exposed in front of their managers. The best ways for managers to ensure that inspections are being conducted effectively are to train their staff in the inspection process, monitor inspection summary reports, and measure the overall quality of work by the number of defects that remain in finished products.

One issue in inspection implementation is whether or not there should be a reader who paraphrases the product. Fagan's [1976a] original process requires paraphrasing during the examination, and the 1988 version of IEEE Std 1028 states that the reader "generally paraphrases." On the other hand, Greg Wenneson [1985], Watts Humphrey [1989], Tom Gilb [1994], and others define inspection processes that do not include paraphrasing. The main advantage of paraphrasing is that it provides an opportunity for synergistically finding new defects that were not found by individuals. The advantage of not paraphrasing is that the meeting can take much less time, which is significant because meetings can consume a great deal of valuable time. Published experiments comparing the relative advantages of paraphrasing versus not paraphrasing are needed.

Another issue in inspection implementation is whether or not the meeting should be eliminated entirely or replaced with depositions (a series of meetings of the moderator, author, and one other inspector). Some experiments have suggested that meetings do not significantly add to the defect detection ability of the inspection process [Votta 1993, Porter 1995].

2.2 Data Collection

Data collection and analysis is a fundamental aspect of the inspection process. Without adequate data collection, it is impossible to demonstrate the effectiveness of inspection. Analysis of inspection data is important in fine-tuning the process, identifying potential problem areas, and evaluating the effects of long-term process improvement. In examining the types of data collected during the inspection process, three categories are consistently reported:

1. *Defects*. The number, type, and severity of defects detected by individual inspections are commonly collected. Causal analysis of these defects can provide extremely valuable information in preventing similar defects. Analyzing the defects found in the field can provide useful information for evaluating and improving the effectiveness of the inspection process. Defects detected by non-inspection processes are also sometimes recorded to compare defect detection efficiencies.

2. *Effort*. The amount of time spent per inspection phase is often recorded. Particular emphasis is placed on the amount of preparation time and the duration of the inspection meeting. Although the effort spent in rework after an inspection can provide valuable information for comparing defect detection processes (such as inspection, static and dynamic analysis, and integration testing), this data is seldom collected.

3. *Size and Type of Work Product*. Data is usually collected on the size of the work product being inspected (for example, lines of code, number of pages or screens). Also, the type of material being inspected (,requirements, design, and code, for instance) is often recorded.

2.3 Implementing Inspections

Several factors can increase the likelihood of implementing a successful inspection program. Management commitment is very important to inspection success. The inspection process requires up-front invest-ment (for example, training and data collection proce-dures) and continued costs (such as the actual cost of meeting and preparation). Unless management is committed to allocating the proper resources toward inspection, the resulting benefits may be substantially lower. Managers who naively question "Why are we spending so much time in meetings? We should be coding!" are not conducive to a healthy inspection process. However, those managers should be exam-ining inspection results to ensure they are gaining the proper benefits from the process.

Pilot programs are an effective method for intro-ducing inspections into an organization. Pilot projects can provide management with a means to evaluate the suitability of inspections before committing larger portions of the organization to the process. Problems with the implementation of the inspection process can be identified early and corrected before widespread use. The criteria for selecting the pilot project should include the project's receptiveness of inspections and the likelihood that successful results will be emulated by other projects.

Data collection and analysis is critical for contin-ued inspection success. Unless managers observe im-provements resulting from the use of inspections, it is unlikely that the process will be continued. Analysis of inspection data provides a quantitative basis for judging the effectiveness of the process. See [Weller 1993] for an excellent treatment on lessons learned during an extensive corporate transition to inspections.

An inspection "champion" is often critical in the first attempts at using inspections. Effective technol-ogy insertion is difficult. In getting inspections in-serted, project managers must be educated. Staff must be trained, data collection forms must be developed, pitfalls must be avoided, and so forth. An inspection champion, who is aware of all of these aspects, can be highly instrumental in making sure the process is im-plemented properly. If corners are cut and the process is not adequately implemented, then inspection bene-fits may not outweigh their cost.

Inspection pitfalls do exist. Fortunately, many of these pitfalls have been documented, so most can be avoided through proper training [Shirey 1992, Weller 1993].

Formal training is important to an effective in-spection process. Although the inspection process is conceptually very simple, there are a number of as-pects that can reduce its effectiveness. Author-bashing, author defensiveness, lack of focus on defect detection, and high inspection rates are some of the potential problems that must be prevented. Books (such as Gilb [1993], Strauss [1994], and Wheeler [1996a]) can aid in understanding how to apply the

inspection process. However, while the problems can be read about in the literature, effective formal train-ing can better prevent their manifestation in practice.

3. Walkthroughs

This section describes walkthroughs. Walkthroughs are a popular form of peer review process, and are gener-ally viewed as not being as "powerful" as inspections.

Walkthroughs are similar to inspections in that they are also peer reviews used to detect defects. Usu-ally, however, the person leading the review meeting and presenting the product is the producer of that product. In addition, most walkthrough approaches are less formal, since data collection is often not re-quired and an independent check of changes might not be made. Walkthroughs also permit suggestions for general improvements to be made during the main meeting, as well as other goals, while inspections con-centrate (during the main meeting) on finding defects.

IEEE Std 1028 defines minimum requirements for a walkthrough [IEEE 1989]. It defines the objective of a walkthrough to evaluate a software element, mainly "to find defects, omissions, and contradictions, to im-prove the software element and to consider alternative implementations." Other important objectives include "exchange of techniques and style variations, and education of the participants. A walkthrough may point out efficiency and readability problems in the code, modularity in the design or untestable design specifications." Note that this permits many different subjects to be raised that are important, but can also reduce the amount of time available for finding de-fects. The presenter (usually the author) then "walks through" the software element in detail while defects, suggested changes, and improvements are noted and written. The roles defined here are moderator, re-corder, and author (who is also the presenter). The author may also be the moderator.

Edward Yourdon has defined a specific walk-through approach under the title "structured walk-throughs" [Yourdon 1989]. Yourdon defines a walk-through as "a group peer review of a product." The reviewers are to find defects, but suggestions that do not involve defects are permitted.

The roles in Yourdon's version of walkthroughs include presenter (usually the producer), coordinator, secretary (who records comments and is not the same as the coordinator), maintenance, standards-bearer, and user (representative). The preparation time for a walkthrough should average one hour. A walkthrough should average 30–60 minutes, with two hours the absolute maximum and less time (for example, 15 minutes) perfectly acceptable. The product size should be 50–100 lines of code, one to three structure charts, or one or two dataflow diagrams plus a data dictionary. No more than two walkthroughs should be held back-to-back. A walkthrough begins with a review of any old actions from previous walkthroughs.

A walkthrough can be scheduled at a number of different points for a particular product—for example, code could be reviewed before compilation, after successful compilation, or after test. Yourdon recommends that walkthroughs be held after successful automatic syntax checking (for example, by a compiler) but before any kind of execution testing.

Management is then given a verdict on the product's disposition that is signed by all reviewers: accepted as-is, revise but no further walkthrough needed, or revise and conduct another walkthrough. Management is not given a count of defects or their type, and is urged not to use this information for performance evaluation (except for the largest outliers). Managers should in general not be present, as they can affect the utility of a walkthrough.

Daniel Freedman and Gerald Weinberg define a walkthrough as a review that is characterized by the producer of the reviewed material being present and guiding the progression of the review [Freedman 1982]. In their approach a walkthrough is performed as a step-by-step simulation of the code with a sample set of input. They state that the advantages of walkthroughs are that a large amount of material can be examined in a short period of time, little time is demanded of the participants, and the review is often educational. Unfortunately, it can be difficult to conduct walkthroughs in a way that explores substantial issues. In addition, the producer's ability to present can be too influential—good presenters may obscure problems, and poor presenters can give poor impressions of good products.

4. Other Review Processes

There are many different review processes. Figure 2 shows a taxonomy of various review approaches that should aid in comparing these [Wheeler 1996b]. Starting from the left, it shows that review approaches may be divided into two basic classes: (1) those that do not limit the number of reviewers (and generally do not limit the amount of material reviewed), and (2) those that permit only a limited number of reviewers (and generally limit the amount of material reviewed). We have subdivided reviews with a limited number of reviewers into four subcategories: inspections, walkthroughs, selected aspect reviews, and other reviews that limit the number of reviewers. Note that nearly any review can be repeated on the same product using

different teams; this would create an N-fold version of the review [Schneider 1992, Tripp 1991].

Unfortunately, terms for reviews are not widely agreed upon, and this has created a great deal of confusion. We have used the terms defined in IEEE Std 1028 as a baseline and added additional terms (such as "selected aspect review") to create this taxonomy. Table 1 shows more detailed characteristics of the four different review approaches defined in IEEE Std 1028 (management reviews, technical reviews, walkthroughs, and inspections). An organization may, however, conduct a review that they term a "walkthrough" but which would fit under the category of an IEEE Std 1028 technical review, or inspection, or some other category. For example, note that Freedman and Weinberg [Freedman 1982] define a review process they call an "inspection" that is very different from the inspection process defined in IEEE Std 1028. Thus even if a review process is called an inspection, it may not be one as defined by IEEE Std 1028.

No such taxonomy can be perfect or complete, because review approaches continue to be developed and modified. For example, recent works have focused on changing detection methods such as modifying checklists [Chernak 1996] and replacing checklists with scenarios [Porter 1995]. The Internet and the increasing internationalization of software development make it likely that new processes will be developed based on groupware applications.

The following subsections briefly describe some of the review processes in these various categories, with the exception of inspections and walkthroughs (previously discussed).

4.1 Unlimited Numbers of Participants

Reviews with unlimited numbers of participants may involve tens or hundreds of people, at which point "crowd control" becomes a significant issue. With so many attendees, the character of the review changes. On the negative side, most attendees cannot discuss at length any particular issue, simply because there is no time for all of the attendees to speak. On the positive side, such reviews permit a wide range of viewpoints to be represented.

Examples of reviews that do not limit the number of attendees include the reviews defined in the US military standard Mil-Std-1521B [DoD 1985] and the management and technical reviews defined in IEEE Std 1028 [IEEE 1989]. Note that the Mil-Std-1521B reviews and management reviews are not usually peer reviews, since management participates in such reviews.

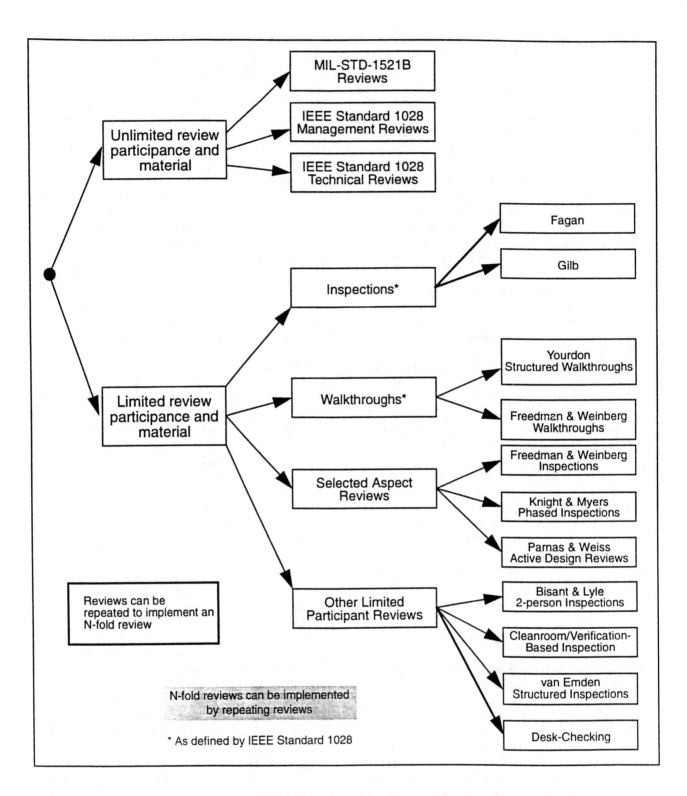

Figure 2. A taxonomy of review processes.

Table 1. Review approaches defined by IEEE Std 1028-1988.[1]

Category and Attributes	Management Review	Technical Review	Software Inspection	Walkthrough
Objective	Ensure progress. Recommend corrective action. Ensure allocation of resources.	Evaluate conformance to specifications and plans. Ensure change integrity.	Detect and identify defects. Verify resolution.	Detect defects. Examine alternatives. Forum for learning.
Delegated Controls				
Decision making	Management team charts course of action. Decisions are made at the meeting or as a result of recommendations.	Review team petitions management or technical leadership to act on recommendations.	Team chooses from predefined product dispositions. Defects must be removed.	All decisions made by producer. Change is the prerogative of the producer.
Change verification	Change verification left to other project controls.	Leader verifies as part of review report.	Moderator verifies rework.	Change verification left to other project controls.
Group Dynamics				
Recommended size	Two or more persons.	Three or more persons.	Three to six persons.	Two to seven persons.
Attendance	Management, technical leadership, and peer mix.	Technical leadership and peer mix.	College of peers meet with documented attendance.	Technical leadership and peer mix.
Leadership	Usually the responsible manager.	Usually the lead engineer.	Trained moderator.	Usually producer.
Procedures				
Material volume	Moderate to high, depending on the specific *statement of objectives* for the meeting.	Moderate to high, depending on the specific *statement of objectives* for the meeting.	Relatively low.	Relatively low.
Presenter	Project representative.	Software element representative.	Presentation by *reader* other than producer.	Usually the producer.
Data collection	As required by applicable policies, standards, or plans.	Not a formal project requirement. May be done locally.	Formally required.	Not a formal project requirement. May be done locally.
Outputs				
Reports	Management review report.	Technical review reports.	Defect list and summary. Inspection report.	Walkthrough report.
Database entries	Any schedule changes must be entered into the project tracking database.	No formal database required.	Defect counts, characteristics, severity, and meeting attributes are kept.	No formal database requirement.

4.2 Selected Aspect Reviews

A "selected aspect review" is what we call a review that is confined to a preselected set of specific aspects. Reviewers look only at these preselected aspects of the product, one at a time. These aspects are usually further broken down into a specific set of items to look for, called a checklist. Even if a detailed checklist is not written, the selected aspects are essentially a higher level checklist of aspects to cover in the review. Generally, selected aspect reviews are performed as a collection of reviews, where each review covers only the preselected aspects of the work product.

Selected aspect reviews bear a number of similarities to the inspection and walkthrough process defined in IEEE Std 1028-1988. Inspections also often use checklists, and selected aspect reviews may even be called inspections by the creators of the review approach. The key difference of selected aspect reviews from inspections and walkthroughs is that the reviewers look only at the pre-selected aspects, one at a time, while inspections and walkthroughs look for all defects in a product, possibly assisted by a checklist. Defects that are not among the preselected aspects are unlikely to be found, and conversely, defects that are the focus of the review should have a high likelihood of detection (though this is unproven). Selected aspect reviews usually do not require paraphrasing of the product. It is quite possible to combine the two approaches, for example, to perform selected aspect reviews as part of the entry criteria for an inspection.

Freedman and Weinberg define a selected aspect review approach that they call an inspection [Freedman 1982] (not to be confused with their walkthrough approach, which was discussed in the previous section). Freedman and Weinberg state that larger amounts of material are generally covered in their review approach, and while sessions may be limited in time (one to two hours) the entire review may take weeks. They believe that the fixed agenda means that the role of moderator does not require much technical ability.

John Knight and E. Ann Myers have also developed a selected aspect review technique called "phased inspections" [Knight 1993]. A phased inspection[2] consists of a series of phases, where each phase addresses one or a small set of related properties (aspects) deemed desirable for the product to have. Phases are conducted in series, with each depending on the properties established in the preceding

phases. Each phase is carried out by staff whose training and experience is appropriate for the phase— some phases may require only rudimentary knowledge. Each inspector is required to sign a statement after the phase that the product possesses the prescribed property to the best of his or her knowledge.

Knight's approach has two basic types of phases: single-inspector phases and multiple-inspector phases. In single-inspector phases one person uses a list of unambiguous checks from a checklist or executes a computer program that checks those selected aspects. In multiple-inspector phases personnel examine the documentation for completeness, examine the product thoroughly in isolation preparing a defect list, and then perform a reconciliation step in which the inspectors' lists are compared. The lists are supposed to be identical.

Multiple-inspector phases bear some similarity to inspections as defined in IEEE Std 1028, but there are a number of key differences: there is no verbal overview (all information must be available in documentation), individual time is spent creating an complete defect list instead of simply preparing for understanding, and the lists created are supposed to be identical before the meeting. This approach does not attempt to use group synergy to find defects missed by the individuals (termed the "phantom inspector" by Fagan [Fagan 1986]), but instead depends on reconciliation to provide the inspectors a challenge and incentive for thoroughness. One important factor in phased inspections is that they were designed to be supportable by computers, and a prototype tool set has been developed.

Unfortunately, as Knight and Meyers note, there is relatively little experimental evidence of the utility of phased inspections. Their review approach is promising, but larger scale experiments are needed that demonstrate the utility of this approach in industrial settings.

David Parnas and David Weiss' "active design reviews" are also a set of selected aspect reviews [Parnas 1987]. In this process, the designers pose questions to the reviewers (the opposite of the usual) through questionnaires. This forces the reviewers to think hard about the product instead of skimming, and also forces them to contribute. Each review has three stages. The first is a brief overview of the module to the reviewers, and if not done already, the reviewers are assigned to reviews and document sections. In the second stage the reviewers review and meet with designers to resolve any questions. In the third stage, the designers read the completed questionnaires and meet with the reviewers to resolve miscommunications. The reviewers may be asked to defend their answers. Little empirical data is available on this review method.

---

[2] Knight and Myers' terminology is slightly different than both IEEE Std 1028 and ours. Knight and Myers use the term "Fagan inspection" where we and the IEEE use the term "inspection," and they use the term "inspection" where we use the term "selected aspect review."

4.3 Other Peer Review Processes

Other review approaches do not fit into the categories above. One is David Bisant and James Lyle's "two-person inspection" approach [Bisant 1989]. This is a review approach for projects that wish to use an inspection-like process but for which larger groups are not available. This approach is similar to Fagan inspections except that it requires only two people (including the author) and there is no moderator. Bisant and Lyle suggest this might be a useful intermediate step toward full inspections.

The Cleanroom process is not simply a review process but an entire software development process that includes a collection of techniques [Dyer 1991, 1992]. One of these techniques is a review process called "verification-based inspections." In these reviews the software's correctness is confirmed, line by line, through informal proof. Each basic programming construct (sequence, if-then, and loop) is examined in turn, and functional correctness questions must be checked for each. This approach changes the meeting goal from defect detection to informal group verification of the product. The intent is to strike a compromise between formality and thoroughness.

Maarten van Emden has also developed a review process for code that is a cross between inspections and a weakened formal verification process, and his process also requires a change in the method for code development [van Emden 1992]. The text of what would be paraphrased in an inspection meeting is included as comments in the code in some suitable formal notation. An inspection meeting consists of determining if the comments are adequate and if the code conforms to the comments. These comments are difficult to add after the fact, so the article presents a method for developing and structuring comments and code simultaneously so this can be accomplished. There is no published experimental data on the cost and benefits of this approach, and the author addresses only code issues in the article (though it is conceivable that it could be applied to other work products).

"Desk-checking" reviews take the limit on participant numbers to the extreme: a single person examines the code in isolation. This approach can certainly find defects but is totally dependent on the reviewer's experience and self-discipline.

We expect that work on groupware support tools will produce many new review processes that take advantage of computing technology.

An active area of research today is focused on using networked workstations more effectively to support work performed by groups. In a Computer Supported Collaborative Work (CSCW) or groupware environment, the work of multiple people is assigned, performed, coordinated, monitored, and combined using workstation and network facilities. Since peer reviews are examples of group work, several researchers have undertaken to provide automated support for them [Brothers 1990, Drake 1992, Gintell 1993, Johnson 1993a]. These systems are still very experimental.

Using this kind of automated support for peer reviews clearly alters certain aspects of the conventional peer review process, and makes processes possible that would be impractical otherwise. Some of these changes may be beneficial but others may be detrimental. For example, eliminating the face-to-face social interaction between participants may reduce the time needed to gather the participants but may also increase misunderstanding. The research to test the effects of these changes is still in progress.

5. Benefits and Costs of Peer Reviews

Unfortunately, there is little experimental data on the costs and benefits of most review processes. Many review processes do not emphasize data collection of costs (such as staff hours) nor do they log results (such as defects discovered) in a way that can be analyzed later. While there have been some efforts to measure the results of the Cleanroom process, it must be noted that the measurements have examined Cleanroom as an entire process and its "Verification-Based Inspections" are only a small piece of the Cleanroom process. This lack of data is in some sense self-perpetuating; without evidence that a given process is beneficial, many organizations are reluctant to spend significant resources on peer reviews.

The primary exception to this lack of data is the software inspection process. A significant body of information is available that describes the costs and benefits of inspections in realistic development environments. The following subsections provide an overview of these reported benefits for inspections, followed by an explanation of these inspection results.

5.1 Benefits and Costs of Inspections

There are many published reports on the use and benefits of inspections from companies such as IBM [Fagan 1976a], AT&T [Ackerman 1984], and Bull [Weller 1993]. NASA's Space Shuttle Program and Jet Propulsion Laboratory have also published positive experiences using inspections [Myers 1988, Kelly 1992]. A host of other organizations have reported positive inspection experiences. including: American Express, AETNA Life and Casualty, the Standard Bank of South Africa [Fagan 1986], Shell Research [Doolan 1992], and Hewlett-Packard [Blakely 1991].

Glen Russell gives the following example of the cost-effectiveness of inspections on a project at Bell Northern Research (BNR) that produced 2.5 million lines of code [Russell 1991]. It took approximately one staff hour of inspection time for each defect found by inspection. It took two to four staff hours of testing time for each defect found by testing. Inspections, therefore, are two to four times more efficient than testing. Later they found that it took, on average, thirty-three staff hours to correct each defect found after the product was released to customers. Inspections reduced the number of these defects by a factor of 10.

5.2   Explanation of Inspection Benefits

To see how these results are achieved, we must analyze several aspects of the software development process. Figure 3 shows a typical breakdown of software development costs, as derived from data published by Barry Boehm [Boehm 1987]. Look at the proportion of time spent on testing. It is commonly held that at least 40 percent of software development is spent on unit, integration, and system testing. Upon closer examination, however, a large part of the testing effort is not actually spent running tests. The extra time is taken up by correcting defects that are found by tests. As much as 40 to 50 percent of typical software development effort is devoted to correcting defects.

Figure 4 shows a profile of the time spent on rework throughout the development process, also derived from Boehm's data. Rework increases in each successive phase because defects from earlier phases are discovered and need to be corrected. By the final integration and system testing phase, twice as much time is spent on rework as on productive testing. Inspections directly attack this growth in rework by minimizing the number of defects at each step.

Figure 5 shows the conventional sequence of software development phases. Beside the boxes are numbers that indicate how many defects are passed on from one phase to the next. The 50 defects per thousand lines of code (KLOC) at the completion of unit testing, and the 10 per KLOC delivered to the field are well-documented industry averages [Jones 1986, Jones 1991]. Anecdotal data from individual projects was used to fill in approximate numbers for defects in the other phases—we are not claiming that these numbers hold for all projects; rather, we are using these numbers to explain why inspections might be as effective as some experiments report.

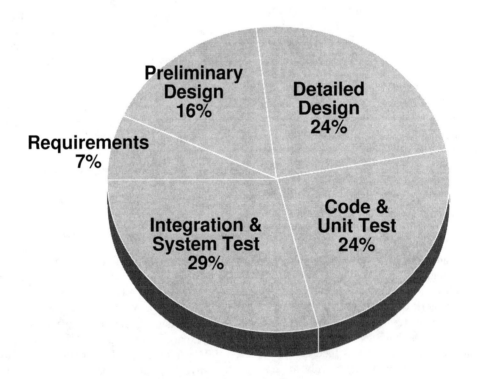

Figure 3. Cost of software development.

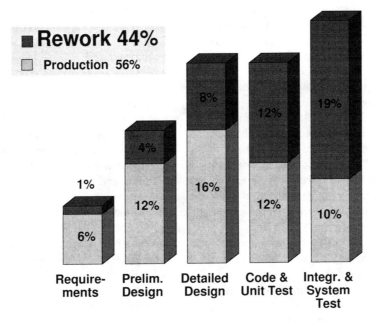

Figure 4. Distribution of rework during development.

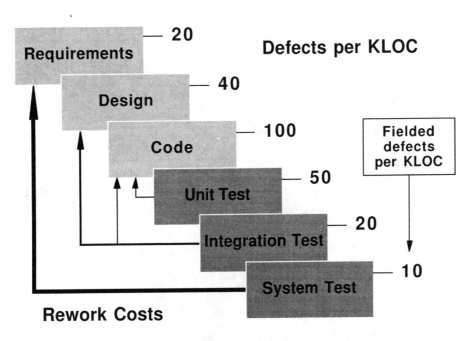

Figure 5. Typical software defect profile.

The width of the arrows in Figure 5 that point back from the testing phases to earlier construction phases suggest the relative costs of correcting defects that were not detected earlier. For example, a misunderstood requirement that is not recognized until the final system testing phase will likely be costly to correct. Late discovery and correction of defects may also delay system delivery.

Figure 6 depicts the introduction of inspections for requirements, design, and code into the development process. The objective of these inspections is to find all the defects at each phase so that development can proceed to the next phase with a completely correct basis. Even though the ideal of completely eliminating defects is rarely achieved, success rates of 80 percent are consistently reported [Fagan 1986]. Therefore, the number of defects passed on to succeeding phases is reduced dramatically (the numbers in parentheses in Figure 6 show the number of defects when inspections are not used.) The cumulative effect of requirements, design, and code inspections along with normal testing, is an order of magnitude reduction in the number of defects in fielded products.

In addition to this gain in quality, there is a corresponding gain in productivity because the amount of rework needed to correct defects during testing is significantly reduced. This reduction in rework is illustrated in Figure 6 by the reduced width, in comparison with Figure 5, of the arrows pointing back from the testing phases. For a comparison of inspections to the work of Deming and Crosby on quality and productivity, see Bill Brykczynski [1995].

Inspections reduce the number of defects in work products throughout the development process. More defects are found earlier, where they are easier and much less expensive to correct. Inspections are also able to uncover defects that may not be discovered by testing. Examples include identifying missing requirements and special cases or unusual conditions where an algorithm would produce incorrect results.

All these benefits are not without their costs, however. Inspections require an investment of approximately 15 percent of the total cost of development early in the process. Figure 7 shows typical spending-rate profiles for development projects with and without inspections. The taller curve shows increased spending early in the project, which reflects the time devoted to inspections [Fagan 1986]. This curve then drops quickly through the testing phases. The broader curve, for projects that do not use inspections, shows lower initial spending but much higher spending through testing, which reflects the 44 percent rework being done [Boehm 1987].

The investment in inspections pays off in a 25 to 35 percent overall increase in productivity. This productivity increase, as demonstrated by Fagan in industry studies, can be translated into a 25 to 35 percent development schedule reduction [Fagan 1986]. In Figure 7, the area under the inspection curve, which represents total development cost, is approximately 30 percent less than the area under the non-inspection curve.

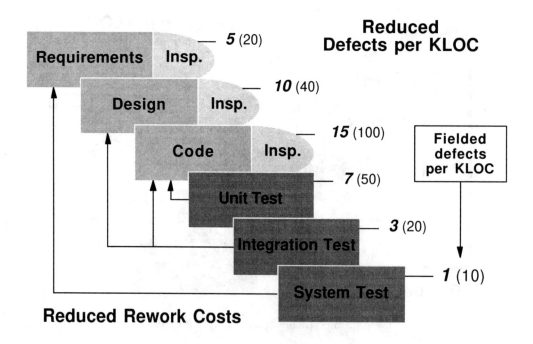

Figure 6. Defect profile with inspections.

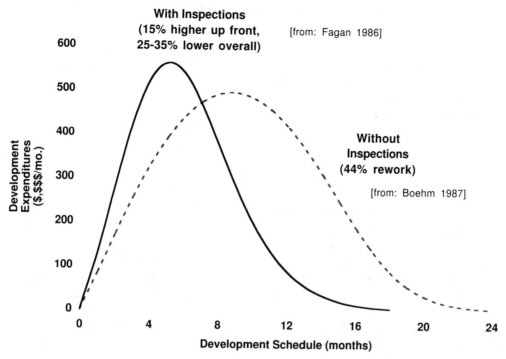

Figure 7. Software development spending profiles.

6. Summary

There are many different kinds of peer review processes. Two of the most common are software inspections and walkthroughs. We believe that walkthroughs are slowly being replaced by the more rigorous software inspection process, though walkthroughs continue to be useful in the early stages of a product's development when alternative approaches are of more interest. The inspection process is often cost-effective, as supported by numerous empirical studies. The cost of the inspection activity is usually offset by the savings through the early detection of software errors.

An inspection is a formal peer review process consisting of a detailed scrutiny of software work products by a group of qualified individuals. Software work products are provided in advance for review team members to examine in detail. The inspection meeting itself has well-defined roles, including moderator, recorder, reader, author, and additional inspection team members. The author is not allowed to control the meeting nor to present the product. The sole goal of the meeting is to detect defects, not to discuss how to repair them nor to suggest alternatives. A limited amount of material is covered in each inspection to allow a thorough and complete examination of the product. Metrics are collected as to the amount of effort required by all team members and the number of major and minor errors found. The errors are catego-

rized to help identify problems with the process. The emphasis is to identify as many major and minor errors as possible before test and delivery. Management commitment is necessary to implement and maintain a healthy inspection process. The inspection process is useful when it is important to remove defects from a product and there is sufficient management commitment to sustain the process. More information on inspections is available in David Wheeler [1996a].

Walkthroughs are a much less formal review process. Someone, usually the author, simply presents the product to his or her peers. The presented product may or may not have been provided in advance. In the meeting the presenter (for example, the author) "walks through" the product providing the rationale behind the technical decisions made. The attendees point out problems in the product or alternatives as they are observed. The goals of walkthroughs vary. Most walkthroughs have several goals, such as detecting defects, discussing how they could be repaired, discussing alternative approaches, and educating the attendees. Problems are recorded by the product's author, if at all, and a follow-up process might not be initiated. Fewer hours are involved in a walkthrough, because peers are usually not required to prepare ahead of time and no specific roles are assigned. The walkthrough process is particularly useful for discussing alternatives, but it can also be used to detect product defects.

There are many different peer review processes that can be used in a software development process. Unfortunately, few have taken the step of developing experiments to determine the costs and benefits of these processes. There is significant empirical evidence for the effectiveness of inspections, which is one reason for their widespread use. It is our hope that more experimentation and examination of peer review processes will occur in the future.

7. References

References with an asterisk (*) are included in [Wheeler 1996a].

[Ackerman 1984] Ackerman, A. Frank, Priscilla J. Fowler, and Robert G. Ebenau, "Software Inspections and the Industrial Production of Software," *Software Validation*, H.L. Hausen, ed., Elsevier, Amsterdam, 1984, pp. 13–40.

[Bisant 1989] Bisant, David B. and James R. Lyle, "A Two-Person Inspection Method to Improve Programming Productivity," *IEEE Trans. Software Eng.*, Vol. 15, No. 10, Oct. 1989, pp. 1,294–1,304.*

[Blakely 1991] Blakely, Frank W. and Mark E. Boles, "A Case Study of Code Inspections," *Hewlett-Packard J.*, Vol. 42, No. 4, Oct. 1991, pp. 58–63.*

[Boehm 1987] Boehm, Barry W. "Improving Software Productivity," *Computer*, Vol. 20, No. 9, Sept. 1987, pp. 43-47.

[Brothers 1990] Brothers, L., V. Sembugamoorthy, and M. Muller, "ICICLE: Groupware for Code Inspection," *CSCW 90: Proc. ACM Conf. Computer Supported Cooperative Work*, 1990, pp. 169–181.

[Brykczynski 1995] Brykczynski, Bill, "The Software Inspection Process-Applying the Principles of Deming and Crosby," *Information and Systems Engineering*, Vol. 1, No. 1, IOS Press, Amsterdam, Mar. 1995, pp. 23–37.

[Chernak 1996] Chernak, Y., "A Statistical Approach to the Inspection Checklist Formal Synthesis and Improvement," *IEEE Trans. Software Eng.*, Vol. 22, No. 12, Dec. 1996, pp. 866–874.

[DoD 1985] United States Department of Defense (DoD), *Military Standard for Technical Reviews and Audits for Systems, Equipments, and Computer Software*, Mil-Std-1521B, 1985.

[Doolan 1992] Doolan, E.P., "Experience with Fagan's Inspection Method," *Software-Practice and Experience*, Vol. 22, No. 2, Feb. 1992, pp. 173–182.*

[Drake 1992] Drake, Janet, Vahid Mashayekhi, John Riedl, and Wei-Tek Tsai, "*Support for Collaborative Software Inspection in a Distributed Environment: Design, Implementation, and Pilot Study*, Tech. Report TR 92-33, Univ. of Minnesota, June 1992.

[Dyer 1991] Dyer, Michael, "Verification Based Inspection," *Proc. 25th Hawaii Int'l Conf. System Sci.*, Vol. 2, IEEE CS Press, Los Alamitos, Calif., 1991, pp. 418–427.

[Dyer 1992] Dyer, Michael, *The Cleanroom Approach to Quality Software Development*, John Wiley & Sons, New York., N.Y., 1992, pp. 96–99.

[Fagan 1976a] Fagan, Michael E., "Design and Code Inspections to Reduce Errors in Program Development," *IBM Systems J.*, Vol. 15, No. 3, 1976, pp. 182–211.*

[Fagan 1986] Fagan, Michael E., "Advances In Software Inspections," *IEEE Trans. Software Eng.*, Vol. 12, No. 7, July 1986, pp. 744–751.*

[Freedman 1982] Freedman, Daniel P. and Gerald M. Weinberg, *Handbook of Walkthroughs, Inspections, and Technical Reviews: Evaluating Programs, Projects, and Products*, 3rd Ed., Little, Brown & Co., Boston, 1982. Previously published in 1977 and 1979 under a different title.

[Gilb 1993] Gilb, Tom and Dorothy Graham, *Software Inspection*, Addison-Wesley, Reading, Mass., 1993.

[Gintell 1993] Gintell, John, John E. Arnold, Michael Houde, Jacek Kruszelnicki, Roland McKenney, and Gerard Memmi, "Scrutiny: A Collaborative Inspection and Review System," *Proc. 4th European Software Eng. Conf.*, 1993.

[Humphrey 1989] Humphrey, Watts, *Managing the Software Process*, Addison-Wesley, Reading, Mass., 1989, pp. 463–486.

[IEEE 1989] IEEE, *IEEE Standard for Software Reviews and Audits*, ANSI/IEEE Std 1028-1988, IEEE, New York, June 30, 1989.

[Johnson 1993a] Johnson, Philip M. and Danu Tjahjono, "Improving Software Quality through Computer Supported Collaborative Review," *Proc. 3rd European Conf. Computer-Supported Cooperative Work*, 1993, pp. 61–76.

[Jones 1986] Jones, Capers, *Programming Productivity*, McGraw-Hill, New York, N.Y., 1986.

[Jones 1991] Jones, Capers, *Applied Software Measurement*, McGraw-Hill, New York, N.Y., 1991.

[Kelly 1992] Kelly, John C., Joseph S. Sherif, and Jonathan Hops, "An Analysis of Defect Densities Found During Software Inspections," *J. Systems and Software*, Vol. 17, No. 2, Feb. 1992, pp. 111–117.*

[Knight 1993] Knight, John C. and E. Ann Myers, "An Improved Inspection Technique," *Comm. ACM*, Vol. 36, No. 11, Nov. 1993, pp. 51–61.

[Myers 1988] Myers, Ware, "Shuttle Code Achieves Very Low Error Rate," *IEEE Software*, Vol. 5, No. 5, Sept. 1988, pp. 93–95.

[Parnas 1987] Parnas, David L. and David M. Weiss, "Active Design Reviews: Principles and Practices," *J. Systems and Software*, No. 7, 1987, pp. 259–265.

[Porter 1995] Porter, A.A., L.G. Votta Jr., and V.R. Basili, "Comparing Detection Methods for Software Requirements Inspections: A Replicated Experiment," *IEEE Trans. Software Eng.* Vol. 21, No. 6, June 1995, pp. 563–575.

[Russell 1991] Russell, Glen W., "Experience with Inspection in Ultralarge-Scale Developments," *IEEE Software*, Vol. 8, No. 1, Jan. 1991, pp. 25–31.*

[Schneider 1992] Schneider, G. Michael, Johnny Martin, and Wei-Tek Tsai, "An Experimental Study of Fault Detection in User Requirements Documents," *ACM Trans. Software Eng. and Methodology*, Vol. 1, No. 2, Apr. 1992, pp. 188–204.

[Shirey 1992] Shirey, Glen C, "How Inspections Fail," *Proc. 9th Int'l Conf. Testing Computer Software*, 1992, pp. 151–159.*

[Strauss 1994] Strauss, Susan H. and Robert G. Ebenau, *Software Inspection Process*. McGraw-Hill, New York, 1994.

[Tripp 1991] Tripp, Leonard L., William F. Struck, and Bryan K. Pflug, "The Application of Multiple Team Inspections on a Safety-Critical Software Standard," *Proc. 4th Software Eng. Standards Application Workshop*, IEEE CS Press, Los Alamitos, Calif., 1991, pp. 106–111.*

[van Emden 1992] van Emden, Maarten H., "Structured Inspections of Code," *Software Testing, Verification and Reliability*, Vol. 2, No. 3, Sept. 1992, pp. 133–153.

[Votta 1993] Votta, Lawrence G. Jr., "Does Every Inspection Need a Meeting?" *Proc. 1st ACM SIGSOFT Symp. Foundations of Software Eng.*, 1993. Published in *ACM Software Eng. Notes*, Vol. 18, No. 5, Dec. 1993, pp. 107–114.*

[Wenneson 1985] Wenneson, G., "Quality Assurance Software Inspections at NASA Ames: Metrics for Feedback and Modification," Proc. *10th Ann. Software Eng. Workshop*, Goddard Space Flight Center, Greenbelt, Md., 1985.

[Weller 1993] Weller, Edward F., "Lessons from Three Years of Inspection Data," *IEEE Software*, Vol. 10, No. 5, Sept. 1993, pp. 38–45.*

[Wheeler 1996a] Wheeler, David A., Bill Brykczynski, and Reginald N. Meeson, Jr., *Software Inspection: An Industry Best Practice*, IEEE Computer Society Press, Los Alamitos, Calif., 1996.*

[Wheeler 1996b] Wheeler, David A., Bill Brykczynski, and Reginald N. Meeson, Jr., "Peer Review Processes Similar to Inspection," *Software Inspection: An Industry Best Practice*, IEEE Computer Society Press, Los Alamitos, Calif., 1996, pp. 228–236.*

[Yourdon 1989] Yourdon, Edward, *Structured Walkthroughs*, 4th Ed., Prentice-Hall, Englewood Cliffs, N.J., 1989.

Software Project Management Audits

L. Bernstein

Bell Laboratories

This paper shows how project audits can be used to un-cover project strengths and weaknesses. Three audits are described and findings of the audit teams are summa-rized. Audits helped identify organizational problems, lacking management discipline, and software testing ap-proaches useful to other projects. The issue of product sales versus disciplined project management was faced in all three audits. How this issue was handled is dis-cussed and related to the success or lack of it for each project.

INTRODUCTION

When a software project is in trouble, a software pro-ject audit can help [1]. Turner's book [2], *Project Au-diting Methodology,* provides a framework for audits. This paper presents the who, what, when, where, why, and how of software project management audits includ-ing tools for the audit team.

Audits do not replace competent management. They provide a snapshot of project status. Recovery plans cannot be expected from the audit team. These are best developed within the development organization. Bot-tom-up plans where developers own the schedules trig-gered with data collected during the audit are most likely to succeed.

Appendix A contains a questionnaire the author used to audit several software projects. A structured meeting schedule is shown in Appendix B. They evolved from experience in four software project management audits.

For its findings to be accepted and trusted, the audit team must be sensitive to the climate within the orga-nization and respect the concerns of line management. Most important, the audit team must not add fuel to an existing fire. There is nothing worse than the audit team stridently defining the problems an organization faces and pronouncing solutions, only to find that the audit

process destroyed the project. Less serious a problem, but a waste of time, is when the project management becomes defensive owing to high-handed audit team methods and rejects recommendations even when they may be useful.

Software project management audits can change the way in which a project is managed. Furthermore, by participating in an audit, auditors can relate software project management theory to real situations without the perils of on-the-job training. Buckle [3] writes that an audit team has "the effect of getting the group being audited to think more about where they are and what they need to do, and gives staff a chance to express their fears and problems without seeming to admit failure to their immediate supervisors." My experience supports his conclusion. Furthermore, those being audited often feel flattered that their opinions are sought.

Those working on the project often know what's right, what's wrong, and how things could be done bet-ter. The audit team acts best as a *catalyst* for drawing out recommendations latent within the organization. One designer said, "Debriefing sessions such as this one should be held by line management whenever a major problem is solved."

Auditors must establish a level of trust with those on the project so that they will speak freely. Witch hunts quickly undermine the usefulness of audits and audits have been destroyed by "preliminary" findings leaking to higher management.

Reviewing findings with project management, ab-stractly enough to protect individuals, *before* submit-ting them to higher management ensures their validity and obtains project ownership. This increases the like-lihood that some action will be taken.

Richard Canning [4] and Ioannis Methodis [5] de-scribe the need for software project management audits and how they might fit into a total auditing strategy. How auditing fits with the software life cycle was re-cently described in *Computer* magazine (March 1982).

Auditors I have worked with were successful project managers, not professional auditors. Firms should es-

---

Address correspondence to L. Bernstein, Bell Laboratories, 6 Corporate Place, Piscataway, New Jersey 08854.

tablish a pool of software project managers, known to be objective, who can be called upon to serve on an audit team. Firms without this capability should hire an outside software consulting firm to conduct the audit.

The audit can be a valuable tool to project managers. They can reflect on their development process and can see how to change their approach. Project managers can use the audit findings to support their position with their management or customer. One audit established that a project manager needed the people required to study system performance even though higher management had previously planned to move them to another project. Project managers can also learn how their people perceive their management style.

WHAT

A software project management audit is a review of the process, tools, and organization employed in developing a software system. The audit focuses on the software development life cycle technology being applied [7,8]. It is not a review of technical or marketing issues. Undoubtedly some of these issues will spill over into the discussions. The audit team, however, must be judicious of its time and not meander onto some of the more interesting byways associated with technology or market strategy. The focus of the audit is on schedule analysis, project management tools, and the emotionally charged issues of working relationships. Audits on technical or marketing issues can also be done [9,10], but those are not the purpose of a software project management audits nor of this paper.

The audit team should look for common themes cutting across organization boundaries and levels of management.

Often those things not said about working relationships and the development process are most important. A project with four levels of management was audited to see how they could improve their software building process in order to shorten test time. In the course of the audit *no* mention was made of the role of the third level managers. Following up on this clue uncovered organizational conflicts which ultimately required the transferring of two managers. Taboos are often those problems which are described symptomatically in terms of "safe" topics. The audit team can bring focus to them by simply mentioning the possibility of a problem and letting people talk about them. Examples of such taboos are discussions of overstaffing, respect for the project manager, bypassing of the management structure for decision making, favoritism in machine allocation, and reward of slackers.

It is useful to explain the catalyst concept at the beginning of each interview and state explicitly that the

audit can be a means for people on the project to express their opinion to their management without fear since their anonymity will be protected.

WHAT IT'S NOT

Top management should not look at the audit as a way to recruit. It is not a vehicle for obtaining a "clean bill of health." It is not a complete view of the state of the project. There is a temptation to appoint someone to the audit team who will later be transferred to the project as a key manager. This can result in distrust of the new manager simply because the confidentiality of the audit process is broken when the auditor joins the project.

Audits should be instituted when needed and not planned as a regular part of the project life cycle. One audit I performed was a successful project that resulted in no change since management took the point of view "why fix things that aren't broken." Furthermore the people audited saw the audit as an intrusion in their time and much of my efforts were spent assuring the developers that their project was not "in trouble." The audit is most effective in an area of the project where there is an actual or potential failure. It is best when the project manager sees the need to bring in outsiders to help define his problems. It is less promising when external forces such as an irate customer cause management to impose an audit. In one case the entire audit was discounted when the audit team questioned the competency of the staff.

THINGS TO LOOK FOR

Here are some clues to project problems found in audits conducted using the techniques purposed in this paper:

1. disagreements between managers on facts
2. disagreements with customer particularly on delivery
3. statements like "The savings are not what was originally projected."
4. statements like "The dumb user isn't trained, that's why . . ."
5. key people being shifted from crisis to crisis
6. key people leaving
7. uncertain roles of managers and developers and poor interorganization relationships
8. few commitments being made and those being made were not communicated to project members; some commitments made before features specified; others being made without a development plan for meeting them
9. shipping to first site before testing was complete and to additional sites without time for an adequate soak-in.

10. absence of module ownership
11. critical items not being tracked, for example, no freeze dates for software deliveries to testing
12. program listings unreadable—too many or too few comments
13. a preoccupation with *enforcing* standards rather than their usefulness
14. bugs found late in the software life cycle
15. program administration ignored
16. a variety of approaches to software design and no apparent correlation between software design and programs

The project may be in serious trouble when the project manager starts saying, "the load is twice what we expected and we need a bigger machine," "the customer is late with the requirements," "yes we have schedules and we must have specific development intervals, but we do not have a written specification of what the system is to do," or "our economics are somewhat worse that we projected."

Audits have identified where a lack of development tools exists, when storage and real time constraints comprised design, and where a test plans design reviews or code reviews did not exist with little appreciation by project management of the consequences of these shortcomings.

WHERE AND WHEN

An audit of a large project employing over 100 people takes 4 to 6 days. It should be held at the development plant, with each session lasting 2 days. Each session should be approximately 2 weeks apart. A full 6-day audit consists of three 2-day meetings over a period of 6 weeks.

To keep the audit crisp, it is essential that propaganda be eliminated. This can be done before the meeting by having information distributed to auditors about the state of the project and the function the project is supposed to perform, including whatever marketing information is available. Furthermore, having an explicit 1-hour discussion of what the project will do as the first topic of discussion recognizes that such a discussion must take place, yet limits its duration through the structured schedule shown in Appendix B.

Teleconferencing is possible for the audit team procedural meetings. Once a level of trust is established, telephone calls to members of the audited organization can clarify issues, without the travel overhead. In order to find out what is going on, it is extremely helpful when an auditor has a previous personal relationship with someone in the audited organization.

WHY AUDIT

Audits normally find problems earlier than they would show of their own accord and give project management more time to circumvent them. They are therapeutic and can give harried managers and developers time out to take stock.

When schedules, feature objectives and/or allocated resources seem unrealistic, audits can be used to support the project manager's cry for relief. On the other hand, audit findings can be used to purge incumbent managers.

HOW

Individual and group interviews are the fundamental tools used in audits. The questionnaire in Appendix A provides a useful outline for structuring the interviews. Auditors should spend at least one-third of their time in informal one-on-one interviews with developers and first line supervisors to gain insight into the workings of the organization.

It is useful to distribute this questionnaire prior to the interview. It is not mandatory that the questionnaire be followed rigorously. It is useful in keeping discussions from going off on tangents. It lets the audit team turn off filibusters. On the other hand, when the audit team finds that a particular topic is illuminating a project management issue, they can depart from the formality of the structure to get to the problem and possible solutions.

WHO

The audit team should consist of three to five people from outside the organization being audited. The leader of the audit team should be someone in a sister organization who has some familiarity with the project and knows project members. It is recommended that some of the auditors have previous auditing experience, but they need not be professional auditors. It is important that they be developers and preferably experienced project managers. At least one of the audit team members should be a highly experienced project manager who can ask penetrating questions and facilitate the identification problems, while being very sensitive to the instabilities that can be caused by the audit team.

It goes almost without saying that the members of the audit team should not report to the same manager as the project manager. In such cases the loyalty of the auditor is divided between his boss and the confidentiality needs of the audit. Those being audited will not trust the audit team and perceive the auditors as doing performance evaluation.

TOOLS FOR THE AUDIT TEAM

The most important tool that the audit team can use is nondirective listening. It is essential to listen carefully to what people are saying and to try to glean from their discussions the common themes.

A second tool is the questionnaire in Appendix A which provides a structured interview plan and focuses on the management issues which may be uncomfortable for the developer to discuss. It is much more pleasant to talk about what the project will do than it is to talk about how people work together, particularly when there is conflict.

The third tool is the structured set of interviews identified in Appendix B. People from all levels should be selected for interviews and given the opportunity to discuss the questionnaire and any other items that come to mind. It is useful to let the project managers select the people to be interviewed. This emphasizes ownership of the results on the project management team. If the audit team feels that the project manager is not being open, they can cut the audit short to a 2-day session and give a bureaucratic report that things "seem to be on the right track."

The fourth tool is public praise and sympathy. It is useful for the auditors to indicate when they are facing the same problems on their projects. Pointing to people's successes and good ideas opens communication. Set up some stress points in the interviews by having two levels of management together followed by interviews with just the lower level manager. This lets the auditors detect the openness with which problems are being faced. These stress situations can demonstrate working relationships, and see how people defend one another, support one another, and contradict one another. The topics that come up in the single level interview and not in the two level one are clues to areas needing examination.

Visit work area to look at logs, computer programming listings, test cases, and demonstrations of the system. Ask people, quite randomly, what they are doing and why. Auditors can quickly get a feeling for how well procedures are being followed and how much compliance there is to standards.

REACTIONS TO THE AUDIT INTERVIEW

Here are some actual comments from people audited: "I feel good about being able to say what's been on my mind," "Nobody ever asked me before," "We were glad to hear that other projects have problems," "This has been very helpful in enabling us to be reflective," "Let me get up on my soap box and tell you what's wrong

with the project"; afterwards, "I really didn't have that much to say."

During the interviews it is important that each person says something and that some questions get directed to those who are quiet. Anybody that comes to the meeting must say something. The audit team must provide a climate of participation and not let one person dominate the discussion. When closing each interview it is useful to go around and have each person state how they feel about the interview.

DEBRIEFING

To establish ownership of the results by the project management team, debrief findings with them, not privately with just an audit team member. It is alright for the auditors to disagree. Disagreements let project management see what supports the audit team findings. This lets them trust the results and leads to action.

Stay clear of evaluations of individuals. The purpose of the audit is to discover those problems facing the organization and hopefully come up with recommended solutions. It is irresponsible to evaluate people based on the brief contacts the audits provide.

The audit team must be quite sensitive in its approach so that it does not destroy the organization it is trying to help. The auditors must be careful not to pontificate about "how we do it better on our project." On one project audit, the audit team indicated that the educational background of the people working on the project was inadequate. Even though the audit team made recommendations pointing to serious problems, the entire audit report was discarded. Short of recommending cancellation of the project, or a wholesale purge, it is important to steer clear of comments on the caliber of the staff.

SUMMARY

Software project management audits are a useful tool in helping a project in crises define its problems and possible remedies. The audit should be used sparingly, with experienced project managers as auditors. People being transferred into the organization should not be on the audit team as a way to learn about the project since confidentiality must be maintained.

APPENDIX A. Audit Interview Questionnaire

1. What is the status of the project?
2. Project objectives/requirements
   A. How do you feel about the requirement? Are they:
      1. too vague;

    2. too specific;

    3. accurate?

  B. Is the priority of individual requirements made clear?

3. Project definition and organization

  A. How is the project being planned?

  B. What is the role of and relationship with the customer?

4. Staffing and laboratory facilities

  A. How and in what proportions is work divided among organizations? Describe the interactions between the various organizations.

  B. How was the project staffed as a function of time (including projection into the future)? (Include experience level of original people both managers and staff.) Are there staffing problems?

  C. What training programs do you have for new employees?

  D. Do you have any special stafflike organizations? If so, what is their role?

  E. How much overtime is worked?

5. Project controls and tracking

  A. What are they and who monitors them? For:

    1. schedules

    2. milestones (include original milestones and current schedule)

    3. design record documentation

    4. user documentation

    5. development techniques

  B. What project parameters are tracked? For example:

    1. schedules

    2. real time

    3. memory usage

    4. I/O bandwidth usage

  C. How are changes controlled?

  D. How are problems uncovered and dealt with?

  E. How much time is spent estimating status?

  F. Who is the highest level manager who ever reads code?

  G. Who is the highest level manager who frequently reads code?

6. Decision making

  A. How are key desicisions made?

  B. How was the most significant crises solved?

  C. What level of approval is required for what kinds of decisions (who's in charge of what)?

  D. What is the role of task forces and committees?

7. Communications

  A. How are intraproject communications (verbally and written) handled?

    1. between each organization

    2. vertically through line management

    3. between peers

8. Project management tools

  A. What are the management tools and techniques that contribute most to this project?

  B. How can they be modified to be more effective?

  C. Are there tools which should be used and aren't?

  D. How is programmer productivity estimated and measured?

9. Technical approach

  A. What are the major risks?

  B. What are the development and execution environments?

  C. How much effort is devoted to software tools? What are they and how useful are they?

  D. How is user documentation developed and what was the role of human performance engineering?

  E. What is the system test approach?

  F. What outside projects did you and are you learning from?

  G. Fill out the attached charts (see Table 1) on usage or project program development techniques.

10. Prognosis

  A. What are the most critical problems the project faces?

  B. How do you suggest they be solved?

11. Additional questions for one-on-one interviews

  A. Describe your assignment.

  B. What are your criteria of success?

  C. What frustrates you about your job?

  D. What satisfies you about your job?

  E. What do you need to make a more significant contribution in your job?

APPENDIX B. Typical Audit Schedule

Situation

You are asked to audit a project with xxx people working on it. The project manager has one level of management reporting directly to him. People in one of his peer's organization are also working on the project. The organization structure is shown in Figure 1

Day 1:

8:15–11:30 Project manager, peer and managers—A 1¾ hour review of organization, architecture, design philosophy, schedules, and plans. A 1½ hour discussion of the questionnaire.

11:30– 1:00 Conference lunch with Big boss, Project manager, Peer, and Managers to continue the discussion.

1:00– 1:45 "One-on-one" sessions with managers.

1:45– 2:30 Tour of the work areas and test facilities. If possible, see a demonstration of the system.

2:30– 3:00 Audit team "taking" stock session.

3:00– 5:00 Discussion of questionnaire with six exempt

Table 1. Project development techniques

	Performance modeling	Function modeling	Project meetings	Problem/ action item lists	Independent test group	Standards	Software manufacturing	Design specifications	Design reviews	Top-down design	Structured programming	Code walk-through	Module ownership	Jackson method	Regression testing
Did you use it?															
How?															
What was the result?															
If not used, should it be?															
Why?															

	Project manager Programmer manager B	Big boss Manager C	Peer Manager D	Manager E
Manager A				
–	Exempt software engineer			
–	Exempt program designer			
–	Nonexempt programmer			
–	Nonexempt programmer			
–	Nonexempt programmer			

Figure 1. The organization structure.

software engineers/program designers selected by the project manager.

6:00   Dinner with three managers, three other exempt employees, and three nonexempt employees.

(Note: One-third of those interviewed should be rated "below average" in performance.)

Day 2:

8:15–9:30   Meet with three exempt people who were at dinner in one-on-one session to discuss questionnaire.

9:30–10:30   One-on-one session with five exempt employees who did not attend dinner to discuss questionnaire.

10:30–12:00   Developer sessions. Meeting with three exempt, two nonexempt, and one contractor employee (if applicable) to discuss questionnaire.

12:00–4:00   Lunch and debriefing session with project manager, peer, and managers. Summary of findings and plans for further meetings.

REFERENCES

1. J. K. Buckle, *Managing Software Projects,* American Elsevier, New York, 1977 (Library of Congress CIP No. 76-53589), p. 94.
2. W. D. Turner, *Project Auditing Methodology,* North-Holland, 1980 (Library of Congress CIP No. 80-23934).
3. J. K. Buckle, in Ref. 1.
4. R. Canning, The Internal Auditor and the Computer, *EDP Analyzer,* Canning Publ. **13** (3), (1975).
5. Ioannis Methodis, Internal Controls and Audits, *J. Syst. Manag.,* **27** (6), 6–14 (1976).
6. W. L. Bryan, S. G. Siegel, and G. L. Whileleather, Auditing throughout the Software Life Cycle: A Primer, *Computer* **15** (3), 57–67 (1982).
7. P. A. Metzger, *Managing Programming Projects,* Prentice Hall, Englewood Cliffs, N.J., 1973 (Library of Congress CIP No. 72-8535.
8. R. W. Jensen and C. C. Tonies, *Software Engineering,* Prentice Hall, Englewood Cliffs, N.J., 1979 (Library of Congress CIP No. 78-15659), Chap. 2.
9. E. F. Miller, A Service Concept for Software Auditing, *Tutorial: Software Testing and Validation Techniques,* IEEE, New York, 1976, pp. 358–376.
10. Ramsperger, GOB/GOD: Which valid program version is running?, *Online* **14** (3), 140 (1976) (German).

The Unit Development Folder (UDF): A Ten-Year Perspective

Frank S. Ingrassia
TRW Systems Engineering and Development Division
One Space Park
Redondo Beach, California 90278

Abstract

This paper is an annotated version of the original 1976 description of the content and application of the Unit Development Folder, a structured mechanism for organizing and collecting software development products (requirements, design, code, test plans/data) as they become available. Properly applied, the Unit Development Folder is an important part of an orderly development environment in which unit-level schedules and responsibilities are clearly delineated and their step-by-step accomplishment made visible to management. Unit Development Folders have been used on a number of projects at TRW and have been shown to reduce many of the problems associated with the development of software.

Ten years of application have not diminished the viability of this tool. This is probably due to the fact that it is a basic, simple, adaptable, and natural approach to software development. Experience has shown, however, that its effectiveness has been uneven. This is not surprising since the effectiveness of any tool is dependent on proper and diligent use. More fundamentally, tools will not resolve or compensate for intrinsic deficiencies in the software development environment. Everyone knows that the most critical aspect in developing software is to have a clear, consistent, well structured, and complete set of requirements at the beginning of the development process. Everyone knows this but many choose to compromise this principle. If you don't know where you are going, tools will not help you get to the right place.

One of the main side effects resulting from the invention of computers has been the creation of a new class of frustrated and harried managers responsible for software development. The frustration is a result of missed schedules, cost overruns, inadequate implementation and design, high operational error rates, and poor maintainability, which have historically characterized software development. In the early days of computer programming, these problems were often excused by the novelty of this unique endeavor and obscured by the language and experience gap that frequently existed between developers and managers. Today's maturity and the succession of computer-wise people to management positions does not appear to have reduced the frustration level in the industry. We are still making the same mistakes and getting into the same predicaments. The science of managing software development is still in its infancy and the lack of a good clear set of principles is apparent.

The problems associated with developing software are too numerous and too complex for anyone to pretend to have solved them, and this paper makes no such pretensions. The discussion that follows describes a simple but effective management tool which, when properly used, can reduce the chaos and alleviate many of the problems common in software development. The tool described in this paper is called the Unit Development Folder (UDF) and is being used at TRW in software development and management.

What is a UDF? Simply stated, it is a specific form of development notebook which has proven useful and effective in collecting and organizing software products as they are produced. In essence, however, it is much more; it is a means of imposing a management philosophy and a development methodology on an activity that is often chaotic. In physical appearance, a UDF is merely a three-ring binder containing a cover sheet and is organized into several predefined sections which are common to each UDF. The ultimate objectives that the content and format of the UDF must satisfy are to:

(1) Provide an orderly and consistent approach in the development of each of the units of a program or project

(2) Provide a uniform and visible collection point for all unit documentation and code

(3) Aid individual discipline in the establishment and attainment of scheduled unit-level milestones

(4) Provide low-level management visibility and control over the development process

Figure 1 illustrates the role of the UDF in the total software development process.

Reprinted from *Software Engineering Project Management*, R.H. Thayer, ed., 1988, pp. 405–415.

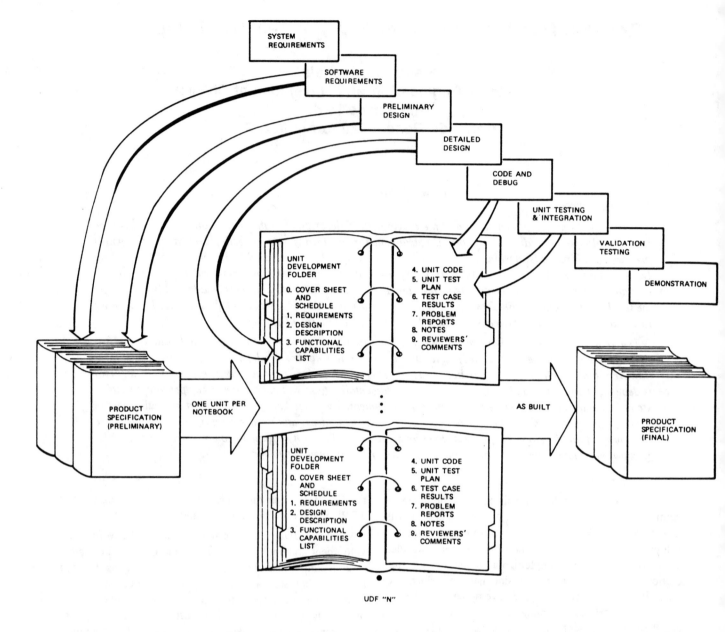

Figure 1. The UDF in the Development Process

If one follows a fairly standard design approach, the completion of the preliminary design activity marks the point at which UDFs are created and initiated for all units comprising the total product to be designed and coded. Therefore, the first question to be answered is, "What is a unit?" It was found that, for the purpose of implementing a practical and effective software development methodology to meet the management objectives stated earlier, a unique element of software architecture needed to be defined. This basic functional element is designated a "unit" of software and is defined independently of the language or type of application. Experience has indicated that it is unwise to attempt a simpleminded definition which will be useful and effective in all situations. What can be done is to bound the problem by means of some general considerations and delegate the specific implementation to management judgment for each particular application.

In retrospect, the preceding paragraph proved to be misleading. The intent was not to introduce and define a new software architectural entity, but a management entity which reflected the partitioning of the development effort. As a result, some people proceeded to define and establish "units" as architectural subdivisions, which often did not represent good functional delineations and were not logically addressable in the detailed description document. A more accurate concept of the UDF is that it encompasses a "unit of work."

At the lower end of the scale a "unit" can be defined to be a single routine or subroutine. At the upper end of the scale a "unit" may contain several routines comprising a subprogram or module. However it is defined, a unit of software should possess the following characteristics:

(1) It performs a specific defined function.

478

(2) It is amenable to development by one person within the assigned schedule.

(3) It is a level of software to which the satisfaction of requirements can be traced.

(4) It is amenable to thorough testing in a disciplined environment.

The keyword in the concept is manageability — in design, development, testing, and comprehension.

A natural question that may arise at this point is, "Why should a unit contain more than one routine?" The assumption for this proviso is that the design and development standards impose both size and functional modularity. Since functional modularity can be defined at various levels, the concept can become meaningless if it is not accompanied by a reasonable restriction of size. Consequently, the maximum-size constraint on routines may sometimes result in multiple-routine units.

There have been various attempts to establish simple, general rules for designating the units. In one situation, it was decided that there would be one UDF per routine. This resulted in a large number of UDFs, each with its own test plan/procedures, and a large number of requirements that were split and allocated to more than one unit. This strategy undoubtably had a negative effect on both cost and schedule since, 1) it increased the number of units and associated paperwork severalfold, 2) it did not take advantage of logical associations for requirements allocation and testing, and 3) it delayed the accomplishment of low-level integration.

In another situation, it was decided that each UDF would contain a Computer Program Component (CPC) as delineated in the preliminary design. Unfortunately, the CPCs were structured along strict, but high-level, functional aspects. That resulted in UDF size variation from one routine to two-hundred routines. This produced some extremely large UDFs that were practically unmanageable and had to be internally partitioned into smaller units. This strategy undoubtably also had a negative impact on cost and schedule due to the complexities and higher percentage of errors that occur as a function of size.

The lessons learned were:

(1) That the apportionment and allocation of software components into units can have a significant effect on cost and schedule results, and

(2) There is no general rule that can substitute for good judgment and planning.

Ideally, to assist both the documentation and the integration processes, it is advantageous if the units correspond directly to CPCs. However, this requires some thoughtful planning during architectural design, and may not always be feasible or practical.

The organization and content of a UDF can be adapted to reflect local conditions or individual project requirements. The important considerations in the structuring of a UDF are:

(1) The number of subdivisions is not so large as to be confusing or unmanageable.

(2) Each of the sections contributes to the management and visibility of the development process.

(3) The content and format of each section are adequately and unambiguously defined.

(4) The subdivisions are sufficiently flexible to be applicable to a variety of software types.

(5) The individual sections are chronologically ordered as nearly as possible.

The last item is very important since it is this aspect of the UDF that relates it to the development schedule and creates an auditable management instrument. An example of a typical cover sheet for a UDF is shown in Figure 2; the contents of each section will be briefly described in subsequent paragraphs.

The UDF is initiated when requirements are allocated to the unit level and at the onset of preliminary design. At this point it exists in the skeletal form of a binder with a cover sheet (indicating the unit name and responsible custodian) and a set of section separators. The first step in the process is for the responsible work area manager to integrate the development schedules and responsibilities for each of his UDFs into the overall schedule and milestones of the project. A due date is generated for the completion of each section and the responsibility for each section is assigned. The originators should participate in establishing their interim schedules within the constraints of the dictated end dates.

The first sentence of the preceding paragraph is badly written and somewhat misleading since it assumes that the software requirements are sufficiently detailed and well structured to allow the UDF definition process to proceed from consideration of the requirements alone. This is not always the case since requirements specifications vary considerably in their depth, structure, and level of detail. It may well be that the units cannot be adequately defined until near the end of the preliminary design phase. The exact time/date of UDF initiation is not as important as assuring that the allocation is reasonable and efficient.

The organization and subdivisions of the UDF are such that the UDF can accommodate a variety of development plans and approaches; it can be used in a situation where one person has total responsibility, or in the extreme where specialists are assigned to the particular sections. However, in the one-man approach it is still desirable that certain sections, indicated in the following discussion, be assigned to other individuals to gain the benefits of unbiased reviews and assessments.

The development of the UDF is geared to proceed logically and sequentially, and each section should be as complete as possible before proceeding to the next section. This is not always possible, and software development is usually an iterative rather than a sequential process. These situations only serve to reinforce the need for an ordered process that can be understood and tracked even under adverse conditions.

SECTION 0
COVER SHEET

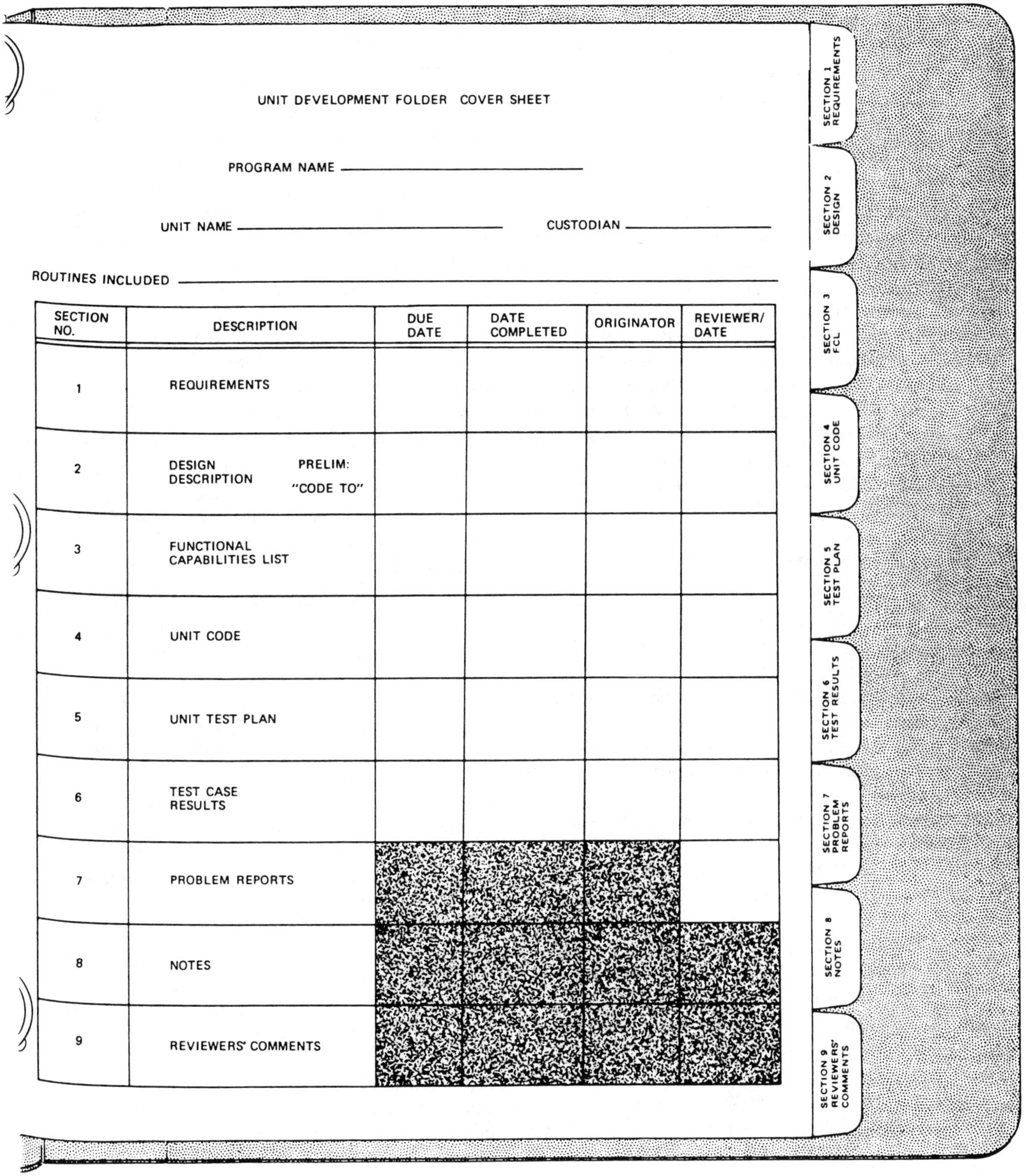

UNIT DEVELOPMENT FOLDER COVER SHEET

PROGRAM NAME _____

UNIT NAME _____   CUSTODIAN _____

ROUTINES INCLUDED _____

SECTION NO.	DESCRIPTION	DUE DATE	DATE COMPLETED	ORIGINATOR	REVIEWER/ DATE
1	REQUIREMENTS				
2	DESIGN DESCRIPTION PRELIM: "CODE TO"				
3	FUNCTIONAL CAPABILITIES LIST				
4	UNIT CODE				
5	UNIT TEST PLAN				
6	TEST CASE RESULTS				
7	PROBLEM REPORTS				
8	NOTES				
9	REVIEWERS' COMMENTS				

SECTION 1 REQUIREMENTS

SECTION 2 DESIGN

SECTION 3 FCL

SECTION 4 UNIT CODE

SECTION 5 TEST PLAN

SECTION 6 TEST RESULTS

SECTION 7 PROBLEM REPORTS

SECTION 8 NOTES

SECTION 9 REVIEWERS' COMMENTS

Figure 2. UDF Cover Sheet and Layout

Once a specific outline and UDF cover sheet have been established, it is imperative that the format and content of each section be clearly and completely defined as part of the project/company standards to avoid ambiguity and maintain consistency in the products. The following discussion expands and describes the contents of the UDF typified by the cover sheet shown in Figure 2.

Section 0: Cover Sheet and Schedule

This section contains the cover sheet for the unit, which identifies the routines included in the UDF and which delineates, for each of the sections, the scheduled due dates, actual completion dates, and assigned originators and provides space for reviewer sign-offs and dates. In the case of multiple-routine units, it may be advisable to include a one-page composite schedule illustrating the section schedules of each item for easy check-off and monitoring. Following each cover sheet, a UDF Change Log should be included to document all UDF changes subsequent to the time when the initial development is completed and the unit is put into a controlled test or maintenance environment. Figure 3 illustrates a typical UDF Change Log.

Section 1: Requirements

This section identifies the baseline requirements specification and enumerates the requirements which are allocated for implementation in the specific unit of software. A mapping to the system requirements specification (by paragraph number) should be made and, where practical, the statement of each requirement should be given. Any assumptions, ambiguities, deferrals or conflicts concerning the requirements and their impact on the design and development of the unit should be stated, and any design problem reports or deviations or waivers against the requirements should be indicated. In addition, if a requirement is only partially satisfied by this unit it will be so noted along with the unit(s) which share the responsibility for satisfaction of the requirement.

For units which comprise a part of a CPC, these will normally be a subset of the requirements that were allocated to the CPC during the preliminary design phase. In some instances, a particular unit of software may be totally or partially the result of a design solution for software implementation and, therefore, not directly traceable to the requirements. This may be the case, in particular, if the unit is composed of utility-type functions and routines. In this event, the lack of requirements should be explicitly stated and explained in this section.

The contents of this section may be a copy of the specific requirements paragraphs from the specification itself or an enumeration of the requirements paragraphs on a composed standard form.

Section 2: Design Description

This section contains the current design description for each of the routines included in the UDF. For multiple routine units, tabbed subsection separators are used for handy indexing. A preliminary design description may be included if available; however, the end item for this section is detailed design documentation for the unit, suitable to become (part of) a "code to" specification. The format and content of this section should conform to established documentation standards and should be suitable for direct inclusion into the appropriate detailed design specification (Figure 1). Throughout the development process this section represents the current, working version of the design and, therefore, must be maintained and annotated as changes occur to the initial design. A flowchart is generally included as an inherent part of the design documentation. Flowcharts should be generated in accordance with clear established standards for content, format, and symbol usage.

When the initial detailed design is completed and ready to be coded, a design walk-through may be held with one or more interested and knowledgeable co-workers. If such a walk-through is required, the completion of this section should be predicated on the successful completion of the design walk-through.

One of the common problems that occurs is in assuring that the design description contained in this section is maintained in current status and is an accurate reflection of the coded product. Whether the design is represented in the form of narrative plus flow charts or in the form of a design language listing, similar problems occur. It is not unusual for the coded product that is developed from the "code to" design to deviate somewhat from that initial design for various reasons. It is also not unusual for programmers to overlook the task of maintaining the design and code in sync. A design/code walk-through at the completion of the coding and test phase for each unit can help assure compatibility.

Section 3: Functional Capabilities List

This section contains a Functional Capabilities List (FCL) for the unit of software addressed by the UDF. An FCL is a list of the testable functions performed by the unit; i.e., it describes what a particular unit of software does, preferably in sequential order. The FCL is generated from the requirements and detailed design prior to development of the unit test plan. Its level of detail should correspond to the unit in question but, as a minimum, reflect the major segments of the code and the decisions which are being made. It is preferred that, whenever possible, functional capabilities be expressed in terms of the unit requirements (i.e., the functional capability is a requirement from Section 1 of the UDF). Requirements allocated to be tested at the unit level shall be included in the FCL. The FCL provides a vector from which

UDF CHANGE LOG

UNIT NAME _____ VERSION _____ CUSTODIAN_____

DATE	DPR/DR Number	Section(s) Affected and Page Numbers	Retest Method	Mod No.

NOTE: This revision change log is to be used for all changes made in the UDF after internal baseline (i.e., subsequent to mod number assignment). It is inserted immediately after the coversheet.

Figure 3. Example of a UDF Change Log

TEST CASE/REQUIREMENTS/FCL MATRIX

REQUIREMENTS DOCUMENT _____

DATE _____

Req'ts Paragraph Number	FCL NO.	TEST CASE NUMBER										OTHER ROUTINES
		1	2	3	4	5	6	7	8	9	0	

INSTRUCTIONS: Mark an X in the appropriate box when a particular test case fully tests a particular requirement. Mark a "P" when a test partially tests a requirement. If a requirement is partially tested in another routine, mark a "P" in the "other routines" column. If more space is required, attach additional copies of this figure.

Figure 4. Example Test Case/Requirements/FCL Matrix

the Test Case Requirements/FCL matrix (Figure 4) is generated. The FCL should be reviewed and addressed as part of the test plan review process.

The rationale for Functional Capabilities Lists is as follows:

(1) They provide the basis for planned and controlled unit-level testing (i.e., a means for determining and organizing a set of test cases which will test all requirements/functional capabilities and all branches and transfers).

(2) They provide a consistent approach to testing which can be reviewed, audited, and understood by an outsider. When mapped to the test cases, they provide the rationale for each test case.

(3) They encourage another look at the design at a level where the "what if" questions can become apparent.

An FCL is particularly important for those portions of the design that are implementation-derived and not directly driven by requirements.

Section 4: Unit Code

This section contains the current source code listings for each of the routines included in the unit. Indexed subsection separators are used for multiple routine units. The completion date for this section is the scheduled date for the first error-free compilation or assembly when the code is ready for unit-level testing. Where code listings or other relevant computer output are too large or bulky to be contained in a normal three-ring binder, this material may be placed in a separate companion binder of appropriate size which is clearly identified with the associated UDF. In this event, the relevant sections of the UDF will contain a reference and identification of the binder with a history log of post-baselined updates. Figure 5 illustrates a typical reference form.

An independent review of the code may be optional; however, for time-critical or other technically critical units, a code walk-through or review is recommended.

Section 5: Unit Test Plan

This section contains a description of the overall testing approach for the unit along with a description of each test case to be employed in testing the unit. The description must identify any test tools or drivers used, a listing of all required test inputs to the unit and their values, and the expected output and acceptance criteria, including numerical outputs and other demonstrable results. Test cases shall address the functional capabilities of the unit, and a matrix shall be placed into this section which correlates requirements and functional capabilities to test cases. This matrix will be used to demonstrate that all requirements, partial requirements, and FCLs of the unit have been tested. An example of the test case matrix is shown in Figure 4. Check marks are placed in the appropriate squares to correlate test cases with the capabilities tested. Sufficient detail should be provided in the test

definition so that the test approach and objectives will be clear to an independent reviewer.

The primary criteria for the independent review will be to ascertain that the unit development test cases adequately test branch conditions, logic paths, input and output, error handling, and a reasonable range of values and will perform as stipulated by the requirements. This review should occur prior to the start of unit testing.

Section 6: Test Case Results

This section contains a compilation of all current successful test case results and analyses necessary to demonstrate that the unit has been tested as described in the test plan. Test output should be identified by test case number and listings clearly annotated to facilitate necessary reviews of these results by other qualified individuals. Revision status of test drivers, test tools, data bases and unit code should be shown to facilitate retesting. This material may also be placed in the separate companion binder to the UDF.

Section 7: Problem Reports

This section contains status logs and copies of all Design Problem Reports, Design Analysis Reports, and Discrepancy Reports (as required) which document all design and code problems and changes experienced by the unit subsequent to baselining. This ensures a clear and documented traceability for all problems and changes incurred. There should be separate subsections for each type of report with individual status logs that summarize the actions and dispositions made.

Section 8: Notes

This section contains any memos, notes, reports, etc., which expand on the contents of the unit or are related to problems and issues involved.

Section 9: Reviewers' Comments

This section contains a record of reviewers' comments (if any) on this UDF, which have resulted from the section-by-section review and sign-off, and from scheduled independent audits. These reviewers' comments are also usually provided to the project and line management supervisors responsible for development of the unit.

Summary

The UDF concept has evolved into a practical, effective and valuable tool not only for the management of software development but also for imposing a structured approach on the total software development process. The structure and content of the UDF are designed to create a set of milestones at the unit level, each of which can be easily observed and reviewed. The UDF approach has been employed on several software projects at TRW and continues to win converts from the ranks of the initiated. The concept has proved particu-

LISTINGS/TEST RESULTS

SEE SEPARATE NYLON PRONG BINDER IDENTIFIED AS

_____ FOR CODE LISTINGS

OR TEST RESULTS.

HISTORY LOG

CODE MOD NUMBER	DATE	REVIEWED BY
_____	_____	_____
_____	_____	_____
_____	_____	_____
_____	_____	_____
_____	_____	_____
_____	_____	_____
_____	_____	_____
_____	_____	_____
_____	_____	_____
_____	_____	_____

Figure 5. Example Reference Log for Separately-Bound Material

larly effective when used in conjunction with good programming standards, documentation standards, a test discipline, and an independent quality assurance activity.

The principal merits of the UDF concept are:

(1) It imposes a development sequence on each unit and clearly establishes the responsibility for each step. Thus the reduction of the software development process into discrete activities is logically extended downward to the unit level.

(2) It establishes a clearly discernible timeline for the development of each unit and provides low-level management visibility into schedule problems. The status of the development effort becomes more visible and measurable.

(3) It creates an open and auditable software development environment and removes some of the mystery often associated with this activity. The UDFs are normally kept ''on the shelf'' and open to inspection at any time.

(4) It assures that the documentation is accomplished and maintained concurrent with development activities. The problem of emerging from the development tunnel with little or inadequate documentation is considerably reduced.

(5) It reduces the problems associated with programmer turnover. The discipline and organization inherent in the approach simplifies the substitution of personnel at any point in the process without a significant loss of effort.

(6) It supports the principles of modularity. The guidelines given for establishing the unit boundaries assure that at least a minimum level of modularity will result.

(7) It can accommodate a variety of development plans and approaches. All UDF sections may be assigned to one performer, or different sections can be assigned to different specialists. The various sections contained in the UDF may also be expanded, contracted or even resequenced to better suit specific situations.

As a final comment, it must be emphasized that no device or approach can be effective without a strong management commitment to see it through. Every level of management needs to be supportive and aware of its responsibilities. Once the method is established it also needs to be audited for proper implementation and problem resolution. An independent software quality assurance activity can be a valuable asset in helping to define, audit, and enforce management requirements.

Software Management Metrics[1]

Herman P. Schultz
MITRE Software Center,
Bedford, MA 01730

1. Introduction

The software management metrics presented in this document provide a top-level management overview of software development status. These metrics are based on government and industry experiences with a previous set of metrics known as "software reporting metrics" and on an evaluation and analysis of their use. The metrics can provide early indications of potential software development problems, and can call attention to and stimulate discussion leading to early resolution of those problems. These metrics are reported by the software developer at each program management review (PMR).

The successful use of the metrics depends on the program manager's enforcement of a serious technical review of the data collected for each metric. The metrics graphs are a tool for escalating the discussion of important progress and status indicators to both government and software developer senior managers.

The metrics graphs show developing trends that may indicate future problems and, when analyzed as a set, can highlight inconsistencies that might otherwise be overlooked. Through senior management reviews and related communications, the significance of the identified trends can be determined and appropriate action taken.

Approximately three years of experience in the use and analysis of metrics have resulted in this report, which includes actual examples as well as comments on the behavior and interpretation of each metric.

This document describes the software management metrics and provides information relating experience on previous software acquisitions. Section 2 discusses metrics coverage, reporting, and analysis. Section 3 describes the software management metrics; each description includes a statement of purpose, typical behavior patterns, data inputs, tailoring ideas, example plots, and interpretation notes.

2. Metrics Coverage, Reporting, and Analysis

The software management metrics described in this document are intended to assure that (1) the metrics are delivered in a manner that assures management visibility into important issues; and (2) most importantly, the metrics reported are effectively analyzed to identify potential software development problems. This section describes the metrics' coverage and provides recommendations regarding their reporting and analysis.

2.1 Coverage

The management metrics should cover all phases of software development. In some cases, the metrics can overlap and cover some development phases more than once. This multiple coverage provides not only better visibility into each development phase, but also an opportunity to verify the correctness of reported data through consistency checks.

Metrics address two aspects of development: progress and planning. Progress metrics indicate deviations between the planned and actual status of software development. Planning metrics influence software development progress. The metrics illustrated in this article address primarily planning metrics.

2.2 Reporting

The metrics should be presented at each PMR where they can provide management with visibility into potential cost and schedule impact problems. In order to focus the PMR discussions, a pre-PMR metrics screening is recommended that should be accomplished in two steps:

---

[1] This article has been adapted and abbreviated from Schultz, H.P., *Software Management Metrics*, ESD TR88001, 1988. Prepared for Deputy Commander for Product Assurance and Acquisition Logistics, Electronic Systems Division (ESD), AFSC, USAF, Hanscom AFB, MA 1988. Interested people should read the entire report.

1. The software developer delivers the metrics to the government at least one week prior to the PMR. At that time, they are discussed in a technical interchange meeting (TIM) or by telephone conference between the government's and software developer's technical staff to identify potential problem areas for discussion at the PMR.

2. The results of this TIM are discussed within the system program office (SPO) at a meeting with the SPO director. The purpose of this meeting is to separate issues to be discussed at the PMR from those to be discussed at TIMs. The recommendations are conveyed to the software developer, who then tailors his PMR presentation accordingly and schedules any necessary TIMs.

2.3 Analysis

The metrics are a mechanism for evaluating the credibility of project plans and for identifying trends—not only in deviations between planned and actual values, but also in projections that can be made from actual values. Two analysis techniques that have proven to be effective are correlation and extrapolation.

2.4 Correlation

During many phases of development, several metrics are being reported. There is also a strong relationship between the reported metrics; that is, changes in one metric should cause changes in others. The analyst should look for inconsistencies within the related group of metrics. For example, if the development progress metric shows that actual development is behind schedule and the personnel metric shows a reduction in planned staffing, then these metrics are not consistent and should be discussed with the software developer. Figure 1 is an example of just such an occurrence on an actual project. In this case, the software developer acknowledged the discrepancy and revised the staffing plan the following month. The correlations shown in the matrix are not meant to be all-inclusive. Specific projects may have other important relationships.

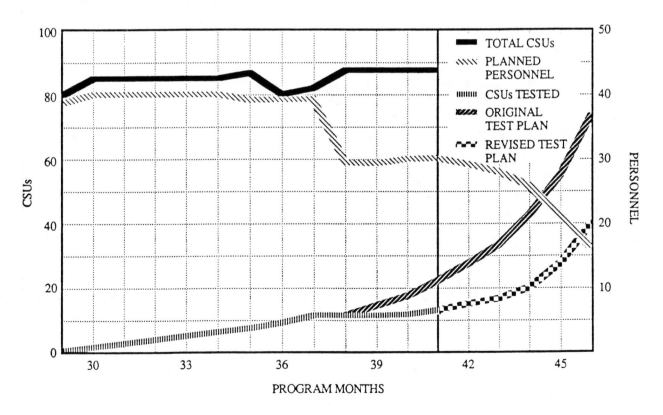

Figure 1. Unit development progress and software personnel.

2.5 Extrapolation

One means of analysis that can provide an early indication of potential problems is extrapolation. Trends in actual data can be projected to evaluate their potential impact on schedules. This applies to progress data for development items such as computer software unit (CSU) design, code and test, and integration, as well as to quantitative trends in software size, errors, and requirements changes.

To show how useful and accurate extrapolation can be, two examples are presented from actual project graphs. These were selected because they contain enough data to show a trend, and in both cases the trend is distinctly different from the plan. Figure 2a is a graph taken from a PMR. Notice that actual progress lags behind the plan. Figure 2b shows an extrapolation based on actual progress to date. This extrapolation predicted the development to be completed around week 55, about 20 weeks behind schedule. In Figure 2c, the actual data for the balance of the development was obtained and plotted. The last CSU was actually developed during week 55.

Another example is shown in Figures 3a through c. In this example, four months elapsed between Figures 3b and 3c. The extrapolation was performed with only the data shown in 3a. Actual data for the intervening four months was then obtained and, as can be seen, it closely follows the extrapolated schedule. Data for the following four months later became available and was added to the graph. Notice how the actual data continues to follow the extrapolated schedule in spite of a replan at month 42.

Figure 4 again illustrates the unvarying nature of an established trend. It shows that an extrapolation made as early as April or May would have been quite accurate.

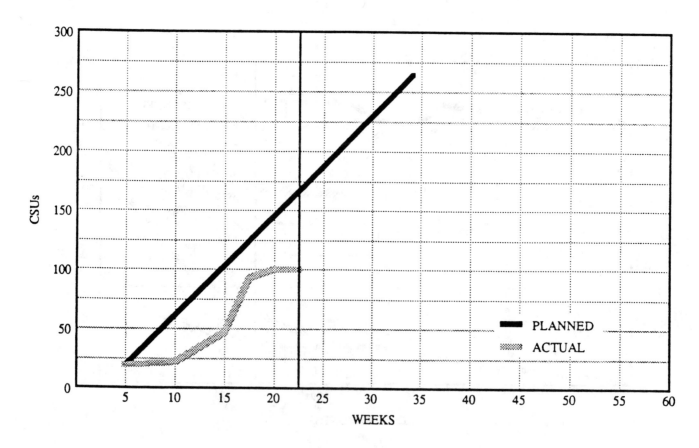

Figure 2a. CSU development progress.

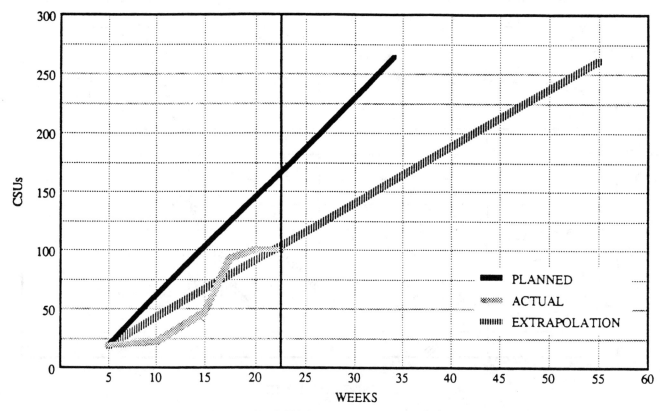

Figure 2b. CSU development extrapolation.

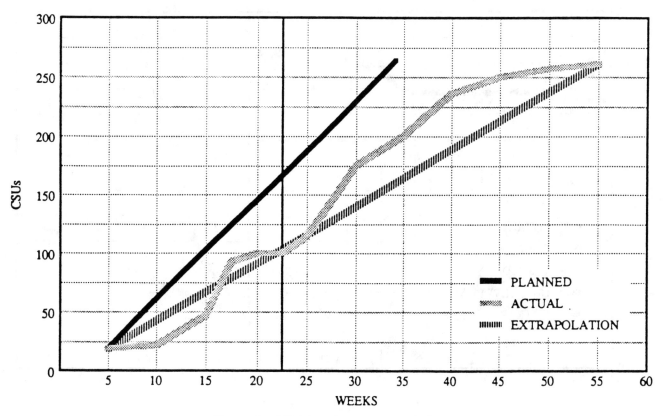

Figure 2c. CSU development completion.

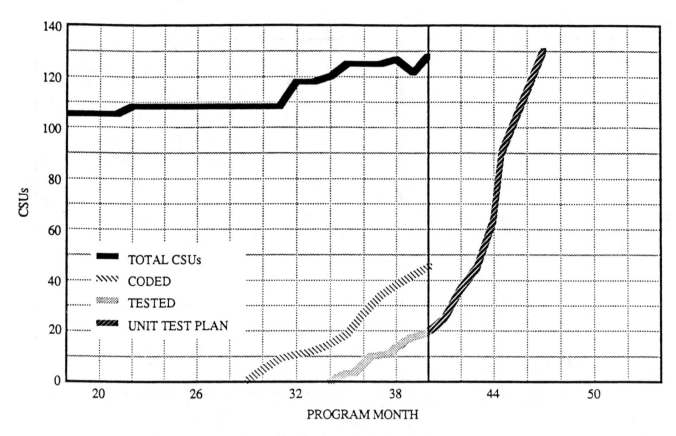

Figure 3a. Code and test progress.

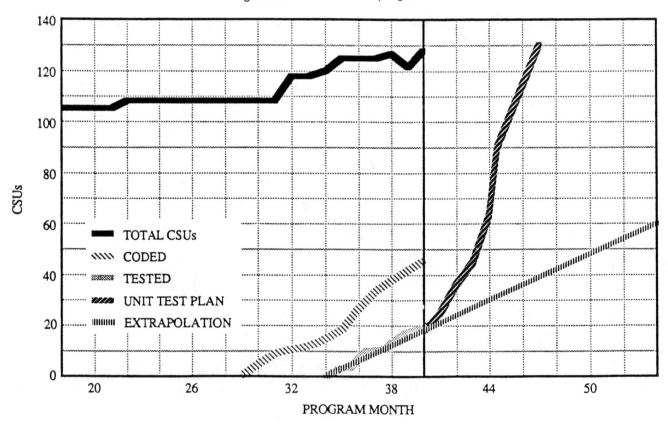

Figure 3b. Test extrapolation.

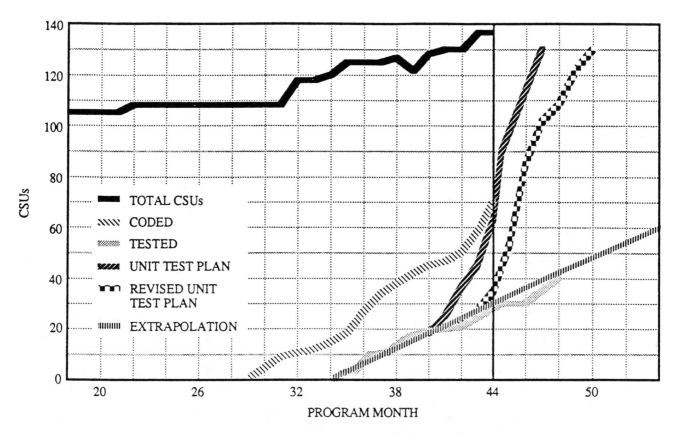

Figure 3c. Test progress with replan and actuals.

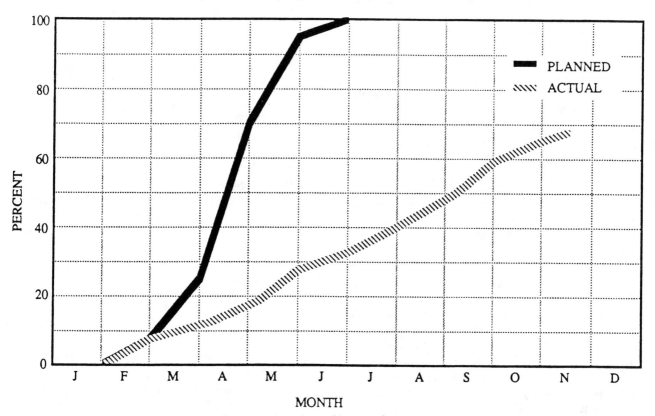

Figure 4. Number of integration tests.

3. The Metrics

Five software management metrics are described in this section. Each metric description includes a statement of purpose, typical behavior patterns, data inputs, tailoring ideas, plotting examples, and interpretation notes. The latter three require some explanation, which is provided in the following paragraphs.

3.1 Definitions of Metric Descriptions

3.1.1 Tailoring. Most of the metrics will apply to all programs. However, there are cases when an individual metric could be deleted or replaced to meet specific needs. Such tailoring also applies to the individual data items collected for each metric. Factors to consider when tailoring include the nature of the software acquisition, high-risk areas, the software metrics currently used by the software developer, the use of more than one programming language, the type of testing, and the number of computer software configuration items (CSCIs). Tailoring suggestions are included with each metric. The resulting set of data input requirements for each metric is then contractually specified in a data item description (DID) referenced by the contract data requirements list (CDRL). The reader is cautioned that the tailored set is merely an example, and that each acquisition must be analyzed to determine which, if any, changes are needed and appropriate.

3.1.2 Ada and Object-Oriented Design. The use of Ada and the use of an object-oriented design methodology affect the collection of certain metrics data. Ada and object-oriented design may be used separately or in conjunction; therefore, the implications of each are noted with those metrics that would require modification.

3.1.3 Plotting Examples. An example plot is included for each metric. The plot format is important and should conform to certain guidelines. Each plot should present at least the past 12 months of planned and actual data and the next 5 months of plan data. Review milestones are indicated on the abscissa. Plan data is the original plan submitted to the government. Revised plans may be added and so labeled, but previous plans may not be removed because important trend data would be lost. A bold vertical line on the chart identifies the current month. The metrics are normally reported at PMRs and therefore have the same reporting period. The example plots are based on a software development initially estimated to require 120,000 source lines of code (SLOC) and 1,200 staff-months over a 36-month schedule. The project milestones are system requirements review (SRR) at month 2, system

design review (SDR) at month 5, software specification review (SSR) at month 8, preliminary design review (PDR) at month 12, critical design review (CDR) at month 17, test readiness review (TRR) at month 27, and physical configuration audit (PCA) at month 36.

3.1.4 Interpretation Notes. The interpretation notes contain specific guidelines derived from experience and from analyses of actual projects. They are intended to be viewed as helpful information, not as inflexible principles. Again, the metrics must be carefully analyzed by staff and by senior managers if they are to have an impact on management decisions and on subsequent software development costs and schedules.

3.2 Software Size Metric

3.2.1 Purpose. The software size metric track changes in the magnitude of the software development effort. SLOC to be developed directly relates to the software engineering effort necessary to build the system. SLOC is also the primary input parameter to almost all software cost estimation models. An increase in SLOC estimates can lead to schedule slips and staffing problems. An increasing trend should trigger steps to counter the trend or to plan for a larger effort. SLOC count is initially an estimate, but as the design matures and code is developed, the count becomes more and more accurate until it represents the actual code at completion.

SLOC is usually tracked for each CSCI as well as for the total system. To be complete, SLOC counts for all commercial off-the-shelf (COTS) and modified off-the-shelf (MOTS) software should also be included.

3.2.2 Behavior. Some programs show increases in estimates of SLOC over time while others show decreases. Increases may be due to a better understanding of the requirements, a better understanding of the design implications and complexities, or an optimistic original estimate, whereas decreases usually result from an overestimate at the beginning of the program and not from changes in requirements. Both may be due to an original lack of understanding and appreciation of the requirements.

3.2.3 Data Inputs. Each reporting period:

- Estimated new SLOC—newly developed code
- Estimated reused SLOC—existing code used as is
- Estimated modified SLOC—existing code requiring change
- Estimated total SLOC—all code (sum of above)

A definition of SLOC that both the software developer and the SPO understand and accept should be used. A recommended example taken largely from Barry Boehm's *Software Engineering Economics* (Prentice-Hall 1981) is that SLOC includes each source statement created by project personnel and processed into machine code. It excludes comments and unmodified utility software. It also includes job control language, format statements, and data declarations. It also includes newly developed support software.

A tighter definition could be developed depending on the source code language.

(Note: An accepted measure of SLOC in Ada is to count all nonliteral semicolons (;) in each package. SLOC counts in Ada may be higher than with other languages due to the specificity and completeness of the language.)

3.2.4 Tailoring Ideas.

- Delete SLOC types not applicable, that is, new, reused, or modified
- Require separate data reporting for each coding language used

- Require separate reporting for each processor and/or CSCI
- Report object code size

3.2.5 Example Plot.
Figure 5 illustrates several changes in coding effort that would not be shown if only SLOC were reported. A month before SSR it is determined that some modified SLOC cannot be used and that new SLOC will have to be developed. This results in an increased effort, but if only total SLOC were reported, the increased effort would not show on the graph. It is next determined that some reused SLOC cannot be used and that new SLOC will have to be developed. Again, this change requires additional effort, but if only total SLOC is reported, it again would go unnoticed. A month prior to PDR, the example shows an increase in new SLOC resulting from a better understanding of requirements. This is the only change reflected in the total SLOC count.

3.2.6 Interpretation Notes.
Software size should not vary from the previous reporting period by more than 5 percent without a detailed explanation from the software developer and related discussions regarding cost and schedule improvements.

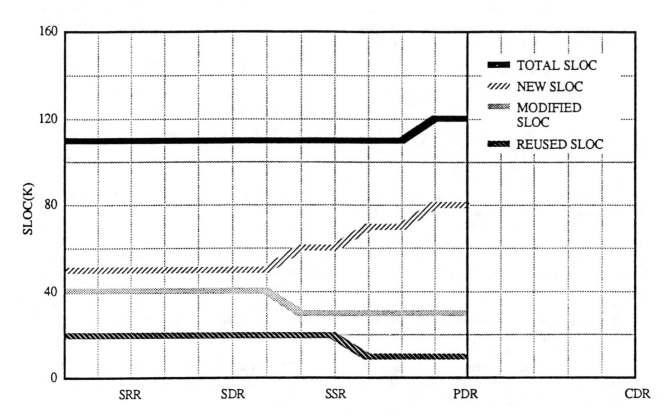

Figure 5. Software size.

495

Changes in SLOC estimates often result from a better understanding of requirements, which is desirable. However, increases in size must be accounted for in the software developer's schedule and staffing plans.

Total SLOC does not linearly relate to effort because modified and reused code require increasingly less effort to develop than new code. If SLOC to be modified are identified and counted at the CSU level (including SLOC that must be understood in order to modify other lines), then the modified code development effort will closely equal that for newly developed code. Similarly, reused code may also require coding effort to be integrated into a new system. Therefore, if the lines of reused code requiring modification are included in the counts of modified code, then the sum of modified and new code will approximate the total software development effort.

3.3 Software Personnel Metric

3.3.1 Purpose. The software personnel metric tracks the ability of the software developer to maintain planned staffing levels and to maintain sufficient staffing for timely completion of the program. The software staff includes the engineering and management personnel directly involved with the software system planning, requirements definition, design, coding, test, documentation, configuration management, and quality assurance. Counts of unplanned personnel losses are maintained so that work force stability can be tracked. An experienced staff is crucial to timely software development. Experienced personnel are nominally defined as those individuals with a minimum of five years' experience in software development and a minimum of three years' experience in software development for applications similar to the system under development.

3.3.2 Behavior. The planned staffing profiles for total software staff and for experienced software staff should be plotted at the beginning of the contract. A normal program may have some deviations from the plan, but the deviations should not be severe. However, a program with too few experienced software personnel, or one that attempts to bring many personnel onboard during the latter stages of the project's schedule, will most likely experience difficulty. The normal shape of the total software staff profile is to grow through the design phases, peak through the coding and testing phases, and then gradually taper off as integration tests are successfully completed. The shape of the experienced staff profile should be high during the initial stage of the project, dip slightly during CSU development, and then grow somewhat during testing. The ratio of total to experienced personnel should typically be near 3:1 and should never exceed 6:1.

3.3.3 Data Inputs. Initial:

- Planned total personnel level for each month of the contract

- Planned experienced personnel level for each month of the contract

- Expected attrition rate

Each reporting period:

- Total personnel
- Experienced personnel
- Unplanned personnel losses

3.3.4 Tailoring Ideas.

- Report staffing separately for each development task, for example, validation and verification (V&V), support software, applications software, testing, and software quality assurance (SQA).

- Report staffing separately for special development skills needed, for example, Ada, database management system (DBMS), operating system, and artificial intelligence (AI).

- Report staffing separately for each development organization.

3.3.5 Example Plot. Figure 6 shows that prior to CDR the actual number of personnel was lagging behind the plan, but that the number of experienced personnel was higher than planned. This may indicate that the software developer was initially having staffing problems and was trying to compensate by using additional experienced staff. Current levels may be appropriate if development schedules are maintained, but the SPO should monitor this closely. Unplanned losses show a nominal trend and do not indicate any internal problems.

A total of 20 staffers, out of an average staffing level of 400, left the project during the past 12 months.

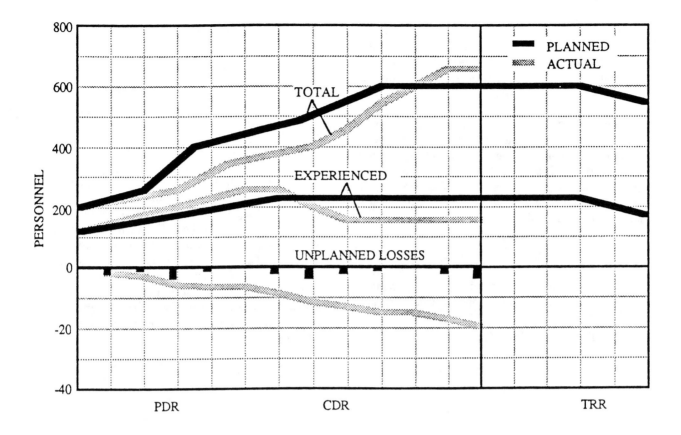

Figure 6. Software personnel.

3.3.6 Interpretation Notes.

- Understaffing results in schedule slippage and, if not corrected, in a continuing rate of slippage. Causal relationships to various progress metrics should be examined.

- Adding staff to a late project will seldom improve the schedule and often causes further delays.

- A program that is experiencing a high personnel turnover rate cannot maintain needed continuity. Losses that would impair the project knowledge and experience base should be discussed with the software developer.

- Initial staffing levels should be at least 25 percent of the average staging level.

3.4   Software Volatility Metric

3.4.1 Purpose. The software volatility metric tracks changes in the number of software requirements and in the software developer's understanding of these requirements. The two graphs used for this metric track requirements changes and software action items (SAIs). The graph of requirements changes tracks the total number of software requirements—typically the number of "shells" in the software requirements specifications (SRSs) as well as the cumulative number of changes to those requirements. The graph of SAIs tracks the number of unresolved requirement/design issues. Both graphs are good indicators of requirement and design stability. Changes in the number of requirements (both additions and deletions) directly impact the software development effort. Changes are expected in the early stages as details of the system's operations are being defined and understood. At some point, however, software requirements must be frozen. The longer this takes the greater the impact on cost and schedule.

Design reviews may have several inconsistencies between the requirements and the design or within the design itself. When this occurs, an SAI is opened. It may be closed by modifying or clarifying the design or by modifying the requirements. An SAI is defined as any discrepancy, clarification, or requirements issue that must be resolved by either the software developer or the government.

3.4.2 Behavior. Changes in software requirements can be expected to be more numerous during requirements analysis and preliminary design phases.

Changes occurring after CDR may be expected to have a significant schedule impact, even if the change is the deletion of a requirement. Therefore, the plot of cumulative changes is expected to rise more steeply prior to PDR and show a leveling off after CDR.

The plot of SAIs is expected to rise at each review and then taper off exponentially. Programs that produce clear and complete specifications will experience less of a rise at each review; and programs that have good communications among the SPO, the system engineer, and the software developer will experience a high rate of decay to the curve.

3.4.3 Data Inputs. Each reporting period:

- The current total number of requirements
- The cumulative number of requirement changes to include additions, deletions, and modifications
- The number of new SAIs

- The cumulative number of open SAIs

3.4.4 Tailoring Ideas.

- Track the longevity of open SAIs, for example. 30 days, 3,060 days, 6,090 days, and over 90 days.
- Track open SAIs by priority.

3.4.5 Example Plots. The graph of requirements changes in Figure 7a shows an upward trend in the number of changes prior to PDR and a leveling off approaching CDR. The changes after PDR may result in a schedule slip for CDR because some computer software component (CSC) and CSU designs in the software design documents (SDDs) may have to be redone.

Figure 7b shows the number of open SAIs peaking at PDR and CDR. The steady decrease after each review indicates the software developer's ability to resolve the issues.

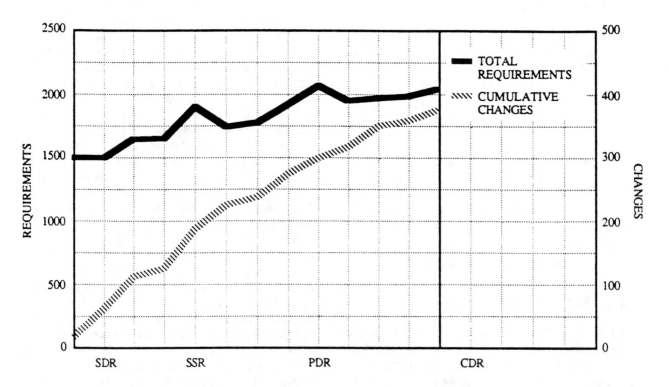

Figure 7a. Software volatility/software requirements changes.

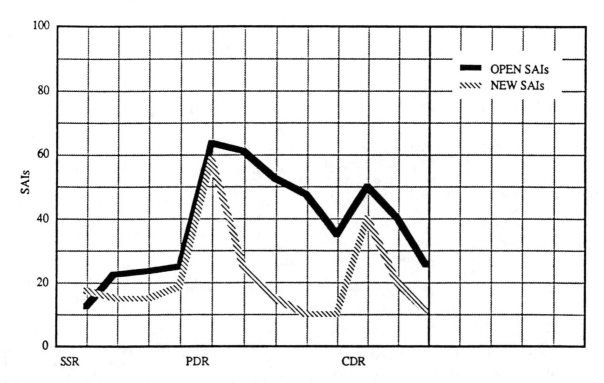

Figure 7b. Software volatility/SAIs.

3.4.6 Interpretation Notes. Requirements volatility between CDR and TRR will result in schedule impacts whose extent must be determined through discussions with the software developer.

SAIs open more than 60 days should be closely examined. They could have significant schedule impacts, especially if they have been termed "unimportant."

3.5   Computer Resource Utilization Metric

3.5.1 Purpose. The computer resource utilization metric tracks changes in the estimated/actual utilization of target computer resources and provides warnings if the limits of these resources are approached. Three resources typically monitored are CPU timing, memory (such as CPU and mass storage), and I/O channels (such as communications or bus). The system architecture (for example, parallel, serial, or distributed) will determine how the resources are monitored, but they must be monitored to assure that the system will fit the planned resources.

3.5.2 Behavior. Most projects experience an upward creep in resource utilization. Large system acquisitions typically specify a 50 percent spare capacity. This means that only one-half of the capacities may be used, leaving 50 percent for growth. If the utilization exceeds 50 percent, the project either has to expand the resource capabilities or change the system re-

quirements. Whenever resource capabilities are expanded, the utilization curves affected will drop to new values.

Dependencies among resources result in parallel movements. For example; an expansion of memory not only decreases its utilization, but also may allow the CPU to operate more efficiently, thus decreasing CPU utilization. The same memory expansion may also allow larger blocks of data to be transported, thus reducing utilization of the I/O channels.

3.5.3 Data Inputs. Initial:

- Planned spare for each resource.

Each reporting period:

- Estimated/actual percentage of CPU utilization.

- Estimated/actual percentage of memory utilization.

- Estimated/actual percentage of I/O channel utilization.

3.5.4 Tailoring Ideas.

- Report combined utilization in a multiresource architecture that uses a load-leveling operating system.

- Report utilization separately in a multiresource architecture that has dedicated functions.

- Report average and worst-case utilizations.

- Report separately for development and target processors.

- Consider memory addressing limits of the architecture when establishing utilization limits.

3.5.5 Example Plot. A 50 percent spare requirement was planned for all three resources. Notice that each of the utilizations plotted in Figure 8 shows a tendency to increase over time. In this example, the CPU utilization was the first to exceed the spare limit and was corrected by upgrading to a faster CPU. If growth in the same computer series is not possible, then impacts may be felt on all computer resources as well as on system and applications software. It is necessary to anticipate growth as early as possible to minimize such changes.

3.5.6 Interpretation Notes.

- Performance deteriorates quickly when utilization exceeds 70 percent for real-time applications.

- Resource expansion should be planned early in the development cycle to take into account the tendency of resource utilization to increase over time.

- Software developers' costs and schedules increase dramatically as computer resources' utilization limits are approached and optimization forces design and coding changes.

3.6   Schedule Progress Metric

3.6.1 Purpose. The schedule progress metric tracks the software developer's ability to maintain the software development schedule by tracking the delivery of software work packages defined in the work breakdown structure (WBS). The program's estimated schedule can be calculated each month by applying the relative progress to date to the program schedule. The calculation is as follows:

$$\text{Estimated Schedule (Months)} = \frac{\text{Program Schedule (months)}}{\text{BCWP} / \text{BCWS}}$$

where BCWP is the budgeted cost of work performed and BCWS is the budgeted cost of work scheduled. The use of cost data to estimate progress requires close coordination with the costing staff to assure that only software costs are used in this calculation and that the software developer is credited only for work performed and confirmed by other progress metrics such as design, CSU development, testing, and incremental release content.

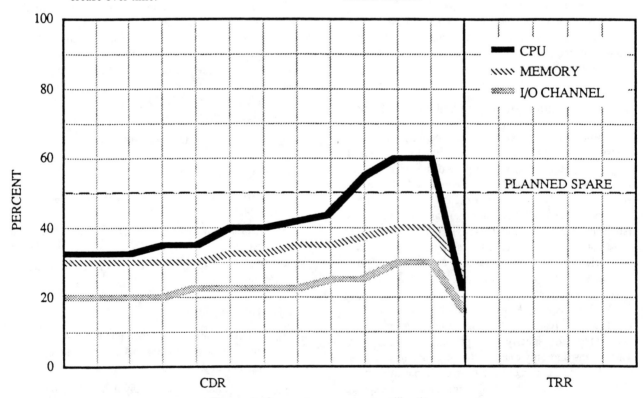

Figure 8. Computer resources utilization.

3.6.2 Behavior. It is not unusual for a program to initially fall behind, because insufficient time is usually allocated to the design process. This trend should level off as the design is implemented, but may again occur during testing due to inadequate test planning and inadequate testing at the CSU and CSC levels. It is important that testing at these levels is tied to WBS elements to assure visibility into its adequacy either directly or through a V&V function. Applying this metric retroactively to certain procurements running 50 to 100 percent over schedule shows the progress to be almost on schedule right up to system testing. This means that credit was given for software development progress that had not occurred. The WBS for software must be tied to each stage of testing so that credit is not given until the adequacy and success of tests at the CSU, CSC, and CSCI levels have been verified.

3.6.3 Data Inputs. Initial:

- Number of months in program schedule.

Each reporting period:

- BCWP for software.

- BCWS for software.

- Number of months in program schedule (if revised).

3.6.4 Tailoring Ideas.

- Track progress separately for each CSCI.

3.6.5 Example Plot. At month 2, the plot in Figure 9 indicates that given the current rate of productivity, it will require 45 instead of 36 months to complete the project. The ratio of work performed to work scheduled was 80 percent, resulting in an estimated schedule of 45 months (36/. 8 = 45). During succeeding months productivity dropped to around 70 percent, resulting in estimated schedule duration of about

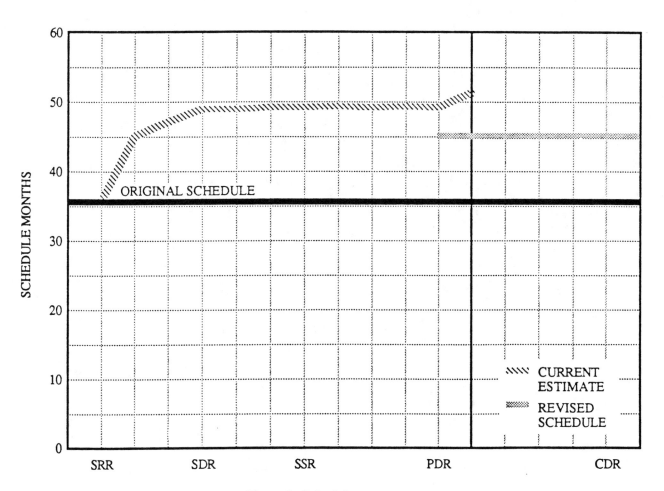

Figure 9. Schedule progress.

51 months. At this point, almost halfway though the original 36-month schedule, the schedule was revised and extended to 45 months. This change does not affect computation results because increasing the schedule by 25 percent also reduces the work by 20 percent, so the estimated schedule months remain the same. However, the plot now indicates a slip of only 6 months versus 15 months from the original schedule.

3.6.6 Interpretation Notes. The plot of this metric can be used to identify and extrapolate trends. If the trend is up, it implies a worsening condition. An extrapolation can be made to predict the estimated schedule by extending the extrapolation until its value intersects with the same value on the abscissa. This is the estimated schedule based on the trend.

If the trend is down, it indicates that productivity is under control and improving, and that the overall schedule can be predicted by extrapolating this plot and again seeking the intersection of the plot value with the abscissa.

Chapter 11

Epilogue: The Silver Bullets

Ed Yourdon, in his foreword to this tutorial, describes software engineering project management as the "silver bullets" of software engineering[1]. These are the silver bullets that can slay the software project "werewolf" of late or over-budget projects that do not satisfy the engineering problem at hand.

Within this tutorial, I have identified the project management tools, techniques, and methodologies that can make a difference in the successful delivery of a software system.

The one paper in this chapter is a summary of the best practices of project management and software engineering. It proposes a list of silver bullets (or perhaps a shotgun blast) developed by the author and Dr. Richard Fairley that are required to slay the software werewolf (in other words to eliminate or reduce software failures). Discussions on how to implement these techniques are contained in the articles in this volume or in the its companion volume, the IEEE tutorial on *Software Engineering*[2].

BY JOVE, CHARLES! YOU'VE GOT THE BLIGHTER.

1. Brooks, Frederick P., "No Silver Bullets: Essence and Accidents of Software Engineering," *Computer*, April 1987.

2. Dorfman, M., and R.H. Thayer, eds., *Software Engineering*, IEEE Computer Soc. Press, Los Alamitos, Calif., 1997.

Software Engineering Project Management: The Silver Bullets of Software Engineering

Richard H. Thayer
California State University, Sacramento
Sacramento, CA 95819-6021

Richard E. Fairley
Colorado Technical University
Colorado Springs, CO 80907-3896

Ed Yourdon in his foreword to the IEEE tutorial *Software Engineering Project Management* [1] describes software engineering project management as the "silver bullets" of software engineering. These are the silver bullets that can slay the software project "werewolf" of late or over-budget projects that do not satisfy the engineering problem at hand.

Project managers have the clear responsibility to deal with any problems that interfere with the successful delivery of a software product. With these silver bullets, a good manager can quickly change directions when environment or requirements change or software engineering methodologies fail, implement innovative ideas when the situation calls for it, and/or withstand pressure from marketing and senior staff who want to put delivery dates and/or product features ahead of quality.

The following is a proposed list of actions to take, products to build, or tools to use that the individuals manager might use to eliminate or reduce software failures. These items are not exclusively project management activities or tools but they are all under the control of the project manager.

The list is partitioned into *project planning* and *project control* functions.

Planning the Project

1. Use *software requirements engineering* to establish the objectives of the project. *Software requirements engineering* is an engineering method for defining the to-be-delivered software product. It involves requirements elicitation, analysis, specifications, verification, and management. Supporting tools are:

   - The *ConOps document* that is designed to reveal the users' and customer's needs, goals, and expectations.

   - *A prototyping* strategy for developing a partial solution to the software system to resolve requirements issues prior to developing the requirement specifications.

   - A *software requirements specifications* document that establishes the technical goals of the project to provide adequate, correct, and measurable requirements information to the software designers.

   - A *requirements traceability* method that assures continuity between requirements and the delivered products.

2. Develop a *project plan* to establish the way the product will be developed, how much it will cost, and when it will be finished. *A project plan* is a description of the essential activities that must be accomplished and the tasks the project must complete in order for the project to reach its goals. A sound plan insures that the project is based on a realistic cost-estimate and schedule.

3. Perform *risk management* (with problem tracking) as a means of anticipating potential problems and mitigating or avoiding them. Use *problem tracking* to insure that management pays constant attention to both existing and potential problems.

4. Use an *Incremental release process model* (with periodic demonstrations) as a process

[1] Yourdon, Edward, Foreword, *Software Engineering Project Management*, 2nd ed., R.H. Thayer, ed., IEEE Computer Soc. Press, Los Alamitos, Calif., 1997.

for establishing reachable short-term goals within the longer term goal of project completion and product delivery. *Periodic demonstrations* provide a method of checking progress toward those goals.

Controlling the Project

5. Develop *work packages* as a means of controlling work to be done by providing visibility of progress toward the project goals. Supporting tools are:

   - A *WBS* as a method of partitioning a large project into small measurable tasks (work packages) that can be assigned to 1 or 2 individuals for 1 or 2 weeks.

   - *Work package specifications* that are mini-specifications that describe the tasks to be done and the required conditions for starting and stopping the tasks.

   - *A binary tracking technique* that is a means of measuring completion of a task whereby a task is either done or not done, that is, the percent complete is not considered.

   - *A earned value tracking technique* that compares the amount of work completed and the cost to date, with the planned cost and schedule for that amount of work.

6. Use *software metrics* as a means of measuring both the product and process of software development. Metrics make it possible to implement effective planning and control procedures.

7. *Use a software configuration management (CM) system* as a means of identifying and tracking the components of a software system and its documentation to guard against unwanted changes. Software configuration management is used to track and control the evolution of the software product within the allocated schedule and budget.

8. *Use a software quality assurance (SQA) process and engineering standards* as a means of controlling the software process to assure a quality result.

9. *Use peer reviews* (either walkthroughs or inspections) as a means of early elimination of errors in software products and processes.

10. *Use independent verification and validation (IV&V)* techniques as a means of assessing and controlling the quality and quantity of the software products.

11. *Require a software engineering assessment* as a means of validating the capability of the development organization to develop software systems and to provide a road map for software process improvements. Capable software development organizations can produce high quality software products within the planned cost budget and development time [2]

Conclusion

If the above 11 techniques are rigorously implemented on a software project, there is every chance that the project will be successful and that the software development werewolf, if not killed outright, will be seriously wounded.

---

[2]   Paulk, M.C., B. Curtis, M.B. Chrissis, and C.V. Weber, "The Capability Maturity Model for Software," in *Software Engineering*, M. Dorfman and R.H. Thayer, eds., IEEE Computer Soc. Press, Los Alamitos, Calif., 1997. Reprinted in *Software Engineering Project Management*, 2nd ed., R.H. Thayer, ed., IEEE Computer Soc. Press, Los Alamitos, Calif., 1997.

Software Engineering Project Management Glossary

Richard H. Thayer
Mildred C. Thayer

Scope

This glossary defines the terms used in the field of system and software project management and supporting disciplines. These definitions have their roots in several management and technical domains: general (mainstream) management, project management, and system and hardware engineering. In addition, there are new definitions and old terms with new meanings. The relationships between these domains and software engineering and software engineering project management can be seen in Figure 1.

The definitions from any domain in Figure 1 usually can be applied to any domain located lower on the hierarchy. For example, a system engineering definition can apply to both system engineering and software engineering, and a project management definition can also apply to software engineering project management. But because of new technologies and meanings, a software engineering definition will not necessarily apply to general engineering.

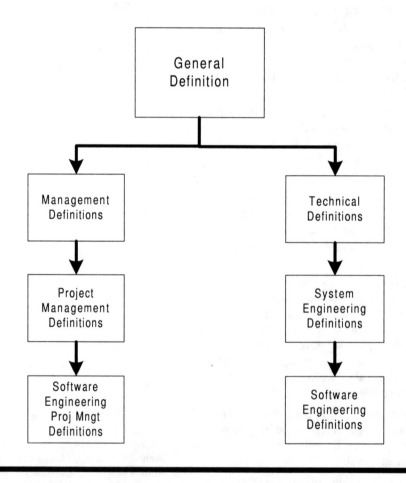

Figure 1. Hierarchical domains of software engineering and software engineering project management definitions.

Definitions for hardware and software engineering and system and software system engineering are so similar that the terms *hardware/software* and *system/software* are frequently used to mean applicability in both domains.

The domain of the definition should be understood or identified in the first sentence of the definition. When the definition was taken from another source and the domain of definition was not obvious, the domain was added.

Glossary Structure

Entries in the glossary are arranged alphabetically. An entry may consist of a single word, such as *requirements*; a phrase, such as *requirements engineering*; or an acronym such as *SQA*. Phrases are given in their natural order (*project management*) rather than reversed (*management, project*).

Blanks are taken into account in alphabetizing. They precede all other characters. For example, *ad hoc* precedes *Ada*. Hyphens and slashes follow blanks. Alternative spellings are shown as separate glossary entries with cross-references to the preferred spelling.

No distinction is made between acronyms and abbreviations. Where appropriate, a term that has a common acronym or abbreviation contains the acronym or abbreviation in parentheses following the term. The abbreviation or acronym might also be a separate entry. The definition is placed with the term or abbreviation, depending on which one has the most usage; and the other will be cross-referenced. For example, *CASE*, an acronym for *computer-aided software engineering*, has its definition after *CASE*. In contrast, *SQA*, an acronym for *software quality assurance*, will have its definition after *software quality assurance (SQA)*.

If a term has more than one definition, the definitions are listed with numerical prefixes. This ordering does not imply preference. Where necessary, examples and notes have been added to clarify the definitions.

The following cross-references are used to show a term's relationship to other terms in the glossary:

- *See* refers to a preferred term or to a term whose definition serves to define the term that has been looked up.

- *See also* refers to a related term.

- Sometimes *synonymous with* refers to a term that may or may not be synonymous with the defined term, that is, it is a nonstandard usage.

- *Synonymous with* refers to a term that is always or nearly always synonymous with the defined term.

- *Contrast with* refers to a term with an opposite or substantially different meaning.

In a few cases, nonstandard cross-references are used to clarify a particular definition.

Sources

In those cases in which a definition is taken or paraphrased from another source or paper, the source is designated in brackets following the definition, for example [Smith 1988]. The use of a source reference does not imply an exact quote, but is an acknowledgment of the source of the definition. A list of all sources used in this glossary is at the end of the glossary.

Acknowledgment

The authors would like to acknowledge the hard work done by all the members of the IEEE Computer Dictionary Standards Working Group, who have worked diligently without compensation to further the discipline of software engineering.

Glossary

A

activity—In project management, a major unit of work to be completed in achieving the objectives of a hardware/software project. Examples of software system engineering activities include requirements, design, implementation, and testing. An activity has precise starting and ending times, incorporates a set of tasks to be completed, consumes resources, and produces tangible results. An activity may contain other activities and tasks in a hierarchical manner. The lowest-level activities in the hierarchy are tasks. Dependencies often exist among activities, so that completion of one activity or task may provide necessary preconditions for initiation of subsequent activities and tasks.

activity network—In project management, a network graph using nodes with interconnecting edges to represent tasks and their planned sequence of completion, interdependence, and interrelationships that must be accomplished to reach the project goals.

activity report—A management report that provides the status of project activities over a period of time.

actual cost of work performed (ACWP)—In software engineering (controlling), it is the actual expenditures for the work that has been completed by the software developers to date.

ACWP—See actual cost of work performed (ACWP).

allocated baseline—The initial configuration identification established at the end of the allocation activity. This baseline is established by an approved hardware/software configuration item requirements specification. *See also baseline document, configuration management.*

analyst—In software engineering project management, an individual who is trained and experienced in analyzing existing systems to determine and describe users' needs as a set of software requirements specifications. *See also analysis, programmer.*

annual performance review—A management appraisal of an employee given annually. *See also appraisal, management by objectives (MBO).*

appraisal—A management process for evaluating and judging the performance of employees' work. *See also management by objectives (MBO).*

audit—1. A management review of a hardware/software project for the purpose of assessing compliance with requirements, specifications, baselines, standards, procedures, instructions, codes, and contractual and licensing requirements. 2. In system/software system engineering, an activity to determine through investigation the adequacy of, and adherence to, established procedures, instructions, specifications, codes, and standards or other applicable contractual and licensing requirements, as well as the effectiveness of implementation. *See also independent audit.*

authority—In management (organizing), 1. The legal or delegated right to give directions to subordinates and to command resources. 2. The discretion given an employee or incumbent of an organizational position to use their judgment in decision making.

B

backup programmer—In software engineering, the assistant leader of a chief programmer team; a senior-level programmer whose responsibilities include contributing significant portions of the software being developed by the team, aiding the chief programmer in reviewing the work of the other team members, substituting for the chief programmer when necessary, and having an overall technical understanding of the software being developed [IEEE SET Glossary, 1983]. *See also chief programmer team.*

balanced matrix—In a matrix organization, a balanced matrix means that both the functional and project organizations that contribute tangible and intangible resources to the project will have equivalent responsibilities, authority, and status. For example, the project manager and the functional manager will have equal pay and rank, equal availability to top management, equal status, equal privileges, and so on. *See matrix organization.*

bar chart—A management tool used to plan and control the time elements and schedule of a program. The bar chart lists the major activities of the project, its scheduled start and ending times, and its current status. The primary advantage of the bar chart is that the plan (schedule) and progress of the project can be portrayed together graphically. *Synonymous with Gantt chart.*

baseline—1. A hardware/software work product that has been formally reviewed and agreed upon, which then serves as the basis for further development, and that can be changed only through formal change control procedures. Each baseline must specify items that form the baseline (for example, software requirements, design documentation, and deliverable source code), the review and approval mechanisms, the acceptance criteria associated with the baseline, and the customer and project organization that participated in establishing the baseline. 2. A hardware/software configuration identification document or set of documents formally reviewed and agreed on at a specific time during the system's/software's lifecycle, which completely describes the functional and/or physical characteristics of a hardware/software configuration item. Baselines, plus approved changes to those baselines, constitute the current hardware/software configuration identification of a product.

Examples [US Department of Defense (DoD) usage] of system/software baselines are:

functional baseline—The initial configuration established at the end of the requirements definition phase.

allocated baseline—The initial configuration established at the end of either the system design review (large projects) or the preliminary design review (medium or small projects).

product baseline—The initial configuration established at the end of system testing.

See also configuration management, baseline document, and milestone review.

baseline document—System/software documents that establish one of the configuration identifications of a hardware/software configuration item. The system specifications, requirements specifications, and design specifications are examples of baseline identification documents. *See also allocated baseline, configuration management, and functional baseline.*

baseline management model—A management and software lifecycle development strategy that integrates a series of lifecycle phases, reviews, and baseline documents into a system for managing a software engineering project. Specifically it uses the waterfall lifecycle model to partition the project into manageable phases: requirements, design, implementation, and test, and establish milestones, documents, and reviews at the end of each phase. *See also baseline, baseline document, lifecycle development model, milestone, milestone review, and waterfall model.*

BCWP—*See budgeted cost of work performed (BCWP.)*

BCWS—*See budgeted cost of work scheduled (BCWS).*

budget—A statement of management plans and expected results expressed in numbered, quantitative, and monetary terms. Money is the only common denominator for expressing all resources required and used.

budget report—A management report that compares monetary expenditures to monetary estimates (budget). Differences between the budget estimates and actual project expenditures are explained.

budget review—A formal meeting at which the monetary expenditures for a system/software engineering project are presented to the user, customer, or other interested parties for comment and approval. The monetary expenditures are compared to the budget, and differences between the budget estimates and actual project expenditures are explained.

budgeted cost of work performed (BCWP)—In software engineering (controlling), it is the amount of the budget that has been "earned" on the work that has been completed by the software developers to date.

budgeted cost of work scheduled (BCWS)—In software engineering (controlling), it is the amount of the budget that has been "allocated" to the work that was planned to be completed by the software developers to date.

C

Capability Maturity Model (CMM)—In software engineering, the CMM is a set of recommended practices in a number of important (key) process areas that have been shown to enhance the capabilities of the software development organization to deliver software on time, within cost, and meeting the objectives of the system and customer.

CASE—Acronym for computer-aided software engineering. *See CASE tool.*

CASE tool—An automated software engineering development tool that can assist software engineering in analyzing, designing, coding, testing, and documenting a software system and managing a software project. John Manley, University of Pittsburgh, is apparently the first person to use the acronym CASE for computer-aided software engineering.

change—In configuration management, a formally recognized revision to a specified and documented program requirement. This may include a change in specification or engineering. *See also configuration control, configuration management.*

change control—In configuration management, the process by which a change is proposed, evaluated, approved or rejected, scheduled, and tracked [ANSI/IEEE Standard 729-1983]. *See also configuration control, configuration management.*

change status report—In configuration management, details the status of all proposed changes to a hardware/software configuration item for which the developer is responsible and for which existing documentation is listed in the configuration index. The purpose of the report is to provide the customer and the developer with a summary of the current status of all proposed and approved engineering change proposals (ECPs). *See also configuration management.*

chief programmer—In software engineering, the leader of a chief programmer team; a senior-level programmer whose responsibilities include producing key portions of the software assigned to the team, coordinating the activities of the team, reviewing the work of the other team members, and having an overall technical understanding of the software being developed [IEEE SET Glossary, 1983]. *See also chief programmer team.*

chief programmer team—A software development team that consists of a chief programmer, a backup programmer, a secretary/librarian, and additional programmers and specialists as needed, and that employs support procedures designed to enhance group communication and to make optimum use of each member's skills [IEEE SET Glossary, 1983]. *See also egoless programming team, project team, project team structure.*

classic management model—The diagrammatic presentation of the five principal functions of management: planning, organizing, staffing, directing, and controlling.

CMM—*See Capability Maturity Model (CMM).*

COCOMO 1.0—*See COCOMO software cost-estimation model.*

COCOMO 2.0—The latest version of the COCOMO software estimation model developed by Dr. Barry W. Boehm. *See also COCOMO software cost-estimation model.*

COCOMO software cost-estimation model—A software cost and schedule estimating method that was developed by Barry W. Boehm and documented in *Software Engineering Economics* [Boehm 1981]. The model is an empirically derived, nonproprietary, cost-estimation model, based on a study by Boehm of 63 software development projects. The model accommodates three categories of software application, has a basic (simple), intermediate, and detailed version, and its primary input parameter is the estimated lines of uncommented source code. The intermediate and detailed versions of the model contain 15 cost multipliers that recognize differences in the project products and environment. Typically only the intermediate version is used.

commercial off-the-shelf (COTS)—In system/software engineering, hardware and software that can be purchased and placed in service without additional development cost for the system or component. COTS systems do, however, come with a significant integration cost.

commitment—1. A term used by managers to indicate the duty of an employee to follow through on an agreed-on plan or program. An obligation owed. 2. To identify with a project, organization, manager, program, and so forth. 3. A commitment is a pact between two or more people who trust each other to perform. Commitments are freely assumed, explicitly defined, and visible. 4. In contracts, a binding financial obligation.

communication—In management (directing), the process of transferring information from one person or group to another person or group with the understanding that the message being transmitted was understood by both groups or by both individuals.

computer program—A combination of computer instructions and data definitions that enable computer hardware to perform computational or control functions [IEEE Standard 610.12-1990]. *Synonymous with software.*

computer-aided management (CAM)—The application of computers to management activities. For example, database management, control reporting, and information retrieval [IEEE CAT Glossary 1986].

computer-assisted project management (CAPM)—The act of managing a project with the assistance or support of a data processing system.

configuration—1. The arrangement of a system or network as defined by the nature, number, and chief characteristics of its functional units. More specifically, the term *configuration* may refer to a hardware configuration or a software configuration. 2. The requirements, design, and implementation that define a particular version of a system or system component. 3. The functional and/or physical characteristics of hardware/software as set forth in technical documentation and achieved in a product [DoD Standard 480B 1988]. *See also configuration management.*

configuration accounting—In configuration management, the act of reporting and documenting changes made to a baseline configuration to establish a hardware/software configuration status. *See also configuration management, configuration status accounting.*

configuration auditing—In configuration management, the process of verifying that all required hardware/software configuration items have been produced, that the current version agrees with specified requirements, that the technical documentation completely and accurately describes the configuration items, and that all change requests have been resolved [ANSI/IEEE Standard 729-1983]. *See also configuration management.*

configuration control—In configuration management: 1. The process of evaluating, approving or disapproving, and coordinating changes to hardware/software configuration items after formal establishment of their configuration identification. 2. The systematic evaluation, coordination, approval or disapproval, and implementation of all approved changes in the configuration of a hardware/software configuration item after formal establishment of its configuration identification [DoD Standard 480B 1988]. *Sometimes erroneously used synonymously for configuration management. See also configuration management.*

configuration control board (CCB)—In configuration management, the authority responsible for evaluating and approving or disapproving proposed engineering changes to the hardware/software configuration, and ensuring implementation of the approved changes [ANSI/IEEE Standard 729-1983]. *See also configuration management.*

configuration identification—In configuration management: 1. The process of designating the hardware/software configuration items (CI) in a system and recording their characteristics. 2. The approved documentation that defines a hardware/software CI. 3. The current approved or conditionally approved technical documentation for a hardware/software CI as set forth in specifications, drawings, and associated lists, and documents referenced therein [DoD Standard 480B 1988]. *See also configuration management.*

configuration item (CI)—In configuration management, an aggregation of hardware/software, or any of its discrete portions, that satisfies an end-use function and is designated by the customer for configuration management. CIs may vary widely in complexity, size, and type, from an aircraft, electronic system, or ship system to a test meter, circuit board, or teddy bear. During development and initial production, CIs are only those specification items that are referenced directly in a contract (or equivalent in-house agreement). During the operation and maintenance period, any repairable item designated for separate procurement is a CI [DOD Directive 5010.19]. *See also configuration management.*

configuration management (CM)—In system/software system engineering, the discipline of identifying the configuration of a hardware/software system at discrete points in time with the purpose of systematically controlling changes to the configuration and maintaining the integrity and traceability of the configuration throughout the system lifecycle. *See also change control, change status report, configuration, configuration accounting, configuration auditing, configuration control, configuration control board, configuration identification, configuration item, configuration management plan, configuration status accounting.*

configuration management plan—In configuration management, a program for carrying out the project, design, or schedule for hardware/software configuration. *See also configuration management.*

configuration status accounting—In configuration management, the recording and reporting of the information that is needed to manage a hardware/software configuration effectively, including a listing of the approved configuration identification, the status of proposed changes to configuration, and the implementation status of approved changes [DoD Directive 5010.19]. *See also configuration management.*

conflict—In management (directing), a clash between hostile or opposing elements or ideas. The state that exists when two individuals or groups have goals that will clash or will affect each other differently.

conflict management—A modern management approach that does not see conflict as inherently bad but inevitable between humans, and as a manageable and controllable force for the good of the organization or activity.

conflict resolution—A management activity for reducing conflict in an organization. The destructive effects of conflict should be avoided and the conflict resolved through the application of problem-solving techniques.

controlling—All the management activities that ensure that actual work goes according to plan. It measures performance against goals and plans, reveals when and where deviation exists and, by putting in motion actions to correct deviations, helps ensure the accomplishment of plans.

conventional development model—*See waterfall development model.*

conventional lifecycle model—*Synonymous with waterfall model.*

conventional organization—An organizational structure that is either a line or staff organization. *Contrast with project organization. See also line organization, organizational structure, staff organization.*

cost center—An organization or organizational entity that prepares its own budget and accounts for its own expenditures. The cost center may or may not be responsible for making a profit.

cost estimation—1. The estimated cost to perform a stipulated task or acquire an item. 2. The product of a cost-estimation method or model. *See also software cost-estimation model.*

cost trade-off—In system engineering and management, that approach to problem solving that compares and evaluates alternatives (technical) solutions, especially where advantages and costs cannot be accurately measured in numbers, by considering costs of alternatives in comparison with benefits derived.

cost-benefit analysis—In system/software engineering, the comparison of alternative courses of action, or alternative technical solutions, for the purpose of determining which alternative would realize the greatest cost benefit.

crisis—*See software engineering crisis.*

critical (detailed) design review (CDR)—In system/software system engineering, a milestone review conducted for each hardware/software configuration item (CI) when the detailed design is essentially complete. The purpose of this review will be to: (1) determine that the detailed design of the CI under review satisfies the functional and performance requirements of the CI requirement specifications; (2) establish the detailed design compatibility among the CI and other items of equipment, facilities, software, and personnel; (3) assess CI risk area (on technical, cost, and schedule basis); and (4) review the detailed design description (specifications) [Mil-Std. 1521B-1985]. *See also milestone review, review.*

critical path—In the critical path method (CPM), a path through the activity net that takes a longer time than any other path. A path is the sum of all the activities on a particular route from the start of the overall activities until it is finished. *See also critical path method (CPM).*

critical path method (CPM)—A project management technique in which the activities that constitute a project are identified, dependencies among the

activities are determined, an estimated time is assigned to each activity, and a sequence of activities taking the longest time (a critical path) is identified, and is used to determine the shortest possible completion time for the overall project [IEEE CAT Glossary 1986]. *See also critical path, PERT.*

D

debugging—1. In software development, the process of correcting syntactic and logical errors detected during coding. With the primary goal of obtaining and executing a piece of code, debugging shares with testing certain techniques and strategies but differs in its usual ad hoc application and local scope [FIPS Publication 101 1983]. 2. In software engineering (testing), the process of locating, analyzing, and correcting suspected faults. *Synonymous with unit testing. See also testing.*

decision—A management (planning) activity for selecting a course of action from among alternatives.

delegation of authority—In management, the passing on, by one person to another, of the responsibility for an activity or task and the right to command resources necessary to fulfill those responsibilities in the accomplishment of the activity or task.

design review—In system/software system engineering: 1. A review that will be conducted on a periodic basis to assess the degree of completion of technical efforts related to major milestones before proceeding with further technical effort associated with a particular element of the system. The schedule and plan for the conduct of design reviews should be included in the developer's program plan and master schedule. 2. A milestone review at which the preliminary or detailed design of a system is presented to the user, customer, or other interested parties for comment and approval. 3. The formal review of an existing or proposed design for the purpose of (1) detection and correction of design deficiencies that could affect fitness for use and environmental aspects of the product, process, or service, or (2) identification of potential improvements of performance, safety, and economic aspects [ANSI/IEEE Std. 729-1983]. *See also milestone review, review.*

directing—All management activities that deal with the guidance and motivation of employees to follow the plan. Once employees are trained and oriented, the manager has a continuing responsibility for monitoring their assignments, guiding them toward improved performance, and motivating them to perform to the best of their abilities.

E

earned value—In software engineering (controlling), it is the budgeted cost of work performed (BCWP). If the earned value is less than actual expenditures, then the project is over budget. If the earned value is less than the planned expenditures to date, then the project is behind schedule. *See ACWP, BCWP, and BCWS.*

earned-value method—A project planning and control technique that compares project expenditures to a project's current earned value and budgeted cost. The earned-value system is initiated by allocating a budget to individual software deliverables, for example, SCIs or software components. The *earned value* at any time on the project is the accumulated value of all the individual budgets from SCIs or software components that are completed. If the earned value is less than the actual expenditures to date, then the project is over budget. If the earned value is less than budget, then the project is behind schedule.

education—The process of developing the knowledge of basics, theory, and underlying concepts of a discipline usually provided by formal schooling at an institute of learning. This is in contrast to training in a skill or process. For example, an individual would be educated in the principles of programming languages but trained in Fortran. Education is usually not needed immediately and is viewed as having a long-term payoff. *Contrast with training.*

egoless programming—An approach to software development based on the concept of team responsibility for program development. Its purpose is to prevent the programmer from identifying so closely with his or her output that objective evaluation is impaired [ANSI/IEEE Std. 830-1984].

egoless programming team—A software engineering project team that practices egoless programming. The egoless team structure was developed by Gerald Weinberg in 1971. An egoless team typically consists of approximately ten members. Discussions and decisions are made by consensus. Group leadership responsibility rotates; there is no permanent central authority [Weinberg 1971]. *See also egoless programming, chief programmer team, project team, project team structure.*

evolutionary development model—A software development process whose stages consist of expanding increments of an operational software product. The directions of evolution are determined by operational experience. The evolutionary development model gives users a rapid initial operational capability and provides a realistic operational basis for determining subsequent product improvement [Boehm, Spiral Model, 1988]. *Sometimes synonymous with evolutionary prototyping. See also software lifecycle model.*

evolutionary prototyping—In software development strategies, the developers construct a partial implementation of the system that meets known requirements. This prototype is then employed by its intended user to help understand the full requirements. Incremental development, on the other hand, implies that one understands most requirements up front, but the system is implemented in subsets of increasing capability. Evolutionary prototyping implies a need to experiment with an operational system or to learn the requirements. Note that in the case of throwaway prototypes, only those aspects that are poorly understood may be implemented, but in the case of evolutionary prototypes, those systems aspects that are best understood are more likely to be implemented. *Contrast with incremental development model, rapid prototyping. Sometimes synonymous with evolutionary development model.*

experience—In management (staffing), the state of having done something before. A person is said to be experienced in some skill or activity if they have been involved in that skill or activity as it occurred.

F

forecasting—The managing (planning) process of attempting to predict future events. Forecasting has two views—view 1 anticipates future events or make assumptions about the future; view 2 predicts future results or expectations from courses of action. To illustrate in project management: the first view requires the forecasting of future events such as availability of manpower, predicted inflation rate, or availability of new computer hardware, and the impact these future events will have on the software engineering project. The second view requires the estimation of how the software engineering project will meet these future expectations and assumptions. Examples are expected expenditure of available resources and project funds against the project.

formal method—In software development, formal methods are mathematically based techniques whose rigorous application enables the correctness of software to be verified against the specification of that software. For this process to take place, there must also be a formal specification. The creation of this specification is itself part of formal methods [IEE/BCS Safety-Related Systems 1989].

function—1. In management, a major activity or group of activities that is continuous. For example, the principal functions of management are planning, organizing, staffing, directing, and controlling. 2. In project management, an activity or set of activities that span the entire duration of a software project. Examples of project functions include configuration management, quality assurance (QA), and project cost accounting. 3. In functional analysis, the system or subsystems under study. The function is the activity or behavior of the system, that is, what it does. 4. In software, a subprogram that is invoked during the evaluation of an expression in which its name appears and that returns a value to the point of invocation.

function point analysis—In system/software engineering, the process of studying a system by partitioning the system into functional entities and function points to be used in estimating the potential cost of the software development. *See function point metric.*

function point metric—In software engineering, a measurement of the functionality of the software product in standard units independent of the coding language. A function point is a measure of software functionality based on the counting or estimated number of "externals" (inputs, outputs, inquiries, and interfaces) of a system plus the estimated number of internal files of a program unit. *See also function point analysis. Contrast with COCOMO.*

functional analysis—In system/software engineering. the process of studying user needs to arrive at a definition of software requirements. *Contrast with object-oriented analysis.*

functional authority—The right or power inherent in a position to issue instructions or approve actions of persons in positions not reporting directly to the person holding such authority; normally it is a limited line type of authority applicable only to specialized areas and representing a delegation to a specialist by a superior manager with authority over both the position given functional authority and the position subjected to this authority [Koontz, O'Donnell, and Weihrich 1984].

functional baseline—In system/software system engineering, the initial hardware/software configuration identification established at the end of the conceptual phase. This baseline is established by an approved system specification.

functional organization—In management, a line or staff organization that is organized around one or more related sets of functions. The functional organization is used primarily to group together individuals with high technical skills such as programmers, engineers, and so forth. Functional organizations are normally continuous.

functional project organization—A project structure built around a functional organization or group of similar functional organizations. A project is accomplished either within the functional organization or, if multifunctioned, between two or more functional organizations. The project is accomplished by passing the project from functional organization to functional organization as the project passes through the lifecycle phases. *See also functional organization, project organizational structure.*

G

Gantt chart—A management technique or tool for planning and controlling projects, activities, and tasks. Developed by Henry L. Gantt during World War I. *Synonymous with bar chart.*

H

Herzberg's motivation theory—A motivation technique based on the theory that a decrease in environment factors is dissatisfying, but an increase in environment factors is not satisfying. However, a decrease in job content factors is not dissatisfying, but an increase in job content factors is satisfying. *See also Maslow's hierarchy of needs.*

hybrid work breakdown structure (WBS)—In system/software engineering, a WBS that includes both process and product WBSs. Contrast with process work breakdown structure (WBS) and product work breakdown structure (WBS). *See also WBS.*

I

incremental development model—A software development lifecycle that involves constructing a partial implementation of a system and gradually adding increased functionality or performance. Each increment is developed using all lifecycle phases from analysis to integration and test. *See also software lifecycle model.*

independent audit—An independent review of a software project by an outside agency or team that is separate from the organization responsible for the project for the purpose of assessing compliance with software requirements, specifications, baselines, standards, procedures, instructions, codes, and contractual and licensing requirements. *See also audit, review.*

independent verification and validation (IV&V)—In software system engineering, verification and validation of a software product by an organization that is both technically and managerially separate from the organization responsible for developing the product. The degree of independence must be a function of the importance of the software [ANSI/IEEE Std. 729-1983]. *See also validation, verification and validation, verification.*

inspection—In software engineering: 1. A semiformal to formal evaluation technique in which software requirements, design, or code are examined in detail by a person or group other than the originator to detect faults, violations of development standards, and other problems. The review members are peers (equals) of the designer or programmer. Traditional error data is collected during inspections for later analysis and to assist in future inspections. Sometimes called a walkthrough or peer review. *See also inspection moderator, walkthrough.*

inspection checklist—In software engineering (inspections), a list of products, processes, and documents to review during an inspection. *See also inspection, inspection defect list, and walkthrough.*

inspection coverage—In software engineering (inspections), the degree to which a software product has been inspected. It is typically stated as a percentage of the product's design statements or lines of executable code evaluated by the inspection process. *See also inspection.*

inspection data—In software engineering (inspections), the data gathered from design or code inspections. This data is of two types: (1) process data which typically includes preparation time, lines of code per hour of preparation time,

errors identified during preparation (by category), hours per error found in preparation, inspection time, lines of code (or design statements) inspected, code (or design statements) inspected per hour, and errors found per inspection man-hour (by category); (2) product data from the inspection, typically includes errors found per line of code (or design statement), action items identified from each inspection, action items closed for each inspection, items needing re-inspection, and re-inspections conducted. *See also inspection.*

inspection defect list—In software engineering, a list of defects found in the products, processes, and documents from an inspection. *See also inspection, inspection checklist.*

inspection moderator—In software engineering (inspection), the individual who is trained in the inspection process and who is assigned to monitor the inspection. The moderator ensures that the participants are properly prepared and that the inspection is efficiently and thoroughly conducted. The moderator schedules the inspection, distributes the material being inspected, facilitates the inspection process, and ensures that the errors in the material are recorded and corrected. The moderator is responsible for recording inspection data, making sure that the actions resulting from the inspection are completed, and for conducting re-inspections where appropriate. The moderator should not be the producer of the inspected item or the producer's supervisor. *See also inspection.*

inspection system—In software system engineering, a set of policies, procedures, and methods for performing inspections. *See also inspection.*

inspection team leader—*See inspection moderator.*

integration testing—1. In system engineering, an orderly progression of testing in which software elements or hardware elements or both are combined and tested until the entire system has been integrated. 2. In software system engineering, activity that interconnects sets of previously tested modules to ensure that the sets behave as well as their independently tested module components did. *See also system testing.*

interview—In management (staffing), to evaluate or question a job applicant.

J, K

515

L

leadership—The management (directing) art of influencing others to willingly work toward the completion of group goals with enthusiasm and confidence. In project management, interpreting the plans and requirements to ensure that everybody on the project team is working toward a common goal.

leading—In management, the art of influencing others to willingly work toward the completion of group goals with enthusiasm and confidence. In project management, interpreting the plans and requirements to ensure that everybody on the project team is working toward a common goal.

lifecycle development model—A model or representation of a software development lifecycle. *See also software lifecycle model.*

line organization—In management, an organization within a larger organization or company with the responsibility and authority to do the work that represents the primary mission of the larger organizational unit. *Contrast with staff organization. See also conventional organization.*

lines of authority—In management (organizing), the connections between an individual, position, or activity and the individual, activity, or activity over which the authority is exercised. *See also authority.*

M

management—All activities and tasks undertaken by one or more persons to plan and control the activities of others to achieve an objective or complete an activity that could not be achieved by the others acting independently.

management by objectives (MBO)—A management and motivation technique that requires an individual employee and the employee's manager to establish and agree on a set of verifiable organizational and individual objectives that both the individual and the manager believe can be met over a given period of time. The employee's success or failure in meeting these goals frequently forms the basis of a performance appraisal. This approach is superior to an appraisal by personality traits and work characteristics, such as promptness, neatness, punctuality, golf scores, and so on. *See also appraisal, annual performance review.*

management function—The set of activities that are continuous in relationship to the goals of the organization or activity. The principal functions of management are planning, organizing, staffing, directing, and controlling. *See also classic management model, function.*

management model—A representation or abstraction of some aspect of management for the purpose of explaining its behavior.

management system—A conglomerate of interrelated and interdependent subsystems and functions. No one management subsystem can perform effectively without the other. Action taken by one subsystem can be traced throughout the complex environment in which the management system exists [Cleland and King 1972].

manager—Anyone put in charge of a group of people, organization, or activity. Someone who is recognized as having the ability to plan, organize, staff, direct, and control resources and personnel in accomplishing objectives. One who undertakes the tasks and functions of managing at any level of enterprise. *See also project manager, software engineering project manager.*

Maslow's hierarchy of needs—The classifications of human needs by Maslow placed in a hierarchical form. Once an individual's needs have been satisfied at a given level, only the needs at a higher level can be motivators.

Maslow's hierarchy of needs is as follows:

Biological survival needs—basics to sustain human life: food, water, shelter, and so forth

Security and safety needs—freedom from physical danger

Social needs—to belong; to be accepted by others

Esteem and recognition needs—to be held in esteem by themselves and by others

Self-actualization needs—to maximize one's potential and to accomplish something

Maslow's motivation theory—A motivation technique based on the theory that human needs can be classified and those satisfied needs are not motivators.

matrix organization—A project organizational structure built around a specific project in which personnel from two or more functional organizations are combined on a temporary basis under a project manager. The matrix organization is a compromise between the functional project organization and the project organization. Project managers are given responsibility and authority

516

for completion of the project. The line or staff functions (usually called resource managers) provide skilled personnel (resources) when needed. The project manager usually does not have the authority to hire, discharge, train, or promote personnel within his project. *See also functional project organization, project organization.*

matrix project organization—*See matrix organization.*

Mayo's motivation theory—A motivation technique based on the theory that interpersonal group values are superior to individual values. Personnel will respond to group pressure. *See also motivation theories by Herzberg, Maslow.*

milestone—In project management, a scheduled event used to measure progress. Examples of major milestones include the issuance of a specification, completion of system integration, product delivery, and customer or managerial sign-off. Minor milestones (sometimes called "inch pebbles") might include baselining a software module or completing a chapter of the user's manual. A manager or an individual project member is identified and held accountable for achieving the milestone on time and within budget.

milestone document—A project management document that describes and documents some part of a software development lifecycle. The completion of the document signals the completion of the milestone. For example, the completion of the software requirements specification (SRS) signals the completion of the software requirements analysis phase. *See also milestone, milestone review.*

milestone review—In software engineering: 1. A project management review that is conducted at the completion of each of the hardware/software development lifecycle phases (a milestone)—requirements phase, preliminary design, detailed design phase, implementation phase, test phase, and sometimes installation and checkout phase. For example, a preliminary design review (PDR) is held at the completion of the preliminary design phase. 2. A formal review of the management and technical progress of a hardware/software development project.

model—A representation of an artifact or activity intended to explain the behavior of some aspects of it. The model is less complex or complete than the activity or artifact modeled. A model is considered to be an abstraction of reality.

N

O

objective—In management (planning), the goals toward which activities are directed. In project management, the technical requirements and management constraints of the project.

object-oriented analysis (OOA)—In software engineering (requirements), the application of an object-oriented method to software requirements analysis. *Contrast with functional analysis, structured analysis (SA). See also object-oriented design, object-oriented method.*

object-oriented design (OOD)—In software engineering (design), the application of an object-oriented method to software design. *Contrast with structured design. See also object-oriented analysis, object-oriented method.*

object-oriented method—A software engineering methodology in which the system is viewed as a collection of objects, attributes of objects, operations on the objects, and messages passed from object to object. *Contrast with functional analysis, structured analysis (SA), structured design. See also object-oriented analysis, object-oriented design.*

on-the-job training (OJT)—In management (staffing), an informal method of training employees on the job through demonstration and hands-on experience rather than in a classroom using models and text books.

OOA—*See object-oriented analysis.*

OOD—*See object-oriented design.*

organization—In management (organizing), a formal or informal framework of tasks, groups of tasks, and the line of authority between tasks for the purpose of focusing the efforts of many on a goal or objective.

organizational position—In management (organizing), a position in an organization designed for individuals to fill. The position should incorporate (1) a clear description of the major duties or activities involved, (2) verifiable objectives, (3) the availability of information and resources necessary to accomplish a task, and (3) the authority granted to accomplish the assigned duties or activities.

organizational structure—In management (organizing), a defined relationship between certain functions, resources, and organizational positions. It is based on determining and itemizing the activities or tasks required to achieve the objectives of the organization and the arrangement of these activities according to type, size, and other similar characteristics.

organizing—All management activities that result in the design of a formal structure of tasks and authority. Organizing involves the determination and enumeration of the activities required to achieve the objectives of the organization, the grouping of these activities, the assignment of such groups of activity to an organizational entity or group identifiers, the delegation of responsibilities and authority to carry them out, and provisions for coordination of authoritative relationships.

P

peer review—In software engineering: 1. A semiformal to formal evaluation technique in which software requirements, design, or code are examined in detail by a person or group other than the originator to detect faults, violations of development standards, and other problems. The review members are peers (equals) of the designer or programmer. Traditional error data is collected during inspections for later analysis and to assist in future inspections. *Sometimes called a walkthrough or inspection.*

planning—All management activities that lead to the selection, from alternatives, of future courses of action for the enterprise. Planning involves selecting the objectives of the enterprise and the strategies, policies, programs and procedures for achieving them, either for the entire enterprise or for any organized part thereof.

PM—Abbreviation for project management, project manager.

policy—1. In management (planning), policies are concerned with predetermined management decisions. They are general statements or understandings that guide decision-making activities. Policies limit the freedom in making decisions but allow for some discretion. 2. In software engineering (structured analysis methodology), a tool of the structured specifications methodology.

position description—In management (organizing), a description of the title, duties, responsibilities, and authority that go with each position identified in the organizational structure.

precedence network—A diagram that expresses graphically the relationship and the requirement that one activity must come before or be completed before another activity begins. When expressed as an activity network, the activities are symbolized by nodes and the precedence by edges. *See also activity network, lines of authority.*

preliminary design review (PDR)—In system/software system engineering, a milestone review conducted for each hardware/software configuration item (CI) before the detailed design process to: (1) evaluate the progress and technical adequacy of the selected top-level design approach, (2) determine its compatibility with the functional and performance requirements of the CI requirements specification, and (3) establish the existence and compatibility of the physical and functional interfaces between the CI and other items of equipment or facilities [Mil-Std. 1521B-1985]. *See also milestone review, review.*

present value analysis—In software engineering it is used in making lifecycle cost comparisons between alternative systems during the feasibility phase, in order to decide on the most cost-effective concept for development [Boehm 1981].

PRICE-S cost-estimation model—A SEPM tool that is used for estimating software costs (from design through implementation). It is a management-oriented non-database tool. The PRICE is available as a licensed product from RCA Limited [NCC STARTS Guide 1987].

problem—In risk management, a problem is a risk that has materialized. *See also risk management.*

process work breakdown structure (WBS)—In system/software engineering, a WBS that partitions a large process into smaller and smaller processes. Each process would generally reduce to tasks that can be assigned to individuals for accomplishment. *Contrast with product WBS. See also WBS.*

product standard—A standard concerned with specific software products, such as compilers and communications equipment. *See also software engineering standard, product standard.*

product work breakdown structure (WBS)—In system/software engineering, a WBS that partitions a large entity into its components. Each one of these components can be identified, resulting in a clearer identification of the larger system. *Contrast with process WBS. See also WBS.*

profit margin—The amount of money and resources remaining after cost has been deducted from the selling price.

program—1. In management (planning), an interrelated set of goals, policies, procedures, rules, tasks, assignments, resources to be employed, schedules, and other elements necessary to carry out a given course of action. 2. In computer science, synonymous with software. *See also computer program.*

program management review—*See milestone review.*

programmer—In SEPM (staffing), an individual who is experienced and qualified to write and document computer programs (software). An individual who is responsible for writing computer programs. *See also analyst, programmer-analyst.*

project—A temporary activity characterized by having a start date, specific objectives and constraints, established responsibilities, a budget and schedule, and a completion date. (If the objective of the project is to develop a software system, then it is sometimes called a software development or software engineering project.)

project management—A system of procedures, practices, technologies, and know-how that provides the planning, organizing, staffing, directing, and controlling necessary to successfully manage an engineering project. Know-how in this case means the skill, background, and wisdom to apply knowledge effectively in practice. *See also software engineering project management.*

project management plan—A project management document describing the approach that will be taken for a project. The plan typically describes the work to be done, the resources required, the methods to be used, the configuration management and quality assurance procedures to be followed, the schedules to be met, and the project organization. *See also software project management plan.*

project manager—1. A manager who has responsibility for planning, organizing, staffing, directing, and controlling a project. 2. In software engineering, a manager who has responsibility for planning, organizing, staffing, directing, and controlling a software engineering project. *See also project management, software engineering project management.*

project organization—A project organizational structure built around a specific project. Project managers are given the responsibility, authority, and resources for completion of the project. (The project organization is sometimes called a projectized organization to get away from the term "project project organization.") The manager must meet his project goal within the resources of the organization. The manager usually has the responsibility to hire, discharge, train, and promote people within his project organization. *See also project organizational structure.*

project organizational structure—A special organization that has been established for the purpose of developing and building something that is too big to be done by only one person or, at the most, a few people. In a software engineering project, the "something" is a software system. The project organizational structure can be superimposed on top of a line or staff organization. *See functional project organization, matrix organization, and project organization.*

project plan—*Synonymous with project management plan. See also software project management plan.*

project team—1. A designated group of people responsible for conducting a successful software development project from its planning through delivery. 2. The project team is a structured organization in which the project leader manages senior programmers, and senior programmers manage junior programmers. The project team is sometimes called a hierarchical team because of its top-down flow of authority. It can be organized by component or phase. Many project teams practice egoless reviews (walkthroughs) and use a programmer support library. Senior programmers ensure quality of the product. *See also egoless programming team, chief programmer team, and project team structure.*

project team structure—In project management, an organized group of 5–10 specialists (team members) with a defined relationship between certain functions, resources, and people. Several project team structures are usually part of a larger project organizational structure. *See also egoless programming team, chief programmer team, or project team.*

projectized organization—*See project organization.*

promotion—In managing (staffing), the transferring of an individual within a company or organization to a position with greater responsibilities that usually requires more advanced skills and knowledge than the previous position. The individual usually also receives greater compensation and greater recognition.

Putnam cost-model—*See SLIM software cost-estimation model.*

Q

R

rapid prototyping—*See throw-away prototyping.*

resource manager—In project management (organizing), the manager of a functional organization who provides resources (people) for the project and matrix organizations. *See also functional organization, matrix organization.*

responsibility—In management (organizing), the accountability for actions taken, resources used, compliance with policy, and the attainment of results. It is "the obligation owed by subordinates to their supervisors for exercising authority delegated to them in a way to accomplish results expected" [Koontz and O'Donnell 1976].

retraining—In management (staffing), instructing workers to become proficient and qualified in a discipline other than that for which they are currently practicing or were originally schooled.

reuse—In software development, the act of using a software product in a different project.

review—1. In system/software system engineering, a formal meeting at which a product or document is presented to the user, customer, or other interested parties for comment and approval. It can be a review of the management and technical progress of the hardware/software development project. 2. In hardware/software engineering, the formal review of an existing or proposed design for the purpose of detection and remedy of design deficiencies that could affect fitness for use and environmental aspects of the product, process, or service, and for identification of potential improvements of performance, safety, or economic aspects [ANSI/IEEE Std. 729-1983]. 3. In the spiral software development model, the review covers all products developed during the previous cycle, including the plans for the next cycle and the resources required to carry them out. The major objective of the review is to ensure that all concerned parties are mutually committed to the approach to be taken for the next phase [Boehm, *Spiral Model*, 1988]. *See also audit, critical*

(detailed) design review (CDR), independent audit, inspection, milestone review, preliminary design review (PDR), software specification review (SSR), system design review (SDR), system requirements review (SRR), walkthrough.

risk—1. In system/software engineering (failure analysis), the likelihood of a specified hazardous event occurring within a specified period or circumstance. The concept of risk has two elements: the frequency, or probability that a specified hazard might occur, and the consequences of it [IEE/BCS Safety-Related Systems 1989] [Sailor 1990].

risk analysis—In risk management, an analysis of the program, as well as any environmental changes, to determine the probability of events and the consequences associated with the potential actions that could affect the program. Many tools exist to aid in the analysis, such as schedule network models and lifecycle cost models. The purpose of risk analysis is to discover the cause, effects, and magnitude of the risk perceived, and to develop and examine alternative options. *See also risk management.* [Sailor 1990]

risk assessment—In risk management, the process of examining a situation and identifying the areas of potential risk. This may include a survey of the program, customer, and uses for concerns and problems. The thoroughness with which this identification is accomplished will determine the effectiveness of risk management. *See also risk management.* [Sailor 1990]

risk assumption (retention)—In risk management (risk handling), the conscious decision to accept the consequences should the event occur. Risk assumption is an acknowledgment of the existence of the risk, but a decision to accept the consequences if failure occurs. Some amount of risk assumption is always present in software development programs. The project manager must determine the appropriate level of risk that can safely be assumed in each situation as it is presented. *See also risk handling.* [Sailor 1990]

risk avoidance—In risk management (risk handling), the process of eliminating or reducing the risk by selecting a non- or low-risk solution. There are many situations where a lower risk choice is available from several alternatives. Selecting the lower risk choice represents a risk avoidance decision. (Not every risk can be avoided). *See also risk handling.* [Sailor 1990]

risk control—In risk management (risk handling), the process of continually sensing the condition of a program and developing options and fall-back positions to permit alternative lower risk solutions. Controlling risk involves the development of a risk reduction plan and then tracking to the plan. This includes not only the traditional cost and schedule plans, but also technical performance plans. *See also risk handling.* [Sailor 1990]

risk exposure—In risk management, a product of probability and cost. *See also risk management.* [Sailor 1990]

risk handling—In risk management, techniques and methods developed to reduce and/or control the risk. There is no risk management if there are no provisions for handling the identified and quantified risk. Techniques for reducing or controlling risk fall into the following five categories: avoidance, control, assumption (retention), transfer, and knowledge and research. *See also risk assumption (retention), risk avoidance, risk control, risk management, risk knowledge and research, risk transfer.* [Sailor 1990]

risk identification—In risk management, an organized, thorough approach to seek out the real risks associated with a program. It is not a process of trying to invent highly improbable scenarios of unlikely events in an effort to cover every conceivable possibility of outrageous fortune. *See also risk management.* [Sailor 1990]

risk knowledge and research—In risk management (risk handling), a continuing process that enables the participants to perform risk handling (along with the other methods) with greater confidence. It consists of gathering additional information to further assess risk and develop contingency plans. This is not a "true" risk handling technique; however, it does supply the other methods with valuable information. [Sailor 1990]

risk management—In system/software engineering, an "umbrella" title for the processes used to manage risk. It is an organized means of identifying and measuring risk (risk assessment) and developing, selecting, and managing options (risk analysis) for resolving (risk handling) these risks. The primary goal of risk management is to identify and respond to potential problems with sufficient lead time to avoid a crisis situation. *See also risk assessment, risk handling, and risk identification.* [Sailor 1990]

risk measured—In risk management, the combined effect of the likelihood of the occurrence and a measured or assessed consequence given that occurrence. *See also risk management.*

risk monitoring—In risk management, the monitoring of potential risks identified in the risk identification and analysis phase. Particular attention should be paid to the "risk triggers," those metrics that have been identified to "sound the alarm" that a potential risk has either now or soon will become a problem.

risk transfer—In risk management (risk handling), the reduction of risk exposure by sharing risk with another agency. Two or more agencies share the consequences should the event occur. For example: type of contract, performance incentives, warranties, insurance. *See also risk handling.*

rule—In management (planning), procedures and requirements for specific and definite actions to be taken or not taken with respect to a situation. No discretion is allowed.

S

scheduling—In SEPM, determining and documenting the start and stop time for each activity and task in the project, taking into account the precedence relations among tasks, the dependencies of tasks on external events, and the required milestone dates. Schedules may be expressed in absolute calendar time or in increments relative to a key project milestone.

SEPM—Acronym for software engineering project management [Thayer, Pyster, and Wood 1981].

significant change report—A management report that identifies and calls attention to significant deviations from the plan.

SLIM cost-estimation model—A proprietary, commercially available, macro software cost-estimation method and software package that is based on Putnam's analysis of the software lifecycle in terms of the Rayleigh distribution of effort versus time. The model accommodates three categories of software application. Its primary input parameters are the estimated lines of uncommented source code, development technology environment, and estimated project development time. The SLIM was initially calibrated on 150 software development projects. It has since been calibrated on over 1,400 software projects. *See also software cost-estimation model.*

software—All instructions and data that cause computers to function in any mode; the term includes operating systems, supervisory systems, compilers, and test routines as well as application programs.

software cost-estimation model—Any one of several quantitative methods of estimating the expected cost (and sometimes schedule) of a software project. Quantitative techniques are generally based on empirically derived cost estimating relationships. Generally the major independent parameter (input) is lines of source code. *See also the following software cost-estimation models: COCOMO software cost-estimation model, PRICE-S cost-estimation model, SLIM software cost-estimation model.*

software design—In software engineering, the process of defining the software architecture (structure), components, modules, interfaces, test approach, and data for a software system to satisfy specified requirements [ANSI/IEEE Std. 729-1983].

software development lifecycle—A software development model/strategy that begins with the decision to develop a software product and ends when the product is delivered. It depicts the relationships among the major milestones, baselines, reviews, and project deliverables that span the life of the project. A project lifecycle model must include project-initiation and project-termination activities. The software development lifecycle typically includes a requirements phase, design phase, implementation (coding) phase, test phase, and, sometimes, installation and checkout phases. *See also software lifecycle.*

software development methodology—In software engineering: (1) an integrated set of software engineering methods, policies, procedures, rules, standards, techniques, tools, languages, and other methodologies for analyzing, designing, implementing, and testing software; and (2) a set of rules for selecting the correct methodology, process, or tools.

software development paradigm—Software engineering examples or models that can be used as a strategy for developing a software system. Examples are baseline management, top-down development, incremental development, rapid throwaway prototyping, and reusable software.

software development plan—*See software project management plan.*

software development process—The process by which user needs are translated into software requirements, software requirements are transformed into design, the design is implemented in code, and the code is tested, documented, and certified for operational use [IEEE SET Glossary 1983]. *See also software development lifecycle.*

software development project—*See software engineering project.*

software engineering—1. The practical application of computer science, management, and other sciences to the analysis, design, construction, and maintenance of software and its associated documentation. 2. An engineering science that applies the concept of analysis, design, coding, testing, documentation, and management to the successful completion of large, custom-built computer programs. 3. The systematic application of methods, tools, and techniques to achieve a stated requirement or objective for an effective and efficient software system. 4. The application of scientific principles to (1) the early transformation of a problem into a working software solution, and (2) subsequent maintenance of that software until the end of its useful life [Davis, *Comparison of Techniques*, 1988].

software engineering crisis—A term used since the 1960s to describe the recurring system development problems in that software development problems cause the system to be late, over cost, and not responsive to the user/customers or requirements.

software engineering project—In software engineering, the set of all activities, functions, and tasks, both technical and managerial, required to satisfy the terms and conditions of the project agreement. A software engineering project is a temporary activity characterized by having a start date, specific objectives and constraints, established responsibilities, a budget and schedule, and a completion date. The project consumes resources and has the goal of producing a product or set of products that satisfies the project requirements, as specified in the project agreement. A software engineering project may be self-contained or may be part of a larger project. In some cases, the project may span only a portion of the software product lifecycle. In other cases, the project may span many years and consist of numerous subprojects, each in itself being a well-defined and self-contained software engineering project [ANSI/IEEE Std. 1058.1-1987]. *Synonymous with software project, software development project.*

software engineering project management (SEPM)—A system of procedures, practices, technologies, and know-how that provides the planning, organizing, staffing, directing, and controlling necessary to successfully manage a software engineering project. Know-how in this case means the skill, background, and wisdom to apply knowledge effectively in practice. *See also project management.*

software engineering project manager—Anyone put in charge of a group of people for the purpose of developing or maintaining a software system. *See also manager, software engineering project management.*

software engineering project plan—*See software project management plan.*

software engineering standard—In software engineering, a standard that sets the procedures and process for developing the software, or descriptions that define the quantity and quality of a product from a software engineering project. *See also standard.*

software functional organization—A line or staff organization that is organized around a number of software skills. Personnel assigned could include software engineers, programmers, analysts, software managers, and sometimes machine operators, data entry, and other support personnel. The organization would provide a center of expertise in the software disciplines and a source of resources for project and matrix organizations. *See also functional organization, matrix organization, project organization.*

software lifecycle—In software engineering: 1. A model of the phases of a software system that starts when a software product is conceived and ends when the product is no longer available for use. It depicts the relationships among the major milestones, baselines, reviews, and project deliverables that span the life of the system. The software lifecycle typically includes a requirements phase, design phase, implementation (coding) phase, installation and checkout phase, operation and maintenance phase, and, sometimes, retirement phase. *See also software development lifecycle.* 2. A strategy for developing a system that includes the development of requirements, product design, and detailed design that involves the development of verification and validation, approval or disapproval, and baselining of each of these specifications. [Boehm, *V&V Software Requirements*, 1984]

software lifecycle model—A representation of a software lifecycle. *See also evolutionary development motel, incremental development model, spiral model, software lifecycle, and waterfall development model.*

software project—*See software engineering project.*

software project management plan (SPMP)—In software engineering project management, the controlling document for managing a software project. A software project management plan defines the technical and managerial functions, activities, and tasks necessary to satisfy the requirements of a software project, as defined in the project agreement. *Synonymous with software development plan, software engineering project plan.*

software quality assurance plan—A project management plan for implementing a software quality assurance program within a company, organization, or project. The plan should include sections on (1) purpose, (2) reference documents, (3) management, (4) documentation, (5) standards, practices, and conventions, (6) reviews and audits, (7) software configuration management, (8) problem reporting and corrective action, (9) tools, techniques, and methodologies, (10) code control, (11) media control, (12) supplier control, and (13) record collection, maintenance, and retention [IEEE Std. 730-1984].

software requirement—In software engineering: 1. A software capability needed by a user to solve a problem to achieve an objective. 2. A software capability that must be met or possessed by a system or system component to satisfy a contract, standard, specification, or other formally imposed document. 3. The set of all software requirements that forms the basis for subsequent development of the software or software component [ANSI/IEEE Std. 729-1983]. 4. Short description sometimes used in place of the term software requirements specification. *See also software requirements analysis, software requirements specification (SRS).*

software requirements analysis—In software requirement engineering, the process of studying user needs to arrive at a definition of software requirements. Sometimes synonymous with analysis, software analysis, software requirements engineering. *See also software requirements engineering.*

software requirements elicitation—The process through which the customers (buyers and/or users) and the developer (contractor) of a software system discover, review, articulate, and understand the users' needs and the constraints on the software and the development activity. *See also software requirements engineering.*

software requirements engineering—In software system engineering, the science and discipline concerned with analyzing and documenting software requirements. It involves transforming system requirements into a description of software requirements, performance parameters, and a system configuration through the use of an iterative process of definition, analysis, trade-off studies, and prototyping. *Sometimes synonymous with software requirements analysis and specifications. See software requirements, software requirements analysis, software requirements elicitation, software requirements management, software requirements specification, and software requirements verification.*

software requirements management—In software requirements engineering, the planning and controlling of the requirements elicitation, specification, analysis, and verification activities. *See also software requirements engineering.*

software requirements review (SRR)—*Synonymous with software specification review (SSR).*

software requirements specification (SRS)—In software requirements engineering, a document that clearly and precisely describes each of the essential requirements (functions, performance, design constraints, and quality attributes) of the software and the external interfaces. Each requirement is defined in such a way that its achievement can be objectively verified by a prescribed method, for example, inspection, demonstration, analysis, or test.

software requirements verification—In software requirements engineering, ensuring that the software requirements specification is in compliance with the system requirements, conforms to document standards of the requirements phase, and is an adequate basis for the architectural (preliminary) design phase. *See also software requirements engineering.*

software specification review (SSR)—In software system engineering, a milestone review conducted to finalize software configuration item (SCI) requirements so that the software developer can initiate preliminary software design. The SSR is conducted when SCI requirements have been suf-

ficiently defined to evaluate the developer's responsiveness to and interpretation of the system/segment level technical requirements. A successful SSR is predicated on the developer's determination that the software requirements specification and interface specifications form a satisfactory basis for proceeding into the preliminary design phase [Mil-Std. 1521B-1985]. *See also milestone review, review.*

software tool—A software system or software package used by programmers or software engineers in the performance of their tasks. Software systems used to help develop, test, analyze, or maintain another software system or its documentation. Examples of these tools are automated design tools, compilers, test tools, maintenance tools, and word processors [ANSI/IEEE Std. 729-1983]. *See also CASE tool.*

spiral model—1. A software development strategy developed by Barry W. Boehm that creates a risk-driven approach to the software process in contrast to a document-driven or code-driven process. The spiral model holds that each cycle involves a progression through the same sequence of steps, for each portion of the product, and for each of its levels of elaboration, from an overall concept of operations documented down to the coding of each individual program [Boehm, *Spiral Model*, 1988]. 2. A software development process model that represents combinations of the conventional (baseline management), prototyping, and incremental models to be used for various portions of a development. It shifts the management emphasis from product development to risk analysis and avoidance, and explicitly calls for evaluation concerning whether or not a project should be terminated [Dorfman 1990]. *See also waterfall model.*

SSADM (Structured System Analysis and Design Methodology)—A United Kingdom (UK) government software development process by Learmonth and Burchett Management Systems (LBMS). Three main classes of diagrams are used in SSADM: logical data structures, which represent the relationship between data elements within the system; dataflow diagrams, which show how data moves around an information system and which processes act upon; and the entity life history, which gives a third view of data showing all events affecting the entity during the life of the system. An entity life history, for example, includes those who created it, those who modified it in some way, and those who deleted it [Williams 1987].

staff—In management (staffing), a group of individuals assigned to one organization or activity.

staff organization—A group of functional experts who have the responsibility and authority to perform special activities that help the line organization do its work. A group of experts in their field that give advice or counsel. *Contrast with line organization. See also conventional organization.*

staffing—All the management activities that involve manning and keeping manned the positions established by the organizational structure. This includes selecting candidates for positions, training or otherwise developing both candidates and incumbents to accomplish their tasks effectively, appraising and compensating the incumbents, and terminating the incumbent when the organizational position is dissolved or the incumbent's performance is unsatisfactory.

staffing plan—In management (staffing) a plan that sees to filling, and keeping filled, positions in the organization structure through defining staffing requirements, keeping an inventory of the available work force, and selecting and training the new hires [Koontz, O'Donnell, and Weihrich 1984].

standard—1. A standard is an approved, documented, and available set of criteria used to determine the adequacy of an action or object. 2. A document that sets forth the standards and procedures to be followed on a given project or by a given organization. *See also process standard, product standard.*

strategy—In management (planning), the determination of the basic long-term objectives of an organization or enterprise, the adoption of courses of action, and allocation of resources necessary to achieve these goals.

structured analysis (SA)—In software engineering (methodology), a state-of-the-art software analysis technique that uses dataflow diagrams (DFDs), data dictionaries, and process descriptions to analyze and represent a software requirement. The technique supports both non-real-time and real-time systems. *Contrast with object-oriented analysis.*

structured design—1. In software engineering, a design technique that involves hierarchical partitioning of a modular structure in a top-down fashion, with emphasis on reduced coupling and strong cohesion [DeMarco 1979]. 2. A disciplined approach to software design that adheres to a specified set of rules based on principles such as top-down design, stepwise refinement, and dataflow analysis [ANSI/IEEE Std. 729-1983].

supervise—In management (directing), the responsibility for overseeing the work and providing day-to-day control and direction to the personnel assigned to the manager or authorized for his control. It is the manager's responsibility to provide guidance and, when necessary, discipline to these people in order that they fulfill their assigned duties.

support personnel—In management (staffing), the staff personnel who provide assistance, advice, and auxiliary tasks in support of the personnel doing the primary duty of the organization.

system design review (SDR)—In system/software system engineering, a system milestone review conducted when the definition effort has proceeded to the point where system requirements and the design approach are defined, and when alternative design approaches and corresponding test requirements have been considered, and the developer has defined and selected the required equipment, logistics support, personnel, procedural data, and facilities. This normally is late in the definition phase. This review is conducted in sufficient detail to ensure a technical understanding between the system developer and the customer. The system segments are identified in the system design specification, and the hardware/software configuration items are identified in the requirements specifications. *See also milestone reviews, reviews.*

system project manager—A manager that has responsibility for planning, organizing, staffing, directing, and controlling a system engineering project. *See also project manager, software engineering project manager.*

system requirements review (SRR)—In system engineering, a system milestone review that ascertains the adequacy of the system developer's efforts in defining system requirements. It will be conducted when a significant portion of the system functional and performance requirements has been established, normally in the definition phase (or equivalent effort). *See also milestone review, review.*

T

technology insertion—*See technology transfer.*

technology transfer—The awareness, convincing,

selling, motivating, collaboration, and special effort required to encourage industry, companies, organizations, and projects to make good use of new technology products. Synonymous with technology insertion. *See also technology transfer gap.*

technology transfer gap—The time interval (measured in years) between the development of a new product, tool, or technique and its use by the consumers of that product, tool, or technique. *See also software technology transfer, technology transfer.*

test—In software engineering: 1. A set of one or more test cases. 2. A set of one or more test procedures. 3. A set of one or more test cases and procedures [ANSI/IEEE Std. 829-1983]. *See also testing.*

testing—In software system engineering: 1. A verification method that applies a controlled set of conditions and stimuli for the purpose of finding errors. This is the most desirable method of verifying the functional and performance requirements. Test results are documented proof that the requirements were met and can be repeated. The resulting data can be reviewed by all concerned for confirmation of capabilities. *Contrast with analysis, demonstration, examination, and similarity.* 2. The process of analyzing a system/software item to detect the differences between existing and required conditions and to evaluate the features of the system/software item [ANSI/IEEE Std. 729-1983]. 3. The process of exercising or evaluating a system or system component by manual or automated means to verify that it satisfies specified requirements or to identify differences between expected and actual results. *Compare with debugging.*

throwaway prototyping—A software engineering strategy (made popular by Gomaa) addresses the issue of ensuring that the software product being proposed really meets the user's needs. The approach is to construct a "quick and dirty" partial solution to the system prior to (or during) the requirement stage. The potential users utilize this prototype for a period of time and supply feedback to the developer concerning strengths and weakness. This feedback is then used to modify the software requirements specification to reflect the real user's needs, and the prototype is discarded. At this point, the developer can proceed with the actual system design and implementation with confidence that they are building the "right" system [Davis et al. 1988]. *Sometimes synonymous with rapid prototyping.*

top management—In management, an expression that equates to senior level management, for example, general manager, vice president of operations, director of computer services. Within a project management context, the project manager might refer to his or her and the customer's managers as "top management."

training—1. In management (staffing), the process of developing a skill, or knowledge on how to use, operate, or make something. This is in contrast to education in a concept of basic theory. For example, an individual would be trained in using Fortran but educated in the principles of programming languages. Training is typically used to satisfy a short-term requirement for skilled personnel on a particular activity or task. It has a short-term payoff. *Contrast with education.* 2. In software quality metrics, those characteristics of software that provides transition from current operations and provides initial familiarization [RADC 1985].

training plan—1. In management (staffing), the career goal for each member of the staff, and the training and education required to achieve those goals. 2. In project management, a description of the training needed by an organization's personnel in order to complete a project. 3. In an engineering project, a deliverable configuration item. *See also education, training.*

trend chart—A management report that shows trends in such areas as budget, number of errors found in the system, man-hours of sick leave, and so on. Trend reports are used to predict the future.

U

unit development folder (UDF)—In software engineering project management, a central depository for recording the progress that has been made toward a "unit's" objectives. A UDF is used by project management for monitoring software work accomplished. A unit can be a single project member or project team. Initial development credited to Frank Ingrassia. *Sometimes synonymous with software development file.*

unit testing—In software engineering (testing), the process of locating, analyzing, and correcting suspected faults in software units or components. *Sometimes synonymous with debugging. See also testing.*

universality of management—From the management sciences [Koontz, O'Donnell, and Weihrich 1984], [Fayol 1949], a concept that means that (1) management performs the same functions regardless of its position in the organization or the enterprise managed, and (2) management functions and fundamental activities are characteristic duties of managers; management practices, methods, detailed activities, and tasks are particular to the enterprise or job managed.

V

validation—In software engineering, determination of the correctness of the final program or software produced from a development project with respect to the user's needs and requirements. Validation answers the question "Am I building the right product?" [Boehm, *V&V Software Requirements*, 1984].

verification—In software engineering: 1. The process of determining whether the products of a given phase of the software development cycle fulfill the requirements established during the previous phase. Verification answers the question, "Am I building the product right?" *See also validation.* 2. The act of reviewing, inspecting, testing, checking, auditing, comparing, or otherwise establishing and documenting whether or not items, processes, services, or documents conform to specified requirements. 3. Formal proof of program correctness. 4. In system/software system engineering, a generalized term that can mean test (using precision instrumentation), demonstration (a functional test), analysis (or simulation), or examination (or documentation) [Sailor 1990].

verification and validation (V&V)—In software engineering, a software quality assurance (SQA) procedure that includes both verification and validation. The basic objectives in verification and validation of software requirements and design specifications are to identify and resolve software problems and high-risk issues early in the software cycle [Boehm, *V&V Software Requirements*, 1984]. *See also independent verification and validation, validation, verification.*

W

walkthrough—In software engineering, a software inspection process, conducted by the peers of the software developer, to evaluate a software element. Although usually associated with code examination, this process is also applicable to the software requirements and software design. The major objectives of the walkthrough are to find defects (for example, omissions, unwanted additions, and contradictions) in a specification and other products and to consider alternative functionality, performance objectives, or representations [Hollocker 1990]. *See also inspection, peer review.*

waterfall development model—*See waterfall model. See also software lifecycle model.*

waterfall model—A software development lifecycle strategy, first developed by Winston W. Royce [1970], that partitions the project into manageable phases (requirements, design, implementation, and test) and establishes milestones, documents, and reviews at the end of each phase. In the model, the successful completion of one lifecycle phase in the waterfall chart corresponds to the achievement of the counterpart goal in the sequence of software engineering goals for the software process. The waterfall model also recognizes the iteration between phases.

WBS—*Acronym for work breakdown structure.*

work breakdown structure (WBS)—In project management, a method of representing in a hierarchical manner the parts of a product or process. A WBS can be used to represent a process (requirement analysis, design, code, or software test) or a product (application programs, utility programs, or operating systems). *See also hybrid work breakdown structure, process work breakdown structure, and product work breakdown structure.*

work breakdown structure (WBS) dictionary—In system/software engineering, a list of components from a specific WBS. Generally, the elements are signed numbers, listed sequentially in the dictionary with necessary identification, definition, objective of element, synopsis of effort required, and the elements' relationship to other elements. *See also WBS.*

work package—*See work package specification.*

work package specification—A specification of the work to be accomplished in completing a function, activity, or task. A work package specification specifies the objectives of the work, staffing requirements, the expected duration of the task, the resources to be used, the results to be produced, and any special considerations for the work.

work product—Any document, documentation, or other tangible items that results from working on a project function, activity, or task. Examples of work products include the project plan, functional requirements, design documents, source code, test plans, meeting minutes, schedules, budgets, and problem reports. Some subset of the work products will form the set of project deliverables.

workload chart—In management, a schedule of work to be done and the estimated amount of man-hours/days scheduled to accomplish the work.

worksheet—In management, a working document that details the analysis of data and information about a proposed plan of action that is used in decision making.

X, Y, Z

References

[ANSI/IEEE Std. 729-1983] *IEEE Standard Glossary of Software Engineering Terminology*, The Institute of Electrical and Electronics Engineers, Inc., New York, N.Y., approved by American National Standards Institute Aug. 9, 1983.

[ANSI/IEEE Std. 730-1988] *IEEE Standard for Software Quality Assurance Plans*, IEEE, Inc., New York, N.Y., 1984.

[ANSI/IEEE Std. 829-1983] *IEEE Standard for Software Test Documents*, IEEE, Inc., New York, N.Y., 1987, approved by American National Standards Institute, Aug. 19, 1983.

[ANSI/IEEE Std. 1058.1-1987] *IEEE Standard for Software Project Management Plans*, IEEE, Inc., New York, N.Y., approved by American National Standards Institute Oct. 6, 1988.

[Boehm 1981] Boehm, B.W., *Software Engineering Economics*, Prentice-Hall, Englewood Cliffs, N.J., 1981.

[Boehm, *Spiral Model*, 1988] Boehm, B.W., "A Spiral Model of Software Development and Enhancement," in *Software Engineering Project Management*, R.H. Thayer, ed., IEEE Computer Society Press, Los Alamitos, Calif., 1988, pp. 128–142.

[Boehm, *V&V Software Requirements*, 1984] Boehm, B.W., "Verifying and Validating Software Requirements and Design Specifications," *IEEE Software*, Vol. 1, No. 1, Jan. 1984, pp. 75–88.

[Cleland and King 1972] Cleland, D.I. and W.R. King, *Management: A Systems Approach*, McGraw-Hill, New York, N.Y., 1972.

[DeMarco 1979] DeMarco, T., *Structured Analysis and System Specification*, Prentice-Hall, Englewood Cliffs, N.J., 1979.

[DoD Directive 5010.19] DoD Directive 5010.19, *Configuration Management*, US Dept. of Defense, Oct. 28, 1987.

[DoD Std 480B-1988] DOD Standard 480B, *Configuration Control—Engineering Changes*, Deviation and Waivers, US Dept. of Defense, July 15, 1988.

[Fayol 1949] Fayol, H., *General and Industrial Management*, Sir Isaac Pitman & Sons, Ltd., London, 1949.

[Hollocker 1990] Hollocker, C.P., "Requirement Specification Examinations," in *System and Software Requirements Engineering*, R.H. Thayer and M. Dorfman, eds., IEEE Computer Society Press, Los Alamitos, Calif., 1990.

[IEE/BCS Safety-Related Systems 1989] IEE/BCS, *Software in Safety-Related Systems*, IEEE and The British Computer Society, Oct. 1989.

[IEEE CAT Glossary 1986] *IEEE Glossary of Computer Applications Terminology* (Draft), IEEE, Inc., New York, N.Y., 1986.

[IEEE SET Glossary 1983] ANSI/IEEE Std. 729-1983, *IEEE Standard Glossary of Software Engineering Terminology*, IEEE, Inc., New York, NY, 1983.

[IEEE Software Engineering Standards 1987] Hardbound Edition of *Software Engineering Standards*, IEEE Computer Society, Los Alamitos, Calif., 1987.

[Koontz and O'Donnell, 1972] Koontz, H. and C. O'Donnell, *Principles of Management: An Analysis of Managerial Functions*, 5th ed., McGraw-Hill, New York, N.Y., 1972.

[Koontz, O'Donnell, and Weihrich 1984] Koontz, H., C. O'Donnell, and H. Weihrich, Management, 8th ed., McGraw-Hill., New York, N.Y., 1984.

[Military Std. 1521B-1985] Military Standard 1521B (USAF), *Technical Reviews and Audits for Systems, Equipment, and Computer Programs*, US Dept. of Defense, June 4, 1985.

[NCC STARTS Guide 1987] The National Computer Centre, Limited, *The Starts Guide*, 2nd ed., Chapter 5, Vol. I, Manchester, England, 1987.

[RADC 1985] Bowen, T.P., G.B. Wigle, and J.T. Tsai, *Specification of Software Quality Attributes*, Vol. II: *Software Quality Specifications Guidebook*, RADC-TR-85-37, prepared by Boeing Aerospace Co. for Rome Air Development Center, Griffiss AFB, NY, Feb. 1985.

[Sailor 1990] Sailor, J.D., *System Engineering Management Guide*, Defense Systems Management College, 1983. (The second [1986] edition of this book can be obtained from the Superintendent of Documents, US Government Printing Office, Washington, DC.

[Thayer, Pyster, and Wood 1981] Thayer, R.H., A.B. Pyster, and R.C. Wood, "Major Issues in Software Engineering Project Management," *IEEE Trans. Software Eng.*, Vol. SE-7, No. 4, July 1981, pp. 333–342.

[Weinberg 1971] Weinberg, G., *The Psychology of Computer Programming*, Van Nostrand Reinhold, New York, N.Y., 1971.

[Williams 1987] Williams, J., "SSADM—System Building Made Simple," *Systems International*, Nov. 1987, pp. 91–92.

BIOGRAPHY OF RICHARD H. THAYER

Richard H. Thayer is a Professor of Computer Science at California State University, Sacramento, California, United States of America. He travels widely where he consults and lectures on software requirements analysis, software engineering, project management, software engineering standards, and software quality assurance. He is a Visiting Researcher and lecturer at the University of Strathclyde, Glasgow, Scotland. As an expert in software project management and requirements engineering, he is a consultant to many companies and government agencies.

Prior to this, he served over 20 years in the U.S. Air Force as a senior officer in a variety of positions associated with engineering, computer programming, research, teaching, and management in computer science and data processing. His numerous positions include six years as a supervisor and technical leader of scientific programming groups, four years directing the U.S. Air Force R&D program in computer science, and six years of managing large data processing organizations.

Thayer is a Senior Member of the IEEE Computer Society and the IEEE Software Engineering Standards Subcommittee. He is Chairperson for the Working Group for a Standard for a Concept of Operations (ConOps) document and co-chairperson for the Working Group for a Standard for a Software Project Management Plans (update). He is a Distinguished Visitor for the IEEE Computer Society. He is also an Associate Fellow of the American Institute of Aeronautics and Astronautics (AIAA) where he served on the AIAA Technical Committee on Computer Systems, and he is a member of the Association for Computing Machinery (ACM). He is also a registered professional engineer.

He has a BSEE and an MS degree from the University of Illinois at Urbana (1962) and a PhD from the University of California at Santa Barbara (1979), all in Electrical Engineering.

He has edited and/or co-edited numerous tutorials for the IEEE Computer Society Press: *Software Engineering* (1997), *Software Requirements Engineering* (1997), and *Software Engineering—A European Prospective* (1993). He is the author of over 40 technical papers and reports on software project management, software engineering, and software engineering standards and is an invited speaker at many national and international software engineering conferences and workshops.

IEEE COMPUTER SOCIETY

Press Activities Board

IEEE Computer Society Publications

The world-renowned IEEE Computer Society publishes, promotes, and distributes a wide variety of authoritative computer science and engineering texts. These books are available from most retail outlets. Visit the Online Catalog, *http://computer.org*, for a list of products.

IEEE Computer Society Proceedings

The IEEE Computer Society also produces and actively promotes the proceedings of more than 141 acclaimed international conferences each year in multimedia formats that include hard and softcover books, CD-ROMs, videos, and on-line publications.

For information on the IEEE Computer Society proceedings, send e-mail to *cs.books@computer.org* or write to Proceedings, IEEE Computer Society, P.O. Box 3014, 10662 Los Vaqueros Circle, Los Alamitos, CA 90720-1314. Telephone +1 714-821-8380. FAX +1 714-761-1784.

Additional information regarding the Computer Society, conferences and proceedings, CD-ROMs, videos, and books can also be accessed from our web site at *http://computer.org/cspress*

Revised 9 November 1999